PRAISE FOR PREVIOUS ORAL HISTORIES
FROM ALTMAN & GROSS

"Mark and Ed tell the fascinating story of that rare Hollywood product that actually means something to mankind."
—Seth MacFarlane

"The authors have done an exhaustive, masterful job of collecting interviews and editing memories, opinions, and reflections of hundreds of creative artists, business executives, critics, and even the occasional social scientist. What emerges is an intriguing look inside the sausage-making process that is television and film production."
—*The Wall Street Journal*

"A page-turner. Longtime fans will find a lot to chew on, and newer fans will feel like old pros after reading this splendidly crafted work."
—*Publishers Weekly*

"Breathtaking in scope and depth, this is a must-read for Star Trek lovers, as well as anyone who wants a better understanding of how television and film production works."
—*Booklist*

"A tantalizing Star Trek tell-all . . . Perhaps the most comprehensive compendium of Star Trek knowledge you'll ever find."
—*Emmy* magazine

"*Slayers & Vampires* is a new primary text to pore over, with plenty of behind-the-scenes tidbits about who hated whom and how TV shows are made."
—*The New York Times Book Review*

"If you're just dying for juicy secrets about the famous franchise, then your search is over. We just know you're going to love this book, resistance is futile."
—*Bookish*

"*The Fifty-Year Mission* is a Ken Burns's *The Civil War*–, Ezra Edelman's *O.J.: Made in America*–class achievement."
—Chris Smith, *Dorking Out* podcast

"An absolute must for any Star Trek fan."
—*Kirkus Reviews*

"An epic tome that's full of so much fantastic information I felt like I was discovering the incredible behind-the-scenes story of Star Trek—and Hollywood, for that matter—all over again. It's a page-turner in every sense of the word and I could not put it down."
—Scott Mantz, *Access Hollywood*

"This is the ultimate chronicle of the shows, movies, and fandom of one of sci-fi's most important franchises."
—*io9*

"A must for genre fans and aspiring filmmakers alike."
—Jesse Alexander, executive producer, *American Gods*

ALSO BY THE AUTHORS

The Fifty-Year Mission:
The Complete, Uncensored, Unauthorized Oral History of Star Trek:
The First 25 Years

The Fifty-Year Mission:
The Next 25 Years: From The Next Generation *to J. J. Abrams:*
The Complete, Uncensored, and Unauthorized Oral History of Star Trek

Slayers & Vampires:
The Complete Uncensored, Unauthorized
Oral History of Buffy *and* Angel

So Say We All:
The Complete, Uncensored, Unauthorized
Oral History of Battlestar Galactica

NOBODY DOES IT BETTER

THE COMPLETE, UNCENSORED, UNAUTHORIZED ORAL HISTORY OF

JAMES BOND

MARK A. ALTMAN

AND **EDWARD GROSS**

WITH ADDITIONAL MATERIAL BY

RICHARD SCHENKMAN

FORGE

A TOM DOHERTY ASSOCIATES BOOK

NEW YORK

This book is not licensed or approved by MGM/UA or Eon Productions and is solely an academic work devoted to the James Bond motion pictures and spymania. The opinions expressed reflect only those of the authors or those quoted.

NOBODY DOES IT BETTER

A Forge Book
Published by Tom Doherty Associates
120 Broadway
New York, NY 10271

www.tor-forge.com

Forge® is a registered trademark of Macmillan Publishing Group, LLC.

The Library of Congress Cataloging in Publication Data is available upon request.

ISBN 978-1-250-30095-9 (hardcover)
ISBN 978-1-250-30096-6 (ebook)

Our books may be purchased in bulk for promotional, educational, or business use. Please contact your local bookseller or the Macmillan Corporate and Premium Sales Department at 1-800-221-7945, extension 5442, or by email at MacmillanSpecialMarkets@macmillan.com.

First Edition: February 2020

Printed in the United States of America

0 9 8 7 6 5 4 3 2 1

In loving memory of Karl Hergensheimer,

G-Section

FROM MARK A. ALTMAN

My mom and dad, who couldn't agree on much, but always let me stay up to watch James Bond movies on *The ABC Sunday Night Movie* . . . even on a school night.

Our jocular editor, **Christopher Morgan**, our very own M.

My *Bond* Girl, **Naomi Altman**, nobody does it better, makes me feel sad for the rest.

Ella and **Isaac**, the spies who love me.

Giles and **Willow**, my cats who help me rule the world.

Sean, George, Roger, Timothy, Pierce, and **Daniel** because they all had a license to thrill in their own unique and incomparable ways (and they all had more card sense than Barry Nelson ever had).

The late United Artists president **David Picker**, who greenlit my childhood.

And the man with the golden pen, **Edward Gross**; I wish he charged a million a shot—because I would get 50 percent.

FROM EDWARD GROSS

My wife and best friend of thirty-two years and counting: *You drift through the years and life seems tame, till one dream appears, and* ***Eileen*** *is her name.*

The "00" section that is our family: **Teddy** and **Lindsay**; **Dennis** and his fiancé, **Yumi**; and **Kevin** and we-all-know-she's-the-one, **Nicole**.

Jay Starr, my friend of forty-five years who goes to see every Bond movie with me and who, like me, when a film disappoints, shrugs and says, "Ah, they'll get it right next time." Indeed, they will.

Bruce Feirstein, who, twenty years between conversations, chats with me like an old friend without missing a beat, talking Bond as well as the joys and frustrations of toiling in our mutual world of journalism.

Christopher Morgan, our editor, and **Laurie Fox**, our agent, for bringing us one step closer to world domination.

And my cowriter, **Mark A. Altman**. Are we supposed to be having this much fun writing these books?

MISSION DOSSIER

"My plots are fantastic while often based upon truth.
They go wildly beyond the probable, not, I think,
beyond the possible."

—Ian Fleming

NOBODY DOES IT BETTER

JUST SAY (DOCTOR) NO. . . .

"Why is it that people who can't take advice always insist on giving it?"

BY **Mark A. Altman**

If you're someone like me who plays "Arrival in Miami" on their iPhone blasting through earbuds as they come in for a landing at Miami International Airport or insists on staying at the Hotel Fontainebleau because that's where Bond first tangled with Auric Goldfinger and drank Dom Pérignon '53 at 38 degrees Fahrenheit with golden girl Jill Masterson, then this book is definitely for you.

And it's decidedly not just "man talk."

There have been a myriad of truly spectacular books written about the only gentleman secret agent with a license to kill—and thrill—over the years (and my bookshelf is filled with them), but for Ed Gross and me, we wanted to do something different and unique in examining the 007 oeuvre, to not only explore the making of these seminal films but also examine why they have had such an incredible impact and enduring appeal for fans as well as an entire generation of contemporary filmmakers who grew up on these movies.

Full disclosure: the first 007 movie I ever saw in a theater, which inspired my lifelong obsession with James Bond, was quite improbably *The Man with the Golden Gun* (although you could argue it was *North by Northwest*, really, which I saw at the wonderful Thalia revival house in Manhattan with my mom, that inspired my obsessive devotion to cinema ever since), which my parents took me to see when I was seven years old. To say it was a life-changing experience would not be an overstatement. Ironically, the film that inspired my passion for 007 is probably now one of my least beloved installments, but I will forever be grateful for its lighting the spark of my imagination as well as immediately sending me to the library, where I began haunting the stacks to check out all the Ian Fleming novels as well.

My story is similar to many of the others you will read about in this book. From then on, it was years of watching the movies, often truncated and out-of-sequence, on the still justly beloved *ABC Sunday Night Movie*. There was something truly magical about Ernie Anderson's stentorian voice announcing, "Tonight, Sean Connery is James Bond, 007, in the one that started it all, *Dr. No*." To me, the famous star tunnel and opening strains of *The ABC Sunday Night Movie* theme are as indelibly a part of *Bond* lore as anything in the films themselves. Strangely enough, I can still remember how they banished *On Her Majesty's Secret Service* (or as *Bond* aficionados and typesetters know it best, *OHMSS*) to Friday nights and was amazed to see the pre-title teaser of *Goldfinger* for the first time on VHS (incongruously following a *Pink Panther* cartoon) since it had been routinely excised on ABC to make the film fit a two-hour time slot with commercials.

Growing up in Brooklyn in the Seventies, there were a few arguments that one routinely had in the schoolyard: Mets or Yankees (Mets!), *Star Trek* or *Star Wars* (*Trek*!), Giants or Jets (I don't care!), and, most importantly, Sean Connery or Roger Moore. I have to admit, I loved them both. As much as Connery was and always will be the most iconic 007, Roger Moore crafted an equally memorable, albeit far different, take on Bond as a debonair gentleman spy. (Other than me, I don't think anyone else in middle school actually knew who George Lazenby was, BTW.)

Of course, I was the proud owner of a Corgi DB5 silver Aston Martin and most of the soundtrack albums, some of which I covertly purloined from my parents' stereo rack, and would religiously buy the *Best of Bond* LPs, which inevitably would be updated every time a new 007 movie came out with the latest title song. I often wondered what would happen when there would be too many songs to fit on one record, failing to anticipate the arrival of the compact disc or MP3s, which allowed you to have both Sheryl Crow's "Tomorrow Never Dies" and k.d. lang's "Surrender" in your *Bond* songs compilation without ever risking running out of space.

In the following years, I've probably spent the equivalent of a small mortgage payment on buying and re-buying all the films on VHS, then laser disc, then laser disc box set, then DVD, then Special Edition DVD, then Ultimate Special Edition DVD, to be followed by Blu-ray, 50th anniversary Blu-ray box set, SVOD, and inevitably 4K UHD.

Watching the opening of any *Bond* movie is special, its always holding the promise that it will be the best one yet; the strains of the "James Bond Theme," the gun barrel logo, the hint of nudity in the always spectacular opening credits. But if *The Man with the Golden Gun* had proven to be my gateway drug into the incredible world of 007, it was seeing *The Spy Who Loved Me* in 1977 at a multiplex in Valley Stream, Long Island, that would make me a lifetime member. In my opinion, the best of Roger Moore's films, *Spy* had it all—except anything lifted from the novel, of course. It was the one book that Ian Fleming demanded the producers not adapt (although there are small vestiges of two of the characters in the film that remain). I never missed the arrival of a James Bond film, and I could tell you every theater I ever saw them at. I vividly remember, on my very first book tour, I played hooky from a book signing while in San Francisco to go see *GoldenEye* opening day at the Castro. As my coauthor Ed Gross once joked in a moment of gallows humor uncharacteristic of him, it's disappointing to know that one day we'll be dead, but they'll still be making *James Bond* films we'll never get to see. That said, it kind of bummed us both out.

And speaking of bummers, I recall being particularly agitated over a decade ago when it was first announced Daniel Craig had been cast as James Bond. I just couldn't square the craggy-faced star of *Tomb Raider* as my favorite gentleman agent with a license to kill. Sure, I loved him in *Layer Cake* and *Munich,* but the rotten son in *Road to Perdition* was no 007. I remember being so irate, and perhaps a tad inebriated, while attending the Sitges Film Festival in Barcelona, Spain, moments after the announcement had come out that I began to ask every British tourist I could find what they thought in the hopes it would buoy my spirits, only to find they were as flummoxed and gobsmacked as I was about this rather odd casting choice. But leave it to Barbara Broccoli to make us all look like complete fools in what proved to be perhaps the most inspired, original, and savvy casting choice since Sean Connery himself was first hired by Cubby Broccoli and Harry Saltzman.

It's a testament that over the course of more than five decades, this unique family business, first under the aegis of the late, great Cubby Broccoli and later daughter Barbara and Michael Wilson, has managed to never miscast a Bond. Sure, there have been better Bonds and worse, but none of them have ever been irredeemably awful or miscast. Every one of them has earned the right to wear that tuxedo and intone, "Bond, James Bond." They left us both shaken and stirred and it's comforting to know that they will for many, many years to come.

And the Broccoli family has given my family a great gift as well. In the last few months of finishing this exhaustive tome, I was forced to give up my prized Sideshow James Bond action figures to my ten-year-old son, Isaac, who has become as obsessed with the films as his father. Like my amazing dad, Michael, before me, I am now passing on 007 to the next generation of *Bond* fan. When he looked up at me after studying a photo of the ornate conference room in *Thunderball* and said, "Do you notice in the briefing that Bond sits in the seventh seat for 007," I couldn't have been more proud. He'd unearthed something even I had never realized. And to listen to him do a mean Donald Pleasence as he returns to his room saying, "We heard you were assassinated in Hong Kong . . . well, you only live twice, 007," made it clear he deserved every one of those action figures, from Dr. No to Oddjob to Pussy Galore to, gulp, Jaws, as painful as it might have been for me to part with them.

So this is not a "making of" book you're now holding in your hands (or tablet). You're going to read a lot of commentary and opinions that will infuriate you, excite you, and absolutely baffle you. That's part of the fun of being a *Bond* fan, and we wanted to bring those conversations to these pages, the same ones you and your friends have over martinis at the local watering hole or over a pint at a nearby pub; we wanted to create a fresh, new take on the 007 films by not only chronicling the making of these movies, but allowing other filmmakers, critics, and fans to share their thoughts about these movies and their impact over the decades.

While you may disagree with a lot of what you read in these pages, we hope the one opinion you will share when all is said and done is that "this *is* the big one, 007." It was for us. Thanks for coming along for the ride. Ejector seat not included.

Maybe Christmas does come more than once this year after all.

Mark A. Altman
October 29, 2018

TOMORROW NEVER LIES

"I'm putting on a little scientific demonstration in Iceland this weekend. Perhaps you could join us?"

BY **Edward Gross**

James Bond wielded the knife with obvious skill. He approached, blade barely glinting in the light, and pounced, the knife coming down to join the awaiting fork. "I usually eat fruit," he said simply, "but today I'm in the mood for a good English breakfast." And with that, he began his meal.

Admittedly it's not stopping Ernst Stavro Blofeld from stealing space capsules, weaponizing diamonds, and authoring all of Bond's pain; preventing Auric Goldfinger from radiating the gold in Fort Knox or having Karl Stromberg and Hugo Drax threaten humanity with extinction, but it was *my* experience with Agent 007 back in 1994.

At the time, I was senior editor at *Cinescape* magazine and writing a cover story on the 17th James Bond movie—and the first one to star Pierce Brosnan—*GoldenEye*. Even more incredibly, I was flown to England to spend a few days on the set at Leavesden Studios, later to be home to the *Star Wars* prequels and *Harry Potter* films.

Back in the day, a set visit was an entirely different experience than it is now. For the most part, these days, whenever you're invited to a movie set it's usually as a part of "genre day," where upwards of 30 entertainment journalists are brought in at *exactly* the same time to speak to *exactly* the same people and get *exactly* the same quotes. But in 1994, I was one of only two journalists who came to the *GoldenEye* set on those select days, and while being ushered around from interview subject to interview subject, was allowed free rein to walk around and take things in while being sure not to interfere with filming.

Oh, okay.

You have to understand how mind-blowing a situation this was for a guy who grew up on the *Bond* films, and whose earliest "movie memories" include Sean Connery as Bond, trapped on that traction machine in 1965's *Thunderball.* From there, as a kid growing up in Brooklyn, New York, I became obsessed with all things 007. Either my parents brought me or I went with my friends (and bear in mind that we weren't even 10 years old—times were *definitely* different) to the movies to see *You Only Live Twice* and *On Her Majesty's Secret Service; Thunderball* and *You Only Live Twice; Diamonds Are Forever* and *On Her Majesty's Secret Service;* and *Diamonds Are Forever* (thank God for double-feature rereleases). Then, one day in 1971, my friends and I went to a matinee at the Marine Theatre on Flatbush Avenue to see a triple feature of *Dr. No, From Russia with Love,* and *Goldfinger*—the first time I had seen *any* of them, so they were like brand-new *Bond* adventures to me.

We moved to Long Island in 1972 (on the night, coincidentally, that ABC ran *Goldfinger* for the first time on *The ABC Sunday Night Movie*). While I had to leave my life in Brooklyn behind, I had taken James Bond with me on the trip, and he's never left. Roger Moore is James Bond? Okay, no problem. He wasn't the same as Sean Connery, but this was James Bond and I wasn't going anywhere (although *The Man with the Golden Gun* seemed to do everything it could to push me away). I saw *The Spy Who Loved Me* at the former Meadowbrook Theatre in East Meadow, New York, the lobby of which was adorned with not only a wide variety of stills, posters, and banners for the film, but had the Lotus Esprit right *there* to be gawked at. Two years later, I was in Manhattan at the Rivoli Theatre, watching *Moonraker* in 70mm, and remember to this day my stunned joy at the pre-credit sequence, which had Bond thrown out of a plane without a parachute, and having to catch up to the baddie who had one to wrestle it away from him.

By the time *For Your Eyes Only* was released in 1981, I was attending college and on the school newspaper, and came into New York to interview producer Michael G. Wilson—and it was pretty amazing to me to be sitting there talking to someone actually involved with the *James Bond* films. Two years later, history would repeat itself, in that I would go and meet with director John Glen for *Octopussy.* Jump ahead two years and I was interviewing screenwriter Richard Maibaum regarding *The Living Daylights*; two years after that I was conducting interviews at the press junket for *Licence to Kill,* sitting right next to Timothy Dalton and asking him questions about his approach to Bond (he was serious) and how his take was different from Roger Moore's (he was serious). Things went on from there as I embarked on my journalism career, once again bringing 007 with me as I conducted various interviews over the years.

Which brings me back to Pierce Brosnan's trailer, chatting with him over breakfast—though it actually wasn't the first time I'd spoken to the actor about James Bond. Back in 1986, while he was promoting his first starring role in a feature film, *Nomads*, there were rumblings aplenty that he would be offered the role, as Roger Moore had wrapped up his time with the character.

"There's no truth," he responded in that first conversation. "I've never been asked to play James Bond. Next question is, would I like to play James Bond? Well, I suppose I would like to have a crack, yes, but it hasn't been a lifetime ambition to play James Bond. But the last year and a half I wish they would make up their minds one way or another, either cast somebody else or go ahead and offer me the damn part, because not a day goes by now without someone saying, 'You're going to make a great James Bond.' 'When are you playing James Bond?' 'We hear you're playing James Bond.' But no one has ever come to me and said, 'Pierce, my dear boy, we'd like you to play Jimmy Bond.' And so that may knock the rumor on its head, but I've said that before and the rumor seems to keep going round."

For the record, he *would* be offered the role shortly thereafter, and signed, but released from his contract when NBC screwed him over by renewing his canceled series, *Remington Steele,* at the last possible moment, hoping to cash in on the *Bond* films' popularity. The *Bond* people were having none of that, so Pierce was released and Timothy Dalton took on the part in 1987's *The Living Daylights.*

In any case, I sat there with Pierce in his trailer for about 30 minutes, barely concealing my excitement as I hit him with what I wanted to be riveting questions. Instead, I came out with the most obvious one you could imagine: "So, how does it feel to finally say for the camera, 'My name is Bond. James Bond'?"

"I suppose," he replied between bites of breakfast, "it's like it would be for any guy in a play. It's not quite on par with Shakespeare, but nevertheless, it is known by the man in the street. The whole world knows it. Perhaps more than 'To be or not to be . . .' Yes, I find myself brushing my teeth in the morning, kind of mumbling the lines. Of course I do. I just practice it, I say it and I crack myself up. It's quite funny, just a breath away from parody, really. I just kept it as simple as possible because I'm very aware that the audience is waiting for me to say it, so I share the moment *with* them."

I also mentioned that the impression I have is that his Bond will be a hybrid of Sean Connery's and Roger Moore's, humor coupled with ruthlessness.

"I agree with that," he said, hopefully not noticing how cool I thought it was that James Bond agreed with my theory. "It really should be pointed out that Roger made the part his own. There's a generation out there that was brought up only with Roger. They didn't know who the hell Sean Connery was, and Roger's films *did* make a lot of money. First impressions, of course, were Sean. There will be people who accept me and those who say, 'He's not Roger. He's not Sean. . . .'"

"He's not George Lazenby," I piped in, being a wiseass regarding the actor who had a one-shot as 007 in 1969's *On Her Majesty's Secret Service.*

"Right," Brosnan laughed, "he's not George Lazenby."

Things went on from there.

Later, special effects supervisor Derek Meddings took me around the area, explaining and demonstrating the virtues of using models over computer effects, giving me a tour of miniature buildings, including the nerve gas facility that opens the film. In mid-sentence, though, Meddings paused, a look of concern crossing his face.

"Oh, dear," he said in his natural British tongue, "you seem to have burst your zipper."

I looked down and, sure enough, the zipper on my jeans had snapped off, revealing my underpants. I immediately looked up, embarrassed, and commented, "My wife told me I'd be so excited, something like this would happen."

He seemed to enjoy that one as we proceeded to the newly added next stop, the costume department, where James Bond's costume designer pinned me up. Hey, can *you* say you were pinned up by James Bond's costume designer?

The following day, I sat down with producer Michael Wilson, who asked me if I wanted to watch the first teaser trailer for the film. *Mikey, are you friggin' kidding me?* (I didn't actually say that, but I thought it.) He brought me into his office and played the trailer that wouldn't be hitting theater screens for another month or so. Needless to say, I was pretty blown away by the fact that Bond was back . . . big time!

Between takes, I interviewed director Martin Campbell, director of photography Phil Méheux, leading lady Izabella Scorupco, and various behind-the-scenes personnel about the film and Bond's place in the modern world of the mid-'90s. Through it all, I was no doubt smiling like a kid in Q's workshop.

Over the course of my few days on the set in England, I managed to travel quite a bit of the globe with the new Mr. Bond. We began in Cuba, at the brim of a secret satellite dish that the film's villain intended to use to destroy society. From there it was about a five-minute walk to Saint Petersburg, Russia, where the bad guys were fleeing in a car, with Bond chasing them in a state-of-the-art tank(!).

Which is about where I left 007—after watching Bond zoom through Russia, I had to catch a cab to Heathrow Airport for my return flight to the United States. But as a parting shot, if you will, through the side window of the cab I was treated to the sight of an explosion in their version of Saint Petersburg, and one thought instantly flashed through my mind: I had survived my tour of James Bond's world. Shaken, perhaps, but not stirred (sorry).

No surprise here, but my passion for Bond would continue through the four Pierce Brosnan films, and then the Daniel Craig efforts, that actor, despite early misgivings, proving himself to be a *really* close second to Connery. My interviews with various people involved with the films, both from the past and in the present, continued, and I even developed a fun rapport with Michael Wilson, stemming from a comment I made to him on *GoldenEye* regarding the fact it felt like it was going to be pretty radically different from what had come before.

"It's not like the bad guy has a scar," I said, to which he replied, "Well, he *does* have a scar." "Okay, but it's not like there's a countdown to destruction at the end," resulting in a sigh and him noting, "There *is* a countdown." At that point, he let out a chuckle and said to no one in particular, "I'm trying to tell this guy how different the movie is, and it's not working out so well." That joke continued over the next couple of films. Then, when *Skyfall* was opening, I was doing a phone interview with him and said, "C'mon, Michael. Make me a happy man. Tell me I've got my gun barrel back at the beginning of the film." "Ed," he said, "you're *not* going to be a happy man," which led to him telling me why there was no gun barrel sequence. I'm *still* not happy about it.

Cowriting *Nobody Does It Better* with Mark has been an amazing experience, and, fueled by our mutual lifelong passion for 007, the definition of a labor of love. As I approach my sixth decade of life, there's something comforting in knowing that the *James Bond* films are close to doing the same. Our journey together will continue.

Edward Gross
January 5, 2019

BOND, JAMES BOND

"The name is Bond, James Bond."

As Pierce Brosnan once famously remarked, "More men have walked on the moon than played James Bond." It's a staggering thing to consider when you realize that the character of James Bond has been with us for over six decades now. From the pages of Ian Fleming's original novels, written on a golden typewriter in his palatial Goldeneye retreat in Jamaica, to the nearly unwatchable live episode of CBS's *Climax Mystery Theater* adaptation of *Casino Royale* to the ongoing and wildly successful film series, James Bond is as familiar a staple of popular culture as such legendary fictional characters as Sherlock Holmes, Captain Nemo, Jay Gatsby, or Luke Skywalker. Ask virtually anyone around the globe who James Bond is and they'll likely be able to tell you he's 007, a British secret service agent with a license to kill, and has done so on numerous occasions . . . or an ornithologist. Either answer is perfectly acceptable.

With 24 official James Bond films produced to date, with more on the way, the franchise shows no sign of slowing down anytime soon. Bond is a character who has captured the imagination of millions and is likely to continue to do so for the foreseeable future.

PHIL NOBILE, JR.

(columnist, *Birth. Movies. Death.*)

Ian Fleming created this avatar of his imagined self who was free of all the things that were swirling around the author and threatening to tie him down forever: stability, loved ones, middle age. In serving the panicked middle-aged man inside himself, Fleming ended up creating a fantasy for an entire generation of postwar 40-somethings who were starting to, in their own minds, outlive their usefulness.

RAYMOND BENSON

(author, *The James Bond Bedside Companion*)

In America, I think most—certainly not all—Bond fans discovered the character through the films. The books were not bestsellers in the US until then-President John F. Kennedy professed liking them, and *Playboy* magazine began to publish Fleming's short stories and serialize his novels. These events in 1960–61 kick-started Bond.

PIERCE BROSNAN

(actor, "James Bond")

Barbara Broccoli gave me a black leather-bound first edition of *Casino Royale*. I read the first chapter, and it's really Bond at the casinos playing, going back to his hotel room, checking to see if the hair he placed in the door was still there and undisturbed. And just as he's falling asleep, he puts his hand under the pillow for the revolver, and the last sentence is, "His face goes into repose. Brutal. Cold." It's good writing. Fleming put things down well; he could turn a phrase. Bond is just the ultimate hero to play, but he's complex enough to keep it interesting. He has enough demons there that he just sits on the whole time, because he *can't* let them out.

TIMOTHY DALTON

(actor, "James Bond")

I always have a very fond memory for *Casino Royale*. That is the first book. It's probably the one that's most evocative of Bond, because it was the one in which he was setting out Bond himself. Once the character was established, the sense of who the man was, was taken for granted, and he concentrated on the stories.

RAYMOND BENSON

I read all the Fleming books at age nine, ten, and eleven, reread them later when I was older, and continue to reread them. My favorite is *From Russia with Love*, but if I had to name some additional favorites, they would be *Dr. No, On Her Majesty's Secret Service, You Only Live Twice, Thunderball*, and *Live and Let Die*.

CHRISTIAN SLATER
(actor, *Mr. Robot*)

Ian Fleming created something very, very special. I remember the first time I saw *Dr. No* and *Thunderball* and all those movies. I was blown away with just how cool, how smooth, and just how amazing a character he was and still is today.

RALPH WINTER
(producer, *Planet of the Apes*)

I *love* the *Bond* movies. The Fleming novels were being passed around when I was in junior high, so we were reading them at the same time the movies were coming out. We devoured *Dr. No* and all those movies as kids. It's just iconic, something you grow up with, like The Beatles. Just that music when it comes on brings back all those feelings as a kid and the excitement of going to the movies and enjoying what they do.

JOHN GLEN
(director, *For Your Eyes Only*)

One of the great beauties about *James Bond* is its history. Audiences expect certain things from a *Bond* movie and you've got to give it to them. You've got to have an exciting sequence and then you've got to have something funny at the end to make people laugh, to get rid of all the tension, and that's part of the art of thrilling people.

ROBERT RODRIGUEZ
(director, *Spy Kids*)

I love *James Bond* movies.

ROAR UTHAUG
(director, *Tomb Raider*)

James Bond was a big influence on me growing up, as well as *Raiders of the Lost Ark* and the early *Alien* movies. I used to watch a lot of *Bond* movies.

GUY HAMILTON
(director, *Goldfinger*)

One thing which I don't think the critics have ever really picked up is that it's no accident that Mr. Big is always a millionaire. You never get Bond going down dark alleys looking for villains. He's always in the lap of luxury; he's always going to exotic places, which takes the audience into marvelous realms.

You don't go down the back streets of Los Angeles; we were always looking for the bizarre, the strange, the sort of thing that you're not likely to encounter every day of the week. Bond doesn't find a girl in a bedroom per se; it's got to be a bedroom that has piranha fish stuck in the wall or something of that nature.

RONALD D. MOORE

(cowriter, *Mission: Impossible II*)

James Bond just defines cool. Even if you haven't seen the movies, you accept it in pop culture that James Bond just lives in that space. It's almost like John Wayne. You know what John Wayne embodies and represents in the American idea of itself. You accept that idea of American masculinity and strength and what we thought of ourselves at a certain period of time.

JOHN GLEN

As a character, Bond is a very strong man. He's also a man with a lot of depth, a man that doesn't let his feelings be known easily. He's suffered a great deal in his personal relationships in the past because of his work. I think in a lot of ways he despises himself in what he has to do. But he has a charm and has panache and tongue-in-cheek humor. He's a man that is able to adapt very quickly. He's a very resourceful person, obviously.

RONALD D. MOORE

"Bond, James Bond." Sean Connery says it so effortlessly. You don't have a sense that he's trying to establish a catchphrase, you know? It's done with such aplomb and is instantly iconic. It's so weird, because, literally, every other actor playing that part has to pay homage to Sean Connery's delivery of one line, because it's really *not* the line. It's the way Connery delivers that line that became this . . . thing.

PHIL NOBILE, JR.

Slice it any way you like; without Sean Connery there's no franchise. He reinvented the British male for cinema, and he essentially originated the pithy, one-liner-spouting action hero.

BÉRÉNICE MARLOHE

(actress, "Sévérine," *Skyfall*)

James Bond really can be like one of the ideal fantasies, for a male or for a female, because it's larger than life. To me, I like that. He's like a superhero, but with no superpower, but with his gadgets, which is more fun because you can really identify with him and have those gadgets, too, if you could get them.

GUY HAMILTON

I think the imitators died out because they believed that gimmicks was a means to itself, and it isn't really. To me, *Bond* is much more *The Perils of Pauline,* which has been the best of movies since they started. Adventure, excitement, suspense, and identification with the hero.

JOHN LANDIS

(director, *Spies Like Us*)

I was born in 1950, so I was a teenager when the first *Bond*s came out. They were huge movies. I really enjoyed them, especially the early ones. *Dr. No* is really fun with the Chinese villain played by Joseph Wiseman. Actors from the Yiddish theater always played great villains, like Paul Muni as Scarface.

RICHARD SCHENKMAN

(editor, *Bondage* magazine)

Like every person alive in the '60s, even though I was a young boy, I was aware of James Bond and the *James Bond* films from popular culture—*Life* magazine, newspaper articles, TV specials, toys in stores, and glimpses of my father's *Playboy* magazines. I even had a *James Bond* attaché case toy, which I played with vigorously in my backyard.

TERRENCE MCDONNELL

(writer, *James Bond Jr.*)

As a high school freshman I began reading *Live and Let Die*, quickly followed by *From Russia with Love*, and then the rest of them one after the other. I couldn't read them fast enough. I loved the whole concept of Bond: how deadly he could be, the exotic locations, the fast, high-end lifestyle, the bigger-than-life characters, and the great, imaginative plotting that the Ian Fleming books provided. I'd even buy *Playboy* magazine and sneak them into the house in order to read the latest short stories from Fleming that the magazine would publish from time to time. That's right. I actually read the magazine for the *articles*. Well, mostly. And I was at the Fairview Theater—in my hometown of Fairview Park, Ohio—one Wednesday night when *Dr. No* made its US debut, then was back again to see it the next night and several more times that week. Couldn't get enough of it.

RAYMOND BENSON

Dr. No appeared in 1963, six months after the UK release. There was a snowball effect that occurred with the second film, and then, of course, *Goldfinger* became what I feel is the most influential film—from a pop culture standpoint—of the 1960s.

RIC MEYERS

(author, *For One Week Only: The World of Exploitation Films*)

Dr. No transported me to a place where a man could be smart, strong, and superior. It was a sordid, exciting, adventurous world with danger, excitement, and power. It was everything I had been reading in mystery, science fiction, and pulp thrillers come to vivid life. I was in love.

RAYMOND BENSON

At the ripe age of nine, my father took me to see *Goldfinger*, and I know it sounds cliché, but it changed my life. I immediately wanted to read the books—which were in plentiful display everywhere you looked as those early colorful Signet paperbacks. The first one I read was *Dr. No*—prior to my seeing the film, which I did just a few months after seeing *Goldfinger* (the re-release double bill of the first two films). The Bonds were the *Star Wars* of the 1960s, so naturally every kid—especially male ones—was attracted to them. They were big, glamorous, cool as hell, and sexy. That last bit was an ingredient we couldn't ignore!

FRED DEKKER

(director, *The Monster Squad*)

It was a new kind of heroism. There were still Westerns when I was a little kid. I didn't really watch them much, but I understood that notion of what machismo was in movies and TV. This was different, because James Bond was so elegant and refined. There was also something that was aspirational about Bond. He always looked good and he always had a great suit. He was unflappable—and when he was flapped, you really felt, "Oh, shit, how's he going to get out of this?" Like when he's on Goldfinger's laser table.

JOHN GLEN

Cubby Broccoli's favorite scene was the laser sequence in *Goldfinger*. Where he says, "I suppose you want me to talk," and he says, "No, Mr. Bond, I want you to die." That was the scene that Cubby loved.

JEFF KLEEMAN

(executive vice president of production, United Artists)

Goldfinger is the movie that solidified what the most signature aspects of a *Bond* film are. It brought them together, maybe better than any other has before or since. If there's a bible for what a *Bond* movie is, *Goldfinger* is as close to that bible as you get.

JOHN LANDIS

Goldfinger actually is the one that I enjoy the most because it's so silly.

TOM MANKIEWICZ

(writer, *Live and Let Die*)

James Bond movies rise or fall not on the huge psychodynamics of the movie, but the moments that people remember. The one-liners. The spots he's caught in. And the gadgets.

ROBERT RODRIGUEZ

The incredible gadgets, the inventive action. It really made an impact, and just about all my movies are filled with cool gadgets. *Spy Kids, Desperado, Machete*; even *From Dusk Till Dawn* is full of neat gadgets and gags, very much a product of the *Bond* movies' influence on me from an early age.

JOHN LANDIS

I love the fascination with hardware. You can see a big close-up of a digital watch; the gadgetry in Bond is like *Star Trek* or *Dick Tracy.* We don't think twice about it now. You don't remember the first time you ever saw GPS was Bond tracking Goldfinger's car.

GUY HAMILTON

You always have to keep a solid foot in reality. Bond is always playing with things that are just conceivably possible. We played with a laser beam when nobody had yet found a use for it. You must never go into things that don't exist.

RICHARD MAIBAUM

(cowriter, *Dr. No*)

We objected to the way that Fleming had it. He had Bond put on a circular saw which was supposed to cut him in half. We thought that was *The Perils of Pauline*, so we came up with the laser beam. And then later, in *Diamonds Are Forever*, we found out during research that the first laser beam had been projected not through a ruby, but through a diamond, and that's how we got the diamond satellite in the sky idea that projected the beam.

ROBERT RODRIGUEZ

The first *Bond* I saw in a theater was *The Spy Who Loved Me.*

JEFF KLEEMAN

When I saw *The Spy Who Loved Me,* there was the Jet Ski, which was something I had never heard of before in my life. But six months after the movie came out, there were Jet Skis actually being marketed and sold. It made me believe that the best *Bond* gadget, as we learned to phrase it, is 30 seconds into the future. It's not ten years away or five years away, it's a gadget that feels exciting and fresh to you. That you could imagine that maybe in six months might be around, which is why the invisible car in *Die Another Day* doesn't work for me. *The Spy Who Loved Me* taught me about what makes a great *Bond* gadget versus what doesn't. When I saw the invisible car, I didn't think in six months those are going to be available in showrooms.

MATT SHERMAN

(creator, BondFanEvents.com)

It's a crazy thing. The first film I can ever recall seeing on television was *Goldfinger.* I was five years old and the family hushed quietly to watch Bond on TV. I still remember that as the film started, I watched a gold hand and body appear on screen with mysterious figures moving over their surfaces. The film was shown out of sequence by ABC Television, eliminating the title sequence as too violent for television with its electrocution scene, so we started with the titles set to song.

JOHN CORK

(film historian; author, *James Bond: The Legacy*)

My first introduction to James Bond, which did not make me a fan, was in the summer of 1965, the rerelease of *Dr. No* and *From Russia with Love.* I went and saw it with my mother, at a place called the Capri Theater in Montgomery, Alabama. I remember only one thing from that, and that was the water catching on fire at the end of *From Russia with Love.* I turned to my mother and asked her how come the water was burning and she told me, "Well, James Bond leaves gasoline all over the water, and he lit the gasoline on fire, and it's the gasoline that's burning." I remember that and this moment of feeling like that's so cool and smart.

But it wasn't until *Live and Let Die* came out in the summer of 1973 when I was 11 years old that a friend of mine and I got on our bicycles, and it was the first time I ever rode my bicycle to see a movie. We saw that movie, and that's when I became a James Bond fan.

RICHARD SCHENKMAN

My parents felt I was too young to see the films, so I didn't actually get to see one until a summer rerelease of *You Only Live Twice,* which I got to see on a rainy day, thanks to the sleepaway camp I attended in Fleischmanns, New York. That made me a fan for life. A couple of years later, in the run-up to the release of *Diamonds Are Forever,* they were rereleasing all of the films in double features, so I got to catch up on the entire series in very short order. Meanwhile, my friend Bob Forlini was a longtime fan who had read all the books, so he lent me his collection and I read them all, in order, over the course of that summer in sleepaway camp. I just inhaled them. I always thought that because I consumed all the movies and all the books at virtually the same time, it affected the kind of *Bond* fan I became.

JEREMY DUNS
(author, *Rogue Royale*)

There was a kind of hype about a comeback when *GoldenEye* came out, and Pierce Brosnan finally got the job, and that contributed largely to that film's success. So I went to see *GoldenEye*, and that's probably when I became more of a *Bond* film fan.

S
(sound editor, *Die Spy Kill Kill*)

Bond movies struck a certain narrative formula that made them the longest-running film series in the world for a reason. There were several trademark things that you only really got from *Bond* films. He was never just an action star; he'd use charm and wit as he dispatched goons in often hilarious ways. Early *Bonds* had a lot of detective work in them as well. He wasn't just handed the villain on a platter all the time.

FRED DEKKER

I think there are five great Bond movies and all the other ones are trying to capture whatever they have: *Dr. No, From Russia with Love, Goldfinger, On Her Majesty's Secret Service*, and *Casino Royale*. All the rest of them, as much as I love them, some more than others, are all are trying to capture some element of one or all of those five.

DANIEL CRAIG
(actor, "James Bond")

Director Marc Forster and I had a long conversation when he came on to do *Quantum of Solace*. We're both big fans of the early *Bonds*, but also of the movies that they spawned in the '60s. They had a direct effect on movies all over. One of the biggest things that the early *Bond* movies did was to go on location. That was unusual at the time. If they were Hollywood movies, usually they shot on a back lot and created sets, which were beautifully done, but when Bond went to Japan, it was shot in Japan.

JEFF KLEEMAN

I really loved *You Only Live Twice* and I attribute a lot of that to writer Roald Dahl, rightly or wrongly, because I felt like it pushed the envelope in some ways of what a *Bond* movie could be.

FRED DEKKER

It's affected my aesthetic about architecture, interest in Japan and Asia, and then the more obvious stuff, which is everything that *Bond* is. It so rocked my world that I've never been the same since.

S

You Only Live Twice was my first *Bond*, and I still love it to absolute bits.

TOM MANKIEWICZ

At the time *Diamonds Are Forever* and *Live and Let Die* were being made, *Bond* movies were *the* event. Then you had the *Raiders of the Lost Arks* and the *Star Wars*, and *Bond* had to compete on a different level.

E
(editor, *Die Spy Kill Kill*)

I've got a soft spot for *Octopussy* . . . and *The Spy Who Loved Me* is one of the best as well. *GoldenEye* is the best modern *Bond* film.

ROBERT RODRIGUEZ

My favorite *Bonds* are *From Russia with Love, Goldfinger, Thunderball, The Spy Who Loved Me*, the opening scene of *Moonraker, For Your Eyes Only, GoldenEye*, and *Casino Royale*.

S

As much as I love *Casino Royale* and have it in the top five, the Daniel Craig films after that one have just lost the magic touch for me.

TOM MANKIEWICZ

James Bond started as a kind of a tough-ass secret agent, then the pictures became, as I say, pieces of entertainment. Then they lapsed into almost being like Disney films, where it was all special effects and so on. The hard narrative was gone with *Moonraker*. Then they tried to get back to a tougher *Bond*.

S

Bond presents a certain wish fulfillment for people about either a guy they'd like to be or be with, but there are loads of movies that do that. I think the main draw was that, much like a beloved TV show, you knew the formula and knew what you were going to get would be reliably entertaining. And that formula saw *Bond* comfortably through right up to around *Licence to Kill*, where they started experimenting a lot more, for better or worse.

TIMOTHY DALTON

Every story is a different story and different from the other, in terms of both style and content. For example, *Dr. No* and *Moonraker*. How would you compare *From Russia with Love* to *A View to a Kill*? I think the valuable question to ask is did you enjoy your two hours in the movie theater?

RICHARD SCHENKMAN

I just thought he was the coolest guy. I loved the witty repartee, I loved the gadgets, the fights, and just how slick, confident, and smart Bond was. And from the books I loved his self-destructive streak, the toll that his work took on him, and the gritty realism of the earlier books especially. And I loved the sex. For example, getting to run a finger over an erect nipple—something Bond did pretty frequently in the books—was well in my future, but I sure liked how it felt to read about it.

CHARLES ARDAI

(editor, Hard Case Crime)

In the books, Bond is a rather unlikable fellow: bitter, angry, violent. The filmmakers had to retain the violence while amping up the man's charisma and appeal. Somehow he had to enter the chrysalis of adaptation and emerge as Sean Connery. Not a small transformation.

PHIL NOBILE, JR.

1962's *Dr. No* offers lo-fi, smaller stakes than you might expect from a movie that launched a 55-year film series, but Connery was never better in the role than he is here. Thirty-two years old, all sex and danger, Connery immolates the then-stereotype of the wan, prim-and-proper British film hero, invents the action star and maybe the action genre, and changes film history forever. The early *Bond* films are glossy, old-school bits of cool, their budgets doubling and tripling with each successive entry, their plots growing more and more outlandish to match, but at the center of each is Sean Connery's absolute sea change of a protagonist, a predator in a dinner jacket, too cool for any room in the world.

FRED DEKKER

Even as an eight-year-old, I knew that Sean Connery was a movie star. It was the first time I looked at somebody on-screen and then wanted to act like them out in the street when I left the theater. I think that was the generation that idolized Connery Bonds as the male role model.

JOHN CORK

Because the last three *Bond* novels were written after Connery was cast as 007, Fleming made minor concessions to Connery's Bond. He gave 007 a Scottish background, for example. But just as importantly, [director] Terence Young was devoted to transforming Fleming's Bond into a cinematic character. That involved some changes, but Young and Connery captured the elegance, humor, irony, and brutality of Fleming's writing with Connery's performance.

ARMYAN BERNSTEIN
(producer, *Spy Game*)

A friend told me a story about how he was with Sean Connery when he was visiting Los Angeles and had locked himself out of his apartment. Instead of asking the building manager to open the door to his condo, Sean climbed outside on a balcony and jumped from one balcony to the next, four floors up, until he got to his apartment. He could've just gotten the key, but that wasn't Sean. He *was* James Bond.

WOODY ALLEN
(director, *Annie Hall*)

I was aware of James Bond. I saw the first picture, *Dr. No,* but unlike friends of mine, I had no interest in it or James Bond after it. I may have seen one more

James Bond picture, perhaps marooned somewhere in a foreign city with no movies to go to. But I'm not a *James Bond* fan, never have been. After *Dr. No,* I may have seen one more of the pictures under duress, but I don't go see them because I'm not interested. I did have dinner and play cards with Sean Connery, whom I liked very much. I found him to be a charming, lovely guy, and a fabulous actor in other pictures. But I never had any interest in *James Bond* movies.

YAPHET KOTTO

(actor, "Kanaga/Mr. Big," *Live and Let Die*)

Most of my favorite *Bond* pictures are all Sean Connery films. It was there in all of the movies that Connery did. It's always there with him. Even in *Never Say Never Again,* it's there. He *is* James Bond.

JOHN GLEN

Sean had a bit of a grievance against the *Bond*s for some reason, and yet he was fantastic as Bond. It made him. He set the standard, without a doubt.

ROBERT SELLERS

There are conflicting stories about Connery's attitude regarding accepting the role of James Bond. He has said it was like a car fanatic being given a brand-new Jaguar car; then there are reports that he took advice from his wife-to-be Diane Cilento, a serious and acclaimed actress, about whether or not he should accept the part.

CHRISTIAN SLATER

I got to work with Sean Connery when I was a kid. I did *The Name of the Rose* with him, and I worked with him again on *Robin Hood: Prince of Thieves* when he played the king. So I've always been pretty much awestruck in his presence and found him to be a phenomenal guy. To get the chance to work with James Bond was quite thrilling.

ALBERT R. BROCCOLI

Ian Fleming is responsible for what we put on the screen. Harry Saltzman and myself, when we first started—being Americans—saw Bond as a more macho kind of guy and yet he had to be British. We were very lucky in finding the type we thought Americans would like as Bond when we came across Sean. When I first met him, it was at a cocktail party, and he appealed to me as a very natural type. We thought he would be good for it.

JOHN LANDIS

[Director] Terence Young was the one who took Connery to his tailor on Savile Row. This whole snobbery was from the books, but they're not very good books. It was like *Playboy* magazine. This false sense of class. He had to have the best of everything: the best cars, the best girls, the best clothes, the best drink.

RICHARD SCHENKMAN

I'm hardly the first person to theorize that one's favorite Bond is directly linked to the actor who was playing Bond when you were first exposed to the character. . . . I mean, we all love the music of our early teen years, no matter how terrible it may have been. Having said that, my favorite Bond remains Sean Connery. Crucially, Connery had a strength and swagger that suited the character. He was physically imposing; you felt that if he hit you, you'd stay down, movie magic or no. The sparkle in his eye sold the humor, but he was deadly serious when the moment called for it, and indeed some of my favorite Connery scenes included the visible transition, as the character realized this was not a time for jokes.

ALBERT R. BROCCOLI

When Sean left our office, and walked across the street, we knew from the way he walked and the way he talked that he was the best possibility. And we presented him to United Artists at that time, for pictures and tests, which, actually, he didn't want to do, so we tricked him. We told him we were testing some of the girls when we tested him. United Artists said, "Well, you'd better try somebody else," and, of course, we didn't. We said, "No, we're going to do it with this fellow." Later on, Fleming said, when he met him, "I don't think he's right." Then, after talking to him for a while, he said, "I like him, he'll do."

JOHN CORK

George Lazenby looked the part, had the arrogance, had the charm, had the physicality, but his weakness was that he wasn't an actor. He fell victim to playing the part of an actor playing James Bond. He figured out exactly how to act to get the role, but that is very different than knowing how to act in the role.

MATT GOURLEY

(cohost, *James Bonding* podcast)

I remember as a kid specifically getting the VHS of *On Her Majesty's Secret Service* and watching it on home video. This guy's being called Bond throughout, and it took me half the movie to realize that Connery or Moore wasn't showing up in this one, that this guy *was* James Bond. Even my dad didn't really remember it. We're like, "Is he, like, an impostor? They're doing an imposter for a bit and then Connery will come out and kill him?" Then realizing, "Oh, no. This guy played Bond one time."

PHIL NOBILE, JR.

Someone had to be George Lazenby. Had Moore taken over from Connery, Moore might have been the one-and-done. Let's be honest: Lazenby was never going to succeed, at least not in the public's mind. Sean Connery owned the role, becoming a household name over the course of five *Bond* films between 1962 and 1967. The franchise made him a star, but he had grown bored of the part and resentful of the piles of money he was making the producers. When he split, Eon Productions forged ahead, convinced that the franchise was bigger than just one actor. They weren't wrong, but this kind of seismic shift couldn't help but have casualties, and George Lazenby was on the front line. Lazenby's one-and-done turn awoke audiences to the idea that the role could and would be recast, opening the door for Roger Moore and the others. But someone had to go through that door first, and that person was always going to take the bullet. Saint George of Lazenby laid down his life as Bond so that the series might live.

JEFF KLEEMAN

Each actor who's taken on Bond successfully has brought a slightly different kind of Bond to the screen. And that's one of the tricks when you move an actor into an established role, which is how do you tailor the role to the new actor while still keeping the role recognizably the role?

GEORGE LAZENBY

(actor, "James Bond")

I can't believe I got James Bond. Never acted before and had never been an actor. I guess that made me more sure of myself. I'm happy because I've had a great life. I went up motocross racing and doing stupid things that people who aren't concerned with acting do. I have great kids and had a lot of fun hanging around the edges of things. If I wanted to work as an actor, I could've worked a lot. But I found that a lot of time, actors just hang around. And I like to do things.

LEWIS GILBERT

(director, *The Spy Who Loved Me*)

Roger Moore is a totally different person from Sean Connery. I directed Sean in *You Only Live Twice* and they'd already made five by then. He really wasn't very much like Ian Fleming described Bond. I think Sean played Bond in his own image. It's like Charlton Heston playing Moses, and I think it was true of Sean Connery's Bond. When Roger came, he didn't try to play Fleming's Bond, he was always forced to play Connery's Bond. I think this was something of a mistake.

ALBERT R. BROCCOLI

Ian's concept of Bond was, in fact, Roger Moore: the school tie, Etonian type.

SIR ROGER MOORE

(actor, "James Bond")

It's very difficult to get in touch with the character by reading Fleming, because there's very little about the person that Bond is, only what he's doing. I sort of did a quick shifting through all the books to try and find out what he was like. I only found one thing and that was that he had a scar on his cheek and looked like Hoagy Carmichael. The only other key to the character was that he had come back from Mexico, where he had eliminated somebody. He didn't particularly like killing, but he took pride in doing his job well. That was the only thing I could find out about Bond. That I don't like killing, but I'm pleased that I do it well.

JOHN CORK

Roger Moore came to Bond with a huge advantage. The world already saw him as a James Bond type. He came with a leading-man persona. Character actors play parts. Leading men play themselves playing a part. Roger Moore made James Bond his own by making James Bond into Roger Moore. And the world was completely ready to see James Bond morph into Roger Moore.

RICHARD SCHENKMAN

Roger was a legendarily charming man; he was so aware of his effect on people that he was perfectly willing—and able—to mock it. He was funny and bright and warm and never took anything seriously.

JOHN LANDIS

I think Roger's attitude was that being a double-O was a job. He would do what was required. He had that wonderful kind of eyebrow thing, where he was almost too good for it. If there were some fiery pit of hell, he would just eventually step over it. He was so elegant. Connery's was a muscleman, and he's dirty and interesting, but not anything like the literary James Bond.

SIR ROGER MOORE

Every time I opened my mouth, someone would ask me what it was like following Sean, and I would just answer, four hundred actors played Hamlet. I always played heroes because I'm six-foot-one-and-a-half, but I never really believed I was a hero, so I always played things tongue in cheek.

PHIL NOBILE, JR.

Even though he's the Bond I "grew up with," my adult self didn't initially take to Moore, and I had to sort of relearn an appreciation of him. Taking him in context, what's refreshing about Moore is that he embraced the role in a way that no other actor seemed to, enjoying the association long after he'd hung up his Walther.

LISA FUNNELL

(author, *For His Eyes Only–The Women of James Bond: Critical Perspectives on Feminism and Femininity in the Bond Franchise*)

Roger Moore was the best brand ambassador for James Bond, because he embraced it and he embraced his fans. You always hear don't meet your heroes, but he was somebody that you would be happy to meet with because he loved being James Bond.

JOHN CORK

I enjoy all the *Bond* actors, even David Niven [in 1967's *Casino Royale*], but Moore needs no carefully lit Connery-style close-ups like Lazenby, no Spielbergian track-in reveals like Dalton, no punch-up introductions like Brosnan or Craig. He is the only Bond, aside from Niven, introduced by his own comic shtick. His performance can best be summed up by his last line in *Live and Let Die*: "Just being disarming, darling."

CHARLES "JERRY" JUROE

(director of publicity, *Octopussy*)

Roger Moore was the prototype of the successful movie actor. He literally wrote the book on how to get along with the public and the press. As long as things were going great, he was great, and he would do almost anything asked of him. He was cooperative to a fault, and he was basically a nice guy, but at heart, he was an actor, and actors aren't like the rest of us. I spent my life around actors, and there are very few that you can say are basically like regular people. It's part of being an actor not to be that way. That doesn't mean they can't be nice and friendly, and absolutely great, but you never know when they're going to turn. As long as you pet them right, and rub their tummy, they're great, but they can turn and snap any minute.

DESMOND LLEWELYN

(actor, "Q")

Roger Moore had the light Bond touch everyone loved, but I think a great deal of who you liked best had to do with whichever Bond you saw first. That sort of fixes in your mind what Bond is. Luckily, when Roger took it on, he made it a completely different Bond, so you couldn't really compare them. Even if you didn't like him, you certainly accepted him and said, "These are bloody good films, but he's not my idea of Bond."

SHANE RIMMER

(actor, "Commander Carter," *The Spy Who Loved Me*)

Roger loved people. He was a great mixer and he enjoyed the business. He had this face that directors loved.

TANYA ROBERTS

(actress, "Stacey Sutton," *A View to a Kill*)

Roger was great at what he did. He really had the Bond character down and he was lovely and always had a joke. He was always in a good mood. I have to say he was one of those kinds of people who was really a total pro and always very positive.

JOHN GLEN

Humor is a great thing about those films, and it's really been the humor that sustained the series over the years, because the spy situation with the Cold War as we knew it was ending.

JOHN CORK

Unlike Connery, one never gets the sense that sex is an animal passion for Moore. It is, instead, a sport that he casually enjoys more for the amusement than the physical pleasure. If Moore's Bond were asked to rank the perks of his job, one could imagine that "I get to have casual sex with numerous beautiful women" would fall somewhat lower than "I get to be a smart-ass."

PHIL NOBILE, JR.

In an era when successfully recasting an iconic role was not a foregone conclusion, Moore's assumption and transformation of the character was indeed an accomplishment, and his mischievous, easygoing manner helped cement the "unflappable playboy" trademark of the cinematic Bond for an entire generation.

RICHARD MAIBAUM

Roger's personality made us take a lighter touch to it. It couldn't have been any other way. That was very good from a commercial standpoint, because Roger's pictures did better than Sean's financially. People in the world loved them, but, as I say, the joke was growing a little tired and it was time to look for other values in the "*Bond* saga."

CAREY LOWELL

(actress, "Pam Bouvier," *Licence to Kill*)

I thought Timothy Dalton was refreshing after Roger Moore because he brought a new humanity to Bond—this is a real person who could have been. Roger was a bit more stylized, he was more of a cartoon character, because he was playing Bond as somebody who could always skate through these dangerous spots unscathed. The situations Dalton's Bond faced are more probable than somebody who wanted to blow up the Earth or wants to stimulate the San Andreas fault and destroy Silicon Valley. It's more realistic and that's more appealing, because the suspension of disbelief doesn't have to be so broad. I think audiences want to go to the movies to be entertained, but they also want to be entertained by a realistic point of view.

MARYAM D'ABO

(actress, "Kara Milovy," *The Living Daylights*)

The books are quite serious. Timothy Dalton wanted to go back to the books. Be a more serious Bond. I think Tim came at a wrong time, since the audience was expecting much more of the humor.

MICHAEL G. WILSON

(cowriter, *The Living Daylights*)

You always want to do something where there will be some surprise. The problem with any sequel or series is meeting that criterion. Roger Moore's talents and abilities worked better in the more humorous and fantastic style. Timothy Dalton's talent worked best in a different style.

JOHN CORK

Timothy Dalton brought 007 back to Fleming. He understood the literary Bond very well, and having met Dalton on a couple of occasions, he is an immensely charming man. That charm does not follow him on-screen in his two *Bond* films. Whether through his own acting choices or via John Glen's directing, he becomes the world's angriest secret agent. At a time where Sylvester Stallone and Arnold Schwarzenegger were creating these hypermasculine heroes, Dalton brought a needed physicality to the role. You believed his Bond didn't need a stunt double.

JOHN GLEN

Timothy Dalton is quite a historian on the Bonds. He goes into great depth with the character—which a great actor always does. He doesn't take anything for granted in a sense, and he does question certain things and one has to give a good explanation of why you have them in the film. He tries to remain true to the Fleming tradition.

TIMOTHY DALTON

One is constantly reminded by Fleming, both from Bond himself and through the mouth of other characters, that Bond really is as bad as the bad guys. He is a killer, but he does have a moral sense of what good is. That throws him into conflict, because of his self-knowledge of who he is and what he does. He knows what he does . . . he's a killer.

RICHARD SCHENKMAN

I loved Timothy Dalton's serious, studied approach to the movies and I'll defend his films to the end, although again, if a "real" director had made them, they'd have been better movies. I deeply respected the way he dove into the source material and tried to play the Bond he found in the pages of Fleming's books.

PHIL NOBILE, JR.

Timothy Dalton is the best Bond actor to never get a great *Bond* film.

DESMOND LLEWELYN

He is a magnificent stage actor and a very good film actor. Every Bond is different, not an imitation of the other, and they are all excellent in their own way.

JEREMY DUNS

Part of the clever thing about them changing actors is that people get high on Bond again, everything becomes a huge success, and then, after a while, people tend to get a bit bored of it. And that definitely happened with the Sean era, Roger Moore, and then Dalton, and then you just got a sense that people were kind of losing interest in Bond and it was just a bit old-fashioned and a bit old hat.

ROBERT CAPLEN

(author, *Shaken & Stirred: The Feminism of James Bond*)

Timothy Dalton's serious, no-nonsense portrayal of Bond was refreshing after *A View to a Kill*, and I would have liked to see him in more films. But Pierce Brosnan, in my view, imbued the character with both Dalton-esque and Moore-esque qualities. Brosnan's whimsy was not as pronounced as Moore's, but he was much more subtle than Sean Connery.

JEFF KLEEMAN

[Writer] Bruce Feirstein and [director] Martin Campbell had a fantastic mind meld in the way they tailored this role to Pierce Brosnan. How do we really make it Pierce's in a way that's distinctive from Lazenby, from Dalton, from Connery, but still hopefully giving everybody a Bond that they say, "This is not Jason Bourne. This is James Bond"?

CHARLES "JERRY" JUROE

It turned out to Pierce's benefit that he didn't do *The Living Daylights* because of *Remington Steele* being renewed. I talked with Pierce about it at the premiere of *GoldenEye*, and he more or less smirked and agreed. He shrugged and said, "Yeah, you're right." He was still very young in 1986. A big difference between 1986 and 1994.

JEFF KLEEMAN

Martin Campbell actually had a list of mannerisms that he'd seen Pierce perfect during *Remington Steele* and in some of his feature work, that he decided he was going to make sure he eliminated, so that you never felt like you were watching the *Remington Steele* version of Pierce Brosnan.

JOHN CORK

Pierce Brosnan was an actor who was already seen as a James Bond–type figure by audiences. That was an important element that he brought, just like

Roger Moore. His absolutely stunning good looks attracted a lot of female fans back to Bond. I enjoyed his Bond, but my favorite performance as Bond by him was when he wasn't playing James Bond at all. It was when he was playing a character inspired by Bond: Osnard in *The Tailor of Panama*.

MATT GOURLEY

I like Pierce Brosnan as an actor quite a bit, but I knew him as *Remington Steele* in the same way that people probably knew Roger Moore as *The Saint*. For me personally, the films after *GoldenEye* just weren't for me. They seemed like too much of a rehash without bringing anything new. For me, the reason I take issue with the Brosnan run is not all that much to do with Brosnan. It's more to do with them kind of trying to strike a tone balance between Connery and Moore. But those things, those are oil and water to me. They don't work. The way they'd go campy and then ask you to believe in the sincerity of the darker moments were nose-bleedy to me. They would just jar me.

RICHARD SCHENKMAN

The Pierce Brosnan movies are such a mixed bag. The first few are great for an hour or so, and then they fall to hell. The later ones are pretty lousy from the beginning, but he's hardly the weak link, so it's unfair to blame him. He has charm to burn, he's intelligent, funny, and dexterous. If they had made a series of movies as good as the first hour of *GoldenEye*, they'd have really had something. As a piece of casting, I think he was actually a fine compromise between Connery and Moore, and just needed some better scripts and directors to support him.

JEFF KLEEMAN

[Writer] Bruce Feirstein gave Pierce a certain kind of elegance, wit, sophistication, and more self-awareness, to some degree, than previous Bonds had had. He had more willingness to occasionally call himself out. There was an exchange at one point in *Tomorrow Never Dies* where Michelle Yeoh was talking about having grown up in a tough neighborhood. And Bond's response was, "I never grew up at all."

MARYAM D'ABO

After 9/11, the world changed. And [producer] Barbara Broccoli was very clever, because she knew that. She knew she had to bring in a completely different Bond.

JOHN CORK

Daniel Craig reinvented Bond. He understands that it is much more important to play the façade of Bond than the emotion behind the dialogue in the script. He is physical, charming, driven, and a damn fine actor.

ROAR UTHAUG

I appreciate what they did with *Casino Royale* when they kind of rebooted the series. It's the same thing that [writer-director] Christopher Nolan did with the *Batman* movies. It took kind of this dark and more edgy turn.

RICHARD SCHENKMAN

I thought *Casino Royale* was spectacular—a brave and powerful reboot when, at least from a financial standpoint, the series was doing just fine. I really admired Barbara [Broccoli] and Michael's [G. Wilson's] choice to chuck it all out and start over, with a *real* actor, a *real* director, and a *real* screenplay.

JEREMY DUNS

No one was expecting it. People thought *Casino Royale* was just going to be another *James Bond* film with some blond guy they'd never heard of. They weren't expecting it to take James Bond to some places that you haven't seen James Bond before.

RONALD D. MOORE

Prior to this, you had to measure the other actors against Sean Connery. But Daniel Craig literally reinvented the role. Suddenly it was a different game, a different Bond, a different universe. I totally accepted him as Bond and didn't feel like it was a competition with Sean Connery anymore. He has a different vibe to him. He's a little more blue-collar than Sean was. He's more vulnerable in a lot of ways. He can be hurt. Daniel Craig definitely gets hurt. You feel his pain.

It's a similar thing to what Harrison Ford does. When Harrison Ford gets hurt on screen, you kind of feel it. Daniel Craig has that ability, too. It was the first time that Bond seemed vulnerable and could actually be hurt or killed. It was a very different take on the character and I really like it. To me, Connery and Craig are my two favorites, and they're just so different. But I can really accept them both and really love them both.

TANYA ROBERTS

I love Daniel Craig. He's my favorite Bond ever. I used to love Sean Connery, but Daniel Craig is my favorite. I love his looks, his craggy face; he's just terrific, and his body—he's really in outrageous shape. Unfortunately, Stacey Sutton could be his grandmother at this point.

MATT GOURLEY

Casino Royale is when *Bond* became truly interesting for me. Bond is not a role model. He's a psychopath, and he's a fascinating character to watch. When I say I'm a fan of the *Bond* films, I'm not a person who wants to dress like Bond and live like Bond. Actually that lifestyle kind of grosses me out a little bit, to be honest. But I want to watch this guy succeed, and I want to watch him fail. I want to watch him make mistakes. Daniel Craig has brought mistakes to this role that really reawaken the franchise, especially for me.

YAPHET KOTTO

There are some moments Daniel Craig has had that were good, but to me I don't see him as Bond. And the 60-year-olds and 70-year-olds are not crazy with the new style because they miss the humor.

MARYAM D'ABO

Everybody has their favorite James Bond. It's a generational thing that goes on, the ones that like Daniel Craig, don't like Roger Moore, for instance. But everybody brings something. Pierce brought his own lightness. And Daniel is very interesting, because the younger generation loves Daniel Craig. Daniel actually said in an interview that he wanted to go back to what Timothy had started as Bond.

RAYMOND BENSON

Most fans cite the first actor they ever saw on-screen as their favorite. That said, I felt Timothy Dalton encapsulated Fleming's literary Bond. You could say Daniel Craig is doing the same thing. The difference is that Dalton resembles Fleming's physical description of Bond. The literary character is cold, ruthless, hard, and mostly humorless. The humor of the novels is in the writing, in the omniscient observations by the author—not in the Bond character. Bond is a bit of a brooder. Dalton did that, and Craig, too.

JEFF KLEEMAN

[Director] Martin Campbell recognized that Daniel needed to be a very different kind of Bond, with a different kind of voice and a different kind of physicality. And so, there again, you see how the actor, in conjunction with a good director and good writing, can define a Bond.

FRED DEKKER

Here's my litmus test for Bonds: "Who do you think is the best Bond?" For me, if you put those guys in a room, who's going to be on the floor and who's going to walk out the door? Connery, Lazenby, and Craig are going to walk out the door. Those other guys are all going to be on the floor. Those are my three favorite Bonds.

RALPH WINTER

For years I thought Sean Connery was my favorite Bond, but I'll tell you something: I think Daniel Craig has taken over. He's just got the swagger, the attitude, but also a broader range of emotions than Sean Connery brought. Sean was definitely a bull in a china shop, and you can see a little more complexity to Bond with Daniel Craig. Personally, I'm going to have a tough time transitioning from Daniel Craig to somebody else.

THE ROAD TO BOND

"You seem to have this nasty habit of surviving."

"I was in holiday in Jamaica in January 1952 . . . and I think my mental hands were empty. . . . After being a bachelor for 44 years, I was on the edge of marrying and the prospect was so horrifying that I was in urgent need of some activity to take my mind off it. So, as I say, my mental hands were empty and although I am as lazy as most Englishmen are, I have a Puritanical dislike of idleness and a natural love of actions. So I decided to write a book."

Such was the mental state of Ian Lancaster Fleming in 1952 when he sat down to write what would become the first James Bond novel, *Casino Royale*. By that point, various chess pieces had already been put in motion, completely unaware of the fact that that action by Fleming—putting word to paper—would ultimately bring all of them together. Producer Albert R. Broccoli had formed Warwick Film Productions with Irving Allen, and they were prepping their first film, *The Red Beret*; future producer Harry Saltzman, together with Rhea Fink, formed the Mountie Enterprises Corporation (soon to be named Rider Amusement Corporation), whose purpose was to manage coin-operated hobby horses in department stores; Terence Young's sixth directorial effort, *The Frightened Bride,* was released; writer Richard Maibaum had written 19 films, with the 20th, *Paratrooper,* being released in 1953; Sean Connery had been a professional soccer player and bodybuilder en route to a career in acting; and Roger Moore, who had scored a number of uncredited film roles, was earning a living as a male model. For all of them, though, the word was "Bond," and Bond was Fleming.

JOHN CORK
(board member, The Ian Fleming Foundation)

I unashamedly love all the Ian Fleming *Bond* novels. Oh, I wince at the racism and the treatment of women, but that's present in virtually all the writing of the era. Fleming was a genius of a writer. You *want* to turn the page. He was often full of hot air, tossing out factoids that were almost true, dazzling you with his seeming depth of knowledge that frequently made real experts cringe. Yet the confidence in his writing wins over the reader. He can build a great paragraph that is both literary and easy to follow. He understands how to construct a chapter, build to a climax, pay off suspense. Reading each novel is like watching a good magic show filled with new tricks. He makes you care, he draws you in, and then he surprises the hell out of you.

RICHARD MAIBAUM
(cowriter, *Dr. No*)

I thought Fleming was a terrific writer, the best of that kind of adventure. I think he's great and I did read them whenever I was working on a script. I was surprised, always, when I went back to see how good they are.

TERENCE YOUNG
(director, *Dr. No*)

Ian was an intensely shy person, which never showed. I don't care what anybody says, he obviously had some wish fulfillment in James Bond; it was something he wished he could have done himself. I'm convinced there was an awful lot of Bond in his own makeup, but there is nobody who was James Bond in his life. Bond was how Fleming saw himself: the sardonic, cruel mouth; the hard, tight-skinned face. Ian was a charmer, though, once you got to know him. He was one of the most delightful people I ever met.

Fleming was born on May 28, 1908, in Mayfair, London, to a wealthy family consisting of his mother, Evelyn, and father, Valentine, who was a Member of Parliament for Henley beginning in 1910. He was also the grandson of Robert Fleming, a Scottish financier who founded the Scottish American Investment Trust as well as the merchant bank Robert Fleming & Co. The Fleming family also included an elder brother, named Peter, who became a travel writer; younger brothers Michael and Richard; and a maternal half-sister–Amaryllis Fleming–born out of wedlock. In 1921, he enrolled at Eton College.

TOM SOTER

(author, *Bond and Beyond: 007 and Other Special Agents*)

He was a poor scholar and a good athlete. He moved on briefly to Sandhurst Military Academy, but decided against the military life. From there, he went to Switzerland to study for the foreign service exam. Later, his mother obtained him a job at the Reuters News Service. Fleming had done some writing privately, and had always been obsessive with detail and had a lively imagination. He had also learned Russian for his foreign service exam, all of which came in handy in 1933 when Reuters sent him to cover a notorious trial of six British spies in Moscow.

STEVEN JAY RUBIN

(author, *The James Bond Films*)

They were accused of sabotage by the Soviet government. In dispatches that won him the respect of his fellow journalists, Fleming carefully avoided a mundane, blow-by-blow account of the trial and concentrated, instead, on the atmosphere surrounding the event and the strange personalities of the men who were making the news.

TOM SOTER

His account of the trial's climax caught the attention of the British public and earned the plaudits of his journalistic colleagues. It also brought him to the notice of the British Secret Service, which requested a secret report from him on the conditions of the Russian capital. His success could have led Fleming to a career in journalism, but his fear of poverty made him take what looked like a more lucrative and secure job as a stockbroker.

He spent 12 years as a stockbroker from 1933 to 45, though in between, during World War II, he was recruited by Rear Admiral John Godfrey, Director of Intelligence of the Royal Navy, to become his personal assistant. As such, he was able to develop plans designed to undermine the enemy while at the same time helping to coordinate strategies of espionage.

THOMAS CULL

(webmaster, *The Literary 007*)

Fleming had a "good war" and it provided him with tremendous inspiration for plots, characters, and even gadgets. His pivotal role as a liaison between

NID, SIS, and SOE meant he was privy to all manner of operations and key players, from naval directors such as Admiral Godfrey to female SOE agents, secretaries, and real-life "Q" Charles Fraser-Smith.

BRIAN LETT

(author, *Ian Fleming and SOE's Operation Postmaster: The Top Secret Story Behind 007*)

My personal view is that Ian Fleming was substantially influenced by the war years, and by what he learned about the early days of the Special Operations Executive [SOE]. As I say in my book, Fleming wrote to Major General Sir Colin Gubbins, head of SOE, after the war, asking him to write the stories of the various heroic agents and what they had done. Gubbins was prevented from doing so by the Official Secrets Act, so Fleming then walked a narrow line between fiction and fact with his *James Bond* stories. Ian Fleming's brother Peter had worked for SOE early in the war, and Ian himself was liaison officer between the Royal Navy and SOE in 1941 and 1942. He perfected the false cover story for Operation Postmaster.

JEREMY DUNS

(author, *The Dark Chronicles: A Spy Trilogy*)

Given Fleming's intelligence involvement in the war, Bond is kind of a composite of lots of commandos and special forces people and stories he'd heard about different operations. They became more glamorous and transformed into a loose plot, and you can see that particularly in *Casino Royale*.

TOM SOTER

One of Fleming's wartime experiences was to serve as the basis for *Casino Royale*. Traveling with Admiral Godfrey, Fleming stopped at a casino in Lisbon where Nazi intelligence leaders reportedly gambled. He decided he would try to beat the Nazis at cards, thereby depleting their secret service funds, which he imagined were being used for gambling. It's not clear whether the card players actually were Nazis, but it *was* clear that they beat Fleming—who only had 50 pounds anyway.

RAYMOND BENSON

(author, *The James Bond Bedside Companion*)

Fleming's experience in the war informed his writing immensely, especially with the first book, *Casino Royale,* in which he used some real events, albeit highly embellished. Being a journalist, he was already an excellent word craftsman, so he knew how to write. He could spin a good yarn. He was also influenced by the types of adventure stories he read as a child—Bulldog Drummond, the Sax Rohmer books—and thus the *Bond*s were not "realistic" in the sense, say, a John le Carré spy novel might be. The *Bond*s were more fantastic and imaginative—just as the films became.

JEREMY DUNS

Not a lot of people appreciate the fact that Fleming came from a privileged background, so it was very unusual for him to be interested in thrillers—but he was a thriller nut. He was also a member of a very exclusive gentleman's club in London where he would spend quite a lot of time sitting in an armchair reading cheap paperback thrillers. His family were bankers and war heroes, essentially. You had to be highbrow, you had to read literature, and Fleming also read literature and had pretentions in that area, but his guilty pleasure, if you like, was thrillers. He read *a lot* of American thrillers; he was into kind of hard-boiled stuff. He enjoyed going on trains and traveling around the place and just taking a paperback thriller with him, which he did for years. The result of this is that he knew a huge amount about the genre.

TOM SOTER

After the excitement and responsibility of the war, Fleming's civilian life seemed mundane. He drifted in and out of affairs with married women and became a foreign desk editor with *The Sunday Times* of London. He also bought a house in Jamaica, an island with which he became enchanted in the '40s. After the war, he often said he would retire there and write the spy novel to end all spy novels.

STEVEN JAY RUBIN

He was hired by newspaper magnate Lord Kemsley to manage the foreign news section of a large group of English papers. He took the job on condition that his contract included a two-month holiday each year.

> Fleming's journey toward James Bond began in earnest when he met and fell in love with a married woman named Ann Charteris, who, when she found herself pregnant with his child, divorced her husband and married Fleming–a marriage that ultimately led to him writing his first novel.

STEVEN JAY RUBIN

When his beach house, which he named Goldeneye, was completed, he began a routine—coming to Goldeneye to write—that was to continue until the end of his life and which produced 13 *James Bond* thrillers. He'd toyed with the idea of writing for nearly six years, but it wasn't until a few weeks before his marriage in 1952 that he decided to write a novel.

THOMAS CULL

In his formative years, he spent productive time with the writer Phyllis Bottome in the Austrian Alps, where he wrote some early short stories. There are many theories as to why he dove into writing *Bond* novels, but I think it was a mixture of escapism from his own life, an innate need to write, and a dash of commercial ambition which drove him.

STEVEN JAY RUBIN

Fleming took the name of his main character from the author of a book that always graced his coffee table, *Birds of the West Indies,* by the ornithologist James Bond.

> As Fleming told *Playboy,* "I wanted my hero to be entirely an anonymous instrument and to let the action of the book carry him along. I didn't believe in the heroic Bulldog Drummond types. I mean, rather, I didn't believe they could any longer exist in literature. I wanted this man more or less to follow the pattern of Raymond Chandler's or Dashiell Hammett's heroes—believable people, believable heroes."

JAMES O. NAREMORE

(editor, *North by Northwest: Alfred Hitchcock, Director*
Rutgers Films in Print Series)

The British tradition of spy fiction is a strong one, beginning prior to World War One with such writers as Henry James, Joseph Conrad, John Buchan, Somerset Maugham, and Erskine Childers (the last of whom was greatly admired by Ian Fleming). This was a period of growing conflict between European Imperialist states, when secret plots by spies created the possibility of mystery and suspense for writers. Maugham, who was a spy for Britain, could probably be described as the inventor of the "modern" spy story, which treats the work of spies ironically and raises implicit questions about the state apparatus. (See such later writers as Len Deighton and John le Carré.) Buchan, on the other hand, was a conservative who specialized in popular adventure. He influenced Hitchcock, Graham Greene, and Eric Ambler, mainly because his technique was understated and his protagonists were ordinary people who found themselves caught up in spy plots.

In the mid-1930s, spy fiction was embraced by Popular Front writers, the most important of whom was Ambler, and it became explicitly anti-fascist. Hitchcock, who adapted or worked with almost half the writers I've mentioned, doesn't explicitly refer to Nazi spies in his films until he gets to America at the beginning of World War Two. With the later Cold War, his evil spies are Russians or Commies, as in *Topaz* and *Torn Curtain*. In general, Hitchcock's spy pictures were distinctive because of his sense of humor and his sly jokes, and because he understood that spy fiction was a form of travel literature. In his films, an ordinary character becomes involved with derring-do—a suspenseful, spectacular chase that also has a quality of a tourist travelogue.

JAMES STRATTON

(author, *Hitchcock's North by Northwest: The Man Who Had Too Much*)

Greta Garbo's *Mata Hari* and Marlene Dietrich's *Dishonored* suggest many of the elements of these early spy films: exotic European locations, World War One time frames, beautiful but treacherous female spies, love interests controlling how the espionage works. Hitchcock used the genre as a frame for his own individual thematic interests, including mistaken identity, interrupted complacency, deception, victimization, betrayal, the violation of private space, the illusory stability of power, and the precariousness of public order. The mechanics of spying and the immediate strategic objective were beside the point. He brought stylistic complexity, visual depth, subtle humor, and freighted male-female interactions to the mix. Also, and I think this is a major point, Hitchcock saw espionage as a matter of social class; his villains (e.g., Alex Sebastian, Stephen Fisher, Phillip Vandamm) are wealthy, well-educated, upper-class patricians. Political espionage is a way of preserving their sense of privilege and control. The heroes who oppose them are more middle-class, more self-made, and less caught up by social conventions.

JAMES CHAPMAN

(author, *Hitchcock and the Spy Film*)

Fleming's *James Bond* books were an important transitional moment in the history of British spy fiction. They were the last of the old-fashioned sensational adventure thrillers in the Imperialist tradition of John Buchan and "Sapper" and at the same time, through the character of the professional spy, anticipated the more realistic work of John le Carré and Len Deighton. We tend to think of *Bond* as being about megalomaniac master criminals, and that's what the books *became*, but *Casino Royale* is a more realist-styled story featuring a double agent and internal treachery within the Secret Service that has some affinity with le Carré.

CHARLES ARDAI
(editor/founder, Hard Case Crime)

Despite being just as cruel and capable of violence as the villains around him, Bond puts his skills to use in the service of his employer—his country. And that makes all the difference in the world. He is helping preserve order, not to create chaos; the bloodshed he indulges in helps keep ordinary civilians safe. In this respect, he's like any other soldier, or like a cop, and that's certainly something he has in common with Philip Marlowe or Hammett's Continental Op. A detective in Chandler's formula is someone who walks the mean streets, but isn't himself mean. Well, Bond is pretty mean. But he's mean for a good cause. And that makes it possible for us to cheer for him. He's our representative in a dangerous, nasty world—like the big brother that keeps us safe from all those neighborhood bullies, with their razor-edged hats and so forth.

JEREMY DUNS

There's been a lot of assumption that the stuff that Fleming has done over the years is his creation, whereas, actually, a lot of this stuff existed already and he was just kind of going back to it, if you'd like. For example, you know the thing that *Austin Powers* parodied a lot where Bond is captured by a villain and the villain then reveals all his plans? That is something we definitely think of as a parody of *James Bond*, but when Fleming was doing this, it was *already* old hat. This was already something that had been parodied by Leslie Charteris in the *Saint* novels where, in the '30s, he had Simon Templar captured by a villain and the villain then says, "I expect you think that I'm going to give you a whole speech about feeding you to the alligators while telling you my whole plan. Well, I'm not going to do that. That's something that only happens in really bad thrillers."

THOMAS CULL

It's fair to say that *Casino Royale,* published in 1953, was a game-changer in the genre. Fleming's influences certainly came through in his writings, but he modernized some of these thriller conventions. In fact, the likes of Eric Ambler, Dennis Wheatley, and Hammond Innes still sold well in the early 1950s, and it wasn't until *From Russia with Love* that Fleming's *Bond* truly hit the zeitgeist. The "adventure thriller" was more popular, but Fleming's entry breathed new life into the "spy thriller," and Bond's arrival meant that Clubland British hero types quickly went out of fashion.

JEREMY DUNS

Another cliché found in Fleming that might seem obvious if you think about it—though many people don't—is in the movie version of *Goldfinger,* with the famous laser scene, which in the book, of course, is a buzz saw. *That's* something from silent movies, like the girl on the train tracks. The secret agent tied down with the buzz saw coming toward him is a very, very old cliché. So there are lots of these things that he took from previous writers. It's not really been written about how much *The Saint* influenced *James Bond,* but I think this is partly because of the confusion of Roger Moore and everything. But *The Saint* obviously predates *James Bond* by quite a way; there was a whole series of successful films in the '40s and he is a dashing, tuxedoed kind of rogue who speaks lots of languages. It's a really obvious influence, but it's kind of brushed aside.

TERENCE YOUNG

When you analyze it—and this is no disrespect to Ian—the novels were very sophisticated "B"-picture movie plots. If someone tells you, "A *James Bond* film," you'd say, "My God, that's for Monogram or Republic Pictures," who used to be around in those days. You would have never thought of it for a serious "A" film. But it had considerable sophistication, and this was very consciously put in by Ian. Ian was a very shrewd writer. He had never written before; when he wrote *Casino Royale,* he did have a feeling of what the public was going to go for. He was not surprised when it was a success. I think he *was* surprised when the *James Bond* film was a success and then his book sales went up something astonishing. He was selling two million copies a month at one time.

The books were like the old MGM style of films where the sets were always white, with white carpets and furniture. Joan Crawford changed her clothes every five minutes and, in a funny way, Ian brought a little of that escapism into a very dreary time in English history. We had food rationing, gas rationing, and life wasn't that gay in good old England. Ian's books reminded you of lovely meals, there was always a very nice car involved, and it was always a very good hotel you went to stay in. You went to exotic places. He didn't give you the kitchen sink school of writing, and I think it came out at the perfect time—he fell into it very luckily at that time.

Whatever his influences, and whoever preceded him, Fleming caught lightning in a bottle with *James Bond,* although it would, admittedly, take some time for others to fully realize its impact. *Casino Royale* was published in 1953, this first adventure pitting 007 against Le Chiffre, the paymaster for a SMERSH-controlled trade union, in what is ultimately a (very) high-stakes game of baccarat in France. On the one hand, he's aided by CIA agent Felix Leiter, while on the other, he's betrayed by double agent Vesper Lynd, despite the feelings that have developed between them.

Nicholas Rankin, in the pages of *Ian Fleming's Commandos: The Story of the Legendary 30 Assault Unit*, observes that 007 was the perfect hero for the times: "No wonder that James Bond started his fictional life as a creature of the Cold War, fighting the Stalinist terror of SMERSH. He emerged in the same year as Queen Elizabeth II's coronation and the British conquest of Mount Everest, a neo-Elizabethan hero for an age where the British Empire was dissolving and Britain struggled to remain at the top table among the world leaders."

Between the arrival of Bond and, then, The Beatles, many would argue that the British Empire would receive the proverbial shot in the arm it needed. Still not aware of what he had in his hands, Fleming pushed forward with yearly visits to GoldenEye and the writing of a new *Bond* thriller, giving the world, between 1954 and 1965, *Live and Let Die, Moonraker, Diamonds Are Forever, From Russia with Love, Dr. No, Goldfinger, For Your Eyes Only* (containing five short stories), *Thunderball, The Spy Who Loved Me, On Her Majesty's Secret Service, You Only Live Twice, The Man with the Golden Gun,* and *Octopussy* and *The Living Daylights* (the last two posthumously, the final book consisting of four short stories). Additionally, in 1958, England's *Daily Express* began adapting the novels into comic strip form that would span 52 story arcs (consisting of adaptations and, then, originals) and run until 1977.

ALAN J. PORTER

(author, *James Bond: The History of the Illustrated 007*)

There were a few existing adventure hero strips running in the newspapers prior to *Bond*, but most, such as *Buck Ryan,* were original characters developed specifically for the comic strips. Perhaps the most notable exception was *Sexton Blake,* a quintessential British hero whose adventures had been published in prose adventure weekly magazines since 1893 and in subsequent novels and collections. He made his comics debut in 1939, but it was in a weekly comics magazine, *Knockout* comics, as opposed to a newspaper. *The Saint*, who originated in the pulp magazines, was adapted as a daily newspaper strip in the US from 1948 onward. British radio originated thrillers such as *Paul Temple* had been adapted in the early 1950s, but I believe that *Bond* was probably the first major thriller adventure novel series turned into a newspaper strip, certainly in the UK.

The British newspaper *the Daily Express* already had a relationship with Ian Fleming after they had serialized a couple of the *Bond* short stories, when in 1957 the paper's managing editor approached Fleming with a proposal for a daily comic strip starring Bond. Fleming was originally reluctant, stating a concern that a comics adaptation would "lower the perceived literary quality" of his novels, and even worse it might tempt Fleming himself to "lower his standards" in any future *Bond* stories. To counter the objections, the *Express* proposed that the series start with a series of adaptations written by the paper's literary editor, Anthony Hern, who had done the earlier prose adaptations. Fleming liked Hern's work and that, along with the promise to "deliver a Rolls-Royce of a job," and a 1,500-pound check per story and a share in future syndication rights was enough to persuade Fleming to give his permission. So it was that Bond made his comics debut on 7th July 1958 in an adaptation of *Casino Royale* written by Anthony Hern and drawn by British artist John McLusky. Despite the promise to Fleming, this strip would be the only one that Hern would script.

THOMAS CULL

The early strips serialized in the *Daily Express* did serve to reach a wider readership. Fleming was reluctant at first for these to be produced and wanted final approval. As it turned out, they were a smash hit and greatly contributed to the spy craze of the early and mid-1960s.

ALAN J. PORTER

It definitely had an impact in the UK of building wider audience awareness of the character in the public consciousness before the movies debuted, and for a couple of decades it was the only source of new *Bond* adventures between the movies. Personally, I would head to the school library every morning to be the first to grab the *Daily Express*. My teachers were impressed by my desire to keep up with current affairs, but in reality it was 007's affairs and adventures I was reading.

> The adaptations of Fleming were well received, particularly given the restrictions of it being limited to three panels a day. The first of them was always a recap, the second moved the plot along, and the third was a cliffhanger to get the reader to return the following day. In a few of the

early adaptations, writer Henry Gammidge had the idea of making Bond the narrator, which wasn't perceived as effective in that it gave the character knowledge of events he shouldn't have. The device was dropped with *From Russia with Love* in favor of a more straightforward style of storytelling.

ALAN J. PORTER

There was also the occasional reworking of some of the more gruesome or sexual plot points given the fact that anyone could possibly pick up the paper and read the strip (including certain schoolboys). The adaptations hit a snag when the *Daily Express* publisher had an argument with Fleming over story rights and ordered the *Bond* strip canceled immediately, right in the middle of *Thunderball.* After a two-year gap, *Bond* returned to the newspaper in *On Her Majesty's Secret Service* and continued on through the canon. The strip was probably the first place that many people encountered Fleming's short stories. It concluded with *The Spy Who Loved Me,* which Fleming had forbidden to be adapted in his lifetime, in which a new original adventure inspired by a single line in the novel was tacked on to the first half of the story, making it the first non-Fleming *Bond* adventure. The officially sanctioned *Colonel Sun* continuation novel was also adapted into a newspaper strip, making it the only *Bond* continuation novel adapted into another medium to date.

By all standards, between the novels and the comic strips, that was an impressive run even *without* the film series, but Fleming knew that as welcome as royalties were, they couldn't compare to the kind of money generated by other mediums.

BRIAN LETT

Ian Fleming always lived in his brother Peter's shadow. Peter was a great success and an adventurer, while Ian was generally a failure or second best to his elder brother. That includes, of course, the war years. When Ian wrote the first *Bond* novel, he suddenly found success and money for really the first time. In my view, he milked *Bond* for all it was worth. Later, the films were vitally important. Ian was absolutely right in seeing that the films would make a lot of money. He had stumbled upon a very successful formula.

TOM SOTER

In spite of his success, Fleming still had many of his old doubts about his abilities, and often felt that he would run out of ideas and then out of money. To insure against this, he had tried to make *Bond* pay off in a big way. He vainly attempted to market his creation to television and the movies. He sold the rights for *Casino Royale* to CBS-TV, and the American network produced an unsuccessful one-hour version.

In 1954, CBS produced *Casino Royale* as a one-hour live television drama as part of their popular anthology series, *Climax Mystery Theater*, which aired three times a month on the network, offering up live dramatizations of popular and classical novels, old and new plays, and interestingly enough, magazine articles. Written by Anthony Ellis and Charles Bennett, who had adapted *The 39 Steps* and *Sabotage* for Alfred Hitchcock, *Casino Royale* starred Barry Nelson as "Card Sense" Jimmy Bond, an American CIA agent, and Peter Lorre as the villainous Le Chiffre. The production aired on October 21, 1954 and was promptly forgotten until it was resurrected many years later on home video by Goodtimes, the bargain-basement VHS label from the mid-'80s.

STEVEN JAY RUBIN

Veteran Broadway producer and film director Bretaigne Windust decided to give the drama an American perspective and cast Yankee Barry Nelson to portray the British agent. Peter Lorre played Le Chiffre, a Russian agent who controls the resources of the world's largest and most famous casino, while Linda Christian became the first *Bond* Girl.

HARRY ACKERMAN

(vice president of programming, CBS Television Network)

It was one of Peter's first, if not his first, live television shows. He had been doing only theatrical movies up to that point, and he regarded it as a challenge and an opportunity to take a step in a different direction. In those days, it was felt that American audiences resented accents, and that they didn't identify with heroes who weren't American—at least in television—which is why we cast Barry. With Linda, we wanted someone in the role who looked exotic without having actually to portray an affair on-screen. In that time, it would have been shockingly impossible to duplicate the kind of eroticism that *James Bond* is known for today.

JAMES CHAPMAN

Some people object to casting an American actor as James Bond—and Bond himself being American. I'd say it doesn't matter—or at least that it didn't matter in 1954. Nobody in the United States had heard of Bond at the time, and even in Britain he wasn't yet the popular culture phenomenon that he would later become. The association between Bond and Britishness came later. And actually, Fleming once said that he saw Bond as being more in the tradition of the "hard-boiled" school of American crime fiction in the mold of Dashiell Hammett and Raymond Chandler than the gentlemanly British Buchan-Sapper tradition.

At the time, Barry Nelson was known for his stage roles as well as the television series *The Hunter* and *My Favorite Husband*, the lightness of the latter causing him to seek something with a little more edge. *Casino Royale*, which would be directed by William Brown, seemed like it could meet those needs. Then he read the script, and his role as "Card Sense" CIA agent Jimmy Bond.

BARRY NELSON

(actor, "Card Sense Jimmy Bond")

To me, the Peter Lorre character was far more colorful. I brought it up to management that—forgetting about whoever was playing it, the personalities involved—it caused an imbalance in the show. They had given me too much exposition to handle. Le Chiffre had all the lively scenes. To my surprise, Lorre agreed with me. "It *is* an imbalance," he said. "You should really bring up the Bond character." I thought his support was delightful. Actors rarely rally that way. But in the end, the character was colorless. There were none of those wisecracks that you see in the *Bond* pictures. It got too talky. There was no action in it. When you take something that's spread out and depends primarily on action, you're in terrible trouble on live TV. There is a shortage of space. On that show we had about three sets, and the baccarat set took up most of our space.

STEVEN JAY RUBIN

It was filmed mainly on a casino set built at Television City in Hollywood. It lacked all the adventure and dazzling location associated with 007. It was essentially a simple duel between Le Chiffre and Bond, with a baccarat table between them. Not surprisingly, Bond's first screen appearance passed almost unnoticed by the critics.

BARRY NELSON

I had damn little to do with Linda. I kissed her, very politely. Yet she was a smoldering kind of young lady in those days. I knew Linda from Metro and she was not without potential as an actress. She looked good, she moved well.

She was a cultured lady with a beautiful voice, a lilting accent. We caught her on this one just as she announced her separation from Tyrone Power, so she was going through quite a tough time. Lorre's performance was excellent; I enjoyed every minute playing with him. It was the highlight of the whole thing. One of the reasons I took the part was because they told me he was going to be in it. He was a formidable player and a nice man to play with.

JEREMY DUNS

Even if you take away the switches of nationality and plot, there was little chance that such a format could get close to Fleming's novel anyway. There was no way to present the almost tangible claustrophobia and fever of the novel, the madness of gambling, the darkness, Bond's lust, the physical torture, and so much else. Lorre is wasted, too, I think, but it's a serviceable piece of television, of course.

HARRY ACKERMAN

We confined the action to relatively fewer scenes than the book has, because we were working in the one-hour form. Had we waited until *Playhouse 90* came along, we probably would have done the whole book, or attempted to.

JAMES CHAPMAN

Sometimes you read that the television *Casino Royale* is crude and primitive. In fact, it's a very good example of live studio drama: the cutting is faster than most contemporary examples (especially effective during the card game, which is very suspenseful) and it has that intense, close-up studio feel that works very well for this particular story.

RAY MORTON

(senior writer, *Script* magazine)

I'm not familiar with Anthony Ellis, but Charles Bennett was a very capable, old-school screenwriter who had worked with Alfred Hitchcock on the scripts of many of his early films, and would later write the terrific supernatural thriller *Night of the Demon*. The Ellis/Bennett adaptation of *Casino Royale* is a solid piece of craftsmanship—a decent enough adaptation of Fleming's basic plot, condensed to fit a one-hour running time.

BARRY NELSON

It was just another piece of material to them. Just another property. And it's awfully tough to condense it into that short period of time, too, where you want to have more extensive development of plot and character. The script was very muted. Had the script had more potential, then maybe I would have gone to my agent and said, "This has a future and shouldn't we try to encourage it along?" But the script was so uninspired, my agent would have been surprised if I had said, "I've got to do this again."

ROBERT SELLERS

(author, *The Battle for Bond*)

My views on this production are not particularly charitable. The biggest flaw, of course, is the presentation of the Bond character, turning him from Fleming's blunt instrument of Her Majesty's government into a gum-chewing private eye–type. It doesn't help that Barry Nelson thinks he's in an episode of *Dragnet*. Although past his prime, Peter Lorre is far and away the best thing in it, and I suppose the producers have to be congratulated for keeping in a torture scene of some kind, not an easy thing to have got through, especially at a time when US television networks were extremely conservative and sanitized.

HARRY ACKERMAN

We were used to negative reviews. When I started *I Love Lucy*, the *Daily Variety* reviewer hated it and said, "This show won't be around six weeks from now." I was able to remind him of that six years later when it was still number one.

BARRY NELSON

Casino Royale was done live, and live shows are never fun to do. I did an awful lot of them, and I can't say I ever really much enjoyed it. You never had enough rehearsal. And they changed things—always at the last minute. Then they'd always be too long and come slashing down, frantically, with a pencil, and also change many camera positions. So you were getting, largely, a mechanical performance. Except where there was an intimate scene that hadn't been touched. Those times you could enjoy.

A week prior to making his deal with CBS, Fleming had also optioned the *film* rights for *Casino Royale* (quite astoundingly, considering that *today* no author would be able to bifurcate the rights between two different mediums) to producer Gregory Ratoff for six months. In 1955, the film rights were purchased outright. Ratoff was close with a number of Hollywood luminaries, among them Famous Artists agent Charles K. Feldman, who would eventually acquire Ratoff's rights from his widow after he died in 1960. This would ultimately result in the 1967 007 spoof version, and, as such, would be one of two competing *James Bond* projects that would come back to haunt both Eon Productions and United Artists for years to come.

The other was in the form of Kevin McClory.

ROBERT SELLERS

Kevin McClory was Irish, from a working-class background, and fought his way up to a position in the film industry where he was doing very well for himself. He was assistant director on some John Huston films, like *African Queen* and *Moby Dick*. He worked with Mike Todd on *Around the World in 80 Days*. It was after he worked on that that he had this idea to do an underwater treasure hunting film. He got John Steinbeck, who wrote *The Grapes of Wrath*, to come on and write a script. That sort of fizzled out.

KEVIN MCCLORY

(producer, *Thunderball*)

I was pretty tired, because *Around the World* went on for nearly two years, so I went to the Bahamas. Prior to working on *Around the World in 80 Days*, I had spent a lot of time underwater. I'm very keen on oceanography; I'm very keen on everything beneath the ocean. So I was in the Bahamas, taking my first holiday in a long time. I remember walking and thinking, "My God, if you took Todd A-O [a recently developed type of wide-screen motion picture camera] cameras underwater, it would be fantastic." No one had made an underwater picture since *20,000 Leagues*, and part of that was shot in the Bahamas. That was by Disney, and they got kind of leery about it: there wasn't that much equipment at the time. I started taking a really good look at this from the point of view of the entertainment business, so I started mulling whether to make an underwater picture or not.

ROBERT SELLERS

Then he had an idea to do this film called *The Boy and the Bridge*, which was a very low-key, sentimental film, almost, about a young boy who lives on the Tower Bridge. He's sort of an orphan living there, and befriends somebody who works there. I've never seen it; it's just a film that's completely forgotten and vanished. He was looking for finance for that movie and he met a guy called Ivar Bryce, who was a financier, philanthropist, and friend of Fleming—significantly.

KEVIN MCCLORY

I started thinking about driving around the world. Eventually I did that; I did it for the Ford Motor Company. They put the money up, and it took us 104 days. We had 26 men, two camera crews, five cars. . . . On the way, I read *Reader's Digest*. There was a little short story by an American writer named Ian Ware, about a boy who ran away from home and made his home on the San Francisco bridge. I read this, and kind of liked it, so on the way back (because the cars got to Saigon, and then we flew back while the cars were shipped to San Francisco, for the final journey to Detroit) I ran into Mike Todd in Hawaii, in Honolulu. He wanted me to come back and work for him, but I had decided I didn't want to work for anyone anymore. You know, it was about time I did something on my own, so I told him. I'll always remember this: he said, "Well, what are you going to do?" and I said, "Make an underwater picture, in very wide screen." But then I'd just read this story and he said, "Tell me about it," so I told him about the boy who ran away from home and all that, and I said, "I think I'll switch it to London; Tower Bridge, and a Cockney kid. It'll have a lot of appeal and human interest." He said, "Kevin, make the underwater picture," and I said, "Why do you say that?" He said, "Well, I know you, and if you make this boy and the bridge film, you'll go to festivals and win a lot of awards. But remember: You can't eat awards." Prophetic words!

ROBERT SELLERS

Bryce wanted to get into the film business and liked the story, so he backed the film. They went ahead and made it and formed a production company called Xanadu. They thoroughly enjoyed their experience, I think. McClory directed, Bryce produced. Neither had ever made a film before. They fell in love with the filmmaking bug. And they decided, "Let's do another one."

KEVIN MCCLORY

I went and made *The Boy and the Bridge*; I produced it, I directed it, I wrote it. I set it up without a distributor, I got somebody to back it, and I made it. And sure enough, he was right. It represented Britain at the Venice Film Festival, and it went to Spain, and the Cook Film Festival. . . . I've got a lot of awards now to remind me of what he said. The box office was absolutely nothing. It got interest from critics, who were divided. It was never seen anywhere outside of England.

It's in black and white. . . . I think it would be an interesting show for children. But that set me back to, "I better make some pennies, otherwise . . ." Well, you know the industry, and unless you're a financial success no one's prepared to back you. I went back to the Bahamas, and then I started writing an underwater story set in the Bahamas. It was at this time I was introduced to Ian Fleming through the man who put up the money for *The Boy and the Bridge,* and this was in 1959.

ROBERT SELLERS

They talked about various ideas. I think they were going to do a film about Alcatraz or something like that. And then one day Bryce just asked him, "Do you know the *James Bond* books?" McClory knew of them, but hadn't read one. Bryce suggested he read four or five of them, which he did. He wasn't entirely blown away by them, didn't think they were particularly good, especially from the point of view of making them into a film. He thought they were a little bit sadistic, which they are, of course. "Sadism for the family." But the central character of James Bond he thought was terrific. He thought, "This is a potentially terrific screen hero."

KEVIN MCCLORY

I read them, and said that I'd like to meet Fleming. Now at that time no one had made a *Bond*. Fleming had sold two of his books: *Moonraker,* which he sold for $5,000 and later bought back for $5,000; and *Casino Royale,* which was bought by Gregory Ratoff, who I used to work for (I did a picture with him). He bought *Casino Royale,* tried hard to set it up, but no distributor, sadly, was interested, and he died, owning the property. The rights passed to his widow, who later sold them to Charlie Feldman. I was very intrigued by it, so I met with Fleming, and I told him that I'd enjoyed reading the books, but I didn't think they were particularly visual; that each and every one of them would have to be rewritten for the screen—written in a visual sense.

ROBERT SELLERS

When you think about it, he was absolutely right about the books not being filmable, because when Richard Maibaum came along and started writing the Connery *Bonds* from *Dr. No* onwards, he heavily adapted them, and changed an awful lot. *From Russia with Love* is probably the closest to the novel. A lot of criticism of the *Bond* films is that they aren't the Fleming books. I mean, look at *You Only Live Twice*—completely readapted. *Live and Let Die* is a completely different film than the book. *Diamonds Are Forever* is as well. If you were to faithfully adapt those books to the screen, I don't think they would have worked. It's the reason McClory said, "Look, let's start from scratch. Just start with Bond and then create a story around him," which is what they did.

KEVIN MCCLORY

James Bond leapt out of the page; he was totally visual to me. "You really have something here," I said, "but what I'd like to do is to take the character and put him in an underwater setting, in the Bahamas. I'm working on a story right now. . . . Let's put him in this opulent setting." In those days, in 1959, the Bahamas was kind of a paradise to people from Europe, and other places where they couldn't afford to get there. Palm trees, beautiful women, multimillionaires, and yachts, private clubs, white beaches and azure seas . . . I mean, the atmosphere was right for *Bond*. And underwater, I was very keen on, and no one had really utilized it, other than Disney.

STEVEN JAY RUBIN

Fleming's new agent, Laurence Evans of MCA, told him plainly that young, inexperienced directors did not attract big-name stars. He advised him to consider another director for the project, and although Fleming took the point Evans was making, plans went ahead with McClory with an entirely new adventure that would feature plot and production values geared to a film audience.

KEVIN MCCLORY

Fleming asked me to reread *Live and Let Die* and *Diamonds Are Forever*, and I said, "But I'd be reading what I read." I had taken these books and gone away and really read them carefully, so I said, "Why don't you collaborate with me; why don't we write together?" And he said, "Okay"—he was interested. He saw *The Boy and the Bridge* and liked it enormously, he said. Then he said, "I'd like to work with you." I said, "Alright, we'll begin whenever you like." That was the conceiving, right then, really, of *Thunderball*.

ROBERT SELLERS

In July 1959, the deal was done. Fleming wrote a letter, which I saw, saying he wanted Kevin McClory, Ivar Bryce, and Xanadu Productions [the company they'd started] to do the first *James Bond* film. They had his permission and that was it.

KEVIN MCCLORY

We worked on a number of treatments and film scripts . . . a six-page outline would be thrown on the side. . . . In one we had the Mafia get Bond.

ROBERT SELLERS

When Fleming actually sat down to write a film treatment, he forgot about SPECTRE, or thought it wasn't a good idea, and replaced SPECTRE with the Mafia. And it was only when he wrote the book that he replaced the Mafia and put SPECTRE back in.

KEVIN MCCLORY

He was using the term SMERSH as the villains then, and I said, "That's kind of old hat, making Russians always villains, and black people always villains, like that. We should consider another kind of organization," and that was the birth of SPECTRE in 1959, which you might find surprising, because you find it in *Dr. No*, and you find it in *From Russia with Love*, but you won't find it if you read the novels. SPECTRE—the organization with Ernst Stavro Blofeld—was created for *Thunderball*. Anyway, we generally developed various stories and ideas, and mulled them about, and changed them, and altered them again, and so a number of scripts were written.

ROBERT SELLERS

They had this meeting in London with this other chap who came from America, called Ernest Cuneo, who, again, was a friend of Fleming and a friend of Bryce. He was an American lawyer, and they had a big meeting, where all these ideas were thrown around. After the meeting, Cuneo wrote a memo, which he sent to Fleming, which is this famous memo that has been reproduced in quite a few *Bond* books, where he writes down a plot for a *Bond* film, from everybody's ideas that were thrown around at this meeting. It's incredible how relatively similar it is to the finished product of *Thunderball* itself. It's the stolen atom bomb, a big underwater fight at the end. It's all there. It's fascinating. Although the villains were going to be the Russians, which, when Fleming read the memo, he thought was a little dated. He thought by the time the film was made and came out, possibly two or three years, the Cold War might be over. So the film would look outdated if the Russians were still the enemy. So he thought of some kind of private organization that were the villains, and he created, then and there, SPECTRE. That's how SPECTRE was created.

RAY MORTON

The core idea for *Thunderball* was devised by Ernest Cuneo. Ian Fleming developed it over several treatments and script drafts, but Fleming wasn't a screenwriter and couldn't figure out how to make the story play for the screen.

KEVIN MCCLORY

Fleming wasn't really a screenwriter, and he was working for *The Sunday Times*, and they had things for him to do, and he kind of did less and less, so I employed Jack Whittingham; that's how he came into it. He and I completed the screenplay for *Thunderball* in 1959.

RAY MORTON

Whittingham was a very experienced, and very good, screenwriter, and was brought in to turn Fleming's story into a workable script, which he did. He developed the narrative, came up with a much more workable structure and plot, and contributed to a number of important set pieces.

ROBERT SELLERS

The fascinating thing of having all the court papers when I was researching my book was that I had about two and a half years' worth of correspondence, of letters. They were writing to each other on a daily basis for two and a half years. So you would have letters from McClory to Bryce, Bryce to Fleming, Fleming to McClory, Fleming to Bryce, and they were all on other sides of the world. And that was absolutely fascinating, because I put them all in order. It took me about four or five days to read this correspondence, but it told the whole story, in their own words. And about halfway through, you can see that the wheels are falling off. You can see that Fleming is starting to put doubts into Bryce's mind about whether or not McClory is the right person, because McClory was going to direct the movie.

Nonetheless, behind the scenes, plans were starting to converge—unbeknownst to McClory—to find somebody else to direct the film. And that somebody else was no less than the Master of Suspense, Alfred Hitchcock.

ROBERT SELLERS

When McClory discovered that, I think the writing was on the wall for him. By this time, the film that he'd made to set the whole thing rolling, *The Boy and the Bridge,* had been released and been a huge flop. So Fleming started to have second thoughts that McClory wasn't a capable director. Also, it was getting a little too big for McClory to handle, because McClory was saying things like he was thinking of renting an American warship, the USS *Indianapolis* or something. "They'll let us have it for a few days." It was getting *really* big.

JAMES CHAPMAN

After *North by Northwest,* Hitchcock was certainly sounded out about the possibility of directing *James Bond of the Secret Service* (the film that eventually became *Thunderball* and prompted the court battle between McClory and Fleming). But Hitchcock was always being sounded out about various projects. It was discussed briefly, but was more an idea rather than a concrete initiative. They knew that Hitchcock's name would bring prestige, but at the same time would mean surrendering control over the film—and in any event, McClory's budget wasn't enough to afford Hitchcock.

ROBERT SELLERS

Hitchcock was actually interested for quite a few months. He was hemming and hawing, and there are lots of letters to and fro. There's one amazing letter where they're saying, "If Hitch does it, he wants James Stewart to play Bond." And Fleming saying, "It wouldn't be so bad if he loses the accent." Ivar Bryce writes back to Fleming and castigates him, and says, "What are you even thinking that James Stewart is the perfect choice for Bond? He's *so* wrong." The other fear was that if Hitchcock did it, he would take complete control, which he did on his films. He produced and directed them, and he cast them. So it wouldn't have been a *Bond* film as such, it would become a Hitchcock film. But the reason they thought Hitchcock would be perfect was because of *North by Northwest.*

JAMES O. NAREMORE

North by Northwest is a mildly anti–Cold War film whose bad-guy spies aren't connected to a particular nation—they prefigure the fantastic Dr. Evils of the *Bond* franchise, but are more understated and realistic. The picture also prefigures *Bond,* because it's a glamorous, VistaVision spectacular involving a handsome Madison Avenue ad man and a seductive blonde; it's a travelogue, and its design is well suited to the emerging world of *Playboy*-style consumer culture. But I find it more witty, sophisticated, and fun than the *Bond* pictures. Though I like very much the first two *Bond*s, *Dr. No* and *From Russia with Love*, the first because Bond sometimes seems a cold-blooded killer, and the second because of its train journey, which has many of the fascinations of trains in Hitchcock.

ROBERT SELLERS

This was for me one of the big revelations of my research for the book [*The Battle for Bond*]: it was Fleming himself who sent a telegram to the director via a mutual friend, the writer Eric Ambler. Hitchcock was genuinely interested, although it was feared by some that his sheer "weight" of celebrity would overwhelm the project. And with Fleming being so willing to accept James Stewart, I think by this stage he was so desperate to get his novels on the screen he would have had J. Edgar Hoover play the role. It really was an insane suggestion, though. Can you see James Stewart driving an Aston Martin or fighting Robert Shaw aboard the Orient Express?

JAMES O. NAREMORE

It's hard for me to imagine what Hitchcock would have done with Fleming—Hitchcock's approach to sex was rarely exhibitionistic: no cheesecake. His violence is more disturbing than Fleming's sadism, and his humor isn't *Bond*-like.

JAMES STRATTON

I don't think Hitchcock and *Bond* would have been a successful match. Hitchcock was more subtle and more interested in ambiguity. *Bond* would have been a bit too straightforward and the tight *Bond* formula would not have allowed for his personal preoccupations.

While for many Bond fans the "what if?" of Alfred Hitchcock is intriguing, there is no certainty that if he *had* directed the first *Bond* film, there would have been any others. He certainly was not known for sequels, and 007 could have very well been a one-off film in a long and distinguished filmography.

JAMES CHAPMAN

I'm pretty sure Hitchcock would not have committed to directing a series of films, so if it had happened, and if it had led to more films, they would in all likelihood have been by other directors.

ROBERT SELLERS

In the letters and telegrams that passed back and forth between the main protagonists, it was only ever mentioned that Hitch would come in to make *Thunderball,* nothing about him carrying on with the series. I very much doubt he would have made more than one *Bond* film. Now, would the film have been a success with Hitch at the helm? Very much so; he was too good a director to louse things up. In many ways he was the perfect director for 007: he had a terrific and dark sense of humor, knew everything there was to know about film suspense—indeed, he invented it!—and was adept at handling action. Witness the amazing climax on Mount Rushmore in *North by Northwest.* Hitch certainly knew how to end a picture.

As a side note, some of the early *Bond* films were described as Hitchcockian by some critics. Also, in *From Russia with Love* there is an homage to the famous crop duster sequence from *North by Northwest* when Bond is attacked by a low-flying helicopter. Or was this an in-joke by the filmmakers, a nod to how close Hitchcock came to directing a Bond film?

As it turned out, those covert discussions with Hitchcock were the least of the problems that McClory would find himself dealing with when it came to the world of James Bond and Ian Fleming. For starters, Gregory Ratoff was actively pursuing development on *Casino Royale*, which was being reported on by the media. Those rights were a revelation to McClory, who, again, had been promised–in writing–the ability to make the *first James Bond* film.

ROBERT SELLERS

He felt betrayed: that the right to make the first *James Bond* film, given to him by Fleming in a signed statement, had been stolen from him by others, and this sense of betrayal was a flame that burned brightly within him right up until his death. To be fair, he exploited the situation, too. When Broccoli and Saltzman came on the scene and made a success of the *Bond* films, McClory *immediately* stepped up his plans to make *Thunderball*, which he announced would go into production at the same time as *Goldfinger*. You could say he was jumping on the bandwagon, hoping either Richard Burton or Laurence Harvey would play Bond. There's a funny story of Honor Blackman meeting Prince Philip at some society ball, and when she revealed she was making a *Bond* film, the prince asked, "Which one?" Miss Blackman politely told him it was the one starring Sean Connery. This was the same society ball that resulted in newspaper headlines the next day saying, "Pussy Meets the Prince," and persuaded the producers that they could get away with using that name in the film without causing a public outcry.

Running out of patience when it came to the movie business, Fleming returned to GoldenEye to start his next *Bond* novel, the ninth in the series.

KEVIN MCCLORY

All that time, I'm not quite sure what happened, and as Ian's no longer with us I don't want to dwell on it very much, but I think at the time he got himself an agent, and I believe the agent said, "You know, we've got producers, we've got directors, we've got this terrific *Thunderball*, we'll do it. . . ." Anyway, for whatever reason, he went away, and he wrote, at GoldenEye, a novel called *Thunderball,* but it was written from *our* screenplay.

STEVEN JAY RUBIN

In the middle of 1958, everything looked promising for the new film. Two years later, everything had changed. Although Bryce was excited about the Whittingham script, he was no longer capable of financing the *Bond* film on his own. McClory and Bryce were pleased with the Whittingham treatment and continued to submit the script to potential backers. Little did they know that Fleming was using the very same Whittingham/McClory material as the basis for the next *Bond* novel.

ROBERT SELLERS

I think Fleming just got fed up with the whole thing. He *hated* showbiz. He hated entertainment lawyers and agents. And the time was coming where his publisher wanted a new *Bond* novel, so off he went to GoldenEye. He sort of sat at his desk and nothing came out. He had a block. He'd lost his inspiration to write a *Bond* novel, but he had to write one, because the publishers were demanding one.

THOMAS CULL

Indeed, as the series went on, he struggled with coming up with even more fantastical plots and fought his own boredom with the character. He experimented with *The Spy Who Loved Me,* which was a commercial and critical failure at the time, but eventually came back strong with the more formulaic *On Her Majesty's Secret Service.* He developed Bond's character with more humor and levity toward the later novels, and despite facing challenges with his own health (in his words, "running out of puff") he still managed to keep the series thrilling and new, almost to the very end. But at the time of *Thunderball . . .*

ROBERT SELLERS

This is in Fleming's own words. In a letter to a friend he says, "Terribly stuck with James Bond. What was easy at 40 is very difficult at 50. I used to believe in Bonds and blondes and bombs. Now the keys creak as I type. And I fear the zest may have gone. Part of the trouble is having a wife and child. They knock the ruthlessness out of one. I shall definitely kill off Bond with my next book. Better a poor bang, than a rich whimper."

PETER HUNT
(editor, *Dr. No*)

Fleming had run out of ideas, or was running out of ideas, and said, "Oh, I might as well write and publish this script as a book." Then, of course McClory said, "You can't do that. You haven't even said that I contributed to it or Jack Whittingham did."

KEVIN MCCLORY

I knew he was writing a novel, but I didn't know he was writing a novel on *Thunderball*. And the next thing I know, it's published, with no credit for Whittingham or myself. We tried to stop publication of the book, because these were our ideas, really, and it led to a lawsuit. And that lawsuit lasted nearly three years. It ended in the London high courts in 1963. I was assigned all the film and TV rights to *Thunderball*. I said to Fleming, "You have the literary rights; you wrote the novel, I don't want you to part with that. But you put in every novel that this is based on a screenplay by us." This is the legend it's supposed to have; some publishers do, some don't. He assigned to us all the other screenplays—there were 10 in all. All with Bond, all with Felix Leiter, all with Q, all with M, all with the characters. Not all of them are SPECTRE; some of them we have the Mafia and other different villains . . . and that is, basically, how I came to own the copyright.

McClory may have owned the film copyright to *Thunderball*, but with the exception of the previously optioned *Casino Royale*, the other novels were still on the market and available to prospective suitors.

KEVIN MCCLORY

In the meantime, Harry Saltzman, while I was back in court, got an option. He was trying, I believe, to set the pictures up on his own. I wouldn't think the option included *Thunderball*; it couldn't, it was in litigation.

STEVEN JAY RUBIN

By the winter of 1960, Fleming, who was anxious to set up a trust fund for his wife and son, was under pressure to make a quick film deal. It was then that Saltzman was advised to put in a bid for the *Bond* books. At their meeting, Saltzman indicated that he might be able to scrape together $50,000 for a six-month option and if the project was picked up by a major studio, he would try to get Fleming $100,000 a picture, plus a percentage. Fleming agreed in principle, arranging for Saltzman to meet his film agent, Bob Fenn of MCA, to work out the deal on paper. Fenn offered Saltzman the seven available books plus options on any other *Bond* novels. For five months, Saltzman tried unsuccessfully to sell the studios the idea of a series of *James Bond* films. It was the old story. The studios wouldn't touch the project without the commitment of a major star, and a major star would not commit himself to more than a couple of films.

KEVIN MCCLORY

He eventually teamed up with Cubby Broccoli to get the financing. Cubby had his setup; he was an established producer.

STEVEN JAY RUBIN

With only 28 days left on the option, Saltzman received an important call from his writer friend Wolf Mankowitz, who told him that London-based producer Cubby Broccoli was interested in the *Bond* project.

RAY MORTON

Wolf Mankowitz is the most important screenwriter in the series—not for his writing talents (which were considerable), but because he is the man who introduced Harry Saltzman to Cubby Broccoli. So a good argument can be made that without Mankowitz, there would be no *Bond* movies as we know them.

ALBERT R. BROCCOLI

(producer, the *James Bond* films)

I had produced 28 films before that. Irving Allen and I developed a company called Warwick Films and we made three pictures with Alan Ladd, which were very successful pictures. As successful as the *Bond*s, in that era, 1952. The three Alan Ladd pictures were the biggest grossers of any other film company at that time.

DAVID V. PICKER

(president and chief executive officer, United Artists)

Cubby was the real thing. His company with Irving Allen, Warwick Films, specialized in quality action pictures made for a reasonable cost—films such as *The Red Beret, Cockleshell Heroes*, and *Hell Below Zero*. He hired talented directors such as Terence Young and Mark Robson, cameramen like Ted

Moore, production designers such as Ken Adam, and screenwriter Richard Maibaum. Cubby's relationship with his partner Allen was edging toward professional divorce, but he figured he'd try one last shot at doing something together. Having read several of Fleming's books on Bond, he inquired about their availability. A meeting was set up with MCA agent Bob Fenn, who advised them that CBS was interested in a TV series on Bond and that Fleming didn't like movies.

Harry Saltzman was a whole different story. He was an outsider to the business, and in meeting with him it was hard to feel totally comfortable. His limited experience made him awkward and he was often forced to rely on Cubby, whose experience much more grounded him. It was hard for Harry to understand that a handshake deal at UA really was a deal. Fortunately, Cubby and Irving Moskowitz, Harry's lawyer, assured him that was the way it worked. Harry's strength was that he did believe in *Bond* and cared about the films, but he wanted to be treated like the equal partner he was. Since humor and style weren't his long suits, he sometimes felt, and perhaps appropriately, that he was an invited guest.

STEVEN JAY RUBIN

Two years before Harry Saltzman met Fleming, Albert Broccoli was given the opportunity to start a *James Bond* project, but while he himself was keen, Irving Allen rejected the idea outright. This incident contributed to the disintegration of their partnership and the final collapse of Warwick Films in 1960.

RICHARD MAIBAUM

Cubby gave me two of the books to read in 1957, because he was thinking about doing them even then. Unfortunately, with all their inherent sex and violence, they just weren't producible at that time. But with the coming of the Sixties, attitudes began to change.

ALBERT R. BROCCOLI

I tried to get them long before Harry and I met, when I was with Irving Allen, just before we broke up. Irving didn't agree on *Bond* at the time, so in our dealings with Fleming we let it go. Much to the annoyance of Fleming.

DAVID V. PICKER

Allen, who never liked the idea, got up and left the meeting. Clearly a *Bond* deal was out of the question for the partnership.

ALBERT R. BROCCOLI

By that time, Harry had an option on it, but he didn't get anywhere with it. He talked and peddled it around, but no one really wanted it. Distributors, people—he spoke to all of them. At least he said he did.

DAVID V. PICKER

Harry may have tried to set the films up, but he certainly never came to United Artists, nor did I ever know that Harry had gotten this option. He either did nothing, or tried and got nowhere. Cubby got movies made, and that's what Harry needed.

ALBERT R. BROCCOLI

He said the studios weren't interested, and when I met Harry, at the time he wanted to do other properties. He wasn't interested in *Bond* at that time, but that was the only thing I was interested in talking to him about. *Not* some of the other deals he wanted to do. So we got together on that basis. If I could get a deal for it, we would go in 50/50. I talked to an agent on the phone and he came in and made a deal for us.

DAVID V. PICKER

Cubby's first call was to Mike Frankovich at Columbia. Mike would do almost anything for Cubby. They were friends, had a long business relationship, and gambled together. The Columbia response was fast: "Cubby, if you insist, we will give you $300,000 to $400,000 to make a picture, but that's it. There's no real belief or support for the project. If you can get more elsewhere, fine, but let us know before you close any deal." Both Harry and Cubby felt the potential of the *Bond* books couldn't be maximized at that budget. Cubby's next call was to UA's Bud Ornstein, who then called me and the meeting was set.

That meeting was arranged by the London office of United Artists, although Picker had not been told exactly what the nature of the meeting was. Intrigued, he agreed to meet with Broccoli, Saltzman, and Saltzman's lawyer, Irving Moskowitz, joined by various execs from UA, including studio chairman Arthur Krim and, of course, his father, studio prez Arthur Picker.

DAVID V. PICKER

In meetings, I always liked to sit on Arthur's left so I could tilt the back of my chair and put one of my long legs against the side of his desk. I used to do this a lot and this day was no different. Introductions were made all around. We sat back to listen, laughing, telling them Bud had refused to reveal anything, even at the potential loss of his job. "We own the rights to *James Bond*," Harry said. My chair came hurtling back to all four legs. "You're kidding." They weren't. "How did you guys get them?" I wanted to know. All they said was, "We got them." I didn't even try to hide my excitement.

Some time earlier, Picker's cousin-in-law suggested that Fleming's *Bond* novels would make good films, and although he had never heard of Fleming, after reading a few of them he readily agreed. Discovering that Fleming was represented by MCA, he arranged a lunch meeting with über-agent Lew Wasserman. At that meeting, he cut to the chase, suggesting that they do a film with Alfred Hitchcock, an MCA client, and he knew the perfect project: one of the Fleming *Bond* novels, and since Fleming was represented by MCA as well, it shouldn't be a problem. Wasserman laughed, agreeing it was a good idea, and pointing out that "Hitch" had thought of it already and ultimately passed. All he knew was that the rights to *Casino Royale* had been bought by producer Gregory Ratoff some years earlier with no ties to other *Bond* novels, and Fleming had just refused to consider any other offers.

DAVID V. PICKER

Since I was the only one at UA that had read the books, Harry, Cubby, and I started to talk about why we liked them and what it would take to translate them to the screen. As we talked, it was clear we had a mutual creative vision. These books were not the run-of-the-mill adventure story. What gave them their special quality was basically two things of equal importance. One was the character of Bond himself—suave, sophisticated, stylish, witty, and sexy. The second was the Fleming touch: the amazing variety of both location and villains.

An agreement was struck for a $1.1 million budget for a first film, and a deal for profit participation to be split 50/50 between the studio and the producers, as well as a cross-collateralization agreement that a series of films–in sets of two–would balance each other out in terms of profits and losses (obviously that never became an issue).

DAVID V. PICKER

Everything seemed to be moving along very well, so we began to talk about which book should be developed first. They suggested *Thunderball,* but, having read the book, I felt the story was going to be too expensive to shoot as the first picture. *Dr. No* lent itself better to the guidelines we set. The two agreed to go back and consider this, and we'd make a final decision.

JOHN CORK

I think Terence Young knew how to make a *James Bond* film. With Ken Adam, [film title designer] Maurice Binder, Richard Maibaum, Sean Connery, Cubby, and Harry all involved, do you really think they would have made a flop even if the first film had been *Thunderball*? I don't.

KEVIN MCCLORY

They got together, and commissioned Richard Maibaum to write a screenplay, and the novel he was given was *Thunderball*. So Richard Maibaum wrote a screenplay on *Thunderball* in 1961. I believe it was taken to United Artists in New York, and they were unable to make it. They couldn't make it—the copyright was in dispute. They say they didn't make it because it was too expensive, but they couldn't have made it because they didn't have the copyright.

STEVEN JAY RUBIN

They changed it to *Dr. No*, but from Fleming's *Thunderball* novel, Richard Maibaum introduced SPECTRE as Dr. No's backers, an independent operation that conveniently sidestepped the political issues of the day. Fleming's reference to Dr. No's financial backers, the Russians, was removed. SPECTRE, as it does in Fleming's novel *Thunderball*, now stood for "Special Executive for Counter-intelligence, Terrorism, Revenge, and Extortion."

KEVIN MCCLORY

It's obvious that elements of *Thunderball* had to come into *Dr. No*: same screenwriter—it's inevitable . . . unless, of course, you used a different screenwriter. This is clearly how SPECTRE came into *Dr. No*. They then got the same writer, Dick Maibaum, to do *From Russia with Love* and into it goes SPECTRE once again—even more of it. More elements of what we called the *Thunderball* format, and it kind of continued. I hadn't realized to what extent this material had been used [for years].

DAVID V. PICKER

Now all Harry and Cubby had to do was find an actor who would carry out the role of Bond and agree to options for additional films, play a suave, sexy character that would explode off the screen and become the next Gable, Grant, or Bogart, and—oh yes, he had to be English, irresistible, wear clothes beautifully, look good in a tight bathing suit, be able to run, jump, fight, and drive cars very fast, seduce every woman he meets, and since he was being given the chance of a lifetime, be very inexpensive to hire, because after all, he was being given the chance of a lifetime.

THE SIXTIES: THE DOCTOR IS IN

"No, Mister Bond, I expect you to die. . . ."

Two decades into the twenty-first century, it's hard to imagine what it was like to first see *Dr. No* in a theater unless you were actually there. It was 1962, only two decades after the end of World War Two. The Cold War was heating up; the Soviet Union signed a trade pact with communist Cuba, triggering a US trade embargo; downed U2 pilot Francis Gary Powers was exchanged for convicted Soviet spy Rudolf Abel in Berlin on the Glienicke Bridge; and astronaut John Glenn became the first American to orbit the Earth. In August, East German border guards murdered 18-year-old Peter Fechter as he attempted to make it over the Berlin Wall, while an assassination attempt was made against French president Charles de Gaulle, escalating global tensions.

Meanwhile, the glamorous Jackie Kennedy took viewers on a tour of the White House in a nationally televised special, AT&T put the first commercial communications satellite into orbit, Wilt "The Stilt" Chamberlain became the first basketball player to score 100 points in one night (and more than likely 100 women as well), Bob Dylan released his first album, and *West Side Story* won Best Picture at the Oscars. Tragically, it was also the year in which Marilyn Monroe was found dead in bed from an overdose of sleeping pills.

Ironically, it was also the year that Air France Flight 007 crashed on takeoff in Paris, while at movie theaters 007 first took off. In October 1962, only weeks before the Cuban Missile Crisis had the world on the brink of a nuclear exchange (and on the same day that The Beatles released their first single, "Love Me Do"), *Dr. No* debuted in theaters. As presidents such as Ronald Reagan and Bill Clinton both said many years later in explaining the appeal of 007, it was very reassuring to audiences to know a secret agent like James Bond was looking out for Queen and country and making the world safe for democracy.

DR. NO (1962)

The milieu in which the early *James Bond* films took place was still remarkably exciting and unfamiliar to most fans. Movies about tradecraft (aka spying) had largely been dour affairs and set in the run-up to or during World War Two in which American and British spies attempted to foil the Nazi or German spies that had infiltrated America. While legendary director Alfred Hitchcock had visited the world of espionage with relish in such films as *Notorious*, *The Man Who Knew Too Much*, *The Lady Vanishes,* and *Secret Agent*, it's his classic 1959 masterpiece, *North by Northwest*, that would in many ways prove the template for over five decades of *James Bond* adventures, filled with a protagonist who travels in high society (in this case, a New York advertising executive mistaken for nonexistent spy George Kaplan); a picturesque travelogue from Manhattan hotels and the United Nations to trains to prairies to Mount Rushmore; a coterie of elegant villains top-lined by James Mason; and, of course, a beautiful woman in danger, the resourceful Eva Marie Saint.

JAMES STRATTON

(author, *Hitchcock's North by Northwest: The Man Who Had Too Much*)

North by Northwest brought lavish production values, attractive leads, and glamour to what had been grittier, film noir–like narratives. Also, unlike the more cerebral, complex narratives of le Carré, the emphasis was on a series of loosely connected thrill-ride adventures. The suggestion that the government was gathering intelligence in a way that was murky and dispassionate would be expanded on by subsequent entries in the genre.

JAMES CHAPMAN

(author, *Hitchcock and the Spy Film*)

Obviously *Bond* would go to some wild places that Hitchcock never would have, but, given *North by Northwest,* does it feel like a natural progression for Hitchcock from his spy films to, at the very least, *Dr. No* and *From Russia with*

Love? I think the look and style of the early *Bond* films were very strongly influenced by *North by Northwest*. Most spy movies in the 1950s, in Britain and Hollywood, were relatively low-budget, black-and-white affairs. Supporting features at best. Hitchcock's film demonstrated that the genre could be mounted on a bigger, more spectacular, A-feature scale.

JAMES STRATTON

North by Northwest gave *Bond* the following: the quickly changing multiple locations, the smart-assed, irreverent verbal reactions, the sophisticated debonair villains, the complicated assaults, the sustained physical abuse of the hero, and the initially distant female character who becomes an ally.

Dr. No from United Artists offered everything *North by Northwest* did and more. In the colorful, globetrotting, and, at times, sadistic film, the sinister Dr. Julius No is working for SPECTRE to topple American rocket launches. One man stands in his way: James Bond, the only gentleman secret agent with a license to kill . . . and thrill . . . as the trailers bombastically heralded Sean Connery's tuxedo-clad arrival.

Played with sinister aplomb by Joseph Wiseman, who feared being typecast in a series of faux Fu Manchu-like roles, Dr. No brings an understated menace to the proceedings with a dash of elegance and class. His lair is hidden on the island of Crab Key; it's exteriors were filmed on the beaches of Ian Fleming's beloved Jamaica, and the stunning Ken Adam-designed interiors—unlike audiences had ever seen before—were created at Pinewood Studios. "Minnows pretending to be whales," muses 007. It depends on which side of the glass you're on.

Although early development revolved around adapting *Thunderball*, plans were abandoned when it became clear to Albert Broccoli and Harry Saltzman that the legal rights were potentially encumbered due to the litigation between Kevin McClory and Ian Fleming. Instead, they chose to develop *Dr. No*, giving birth to the world's greatest movie franchise along the way.

RICHARD MAIBAUM
(cowriter, *Dr. No*)

Deciding to go with *Dr. No* first was one of the best things that ever happened. At that time I went to England and was put to work. I was told to collaborate with Wolf Mankowitz. We read the book again and fell on the floor and said, "What is this? This guy? A Chinaman with two hooks? Fu Manchu and all that kind of stuff, that's gone out with long winter underwear." We decided that Dr. No would be a monkey that sat on the shoulder of the villain, who was going to be the professor. That's the way we wrote it.

RAY MORTON

(senior writer, *Script* magazine)

Mankowitz's contributions to *Dr. No* appear to have been minimal. He worked with Maibaum on an early treatment and apparently had a hard time taking the assignment seriously, since he was allegedly the person responsible for transforming the character of Dr. No into a monkey carried around by Buckman, a more mundane bad guy he created, because he felt Fleming's Fu Manchu–style villain was ridiculous. Mankowitz's presumption ticked off Cubby Broccoli, so Mankowitz withdrew from the project, leaving Maibaum to carry on alone.

WOLF MANKOWITZ

(uncredited cowriter, *Dr. No*)

There were many disagreements with the producers, one of them on the tone of the script. I always intended it to be a spoof. In fact, I wanted Dr. No to be an ape.

RICHARD MAIBAUM

When we handed in the treatment, both Cubby and Harry Saltzman screamed and hollered and yelled and said, "No, this monkey is terrible. We want the Chinaman with the hooks." Wolf Mankowitz didn't like what happened and quit. I was there alone, and the monkey was out. Though whenever Cubby and I had an argument about something, he would yell at me, "Dr. No was a monkey!"

While the script was being written, the search began for a director. Although Terence Young would eventually get the gig, first up was Guy Hamilton, whose most recent films at the time had been *An Inspector Calls* (1954), *Charley Moon* (1956), *Manuela* (1957), and *The Devil's Disciple* (1959). But family issues prevented him from being able to commit to the shooting schedule in Jamaica and he bowed out. The job fell to Young, who was born on June 20, 1915, in Shanghai, China. His pre-*Bond* directorial credits include *Corridor of Mirrors* (1948), *Safari* (1956), *Action of the Tiger* (1957), and *Black Tights* (1961). After directing *Dr. No, From Russia with Love* (1963), and *Thunderball* (1965), he moved on to such projects as *Wait until Dark* (1967), *Red Sun* (1971), *The Valachi Papers* (1972), *Bloodline* (1979), *Inchon* (1981), *The Jigsaw Man* (1984), and *Run for Your Life* (1988).

Early on in his career, Young received training as a writer and sold several screenplays. In World War Two he was a part of the Guards Armored Division and was wounded twice in battle. His feeling was that the experience provided a more rounded understanding of men in action. Later, in 1948, he encountered playwright Sherwood Anderson, from whom he learned the fast-moving style that would later be utilized by him in the *Bond* films.

TERENCE YOUNG
(director, *Dr. No*)
I learned not to use up time and attention introducing characters and getting them started. He also taught me the importance of strong "go-outers," which is the line you write to take someone off the scene in an unforgettable way.

DAVID V. PICKER
(president and chief executive officer, United Artists)
As I'm sure is the same with everyone else in the world, I found Terence to be a charming, witty, extremely literate, and pleasant gentleman. I appreciated his time and his willingness to talk openly about his friendship with Ian Fleming and his observations of the world of James Bond. Certainly no one knows more about the creation of the cinema's 007 than the man who defined a genre, creating *Dr. No*, *From Russia with Love*, and *Thunderball*, three of the first and probably best films in the series.

PETER HUNT
(editor, *Dr. No*)
Terence was extremely instrumental in the whole style of the films. He was extremely encouraging to me in our early style of *Dr. No* and *From Russia with Love*, and one cannot underestimate the personality of Terence that was interjected into the character of James Bond and Sean Connery's playing of it in the early films. There's no doubt about it, and he was the right man for the job at the time, a very good filmmaker.

RICHARD MAIBAUM
I think Terence is not a meticulous director, but he's an inspired one at times. Although there are things in his pictures that are even sloppy, still, I think he's almost the best that we've had in doing the romantic scenes. I don't think he's been given all the credit that he deserves, especially not these days, where it's a long time ago.

DAVID V. PICKER

Had he been some years younger, Terence could have played James Bond. Years after I left UA, I produced a film directed by Terence. Terence dressed from Savile Row. Terence ate at Les Ambassadeurs, the poshest place in London. If he had money, he spent it. If he didn't have any, he spent it. If he saw a beautiful woman, he went after her, but with class and style. And that's what Sean needed to become James Bond. He needed Terence Young, and that's who he got.

Young came to the project already knowing both Cubby Broccoli and Ian Fleming, which helped in no small way in terms of his comfort level.

TERENCE YOUNG

I knew Ian, but I didn't particularly like him. We became, eventually, enormously good friends, but I thought he was a pompous son of a bitch, immensely arrogant, and when we saw him after I'd been signed to do the picture at some big press show put on by United Artists, he said, "So they've decided on you to fuck up my work." I said, "Well, let me put it this way, Ian. I don't think anything you've written is immortal as yet, whereas the last picture I made won the Grand Prix at Venice. Now let's start level." He said, "My, you're a prickly guy, aren't you?" and I said, "Yes, I am, now let's go and have dinner." We left the party and went off and had dinner. Ian was a charmer once you got to know him. He was one of the most delightful people I ever met.

One of Young's first challenges, according to the director, was the screenplay itself, which wasn't close to being ready to shoot.

TERENCE YOUNG

We had, at one time, I believe, five different scripts on *Dr. No*, including one in which Dr. No was a monkey. It was the craziest thing, and finally Cubby Broccoli nearly killed Harry. I mean physically. He got in a rage, and Cubby's a very quiet, tranquil man, but by God he was inflamed, and he said, "Look, we've paid all this fucking money for this *James Bond* book and we're not using a word of it. Now, Terence is a writer; he's the quickest writer I know. He's got 10 days to put it back; he can take all the scripts we have and collect them, and whatever he writes we're going to be stuck with, and Harry, if it's bad, it's *your* fault." He blamed Harry, because Harry was in charge of the script. Cubby was doing other things. That's how this girl, Johanna Harwood, who was my continuity girl on a previous picture, got in it with me. We took a room at the Dorchester Hotel, and we worked day and night. I used to give her things to write, like I'd say, "James Bond comes out of this, gets in the car, and drives off. Just put it in, wearing this . . . ," and I'd go on writing another scene with dialogue. She did that and she did it very well.

RAY MORTON

Johanna Harwood was the first screenwriter of the Eon *Bond* movies. She penned the original treatment for *Dr. No*—by her own account, a very straightforward adaptation of the novel—which was used to get things rolling, but was apparently discarded by Maibaum and Mankowitz when they came on board. She was also the final screenwriter on the movie, doing a final edit and polish on the script in conjunction with director Terence Young just prior to the commencement of principal photography. So she was responsible for the final shape of the narrative and also contributed the great visual gag showing the recently stolen *Portrait of the Duke of Wellington* by Goya in Dr. No's lair, suggesting that No was responsible for its theft.

With the script being finalized and Young signed as director, the most important challenge was finding an actor who could bring James Bond to life. While the initial instinct may have been to cast a "name," Broccoli and Saltzman strongly believed that 007 needed to be played by an unknown for two significant reasons: they wouldn't be bringing the baggage of other roles to this film, and, more importantly, an established star likely wouldn't sign for multiple films and would be too expensive. The answer ultimately came in the form of Sean Connery.

TERENCE YOUNG

I first met Sean in 1957 when I was making *Action of the Tiger,* which starred Van Johnson and Martine Carol. He was a rough diamond, but already he had a sort of animal force. Like a younger Burt Lancaster or Kirk Douglas. The interesting thing is that Martine Carol, who was a very famous French actress at the time, said, "This boy should be playing the lead instead of Van Johnson. This man has big star quality."

ROBERT SELLERS

(author, *The Battle for Bond*)

My feelings are that Connery wanted the role, but the hesitancy came from having to sign another long-term contract. And as we know, by his third or fourth *Bond* film this became a bone of contention between the actor and the producers.

DAVID V. PICKER

Names started to filter back to us from London. Patrick McGoohan was mentioned. Then a bright young actor named Robert Shaw. Finally, Harry Saltzman called me from London to say he was coming to New York with some film and stills on their choice. His name was Sean Connery. He was a Scotsman. The clips Harry brought were from two films Connery had made for American companies, *Darby O'Gill and the Little People* for Disney, and *Another Time, Another Place* for Paramount, both in small roles. I saw the clips. He was attractive. He had what I thought was an Irish accent in *Darby O'Gill*, and in the film with Lana Turner, he sounded more English. I was neither over or underwhelmed. I asked Harry if he was the best he could find, and his answer was, "He's the richest man in the poorhouse." "If he's the best you can find, then let's go with him." It was as simple as that. The deal for Connery's services was made by Harry and Cubby with Richard Hatton, an agent I'd found in previous dealings to be most approachable and fair.

ROBERT SELLERS

Connery's mistrust of long-term contracts was as a result of his misuse at the hands of 20th Century Fox when they signed him up in the '50s. There he was made to feel like a piece of meat, loaned out to other studios for his bosses to make money. It was a situation that influenced how Connery would always feel about studios and producers and the reason why he carved out a career for himself suing them. Connery also had the recent example of his British contemporary Albert Finney, who had rejected the role of Lawrence of Arabia because he didn't want to sign a five-picture deal with its producer, Sam Spiegel. This might also have crossed Connery's mind as he debated whether to sign on the dotted line to play Bond. "Is this part worth all the shit I'm going to get?"

STANLEY SOPEL

(associate producer, *Dr. No*)

I think they always knew from Day One that Sean Connery was going to play James Bond. He was recommended by a lady journalist who worked for the *Daily Express*. We saw him—he didn't look like anybody's idea of Bond when we first saw him—but there was something there, and Harry and Cubby were pretty certain this was the man they wanted. We did go through the motions of screen-testing some 15 or 20 hopefuls of everybody's idea of what Commander Bond should look like: 6′2″, British upper crust, with the sort of chiseled face. Had a genius come out of that testing, Sean probably wouldn't have gotten the part, but he was it from the beginning.

JOHN CORK

(author, *James Bond: The Legacy*)

The first thing to understand about the cinematic James Bond is that Sean Connery was perfect for the role. He wasn't simply *good*. He was John Wayne in *Stagecoach*. He was Humphrey Bogart in *The Petrified Forest*. He was Marilyn Monroe in *Gentlemen Prefer Blondes*. Everything Connery brought to the role was right.

ROBERT SELLERS

When Sean was cast, people said that was terrible casting. Why are you casting a Scottish truck driver as an Eton-educated English spy? They thought the choice was terrible. But, of course, it was the perfect choice, because to some extent, the Sean Connery film Bond is not the Fleming Bond. He's not the Bond of the novels. He's a different animal altogether.

TERENCE YOUNG

Sean has always hated the press, because they were very snide when he first got the job. They kept saying, "Mr. Connery, would you call yourself an Old Etonian? How did your training driving a milk truck prepare you for this picture?" They were very, very cruel when he started, and Sean from that day on never wanted to have anything to do with the press. I remember when we were doing *Thunderball*, people were saying, "Now that he's important, he won't do any press interviews"—I used to have to twist his wrist to get him to go see the press—and people would say, "Why is he being so unpleasant?" I said, "He's not unpleasant, you were. You started it. After all, Sean's never changed. He's been like this all the time and you're the people that provoked him. You tried to make a monkey out of him and now he doesn't need you."

BOB SIMMONS

(stunt arranger, *Dr. No*)

I used to work with Sean very carefully. He used to say, "What do I do, and what do you do for me?" As the film was progressing, I'd say to Sean, "I want you to come and look at this sequence; I'll show you something." He'd say, "Okay, let's work on it." Sean would be on the set until ten o'clock at night; we'd stay there on the set with just the house lights on, when everybody else had gone. Just the night watchman was there. Sean was so keen; so good.

TERENCE YOUNG

Sean caught on very quickly. I actually took him to Jamaica a week or two before the picture started and we played a little golf. I taught Sean to play golf, actually, and now he can kick the hell out of me, because he's very good. He'd never played before and he didn't like the game; he just went round with me a couple of times. Then when he was doing *Goldfinger,* he had to learn to play properly and he became an absolute golf nut. He's probably the craziest golf enthusiast I've ever met. So Sean came and spent a few days in Jamaica. He's a very shrewd person—he's not clever, he's intelligent. In one week he got the whole thing summed up: how he was going to play Bond, how he was going to look, and all that. He's a very quick study, believe me.

STEVEN E. DE SOUZA

(screenwriter, *Die Hard*)

I knew Connery from *Tarzan's Greatest Adventure*, where he was, essentially, Red Grant to Gordon Scott's almost Bondian Tarzan. Because I had read the novel after I already knew the movie was in the pipeline, I visualized Connery from the very first chapter. In my humble opinion, after him, Timothy Dalton came the closest in appearance to the character described in the books and is tied with Daniel Craig and Connery's first three outings in bringing Bond to plausible life as a living, breathing character.

ROBERT SELLERS

I think Connery was hired for the same reason Fleming and McClory wanted someone like Richard Burton to play Bond in their movie: they could see that if Bond on-screen was played by, let's say, a David Niven–type English actor, it just wouldn't have worked. By the time the *Bond* films came to be made, there had been a revolution in screen acting, instigated in America with the Method and actors like Marlon Brando and James Dean. That style of acting, blue-collar acting if you like, didn't permeate into England for quite a few years.

British film and theater remained the preserve of the middle classes, with about as much dynamism as a slab of pork luncheon meat. There was no virility in British acting at all. Then along came the "kitchen sink" actors who all hailed from the working class: Michael Caine, Albert Finney, Richard Harris, etc., and of course Sean Connery. These actors were macho, virile, uncompromising; their heroes were Bob Mitchum, not Laurence Olivier. In other words, had Bond been played by a middle-class actor, a Dirk Bogarde type, it would have been a gigantic turnoff, especially with American audiences. I think Richard Maibaum said it best when he was asked why Connery worked so well—it was the fact that the producers cast an actor who looked like he was a truck driver, but gave him all the attributes of an English establishment figure, and it was this clash of cultures that made Connery's Bond so fascinating. He was a brute in a Savile Row suit. Daniel Craig has exactly the same appeal.

RONALD D. MOORE

(cowriter, *Mission: Impossible II*)

Sean Connery and *Dr. No* is where it all begins with me. I return to that movie over and over again in my love of the *Bond* franchise. I kind of came to it a little late; I wasn't the dyed-in-the-wool *Bond* fan from an early age. I didn't discover it until high school in the late '70s or early '80s. We had a Betamax and I was madly recording things on network television, and one of them was *Dr. No*. I recorded it from network television and watched it over and over again.

FRED DEKKER

(cowriter, *The Predator*)

Connery was supremely confident. I realize this is what makes a great movie star. If you look back at Steve McQueen or Clint Eastwood or any of those guys, they exude confidence, and there's something magical about that for a schmoe like me going into the movies and wanting to be that.

STEVEN E. DE SOUZA

That moment when he introduced himself in the casino as "Bond, James Bond"—it struck me as simple and classic and, as I was a precocious film buff even at 13, an echo of the introduction to Rick Blaine in *Casablanca*.

LISA FUNNELL

(author, *For His Eyes Only: The Women of James Bond*)

To me, this is one the greatest cinematic introductions. Our first encounter with Bond is through his hands as his face is obscured. We observe his keen sense of touch as he defeats his opponent with ease at the card table. Only when Sylvia Trench asks for his name do we get a shot of Connery, who looks dapper in his tuxedo while smoking a cigarette, and delivers the classic line, "Bond, James Bond." This moment is iconic and many people on-screen and in person have mimicked this mode of personal introduction!

SEAN CONNERY
(actor, "James Bond")

In the beginning, there was one kind of Bond very well known to many people who read the books and had a very definite opinion. For instance, the lock of hair that would fall forward, the blue eyes, cruel to some, sadistic to others, and an athlete. Just many dimensions. That sort of success was there before I even touched it, or even read any of the books. Then when I became involved with the film, I felt that there was a lack of humor about it. Within a year I became quite friendly with Ian Fleming, and what I admired more than anything else about him was his curiosity about *everything.* When I mentioned the business of humor, he was quite surprised, because he felt he was quite humorous. He was, as a man, humorous, but in writing the character, he wasn't.

JOHN CORK

Connery was the closest to Fleming's Bond by a wide margin. It is the Connery of *Dr. No* and *From Russia with Love* who is Fleming's Bond—the Connery who stays out too late at a casino, who has flashes of real anger, who has genuine distaste for the senseless deaths that are too often part of the job. Because the last three *Bond* novels were written after Connery was cast as 007, Fleming made minor concessions to Connery's Bond. He gave 007 a Scottish background, for example. But just as importantly, Terence Young was devoted to transforming Fleming's Bond into a cinematic character. That involved some changes, but Young and Connery capture the elegance, humor, irony, and brutality of Fleming's writing with Connery's performance.

LISA FUNNELL

Connery was an interesting choice for the part. Ian Fleming wanted to cast David Niven in the title role, but Albert R. Broccoli wanted Bond to convey a more mid-Atlantic image with less jarring English mannerisms in order to appeal to the American market. Connery was certainly able to achieve this. However, my primary issue with Connery's Bond is the way in which he interacts, often violently, with women. He manhandles them (like when he tells Honey Ryder to leave the island and pulls her toward her boat) and his sexual encounters are often coercive and devoid of consent (as in the case of Miss Taro, who clearly doesn't want to sleep with Bond but is coerced). If the character of Bond stems from the British-lover literary tradition, then why does he need to use force to get women to comply with his wishes? For me, this detracts from his heroism. In fact, my students describe Connery's Bond as being "rapey," and I find this to be extremely problematic.

TERENCE YOUNG

People have said I put a lot of myself into Bond. I sent Sean to my shirtmaker, I took him to my tailor, I used to make him go out in these clothes, because Sean's idea of a good evening out would be to go out in a lumber jacket. One thing, in fact—and I don't know whether one should talk about this—Sean is not a very polite eater. In *Dr. No,* in that scene in the dining room, Sean sits down and they have dinner. I kept saying, "Sean, you've got to eat with your mouth closed," and he kept saying, "Well, I can't breathe if I do that!" So I changed the thing and we brought in the champagne and Sean had a little bit of one-upmanship by saying, "Ah, the 1951; I prefer the 1952," or something like that. Of course, by the time we did *Thunderball,* Sean *was* James Bond as no one else will ever be.

Beyond Connery, Bernard Lee and Lois Maxwell were cast as Bond perennials "M," his superior, and M's secretary, Miss Moneypenny; Joseph Wiseman was cast as Dr. No, Jack Lord as CIA agent Felix Leiter, and Ursula Andress as the first "*Bond* Girl," Honey Ryder.

RICHARD MAIBAUM

Joseph Wiseman was sensational. I owe a great deal to him. When he read that line "You disappoint me, Mr. Bond. You are nothing but a stupid policeman. . . ." I just *knew* that was the tone that all the villains had to take. A touch of elegance and so forth.

GLEN OLIVER
(pop culture commentator)

Joseph Wiseman did less to set "the template" than the overall conception of his character. His mega-baddie moves were so pointedly archetypical from the outset, I'm not sure how the role might've been played differently. My understanding is that the *Bond* creative team at that time was big on revisiting notions and gags which were previously proven to have worked. Wiseman ran the program vividly and memorably. As a result, the archetype was proven valid, and subsequently revisited for future pictures. That's my read on the matter, at least.

LISA FUNNELL

It is hard for me to talk about Dr. No as a villain without first addressing the use of yellowface in the film. All the major Asian characters—Dr. No and Miss Taro—are depicted through this racist representational mode. Even though the character of Dr. No is multiracial, they still rely on racist stereotypes in his representation. The film is also ableist [biased in favor of the able-bodied] in its vilification of Dr. No, and this set the precedent for the following films to do the same. While Bond is presented as able-bodied and physically capable, he often comes up against villains and hench-people (men specifically) who have some form of physical impairment. This taps into a longstanding cultural tradition of vilifying people who look and/or move differently. Blofeld is a good example, and his eye scar has been used in the depiction of other villainous characters, like Scar (who is essentialized by his name) in *The Lion King*.

JOHN CORK

Terence Young worked very closely with Wiseman to develop the performance you see in *Dr. No.* Young instructed Wiseman to move like a robot, to speak like a robot, to avoid blinking. Wiseman, a skilled actor, turned in a great performance that gave Terence Young exactly what he wanted.

GLEN OLIVER

Jack Lord was an extremely legit Felix Leiter. Of course, Lord had a way of legitimizing anything—he was basically a smooth, finely tuned "cool" machine. I mean, his name was Jack Lord, which in itself sounded like a "Don't fuck with me" throw-down before he even had a chance to speak a line. The bitch of it for Jack is, when viewed from a historical perspective, it's nearly impossible to separate Lord's Felix from his later role as Steve McGarrett on *Hawaii Five-O.* Which isn't fair at all, but is a tricky pitfall to avoid when looking back across the decades. Lord's Felix was a great McGarrett and vice versa. Nonetheless, Lord strongly complemented Connery's harder, cooler demeanor. He was one of the few Felixes who felt like he might feasibly be a worthy counterpart to Bond. He felt like someone who might actually be capable of working alongside Bond—someone who was perhaps even close to being an equal to 007.

RICHARD MAIBAUM

The best Leiter we ever had was Jack Lord, but he wanted so much money to continue that they couldn't do it. He probably wouldn't have stayed anyway, because he went off and did that Hawaiian thing, which was a great success. But I liked Jack very, very much.

LISA FUNNELL

Felix Leiter is set up as Bond's equal in the CIA. When working in the US, Leiter has access to material resources and personnel while Bond is shown to be mobilizing and/or directing them. So while initially presented as equals—

with Jack Lord looking notably similar to Sean Connery in terms of their facial features, mode of dress (in tan suits), and even posture—Bond appears to be a more capable and competent agent. This is a *James Bond* film, after all. But this, in turn, creates the impression that the UK is comparable to the US, if not superior, when it comes to safeguarding Anglo-American interests.

JOHN CORK

Until *Casino Royale* and the fantastic casting of Jeffrey Wright, Felix Leiter was the bastard stepchild of the *Bond* films. Jack Lord could have been a great reoccurring character in the films, but he was unavailable for *Goldfinger.* Regardless, these are *Bond* films, not buddy-cop movies. Felix, invariably, was treated as an afterthought by the screenwriters and the directors. He's left basically saying lines that no actor can sell. No straight man can do much with, "On you everything looks good." Leiter serves the purpose of tossing off bits of generally ill-informed exposition and making James Bond look smart, suave, and irresistible. I liked David Hedison's Felix in *Live and Let Die*. In that film, Tom Mankiewicz was very smart in how he let Leiter play the guy who had to go around cleaning up the messes that Bond leaves behind. The scene at the Royal Orleans where Felix is handling the angry phone calls from Mr. Bleeker while Bond is meeting with a tailor is perfectly handled by Hedison. He's exactly right for *Live and Let Die*. On *Casino Royale,* Jeffrey Wright is not only a fantastic actor, but thankfully the filmmakers worked hard to give him something to do. All those early actors had one job: find a way to look admiringly at James Bond, give a knowing sigh, and convey that "gee, what a guy" expression without looking like they had a crush on 007.

RICHARD MAIBAUM

As Moore got older, and as Connery got older, some of the Leiters had to get a little older. I don't think it had much effect.

GLEN OLIVER

Being an equal or near equal to Bond was a critical component of making the Leiter role work at all, and an element many of the films featuring Felix struggled with. So many of the Felixes in later films were cast with lesser personalities, or weaker presences, when compared to the Bond du jour. Which in my mind at least, begged the question: how did these numpties end up on such a high-end assignment, working alongside the world's best secret agent? Their personality and energy made no sense within the *Bond* universe and playbook. David Hedison, for example, was an extremely likable presence—

and he was certainly an eminently accessible Felix. But, at the end of the day, watching him run around as an action guy with 007 was every bit as discordant as imagining Regis Philbin as John Wick.

And then, of course, there's Ursula Andress. Playing the voluptuous Honey Ryder, her emergence from the waters around Crab Key–in nothing but a barely there white bikini–remains one of the most memorable sequences (not to mention bathing attire) in the history of cinema. Despite being dubbed by Nikki van der Zyl, Andress epitomized everything a *Bond* Girl is and would become: beautiful, resourceful, and deadly, having murdered, in a most sadistic fashion, the man who raped her as a girl. Although Fleming writes the scene with Honey emerging from the water nude, it's hard to imagine the filmmakers could have crafted a sexier scene than this one. It was so memorable that it would get revisited in *Die Another Day* and *Casino Royale* with Halle Berry and Daniel Craig, respectively, emerging from the water with nearly as dramatic an effect.

JOHN CORK

Ursula Andress was one of the most beautiful women in the world, yet few knew her name or what she looked like. It is one of the greatest entrances in film history. When Cubby called Max Arnow at Columbia Pictures to see about casting Ursula Andress as Honey, Max told Cubby that no photograph could do this woman justice. She was beautiful beyond compare, but, he added, "She has a voice like a Dutch comic." Cubby and Harry were undeterred. They were not trying to cast stars. They were trying to create "*Bond* Girls." These were women that were not going to exist in reality.

ROBERT CAPLEN

(author, *Shaken & Stirred: The Feminism of James Bond*)

On the surface, the *Bond* Girl represents pure sex appeal, a fantasy of the archetypal woman: attractive, somewhat resourceful, and worldly (but not too much to be deemed a threat to the patriarchy), intriguing and susceptible to the power of persuasion. She is, in many respects, escapism for both male and female audiences. Men want to seduce her, and women want to be her.

JOHN CORK

They wanted women who were "exotic" in many of the roles, and by that they simply meant that these were women who were not generally English or American. Those types of actresses spoke with accented English and they were often dubbed in both British and American films. Plus, with both Nikki van der Zyl (who dubbed over a dozen women in the *Bond* films through *Live and Let Die*) and Barbara Jefford (who provided the voice of Tatiana Romanova in *From Russia with Love*), they had actresses who could imbue every line with a level of sensuality. A third factor was editor Peter Hunt, who wanted to move into directing. He supervised the rerecording sessions and, working with the host of actors and actresses who were dubbing so many of the parts, he had the chance to direct performances. He loved reshaping scenes in post-production with the dubbing performances.

LISA FUNNELL

When you ask people about *Bond* Girl imagery or who they look back at, Ursula Andress is the one that they talk about: this notion of just emerging from the sea with Bond watching her. For me, it is typical of this type of gaze that you get in film. There's a scholar, Laura Ulvey, who talks about the gaze in film, and she argues that in film, basically you have a male active gazer, the one who looks, and that women are presented as these objects of pleasure that are being gazed upon. It is exactly that scene where Bond stops literally whatever he's doing to watch her as she moves toward him. Then Quarrel comes down the beach trying to warn about, whatever, that machine is coming, and he does the same thing where he just stopped and gawked at her and at her beauty. When I teach, that is the scene that I use to talk about the gaze in our media, the gaze in film, and it is *that* iconic. I think that as a character, she's very interesting. Hopefully, I'm not going to blend the novel and the film together, but you have this woman who is self-educated, you have this woman who is trying to be self-sufficient, and yet also express vulnerability to it. There's that notion of strength and vulnerability.

ROBERT CAPLEN

Despite her perceived independence, Honey Ryder really doesn't have a profession. Sure, she's a seashell entrepreneur on an exotic island in the Caribbean and educated herself by reading an encyclopedia, but she is ultimately not an independent or reliable character. My study on Honey reveals some interesting—and questionable—character traits. As a fantasy character, Honey Ryder is much different than female characters in other spy films, who might be seen in functional roles akin to Miss Moneypenny. Helen Smith in *Calling Bulldog Drummond* and Eve Kendall in *North by Northwest* come to mind. *Bond* Girls are, for the most part, aesthetic accompaniments, important to Bond's mission, but ultimately objects of affection and dispensable.

STEVEN E. DE SOUZA

Dude, I was 13 and she may as well have stepped out of a *Playboy* centerfold. All that was missing was the staple in her navel. I did notice that, unlike the book, she didn't have a broken nose. Fleming had a thing where all the *Bond* Girls were slightly damaged—one foot shorter than the other, different colored eyes, etc.

LISA FUNNELL

She had me until her pants come off. What happened to her pants when the guards took her away in Dr. No's lair? You can't chain her up without taking off her pants? There's this other really awful trope that happens in film where women get kidnapped by villainous men and they basically take away their agency and dress them in whatever sort of costumes or designs that they want. This happens all the time with women. Like they're *that* disempowered that what they look like is decided for them. You have to be an object of pleasure for this person. That, for me, just taps into the notion of, "Take off her pants, because we've decided that she's imprisoned." Think about Tiffany Case on that rig in *Diamonds Are Forever,* wearing a bikini. Or Mary Goodnight in *The Man with the Golden Gun,* where Britt Ekland is put into a bikini by Scaramanga. It's just an interesting, problematic, repetitive trope.

TERENCE YOUNG

The first time Ian Fleming came to the set, he was walking down the beach when I was shooting the scene with Honey Ryder coming out of the water, which I suppose is the greatest woman's entrance in a picture. The best man's entrance is Omar Sharif in *Lawrence of Arabia,* and the best woman's is Ursula's. I was shooting this scene and I saw some people ruining my shot, walking down the beach toward me. We waved at them and screamed, "Lie down, you bastards!" They all lay down, and we had shot the scene and forgot about them. We went on shooting a scene. Half an hour later, someone said, "Whatever happened to those geezers on the beach?" And I said, "You'd better go see," and he came back with Ian Fleming, Noël Coward, Stephen Spender the poet, and Peter Cornell the critic. Those were the four; it was quite a bridge game.

CHARLES "JERRY" JUROE
(publicist)

Ursula Andress was the first one. She was not a *Bond* Girl—she was *the Bond* Girl. Daniela Bianchi was the next *Bond* Girl, and then it evolved. There were the *Bond* Girls, the many pretty ladies in the movie, and they became the *Bond*

Girls. A *Bond* leading lady was a *Bond* leading lady, except the press said she was a *Bond* Girl. What the press called her, we couldn't control.

Other *Bond* Girls in *Dr. No* were Eunice Gayson as Sylvia Trench, who Bond meets while playing baccarat at the beginning of the film (and was set up as a sort of running joke in this film and *From Russia with Love* as the person Bond would keep abandoning for assignments from M, a conceit dropped by Guy Hamilton in *Goldfinger*), and Zena Marshall as the treacherous Miss Taro, Dr. No's henchwoman.

LISA FUNNELL

I didn't see Sylvia Trench as a running joke. Instead, she is the first of many female secondary characters who are there to convey the impression that Bond is sexually desirable. This feeds into the lover model of masculinity that defines the title character. She has a name and makes her own choices, which is more than I can say for some of his other lovers/conquests. She appears to have bodily autonomy and consents to their sexual encounter. This seems representative of the sexual revolution of the Swinging Sixties and I don't think that women should be judged or ridiculed for their sexual desires and activities (i.e., she initiates the sexual encounter and clearly consents). I am more disturbed by Bond's encounters with Miss Taro and the use of racial stereotypes in her representation as well as yellowface.

Bond's relationship with women depends on who they are in terms of their narrative position (i.e., primary vs. secondary figure, good vs. villainous) and social locations (i.e., primarily race and ethnicity but sexual orientation and professional standing also factor in). For instance, the unnamed photographer in *Dr. No* is a woman of color who works freelance. She is physically assaulted by Quarrel on Bond's order and thrown out of the club. She has little value to Bond and is treated as such. Bond also treats Miss Taro poorly, unlike other female hench-people in the Connery era and *Bond* franchise at large. He coerces her into having sex with him knowing that everyone working for Dr. No is fearful for their lives and she will have to comply. She is presented as a dragon lady, and her sexuality and sexual desirability (from her costuming to the application of her makeup) are emphasized. By comparison, white women in the film are depicted differently and Bond treats them with more respect. It is important to untangle the web of women presented in each film and the franchise at large instead of relying on the colloquial descriptor of "*Bond* Girl" to refer to every woman who appears in the film. There are different types of characters, and the representational politics matter as gender intersects with race, ethnicity, sexual orientation, class, ability, etc.

Highlighted by his playing Henry Higgins to Sean Connery's Eliza Dolittle, Young assembled a film that, even after over 50 years, still holds up remarkably well (despite some dodgy rear projection). Even with a budget of only a little over $1 million, the film has enormous scope and began to put into place many of the iconic 007 elements that are still with us today: Despite the lack of a pre-title sequence, the Maurice Binder–designed credits anticipate the far more sophisticated and memorable titles to come; John Barry's orchestration of Monty Norman's "James Bond Theme" is layered throughout the film (perhaps a tad too often and a bit too bombastically); and then there's Ken Adam's remarkable sets, all of which belie the film's limited budget.

Insofar as Adam is concerned, there are several moments that highlight the unique style of production design he brought to the film. The first is the moment when Professor Dent comes to see Dr. No in a fairly bare set and is given a tarantula that he is to use on Bond.

KEN ADAM

(production designer, *Dr. No*)

It was a low-budget film; the whole film was done for just under a million dollars and my set budget originally was 12,000 pounds, and I said, "I can't do the sets for that." The two producers said they had some money stashed away somewhere and gave me another 6,000 pounds. It was very low, and nobody, of course, expected the success of this movie, and that set was really an afterthought, because I had run out of money and completely forgotten about that set.

BRUCE FEIRSTEIN

(cowriter, *GoldenEye*)

He designed that set so it could only be shot from one angle, and that was a last-minute addition to the film, I was told. Yet that scene and that room, and that set design, was one of these iconic things about the film. What Michael Wilson told me is that it was the necessity of the budget that caused them to create this tiny, little room that they shot from one angle that we remember so clearly. And it wasn't about planning out a $10 million action scene, it was off-the-cuff, quickly done, and yet it stayed with us. Ken Adam, who I did manage to meet and spend some time with, was just amazing.

KEN ADAM

Three or four days before we finished shooting at Pinewood, Terence Young reminded me about the set, and I said, "Oh my God." I had 570 pounds left, and so I came up with this set built in perspective on a sloping platform, and a sloping roof, because in order to get the whole circle of that grill in, I had to do it like that. The cameraman, who was a friend of mine, managed to get this incredible spider effect on the walls, and in a way it was the first minimalistic type of film set, certainly in the *Bond*s . . . a chair, a door and the circle, and the tracking back to the foreground table with the tarantula. A number of critics eventually said that they thought it set the style for all the future *Bond*s.

The next major set was Dr. No's lair, adorned with a large aquarium with huge fish swimming around in it.

KEN ADAM

I sort of mixed the dressing of the design with some antique furniture, because I thought with the tree in the middle of it, it would work. The one problem I had, because we had no money, was we asked for stock shots of fish. But we wanted sharks or something, and instead they were sort of goldfish size. It was a disaster. I had designed this big space to rear project or front project these fish onto, and suddenly these small fish became enormous and completely unbelievable. That's why we had to introduce appropriate dialogue and the magnifying effect. It's something we learned, because, eventually, of course, the budgets of the *Bonds* became larger and I didn't make that mistake again.

BRUCE FEIRSTEIN

What Cubby told me was that it was a mistake, that the prospects that they have put on the glass magnified, which it was supposed to do. On the set, Maibaum wrote the line about it making things look bigger than they are.

KEN ADAM

It was an age of invention, and nobody was really watching me, because I was by myself at Pinewood while the units were shooting in Jamaica. Terence had complete confidence in me provided that I give him the right entrances and exits for the actors. He said, "I leave the style to you," and I got away with it somehow.

Another element that began with *Dr. No* was an innovative style of editing introduced by Young and Peter Hunt, and the start of action sequences that would evolve like in no other films before it.

PETER HUNT

I was a top English film editor in those days. Harry Saltzman, who came across to England, where the first film he made was *Look Back in Anger,* which starred Richard Burton, had been connected to theater and various things during the early '50s. The war was over, and I was editing, and Harry had always wanted to use me. When he made a film he'd call me and say, "Come on, let's make a film together," and each time I was either in the middle of a film or about to do another film, so I had never been able to do it. But we kept on good terms, and it was Harry who got ahold of me when he was doing *Dr. No.* It happened that I wasn't doing anything else at that time. I've known Terence since I was a boy; I'd been assistant on several films with him, and I'd always liked him. So all of that sort of slotted into place, and I found myself editing *Dr. No.*

STANLEY SOPEL

Peter Hunt hadn't been the first choice, but right away we could see he had the right feeling for what we wanted to do. I remember shouting matches between Peter and Terence Young and other directors when he implored them to keep the scenes short, and avoid long speeches. "This is an action picture, not Shakespeare!" he would tell them. I think his contribution is almost as great as Terence's.

PETER HUNT

Of course everybody has forgotten it now, because we've all fallen into that idiom in the way of presenting films—we always cut films in the way I did *Dr. No*—but at that time that was something completely different to do. If you looked at any films made before 1961, even American films, they always have the guy walking down the steps, through the gates, getting into the car, and driving away. We don't do any of that anymore. The fellow says he's going, and he's there. You cut to the chase, which is what I did in *Dr. No* in order to make it move fast and push it along the whole time, while giving it a certain style. Now, of course, that style is standard for everything.

TERENCE YOUNG

Nobody had ever cut pictures the way we did the *Bond* films. *Dr. No* and *From Russia with Love* were an absolute breath of fresh air in the cutting rooms. Even the director David Lean, who's one of the best cutters in the business, used to come and watch *From Russia with Love* on the Moviola while we were cutting it. He was cutting *Lawrence of Arabia* in the next room at the same time, and often used to say that he wished we could swap films.

PETER HUNT

Now on *Dr. No*, of course, they had a lot of production problems; it was a very cheap production, completely unlike the amount of money they spend today. There were an enormous amount of challenges and problems. They had terrible weather in Jamaica, and they didn't shoot half of what they were supposed to shoot, so there was a great deal of ingenuity and creativity that went into the making of the film. That's really how *Dr. No* was born, as it were, and at that time, in fact, nobody gave much thought to the film. They just thought it was a cheap film being made at Pinewood. All cutters, editors, and people like that are cynical beings, because they see the material so much, so often, but we thought *Dr. No* was marvelous fun, and we tried to make it more amusing wherever we could. Terence wasn't quite so sure about all of that. He thought we were setting him up with this film. Anyway, he went along with it and various things that I suggested, because we had to get it moving as a film and make it all work. Out of necessity, the problems of production, *Dr. No* was born.

BOB SIMMONS

Peter Hunt was wonderful! He'd walk on the set and say, "Just let Bob go through it and let him do anything. If it's going left to right, right to left, upside down on the ceiling—let him do it, and I'll cut it into the picture." And this is the kind of editor you need for an action sequence.

PETER HUNT

I don't think that before *Dr. No* was run with an audience, anyone knew what we had, and it was only when a large audience at the London Pavilion saw it, and they fell about and enjoyed it, that it suddenly dawned on them what we had here. We had an entirely new type of film. You must remember that the climate of the audiences at the time was very "kitchen sink." It was all for actresses doing the washing up, and the housework, the sleazy back room about hard lives, which I guess the audience had become a bit bored with. Here was an absolute breath of fantasy, glamour, and they loved it. Like everything, it had a certain amount of luck when it came out, which is why I guess it took off. That's what I think, anyway. Then, after the opening, it was very successful, and United Artists was pleased, although I don't think they originally thought too highly of it. Then, when the returns started to come in, they seemed *very* pleased.

TERENCE YOUNG

It changed styles of filmmaking. There was a very interesting article by the head of the Cinémathèque, in France, in which he said that *Dr. No* was one of the great innovative films. He made a very shrewd comment when he said, "Years from now, all films will be made like this." He said that they'd even be making them like that on television, which I think is very true.

PETER HUNT

It all helped, as it worked out. I really have to point out that at that time we had had many serious films, and I got a feeling that audiences were getting bored with them. The films were about angry, earthy people, and here was something that had suddenly gone back to sort of a 1940s' glamour Hollywood-type style film, with a special film style.

TERENCE YOUNG

I realized there were an awful lot of plot holes in *Dr. No,* but I worked out that if you could entertain an audience for a couple of hours, they wouldn't really start being difficult about the story till they were on the way home, and then the wife would probably say to her husband, "Well, why don't you shut up; you enjoyed it!" That was always the technique we would try to keep in it. To keep the thing moving so much, and Peter Hunt did a wonderful job of editing. It's the first time, in *Dr. No,* that you cut in the middle of pans, in the middle of tracks. Peter was horrified. He said, "I'll never get a job. If you want me to do it, I'll do it, but it'll look awful, and furthermore, I'll never get another job—they'll just think I can't cut." But I said, "Let's have a go." When the picture was finished and we ran it, without soundtrack, Peter was absolutely delighted. And on *From Russia with Love*, he was doing things that had me saying, "Peter, for God's sake, you don't do that! That's not editing!" and he said, "Who's talking?" He really was the most perfect editor for that picture, because he was young enough to be enthusiastic and to try things, whereas somebody else with a great reputation would have been more prudent.

Insofar as the action in the film is concerned, much of that fell to stunt coordinator Bob Simmons, who was also the silhouetted figure walking into the gun barrel in the beginning of the first three *Bond* films.

BOB SIMMONS

I used to watch action sequences and think, "They're not very good. I can do much better than that." Cubby Broccoli actually gave me my first opportunity.

He was then attached to Warwick Films with Irving Allen. I went down to do *Red Beret*. I was taken down by Paddy Ryan, a famous old stuntman—one of the greatest of that era. Paddy introduced me, and I started working. After doing one-third of the picture, Cubby told me he'd employ me on all his pictures. They used to bring over a stunt arranger from America, and after I'd worked on a picture, they didn't bring him over anymore. I got the job. And I was always looking for a better way. I admired the American way of working. It's terribly professional, and that's what I've tried to push into the people who work for me. I know damn well if it hadn't been for the Americans, we wouldn't be in the film industry today.

LISA FUNNELL

The *Bond* films are among the first in the action genre, and over time they become more action-oriented. The fight sequences in *Dr. No* are very short. They usually center on combat between Bond and a single opponent or small group. The fight sequences are short, ranging from 5 to 30 seconds (if that). And the fighting style is straightforwardly American fisticuffs. Over the course of the franchise, the fight sequences become more complex, pulled from a greater range of fighting (like kung fu in *Man with the Golden Gun*) and athletic/sport (like parkour in *Casino Royale*) traditions, and the duration of the sequences increases. For me, the tensest moment is when the tarantula is crawling on Bond's body. The music plays a tremendous role in conveying tension and apprehension. And Bond's killing of the spider with his slipper is punctuated by instrumentation. I'm not sure if this necessarily qualifies as a fight sequence (i.e., Bond vs. the spider), but it is one of the highlights of the film.

RIC MEYERS

(author, *For One Week Only: The World of Exploitation Films*)

The action and fight sequences in *Dr. No* were more physical and visceral, sometimes even bordering on garish—especially for an impressionable nine-year-old, who saw it as their first "adult," non-kiddie-matinee movie the day after it came out. At the start of *Dr. No,* the cold-blooded killing of Strangways—and, especially the blood-splattered execution of his secretary—made me sit up. And I stayed that way during all the sordid, strenuous action highlights: Bond—not a stuntman—grabbing the fake driver's kick and hurling him away in one unbroken shot; the club photographer breaking and scraping a flashbulb against Quarrel's face; Bond viciously hand-gagging and knifing a swamp-searching guard in the kidney . . . all were designed and presented in a blunt-force way. And, of course: "You've had your six." Thump-thump. Unforgettable. Life-changing.

BOB SIMMONS

I used to see people doing fight sequences in bars, and they could never do it in one take, because it wasn't rehearsed. I started choreographing fight sequences, so you could repeat every movement. You could tell the director where to put the camera, because you knew where the action was going to be. This is what I've always concentrated on: giving the best pictorial value, and being able to repeat it. Make it look absolutely fantastic, but nobody should get hurt. If you *do* get hurt . . . well, this is what you're paid for.

> The film also featured a highlight moment that the producers were reluctant to repeat too often over the series' history. When one of Dr. No's henchmen, the ineffective Professor Dent (Anthony Dawson), attempts to get the better of Bond, 007 responds in such a way that it would cement him as being both a clever and ruthless secret agent, capable—when necessary—of cold-blooded murder.

RONALD D. MOORE

The bad guy comes in and thinks Bond is in the bed and he shoots a bunch of shots into the bed. Then Bond trips him up and they have this whole conversation as Bond is just sitting there. He's, like, "Tell me about Dr. No." The guy sees his weapon on the floor and he's edging it over to him slowly, thinking Bond hasn't seen it. He keeps edging this carpet over so that he can grab the gun at a certain point. The guy eventually says, "Well, you'll never find out, so I might as well tell you . . ." and he grabs the gun and it goes "click." Bond just looks at him, cocks his head, and calmly says, "That's a Smith & Wesson, and you've had your six," and he shoots him. I was, like, "Oh my God!" I was *so* blown away.

STEVEN E. DE SOUZA

I saw the movie with other teenaged friends and we lost our minds in that moment. No movie hero had ever done that; it was a palate cleanser after a postwar childhood of watching good guys following Queensberry rules and discarding their weapons facing unarmed opponents.

RONALD D. MOORE

It's such a cold-blooded killing. Don't make any mistake about it. But it was, like, "Wow, a license to kill means something." The way he played that and the cool demeanor and his complete confidence in that moment . . . He never was out of control in the scene, never worried for a second.

STEVEN E. DE SOUZA

It grounded the movie in the real world and established Bond as cold-blooded, practical, and deadly. You can trace a direct line from "You've had your six" to John McClane's "That's what my captain always tells me" before he blindsides the first terrorist he meets in *Die Hard*. (And while we're on the subject . . . *Han shot first.*)

RONALD D. MOORE

That was the scene that defined the character to me. Yes, he got the girls and he could make these witty remarks, and he was always one step ahead of the villains, and there was always the cat and mouse, and there's a lot of other things to love in it, but, man, that scene. I had never seen a hero do anything like that, and I'd never seen anyone as calm and cool as the way Sean Connery played that scene. And it's a moment that kind of stands alone in the series. It was the first movie, so you can see they were sort of trying to figure out how far they'd go with it. They set that marker and then they never exceeded it again.

TERENCE YOUNG

That caused a lot of heartache. United Artists was not happy about it. I said, "Look, this son of a bitch has just tried to kill him in bed; he's had him waylaid up to this palace with the girl and all that to do him in. And you're saying he's behaving wrongly? The man is an executioner. We should never lose that." I think they got further and further away from the character as created by Ian Fleming. It was no longer a character from his books. It's a character from the *James Bond* films.

RIC MEYERS

This scene brings up something not to look for, but to *listen* for: the way the fight sound effects were heightened in the first five films. It's especially noticeable in *You Only Live Twice* during the Osato headquarter building fight scene where Bond uses an entire sofa as a lance against a sumo-size attacker. Suffice to say, the Connery of these five films is totally different than the Connery of what I call his revenge film, *Diamonds Are Forever,* where he mostly runs, flails, and slaughters. But more on that later.

TERENCE YOUNG

I've been accused of being sadistic—the guy pumping bullets into him . . . you know, once you've fired one shot, you may as well fire six. I was a soldier in the war and I was wounded four times. If one bullet hits you and you're still alive, then it matters, but if one bullet hits you and you're dead, they can fire another 20 at you and it isn't going to make you feel any worse.

While it may not have been as visceral as having Bond murder his opponent in cold blood, another innovation of *Dr. No* came in the fledgling world of product placement, which would become an ever-more integral part of the entire *Bond* franchise over the decades.

TANYA NITINS
(author, *Selling James Bond*)

Prior to the *James Bond* film series, product placement in films was a lot less structured. It was always there, though. MGM even had its own product placement office as early as the 1930s; however, the practice was rather sporadic and typically relied on a prop master seeking "donations" of products to be featured as props in a film. What was seen throughout the *James Bond* franchise was a much more systemic approach that saw the practice of product placement become an industry in its own right. James Bond has become one of the few fictional characters to become lodged in our cultural memory banks—even if you have never seen a *James Bond* film or read one of the books, chances are you know who the character of James Bond is. It is this level of global recognition that many brands seek to achieve, making the series a prime site for collaboration.

The fact that product placement was a part of the series right from the start actually isn't that surprising considering Fleming's approach to the literary Bond.

TANYA NITINS

Ian Fleming drew upon specific brand associations for character development. Fleming would spend a great deal of time describing the type of clothing James Bond was wearing, what he was eating, what he was drinking in a specific scene. When *Dr. No* was filmed in 1962, there were 11 separate products featured with 25 actual placements. Over half of these product placements, however, were what I classify as "clutter"—placed in the background of a scene with little to no specific focus placed on them. This was fairly standard practice at the time.

This was also likely a result of James Bond and Sean Connery being fairly unknown entities. Charles Juroe, marketing director for Eon Productions, sought to change this through a series of staged publicity events. Sean Connery was sent on a Continental tour where Juroe enlisted the help of an Italian casino for a publicity stunt in which it was reported that an actor playing an English spy had "broken the bank," which became front-page news around the world.

As noted, *Dr. No* was released in 1962 and was not an immediate hit in America, although ultimately, through various rereleases, it grossed over $16 million on United Artists' $1 million investment. Adjusted for inflation (even without doing so), that is an enormous success. But the truth is, no one had an inkling of what they had unleashed on the world or the success that 007 was destined for in the years to come.

CHARLES "JERRY" JUROE

The first release of *Dr. No* in America, the distribution was basically to drive-ins in Texas and places like that, and it just didn't work. There was not even an upmarket East Side New York release. I wouldn't say that it was mishandled as much as I'd say that they just didn't know what they had. But it was turned around by the success in Europe. It was *so* big in Europe, and then of course, the thing about Kennedy being a big fan of Ian Fleming was a big help. We got a tremendous amount of publicity out of the releases in Europe and eventually in America.

The thing we've got to realize, for United Artists it was just another movie. You've got to separate before it was made and the success it became. It had its positive elements, which any film that gets the green-light situation has to have some spark somewhere that somebody in the company on the production side felt that it was worthwhile putting money into.

JOHN CORK

Dr. No, I believe, was a perfect novel to adapt as the first *Bond* film. The strategic importance of the Caribbean was constantly in the headlines with Castro's takeover of Cuba in '59 and the Bay of Pigs invasion in '61. The space race was in full swing. The story played into these headlines and, of course, the film was released in the UK just before the Cuban Missile Crisis set the world on edge.

FRED DEKKER

The film's low-rent trappings are charming. It's also extremely British. It's in some ways the closest to Fleming, because they were just making a British movie, but the stuff they came up with ended up being ripped off right up until now—which is *not* the things they were thinking about. What they were thinking about was being true to Fleming.

GLEN OLIVER

From very early on, there was a clear sense of who and what Bond was. A sharply focused "vision" of the character's place in the world, of how he relates to the world, and of the overall world he inhabits. It's important to view all of these elements as distinct, by the way, which people often do not do. Bond's "world" doesn't just "happen" or "exist"—it's very much a considered and deliberate construct. In my experience, many folks tend to weigh Bond almost exclusively on their like or dislike of a given leading man. Which is, perhaps, an unavoidable phenomenon given how front and center—and almost iconic—the role is. But when one digs deeper, the truth of the matter is that the overall Bond "universe" is every bit as specialized, defined, and rule governed as *Star Trek* or *Star Wars*—it's just not as obviously so. I think this happens because of, and is a statement to, the charisma of the franchise leads, and the fact that so much of *Bond* feels "real world" and natural at face value, even though the *Bond* world has actually been playing by certain guidelines and definitions for many decades now. Another word for this might be "formula," but the conception and execution of the *Bond*-verse runs deeper than that. It's more like a style guide—more like a "bible."

RICHARD MAIBAUM

We certainly knew there was something different about *Dr. No* from your average spy story. Like when Bond edges a hearse off a cliff and is then asked, "What happened?" and he says, "I don't know. I think they were going to a funeral." Well, now you know *that* was meant to be funny, and humor became an important part of the pictures from the start. *Dr. No* actually told us what the audience liked, what they sparked to.

TERENCE YOUNG

An awful lot of the funny bits in *Dr. No* were knocked up on the set. I supposed I did half, and Sean did at least half himself. He had some very sweet lines and ideas; some of them worked and some of them didn't. One of the lines that got one of the biggest laughs in the picture is when the hearse goes over the cliff, having tried to knock Bond off the road. The construction worker comes up and says, "What happened?" When we had that in the preview, the audience burst out laughing the wrong way, so we changed it. It doesn't lip-sync very well, if you look closely. What he says now is, "How did it happen?" and Sean says, "I don't know. I think he was on his way to a funeral." It's so funny that just transforming a line like that makes it into a belly laugh instead of a laugh *against* us.

RAY MORTON

For me, the Eon *Bonds* break down into two basic categories: relatively realistic and straightforward spy thrillers, and larger-than-life fantasy adventures. The finished script for *Dr. No* is a perfect prototype for the second category: a story that starts with a small incident (in this case, the murder of Strangways) that Bond is sent to investigate and that eventually brings him into both contact and conflict with a megalomaniacal supervillain (in this case, Dr. Julius No), who is assisted by a bizarre henchman (in this case, the Three Blind Mice) and who is planning to implement a world-threatening scheme of some sort, usually one with science-fiction overtones (in this case, missile toppling). This style of *Bond* film usually climaxes with an attack on the villain's lair and ends with Bond killing the bad guy and falling into a final clinch with his leading lady (all of which happens here). The only major difference between *Dr. No* and the subsequent fantasy *Bond*s—thanks primarily to Richard Maibaum, whose main goal was always realism and believability—is the fantasy elements are downplayed in this script, whereas they are amplified in the others.

GLEN OLIVER

Much of *Bond*'s bible was firmly implemented in *Dr. No* and is still very much in play today. This makes *Dr. No* absolutely indispensable in the *Bond* pantheon. It's not one of my favorite *Bond*s, but it *is* the birth of cinematic *Bond*, without a doubt. And what it birthed remains largely recognizable today despite a number of cosmetic makeovers. I think a fascinating point of exploration would be: if *Dr. No* hadn't come out of the gates with such clarity and sure-footedness, what might the resultant *Bond* look like today? Or, would *Bond* still be around at all?

JOHN CORK

The film's tone reflected a ruthlessness and sensuality not seen in most films of the era. One did not have the hero shoot an unarmed man, or, for that matter, coerce a woman into sex when he knows she has been given orders to do whatever it takes to keep him at her home. *Dr. No* reflected the ethos of Ian Fleming's fiction, which was starkly different than what was appearing in cinemas.

RONALD D. MOORE

As you start getting into *Bond,* you see that so much springs from *Dr. No.* The way the villain is played, the supervillain with the giant master plan, having dinner with Bond and talking with him, and the repartee; the gorgeous girl and the exotic location, and getting the mission up front. It's interesting that when he gets the mission from M at the beginning, he's being scolded for having the wrong handgun. What I liked was that it conveyed he *wasn't* a super-agent within the agency. He was just another agent, and actually like a knucklehead who was using the wrong fucking gun. I like that sense of, "Oh, Jesus, it's Bond again with that stupid Beretta." You watch Bond start to become larger than life over the course of all the movies in all the iterations. He's like the greatest spy of them all, but at the beginning he was just another spy. You kind of felt like, "Well, all the double-Os must be really cool; they're all probably interesting and cool and have all kinds of different skill sets, and Bond was just one of them." It kind of grounded it in a different way.

RAY MORTON

The script's other great triumph is that it does a marvelous job of introducing the character of James Bond to the screen. The Bond in this film is a serious fellow who displays much less of a sense of humor than he would in later movies, but his other cinematic traits—his ruthlessness, his wit, his dashing, self-confident manner, his intelligence and resourcefulness, and his incredible sex appeal—are all on prominent display throughout this first adventure.

LISA FUNNELL

Dr. No looks and feels like a different *Bond* film, because it was released before the *Bond* formula was established. It has less action and focuses more on espionage and spy-craft. I really enjoy the scenes where Bond is surveying his surroundings and setting up his hotel room to detect intruders. It shows that he is more than just a "gun for hire" or "strongman" hero. He needs to use his senses to get the job done. I really like how the inaugural film stresses the haptic and sensual qualities of Bond.

RICHARD MAIBAUM

I didn't expect the tremendous reception that *Dr. No* got. I thought it was a very good job on the basis of the script and Terence Young's work. Incidentally, while we're talking about Terence Young, I think that he has not been given the great credit he deserves for the style of the films. Of course, I take a little credit myself, but I think Terence had a great deal to do with that.

STANLEY SOPEL

When the crew went to Jamaica to shoot *Dr. No*, things had been different. It was just another movie being shot with this big Scottish chap; who the hell had ever heard of Sean Connery, or James Bond for that matter? He was just the hero of another book that had not become terribly famous. Film crews don't ever think that they're doing great things.

TERENCE YOUNG

Without being arrogant, the style of the film was established very simply, on the floor, by me. I knew what I wanted. I didn't think the picture was going to be anywhere near as popular as it was. I thought it was going to be a thing for rather highbrow tastes. I thought an awful lot of the jokes were going to be in-jokes. But I guess it caught on very well.

FROM RUSSIA WITH LOVE (1963)

A beautiful Russian cipher clerk in Istanbul claims to have come across a photo of England's only gentleman secret agent with a license to kill, and has decided to defect to the West–through only him–with the Russian's Lektor decoding machine. Absurd? Quite. And yet the premise is at the heart of one of the most grounded, nail-biting 007 adventures of all, the brilliant espionage thriller *From Russia with Love*.

A little over a year after *Dr. No* exploded onto movie screens–October 11, 1963–James Bond was back, as the one-sheets exclaimed with a plethora of exclamation points. It wasn't a surprise why Albert R. Broccoli and Harry Saltzman picked this title to adapt after President John F. Kennedy had hailed to *Life* magazine that the Fleming novel was one of his 10 favorite books of all time. (Tragically, on November 20 and prior to leaving for Dallas, *From Russia with Love* was the last film President Kennedy ever saw.)

JOHN CORK

(author, *The James Bond Encyclopedia*)

The oft-repeated story is that once JFK listed *From Russia with Love* as one of his favorite books, sales of the *Bond* novels soared in the United States. In fact, it was much more complex than that. JFK's endorsement in March 1961 sparked Signet to redesign their *Bond* titles and start releasing them in a uniform style, but the first of those wasn't released until November. Viking Press, which had the hardback rights, heavily promoted *Thunderball,* including having it serialized in US newspapers in early 1962; and Fleming's article on "The Guns of James Bond" in *Sports Illustrated,* plus his appearance on a CBS public affairs program, all worked together to ignite the sales of the *Bond* novels. That really coalesced in early 1962, many months after the appearance of *From Russia with Love* in *Life* magazine on JFK's favorite books list. *Bond* became a phenomenon because of some very hardworking, very smart folks in the book business. They capitalized off of JFK's endorsement, but it took almost a year for that to happen.

STEVEN JAY RUBIN

(author, *The James Bond Films*)

The critical and commercial success of *Dr. No* guaranteed the continuation of a *James Bond* series of films. To reinforce this, the producers had included a brief note at the end of their first film. It read, truthfully: "The end of *Dr. No,* but James Bond will return in *From Russia with Love.*"

DAVID V. PICKER

(president and chief executive officer, United Artists)

We all agreed that *From Russia with Love* was the logical choice. It was a good story for the second in the series, and it could be made for a reasonable cost. The team went to work again, and they did a brilliant job with a bigger budget—$2 million, no questions asked. Cast in the roles of the two villains were Robert Shaw, who had been considered for Bond, and Lotte Lenya, the grande dame of Bertold Brecht musical history.

CHARLES "JERRY" JUROE

(publicist)

With *From Russia with Love,* we were already pretty aware that we had something special—"we" meaning the distribution company, United Artists, who I was with. With rare exception, everything after *Dr. No* became bigger and better, and Sean became bigger and better with it. That was the nature of the way they kept improving the films.

STANLEY SOPEL

(associate producer, *From Russia with Love*)

The crew did grow to love Sean Connery because of his professionalism and his concern for their problems. If the call was for 8:00 A.M., he was on the set at 10 minutes to. He made it a point to learn about their equipment and their problems. He learned about what the cameraman does, not because he particularly wanted to be photographed well, but because he was *interested* in knowing what the cameraman did.

PETER HUNT

(editor, *From Russia with Love*)

On *From Russia with Love* they had more money then, and then I had the bit between my teeth. I knew we were going to be okay, and I was determined that it was going to be okay. *Dr. No* had been made for just under a million dollars. You couldn't possibly make it today without it costing so many millions more. The returns, again, were greatly increased. The funny thing is that they make such a big deal about every latest *Bond* breaking all the records. They break the records because the price of tickets has gone up. For instance, *Thunderball* was the most successful. I don't know if you remember, but they ran it 24 hours a day in New York. It was *amazing*.

TOM SOTER

(author, *Bond and Beyond: 007 and Other Special Agents*)

When Broccoli and Saltzman selected this for their second *Bond*, they attempted to repeat many of the ingredients from *Dr. No*: action, women, and a larger-than-life villain.

TERENCE YOUNG

(director, *From Russia with Love*)

One had to persuade Sean and everybody on the first picture that this picture was going to have a certain style, but you must not take the mickey out of—"taking the mickey out of it" is an English phrase for making a fool of it. It's not satire, it's tongue in cheek, but no more than that. You had to play it with a straight face, but the audience had to realize that there was a little sense of humor flying around the picture. Then they went with it, and they moved with it all the time. We carried that over to *From Russia with Love* and beyond.

PETER HUNT

From Russia with Love was the third film of the deal made between the producers and United Artists. *Dr. No* was a big success, and even their comedy *Call Me Bwana* wasn't a bad success. Bob Hope once told me that it was the only one of his films at that time that had made him money. We were in great, confident spirits at that time, and while we couldn't go mad, I don't think there was a problem regarding production or money. If we needed another day or some extra shots, we got them and did them. So the production was a far better laid out production, although it was entirely the same crew. I think that's what happened, and that there was a great deal more confidence. We were also much more respected by the studio then. They no longer thought of us doing a little crappy picture; suddenly we were the big boys, and demanded all sorts of things.

Once again directed by Bond's auteurist doppelgänger, Terence Young, the film's script was credited to Richard Maibaum and Johanna Harwood, based on the crackling 1957 novel by Fleming. The story seemed tailor-made for the screen and boasted the exotic Istanbul, Turkey, as the center of its Cold War action.

TOM SOTER

From Russia with Love was Fleming's attempt to give his creation a stronger identity and then be done with him. At Raymond Chandler's suggestion, he attempted to paint a more complex Bond—moody, brooding, less of a cardboard figure—and then killed him off in the climax (though he had second thoughts and revived him the following year).

RICHARD MAIBAUM

(cowriter, *From Russia with Love*)

Dr. No told us what the audience liked, what they sparked to. So when I wrote the second film, I think we crystalized the kind of thing that the *Bond* movies should do. That film was the one in which we set the style. In fact, I wrote that script in just six weeks. The others have taken considerably longer—but it still remains my favorite.

RAY MORTON

(senior writer, *Script* magazine)

From Russia with Love is the first of the "thriller" *Bond* films. This second 007 script gives Bond more humor and (if possible) even more charisma than he was given in the first. Richard Maibaum does an excellent job of adapting Fleming's story, retaining the villainous scheme to manipulate and ultimately destroy and defame Bond while changing the villainous organization behind that scheme (SMERSH in the novel, SPECTRE in the film). It also features one of the series' best and most impressive *Bond* Girls, one who plays a vital role in the plot and provides the opportunity for genuine romance. The action in the script is spectacular while always remaining grounded and real. This is also the script that introduces the pre-credit teaser, which would become a staple of the series from then on; and the first Bond "gadget"—his multipurpose briefcase. For my money, Maibaum's script for *From Russia with Love* is—along with his script for *On Her Majesty's Secret Service*—the best and most faithful direct adaptation of a Fleming novel.

TERENCE YOUNG

This was, in my feelings, the best of the *Bond* pictures. Not because I directed it, although I think it's well directed, but because it was the best subject for a *Bond* film. It had a couple of exotic locales, it had the ingredients of the book itself. I think it's the most readable of the books and it's certainly the most agreeable *Bond* picture to sit through and watch. It also had two or three terribly good supporting roles.

STEVEN JAY RUBIN

Richard Maibaum loved this Fleming novel, with its fascinating characters. They were already larger than life, especially the three Russian master spies: Rosa Klebb, the head of operations for SMERSH; Red Grant, the assassin; and Kronsteen, the master planner. Such three-dimensional characterizations, combined with the fantastic blackmail plot and the exotic locale of Istanbul, made the story immediately cinematic. However, as was to be the case in all the *Bond* screenplays, Maibaum was ordered to make changes. Broccoli and Saltzman had decided that the Russians could no longer be the heavies in the film since it was felt strongly that Bond should never get involved in politics. His enemies once more became SPECTRE. Having lost their operative, Dr. No, in the first film, it was only logical to offer them another shot at Bond.

JOHN CORK

SPECTRE is often described as a replacement for SMERSH, the old Soviet internal secret police force that arrested and assassinated those who either betrayed the Soviet Union or who had simply become security risks. When plotting out *Thunderball* as a potential film project, Fleming came up with

SPECTRE, but in all those early scripts, whether it is SPECTRE or, in the drafts managed by Kevin McClory, the Mafia, the organization always has something of a Mafia-type feel, hence all the Italian characters in the novel and the film. But Fleming didn't have a problem with the Russians as adversaries. Russia plays quite a nefarious role in his last two novels, *You Only Live Twice* and *The Man with the Golden Gun*.

For the filmmakers, SPECTRE was a great substitute for Russia right from *Dr. No* on. The Soviet Union was an enemy, sure, but not *the* enemy. It was a great development by Richard Maibaum to structure those early films as being stories where SPECTRE was trying to exploit tensions and capitalize off of them. China, though, is blamed for all sorts of mischief—an atomic device in Fort Knox in *Goldfinger,* Blofeld's volcano rocket base in *You Only Live Twice,* Scaramanga's island hideaway. *The Living Daylights,* like *Octopussy,* plays into the same mold. The films have both good Russians and a bad Russian who is determined to exploit tensions with the West for his own purposes. In none of these films are the Soviets portrayed as anything other than a cultural and geopolitical rival. They are mocked, but respected. One of the best scenes in any *Bond* film is Bond's attempt to assassinate General Pushkin in his hotel room in *The Living Daylights*. We may celebrate the freedom fighters later in the movie, but at that moment, we see the respect and trust Bond has for the Soviet version of M. 007 doesn't believe the Soviets are killing British agents, and he is right.

The cast in *From Russia with Love* is impressive. Lotte Lenya portrays Klebb, and she creates a chilling portrait of the former SMERSH agent now working for SPECTRE and manipulating Tatiana Romanova to carry out their secret agenda. Born October 18, 1898, in Vienna, Austria-Hungary, Lenya enjoyed a career in the world of classical music (performing the songs of her husband, Kurt Weill) as well as acting in English-language films. She was nominated for an Academy Award for 1961's *The Roman Spring of Mrs. Stone*. Beyond the world of music, she appeared in a total of eight films (the last was 1980's *Mahagonny*, released a year before her death from cancer at the age of 83). She also appeared in many stage productions, having originated, on Broadway, the role of Fraulein Schneider in the original 1969 Broadway run of *Cabaret*.

Comments author Donald Spoto in his book *Lenya: A Life*, "As it happened, Lenya's role in *From Russia with Love* introduced her to the widest audience of her career and forever sealed her public image for a new generation as the angular, steely, deadly female. . . . In the film's most famous sequence, Lenya is disguised as a hotel maid bent on killing Bond by jabbing him with poisoned knives that spring neatly from the tip of her sensible shoes. She does a properly graceful feint-and-parry with Connery, kicking and darting round him like a proficient picador. Her death scene is deliciously overplayed, as required by the cartoonlike tone of the *Bond* films."

Vladek Sheybal was the manipulative Kronsteen who foolishly convinces himself that he's pulling 007's strings. Not exactly the case. The actor was born March 12, 1923, and appeared in a wide variety of films from 1957 to 1992 (he died on October 16 of that year), including the 1967 *Bond* spoof, *Casino Royale*. The actor related to ufomagazine.com that it was Sean Connery who wanted him to take the part of Kronsteen. "Why?" he asked rhetorically. "Because I met Sean Connery when he was the boyfriend of Diane Cilento, who was an actress. I was directing a television play with her, and he was always coming to the rehearsal to pick her up and the three of us would go for a drink, and then Diane would try to sell him to me. She would say, 'Look at him! Isn't he sexy? Doesn't he have star quality? Do you see a part for him?' because nobody wanted him. And two years later he was James Bond and Diane Cilento went into decline or whatever–this happens. So, anyway, when I refused flatly to play this part, suddenly there was a telephone call from Sean Connery saying, 'This is something which is going to change the world! It's a new series–*James Bond*–and it's going to be next episode and next episode, and if you take a part in it, you are in a cult thing.' So I signed to do it. He was very kind, because he was waiting personally for me at the doorstep of the studio and he said, 'Welcome to *From Russia with Love*.'"

One of the true highlights of the film is Robert Shaw, whose portrayal of assassin Red Grant is absolutely chilling. Born in Ireland on August 9, 1927, Shaw became known as an actor, a novelist, and a playwright. He received Oscar and Golden Globe nominations for the 1966 film *A Man for All Seasons*; he wrote the novels *The Flag*, *The Man in the Glass Booth*, and *A Card from Morocco*, achieving tremendous acclaim for turning *The Man in the Glass Booth* into a stage play (it was subsequently adapted to film as well). He is, of course, remembered for his roles in such films as *The Sting*, *The Taking of Pelham One Two Three*, *Jaws*, *The Deep*, and *Black Sunday*.

TERENCE YOUNG

I thought Lotte Lenya had an extremely interesting role. Robert Shaw's character was much thinner than in the book, but it still came across as a good character. He was sufficiently *different*.

John French, writing in the biography *Robert Shaw: The Price of Success*, notes, "Shaw's role of Grant is certainly well remembered. His sneering dismissal of the effete Bond ('You may know which wines to drink with your fish, but it's you who are on your knees') and his silent threatening presence through the first two-thirds of the action brought out Shaw's best characteristics as an actor–the ability to suggest a capacity for unlimited violence in a character on the lower rungs of life, in conjunction with some sort of moral, physical, or spiritual superiority, however fleeting. . . . The character was central to the development of the plot of the film. The fact that everything leads up to the confrontation [between him and Bond] on the Orient Express in Yugoslavia, until which time Grant is given no dialogue, gives the part its impact. A comparatively small but crucial part may often count for more than a good performance in a large part which is less integral to the film."

From Russia with Love introduces the man who would ultimately be James Bond's Moriarty or Lex Luthor, Ernst Stavro Blofeld. Anthony Dawson, who played the squirrelly Professor Dent in *Dr. No* and was an old friend of Young's, played the obscured SPECTRE chief, then known only as "Number One," stroking his white cat, his voice dubbed by Eric Pohlmann, remaining to many the definitive portrayal of the character.

JOHN CORK

The real genius of Blofeld came from Terence Young's direction. He focused on using the white cat as Blofeld's alter ego. Eric Pohlmann's voice made Blofeld sound like the most magnificently evil man ever. What a great combination to pair that deep, booming voice with images of a contented soft, white cat. Blofeld was a great go-to villain until Kevin McClory, who had ended up with the rights to *Thunderball*, saw the script for *The Spy Who Loved Me,* and decided it infringed on those rights. The *Bond* producers responded by removing SPECTRE from the script for *The Spy Who Loved Me* and then having a Blofeld-like character appear in the pre-credits of *For Your Eyes Only* to be killed (supposedly). There were arguments on both sides about whether McClory actually could prevent Eon Productions from using Blofeld in future *Bond* movies, but Eon had the right to create new villains, so until they purchased McClory's rights from his estate after *Skyfall*, they didn't feel they needed Blofeld.

Stepping into the position of *Bond* Girl was no easy task when you consider that the leading lady of *From Russia with Love* was being asked to follow *Dr. No*'s Ursula Andress. But the producers were confident that they achieved their goals with the casting of Italian actress Daniela Bianchi in the role of Tatiana Romanova. Born January 31, 1942, she appeared in a total of 16 mostly Italian films, including the 007 knockoff *Operation Kid Brother*, which starred Sean Connery's younger brother, Neil. In 1960, she was the first runner-up in the Miss Universe contest. What Daniela brought to the part of Tatiana was a certain innocence, and the belief that she really could have been a woman taking on this assignment, but then truly falling in love with her target. One additional point: like many of the *Bond* Girls of the 1960s, Daniela's voice was dubbed by another actress, in her case by Barbara Jefford (who would also dub Molly Peters in *Thunderball* and Caroline Munro in *The Spy Who Loved Me*).

RICHARD MAIBAUM

Daniela Bianchi is my favorite *Bond* Girl of them all, though she didn't really want much to be an actress. She'd sit on the set reading an Italian novel and eating chocolates, and then when Terence Young would walk in, he would get peeved with her and scream, "You cow!" She would just shrug and laugh. But, my God, that scene with Sean in the stateroom is probably the sexiest scene in the *Bond* films. The other great thing about her is that, honestly, could there be anything more ridiculous than Tatiana's plot? A cipher clerk working for the Russians sees a picture of Bond and falls in love with him. That's kind of bullshit, but she made it stand up. She seemed to be the kind of a girl who could have done that.

TERENCE YOUNG

Each picture was more successful because of the previous film's setup. A silly example, a line that is certainly not funny the way it was written, and nobody thought it would be funny until we played it with an audience, took place between Sean and Daniela. Romanova is sitting up in bed, wearing a black velvet ribbon around her neck and some silk stockings. In comes Bond wearing a towel, which I had to shoot about three times, because Sean was rather overweight at that time and his belly was showing. I had to say, "Go in and hold your breath and we'll try again." Sean, holding his breath, said in a high-pitched voice, "Now I know how Tarzan feels!" He came in and he did it, and the line she says is, "Romanova," and she puts her hand out. He shakes it and says, "Bond, James Bond," and gets straight into bed. Now it was never thought of as a funny scene when we wrote it, but it just killed the audience straightaway, and that was because Bond had already established a tradition of womanizing, of being a lady killer; that he just had to look at a woman and she just fell into his bed. It was funny, I got the humor, but I didn't see it at the time we were shooting it. It's the strange alchemy of the movie business.

JOHN CORK

After the success of Ursula Andress in *Dr. No,* the producers thought they could cast another unknown. Daniela Bianchi, like Andress, was beautiful and could act, but she also could not speak English very well. The filmmakers were completely ruthless, planning on dubbing her before she shot her first scene. I think Bianchi turns in a great performance.

TERENCE YOUNG

When Bond and Tatiana are in bed, we saw that they were being filmed through a two-way mirror by SPECTRE. That was considered very indecent, very immoral, very sexy and all that. I don't know why. I think you could show it now to a Methodist clergy meeting. We got away with it, because I cut to the guy waving his hand to himself. Actually he was doing it because it was meant to show it was very hot in there. The censor took it as he was saying, "Boy, this is a hot scene going on," and we got a laugh from the censor and got it cleared. I think we had to make it one point darker, or take out two frames just to make him happy.

CHARLES "JERRY" JUROE

The only thing about *From Russia with Love* that wasn't as big or bigger than *Dr. No* was the leading lady, and that wasn't the fault of Daniela Bianchi. It was just that, who *could* hold their own with Ursula Andress? Even though the character of Tatiana was a better-drawn one, it's just that as pretty and as striking as she was, she *wasn't* Ursula Andress.

One of the questions about the character of Tatiana was whether or not Bond—and therefore the audience—could *really* trust her.

RICHARD MAIBAUM

We never showed for sure until the scene where Rosa Klebb has come in as the chambermaid at the end, and then she pulls the gun on her, he pins her up against the wall with that chair. Klebb is kicking Bond with that poisoned blade from her shoe. Well, there's the gun that just got knocked out of her hand. The girl picks it up and shoots her. That was actually created when we were shooting the scene. The way Fleming had it, actually, Bond kicked back and deflected the poison thing in her shoe into Rosa Klebb's ankle, and she died. They tried to film it, but they couldn't get it. I was standing there with Cubby on the set, watching them shoot the scene. I said to him, "Cubby, for God's sake, there's a gun lying there on the floor. Have the girl pick it up and shoot her." He looked at me, walked up to Terence, and eventually Terence said, "Okay, let's do it." But not until that moment was that created. Which shows why sometimes a writer should be on the set.

ROBERT CAPLEN

(author, *Shaken & Stirred: The Feminism of James Bond*)

Tatiana is, in effect, reduced to a mere object: her mission is to be used by both SPECTRE and Bond, fall in love with Bond—and obey his every command—and, in the process, deliver the Lektor sought by both Klebb and MI6. Both Klebb and Bond physically assault her, and Bond allows her to be drugged. But Bond cannot release Tatiana from bondage, and it is for that reason that Tatiana herself must kill Klebb—*and* overcome her aversion to guns, which, as we know, "upset" her. The same is true for Domino in *Thunderball,* a kept woman who is abused and assaulted by Emilio Largo and later used by Bond for his pleasure and to get to Largo. She, too, must free herself from bondage, killing Largo.

Bernard Lee and Lois Maxwell return in their roles as M and Miss Moneypenny, respectively. This time they're joined for the first time by Desmond Llewelyn as Bond's weapons/gadgets quartermaster, Q. Born September 12, 1914, in England, he appeared in quite a number of films in minor roles, but became a 007 mainstay as he played Q in a total of 18 *Bond* films, being the only person to interact with every actor who played the lead, with the exception of Daniel Craig.

DESMOND LLEWELYN

(actor, "Q")

Peter Burton was just an ordinary, straight performance [as Major Boothroyd in *Dr. No*]. I don't know what happened to him and why he didn't play in *To Russia with Love*, but I'm very grateful he didn't. *From Russia with Love* certainly is one of my favorites.

And then there's Pedro Armendáriz, who plays Kerim Bey, Bond's contact in Turkey, who is someone that 007 strikes up an immediate friendship with. Born May 9, 1912, in Mexico, throughout the 1940s he became extremely popular, and acclaimed, for a number of Mexican films. Toward the end of that decade he was brought to Hollywood by veteran director John Ford for the films *The Fugitive, Fort Apache,* and *3 Godfathers. From Russia with Love* would turn out to be his last film, for tragic reasons.

TOM SOTER

Armendáriz's performance is even more remarkable when one realizes that he was suffering from a painful cancer at the time. Young shot all of the actor's studio sequences early in the production. His close-ups were filmed in two weeks; Connery finished the scenes weeks later with Young standing in for Armendáriz.

STEVEN JAY RUBIN

Armendáriz was desperate to complete the film for his wife's [financial] sake. Young, who felt he could not do the film without Armendáriz, convinced the producers that he could shoot all the Pinewood sequences with Kerim Bey in one lump. The atmosphere was heavy at Pinewood Studios during those last weeks of May 1963.

TERENCE YOUNG

Armendáriz finished the picture; we'd shot all his scenes out of continuity. We did the gypsy encampment scene last, and as we got the last shot, the rains came and it rained for four days. We'd literally got the last shot in the can and I'd said, "Cut. Print it. On your way, Pedro. Go home and get some sleep." That was on a Saturday evening, and it rained till the following Wednesday. We didn't get another shot in for four days.

STEVEN JAY RUBIN

On Sunday, June 9, Terence Young held a going-away party for Armendáriz at his London town house. Most of the production crew were there, and Ian Fleming, himself seriously ill, arrived in the late afternoon.

STANLEY SOPEL

Ian was always terribly interested in the production of the films. He came out to Turkey when we were shooting out there. I think he just wanted to have a look around; I know he knew Turkey pretty well, and he wanted to see what we were doing. It wasn't publicity—he just wanted to see what the hell we were up to. I think he stayed about a week, enjoyed himself, and said, "Carry on, fellows," and away he went.

TERENCE YOUNG

I'd managed to save some caviar from when we were in Turkey, because you bought it there very cheaply, and I invited Pedro and his wife to have lunch. I invited Ian; I think Sean was there. There were about half a dozen people, and my wife, whom Pedro adored. They used to go looking at architectural ruins and all that every time he was off duty in Turkey. He was sitting on the sofa after lunch. We were smoking cigars and drinking brandy, that sort of thing. Pedro was telling Ian of the last time he'd seen Hemingway. Papa Hemingway had committed suicide a few weeks earlier. He said, "I went to see him in Cuba. When I said goodbye to him at the house, he ran after the car, made me stop, and got in, and we drove together to the jetty, where I had a small motorboat waiting. He embraced me again and he started to weep. As the boat started away, he turned and tried to jump into the boat, and he nearly fell in the water. We hauled him in, and he said, 'I don't want to say goodbye to you.' We had to put the boat back to shore and get him off. I knew then I'd never see him again. I knew he was going to kill himself." Ian said, "Why did he do it?" and Pedro said, "It's the only thing a man had left to do in that condition." I often think that the death of Ian Fleming was very much conditioned by the death of Armendáriz.

STEVEN JAY RUBIN

Ian and Armendáriz had met for the first time in Istanbul, and taken a considerable liking to one another. At that gathering, they spent much of the afternoon in Young's living room discussing Hemingway.

TERENCE YOUNG

So Pedro goes back to America, and he's supposed to have lunch with his wife and his agent. He was in the hospital at the time. I think he was in Cedars of Lebanon. He told his wife to go on and meet them, that he'd arrive a little bit late.

STEVEN JAY RUBIN

He's lying deathly ill in a hospital bed in Los Angeles, and he took a pistol from under his pillow and killed himself.

TERENCE YOUNG

Nobody knows how he smuggled it in there. I was having lunch with Ian Fleming in the Mirabelle when we were told about this. Ian said, "It's funny, you know, when he was talking about Hemingway. Did you think he was preparing the way?" I said that I did. Now, Ian knew that Pedro had cancer and he said, "It's the right way to go."

Although Fleming would live until August 12, 1964—visiting the set of the third Bond film, *Goldfinger*, but not seeing its release—there was a certain defiance in how he dealt with his illness, though Young remembers things differently than others. By all other reports, yes, Fleming was very ill, and he pretty much ignored his doctor's advice when it came to drinking and smoking. But he suffered a heart attack on August 11, 1964, and on the way to the hospital apologized to ambulance drivers for being such an "inconvenience."

TERENCE YOUNG

Ian got very sick; he had a heart attack. He had a nurse who told him he mustn't do this and he mustn't do that. Finally he said one day, "I'm going to go down and swim," and she said, "The doctor won't let you, Mr. Fleming." He said, "My dear, I'm not just going to swim, I'm going to swim two lengths underwater." He got about one length and floated up, dead. I'm damn sure it was a voluntary act. It all comes back to Hemingway—from him to Armendáriz, to Fleming.

Despite the rush to get the film into production and to theater screens in late 1963, *From Russia with Love* is almost flawless in its execution. Beyond the brilliant casting, it also established a number of elements that became integral to the world of James Bond. For starters, the idea of the pre-credit sequence, an opening mini-adventure that would expand in scope as the series went on. In this case, it shows Red Grant in action, stalking what appears to be an uncharacteristically nervous James Bond, ultimately strangling him to death. A moment later, a face mask is lifted from the corpse, revealing that it wasn't Bond at all.

TERENCE YOUNG

We didn't know what the pre-credits would become. The best one I've ever seen is *The Spy Who Loved Me*, which I thought was just marvelous. I haven't seen many *Bond* films, funnily enough, and I just sat back and yelled. I thought it was wonderful. Only a *Bond* film could have that. Somehow having that scene *after* the titles seemed to lengthen the picture, that's all. Putting it in front changed the picture very much and it's been used ever since.

JOHN CORK

The pre-credit sequences were really the brainchild of Harry Saltzman. He constantly wanted to start the *Bond* films off with a scene where James Bond would be killed before the opening titles. *From Russia with Love* was the first of those. *Thunderball* opens on a casket that looks like it could be Bond's. *You Only Live Twice* opens with Bond's death. In *Diamonds Are Forever*, Saltzman urged reversing this so that Blofeld, the film's central villain, would die in the opening. And, of course, it appears that Bond is being shot by Scaramanga in the opening of *The Man with the Golden Gun*. All these were the result of Harry Saltzman wanting to pull the rug out from under the audience right from the top.

TERENCE YOUNG

The pre-credit sequence in *From Russia with Love* was a very good sequence. It was Harry Saltzman's idea; he wanted to set the killing of James Bond in that training school. We had a lot of arguments about it, and eventually they were all in America and I shot it in the back lot at Pinewood. I'd just seen a picture which I thought was very pretentious, but very beautifully made, called *L'Année Dernière à Marienbad*, and this was my taking the mickey out of that. We set it in the garden with the statues and the moonlight, and it worked awfully well. It didn't blow the game when we used that training school thing later as a throwaway thing, instead of making too much out of it—they just walked through it. That's where Rosa Klebb meets Grant. Harry had some very good ideas, I must say. Also, he had some of the *worst* ideas I've ever seen. If you've sense, you discard the bad ones, and if you're intelligent, you keep the good ones. But he was a terrific idea merchant. That was definitely one of his best.

GLEN OLIVER

(pop culture commentator)

The pre-credit sequences in a *Bond* picture may be best regarded as a pre-show, if you will. An "opening act." They may or may not relate directly to the story which will follow in the actual film, but they sway you into the spirit of *Bond*. In many instances, they are often more compelling than the films themselves, but a few of them have risen to truly great, brilliantly encapsulated cinematic moments in their own right. Two of them are arguably classic, for different reasons and thanks to different levels of iconography. In *The Spy Who Loved Me,* the ski chase culminating in the Union Jack parachute jump, which was, evidently, initially suggested by George Lazenby for *On Her Majesty's Secret Service.* And that transition into the title sequence—the slowly descending Bond, the silhouetted hands of Maurice Binder's opening credits closing in around him? That's pretty great cinema by any measure. Then in *Die Another Day,* there's so much going on in that pre-credit sequence. So much plot being set into motion. Characters and ideas being introduced, which resonate later in the film. The aesthetic of David Tattersall's photography—almost dire and apocalyptic—portending the 14-month stretch of brutal torture Bond is about to endure. And the powerful imagery of those militarized hovercraft. All segueing into a title sequence which, for the only time in the franchise, was actually a component in the film's narrative. All incredibly smart narrative structuring, reflecting hugely competent filmmaking prowess. *Die Another Day*'s opening would be an amazing template for future *Bond* openings to study and build upon.

While it may have been Monty Norman who wrote the original basis for the "James Bond Theme," it was John Barry who turned it into the iconic bit of music that it became and remains. The score in *Dr. No* was effective, with music becoming an integral part of *Bond* films beginning with *From Russia with Love*, and that's largely thanks to Barry. Born November 3, 1933, in England, in 1957 he formed his own band, The John Barry Seven, where he scored several hit records. Two years later he was being commissioned to arrange music for other acts, which gradually led to his composing the scores for the films *Beat Girl* (1960), *Never Let Go* (1960), and *The Cool Mikado* (1962) before coming aboard *Dr. No*. He would ultimately end up scoring a total of 12 *Bond* adventures, among many others, including his Academy Award–winning scores for *Born Free* (1966), *The Lion in Winter* (1968), *Out of Africa* (1985), and *Dances with Wolves* (1990).

JOHN BARRY

(composer, *From Russia with Love*)

I'd had several successful instrumental records in England, with my own group and orchestra, The John Barry Seven. I received a phone call on Friday evening from the head of United Artists Music, and I was just getting started in film music so I was willing to write anything. He said, "We made this movie, *Dr. No*, of Ian Fleming's James Bond," and I didn't know anything about it. He told me a gentleman had been asked to write the score, but it wasn't working out. They needed the main theme very quickly. They asked if I could meet on Saturday morning at their office and he'll play what he's written. So we met and I said, "I can't do anything with what he's written." So it was like, either you just let me write it or I can't help you, and I went home that weekend and booked the orchestra, and we were in the studio on Wednesday, and I never saw any of the film. The only thing I knew about James Bond was a cartoon strip that had been in one of the English dailies. I was given the timing from Maurice Binder, who designed the title, and I went away and wrote and recorded it and was paid 200 pounds for my work on that. When it opened, I stood on line on Sunday afternoon and watched it, and the thing is all over the movie. So I then call United Artists and he tells me, "I've been waiting for this phone call. I knew this was going to happen." And he said if it was a success, they'll be making more and I would be involved in the sequels. So I said, "Okay, fine." That was my introduction to James Bond.

GLEN OLIVER

John Barry was, excuse the pun, absolutely instrumental in establishing the "vibe" of *Bond*. I'd even argue that he helped shape general acceptance of the *Bond* universe more than many other factors. A great deal of Monty Norman's *Dr. No* score involved "the theme"—that iconic, unmistakable, "This is James Bond!" music. Clearly the tune has an amazing hook and undeniably memorable and fun melody line, but that theme was very much front and center. It was, to a large extent, *Dr. No*'s actual score, recurring far more than it should have throughout the picture. Which was a bit exhausting—there wasn't a great deal of range evident within that first 007 score. No "aural road map or footprint"—if you will—to better provoke or guide our responses to the *Bond* universe.

JEFF BOND

(editor, *Film Score Monthly*)

Monty Norman famously won the legal case of who wrote the "James Bond Theme," but there's an argument to be made that he won the case because he was just better at lawsuits than John Barry was at the time—from what I've read, Barry was not a great witness in his own defense. Norman basically proved that he wrote the actual notes of the famous guitar lick, which came out of some musical he'd done where an Asian character was singing in pidgin English. So Norman's background was more musicals than action movies, which I think is why *Dr. No* is such a strange hodgepodge, with a bunch of songs and even Bond singing for a minute. Then, if you listen to Norman's actual dramatic music, it's like a bunch of 1950s library music.

The only part of the music that speaks to what *Bond* would become, and to the 1960s that the *Bond* films sprang out of and reflected, is the "Bond Theme." And the *sound* of the "Bond Theme"—that big band/rock arrangement—was all Barry. So Norman might have created the notes of the theme, but Barry created its indelible sound, and the *Bond* producers clearly recognized that and hired Barry to do *From Russia with Love.* I think Barry wanted to create his own *Bond* theme to supplant Norman's once he realized that Norman was going to get the credit and the money for the original "Bond Theme," so Barry wrote the "007" action march you hear in *From Russia with Love,* and which forms the basis for most of the action music in *Thunderball.*

RICHARD MAIBAUM

I personally adore John Barry's work. He was hip and all that sort of stuff, but he also had a symphonic touch when it was needed. Gave the thing a base and a beauty. There's some stretches of the music that are just magnificent.

JOHN CORK

John Barry's sound became essential for *James Bond* with the appearance of the "James Bond Theme" in *Dr. No.* Even though written by Monty Norman, Barry's arrangement of the "James Bond Theme" told us everything we needed to know about 007's character through music. That's an amazing accomplishment. Over the next five *Bond* films, Barry defined the genre of action film music. He did more than influence *Bond.* He helped redefine film music.

GLEN OLIVER

Like he did with many of his scores, Barry seemed to always treat the filmed material as sacred or worthy, no matter how idiotic the actions unfolding on screen. And let's face it, even the most staunch *Bond* lover would have to admit that there were some truly daffy—perhaps even embarrassing—moments occurring throughout the franchise. But Barry stayed the course, enhancing the elegance of scenes which were already lovely, lifting up scenes which might otherwise have played as shallow or frivolous, and suggesting an emotional context for sequences which might sometimes have been perceived as cold or sterile. Most importantly, in *Bond* and elsewhere, Barry was masterful at adding legitimacy to sequences which might otherwise have been perceived as awkward or clunky. More than whoever played Bond, or whoever was director of whatever specific picture, Barry was a glue which held the disparate ingredients of the *Bond*-verse together. He even brought them into harmony. He was "the makeover"—making the pictures seem more elegant and beautiful than they actually were.

ANDREW MCNESS

(author, *A Close Look at 'A View to a Kill'*)

Barry's '60s *Bond* scores were such groundbreakers. *From Russia with Love* and *Goldfinger* were stunning for their boldness and brassiness, while *You Only Live Twice* and *On Her Majesty's Secret Service* had an unforgettable sweeping romanticism. By *Bond*ian standards, Barry's '80s scores were low key. Does that make them lesser scores? They certainly stir the soul, and Barry's score for *A View to a Kill,* for example, is, I think, a fantastic melding of the foreboding with the majestic. To me, filmmaking doesn't get much better than the moment where Bond is given an impromptu tour of San Francisco, via the mooring rope of Zorin's blimp, and Barry accompanies these fanciful dramatics with a doomy rendition of the film's tinkling, melancholic romantic theme.

JEFF BOND

Barry's *Bond* scores are totally unique, and in those 1960s scores he really fills out the whole world of 007, from those silky, high-pitched strings to the wall-of-sound brass. He was an absolute genius at orchestrational effect—the clang of brass and percussion that said "golden" in *Goldfinger,* a signature for the villain and the villain's fetish for gold; or the flourish of woodwinds that stood in for the luster of diamonds in *Diamonds Are Forever.* He wrote these classic songs for *Goldfinger, You Only Live Twice*, and *Diamonds Are Forever,* but he could also perfectly characterize the movie with just an orchestral theme for *On Her Majesty's Secret Service*. Sometimes in interviews he'd dismiss his *Bond* scores as "Mickey Mouse action music," but Barry's Mickey Mouse action music, like the elevator fight in *Diamonds Are Forever,* is some of the most exciting ever written. You can say he started getting tired of doing *Bond* films after years of it, and *Octopussy* and *A View to a Kill* are less vibrant than his earlier scores, but then he could come back and do something like *The Living Daylights,* which is tremendous. Barry had an instantly recognizable voice as a composer and his *Bond* scores will always be classics.

GLEN OLIVER

Other composers have attempted interesting approaches across the franchise, but the only other composer besides Barry who seemed to fully understand what needed to be done to properly support a *James Bond* picture was David Arnold. He'd clearly studied why the Barry *Bond* films worked so well, and very deftly folded Barry's "any scene is worthy of a carefully considered score" approach into the energetic requirements of the more adrenalized Brosnan/Craig era.

There is so much to love about *From Russia with Love*, but it's no doubt the fight between Bond and Red Grant aboard the Orient Express that showcased what separated 007 from other big-screen action heroes at the time. Bond and Tatiana are on what is supposed to be the final leg of their journey with the Lektor, while Grant pretends to be an ally, drugging her into unconsciousness and holing up in a train compartment where he reveals his true identity and intent to 007. The adrenaline-fueled battle that follows within the claustrophobic confines of the train cabin truly establishes the *Bond* franchise for the ages.

PETER HUNT

Terence, I think, was a little nervous, because it was the second one and he wasn't sure how it was all going to come out. He soon overrode that, and the confidence came back, helped, in no small way, by one of the definitive fights of all time on the train. The carriage was built on the set, and we had three cameras filming that scene, which was great. The scene took a lot of manipulating in the cutting, but anything good almost always does.

STEVEN JAY RUBIN

It's one of the most bloodthirsty examples of hand-to-hand combat ever filmed. With Richard Maibaum's script linked to Peter Perkins' choreography, it was James Bond at his best.

TERENCE YOUNG

The only reason I used to get away with a lot of what I did was because I always used to try and make a laugh at the end of a violent scene. That was one of the traditions I set up, that you could be as violent as you like, provided at the end there was something like when he kills Grant on the train. You remember Shaw kept calling him "old man"? His money's been taken off him by Robert Shaw and he put it in his pocket, and there's the dead man down on the floor. Bond leans across and says, "I don't think you'll be needing this . . . old man," and he takes it. It got a laugh and it took care of the censor. The censor let it through on that strength. He'd been saying, "Oh, no; oh, no!" I was there when they were running it; they told me to go sit with him. He giggled and he laughed and he let us get away with it.

RIC MEYERS

(author, *For One Week Only: The World of Exploitation Films*)

The fights in *Dr. No,* even the climactic one with the metal-handed title villain, were frosting on the action cake. The train fight in *From Russia with Love* was clearly the central highlight of the entire film. Everything that comes afterward pales in comparison. That, as far as I can tell, was done purposely and with malice aforethought. Director Terence Young apparently wanted to do the sequence as Hitchcock would have done it—a supposition supported by his choice to have no music, bathe most of the scene in blue light, and have villain Red Grant break the train window so sound effects would flood the compartment. According to reports, Young himself, not second unit director David Anderson, rehearsed with Connery, Robert Shaw, and their stunt doubles Jack Cooper and Peter Perkins, for two days before filming the action with three cameras. Then he unleashed editor Peter Hunt on the footage.

TERENCE YOUNG

I've never been a particular Hitchcock fan. I've liked some of his films, I've liked some others less. I think he made the most beautifully *constructed* films ever. The workmanship of a Hitchcock film is a piece of jewelry. It's not filmmaking, it's diamond polishing—this wonderful quality that he had in his work. But I'm not like Truffaut or Mel Brooks or the other crazy Hitchcock fans. I just thought that what we put into the picture was the sort of scene that was needed at that particular time.

BOB SIMMONS

(stunt arranger/stunt double, *From Russia with Love*)

If you look at that scene over again, you will see it isn't so much the action, but it is the sound effects: everything builds up, and it isn't so much the visual action as what you're listening to.

PETER HUNT

I was much more confident by then. I now knew that what I had done was good and that it had worked, so there was no holding me back.

STEVEN JAY RUBIN

At first, Young intended to use only two stationary cameras to catch the action, one on a dolly, tracking down into the compartment, and one on ground level. Peter Hunt suggested that a free third camera also be used. It was a good suggestion and Young put it into play. Hunt's free camera later picked up some excellent shots of Bond and Grant spilling on to Tatiana's sleeping form.

PETER HUNT

The pacing overall was the most important thing. If you analyze the story, it's an impossible one. Why did they go by train? Why didn't they take an airplane [*laughs*]? It had to move fast in order to hold you. The whole idea of the *Bond* films—and I don't know if they haven't lost a bit of that now—was that they were paperback films, as it were. They were the sort of thing that the commuters and the average guy working in New York and living outside read on the train. They were this fantasy world because of the way Fleming wrote them. They were all about good wine, well-dressed spies, and all that sort of thing. He brought into the book "style": great lengths of description regarding the shoes and the cotton shirts, ties, the food that James Bond was eating; and the beautiful girls; and all that—if you analyze it—incredible, but superficial grammar that rubbed off the page onto all of these people. And they were enjoyable because of that. I think we had to get the same thing into the films. My feeling was always that one should make the films seriously, but never take them seriously, if you see what I mean. The humor of the thing has to come out of the film itself. You can't sit down and say, "How can we make this funny?" In other words, it has to be there and work itself out.

RIC MEYERS

Not surprisingly, the result is a landmark classic in the annals of action cinema, but also not surprisingly, it didn't change the genre. Fight scenes went wandering back to their roundhouse ways, and even *Bond* really wouldn't try to re-create the effect until Hunt got into the *On Her Majesty's Secret Service* director's chair. Understandably, as strong as the train fight was, ultimately the producers may not have appreciated how it made the rest of the film seem diminished. In retrospect, it would have been better to save the Red Grant confrontation for the finale—just as they should have saved Le Chiffre for the finale of *Casino Royale*. I thought his and his crew's off-screen execution was that classic's single flaw.

From Russia with Love is perhaps the best of the *James Bond* espionage thrillers before the series succumbed to a subsequent overabundance of gadgets, girls, and guns. Not to mention sheer spectacle. Over the ensuing decades, the filmmakers would pay lip service to *From Russia with Love* being their template for future *Bond* plots despite the fact it was really *Goldfinger* that served as the series' future inspiration—its myriad gadgets, elaborate Ken Adam sets, and *Bond* Girls with outrageous names proved to be an intoxicating mix. But as masterful as *From Russia with Love* is, it's unlikely the *Bond* series would have endured for five decades had it not evolved from being a straight spy thriller more akin to Richard Burton's *The Spy Who Came In from the Cold*, or Harry Saltzman's own *Harry Palmer* series, into what it eventually became: an event film filled with ample eye candy and nonstop excitement.

DAVID V. PICKER

From Russia with Love had a total film rental over $25 million, twice that of *Dr. No*. It was clear we had a very good start in building the franchise. It was not long after the opening of *From Russia with Love* that Irving Moskowitz and Norman Tyre, the producers' attorneys, suggested that their clients' deal be renegotiated. That in itself was not unusual, although any changes would usually be tied to a new deal with new pictures. Here, after only two films, the producers were already pushing for a change. One of UA's strongest assets was the style with which they dealt with their filmmaking partners. In this case, Arthur Krim agreed to a modest adjustment from the 50–50 partnership on the back end, as well as an increase in producing fees that satisfied the lawyers for the moment. However, it was clear that with any continuing success there would be continuing renegotiations. And there was one other thing that at the time was not apparent, at least to us. With the success of these first two films and the renegotiated producers' deal, how were Harry and Cubby handling Sean Connery? He was, after all, carrying the load, and had created, with his style and demeanor, a character with increasing worldwide box-office success.

TERENCE YOUNG

I think *From Russia with Love* shows *Bond* to the best advantage. The tone was set in *Dr. No*, but completed in *From Russia with Love*. I have heard that during the filming of the other pictures, my successors have watched my films to see what they could find in them to cannibalize. Mind you, it was easier for those of us who started the whole thing.

GOLDFINGER (1964)

Ask nine out of ten dentists—let alone pretty much anyone else—what *Bond* movie they prefer, and they're likely to say *Goldfinger*. It's an assessment that's hard to quibble with when you consider that *Goldfinger* has it all, from a larger-than-life villain (Gert Fröbe's Auric Goldfinger) to a literal golden girl (Shirley Eaton as Jill Masterson), the introduction of Bond's iconic gadget-laden Aston Martin DB5, an equally iconic henchman (Olympic Silver Medalist in weight lifting Harold Sakata's Oddjob), and Shirley Bassey singing the title song for the John Barry soundtrack. All of which gives this third film the hat trick, so to speak.

STEVEN JAY RUBIN
(author, *The James Bond Films*)

In his biography of Ian Fleming, John Pearson points out that after *From Russia with Love*, Fleming decided to abandon the thought of elevating the literary quality of 007 and instead returned to writing basically the same book over and over again, with only setting changing. On the verge of writing the script of *Goldfinger*, Richard Maibaum found himself in a similar predicament. *From Russia with Love* would always be his favorite *Bond*, but he knew instinctively that its semi-straight approach was not the direction in which Broccoli and Saltzman intended to take the series. It was not the plot or the setting that was going to make *Bond* unique. It was the *presentation*.

RICHARD MAIBAUM
(cowriter, *Goldfinger*)

From Russia with Love is my favorite, but *Goldfinger* is right *there*. I thought *From Russia with Love* was as far as we really could go, spoofing a little bit, but also staying real and keeping a frame of reference. But *Goldfinger* is the most successful, as I see it. It's like when you're a bowler, you bowl the ball down the alley and all 10 pins go "wham!" It worked, and was successful. Sean was magnificent in that picture. Absolutely marvelous. He was *so* good.

He was also getting *so* restless. The first two *Bond* films had been giant hits, with *Goldfinger* destined to surpass them both, and producers Broccoli and Saltzman were intent on turning out one of these films a year. For his part, Connery was already starting to feel a bit trapped; he needed to do something to show the world that he was capable of playing more than 007.

STEVEN JAY RUBIN

Between *From Russia with Love* and *Goldfinger*, he worked with Ralph Richardson and Gina Lollobrigida on *Woman of Straw*, and played the hero in Alfred Hitchcock's *Marnie*. John Ford also offered him the part of playwright Sean O'Casey in a film biography, but Connery had to decline because of *Goldfinger*.

One person who declined to be involved with the new *Bond* film was director Terence Young, who had done so masterful a job on *Dr. No* and *From Russia with Love*. Part of it was over money–he wanted more of it, and the producers didn't want to pay him–but there was another factor in his decision as well.

TERENCE YOUNG
(director, *Thunderball*)

We did a lot of pre-production work on *Goldfinger*. Quite a lot of the casting was done at that time, but I kept saying that I thought for a director it was a dead end. The idea of going on and making a *James Bond* film a year for the next 10 years, it's just not my bag. I wanted to do something else. I've been blamed many times for not having a style of my own. They say it's because I'm always doing something different, but that's what I like doing. Jack [John] Ford developed a style, because he made 30 Westerns. But it's very difficult to find any style with Howard Hawks; he made every different picture under the sun, and that's what appeals to me. I've done a Western, I'd like to do another. I've done what is, I think, a pretty good suspense picture called *Wait Until Dark*, and I'd like to do another of those.

Replacing Young was Guy Hamilton, who had previously been asked to direct *Dr. No*. Born September 16, 1922, in Paris to English parents, he found his first job as a clapperboard boy at Victorine Studios in Nice. When World War Two broke out in 1939, he managed to escape from France with 500 other refugees, eventually arriving in London. He was commissioned to the Royal Navy during the war, but afterward became an assistant director on films, making his directorial debut on 1952's *The Ringer*. Other films prior to *Goldfinger* include *An Inspector Calls* (1954), *Charley Moon* (1956), *Manuela* (1957), *The Devil's Disciple* (1957), and *The Best of Enemies* (1961).

GUY HAMILTON

(director, *Goldfinger*)

In the early '60s, *Bond* was at the top of every schoolteacher's league for sex, violence, and sadism. However, with *Goldfinger* we introduced fantasy. It seemed to me that going on from *From Russia with Love*, Bond was in danger of becoming Superman. He was *too* clever. There was now no suspense, because if somebody pulls a gun on him, you know that he's going to kick it away before the scene's over. Bond is as good as his villains. Let's spend more time worrying about the villains and make *that* important. Let's have fun with Mr. Big, who's an intelligent man, so that there can be intelligent conversations with Bond that always end up with, "I can't stand the sight of blood, so excuse me while I hand you over to Oddjob."

STEVEN JAY RUBIN

With increased attention to style and pace, the writers began, for the first time, to lose sight of Fleming's *Bond*. If the novels had at times resembled comic strips, they still included their brief studies of a man undergoing extreme pressure. Fleming's Bond went through typical middle-age hang-ups. He had health problems, bouts of sexual melancholy, an obsession with drink and cigarettes, and doubts about his own effectiveness as a human being. He was human and he fought against an inhuman world with his own wits and a few surprises. With *Goldfinger*, the *Bond* writers created a new agent, an indestructible man who would survive any situation. It was no longer a question of whether Bond would survive, it merely became a case of which button he would push, or what he would say.

RICHARD MAIBAUM

It is true that with *Goldfinger*, we were getting wilder. The whole business was becoming larger than life. We also took into consideration the audience's growing sophistication. We dared to do something seldom done in action pictures, by mixing what was funny with what was serious.

The original Fleming *Goldfinger* novel—seventh in the series—had a similar, but divergent plot to the one that would be introduced on the big screen. As described on ianfleming.com, "Auric Goldfinger is the richest man in England, though his wealth can't be found in banks. He's been hoarding vast stockpiles of his namesake metal, and it's attracted the suspicions of 007's superiors at MI6. Sent to investigate, Bond uncovers an ingenious gold-smuggling scheme as well as Goldfinger's most daring caper yet: Operation Grand Slam, a gold heist so audacious it could bring down the world economy."

Tasked with adapting that story to film was, as noted, Maibaum, as well as Paul Dehn, a poet turned screenwriter, born on November 5, 1912, in England. His other script credits include *Seven Days to Noon* (1950), *The Spy Who Came In from the Cold* (1965), and the three *Planet of the Apes* films from 1971 to 73.

RICHARD MAIBAUM

Fleming never bothered his head about how long it would take to transport the gold from Fort Knox, or how many men and vehicles it would require. Obviously it would take weeks, hundreds of trucks and hundreds of men. The problem we faced wasn't an easy one. Why, we asked ourselves, would a man want to break into Fort Knox and not carry anything away?

TOM SOTER

(author, *Bond and Beyond: 007 and Other Special Agents*)

The screenwriters' ingenious solution was to have Goldfinger plan to explode a nuclear device in Fort Knox, which would contaminate the gold supply of the US for 97 years, thus increasing the value of Goldfinger's gold and causing economic chaos in the West, something desired by his Red Chinese allies who supplied the nuclear device.

RAY MORTON

(senior writer, *Script* magazine)

For me, Paul Dehn is the most important screenwriter for the Eon *Bond* films, because he is the one who introduced fantasy to the series. Fleming's novels had some fantastic elements in them, but Richard Maibaum—who was primarily a realistic writer—tended to downplay or eliminate them in his screenplays. *Dr. No* was a pretty far-out tale, but Maibaum's adaptation tones down the fantastic elements to the point where the story almost seems realistic. Dehn, on the other hand, not only retained the fantastic elements from the *Goldfinger* novel, but also enhanced and expanded upon them.

RICHARD MAIBAUM

On *Goldfinger*, I did a first draft, Harry Saltzman didn't like it, and he brought in Paul Dehn, a good writer, to revise. Then Sean Connery didn't like the revisions, and I came back to do the final screenplay. That was the first time that happened, where I was followed by someone and then called back to finish up.

RAY MORTON

Dehn was the writer who had Bond discover the dead body of Jill Masterson covered in gold paint (Jill's fate was talked about in the novel, but never depicted), gave Oddjob superhuman powers by having him crush a golf ball, and, most importantly, introduced the gadget-laden Aston Martin, complete with ejector seat. These bits, along with many other additions, resulted in a film that was much less realistic than the two that had preceded it.

STEVEN JAY RUBIN

With *Goldfinger,* Maibaum and Dehn were to write what was to be the key script in the *James Bond* series and which later became the blueprint for all future *Bond* films. *Goldfinger* was the first of the stylized *Bond* thrillers where virtually every scene was planned with tongue deep in cheek. It was a romp, but with a very important twist: the writers never forgot the one element that would expertly balance the comedy—danger. Without Bond falling into constant danger, the humor would upset the balance of the film.

RAY MORTON

Maibaum objected to many of Dehn's contributions, especially the tongue-in-cheek humor, feeling they were too broad and unrealistic and would derail the series. However, the producers liked them, and while some of Dehn's more outrageous notions were toned down or eliminated in the final draft, most were retained and became key staples of the series from then on. And it was these elements—the larger-than-life fantasy and the self-aware humor—that added to the more down-to-earth gun-and-run spy material that made the *Bond* movies so unique and so much more than just ordinary thrillers. Dehn only wrote one *Bond* screenplay, but he should definitely be considered one of the key architects of the "*Bond* formula."

There are many elements that come together beautifully in *Goldfinger,* starting with what is a sterling cast. Gert Fröbe–born Karl Gerhart "Gert" Fröbe on February 25, 1913, in Oberplantz (now known as Zwickau), Saxony, German Empire–is the epitome of the *Bond* villain as the title character. He had been a member of the Nazi party from 1929 when he was 16 and left in 1937, reportedly aiding a pair of German Jews in their attempt to hide from the Gestapo. In 1944, he was drafted into the German army, where he remained until the close of World War Two. Following the war, he appeared in several acclaimed German films, and actually came to the attention of Saltzman and Broccoli for his role as a serial killer of children in *It Happened in Broad Daylight*. While Fröbe cuts an imposing figure as *Goldfinger,* one of the challenges is the fact that he didn't speak any English beyond a few common pleasantries (despite his agent assuring the production otherwise). In the final film, his voice was dubbed by British actor Michael Collins.

Although Fröbe was Harry Saltzman's choice, the filmmakers had considered Orson Welles for the role, but his salary demands were too steep (he would eventually get his *Bond*-ian moment in the 1967 007 spoof, *Casino Royale,* as La Chiffre, in which the only ones to weep blood were the audience members that paid to see it). Theodore Bikel was also considered.

RICHARD MAIBAUM

Gert Fröbe had the great advantage that the English-speaking world did not know anything about him—he'd played in some German pictures—which is what made it the most brilliant casting of all time.

GUY HAMILTON

He had a dialogue coach and he studied his scenes very hard. I made a point of not making them too long and had lots of cuts in them. He learned his dialogue phonetically. The only thing I had to do was get him to speed up, because he was enunciating everything very slowly. The main thing is that the mouth is moving at the right tempo. Michael Collins did a tremendous job of imitating Gert.

JOHN CORK

(author, *James Bond: The Legacy*)

There is a lot of redubbing that goes on that no one ever hears about. Minor actors may not be available for ADR [Automated Dialogue Replacement] work, which is essential in modern films. Women, in particular younger, attractive women, were often redubbed if their voices came across as "harsh" or "not sexy." Mostly, foreign actors with thick accents were redubbed in English-language films. The *Bond* films were not unique in this. They are just high-profile examples. Michael Collins, who dubbed Gert Fröbe in *Goldfinger,* did a great job, but he followed Fröbe's performance, cadence, and pitch very closely. Had Fröbe not been perfect for the role, nothing Collins could have done would have mattered. Fröbe was voice-coached by Nikki van der Zyl on the set, and so he was able to deliver a fantastic, properly paced performance with the right emphasis on the right words, but it was a performance that merely parroted the English dialogue. It's one of the greatest redubbings in film.

Noted Collins himself in a BBC interview at the time, "It wasn't *my* performance, it was Gert Fröbe's performance. Let's say it's like a crossword puzzle. Mr. Fröbe knew all the answers, produced them pretty well, but his vocal pencil was blunt and I just outlined what he said."

Playing Pussy Galore–give Fleming credit for that name–is Honor Blackman. Born August 22, 1925, in Britain, she had starred as Cathy Gale on the television series *The Avengers* (on which she appeared for two seasons from 1962 to 64, and preceded future *Bond* Girl Diana Rigg) and appeared in the 1963 feature film *Jason and the Argonauts*. Pussy works with Goldfinger, and her team of female pilots–making up "Pussy Galore's Flying Circus"–plays an integral role in the film by carrying out his plan. As conceived by Fleming, the character is presumably a lesbian, and the film doesn't do much to dissuade that–until she ultimately succumbs to Bond's charms.

HONOR BLACKMAN
(actress, "Pussy Galore")

Early on, I played sweet, innocent, English, peaches and cream. . . . I couldn't help it; I was those things. I took an awful long time to grow up, I think. I was always looked upon as terribly kind and understanding, and I never got any lovely bitch parts and I was never really playing someone intelligent. I was always the one who says, "Darling, I'll make the cocoa and you just go to bed. Don't worry about it." I was a nit all the time. But in this film, the fighting, from *The Avengers* to *Goldfinger*, was really quite easy compared to the television series. It was sheer dream world when I came into the film industry to do it with Sean. A, he's a lovely gent, and who *doesn't* want to fight in the hay or do anything in the hay with Sean? Secondly, they provide you with the hay; they provide you with the soft stuff. In the television studio, you're bouncing around on the cement, all over the place. And in the film studio, there were bales of hay: "Is that alright, Honor? Would you bounce on that?" Oh, it was heaven. I loved it.

There were occasions, of course, where I did get knocked about for real. You don't have to wait until you get to the fighting scenes with Sean. He just says, "Ah, just a minute," and gets hold of you and you've gone through to the bone, you know, because he really is so tough. There is one scene where he just has to yank me back, and this arm was in a disgusting condition for about week, simply because of the brute force.

RICHARD MAIBAUM

Goldfinger may have been a little sexier than the first two pictures, but, remember, we still had the censors to contend with. For example, for the scene in the plane where Bond wakes up and sees gorgeous Honor Blackman, I first of all had him say, "Who are you?" She says, "Pussy Galore." And he says, "I know, but what's your *name*?" I had to change that last line to, "I must be dreaming," but it still got a big laugh. Actually, we were able to get away with "Pussy Galore," because that was her name in the novel.

HONOR BLACKMAN

I wasn't really shaken by this character until I went on the promotion tour of the States with the picture and hardly any of the interviewers would call me by my character's name. They said, "How do you feel about playing a character with this name? Don't you find it rather distasteful?" and all this. They really took it *so* seriously, you know? I set them up rotten. It was awful, because they'd been given instructions from above that they mustn't say "Pussy Galore."

Other actresses in the film in more supporting roles are Tania Mallet as Tilly Masterson, the sister of Jill; Margaret Nolan as Bond's lady friend early on, Dink; and British-born Shirley Eaton, who, as Jill Masterson, betrays Goldfinger for Bond and ends up lying dead, covered in paint. Gold paint. Over 50 years later, the image of that golden woman remains one of moviedom's most iconic.

SHIRLEY EATON
(actress, "Jill Masterson")

Prior to *Goldfinger*, I'd made 21 films, and the producers just called my agent to have an interview with me. They asked me if I minded being naked and painted gold, to which I replied, with a smile, "Fine, if it's done tastefully." When I was painted gold, it was very, very hot. Very uncomfortable. Because I was lying down, the whole middle part of my front was *not* painted gold. It didn't take long to get it on—about an hour, I think—but getting it off was awful. I had to scrub it off with soap and water, then have several Turkish baths. I must say, I only had two scenes with Sean Connery, who was attractive and studious. It was only a week's work, so I never imagined that the film and my role would have such a lifelong iconic existence.

PIERCE BROSNAN
(actor, "James Bond")

As a boy of 10 years old when I left Ireland in 1964, the first film I ever saw was *Goldfinger,* which, for a young lad from Ireland, was the most incredible thing

I'd ever seen. There was this gold lady laid out in the bed, naked. So *James Bond* has been part of my cinematic heritage, as it were, as an actor.

As Goldfinger's mute but formidable henchman, the film features Hawaiian-born Harold Sakata (who joined us on July 1, 1920) as Oddjob. Prior to being cast in *Goldfinger*, he was an American Olympic weight lifter (he won a 1948 silver medal) and professional wrestler. Also, Cec Linder as CIA agent Felix Leiter; and a series-defining return performance by Desmond Llewelyn as Q, the man who supplies Bond with his gadgets.

GUY HAMILTON

We were *very* lucky to get Harold Sakata as Oddjob. I'd seen him on a wrestling program, and he was just ideal casting, and away you go. With Desmond, he had been in *From Russia with Love*. He only does one or two days' work, and he's very nervous and bad at his lines, which are all gobbledygook. So we're shooting down in Q's quarters and in comes Bond and Desmond starts to genuflect. I looked at him and said, "You hate the bugger." He says, "Why do I hate him?" "Think about it. He comes down here, pays no attention to what you say, takes your props away, uses them in completely different ways than you intended, never returns them. I mean, the man's a menace as far as you're concerned, and the sooner 009 turns up, the happier you'll be." "Oh, yes, I suppose that's true." So we rehearsed the scene and now it's *really* just flying.

GLEN OLIVER
(pop culture commentator)

Early on, Q was a figurehead: an eccentric, cranky scientist/engineer toiling about in his lab, creating gonzo prototypes and perfectly funky (but usually cool) espionage technology. As such, he was a bit of a cliché. He was, principally, a straight man. A springboard for Bond's frat-boy derision, and the target audience of 007's exceptionally shitty puns. Initially there was a cantankerous, one-dimensional joylessness about Q which Bond seemed hell-bent on zinging—and possibly even breaking through. This was all amusing enough, but after a while, the shtick became a nonstarter. There was only so far it could go, and a chief rule of any successful humor is to never overstay one's gag. They broke that rule, and Q's visits started feeling tepid; a welcome familiarity, but also a touch stale.

JOHN CORK

Desmond Llewelyn was a fantastic character actor. He was wonderful in *From Russia with Love*, but it was Guy Hamilton who made Q such a great part of the *Bond* universe. After seeing a run-through of a scene, he told Desmond to play it as though he hated Bond. That's what makes Desmond's appearances so much fun.

GLEN OLIVER

Q eventually became something different, especially in his final few appearances. More akin to a beloved uncle who doesn't wear his affections overtly, but loves those around him all the same. Perhaps more so, he was a father figure to the endlessly bouncy, tirelessly snarky Bond. And, much like a beleaguered father, Q was flat-out fatigued by his association with 007, but also deeply invested in his well-being on a very genuine level. This was especially true in the Brosnan years, during which 007 and Q formed a pointed kinship which both wore openly. A familial connection, of sorts.

Beyond the sterling—or should we say, golden—cast, there is so much more to applaud about *Goldfinger* and its contribution to the overall franchise. For starters, there's the pre-credit sequence, which has Bond emerge from underwater, having used a fake duck as a disguise. He's clad in a wetsuit, and once on land goes into action, planting explosives in a drug manufacturing plant, stripping off his wetsuit to reveal a white tuxedo with a red carnation—which he wears into a local club where he meets his contact. He waits calmly for the inevitable detonation, signifying the success of his mission. Satisfied, he returns to his hotel room, where he begins a romantic encounter with Bonita (Nadja Regin), who attempts to betray him to an assassin—whose image Bond spies reflected in Bonita's pupil as he approaches. Their fight culminates with Bond's would-be assassin thrown into a bathtub full of water, in which Bond knocks a fan, thus electrocuting him. Uttering the words, "Shocking. Positively shocking," Bond leaves the room, which segues into Shirley Bassey's title theme. All in all, a mini-movie that, as effective as the pre-credit scene in *From Russia with Love* had been, truly sets the standard that the series follows to this day.

GUY HAMILTON

The pre-credits were sort of sniffed at in the two previous pictures, but I thought you've got to really go for it now. I would like it to be how I want you to see the picture as the audience. I mean, if you think it's funny that a man under a diving suit has a white dinner jacket on and he's got a carnation in it, or that he can see the villain reflected in the girl's eye as he's about to give her a kiss . . . If you think that's funny, good, because I've got lots more of this nonsense. The great thing is leave your brains under the seat and we'll all go for a great, big ride. Just don't ask too many questions.

STEVEN JAY RUBIN

Fleming had opened the novel in a Miami airport lounge where Bond is contemplating the recent killing of a South American drug smuggler. This reference inspired Maibaum and provided the basis for the teaser. It's said that on the night the sequence—when the bird rises out of the water and we realize it's a rubber decoy perched on Bond's head—was shot in the big tank at Pinewood Studios, a number of crew members told Hamilton that they found it too silly. It's certainly the first time in the series that Bond courts direct laughter by his actions. If we compare the *Goldfinger* teaser with that of *From Russia with Love*, it's easy to see the change that had come over the world of James Bond.

GUY HAMILTON

I couldn't take *James Bond* seriously, and it seemed to me that the pre-credit sequence was absolutely vital for my way of thinking. If you take that whole sequence seriously, right up to the point where he electrocutes the guy, you need your heads examined. What I'm trying to say is that if you enjoy that, then I'm going to play games with you. I'm going to put James Bond in the snake pit and give you 30 seconds to figure out how he gets out. Come on, come on, *quick*! And it's lovely to watch you fail. But the thing is, I've given you 30 seconds and it took the writer and I three months to figure it out, so that's not cheating. And, yes, keep the adventure going, keep a bit of sophistication, let's have us a little bit of wit and style, but tongue firmly in cheek.

Another highlight of the film is the famous sequence in which Goldfinger has Bond strapped to a table with a laser slowly inching its way toward 007's crotch and literally threatening to split him in half. The sequence gives us that wonderful bit of dialogue where Bond asks, "Do you expect me to talk?" to which Goldfinger responds, "No, Mister Bond, I expect you to die." And he comes pretty close to doing just that. As conceived by Fleming, it was actually a buzz saw threatening Bond's manhood.

RICHARD MAIBAUM

Somehow in the reading, because Fleming writes so effectively, *The Perils of Pauline* did not immediately occur to me. Vividly depicted on the screen, however, we were sure audiences would find the episode old-fashioned, hackneyed, and ludicrous. We substituted an industrial laser beam.

GUY HAMILTON

Harry Saltzman was the boy with the toys. He adored them and was getting them from all over the place. We had somebody in the Pentagon who was leaking secrets of whatever the latest American toys were. And he said, "There's a laser beam," and Harry sent for me. He said, "There's a laser beam," and I said, "What's a laser beam, Harry?" He said, "It's like a light, but you can see it on the moon." I thought that was very interesting, but because we didn't know what it was, we didn't know what to use it for. Dick Maibaum said, "We could use it to cut gold, because Mr. Goldfinger is knee-deep in gold and that'll be a good use for it. And we could use it to cut off Bond's private parts, instead of a circular saw, which was the standard thing." And that, of course, was a good idea.

Today, of course, much of that sequence would be handled with CG, and while the laser beam itself was an effect added later, the rest of it was done for real on set.

GUY HAMILTON

Oh, it was real high tech [*laughs*]. The special effects people got a sheet of metal and they cut it in half, then they welded it together again and painted the whole lot. And James Bond is tied on the thing and I say, "Action!" There are two special effects men. One is underneath with a torch [light] and the other one's got a blowtorch and you can see the weld. So the line is there and I wait, but nothing happens for a bit. There's Sean sitting up, having a look. Eventually, though, the blowtorch starts to work and the weld starts to melt. I said, "That's good. But quicker!" So Sean lies down and he's trying to watch, and it's marvelous because some smoke comes out of the spot. I said, "Quicker, quicker, little quicker . . . actually, now slow down." You look at Sean and you're talking about *sweat*. That was real sweat, because he's thinking, "When is that son of a bitch going to say, 'Cut'?" Because he knows that the two technicians underneath, one with a torch to show the other guy with the blowtorch which way to go, they don't know where Sean's crotch is, they're just going along. It was a great sigh of relief to Sean when I did say "Cut."

Although he wasn't a part of *From Russia with Love*, Bob Simmons was back on *Goldfinger* to oversee the stunt work and serve as a stunt double.

RIC MEYERS

(author, *For One Week Only: The World of Exploitation Films*)

Goldfinger was Bob Simmons' show all the way, but, as Peter Hunt has said, the production was a bit of a mess, which I personally feel was reflected on-screen. Apparently Connery was also perplexed as to why Bond was basically a supporting character throughout, and had to pretend that he couldn't soundly and quickly beat his physically limited adversaries. But by this time they were all holding on to a very fast-moving train, so Connery made the best of it and, again, was reportedly surprised by the public's overwhelming reaction upon the film's release. Nonetheless, it's a great example of Bob Simmons' skill in that he was able to make all the fights into well-structured, enjoyable, even credible sequences. Again, the impression I got was that the action in *Goldfinger* was done with tongue firmly in cheek, and then shaped, even rescued, in the editing room. I'm surmising Bob Simmons mounted a nice give-and-take with Bond and "Push-ee" in the barn, as she gives tit for each of his tats.

BOB SIMMONS

(stunt arranger/stunt double, *Goldfinger*)

What I do is take the two characters, then I read the script, then I ignore what it says in the script. I like it when it says, "A battle ensues." I work on it, and develop it from there. When I get a script, I read throughout and then I read it through a second time. First I read it as a story, and then I read the script and start breaking it down; breaking it up in action pieces. Then I break it down a third time, and start taking out sheets and sheets of paper. Then I start making sketches. The next thing I want to do is to get with the art department and special effects, and see what they have. I put my ideas over to them, and the three of us blend. Then you get with the property department and start working out your props. So there's really no such thing as, "*I* did this, or *I* did that." It's the whole team.

RIC MEYERS

If you watch them not as action scenes, but stunt choreographer's challenges, you can see Simmons' smarts: making each into a series of clearly discernible actions and reactions that have an understandable beginning, middle, and end, but ones that require Bond to be vulnerable, even beatable—something, apparently, Connery did not appreciate. He liked his Bond to be in charge and on top of things (as it were) and if you'll notice, the 007 in *Goldfinger* is constantly being bested, captured, failing, showing concern, and even, when lasered, sweating.

BOB SIMMONS

I'm also there when the set construction begins, so I can see how the fights are going to go. From the time they start building that set, you have in mind what you're planning. You build your ideas while they're building that set. You say to the art department, "Wouldn't it be better if you could give me an opening there, or a little piece of equipment over there, some extra set over there." That's what I mean about teamwork. In the master shot of overall action and movement, you must show what the producer paid for—the whole set. You've got to be able to show the whole set, and then cut in for the individual pieces of action. The producer will say, "How much did that set cost me? I want to see it on the screen."

The production designers of the *James Bond* films, from Ken Adam to Syd Cain, Peter Lamont, and beyond, have played an extremely significant role in the franchise's aesthetic distinctiveness from the very beginning. But it really was with *Goldfinger*–and the design work of Adam–that it became apparent.

JOHN CORK

Ken Adam approached set design like Hemingway approached a novel. Everything was there for a reason. Nothing was wasted. Nothing was a flourish. Every detail had been thought out. The result felt grander than the mere sum of the parts. His sets became characters in their own right. He knew Bond's world needed to be bigger than life, so his sets were bigger than life. But like other important production designers, he did much more than create sets. He worked with the costumers to select a color palette for the film. It is no accident that Bond is wearing the baby blue jeans and polo shirt in *Dr. No* and the exact same color in the terry-cloth jumper in *Goldfinger*. Ken liked that color on Connery. Ken paid attention to the smallest details. For some, Ken's cockiness and the way he took his work very seriously got under their skin. He did not suffer fools gladly. He often fought with cinematographers who blanched when they saw the scale of his sets, knowing they would be a nightmare, taking forever to light. [Director] Lewis Gilbert commented that Ken added 10 minutes to a *Bond* film just taking into account how long it would take characters to enter and exit his mammoth sets. But when you think of *Bond*, you think of the world Ken Adam created.

GUY HAMILTON

Ken Adam, Cubby, and I went to Fort Knox, and it was quite amusing, because we were only allowed up to the fence. We said, "Can we come in now and look around?" and they told us, "No, you may not come in and have a look around. Even the president of the United States is not allowed to come in and have a look around." "Oh, why not?" And he said, "Well, it's in the Constitution to prevent a villainous president from putting gold bars in his pocket and walking out the gate." So we realized that nobody had ever been in Fort Knox; there are no pictures of it. Which actually made it an art director's dream.

KEN ADAM

(production designer, *Goldfinger*)

I said, "The audience wants to see the biggest gold depository in the world," so I piled up gold 60 feet up, which is completely impractical, because gold is much too heavy, but in the film you get away with it. After the film, United Artists got over 300 letters from irate Americans who said, "How was it that a British film unit and director were allowed inside Fort Knox when our president isn't allowed?" So they believed it. You see? Completely impractical, but it worked.

GLEN OLIVER

(pop culture commentator)

The production design of *Bond* films is a compelling case study for a number of reasons—*not* just because of the obvious scale and spectacle people like Ken Adam, Syd Cain, or Peter Lamont brought to the equation. I submit that *how* their production design is utilized is every bit as compelling as their actual work. Meaning, in many of the *Bond* films, there are two "worlds"—and 007 moves between them. The first world is the "real" world Bond inhabits: streets, airports, highways, all of the mundane settings that are easily and naturally taken for granted by viewers.

JOHN CORK

In *Dr. No,* the moment where Professor Dent comes in to collect the spider, and the audience sees that huge, stark set, the film shifts. Ken Adam knew how to mesh reality with modern design with elements of German Expressionism. With that one set, Ken Adam made *James Bond* films look and feel different from everything else out there. It's a brilliant moment from a brilliant designer.

GLEN OLIVER

Sometimes *Bond* films take place chiefly in this "identifiable" world. *The Living Daylights, For Your Eyes Only*, and much of *Licence to Kill*, for example, were largely set in places any number of colorful characters, or heroes, or villains might've inhabited. Many other *Bond* films featured movements grounded in this "everyday" world as well (*Diamonds Are Forever*'s Vegas setting, for example, or *Live and Let Die*'s New Orleans locations).

On the flip side of this, however, is the "other world" of the movies. And this "world" is a world unto itself. Almost like, but not literally, a Phantom Zone, or Dark Dimension. A Mirror Universe, if you will. This is the flip side of our everyday world. This is where embarrassingly wealthy mega-millionaires live in cavernous estates which dwarf the physicality of their owners. Where cackling, cat-holding bad guys dwell in spaceship-launching volcanoes. Where supertankers capable of devouring multiple nuclear submarines are constructed beyond the eye of global intelligence communities. Where secret orbital platforms able to gas the entire surface of the Earth are built in space without ever being detected.

This particular world is largely a world of excess. Of corruption. Of misguided ambitions. Of broken compassions or fractured humanity. There's always a hard elegance to it—an allure, a seduction. But, like the dark side of the Force, in this world lies nothing but a negative spiral—peril, heartbreak, and perhaps even apocalypse. If James Bond 007 is driven by any thematic at all—and I'm not sure that the franchise is, nor am I certain that it isn't—I contend that it lies in this disparity. That everyday life is filled with challenge and danger and struggle enough. That excess leads to overreach and greed and megalomania and misguided ambition. *This*, in my mind at least, is the chief importance of Adam and Cain and Lamont's contributions. They manifest all of these negative qualities of this dark world physically—via imposing architectures, oppressive technological design, chilly chrome-and-glass partitions. Their artistry is beyond reproach, and is absolutely invaluable. But how their artistry delivers other worlds, which are often darker and more wicked, on a subversive, narrative level is deeply critical to the heartbeat and personality of the franchise.

JOHN CORK

Ken and Syd were codesigners on *Dr. No,* but Syd's name got left off the credits. Syd did the design work in Jamaica while Ken built the sets at Pinewood. When everyone came back to those sets, they somewhat forgot that Syd existed. With Ken working on *Dr. Strangelove* in 1963, Syd Cain did the production design for *From Russia with Love.* He did a fantastic job, but he didn't have Ken's flair for creating sets that made audiences gasp. Syd's work on *On Her Majesty's Secret Service* and *Live and Let Die* demonstrate that he had a great eye for clever designs. Late in life, he designed the *GoldenEye* key for Pierce Brosnan's first *Bond* film. Peter Lamont started working in the art department on *Goldfinger.* Few have the depth of knowledge about set design, set dressing, managing a massive production, and meticulous research into design like Peter. He not only worked on *Bond,* but he worked on *Titanic,* a grueling production where he had to create almost every square inch of that ship in stunning detail. Peter knew every craftsman, propmaker, plasterer, supplier out there. There was hardly a problem he couldn't solve on a set. He also has a near-encyclopedic memory. He's one of those people you could ask what he ate on some random day 40 years ago, and he would likely be able to tell you. He had learned from the best, yet he had his own style. He could do a Ken Adam–style set like the Soviet war room in *Octopussy,* for example, but he preferred verisimilitude.

And then, of course, there is the ultimate *James Bond* gadget, the Aston Martin DB5, introduced for the first time in *Goldfinger* and enhanced with, as Q would say, certain modifications, among them oil slicks, bulletproof screens, and, of course, the ever-popular ejector seat.

TANYA NITINS
(author, *Selling James Bond*)

Actually, you can thank Mr. Ian Fleming for the association. He first mentioned Bond driving an Aston Martin in *Goldfinger,* but Fleming regularly used brands in his stories and would describe them in elaborate detail in order to show insights into a character's personality. I'm not 100 percent sure *why* Fleming chose Aston Martin specifically, although being such a prominent English luxury brand, it certainly isn't surprising that he chose the model. Interestingly, the Aston Martin DB4 was released in 1958, and Fleming published *Goldfinger* in 1959. Apparently, its new shape caused quite a sensation when it was revealed at the 1958 Motor Show, so it was probably the "car to have." This may have motivated Fleming to associate it with his spy that would only have the best of the best.

GUY HAMILTON

It was fun reinventing the Aston Martin. I think Richard Maibaum came up with a couple of the gadgets involved with it, but my stepson came up with the ejector roof, which was *really* high tech—we had a rubber band and a dummy, and a prop man cut the band and the entire went thing went up and out.

KEN ADAM

In creating this Aston Martin, you have to remember I, by this time, had a brilliant team of assistants. With all the gadgets, I can come up with the ideas, but somebody has to build them and so on. I had a wonderful assistant, Johnny Stears, who did all of that. And the Aston Martin made it very easy to get rid of my frustrations, because, having had a sports car at the same time, and the E-type had that long nose, every time I parked it somewhere, somebody bashed in part of the nose. You see? They disappeared, so I put machine guns on and so on. It was a wonderful way to deal with road rage.

GUY HAMILTON

In the scene where Desmond is explaining the car to Sean, Cubby was on the set, which is very, very rare. You're sitting there and he said, "Aren't you going to tell him about the ejector button?" I said, "No, Cubby. I've said that there's a bit of this and there's a bit of that, and so on, but I want the ejector seat to be a surprise. I think it will get a big laugh." And he says, "It'll get a big laugh anyway, but tell the audience what you're going to do and then do it." You never argue with Cubby; you're wasting your time. So, I shot all the rest of the dialogue and in the end the scene stayed in, and Cubby was absolutely right: "Tell 'em what you're going to do and then do it."

There is so much that, obviously, *Goldfinger* does right, that it's almost unfathomable to believe that there were myriad behind-the-scenes problems, particularly in terms of editing the shot footage.

PETER HUNT

(editor, *Goldfinger*)

I got a little angry with *Goldfinger*, because I didn't think it was being made properly. In fact, I did quite a lot of work on that insofar as second-unit shooting. I just didn't feel that it was coming out the way it should have been coming out. We changed the theme a bit, there was a different director . . . I just felt it wasn't quite right. I must say that from the producers' point of view, they must have thought the same thing, too. They really let me have a much freer hand on that in every way. The whole car chase was actually a good lesson in editing. It was cut and edited and made to be entirely different from the way it was shot. It was very interesting, actually, but you wouldn't know, of course. Again, one of my favorite sayings is, "Thank goodness the audience hasn't seen the script."

TERENCE YOUNG

After *From Russia with Love,* I went off and made a film called *Moll Flanders,* which couldn't have been more different, because it was almost like a Restoration, eighteenth-century romp like *Tom Jones.* And apparently they didn't like *Goldfinger* when it was finished. They thought the picture was not going to be a success. One of the big problems with the film was that Bond got captured and put in jail very early in the film. I went back and I did a little work on it with Peter Hunt, and what we did was try to take some of the scenes that came later, and put them before, so that he wasn't captured until about the fifth reel. In the films that we'd made to date, he got into the villain's hands in the last reel or two of the picture, but certainly an hour had passed before he was in jeopardy. In that one, he was captured in the first 30 minutes. I thought it was a defect in the storyline.

PETER HUNT

What was being shot was very poorly done, in my opinion, but eventually it came out right. As I say, that's all part of filmmaking, I guess. Oh, I remember another reason it was so tough. I had given up smoking, and I was a real bull in a china shop at that time, saying, "No, no, no, no. That's *not* the way it should be done!" I was very autocratic about it all, although in fact it worked in the film. I had to pummel it into the same sort of style that the other two films were, taking what I was given and shaping it like the other two. It was not coming out like them, and my confidence was based on what I had already done. I must say, because it's definitely true, that those two producers always stood behind me very well. They were extremely cooperative and extremely appreciative of all the hard work I did. It *is* hard work, especially when you consider that the films are 90 percent hard work and 10 percent cleverness. They were extremely hard work, and some were more difficult than others. *Goldfinger* was one of them. But as it worked out, it became one of the better ones.

TERENCE YOUNG

The idea was that I was brought back to do *Thunderball,* and they were going to put *Thunderball* out before *Goldfinger.* The idea was to run *Thunderball* and then put *Goldfinger* out a week later or something like that. It just shows how much people *don't* know, because *Goldfinger* became the most popular one they had up until then. They re-edited . . . in fact, I consoled them. I saw the film and I told them I thought it was a damn good picture. I told them I thought they should make some cuts, which they did.

PETER HUNT

I don't know anything about that, but I don't think that can be true, because *Thunderball* was going through litigation at that time. Remember, it belonged to Kevin McClory. That was one of the ones that *didn't* belong to Broccoli, Saltzman, and United Artists, because Fleming had written the book *Thunderball* from a screenplay which Kevin McClory claims—and he won the case—he and Jack Whittingham wrote, which was not a book, but because of that they could never get it lifted off as a film. *Thunderball* interested me insofar that until the court case was settled, they wouldn't touch it at all, and the case was still going on while we made *Goldfinger,* so I don't know what events Terence is talking about.

Obviously, whatever the truth is in this *Rashomon*-style tale (and it's unlikely there's much truth to Young's version of events), they worked it out, with *Goldfinger* being released to theaters on December 22, 1964, and proving an absolute box-office sensation. The $3 million film recouped its production costs in just two weeks, scoring over $51 million at the domestic box office, and left no doubt that James Bond was here to stay. It also marked the introduction of myriad 007 merchandise, including Corgi's Aston Martin DB5, which became the number one selling toy of 1964 and still holds a place of honor on the authors' shelves, and paved the way for the direction the franchise would follow for years to come.

RAY MORTON

This is the screenplay that introduced larger-than-life fantasy and tongue-in-cheek humor to the *Bond* series, and is, along with *The Spy Who Loved Me,* the best of the fantasy *Bonds*. It is also the script that introduces the antagonistic relationship between Bond and MI6's quartermaster, now known as "Q." This script features the best *Bond* villain (Goldfinger) in the entire series, the greatest henchman (Oddjob), the most memorable gadgets (especially that fully equipped Aston Martin DB5 with modifications), one of the best pre-credit sequences, and one of the most striking images (the gold paint–covered corpse of Jill Masterson) of all the movies.

JOHN CORK

I don't think *Goldfinger* changed everything. All the ingredients were in place prior to *Goldfinger. From Russia with Love* had become the highest-grossing film ever released in the UK, and the novels were selling as fast as Pan and Signet (the UK and US paperback publishers) could print them. So much of the commentary on the *Bond* films and novels were about how much fun they were, how they were silly, adolescent "hokum" not to be taken seriously. After *From Russia with Love*, there was only one attempt to make a truly serious *Bond* film (*On Her Majesty's Secret Service*) for almost two decades. The *Flint* films and the *Matt Helm* films went into development before *Goldfinger* was released. *The Man from U.N.C.L.E.* television series premiered in the US a week after *Goldfinger* opened in London. Cubby and Harry knew what was coming, and the only way to compete was to be bigger, better, and cleverer. *Goldfinger* merely reflected that sensibility.

RAY MORTON

The "*Bond* Formula" is perfected in *Goldfinger*: an exciting pre-credit sequence that kicks off the movie in high style; Bond being called into M's office and given an assignment that will eventually bring him into conflict with the villain; a scene in which Bond is equipped with some spectacular gadgets by Q; his encounters with three different women—the first a sacrificial lamb, the second a "bad girl" in cahoots with the villain (and who sometimes changes sides and becomes a Bond ally), and the third the leading lady/damsel in distress; an intriguing plot that features a new "bump" (Cubby Broccoli's term for spectacular action sequences) every 10 minutes or so; a final fight between Bond and the henchman; a final battle between Bond and his allies and the villain and his supporters; a final showdown between Bond and the villain; and a fade-out in which Bond and the leading lady get together. Because of this, the *Goldfinger* screenplay established the blueprint for most future Eon *Bond* movies.

TOM MANKIEWICZ

(screenwriter, *Diamonds Are Forever*)

I think what turned the *Bond* pictures around—and long before I got on them—was that car in *Goldfinger.* I think the minute Sean pressed the button for the ejector seat and the audience roared, the series turned around. The audience saw outlandish things they had never seen before, and the natural response of anybody—a writer, a filmmaker—is to give them more of what they want. And there's a constant pressure as the films gross a great deal of money to make each one bigger and "more" than the last. That car was the first enormous piece of hardware that just opened the dikes. After that car, *anything* went. If you could believe that, you could believe anything.

THUNDERBALL (1965)

Bondmania.

There is no more apt a word to describe the pop culture response to the release of the fourth *James Bond* film, which struck in 1965–*exactly* like *Thunderball*. From its first screening, it was proving itself to be nothing less than a phenomenon, elevating 007 to his highest plateau yet and absolutely rivaling The Beatles in terms of the fervor surrounding the franchise.

PETER HUNT
(supervising film editor, *Thunderball*)

You have the luck of timing and that type of thing. Then you come back to the point that this was the middle of the Sixties and *Thunderball* came out at a time when The Beatles were now the big success, and suddenly everyone—I presume—had a great, euphoric attitude about the British and British products, which happens whether it be British here or America in London. There are areas where it suddenly goes through, and we were in the middle of it by the time *Thunderball* came out here. It just automatically took off. I remember once coming to America to run the film, or something, for United Artists executives. I was in the cab from the airport, when the cabdriver—who had heard my English accent—wanted to talk to me about a great little British film he had seen, even though he had no idea that I had anything to do with the film industry. That great little British film he had seen was called *Dr. No*, which thrilled me. I'll never forget that, because I found it so strangely interesting.

With the departure of Guy Hamilton, Terence Young was lured back into the director's chair for his third (and ultimately final) 007 adventure. *Thunderball*, originally intended as the first *James Bond* film–though in retrospect it would have been an impossible production at the time given the miniscule budget that would have been available to produce it–finally landed in theaters thanks to a brief thaw in the dispute over the film rights to the novel. Two years earlier, producer Kevin McClory had been granted film rights to the Ian Fleming novel *Thunderball* by the London High Court. This in the aftermath of an acrimonious lawsuit with Fleming that was settled over the use of plot elements McClory, Jack Whittingham, and Fleming had developed in their planned 1959 James Bond adventure. One reason behind McClory's ceding his rights to Albert R. Broccoli and Harry Saltzman to make the film as an official entry in the Eon series was his being granted sole producing credit and the two Danjaq partners taking executive producer credits instead. It's a title often accorded to financiers and line producers, but not creative partners as Broccoli and Saltzman had been on the rest of the *Bond* series. In the end, the final screenplay is credited to Richard Maibaum and John Hopkins, based on the original script by Whittingham from a story by McClory, Whittingham, and Fleming.

STEVEN JAY RUBIN

(author, *The James Bond Films*)

In February 1964, with *Thunderball* lost to McClory and *Goldfinger* already nearing completion, it was time to plan Eon's next *Bond* thriller. The producers chose the best of Fleming's later *Bond* stories, *On Her Majesty's Secret Service.* Arrangements were made to return to Switzerland—where parts of *Goldfinger* had been shot—that winter to scout locations for the new film, which takes place almost entirely in the Alpine snows and involves Bond in a search for Ernst Stavro Blofeld, the missing head of SPECTRE.

ROBERT SELLERS

(author, *The Battle for Bond*)

McClory obviously won the film rights to *Thunderball*. This was in 1963. *From Russia with Love* had just opened and been a huge success, and then *Goldfinger* the following year was just a blockbuster. *Bond* was the biggest thing in the world, and McClory had the rights to make his own *Bond* film, which he actually went ahead and tried to do.

KEVIN MCCLORY

(producer, *Thunderball*)

I thought Sean was great in *Dr. No* and *From Russia with Love*, but they had him under contract, so I went in a different direction at that time, with Richard Burton, who was very, very fit. A very strong actor. I needed somebody who was very strong if I was going to come up with someone else other than Sean.

ROBERT SELLERS

Back in 1959, Richard Burton had been a key choice. In my research for *The Battle for Bond,* I came across a letter in which Fleming states his preference for Burton. McClory was also thinking about Richard Harris. In other words, working-class, non-English actors. Burton was Welsh, Harris was Irish. I don't think they really wanted a David Niven–type actor who had those upper-class English attributes. They wanted a ballsy, blue-collar type of actor that working people could relate to around the world. Of course, Broccoli and Saltzman later came around to the same way of thinking when they cast the Scottish and working-class Connery.

What also interested me about the casting process was how much the public had gotten involved. McClory's office was inundated with hundreds of letters from people nominating their favorite actor to play the role. Stars like William Holden and Stanley Baker; some ludicrous choices, too, such as Peter Cushing! Housewives also sent in photographs of their husbands, saying how much they should play the part. And a lot of ex-servicemen and ex-policemen also sent in their particulars. But in 1964, he went back to Richard Burton—who they'd had discussions with previously—and he said yes. He was playing Hamlet on Broadway and McClory went to see him in his dressing room. Burton said, "Yes, I'll do it." But then Broccoli and Saltzman made a deal.

KEVIN MCCLORY

Deep down I knew I wanted Sean. Eventually, the way for me to do that was to get together with Cubby and Harry, which I did.

STEVEN JAY RUBIN

Throughout the autumn of 1964, McClory kept his own production hopes alive, but with United Artists now backing *Goldfinger* with a high-powered prerelease publicity campaign emphasizing the merits of Sean Connery as Bond, it looked as if *Thunderball* was a doomed project. In view of this, McClory took the obvious step and contacted Broccoli and Saltzman with an offer. Since they had been so keen on *Thunderball* for their own series, perhaps they would be interested in going into the venture as partners. To Broccoli and Saltzman, the deal did not seem all that attractive. There were more than enough *Bond* books around. However, Broccoli decided not to pass up the offer, believing that if anyone else made *Thunderball,* it would have a damaging effect on their own series.

ROBERT SELLERS

One must feel a little sorry for Broccoli and Saltzman, in that their huge gamble with *Dr. No* had paid off handsomely, their blood, sweat, and tears had created a worldwide phenomenon, and now here was McClory coming out of the woodwork saying he was going to make his own. At the same time, they knew that *Casino Royale* was coming. They knew a version of it was going to be made, which they eventually did in 1967—and which is one of my great guilty pleasures. I mean, it's *awful*, it's terrible, but brilliant at the same time. So Broccoli and Saltzman knew this was on the horizon, and now, with McClory representing a second unofficial *Bond* film, it could kill the franchise stone dead. So they had to make a deal with the devil. I'm pretty sure had [*Casino Royale* producer Charles] Feldman *not* been around, Broccoli and Saltzman would not have made a deal with McClory to coproduce *Thunderball*. But two rogue *Bond* movies coming out at the same time would have been too much.

STEVEN JAY RUBIN

Plans for *On Her Majesty's Secret Service* were dropped and *Thunderball* became the next *Bond* production. McClory was delighted at the prospect of his film going into production during the height of the *Bond* fever. During the past five years he had rewritten his script a dozen times and had covered every foot of the Bahamas, searching for possible locations. He was an expert diver and underwater explorer and his expertise was invaluable on a film which emphasized underwater effects.

RAY MORTON

(senior writer, *Script* magazine)

It was McClory's idea to create an all-new story for the first *James Bond* film, rather than adapt one of the novels, so without him there never would have been a *Thunderball* story and therefore no *Thunderball* novel or 1965 *Thunderball* film or 1983 remake in *Never Say Never Again*. As to the story itself, it was McClory's idea to set the story in the Bahamas and to have it climax with an underwater battle. He also devised a number of additional narrative elements and scenes. So his contribution to the *Thunderball* story in all its versions was quite significant, although he did none of the actual writing on any of them. He was an idea man rather than a writer. Fortunately, many of those ideas were good ones.

ROBERT SELLERS

One has to give credit to that final shooting script from Jack Whittingham, which is a terrific script. It zips along and feels like a *Bond* film, and without a doubt it was the blueprint for what followed, which has made them always maintain that Richard Maibaum never saw that script. But you look at the *Thunderball* film, and also elements of *Dr. No, From Russia with Love*, and *Goldfinger*, and the Whittingham Bond is there, because what Whittingham did—when you talk about the Connery Bond and the difference of the Fleming novel Bond—was create a Bond for the screen that was acceptable. And that *wasn't* the Fleming Bond. He was a killer, but without a sense of humor. He was quite a sad, flawed individual, in many ways prone to the melancholy.

There's the opening of the *Goldfinger* novel where he's just come back from a killing and is just about to get on a plane. He's the Daniel Craig Bond that we have now, isn't he? I don't think that would have worked in the '60s. You needed this sort of international playboy-type character, which Connery personified brilliantly. So Whittingham rewrote Bond for the screen, and Maibaum carried that forward. He created the cinematic Bond, because the Bond of the films is patently *not* the Bond of the novels. And *that* Bond was created with his scripts.

TOM SOTER

(author, *Bond and Beyond: 007 and Other Special Agents*)

The plot of *Thunderball* was not substantially different from the screenplay McClory had coauthored with Fleming and Jack Whittingham in 1958–59, although it incorporated many of the novel's elements, particularly the health clinic sequence at the opening, as well as adding a few of its own. The story involves the kidnapping by SPECTRE of a NATO jet fighter containing two nuclear bombs. The plane crash-lands underwater in the Bahamas and the bombs are stored aboard the villain's yacht, the *Disco Volante*. SPECTRE gives NATO an ultimatum: either pay a ransom of one hundred million pounds in diamonds or two Western cities will be destroyed. The British Secret Service is one of many agencies attempting to locate the bombs before time runs out. Bond is assigned to the Bahamas—a lucky noncoincidence since the area was McClory's home.

JOHN CORK

(author, *James Bond: The Legacy*)

Kevin McClory had a huge influence on *Thunderball*. He wanted certain elements. He wanted it shot in CinemaScope. He wanted big, elaborate underwater scenes. He wanted the film to be long, possibly released as a roadshow film with an intermission. One of his mentors was Michael Todd, the showman whose name was on the Todd-AO widescreen process. Kevin had been instrumental in convincing Fleming, Ivar Bryce, and their partner Ernest Cuneo that doing a big underwater epic was the road to success.

Two early hits of the widescreen era were *Beneath the 12-Mile Reef* and *20,000 Leagues Under the Sea*, and Kevin wanted to emulate the success of those films. When Cubby and Harry made the deal with Kevin for *Thunderball*, Cubby recalled how much he loved another film with extensive underwater scenes, *Boy on a Dolphin*. Kevin also secured a lot of the locations for *Thunderball*. But all too quickly, Kevin got on the nerves of Cubby. Even before shooting began, there were some major fights. Cubby successfully kept Kevin in Nassau during most of the early production in the UK and France, and then after principal location photography was over, Cubby convinced Kevin to stay with the underwater unit. Likely because Kevin was not deeply familiar with post-production, he largely stayed away from the editing of the film, and by that point Cubby and Harry were glad he did.

Thunderball is frequently derided for its lugubrious underwater sequences and lethargic pace, but that does a disservice to an otherwise terrific film. Are the underwater battles slow? You bet. Does that make it a bad *Bond* movie? Not by a mile. French actress (and a former Miss France) Claudine Auger may be the most beautiful *Bond* Girl to ever grace the silver screen. Playing the sister of François Derval, a victim of SPECTRE's plan, she is the "ward" of villain Emilio Largo. Though she's wonderful in the role, one has to wonder how Cubby Broccoli's original choice–Julie Christie–would have fared, though it was said he did not find her well-endowed enough for the role, prompting him to seriously consider the more voluptuous (but less-gifted actress) Raquel Welch as well as future Oscar winner Faye Dunaway. As was now par for the course, Auger would be dubbed by a returning Nikki van der Zyl, who had looped Ursula Andress in *Dr. No*.

Luciana Paluzzi, who originally auditioned for kept woman Domino, is sexy and deadly as SPECTRE assassin Fiona Volpe, taking great glee in her venality (presaging Famke Janssen's Xenia Onatopp three decades later in *GoldenEye*), prompting one of the great *Bond* one-liners of all time. As Connery gently sets Volpe down on a chair at a nightclub after her own men inadvertently shoot her following a fevered pursuit of 007 through the Junkanoo celebration in the Bahamas, he remarks dryly, "Do you mind if my wife sits this one out? She's just dead."

Fans of '60s cinema will, of course, recognize Martine Beswick, back after *From Russia with Love,* where she was one of the fighting gypsy girls, this time playing it cool as Paula Caplan, Bond's loyal ally in Nassau.

CLAUDINE AUGER

(actress, "Domino Derval")

I started acting when I was about 17 in theater, movies, television. The biggest part in all of my life was *Thunderball*. After the test [for the film], I expected to know the answer in a week. I was quite sure it could be me. And then, when I *knew* it was me, I couldn't sleep for two or three nights. It felt like I was dreaming, that it couldn't be possible. It was so marvelous and it lit a fire inside me. I was just walking along, smiling at nothing in the street. I couldn't imagine it would happen so quickly. I think *Bond* is a challenge for every woman in the world, and I was one.

The test was in a bathing suit that's meant to be sexy. It was a bathing suit open in front with mesh—very sexy. And they made a beach in the studio, at Pinewood, because the first meeting is there in the movie, and then there was a scene where she falls in love with him in the casino. She's gambling with humor, and being provocative. I was supposed to make all the men feel that you love them, but not to show it. They must have a feeling of it. I don't mean you are sexy because you're nude, but sexy in your mind is more important. I think you have to be sexy first of all in your heart, and your mind, and your body, of course, too. But your body follows if you are loving men—and you are loving life.

LISA FUNNELL

(author, *For His Eyes Only: The Women of James Bond*)

The *Bond* Girl is Domino Derval. What I find interesting about her is she is a character who is, yes, a kept woman. Her brother was murdered and she's being tortured by Largo. In the end, she saves Bond. She takes the harpoon gun, she shoots Largo and kills him. She's actually sort of the knight in shining armor and then the two of them can escape. I think that is also important, that women can have that type of representation, even in the 1960s.

MARTINE BESWICK

(actress, "Paula Caplan")

My very first interview when I returned to Jamaica to London in 1961 was for *Dr. No*. Terence Young, who became a great friend and my future champion, realized that I was totally green and told me to go and get experience as he had a part for me in his next film, and he kept his word. I did not read any of the Fleming novels. In fact, I had never even heard of him before going up for *Dr. No*. When I started on *From Russia with Love*, it was with three weeks' rehearsals for the gypsy fight. And my return for *Thunderball* was because of

Terence Young. Harry Saltzman and Broccoli had made it very clear that no *Bond* Girl could be used twice; however, as the part of Paula Caplan called for an island girl . . . well, Terence fought and won. All of the *Thunderball* locations in the Bahamas were some of the most fabulous places I ever visited for a film set.

ROBERT CAPLEN

(author, *Shaken & Stirred: The Feminism of James Bond*)

Fiona Volpe is truly an evil woman. A fiery redhead (contrasting with blondes and brunettes), she was the most dangerous female character presented in the film series at the time. She acted, in essence, like a female equivalent to Bond, an agent (assassin even) who uses her sexuality as a weapon. She and Bond share a bed with a headboard representing a cage. She is wild (as her hair suggests) and immune to Bond's charms, berating him that she is not one of his conquests who "starts to hear heavenly choirs singing" after their rendezvous. She may appear in control, but she is ultimately weak. She works for and answers to male authority, Ernst Stavro Blofeld; unilaterally acquiesces to Angelo Palazzi's demand for higher payment, which draws ire from Blofeld; and, after failing to kill Bond, allows herself to become a physical shield that Bond uses to prevent a bullet from hitting him.

Although the cat-stroking Blofeld was back physically, portrayed by Anthony Dawson and voiced by Eric Pohlmann, the primary villain of *Thunderball* is Emilio Largo, as played by actor Adolfo Celi. Born July 27, 1922, in Sicily, he appeared in dozens of films, though in America the one that made the biggest impact was, of course, the *Bond* film. As was par for the course, Celi had his voice dubbed, this time by Robert Rietty. On the flip side of the coin, working *with* Bond is CIA agent Felix Leiter, this time played by Rik Van Nutter (representing the third actor to have done so by this point).

ADOLFO CELI

(actor, "Emilio Largo")

I was traveling back from Hollywood where I had finished *Von Ryan's Express* with Frank Sinatra, and in New York I purchased the novel *Thunderball* by Fleming. I hadn't seen the movie *Dr. No*, but I had heard about it. Anyway, I read the book on the plane during my flight from NY to Spain, where I had to shoot a film with Jean-Paul Belmondo, and I thought, "How nice it would be acting in a film from this book . . . but probably they will never call me." I made the film in Spain and then I got to Rome with some money and decided to go to Paris. I was leaving when my agent told me to go to the George V, where there was a producer who wanted to see me. The producer turned out to be Saltzman; a bit of discussion and we landed it. I got to the hotel attired and with a bit of makeup suggestive of Emilio Largo, as I knew everything on the character, and this was some help.

I feel that it was good. I remember it with pleasure and I enjoyed it enormously, as I considered the role an amusing one, made to entertain and not to be considered very serious. Many people keep calling me "Goldfinger." It's something I can't get rid of. There are two instances, actually. One is that they call me Goldfinger, and I keep saying, "No, you are wrong. It is the other one." The other one is that they ask me, "And the cat? The white cat?" Now, as you well know, the white cat was kept in his hands by a technician until Blofeld appeared in *You Only Live Twice*, but I have been identified as the man with the cat so much that they keep saying to me, "Ah, the way you were fondling that cat . . . !" Well, that's the power of illusion.

GLEN OLIVER
(pop culture commentator)

I'm shocked that Rik Van Nutter's performance remained in *Thunderball*. He's impressively inadequate in that role. He couldn't have conveyed less charisma, dimension, investment, or any semblance of defined personality if he'd tried. His style and delivery is porn-star level at best, but without any of the payoff.

Gadgets, of course, were everywhere in *Thunderball*, starting with the return of the Aston Martin DB5, utilized as a getaway vehicle in the precredits sequence (which Bond reaches by *flying* from a terrace high above via an operational, courtesy-of-the-military jet pack). Observes John Brosnan in his book *James Bond in the Cinema*, "He lands in the road where the girl we saw earlier and the Aston Martin wait for him. Flinging the jet pack in the trunk, they climb into the car, but, before they can drive away, the guards arrive on the scene, guns firing. Up goes the Aston Martin's rear bulletproof screen and out of the twin exhaust pipes comes two streams of water at such pressure that the gunmen are knocked off their feet. The car roars away and the credits begin to roll. Well . . . to be capable of squirting out that much water at such a high pressure, Bond's car would need to contain a storage tank of vast proportions. When we remember all the other infernal devices that it's supposed to contain—machine guns, ejector seats, etc.—it's surprising that there's still room for the engine."

There's also an underwater breather that provides about four minutes of air—a device that comes in perfectly handy for 007—and Largo's yacht, the *Disco Volante*.

STEVEN JAY RUBIN

Floating out in the harbor in Nassau were two mammoth luxury yachts, both of which were dubbed the "*Disco Volante*." One was the special creation of art director Ken Adam. The *Disco Volante* was the gleaming super yacht of Emilio Largo, but hidden beneath Adam's calm 100-foot exterior lurked a hydrofoil boat, a craft that operated on hydraulic skis that lifted the entire hull out of the water, propelling it along at 45 miles per hour.

KEN ADAM

(production designer, *Thunderball*)

For Largo's superfast yacht, I found a hydrofoil down in Puerto Rico and bought it for $10,000. We took it back to Miami and I redesigned it and doubled its length by building the 50-foot catamaran that cocooned around it. All the naval experts were worried and didn't think it could work. But I used two one-inch slip bolts on either side that held the cocoon to the hydrofoil so they could move independently. Once they separated and the hydrofoil was revealed, the cocoon became a floating arsenal with the type of armament you found on a destroyer ship, like the antiaircraft cannon, armor plating, and machine guns. Everyone said we were going to have a disaster, but it worked beautifully.

There were, of course, what had become the usual fisticuffs, as well as an epic underwater battle between SPECTRE frogmen and Bond's team, desperately trying to retrieve the stolen nuclear bombs.

RIC MEYERS

(author, *For One Week Only: The World of Exploitation Films*)

I loved the pre-credit fight, with Bond's adversary, Jacques Bouvar (note the initials), played by Sean's shorter doppelgänger, Bob Simmons. This may be the second best Connery mano a mano fight (following the Red Grant Orient Express battle), because it's Connery versus his stunt double and stunt arranger. It is also the optimum in Connery's casual brutality and gladiatorial he-man fisticuffs.

GLEN OLIVER

Underwater action in nearly any film—under circumstances which are even vaguely realistic—isn't inherently exciting or fun. It's like watching combatants sludge through molasses. In *Bond* movies, the underwater action which *worked* was generally gadget based and conceptual. For example, it's hard not to get a little bit turned on by *The Spy Who Loved Me*'s weaponized submarine car. When broken down from a filmmaking perspective, the action in that sequence wasn't particularly well mounted, but the spirit, essence, and uniqueness of the idea driving the set piece made the whole affair feel fresh and provocative. There have been a few cinematic instances in which filmmakers have managed to edit and/or direct their way out of this morass—John McTiernan's *The Hunt for Red October* and James Cameron's *The Abyss* spring to mind as "underwater" films which found the necessary sensibilities to sustain large amounts of time underwater (chiefly by exploiting suspense and atmosphere). Alas, Terence Young was a bit more pedantic, and less exploratory, in his approach. The result was a plot hinging on big action which was inherently decelerated and muted. Thus, the energy of the film came crashing down at junctures when the picture should've been at its most exhilarating.

PETER HUNT

I liked the film, particularly the underwater material, because it was a great challenge to me as an editor. I was out in the Bahamas with them, and a great deal of responsibility was laid on my shoulders by them in the making and finishing of the film. But there was a tremendous amount of underwater material, which is very difficult to edit to make move along and make a good story out of it. Underwater by its nature is slow and therefore trying to keep a pace going all through it is the difficult thing.

JOHN CORK

I love *Thunderball*. I love the underwater sequences. They are not too slow for me, but that's somewhat because of John Barry's great score. The one really slow scene is the theft of the bombs and the covering of the Vulcan bomber with underwater camouflage. The huge battle in Biscayne Bay at the end is just magnificent. The scene just gets bigger, wilder, and more frantic until there is so much blood in the water, the sharks come in to attack. That's crazy. As Frank Sinatra used to say, "If you don't like that, you don't like black-eyed peas."

RIC MEYERS

Once again, editor Peter Hunt does his best with both the now-wearying climactic conflict cliché of having a villain clearly physically inferior to the hero, as well as the literally film-sinking underwater ballet battle. Need a surefire way to slow your action movie to a crawl? Stick a battling army in the screen equivalent of Jell-O. To their credit, they try to make lemonade by having the final fight in a lurching, sped-up yacht rather than a crash-diving plane in *Goldfinger,* but the slap-fest between Bond and Largo does not make an equitable bookend to the opening fight with Jacques Bouvar. To add insult to Bond's injury, his bacon has to be saved by the tormented heroine, deserving though her revenge on her tormenting captor is.

TERENCE YOUNG

I don't think the underwater lends itself to a *Bond* picture. The rhythm and tempo . . . For instance, you cannot move somebody underwater at more than four miles an hour without his mask coming off. Even when we had those little machines towing people, they were only going around five knots. Well, at five miles an hour, you've got everybody in the audience saying, "What happened to the guy they left behind and this . . . ?", and so on, and they're starting to pick holes in the scripts . . . and there are a lot of holes in all the stories. You should never give them time until they're on their way home.

GLEN OLIVER

Thunderball is a bit of a mess on the whole. It has a helluva hook—Bond chasing down stolen atomic weapons—but the picture brings zero sense of urgency to the equation. There's an inordinate quantity of standing around, gabbing, and dithering about—no sense that these two missing nukes are actually a particularly pressing concern. And when the folks on-screen don't seem terribly invested in the crisis, why should the audience become invested? *Thunderball* is a funky anomaly. In many regards, it feels like it is one of the more highly visibly and recognized *Bond* films. But it's also one of the clunkiest and one of the least fully realized 007 pictures. Which makes the Kevin McClory mess even more surreal and ironic—he fervently claimed rights to a narrative which, on the whole, was rather lackluster and even a little shabby.

The huge success of *Thunderball*—which debuted in December 1965 supported by the airing of the NBC special *The Incredible World of James Bond*—helped usher in the era of spymania for the rest of the decade. While shows like *The Avengers*, *The Ipcress File*, and *The Man from U.N.C.L.E.* had preceded *Thunderball*, by the time it left theaters the floodgates were open for a spy invasion, including a very different interpretation of James Bond, 1967's *Casino Royale*. *Thunderball*, for its part, would go on to gross nearly $66 million domestically, which, adjusted for inflation, is nearly $684 million.

RAY MORTON

The core idea of *Thunderball*—villains hijack nuclear bombs from a NATO aircraft and use them to hold the world for ransom—is terrific and has the potential to make a terrific thriller-style *Bond* film. However, I'm not a big fan of this screenplay. The villain isn't very interesting; the story takes far too long to get started; the entire Shrublands sequence is long, confusing, and ultimately pointless; there's not enough action—the narrative spends a lot of time spinning its wheels in the Bahamas; and the story's all-important ticking clock (the threat to detonate a bomb off Miami Beach if the ransom isn't paid by a specific time) gets lost amid all the meandering. There are a few strong elements: the villainous character of Fiona Volpe is terrific, and her scenes with Bond have genuine sizzle. Likewise, Domino is an interesting character and there's an appealing tenderness in her relationship with Bond; and some of the one-liners are great—especially "Wait till you get to my teeth," "No, but I know something about women," and "He got the point." Oh yeah, and it has a jet pack. But for me, these positives are not enough to outweigh the script's negatives.

FRED DEKKER

(director, *The Monster Squad*)

In a way, *Thunderball* had a really tough act to follow in terms of *Goldfinger*, and I think it follows it beautifully. Connery's great, the sets are wonderful, the locations are wonderful, Domino is my favorite *Bond* Girl—Tracy in *On Her Majesty's Secret Service* is more interesting and fully rounded, but if I'm just going to have a girl to look at following Bond around, it would be Domino. My only complaint is that the underwater sequences are a little lethargic. Peter Hunt does his best to speed things along, but I think it's just a little bit too long. Other than that, I'm a big fan.

TERENCE YOUNG

I honestly don't know *why* I did *Thunderball*. I don't particularly like it. It's about the most successful *Bond* picture in terms of sales of tickets. It was very successful, but to my mind all that underwater stuff was *anti*–James Bond, because it was slow motion. People swim slowly and you couldn't have them going very fast; we undercranked some of the shots and they looked ridiculous—the water was wobbling around so much it suddenly became stupid. On the whole, I would say it's *not* my favorite picture by a long way. It's a very efficient picture, but already the hardware was creeping into the stories.

ROBERT SELLERS

Over the years, I've had quite a few favorite *Bond* movies. I seem to remember as a kid I loved *Diamonds Are Forever* the most. I don't know why; it's a fun, campy kind of movie, but it's far from the best of the series. For me, *Thunderball* hits pretty much all the buttons and the production team is operating at their absolute peak. For starters, it's Connery's best performance as Bond, John Barry's score is amazing, Ted Moore's photography is sumptuous, and I think the script is pretty clever and features some of the best bits of dialogue in the series. Some of the best jokes, too. For me, *Thunderball* is the bridge between the *From Russia with Love* type of *Bond* movie—all suspense and espionage—and the more all-out escapism *Bond* movies. I think it satisfyingly blends both of these worlds.

PETER HUNT

It was the biggest film of the lot. Funnily enough, it doesn't matter to the audience. What matters to them is whether it captures them or not. It was the most successful at the time, and it was also the most expensive. I think the final negative cost was about $11 million, which was a tremendous amount of money in those days.

RICHARD MAIBAUM

(screenwriter, *Thunderball*)

In *Thunderball*, it really did become larger than life. The production became enormous, more fantastical, almost comic strip. And once we'd done that, there was just no way of bringing them down. With *Thunderball*, the movies became documented fantasy.

TERENCE YOUNG

If you look at the way Sean was equipped underwater, I thought if we were going to make this underwater stuff, we've got to make it like he's wearing everything *including* the kitchen sink. I thought if we're going to do this, let's do it properly. And they did. They piled on as much as they could, but that's why I said after *Thunderball,* "I think you don't want a director anymore, you want an MIT graduate to handle all the machines."

DAVID V. PICKER

(president and chief executive officer, United Artists)

For the opening in New York's Times Square, I suggested that we run the picture 24 hours a day, at least through the holiday season. To our knowledge this had never been done before for a first-run major film, but the exhibitor agreed. Opening night I had a late dinner. The early shows had all been full. When I went by the theater after the midnight show and saw the lines waiting to get into the late-late shows, I knew the idea had worked. *Thunderball* was such an enormous hit that we knew it was time for another renegotiation with the producers. Once again, Arthur and Bob worked it out. It was only a matter of how the profits would be shared, how big the producers' fees would increase, and so on. Greedy, yes; but *Bond* was a big franchise and UA knew an accommodation was necessary.

PETER HUNT

One thing I said at the time of *Thunderball,* and again later on, was that we had to be careful that we didn't become imitators of our imitators, because by then *everybody* had gotten on the bandwagon. So we had to be very careful of copying them, because that would have been a disaster. But they seem to have outlived everything and gone on and on and on, although they've changed tremendously. They're certainly *not* the sort of thing that Ian Fleming wrote.

KEVIN MCCLORY

We agreed that I would produce the picture; the idea was that all three of us would produce the picture. I agreed to do this, and we worked out what our deal was to be, with the understanding that 10 years after the first domestic release of *Thunderball*, all the copyright in the screenplays of *Thunderball* would revert back to my company, automatically and irrevocably. That is in this contract. This is signed by Saltzman and by Broccoli, so they were well aware of the situation. As for the other rights, to the other screenplays, I agreed, in this contract, that I would not make another *Bond* film for 10 years. I believed at the time that *Bond* would be very much alive in 10 years from then.

ROBERT SELLERS

I've always said that McClory must be applauded for his foresight in being one of the very first people to realize the potential of Bond as a cinematic character, and actually trying to do something about it. And getting mightily damn close, too. Yet he was demonstrably the wrong man for the job. He was too inexperienced, too headstrong, and too much of an egoist. In the end, the right people came along, and they were Broccoli and Saltzman. But it's still a very tragic story. McClory felt that Saltzman and Broccoli stole his thunder. He felt that he should have been doing those *Bond* films. It was his idea first and he got to Fleming first, as it were. That's another reason I believe he pursued this to the end. Actually, to the grave. That's what he wanted; not just the right to make a *Bond* film, but the right to be called the originator of the screen Bond.

YOU ONLY LIVE TWICE (1967)

You Only Live Twice began the trend—with few exceptions, *On Her Majesty's Secret Service* and the 2006 version of *Casino Royale* among them—of largely discarding the Ian Fleming source material, in this case his 1964 novel of the same name. Additionally, it wasn't originally intended to be the follow-up to *Thunderball*—*On Her Majesty's Secret Service* was.

STEVEN JAY RUBIN
(author, *The James Bond Films*)

The novel takes place entirely in Japan. James Bond is sent to the Orient to meet the head of the Japanese Secret Service and gain, for England, the secrets of Magic, a decoding apparatus that is systematically intercepting Russian diplomatic traffic. The chief of Japanese intelligence is ex-kamikaze pilot Tiger Tanaka, who offers Bond the Magic ciphers if he will assassinate the evil Dr. Shatterhand, a Swiss citizen who has created a lethal garden of poisonous plants and insects in the remains of an old castle in northeastern Kyushu. There, hundreds of suicidal Japanese are finding a deadly salvation. But Shatterhand is none other than Ernst Stavro Blofeld, who, after many years of evildoing, has come to Japan to retire. His peculiar form of gardening is destroying the flower of Japanese youth and Tanaka sees Bond as Japan's only hope.

PETER HUNT
(second-unit director, *You Only Live Twice*)

On Her Majesty's Secret Service should have come before *You Only Live Twice* in the series of events that Fleming wrote. At the end of *On Her Majesty's*

Secret Service, the wife is killed, and then in *You Only Live Twice* he is sent to Japan to extract revenge from Blofeld. And the series went on from there. But they did it the other way around.

TOM SOTER

(author, *Bond and Beyond: 007 and Other Special Agents*)

You Only Live Twice was an odd choice. Throughout most of it, 007 wanders around Tokyo, taking in the sights and recuperating from the death of his wife. Near the end of the story, he uncovers evidence that his old foe, Blofeld, is running an "island of death."

STEVEN JAY RUBIN

Bond's thirst for revenge is satisfied in the final chapter of *You Only Live Twice* when he breaks into Blofeld's loathsome castle fortress and kills the ex–SPECTRE chieftain. The castle itself, with its volcanic fumaroles, deadly creeping plants, and poisonous insects, was the highlight of a book that was more of a travelogue than a *James Bond* adventure.

TOM SOTER

The climax is bizarre: Bond, in fisherman's gear, battling Blofeld, in a samurai outfit. The tale ends with the reported death of 007, but he actually has amnesia and retires to the simple life of a Japanese fisherman.

The change in order arose partly because the best weather in Switzerland—where much of *On Her Majesty's Secret Service* was set—had passed, but it also indicated problems in the *Bond* machine. The rifts in the partnership between Broccoli and Saltzman were beginning to show. Both had produced their own films, but neither man found the incredible luck alone that they had together. Their solo efforts were *not* blockbusters. And *You Only Live Twice* was a transitional picture for the *Bond* series. Terence Young announced he was tired of the films and wouldn't return, Richard Maibaum became tied up with an MGM movie and was unavailable for screenwriting, and it was the last appearance of Peter Hunt as editor.

Brought in to replace Terence Young as director is Lewis Gilbert, born March 6, 1920, in London. Prior to *You Only Live Twice*, he had directed an astounding 28 films, among them *Ferry to Hong Kong* (1959), *Sink the Bismarck!* (1950), *H.M.S. Defiant* (1962), *The 7th Dawn* (1964), and, most notably, Michael Caine's *Alfie* (1966).

LEWIS GILBERT

(director, *You Only Live Twice*)

At first I declined the film when Cubby offered it to me. I could only copy what had gone before and there was nothing in it for me, really. Supposing I made a good *James Bond* film, nobody's going to say, "Oh, isn't it wonderful he's made this marvelous *Bond* film?" They were well known by that time. The big thing was, of course, I was very fond of the Broccoli family; they were very nice to me and they were very good, so I got on very well with them, which was lucky.

ROALD DAHL

(screenwriter, *You Only Live Twice*)

I've written quite a few films, and Lewis Gilbert is the only director I ever worked with who is any kind of a decent fellow. He was absolutely splendid. He not only helped in script conferences, but had some good ideas and left you alone, and when you shot the finished thing, he shot it. Other directors have such an ego that they want to rewrite it and put their own dialogue in, and it's usually disastrous. What I admired so much about Lewis was that he just took the screenplay and shot it. *That's* the way to direct. You either trust your writer, or you don't.

SHANE RIMMER

(actor, "Hawaii Radar Operator")

Lewis Gilbert was great. I think that the selection of the director was just as important to them as who the main star was. Being on *You Only Live Twice* was like a vacation, because of some of the things you ran into in other productions. There was a lot of go-between between actors and directors and that helps. But the *Bond* family in general was quite different from any other, as I found out later. There was a lot of concern that their actors were in the right place, a comfortable place, and this was followed through on every picture that they made, which I discovered a bit later.

ROALD DAHL

I can remember Tokyo when we were shooting some of those later sequences, and they needed another scene or a rewrite. I met with Lewis down in the bar in the Hilton Hotel and gave them something like 20 pages. He literally flipped through them and then said, "That's fine." And that's it. He still had complete control of everything. I was most impressed. And, of course, I was impressed with the fact that when they do dangerous things like lifting cars up with magnets, they shoot them live! They don't use models unless they have to.

LEWIS GILBERT

Part of the attraction is that it was something that I had never done. I'd never made a film as big as that. It was a big film and I thought, "Well, I'll have a go and see what kind of mess I'd make of it," but I knew enough about films to know that I'd be alright. That I'd come through okay. The good part of me is that I've always been confident and believed in myself that I could do it. Directing could be a frightening job, because you've got a whole unit depending on and waiting for you, and what you're going to tell them.

While Gilbert was being brought aboard, and with the recognition that the Fleming novel wasn't cinematic enough, the producers began looking for screenwriters to come up with a new story. First up was the American Harold Jack Bloom, whose credits include the 1953 Western *The Naked Spur* (which scored him an Oscar nomination) and a variety of television series, notably *The Man from U.N.C.L.E.*, *Bonanza*, and *Emergency!*.

Following Bloom, attention was turned to writer Roald Dahl. Born on September 13, 1916, in Wales, Dahl served as a Royal Air Force fighter pilot during World War Two, and was injured while flying over the Libyan desert. It was *Horatio Hornblower* novelist C.S. Forester who suggested that he write a story about his experience, which he did for *The Saturday Evening Post*. This would lead him to write children's books (*The Gremlins, Charlie and the Chocolate Factory, James and the Giant Peach, The Witches*, and more), screenplays (*You Only Live Twice, Chitty Chitty Bang Bang, Willy Wonka & The Chocolate Factory*), and television (*'Way Out*, a science fiction and horror anthology series that preceded *The Twilight Zone*; *Tales of the Unexpected*).

RAY MORTON

(senior editor, *Script* magazine)

Harold Jack Bloom was an Oscar-nominated screenwriter who worked mostly in American TV and was certainly a solid enough craftsman. He wrote the first draft of *You Only Live Twice,* which Cubby apparently didn't care for. He was replaced by Roald Dahl, although a number of Bloom's key ideas were retained, including the use of ninjas as well as Blofeld's volcanic lair, hence the "additional story material" credit.

JOHN CORK

(writer/director, *The Long Road Home*)

Roald Dahl, who wrote the vast majority of the script, had been good friends with Ian during the war and after. They had shared story ideas. But Dahl had been famous since the war, having been stranded behind enemy lines as a pilot. After recovering, he went on to the US, where he played a key role in British intelligence that was rather more impressive in many respects than Ian's. He had been stationed in Washington, D.C., had become personal friends with F.D.R., and had been a vital back-channel conduit for F.D.R. to signal Churchill policy positions that might be coming. Dahl was already a noted author before Ian Fleming started publishing the *Bond* novels. He, like many of Ian's friends, was somewhat baffled at Ian's incredible rise to fame with *Bond*. This occurred just as Dahl's career hit a brief dry patch before he started writing moderately selling children's books (that would later sell in the millions).

ROALD DAHL

Albert R. Broccoli and Harry Saltzman thought of me and I got a call from Broccoli: "Would you do a *Bond* script?" I said, "Yes," and went up to see them. There were Broccoli and Saltzman and they said, "You know, it [the script] will be completely invented. You can use the Japanese scenes and the names of the characters, but we need an entirely new plot." It was Ian Fleming's worst book, with no plot in it which would even make a movie. They picked up the phone, called Swifty Lazar, my agent in California, and closed the deal. I went away and starting writing it. That's how I got the job.

JOHN CORK

Roald Dahl came to *Bond* through very strange channels. Ian Fleming's closest friend was Ivar Bryce, who set up the deal that brought Kevin McClory into the world of *Bond* in the late 1950s. Bryce was friends with Dahl, and in fact, Dahl and Fleming were not only friends who knew each other from the war, but they used to see each other at Ivar Bryce's wife's estate in Vermont in August sometimes. When Cubby and Harry made the deal to make *Thunderball,* it really galled Ivar Bryce. Bryce felt that Kevin had acted very badly, and he also knew that the deal would have never been made with Kevin if Ian Fleming were still alive. When Cubby discovered these hard feelings, he reached out to Ivar Bryce to make amends. He asked Ivar Bryce if there was anything he could do for him, and Ivar Bryce mentioned Dahl.

Since 1960, Dahl had lost one child to disease, another had been badly injured, and his wife (actress Patricia Neal) had nearly died of a cerebral hemorrhage in 1965. She had collapsed while they were in Los Angeles, and the medical bills left them in some serious financial straits. Dahl had written *James and the Giant Peach*, *Charlie and the Chocolate Factory*, and another small children's book, *The Magic Finger*, but these had not sold well enough to solve his financial problems. A film deal for a World War One story had fallen through. Ivar Bryce asked Cubby if he could find some work for Roald. Cubby immediately arranged to hire Dahl to replace Harold Jack Bloom, an American writer who had done an initial draft. It was the kind of generous act that Cubby often engaged in. He had approved hiring Lois Maxwell when he found out her husband had suffered a massive heart attack and she needed income to support her family. He approved hiring Pedro Armendáriz, who had been diagnosed with cancer, so that the actor could leave something to his family.

RAY MORTON

In writing this script, Roald Dahl seemed to have no interest in reality or believability—every sequence in his script is bigger and more over the top than the one before it, and that's fine. The goal of this screenplay is to be outrageously entertaining and at that it succeeds. There isn't much of a story, and what narrative there is serves mainly as a thread up on which to hang the film's action set pieces, but those set pieces are mostly inventive and fun, so we really don't mind.

JOHN CORK

Dahl didn't have any compunction about chucking out Fleming's work and making *Bond* his own. *You Only Live Twice* became the *Charlie and the Chocolate Factory* of *Bond* films, filled with trapdoors, TVs, and clever, nonsensical contraptions, and even accusations of industrial spying. It is Dahl's work that did more to shift the tone than anything else.

ROALD DAHL

I was given a formula to write a *Bond* film: Bond has three women throughout the film. If I remember rightly, the first gets killed, the second gets killed, and the third gets a fond embrace during the closing sequence. And that's the formula. They found it cast-iron. So, you have to kill two of them off after he has screwed them a few times. And there is great emphasis on funny gadgets and lovemaking. The main problem was the plot. I didn't know what the hell Bond was going to do.

Broccoli told me to start with Bond's "death" and burial at sea, staged to fool his enemies. My guess is that it was the idea of Mr. Bloom. They had probably—and hadn't told me—commissioned a screenplay from him, and it hadn't been any good, but they picked out that idea and possibly one or two others which they had asked me to put in.

ALBERT R. BROCCOLI

(producer, the *James Bond* films)

I'd like to say, it's an iffy state about writing a *Bond.* Whatever anyone thinks of the *Bond* scripts or the *Bond* pictures, there are people on the "committee" who come up with the ideas on writing. It's interesting. You can give a script to a terrific writer, but you can't let him go away and do a *Bond* script without us. These kind of writers, they prefer to work alone. They go away, and they come back and present you with a screenplay, but it would not be what we want. We have to be there all the time, talking to them, consulting on locations, the whole thing, and it's the way it has to be done.

ROALD DAHL

Harold Jack Bloom had a right to some kind of credit. I never worked with him. The first time I heard of Bloom wanting a share in the credits was after the film had been cut and I was told that there would be a share. I said, "Well, there's no way anyone's going to share the full credit." There was a fight about that, and then they gave him what you see.

RICHARD MAIBAUM

(screenwriter, *On Her Majesty's Secret Service*)

The idea of the scripts being written by committee is cockeyed. In the final analysis, the writer, or writers, have to sit down and are responsible for putting all the suggestions together. I don't like the idea of writing by committee, because there isn't a committee. There's input, as there should be on any sensibly set up production. You get as many opinions as possible.

LEWIS GILBERT

Very often the script totally changes. Sometimes Ken Adam comes up with a set, and you look at this set, and suddenly it sparks a whole new series of ideas, just because of the design of this set. So it's very difficult for a writer to imagine what's going to happen. Normally a writer has a book to work from; well, on a modern-day *Bond,* there just aren't the books.

What they ultimately concocted was a story that began with an American spacecraft hijacked by a mysterious capsule in space, which disappears in the Sea of Japan. With a second mission on the books, M dispatches

Bond to investigate as those silly Americans beat the drums of war, accusing the Russians of stealing their missing spaceship. With the help of Tiger Tanaka, the head of Japan's Secret Service, Bond, after engaging in a sham wedding and being physically altered to be turned Japanese (an extended and ultimately pointless sequence of events), begins a search to find who's responsible. That search leads him to discover SPECTRE's hidden base located *inside* an extinct volcano in Pinewood . . . um, Japan. It was a brilliant conceit, given the original plan had been to base SPECTRE in a Japanese castle by the sea, but that idea ran into logistical difficulties.

ALBERT R. BROCCOLI

We had a writer who came up with the idea of having these ninja-like Japanese characters crawling all over Tokyo, and it just wouldn't work. So we had to reject that, and we had to find an an alternate idea. So we flew all over Japan with a fleet of kamikaze pilots (that's true: there were a couple of kamikaze pilots flying us all over Japan) to find some clue to the plot.

LEWIS GILBERT

We all had helicopter pilots who we didn't know only spoke Japanese, which wasn't exactly easy. I'm sitting in the helicopter and the oldest Japanese man you've ever seen climbed in beside me. The first words he spoke when he got in was, "Me kamikaze," and we thought, "We've got the oldest one who's a kamikaze and still alive."

PETER HUNT

Every day we went out in a helicopter looking for a castle on the island, which is how Fleming's book ends, but there was no such thing in Japan. But one day we were flying over this area that had about 21 defunct volcanoes. I suddenly said, "Why don't we use these?" They just looked so spectacular from the air. Out of those conversations came, "Why can't Blofeld be headquartered underneath a volcano?"

KEN ADAM

(production designer, *You Only Live Twice*)

We were in trouble, because we found that Fleming hadn't really been to Japan. We had two helicopters for three weeks flying over Japan, and we couldn't find *any* of the locations that Fleming talked about. Luckily we went over Kyushu, the southern island, and found this area of actual volcanoes. It was incredible, and *that* triggered off the idea, "Wouldn't it be fun if the villain has his headquarters inside an extinct volcano crater?" I did a quick scribble and Cubby said to me, "How much is this going to cost?" I said, "Cubby, don't ask me how much is it going to cost. I have no idea." So he said, "If I give you a million dollars, can you do it?" I said, "Yeah," and then, of course, all my worries started, because even though a million dollars in 1966 was a fortune, my ideas were rather grandiose. I thought I was going crazy, actually, and a lot of my assistants thought that, but I had a very good team around me.

ALBERT R. BROCCOLI

We talked with Ken about building the set, and the committee talked about how it worked, with the sliding roof, and the lake, and the whole thing. And then Ken built this marvelous set, which was where the helicopter flew in, and everybody had the fight down below, and the rocket's going up, and all that sort of thing. It was our first conquest with rockets.

LEWIS GILBERT

Big sets certainly do present certain problems, and, indeed, because of my three *Bond* films, I've probably filmed on more big sets than any other director in the world. In *You Only Live Twice,* the volcano was the size of a football field. The big problem big sets create is one of time—not time in shooting, but time in film. If you have someone walk across the set and it takes 10 seconds, well, just multiply that by 500 times and you've got a film running for four or five hours. So the cutting has to be nipped along faster. Also, you're tempted with a big set to do more in it. You think to yourself, "My God, this has cost so much money, I *must* try to justify it." Ken's designs will sometimes bring a whole new dimension into the story. So there's no doubt large sets are difficult to film in, but they definitely contributed to *Bond* films.

KEN ADAM

We managed to build that lake up there to be the top of the volcano out of fiberglass 120 feet up, and those poor plasterers, who had safety belts, had to work day and night to get it ready. And as fate often happens, in my experience with the most difficult or bigger sets, less things go wrong than go on with the set of a room. You suddenly find there is a close-up of somebody in front of a badly painted door, but those big sets, which cost over a million dollars, everything worked. Even though I had several heart attacks. Not actually, but a helicopter flying into an enclosed space? Nobody had ever done that, and I didn't know what was going to happen. The producers had already committed ahead of time to 4,000 cinema showings, and we had *nothing,* so of course they couldn't argue about money at that time. Fortunately, we found this area that triggered the idea.

STEVEN E. DE SOUZA

(screenwriter, *Die Hard*)

The early pictures with Sean Connery, the first three especially, had a tremendous reality to them, as fantastic as they were. The villains were bad and Bond was refreshing, because he was the first hero who could be as immoral as the villains. Up until then, the villain would be unarmed and the hero would say, "Alright, I'm taking you to jail now." Then the villain would make his move for the hidden knife and *then* you could shoot him. Bond would have just shot them, because he knew they would make a move for the hidden knife. By the time you go to *Moonraker* and some of those later pictures, they got completely ridiculous. A lot of that started with the volcano in *You Only Live Twice.*

RAY MORTON

Roald Dahl was *Goldfinger*'s Paul Dehn on steroids—his screenplay for *You Only Live Twice* amped up the fantasy element of the *Bond* formula to the nth degree and dispensed almost completely with anything even remotely resembling realism. Of course, I'm sure that was what the producers were expecting when they hired a crafter of modern family tales to write a *James Bond* screenplay.

STEVEN E. DE SOUZA

All those guys in orange jumpsuits . . . I always wondered, where do they come from? There are all these guys living in the barracks of a volcano. Do their relatives know where they are? How did they get this job? I could say to you, "Listen, I've got a great job for you. There's a great health plan, it even includes dental, and there's two weeks' paid vacation. But you've got to leave your family and live in a volcano for 10 months." It just seems to be a real vague situation.

On the acting side of things, we were greeted by the returning presence of Bernard Lee as M, Lois Maxwell as Miss Moneypenny, and Desmond Llewelyn as Q. The producers' original choice for Tiger was the legendary Japanese actor Toshirô Mifune, but when he passed to do John Frankenheimer's *Grand Prix* instead, Broccoli and Saltzman gave the nod to Tetsurô Tanba, who was already helping them work with some of the

Japanese actresses who would eventually be cast and need a whirlwind English immersion course (not surprisingly, they would both inevitably be dubbed, as would Tanba himself). Akiko Wakabayashi is Japanese SIS agent Aki, who works with Bond and even pretends to become his wife as part of his cover, though she is poisoned in the night and dies; and Mie Hama is Kissy Suzuki, an Ama diving girl who takes Aki's place in helping Bond. On the SPECTRE side of things, Karin Dor and Teru Shimada play, respectively, Helga Brandt (who, after failing to kill Bond, is fed to piranha) and Mr. Osato.

UNKNOWN TOUR GUIDE
(Shark Reef Aquarium at Mandalay Bay Resort & Casino)

Piranha could not actually eat you alive. They probably would ignore you unless there was blood or open sores and then they would bite you and it would hurt, but they would not rip the flesh from your bones like in the movie.

Most importantly, this film finally revealed the character of Ernst Stavro Blofeld, though Harry Saltzman had made the misstep of casting actor Jan Werich in the role. Later, Lewis Gilbert described the actor as resembling "a poor, benevolent Santa Claus." Not exactly the image fans had conjured in their minds since *From Russia with Love*, having only heard a sinister voice as his cloaked figure ominously stroked a Persian cat. *Austin Powers* so savaged this conceit that it wasn't until the emergence of Thanos at the end of the first *Avengers* that any film series would attempt holding off on the reveal of a major villain over the course of so many movies. Eventually, though, Werich was out and Donald Pleasence (Dr. Michaels in *Fantastic Voyage* and Dr. Sam Loomis in the *Halloween* films, among many others) was brought in.

CHRISTOPHER GULL
(author, *The Films of Donald Pleasence*)

By 1967, Pleasence was already a well-known and respected actor, starring in big-budget films such as *The Great Escape, The Greatest Story Ever Told*, and *Fantastic Voyage*. The *James Bond* producers felt that Pleasence exuded the right amount of menace for Blofeld (especially important as this was the very first time the audience would see the *Bond* villain's face), and they contacted his agent, Joyce Jameson. Pleasence was very quickly brought into the film to replace Werich. This wound up having both positive and negative consequences.

TOM SOTER

Pleasence, five-foot-seven, bald with a soft, silky voice, seemed an unlikely *Bond* villain. He was heavily made up in *Twice,* spending hours in the dressing room. A large scar going down the left side of his face gave him the appearance of a cracked egg—which may or may not have been intentional. Although his characterization bore little resemblance to Fleming's, it is the definitive screen Blofeld.

ROALD DAHL

I had little to do with Blofeld's creation on-screen. I simply wrote, "Blofeld." It was, to my mind, the director's job, along with Cubby, to decide how the first sight of Blofeld in the film is presented.

CHRISTOPHER GULL

Pleasence felt uneasy playing the character, as he seemed to pick up that the producers were not crazy about his appearance in the role. His role involved a three-week shoot and from Day One he was calling his agent to give her updates. Pleasence told her, "They're shooting me in shadow," and "They're shooting over my shoulder." From these comments that he told his agent, it's evident he realized he would probably *not* be repeating his character.

TOM SOTER

Only his legs were shown for the first two-thirds of the story—partly because Pleasence did not join the cast until late in the picture. Most of his scenes were done last.

CHRISTOPHER GULL

In a 1995 interview, he said he devised Blofeld's facial scar and other little quirks, because the producers liked his performance, but didn't find him physically imposing, so the makeup and costuming helped quite a bit. As a matter of fact, some of the shots weren't him at all; they were just the uniform and what was supposed to be his legs and arms.

One person unimpressed with Bond's first face-to-face with Blofeld was the late journalist and critic John Brosnan, who comments in his book *James Bond in the Cinema*, "I thought the occasion should warrant something special in the way of dialogue, but there's not even a single, 'So we meet at last!' After all that Bond has done in the past to upset Blofeld's elaborate schemes, I would have expected a bigger reaction from Blofeld at having Bond in his power. I rather hoped that he might fling himself at

Bond in a terrible rage, yelling things like, 'This is for Dr. No . . . (kick) . . . and this is for Largo! . . . (kick) . . . and this is for that fleet of launches you blew up in the Gulf of Venice . . . (kick) . . . and those four helicopters you shot down only yesterday!' But no such luck."

CHRISTOPHER GULL

I happen to think that Pleasence sort of set the role for future portrayals of Blofeld and that none topped him. He had such a fantastic, menacing look in the film that it's little wonder why Mike Myers copied him for the Dr. Evil character in the *Austin Powers* series. Pleasence had a very long career, but there are only really two iconic characters that he is known for: Blofeld and Dr. Loomis. Had he never appeared as either character, he still would have been acting in film, television, stage, and radio. He was truly one of the best character actors who ever lived. But I'm sure he appreciated the chance to play such a great villain as Blofeld during his career.

Beyond casting, there is, of course, lots of action, not only with Bond's team launching an assault against SPECTRE's agents within the volcano base, but in terms of having Bond undertake martial arts lessons as a part of his training in Japan.

RIC MEYERS

(author, *For One Week Only: The World of Exploitation Films*)

You Only Live Twice didn't introduce martial arts to movies. *From Russia with Love* did that, not to mention 1945's *Blood on the Sun* and 1962's *The Manchurian Candidate*. But it did introduce ninja and Japanese samurai/chambara skills into English-speaking films almost 15 years before 1981's *Enter the Ninja*. The stunt team was filled with exceptional Westerners like Bob Simmons, George Leech, and Vic Armstrong, but Samoan wrestler Peter Fanene Maivia (the grandfather of Dwayne "The Rock" Johnson) is unofficially credited as fight choreographer, which I find unlikely. Much more likely is that he either choreographed, or helped Bob Simmons choreograph, the fight he had with Bond in Osato's office, which included the memorable moment when Bond uses an entire sofa as a battering ram. The person most likely responsible for the samurai/ninja fight choreography is Masaaki Hatsumi, currently a Japanese martial arts Grandmaster and ninja historian. Or even any number of "Tiger Tanaka" actor Tetsurô Tanba's associates, since he had appeared in about a hundred Japanese films before this, including such action classics as 1962's *Harakiri* and 1964's *Three Outlaw Samurai*.

BOB SIMMONS

(stunt arranger/stunt double, *You Only Live Twice*)

In *You Only Live Twice*, you had Bond coming into the volcano and walking across the ceiling with suckers. Well, that was a last-minute idea of mine, and the actual suckers I used were toilet plungers. We actually shot that on the floor and turned the camera around. The prop man went down half an hour before we shot that and bought these plungers. We put them on Sean's hands and then we shot up at the ceiling where a double was crawling across. Because we have a great director like Lewis Gilbert, you can do things off the cuff like that.

I've been in bed here at two, three o'clock in the morning and suddenly I'll get an idea. I'll ring Ken Adam or Johnny Stears or Derek Meddings, and nobody says, "What? It's three o'clock in the morning!" They say, "Yeah, great idea. Let's develop it. What time are you going to the studio?" You go in and you start working. This is the whole success secret of *Bond*. You have a *Bond* "team," which is most unusual. No one says, "My finishing time is 5:30 and I don't want to know about it until 7:30 or 8:00 tomorrow morning." Everyone says, "Let's go. Let's do it. Let's make a great picture." Each *Bond* we tried to make better and bigger.

And then there are the requisite gadgets, which are pretty much limited to a bullet-shooting cigarette (which plays a part in Bond's starting to disrupt Blofeld's plans) and *Little Nellie*, a one-man "gyrocopter" with some pretty heavy destructive power. It's part of one of the film's highlights, which, behind the scenes, was tragically marred by the severing of aerial photographer Johnny Jordan's foot while shooting it.

ROALD DAHL

The whole thing was gadgets. I came in one morning and said to them, "Wouldn't it be rather fun when Bond goes in the office of the bad guy, and the person at the typewriter is pressing the keys and moving the lamp from the ceiling, which is a camera, and keeping it on Bond the whole time?" They said, "Great! Have it in." They *loved* gadgets.

PETER HUNT

I had the idea for a helicopter chase. Harry Saltzman said, "Great! Bond can be chased by five helicopters"—which was typical of how Harry was. No idea was too fantastic. He said, "If he's Bond, he's got to be chased by more than one helicopter." I realized what a big job it was going to be. So we started to write it when Harry went back to London and picked up *Aero* magazine and saw the gyrocopter. He picked up the telephone and said, "I want this gyrocopter. Get it down to Pinewood. I want to look at it."

ROALD DAHL

After I finished the screenplay, Cubby had seen this extraordinary helicopter. It had nothing to do with the *Bond* films at all. This thing was amazing. Cubby had happened to see it and he said, "We've got to have this in the film. It's *so* good." He showed it to me and said, "Go back and put it in." That was actually good filmmaking; it was one more gadget. Of course I knew that you couldn't take that to bits and put it together again in a suitcase the way they did in the movie. That's a bit of artist's license, so I said the only way to do this and have fun with it is to have it in a box. But the fact remains that it's a marvelous little airplane.

KEN ADAM

When I saw this gyrocopter at Pinewood, I thought, "I'm going to make a war machine out of this." I don't know why, but I always had a knack for designing things like planes, cars, boats, and underwater craft. And at the time my wife was designing handbags in Italy and exporting them, and she said, "Wouldn't it be funny if you did the gyrocopter like a do-it-yourself kit, all very chic crocodile baggage with velour inside." Everyone was getting into the spirit of things.

LEWIS GILBERT

We had *Little Nellie* and the chap who invented it—Ken Wallis—for the film to go in the real volcano and fly around to see what it looked like. The only snag was that I was saying, "Okay, come out now," and he couldn't get out, because he was just below the surface and there was no lift. The helicopter he was in was only a toy, really, and it didn't get lift, so he was stuck going round. Oh, that was *really* bad; very nerve-wracking, because none of us could help him. We didn't know what to do. But he suddenly jumped . . . he must have suddenly hit a patch. It jumped and he quickly got over the side and was saved.

There's no denying the ultimate success of *You Only Live Twice*, but Bond-mania had definitely peaked with *Thunderball*, which had pulled in over $67 million at the domestic box office. *You Only Live Twice*, which was released on June 13, 1967, pulled in "just" $43 million. In 1960s dollars, that $24 million was a *huge* difference. Still, the film—no matter what its strengths or weaknesses—is significant in terms of its impact on the spy genre, its sheer scope, and the fact that, for a variety of reasons, it marked the last of the *Bond* extravaganzas until *The Spy Who Loved Me* a decade later. Of course, nobody knew that at the time.

RAY MORTON

This is the first *Bond* screenplay that makes no attempt at all to adapt the Ian Fleming source novel—it basically takes the title and the setting and a few of the character names and uses them in an entirely new story. The new tale has little to do with Fleming, but everything to do with the *James Bond* movie phenomenon that was then at its height and the elements of that phenomenon that audiences were most enthralled with. As has been noted many times, the character of Bond does tend to get a bit lost amid all of the action and set pieces.

GLEN OLIVER

There was a classiness to *You Only Live Twice* which I think subsequent films in the franchise would sometimes reach for. Some achieved it, some fell short, but a broader awareness of what *Bond* "could" be was definitely at work here. Director Lewis Gilbert shifted from the somewhat "workmanlike" qualities we'd seen in previous films toward a more elegant approach. The whole *Bond* "vibe" felt smoother—more well considered—like it was taking itself seriously, was guardedly over the top and being careful not to overplay its fantastical trappings. There was a scale here which hadn't been fully touched on previously—and it was deftly balanced.

More notably, *You Only Live Twice* marked the arrival of the bigger "our whole world is in jeopardy!" *Bond* films—which seem to be the ones that are most remembered, although there were, actually, comparatively few of them throughout the franchise. This same "oversized" approach would be revisited most overtly in *The Spy Who Loved Me* and *Moonraker*. Which were, not coincidentally, also directed by Gilbert. He was, it would seem, their kitschy-cool-shit, end-of-the-world specialist.

RAY MORTON

When people spoof the *Bond* films, this is the one they reference the most: the bald, scarred villain with the Nehru jacket and the white cat; the elaborate secret hideout constructed inside a dormant volcano; the army of jumpsuit-wearing soldiers ready to do the villain's bidding; disposing of ineffective subordinates by dumping them in a pool full of piranha; and so on. For Fleming purists, Dahl's screenplay is arguably the least *Bond*ian of the *Bond* scripts, but in the popular imagination, Dahl's version of 007 is perhaps the most *Bond* of them all.

LEWIS GILBERT

Everything was new on a *Bond* picture, because they had unlimited money. That was the big thing with them; they had literally unlimited money, because the other *Bond*s had made so much. Cubby and company were pretty rich.

ROALD DAHL

I think the *Bond* movies were at their peak then, because they had practiced with four of them already and everyone knew exactly what to do. It was a very well-oiled machine by then. You also had the feeling that they had the money in the bank and they were going to make a fortune, so no money was spared in its making. You went everywhere by helicopter. If the location was 10 miles away, and rather hard to go to—like a Japanese fishing village—you would go there by helicopter and find that they had already dug a helicopter landing pad out of a cliff. It was well organized; they were in on a gold mine and knew it. They quite rightly never skimped on the money. Never.

An exception, one could argue, was the financial arrangement that Broccoli and Saltzman had with Sean Connery, and the fact that he wanted a bigger piece of the *Bond* pie and they weren't willing to serve it up. This, combined with the actor's frustration with the extended shooting schedules of the films that prevented him from getting much in the way of outside roles, and massive media intrusions in his life, had pushed him to the breaking point. He wanted out and, as far as he was concerned, *You Only Live Twice* would mark his final turn as 007.

STANLEY SOPEL

(associate producer, *You Only Live Twice*)

I remember the press conference for *You Only Live Twice* in Japan very well. We had this conference in the ballroom of the hotel in Tokyo. An enormous great room; there must have been five or six hundred Japanese pressmen and photographers. I never saw so many Nikon cameras in my life. Sean was on the stage with our publicity chairperson and Japanese interpreter. They asked what I thought were very personal, almost rude questions, but then press people do, let's face it. Sean is short-tempered and said what he thought, which possibly he shouldn't have said (he could have been diplomatic, but he wasn't). The more diplomatic of the press corps suddenly realized perhaps they shouldn't be asking these kind of questions, they should confine the questions to the movie side of the business, and then it all calmed down. In point of fact, he got good press. But when we were actually shooting, they used to descend on us in absolute *hordes*. There could be two or three hundred chaps with their cameras, which would absolutely interfere with the shooting. There was no way to control them.

ROBERT SELLERS
(author, *The Battle for Bond*)

It's well documented that Sean came to hate not so much the character of Bond itself, but the effect his playing it had on the public. There's the story of him arriving at an airport and being asked for his autograph by an elderly lady, only for her to turn around exclaiming that she wanted him to write "James Bond" and not his own name. An intensely private man, people started scaling the walls of his London home, and he really couldn't go anywhere without being hassled. He was, let's not forget, one of the most instantly recognizable people on earth in the Sixties.

STANLEY SOPEL

I had to virtually every day make a deal with the press that they would *not* interfere with shooting, with the understanding that they could get at least one half hour of Sean's time where they could take pictures of him. It got so ridiculous that even when he went to the lavatory, they'd be poking the cameras through the window. And if ever there was an invasion of privacy, it was *that*.

JOHN CORK

When Connery signed with Cubby and Harry, he was under contract to them. They loaned him out to Hitchcock for *Marnie*, for example. He had renegotiated his contract during the shooting of *Goldfinger*, and was committed for two more *Bond* films after *Thunderball*, but he didn't want that. He was angry that Dean Martin was making more doing the *Matt Helm* films than Connery himself was making doing *Bond*. The negotiations before the location shooting in *You Only Live Twice* included a very big set of demands.

First, Connery had very much wanted Terence Young back to direct *Twice*. Young had been basically fired by Cubby and Harry after cost overruns on

From Russia with Love, and then, when confronted with a bill for what Cubby and Harry felt was excessive spending in the Bahamas on *Thunderball*, Young walked off the film in post-production. Cubby and Harry didn't want Young back, so they had hired Lewis Gilbert. Connery complained to his agent. He wasn't paid enough money. He didn't have approval over the director. He didn't share in the profits under the same formula as Cubby and Harry. He felt the films were shot inefficiently in ways that wasted his time. So his reps laid down the gauntlet: Sean would sign on for more *Bond*s, but as a full partner with Cubby and Harry. He would have approval over director, script, schedule, other casting, and he would share equally with Cubby and Harry in the riches of *Bond*.

ROALD DAHL

I don't think Sean behaved very well on this film. He was a very foolish fellow to get bored by *Bond*, because it made him. It made his life and it made his fame. If it had been me, I wouldn't have gotten bigheaded and gone off and said, "I'm going to do my own thing now. You can all go to hell." I would have stuck with them and seen it through. Not let them hire some other actor.

JOHN CORK

Cubby and Harry would *not* make that new financial deal with Connery. They had just made a frustrating deal with Kevin McClory to make *Thunderball*. There was a competing *Bond* film in the works (the 1967 version of *Casino Royale*), and both Cubby and Harry found their own partnership personally unsatisfying. So Connery announced he was out as Bond after *Twice*.

DAVID V. PICKER

(president and chief executive officer, United Artists)

We had approval of the basic deal with any stars and, in the case of Connery, we knew there was a clause covering his additional options, but we truly did not get involved with the negotiation of the details. We had approved Connery, and the producers had options they could exercise for subsequent films; that's all we cared about. Broccoli was experienced, reliable, and knew his business. During the course of actual filming, we had no presence other than an auditor checking the financial cash flow. We had nobody on the set watching any of the day-to-day trials and tribulations that occur on any film. We simply awaited delivery. It may sound like an odd way to do business, but it was exactly the philosophy that attracted filmmakers to us, and it worked—most of the time.

In the case of the *Bond* pictures, there was little, if any, awareness that there was trouble brewing between Sean and the producers. They never advised us of any problem, and Richard Hatton, Sean's agent, never called to tell me of any difficulty. Harry and Cubby's representatives during the deal renegotiation never indicated that there was a Connery problem. So when Harry and Cubby told us Connery had said that the last of the options was the last *Bond* he would do, we strongly suggested that they get him to agree to additional pictures. *You Only Live Twice* was the last one. Obviously this was a problem, and a big one. United Artists relied on our producers to deal with problems on their films. In this case, Harry and Cubby simply said that Connery wanted out and wouldn't do another *Bond*. They didn't ask for our help and, clearly, losing Connery was hardly to their benefit; we accepted that they had made their best efforts to keep him and had failed. That's the way we worked.

JOHN CORK

Could all of that have been avoided if Cubby and Harry had been more generous with Connery from the start? We'll never know. Connery's frustrations were not limited to money, but certainly money was a big part of it.

James Bond would return, but Sean Connery wouldn't. Not right away, at least.

"THIS NEVER HAPPENED TO THE OTHER FELLA"

"You can't shoot me! I have a very low threshold of death. My doctor says I can't have bullets enter my body at any time."

CASINO ROYALE (1967)

The story of the making of the 1967 *Casino Royale* deserves its own movie and is far more interesting than what eventually appeared on-screen that year. A chaotic, insane, nearly incomprehensible mess with a myriad of stars, including numerous veterans from the official Eon film series, the movie was über-producer Charles K. Feldman's follow-up to his blockbuster farce, *What's New Pussycat?*, which starred Peter O'Toole, Peter Sellers, and Woody Allen in one of his earliest film roles after emerging on the New York stand-up scene as a brilliant comedian and gag writer.

After abandoning plans to produce a serious adaptation of *Casino Royale* written by Ben Hecht, in which the character of James Bond is not even featured (instead it follows a poker-playing American gangster named Lucky Fortunato), Feldman pursued a lighter tone for the film in the vein of *Pussycat*. His intention was to satirize the entire *Bond* franchise and the spymania which had enthralled Sixties film and TV audiences with such productions as *The Man from U.N.C.L.E.; I Spy*; the *Derek Flint* films; the *Matt Helm* films, produced by Broccoli's ex-partner, Irving Allen; and the *Harry Palmer* movies, produced by Harry Saltzman, among others.

At the time, Woody Allen, who had starred in and polished the *Pussycat* script, contributing many of its biggest laughs, in correspondence to his manager's publicist noted, "We demanded a letter saying my name cannot appear on-screen as writer. This because everyone who contributed a comma is demanding his name on the film and the writers list looks like Terry Southern, Ben Hecht, Michael Sayers, Frank Buxton, Mickey Rose, Peter Sellers, Val Guest, Wolf Mankowitz, etc." In addition, *Catch-22*'s Joseph Heller, *The African Queen*'s John Huston, and *The Apartment*'s Billy Wilder, who was going to make the film with Shirley MacLaine, also labored on the script, along with former MGM majordomo Dore Schary.

Eventually, the film would also have multiple directors, including Huston (filming David Niven's early scenes, in which Huston also appears on-screen as M), Joseph McGrath (who shot Peter Sellers' scenes along with those of Ursula Andress and Orson Welles), Robert Parrish, Val Guest (the coda with Woody Allen and additional photography), Ken Hughes (the Berlin sequences), and an uncredited Richard Talmadge, the codirector of the film's elaborate final sequence in which the cavalry arrives, literally, along with a succession of star cameos and carnage, including Jean-Paul Belmondo, George Raft, and David Prowse as Frankenstein's Monster (originally intended to be a giant Winnie the Pooh).

ALBERT R. BROCCOLI

(producer, the *James Bond* films)

When the first deal was made with the Fleming estate to make *Bond* films, *Casino Royale* was already sold. Fleming had sold it to a very famous old director-producer, Gregory Ratoff, who couldn't interest anyone in doing a *James Bond* movie. He went all over the place, to all the studios. It was part of his estate when he died, and it was acquired by a very dear friend of mine, Charlie Feldman, who made a botch of it.

Despite attempts by Feldman to interest Broccoli and Saltzman in producing an officially sanctioned Eon adaptation early on, negotiations were unsuccessful and Feldman went ahead and developed the property on his own after efforts to entice Sean Connery and John Barry also failed. In a version that was dramatically different than the final release, Feldman hired Ben Hecht to write a serious adaptation of the book for him. Apropos of the already cursed project, Hecht finished his final draft of the script in 1964, two days before he suffered a fatal heart attack. Subsequently, legendary director-writer Billy Wilder did a page one rewrite on Hecht's screenplay.

JEREMY DUNS
(author, *Duns On Bond*)

The final draft is April 1964; that's the most complete draft that he did, which is just phenomenal. He worked at least four months on adapting Ian Fleming's first novel, which doesn't sound like very much, but that's a hell of a lot for Ben Hecht. He worked really, really fast. Four months was a long time for him. He did scripts in two weeks. Eventually, what he wrote was pretty much the book, but when he started out it veered a lot away from *Casino Royale* with other ideas about some scientist's daughter's been kidnapped and all sorts of other things. There's all kinds of avenues and ideas in there. I mean, there's enough for several films. He didn't just read the book and do a straight adaptation.

He really thought about it, because one of the problems with the book is it's just too short; you just have to have more stuff happening, so he figured out like a whole kind of thing where the standoff between Bond and Le Chiffre isn't when they meet. He creates a whole backstory in the first act whereby there's a reason why Bond needs to get back at Le Chiffre and vice versa, so he creates this revenge angle.

He thought through the structure of it and came up with several ideas, discarded some and then went with some. I would say it's a pretty astonishingly well-thought-through idea, because prior to 2006 a lot of people said *Casino Royale* was unfilmable. It's essentially a novella, it doesn't kind of globe-trot very much, and a lot of it's a card game. How on earth are you going to film the torture scene? You know, it ends with this line: "The bitch is dead." The conventional wisdom was you can't do it, but he did it in 1964.

To a degree, Hecht had already anticipated the direction that they were going to take with later films, because *Dr. No*, *From Russia with Love*, and I think *Goldfinger* was just around the time when he was writing this, but what he does is expand the settings. He has more globetrotting and he adds more set scenes, more action scenes, he has a Jet Ski chase where two people try to assassinate Bond. The films it's most like are *From Russia with Love* and *On Her Majesty's Secret Service*. It's got much more of the Fleming DNA, particularly in the character, and you just feel that this is someone who really understood the *novel Casino Royale,* and then they really understood how to make a Sean Connery *Bond* film and combine those two things.

Ultimately all that remained of Hecht's *Casino Royale* was one concept, which became a centerpiece of the comedic *Casino Royale*: the idea that the name "James Bond" was given to a variety of agents as a code name, a notion often misattributed to writer Wolf Mankowitz. In the case of Hecht's script, this happens after the death of the original James Bond, which, as his M puts it, "not only perpetuates his memory, but confuses the opposition." It is also a fanciful concept some fans of the official Eon series have adapted as a theory to explain the evolving nature of *James Bond* actors throughout the series—they believe each are different characters assigned the code name "James Bond 007" by MI6. It was a theory that was briefly embraced in the development of *Skyfall*, in fact, when consideration had been given to casting previous *James Bond* actors for the film's finale in which Daniel Craig battles Silva, capping off the franchise's 50th anniversary. It was not to be, and ultimately Albert Finney was cast as Kincade in lieu of Sean Connery.

JEREMY DUNS

Ben Hecht's *Casino Royale* was more Hitchcockian, very *Notorious*. It feels like that kind of film. Would Eon have let him make a film like this? I don't know. There weren't any threats from Eon about the spoof version of *Casino Royale*. To me, it's almost surreal that these scripts exist. Even now, it feels quite strange that they had this stuff and chose to make the film they did, because it's a real mess.

WOLF MANKOWITZ

(cowriter, *Casino Royale*)

Everyone got too greedy, and Charlie became bitter. He became spiteful against Broccoli and Saltzman.

TOM MANKIEWICZ

(screenwriter, *Live and Let Die*)

There's the terrible problem if you're producing the picture at that time. If you make it straight, then you're going into competition with Sean Connery as Bond. And the world had only known one Bond until then and loved him. You take a big chance. People get so used to one person playing the character, and he's so personally identified with it, that it becomes a flesh-and-blood person to the audience. Then you spring a new guy on them and he says, "My name is Bond, James Bond" and the audience says, "No, you're not. I remember James Bond."

ROBERT SELLERS
(author, *The Battle for Bond*)

Many years ago I interviewed the director Clive Donner. He told me that after the release of his critically acclaimed film *The Caretaker,* he was something of a "hot" property. Charlie Feldman was in London at the time and invited Donner over to his suite at the Claridge Hotel. Feldman said he had three projects on the go and Donner could choose whichever one he wanted to direct. One was *The Group,* which Sidney Lumet ended up making; another was a wacky comedy; and the third was *Casino Royale.* The script Clive was given was by Ben Hecht and was a serious attempt to adapt the novel. Clive had read the Fleming original and, although he liked it, he did feel that its main problem was that almost half the book is the buildup to the big game in the casino, and after that it was a bit of an anticlimax. "You haven't got a show there, Charlie," Donner said.

So, turning down *Casino Royale,* Donner asked about the wacky comedy. "It's by this kid," said Feldman. "Never done a movie before." Donner read it, loved it, and ended up making it. The young kid was Woody Allen, the movie was *What's New Pussycat?* Interestingly, the success of *What's New Pussycat?* must have influenced Feldman to turn *Casino Royale* into a way-out comedy, a sort of *What's New Pussycat?* meets *James Bond.* Indeed, he used three of the same cast in both films—Sellers, Andress, and Allen. Peter O'Toole also makes a cameo in the *Bond* spoof.

WOLF MANKOWITZ

The initial concept to satirize what was already a satire was perhaps a little ill-founded. But Charlie was fighting to the death—literally—over the ownership of the Bond character, and this seemed to him to be a way of railroading the Saltzman-Broccoli wagon off the track.

TOM MANKIEWICZ

Charlie Feldman was a tremendous wheeler-dealer himself, and certainly someone on a par with Cubby and Harry. He had founded his own agency, Famous Artists. He had produced many pictures. He was part of show business royalty. So it wasn't like when Cubby and Harry could go to Kevin McClory and say, "Look, let us help you out, while you help us out."' Kevin had never produced a picture before. He needed them and their expertise, and they needed that story. Charlie Feldman, I know, was personally convinced that he would have a gold mine in *Casino Royale.*

ROBERT DASSANOWSKY

(professor, Film & German Studies, University of Colorado Springs)

Charles K. Feldman's original idea was that each director would bring their own style to the film. It was to have been like the omnibus or anthology films that were popular in Italian and French film during the 1960s, where three or four directors would be responsible for short films united by an overarching theme but different plots, styles, casts—like *Boccaccio '70* (1962), *Six in Paris* (1965), or *Spirits of the Dead* (1968), which includes Fellini's psychedelic short masterwork, *Toby Dammit.*

KEN HUGHES

(director, *Casino Royale*)

Casino Royale was one of the best *Bond* novels. I saw it as a serious movie. But Feldman couldn't get Connery in as Bond, and he felt if he couldn't make a serious film without Connery, he wanted to make a spoof. I walked away at that point and said, "I don't want to know."

WOLF MANKOWITZ

We wrote a very funny story which at that point was supposed to cost $2.5 million.

RAY MORTON

(senior editor, *Script* magazine)

As a writer, Mankowitz seems to have been better suited to writing a satire of *Bond* rather than a straight adaptation, because a satire allowed him to make fun of material he found it difficult to take seriously.

ROBERT DASSANOWSKY

Unable to get Sean Connery—and John Barry—or crack a deal with Saltzman and Broccoli, the script went through Hecht's Noir phase, and then Billy Wilder's social satire touch, but absurd tragicomedies and mod comedies blended with a return of the screwball. And influenced by Fellini, it took on the surreal/psychedelic aesthetic that was the focus of the time.

Columbia eventually approved a then-pricey production budget of $6 million. However, production delays and schedule overages of many months led to the budget ballooning to over $12 million, which exceeded even the $11 million spent on the massive *Thunderball* or the more recent

You Only Live Twice. The latter came out only months prior to *Casino Royale* and cost $9.5 million.

TOM MANKIEWICZ

The central problem with *Casino Royale* is that it tried to spoof a spoof. If *Bond* is written properly, you make the audience your partner, which is what the Broccoli-Saltzman *Bond*s did. You present everything as if it really could happen and was happening, but at the same time, you let the audience in on the joke and you're both in on it together. *Casino Royale* was not an affectionate takeoff on the *Bond*s. It tried to be its own movie, almost without acknowledging everything it owed to the *Bond*s.

WOODY ALLEN

(actor, "Doctor Noah/Jimmy Bond")

You could never trust Charlie Feldman, and he was a charmer. My feeling was that he wanted me on *Casino Royale* because he wanted to have me around as a writer. If things went wrong, he always loved that I could write fast and write funny jokes. But he never used me as a writer or anything. I was in my hotel room all day working on my play *Don't Drink the Water*. I socialized in the evenings, played poker, and enjoyed London. I went to the discos; ate at Wheeler's, a good steak restaurant; Trader Vic's; and had a very nice time. The weather was always beautiful, cool and gray. I'd walk the King's Road on Saturday mornings and see all these beautiful girls in miniskirts. It was what they called at the time, Swinging London.

WOLF MANKOWITZ

The film ended up costing God knows how many millions; it was a runaway production and came damned near to destroying the company involved with it. Without a doubt, it killed Feldman. Eighteen names finished up on the script, so nobody was going to blame me for writing the original screenplay.

ROBERT DASSANOWSKY

The writers were no doubt influenced by Billy Wilder's original Cold War screwball satire *One, Two, Three* (1962), Kubrick's *Lolita* (1962) and *Dr. Strangelove* (1964), Tony Richardson's *The Loved One* (1965), George Axelrod's *Lord Love a Duck* (1966), Clive Donner's *What's New Pussycat?* (1965), and Joseph Losey's *Modesty Blaise* (1966).

RAY MORTON

As a movie, the 1967 *Casino Royale* is a fascinating mess—the sprawling, gigantic production; the star-studded cast; and the sheer amount of excess and wastefulness in every aspect of the piece are fascinating to watch even if what you're watching doesn't make much sense. But as a screenplay, it's just a mess. There's no story—instead it's just a collection of scenes and sketches loosely connected by narrative material that doesn't make much sense. It's allegedly a comedy, but it's never very funny. And it's not a very good spoof of *Bond*—either the novels or the movies. The script just uses *Bond* as a jumping-off point for a lot of nonsense that doesn't have much to do with the character or phenomenon it's allegedly spoofing, so ultimately the whole thing is really just pointless.

MARTIN CAMPBELL

(director, *Casino Royale* [*2006*])

Five different James Bonds and five different directors. It's almost unwatchable. I couldn't get through it. It's *so* bad.

WOODY ALLEN

I was not working on the script. I didn't even know what the script was. I was working with Val [Guest] just on that small piece that I was in. I was trying to, you know, give myself a joke or two to say here and there, but nobody knew anything about what was going on. I mean, it was just a chaotic situation. They were changing things around. I had no idea. I didn't meet three-quarters of the actors in that movie.

ED SIKOV

(author, *Mr. Strangelove: A Biography of Peter Sellers*)

It wasn't planned that way. The *story* was supposed to be chaotic—five men *and women* played James Bond, after all! But the production wasn't. The directors didn't have unique styles, particularly—at least on *this* film. Joe McGrath had never directed a feature film before; Robert Parrish was brought in as much for his editing skills as for his directing abilities because by that point they had tons of disparate footage and no idea how to put any of it together; John Huston showed up, too. So did Val Guest and Kenneth Hughes.

WOODY ALLEN

There were always rumors circulating that [John] Huston had dropped a lot at the gambling tables and Charlie [Feldman] picked up the tab on it, and so

Huston agreed to do the thing in the movie. But I don't know if any of that's true or not. All that scuttlebutt always circulated. I do remember that Charlie was thrilled that he was able to make a deal with John Huston to do some stuff.

ROBERT DASSANOWSKY

What made *Casino Royale* different from the anthology models, aside from the single narrative, was that the other directors were less notable than John Huston, who provided an ironic, melodramatic cornerstone for the film with the introduction of Sir James [David Niven], his history, the crisis of the four post-war representatives, and the platonic love story with Agent Mimi/Lady Fiona [Deborah Kerr] that emerges from the parody of the 007-style eroticism in the Scottish castle segment. Huston's segments tended to play with archetypes from romantic literature, while the other directors created more direct meta-filmic frames for their portions of the script. Val Guest, who did spy films before and after *Casino Royale,* understood the possibilities of the genre and was less grandiloquent than Huston in using Niven as the through line of the film after the departure of Sellers, although the striking eccentricity of the Indian temple sequence for Mata Bond seems to be a response to Huston's Scottish castle sequence. More like Billy Wilder—whose unused script contributed aspects to the finished project, most notably the naming of all agents as "James Bond 007" and the "nobody's perfect" phrase used throughout the film—are the witty and beautifully shot Sellers-Andress seduction sequences by Joseph McGrath, whose ease with the non sequitur came from working with Richard Lester on the Beatles' films and promotional music clips.

McGrath was Sellers' personal choice and allowed him the greatest possible leeway with his role and the dialogue, which also explains Sellers' segue from tragicomic hero into a sampling of self-scripted characterizations. *Casino Royale* literally launched McGrath's style for psychedelic satires to follow, such as Terry Southern's *The Magic Christian*. Southern was also a writer on *Casino Royale* for Kenneth Hughes' segment, the expressionistic *Dr. Caligari* setting for Le Chiffre's military blackmail "art" auction in Berlin, which quickly dissolves into a *Dr. Strangelove*–inspired World War Three scramble, with a melee akin to the concluding pie fight that Kubrick cut from his film, which is done here with fire extinguisher foam. It completes with a quick snippet of the theme song to *What's New Pussycat?*, the film's nominal stylistic precursor, and with *the* Cold War fantasy moment of the 1960s, the detonation of the Berlin Wall. Actor, editor, and director Robert Parrish came out of the Hollywood studio tradition and film noir, and it clearly shows in his presentation of sequences that actually originated in the novel—the Sellers-Welles scenes in the casino and the torture room, in which he reinvents Fleming's physical torment into a high-tech LSD-tinged nightmare that reconnects with Huston's Scottish scenes and allows for Sellers' exit from the film. Richard Talmadge, a German-born stuntman and director, revisioned *Bond* film finales into an absurdist cowboys and Indians saloon brawl, which effectively indicates the filmic origin of that element in the series, and also made it a showcase for stunt actors.

KEN HUGHES

The money was very good. Months after I had walked away, Feldman said, "Would you do a piece of it?" I didn't have the script, but I said, "Okay." Three film studios were going at once for the making of the movie: the MGM, Pinewood, and Shepperton Studios. None of us knew what the other guy was doing. When you've got six directors, you've got continuity problems. I'd have to call up and find out what an actress was wearing in the sequence before mine. You'd often find, however, that people would walk through the door and have different clothes—and different characters as well.

BARBARA BOUCHET

(actress, "Miss Moneypenny")

The sets were really way out and some of them were built, but just never were used.

JEFF KLEEMAN

(president of production, MGM/UA)

I got to say, there are things that make me laugh in *Casino Royale*. I don't know how they got Peter Sellers to do the film.

ED SIKOV

Seven hundred and fifty thousand dollars in 1965 dollars, a ten-thousand-dollar expense account, and a white Bentley.

KEN HUGHES

Peter Sellers was to have played a kind of inept James Bond, sort of like the Inspector Clouseau character from *The Pink Panther* films.

ROBERT DASSANOWSKY

Sellers wanted his characterization in *Casino Royale* to be in the style of the elegant and witty comedy of Cary Grant, perhaps knowing that Hitchcock's

North by Northwest was the influence for the style and structure of the early 1960s' *Bond* films. He was less than confident about this decision, but his Evelyn Tremble characterization does emerge as the most tragicomic in the film. Sellers' Tremble/Bond is a man whose own insecurities as a common gambler with intellectual pretentions force him to resort to impulsive silliness to tolerate the agency of the woman that converts him to Bond. The insecurity of the actor and the character blend.

ED SIKOV

Knowing members of the royal family was extremely important to Peter. It was the ultimate statement that he had *arrived*. So one day HRH Princess Margaret came to the set. Peter had invited her. But when she showed up, she swept right past him, went over to Orson [who she had known since he performed *Othello* on the stage in England], and said something on the order of, "Orson! I haven't seen you for days!" Sellers was humiliated. Orson was jubilant.

ROBERT DASSANOWSKY

Having admired Welles as a filmmaker, Sellers had apparently discovered that Welles found him uninteresting and had received a coterie of important visitors to the set, including Sellers' friend Princess Margaret. Sellers was intimidated and simply refused to face Welles in the casino duel. It mirrored the psychology behind the relationship of their characters and gives the sequence, even with a split screen in which they filmed their confrontation with standins, a curious, almost improvisational frisson.

ED SIKOV

It manifested itself to the point that whoever happened to be directing Sellers and Welles at the moment had to shoot them in separate shots. Sellers was deeply neurotic, and finding himself forced to act with the director and star of *Citizen Kane* was more than he could handle. Sellers would drive around outside the studio and call in to see where Welles was; Welles would drink champagne all day and not leave the set. So nothing got filmed. They shut down the production, and Welles flew off to Spain. Robert Parrish's wife told me that Parrish was nervous at the prospect of informing Welles that Sellers was refusing to film any scenes with him. So Parrish flew to Spain. Orson listened, got up from the table, kissed Parrish square on the lips, and said it was the best news he had ever heard.

WOODY ALLEN

I met Orson Welles at one lunch in the Plaza Athénée with about six or seven people and, of course, he was holding court. I never saw him on the screen and never met him in the studio. I didn't have any time to speak to him privately or have any moments with him. That was my only contact with him.

BARBARA BOUCHET

I was under contract to Otto Preminger and I was not allowed to leave Los Angeles and he wasn't using me. I told him, "Please free me because I want to work and you don't need the money but I do. And I want to go ahead with my career." And he freed me without any problems because we spoke in German. We had kind of a bond. So, with me he was never bad. He held me up to others and said, "Why can't you be like Barbara Bouchet?"

So I went to the South of France with another producer I had met who took me there. I can't for the life of me remember his name. He was the ugliest creature in the world. And we flew to Paris and he put me up in a hotel. And then he took me to the Eiffel Tower. The only time I've ever been there. And he says, "Okay, now, tomorrow, you can go shopping." "Shopping for what?" "Well, for some clothes and a fur coat or whatever." I said, "Isn't a wardrobe lady supposed to do all of that?" And he says, "No, no. This is for you." "Ah," I said. "So what do you want from me?" "Well, when we get to the Cannes Film Festival, I reserved a suite for us." I said, "Well, you cancel the suite and I will not buy even a needle. Nothing! Okay?" So, we went to Cannes. I got there. The suite was still there and they ushered me into it. And I went in the bedroom, took a cushion, took it out into the living room, put it on the couch, and shut the door. I said, "Since you did not cancel, you sleep on the couch. Okay?"

So, when I went downstairs one day, a man came up to me and he said, "Are you Barbara Bouchet?" And I said, "Yes." "My name is Carlo Ponti." Now, I knew about him, because Sophia Loren was the president of the festival we were attending at the time. And so, he says, "I would like to talk to you about a project." I said, "Okay." "So, can you please come to the Carlton Hotel later . . . Sophia's going to be there." And so I went. Well, Sophia was nowhere to be found. But he just said, "What does your body look like?" I said, "Fine, thank you." And I guess, he figured I was going to go lift my shirt or whatever and show it to him. I did not. He said, "Well, it will be the director who makes that decision." I said, "I guess so." And so, I was being sent off to London to meet [director] Michelangelo Antonioni. At the airport, another gentleman comes up to me and says, "Are you Barbara Bouchet?" I said, "God, I'm famous in this country." And he said, "My name is Charlie Feldman." "Ah," I said. Uh-oh, here we go. "Okay, what are you doing?" "I'm going to London to meet this Italian director." "Well, I'm going to London too." So, while we're on the plane, he hands me some pages to read. And he says, "This is the film that I'm about to make. If it doesn't work out with the Italian, I'd like to offer you the part of Miss Moneypenny in *Casino Royale*." I said, "Okay. Fine."

I went to London. To the Carlisle Hotel to meet Antonioni. He has a tic. He always shakes his head, kind of thing. And, I'll never forget, it was a rainy day and we sat in a bay window. Him in front of me and him ticcing away. And I said, "So, what is the part about? And what is the film?" And he looked at me and says, "I am very tired right now." I said, "Okay. It was nice meeting you. Goodbye." Ran downstairs in the hotel, called Charlie Feldman, and said, "Okay, I'm in!"

He said, "Great. Have your agent call me." I called my agent at the time, Paul Kohner in L.A. I tell him, you know, make the deal. He says to me, "Yes, sure. You and another thousand girls that he's testing." I said, "I didn't test. I got the part." "Oh, no, no. Don't worry about it. You didn't get nothing, because he's testing every beautiful girl in town and out of town and around the world." I'm like repeating, "I didn't test. I met him. He offered and I accepted. Now make the contract." He wouldn't! So, I called the agency in New York and I said, "Okay, *you* make the deal!" Well, the deal was another seven-year contract that I'd just gotten out of. Another seven-year contract with United Artists to play Miss Moneypenny. And off I went to London to start work. And the filming lasted a year and a half.

In the film, following the decimation of the intelligence operatives of the four postwar Allies who come to David Niven's Sir James for his help, he must be bombed out of his lordly retirement to face the threat. He becomes the new M and intends to crush SMERSH's Control (which is in the novel and explained in *The Living Daylights* as a "death to spies" order under Stalin). To confuse SMERSH, everyone in MI6, male or female, becomes James Bond 007. Le Chiffre (Orson Welles) is one of the main targets, and Evelyn Tremble (Peter Sellers) is brought in by Vesper Lynd to destroy him on the gaming tables, as Mata Bond (Joanna Pettet) ruins his operation in East Berlin. The force behind it all is revealed to be the *nefarious* Dr. Noah, aka Jimmy Bond (Woody Allen), whose dream of outshining his august uncle with world domination and sexual prowess backfires.

BARBARA BOUCHET

David Niven would joke all the time. He would make me laugh. He was actually the one who sort of saved me from working there for a year and a half, because it was fun to be with him.

WOODY ALLEN

I always loved David Niven. He was very strict. He expected that you were on the set punctually, that you knew your lines. He was very nice, very charming and amusing. Every Friday he would go directly from the set to the airport from London to the South of France where he had a house. He told me within an hour and 15 minutes' time from London he could be in his swimming pool.

BARBARA BOUCHET

After a year and a half in rainy and cold London, I just couldn't take it anymore. One ray of sunshine came out and I took my bikini and went into Hyde Park and just basked in the sun. I got arrested. So I told David [Niven], I really miss the sun and, bless his heart, he was really the funniest, gentlest, greatest human being. He said, "There's no problem. I have the right to go any weekend to Cap Serrat to see my family. You get on the same plane. Have your weekend in the South of France and take the same plane back with me. So if the plane crashes, well, you know, they don't have me, they don't have you. So what?" So, I did. But I was a stupid little girl and just lay out in the sun. When I got back, they really hit the ceiling because I was suntanned and it did not match any of the previous shots. So they got mad and had to postpone my shots until I lost my tan.

WOODY ALLEN

I remember Barbara Bouchet. She was a very beautiful young actress on the movie. There were a number of them on that movie that were those beautiful girls from the '60s. Charlie always packed the movies he made with beautiful women, which was a very commercial stroke. Apparently he was right, and most of his films made money. I was excited doing them, because I was worming my way into the movie business. And at least when I went out with my script for *Take the Money and Run,* I could say, "Well, I was in *What's New Pussycat?* and I wrote it, and I did a little thing in *Casino Royale*." I had a gram more of credibility with backers and I could finally get a company to take a chance on me with *Take the Money and Run.*

BARBARA BOUCHET

A few years ago in Rome, I got a part in Woody Allen's *From Rome with Love.* When I came up to the set, I just went up to him and I said, "Hi, Jimmy Bond!" He looked at me and said, "How come you're looking so great and I'm not?" I said, "Well, you know, you kind of play on that." I ended up on the cutting room floor, though.

Another of the stunning women in the film was Israeli actress Daliah Lavi, who played the Detainer—but she made a quick exit when filming ran long and she had to be on the set of another movie.

WOODY ALLEN

She was a very beautiful girl. I wanted to get through a scene to go home early one day and she really helped me, because I had some errand to do and I sent her like a hundred roses as a present and she was overwhelmed by it. She was even more overwhelmed by the fact that I could write her name in Hebrew. She was Miss Israel, or Miss Tel Aviv, I think. But I could write Hebrew so it was very good. If I was taller and more charming, I might've been able to romance her.

ROBERT DASSANOWSKY

Allen clearly used Dr. Noah as a rehearsal for all the over-preening nebbish characters to come, but no one could have played the sexual insecurity, small-man mastermind, and father-figure-revenge aspects of his character to the pitch of Freudian terrors as he did. Allen claims he detests the film, but it gave him the roots of so many future comedic directions. The thought that his Dr. Noah would be a nephew of Niven's Sir James is another deconstruction of mainstream narratives that points to the unique illogic of the spy film. Think Austin Powers and his brother, Dr. Evil, followed by Craig's Bond and his adopted stepbrother, Blofeld.

ED SIKOV

Woody Allen was a big fan of Sellers, but Sellers treated him like dirt. There was no reason for Sellers to have been jealous. Sellers was an international superstar, and Allen was a supporting player.

WOODY ALLEN

I was not aware of that. My contact with Peter was very minimal and he was always very nice when I was in contact with him, always very friendly and nice. I always considered Peter one of the few authentically funny people. I thought Peter was authentically a comic genius. That word is thrown around so meaninglessly in show business and 25 people are called comic geniuses who are not even good, but Peter Sellers was a brilliant, brilliant funnyman, so I was in awe of him. But he was always very nice. It was always very easy to be around him. I never felt any tension, He was a gigantic star, I certainly was not. I had not done any movies of any significance and had no track record in movies and he was a huge and well-deserved star.

At the time, Woody Allen commented in a letter to Richard O'Brien, the publicist for his managers, Jack Rollins and Charles Jaffe, "*Casino* is a madhouse. I am still waiting to shoot and will begin finally tomorrow. I think the film stinks as does my role. There is no involvement or story or importance to any of it. It is silly like an old [Milton] Berle sketch as opposed to a fine Nichols and May sketch. There is no seriousness or maturity of approach. It is unfunny burlesque." Meanwhile, David Niven, an original choice of Ian Fleming's to play James Bond in the Eon film series, reportedly commented, "*Casino Royale* is either going to be a classic bit of fun or the biggest fuck-up since the Flood. I think perhaps the latter."

WOODY ALLEN

You didn't have to see it to know that it was a train wreck, because you could tell from everyday things that were happening. News would come in, well he's hiring this person and they're changing this, now they want to shoot a scene here and somebody else is writing this scene and they've hired Charles Boyer and he's doing something here. It was just *insanity* and I was sitting in my hotel room in The Dorchester and I just was writing my play *Don't Drink the Water* most of the time. And then in the evenings I would play poker with the guys, we would all meet, and play poker until the sun came up really. Then go home and sleep till twelve or one o'clock. Nobody ever needed me for anything or called me for anything. And when they finally *did* get around to me, my contract had expired and I was making extra money.

KEN HUGHES

Trying to hold it all together nearly killed Feldman. He was unable to supervise everything. I remember I hadn't seen him in four weeks, so I sent him a map of London showing him how to get to the studio. I was in the office when Columbia pulled out for two hours. Charlie called them back and said, "Okay, I'm glad you're out. I've got full funding from Paramount." They came back, but he had to keep doing things like that to keep the movie going.

The final indignity for Sellers, who already refused to appear on set with Welles, may have been when Columbia executive Leo Jaffe reportedly confused the actor with Woody Allen and confessed in hushed tones, "Don't worry about that guy Sellers. We'll take care of him. I'm sorry we ever hired him. But you're a gentleman, Woody."

WOODY ALLEN

That's an embellishment that has a kernel of truth. I resembled Peter Sellers in a certain way physically if you didn't know any better. He did run into Sellers at the magazine stand or something in the lobby of one of the hotels, and for a moment, thought it was me. All the rest is apocryphal about saying that I was great and they were going to get rid of Sellers. None of that happened. He just thought it was me and made that mistake. Britt Ekland made the same mistake once. After all, I looked more like Peter than I looked like Charles Boyer.

Ultimately, Sellers disappeared from set, having taken up residence with girlfriend (and future *Bond* Girl) Britt Ekland's mother in Sweden. After Sellers fled the production, only to later be fired after his self-imposed and unauthorized hiatus, Val Guest was charged with making sense of the footage and creating an exit strategy for Sellers' Evelyn Tremble with previously shot footage that resulted in the character's abruptly exiting the finished picture in a race car. At the request (and expense) of Feldman, Woody Allen returned from New York and took up residence again in his suite at the Dorchester Hotel in England, the site of many an official *James Bond* press conference, where he and Val Guest attempted to concoct a suitable ending for the picture.

WOODY ALLEN

I liked Val Guest very much. He was another guy who was a sweet guy, really nice, but lost on the project. Not his fault. He was perfectly capable of directing a movie and directing one well, but nobody knew what was going on. Even great veterans like John Huston were lost. No one had any idea what was happening.

ALBERT R. BROCCOLI

Operation Kid Brother and *Casino Royale* were, in my opinion, abortions. Really badly done. No attempt to give Bond any stature. Merely they thought by "taking the mickey," as they say in England, poking fun at us, they were going to really do a mint of money. It's the reverse. The public is not stupid.

The fans and the public really find it offensive. To try to have three or four Bonds in one picture—one a girl, one a man—it's stupid. And it's surprising to me, because Charlie Feldman, who is not only a dear friend but a very intelligent man, would be talked into it.

When I spoke to him and I advised him, when he had the property, I said he should make a straight *Bond*, find a new actor, and have one shot and he'd make a lot of money. Which he could have, by copying the book, because the book was a good book. And they screwed it up by listening to all the so-called geniuses—the directors, the writers, the whole complex.

ROBERT DASSANOWSKY

The film was not "loathed" during its release—it was a hit with most audiences and received mixed critical judgments. But consider some of the slams that have been given to films that much later would be considered classics. The lore of mass rejection was evolved from the comments of *Bond* purists that believed that if the film originates from a *Bond* novel, it had to fit into strict *Bond* canon. And *Casino Royale*, which was about many more things than just *Bond*, was canonic in some places and deconstructive at the same time.

MATT SHERMAN

(author, *James Bond's Cuisine*)

The spoof *Casino Royale* is Hollywood legend with its bizarre plotlines and countless cameos from the biggest stars of its day. The film wields many jokes at the Eon films and also Fleming's Bond. Most *Bond* fans despise this film, saying it's transgressive from "the real *Bond*" and too spoofy, but some of us, okay, a very few of us, relish it.

ROBERT DASSANOWSKY

Casino Royale took on far more than *Bond*. Its references to various cinema genres and styles, tropes; its sophisticated collection of art, film, music, and historical references; and ultimately its attempt to utilize countercultural aspects in a traditional establishment genre of the Cold War spy saga, prove this. It deconstructs or revisions politics, war, gender roles, women's agency, the myth of the male hero, and the absurdity of "dancing on the edge of the volcano," as the Cold War at its height was often referred to. This is what makes it unique, memorable, and a subject of critical revision. It is a constructed filmic "happening" and its incongruities and missing pages, and its evolution of the narrative, is plainly seen on-screen. No wonder film critic Andrea LeVasseur called it both a "zany disaster" with regards to its mainstream reputation, but also "a psychedelic, absurd masterpiece." Unfortunately, the criticisms by *Bond* purists of it as a purely incoherent, non-canonical *Bond* film have survived and influenced later generations, especially those who have never seen it or cannot place it in time and film.

Similarly, the myth of the film as a financial disaster that bankrupted Columbia Pictures is linked to this. While the sprawling and expensive film did not generate as much as *You Only Live Twice* that same year—but why *should* it have; it was not a *Bond* film per se?—it broke box-office records in London, and went on to be the 13th-highest-grossing film in North America in 1967. The long production on the largest soundstages of three British studios—it was to have been released for Christmas 1966 and emerged in March 1967—gave impetus no doubt for the creation of the immense volcano hideout for *You Only Live Twice* and the later Piz Gloria sets in *On Her Majesty's Secret Service.*

JOHN CORK

(author, *James Bond: The Legacy*)

I do not consider *Casino Royale* 1967 an imitator. I consider it to be a farce—and a *James Bond* film without James Bond. They never give you the character of James Bond. But I love the music in that, I love the sets in it, I love the costumes in it, I love the women in it, I love Orson Welles in it, I love Peter Sellers in it, and I love Woody Allen in it.

ROBERT DASSANOWSKY

In the 1967 film, the first image to meet the audience's eye is the graffiti scrawl announcing "Les Beatles." That is the intended manifesto of the film—the band's non sequiturs, visionary tableaux, dry humor, outrageous spectacle, in-jokes, the mod, the now, the then, the later.

FRED DEKKER

(cowriter, *The Predator*)

Even on its own terms—5 directors, 15 screenwriters, 40 James Bonds—it's a total mess.

DICK CLEMENT

(uncredited screenwriter, *Never Say Never Again*)

From the stories I've heard, the first *Casino Royale* might've been even more chaotic than the making of *Never Say Never Again*, because that sounded absolutely insane. Five different directors doing different bits? It's amazing that that one survived.

ROBERT DASSANOWSKY

Today in postmodern film, superheroes change eras, styles, personalities, basic values, and even hop across dimensions and different "universes" with little criticism. The ahistorical satire of Tarantino, for instance, is able to rethink the original (be it history or legend) with praises. *Austin Powers: International Man of Mystery* is not so much a spoof of *Bond,* but a spoof of a '60s-era spy satire, in that it clearly uses many of the narrative points of *Casino Royale* uncredited and folds it into a self-conscious and somewhat Mel Brooks–influenced broad comedy. Brooks also copied Talmadge's finale for his *Blazing Saddles* and it is recalled as unique and comedically satisfying by audiences and critics alike.

JOHN CORK

I saw it at a drive-in 1967. I wasn't a *Bond* fan at that point. My aunt used to take me to drive-in movie theaters and we would see a lot of movies, so *she's* to blame for what I do. We saw it, and I'm not even sure I stayed awake till the end, you know, because I'm a little kid at that point. The next day, we went to the local record store, and she bought the soundtrack. I actually still have that record that has her name and my name written on the label. Unfortunately, she bought the mono soundtrack. I, of course, have the stereo, which is considered one of the greatest record pressings in the history of record pressings.

ROBERT DASSANOWSKY

While the [Burt] Bacharach/Herb Alpert "TJB" [Tijuana Brass] theme music actually made it to the top of the charts, "The Look of Love" was less admired than it is today, and lost to the insipid "Talk to the Animals" for the Best Song Oscar of 1967. Perhaps this was the result of the fact that the *Doctor Dolittle* fantasy was the sole traditional studio film among all the edgy, topical independent New Hollywood films nominated that year. They had to give it something to balm the threat of the "new"—and *Casino Royale,* which was a comedy, a genre not usually given the same respect as drama by the Oscars or BAFTA [British Academy of Film and Television Arts], took the fall. Truly, how can the amazing costumes and the stunning and innovative production design by Michael Stringer *not* have been praised?

Very little is ever said about the title sequence by animator Richard Williams, who along with Val Guest (the "coordinating director," a title he refused) accomplished much for the cohesiveness of the core Ian Fleming novel–based casino story (Sellers, Andress, Welles) with the Sir James frame (Niven, Kerr, Andress, Bouchet, Pettet, Allen, Lavi). The animated illuminated manuscript titles, which are themselves a spoof of the art in their pop-ish, art nouveau that suggests the various styles of the casino, underscore the knightly epic that this long, multifocal, mythical, and self-conscious film ultimately became. And the mission to bring a legendary knight out of retirement to help a failing Cold War order with "his morals, his vows, and his celibate image" at once gives the narrative an adventurous flow, complete with the location bumps of a traditional *Bond* film, and makes sense of the apocalyptic fight at the end of the film, in which evil is punished and the good ascend to heaven. Moreover, this literary frame exposes the '60s' spy film trend as a response to the anxieties of the nuclear age.

Dassanowsky notes that *Casino Royale* influenced a variety of spy spoofs and psychedelic comedy films into the start of the 1970s. While the aesthetic burned itself out–with films like *Skidoo, The Magic Christian, Catch-22,* and *M*A*S*H*–the 1967 *Casino Royale* was, in fact, a powerful trendsetter.

ROBERT DASSANOWSKY

As a mainstream entertainment film it was as revolutionary in its qualities as were the European new waves of the moment. It was, however, not given credit for this, because it was understood to be just a "*Bond* comedy," and emerged from traditional studio production.

One might recall that the great French auteur Jean-Luc Godard's *Weekend* arrived the same year as *Casino Royale*, 1967, and while the dark comic aspects of his surreal, hallucinogenic condemnation of the hedonistic and immoral Parisian bourgeoisie in the face of Vietnam, racism, counterculture shifts, abusive capitalism, and third world poverty is serious, it is no less intentionally incomplete, incoherent, episodic, and metafilmic than the more pop *Casino Royale*. Both deconstruct the traditional entertainment film themes and both utilize art and culture in highly ironic ways.

Although not a comedy, one of the best of the *James Bond* imitators were the *Harry Palmer* films, starring Michael Caine, from *Bond* producer Harry Saltzman, which began with *The Ipcress File* in 1965, from author Len Deighton's novel and directed by Sidney J. Furie. It was followed by Guy Hamilton's *Funeral in Berlin*, a crackling Cold War espionage thriller, and the zany 1967 Ken Russell–helmed *Billion Dollar Brain*.

JOHN CORK

Sean Connery once said that Cubby and Harry would sit across the huge partner's desk from each other and think, "That S.O.B.'s got half my money!"

Harry hadn't been the one passionate about *Bond*. He, like Cubby's former partner, Irving Allen, saw the success of *Bond* and thought it was all going to be so easy to do on his own. Whereas Allen scooped up the *Matt Helm* novels, Saltzman grabbed Len Deighton's books. They are fine movies, mostly thanks to Michael Caine's performances, but they don't hold a candle to *Bond*.

Deighton, who also had been an uncredited writer on the scripts for *From Russia with Love* and, later, *Never Say Never Again*, told the Deighton Dossier, a website devoted to his work, the following about the Saltzman-produced film series: "I knew Michael before he made *The Ipcress File*. Peter Evans, a mutual friend, introduced us and I found Michael an unassuming and entertaining friend. He was, of course, a tremendous asset; he developed the characterization and was largely responsible for the success of the film.

"When *Ipcress* went into pre-production, we conspired to persuade Harry Saltzman, its producer, to let Michael wear spectacles on the screen. Michael and I both wore glasses and so did Harry Palmer in my book. Harry Saltzman was opposed to this. One evening, when Harry and his delightful wife, Jacqui, entertained me and Michael to dinner in their Mayfair home, we brought it up again. Harry sighed. 'No, no, no. What film star have you ever seen wearing glasses?' he asked rhetorically. But wives are apt to answer rhetorical questions and Harry's wife said: 'Cary, darling. Cary Grant looks lovely in glasses.' This was one of the very few times that I saw Harry at loss for words. 'Very well,' he said eventually. I looked at Michael. Michael looked down at his plate. We had won. My disagreement with the depiction of Harry Palmer on the screen was the implausible suggestion that Harry was blackmailed into working for the secret intelligence service. Blackmailed! This is the old-boy network. These are people with tailored shirts and lace-up shoes. Despite the disrepute it suffered from harboring traitors such as Philby–Westminster, Cambridge, and the Athenaeum–the SIS retained this policy. Blackmailing a Harry Palmer into the service would have been unthinkable."

FRED DEKKER

The Ipcress File is one of my favorite movies of all time. Ken Adam designed it. John Barry did the score. It's got one foot in this weird brain drain science-fiction element. Other than that it's a very bookish, kind of by-the-numbers, espionage thriller.

If Bond was the room we were having the party in, there's a door in the corner and that was *The Ipcress File,* and once I went through that door, now there's another party. It's a little more sedate, a little more grounded, but I love that one, too.

RAYMOND BENSON

(author, *The James Bond Bedside Companion*)

I enjoyed them, especially the first two. I'm not surprised that any spy movie franchise has not endured in the way *Bond* has. *Bond* came at the right time in our history, and the quality control was excellent.

The American answer to *Bond* along with Irving Allen's *Matt Helm* films were the *Flint* duology from star James Coburn, which began with 1966's *Our Man Flint* and continued in 1967's *In Like Flint.*

ROBYN COBURN

(author, *Dervish Dust: The Life and Words of James Coburn*)

The *Flint* movies were more lighthearted than the early *Bond* movies, although perhaps less silly than the *Bond* franchise became for a while later, during the Roger Moore years for example. It feels a bit like the attention to "science" and high tech in *In Like Flint* was something that *Bond* films also picked up. The character of Flint was influenced in the sense of being a reaction to that type of spy, and wanting to find an all-American conception of an individualist. Flint did his "spy work" for the public good, and for his own personal safety and that of his friends.

JOHN CORK

I love the *Flint* films, not because I think they're particular brilliantly directed, but James Coburn is just so wonderful.

ROBYN COBURN

Jim [Coburn] had recently completed *High Wind in Jamaica*, directed by Alexander Mackendrick and produced by 20th Century Fox, so he had a connection with the company. He did a lot of publicity for the film, and it was the first time he had been credited on the same title card as the star. At the same time, he and his wife, Beverly, had been talking about the kind of characters that he was interested in portraying, and he himself expressed the idea that he was ready for "the brass ring of leading man." He formed his first production company expressly for the purpose of developing the first *Flint* script with those two and the writers Hal Fimberg and Ben Starr. Coburn's newly formed production company, M.O.F.F. (Mother's Old Fashioned Films), joined with director Daniel Mann and producer Saul David to develop *Our Man Flint,* which 20th Century Fox hoped would be a megahit and possible franchise for the studio.

JAMES COBURN
(actor, "Derek Flint")

Every chance we had, we would put our two cents in and take ideas on a trip. We were all able to contribute. That was the fun of it. We had an open end. We didn't have any literature to follow, so we took the theme of the ideal individual, doing, learning. Everything he knew, he learned how to do. It wasn't one of those magical things where you were endowed with powers.

ROBYN COBURN

So he had a lot of opportunity to really shape the character, and it was tailored to him in as many ways as possible. Meanwhile, in order to make the film, he had to buy out his multipicture contract with Marty Ransohoff. Then he signed a multipicture deal with Fox. I don't know if he was a fan of the *Bond* films themselves, but he definitely had a vision of the character that was different from James Bond. He saw Bond as being in bondage to the government, as a spy, while he took a humanist approach to Flint, who was his own man, and an extraordinary man.

JAMES COBURN

If I had known Bruce Lee when I made [the *Flint*] films, the fight scenes would have been fantastic. Bruce was a great teacher. He taught from your perspective, from your talent, which would then become the center of your technique—whether you had a good side kick, speed, a good punch, whatever it was. That's what a good teacher does. They have you work with your particular point of view or talent. My talent was a strong running side kick. I had a pretty good punch, too. That's all good teaching really is—teaching from your talents.

ROBYN COBURN

The *Flint* movies were made before Jim met and started training with Bruce Lee. The stunt people he worked with, led by Buzz Henry, helped him by choreographing stunts to his talents, but in later years Bruce Lee was not complimentary about the fights and Jim himself did say that the fight scenes would have been much better had he known Bruce earlier. It was his one regret about *Our Man Flint.*

JOHN CORK

Like I said, I love the *Flint* films. James Coburn is so much fun to watch. The movies have no depth, and the second one is one of the most offensive premises of a feature film ever. In it, women try to take over the world, but Flint convinces them that they should leave global leadership up to men.

JAMES COBURN

We didn't have a chance to really finish the script, because they wanted to get it out. We had to start shooting before we wanted to, and we never quite got the ending right, but it turned out okay. The ideal individual versus the women taking over the world. They don't even use hair dryers anymore.

ROBYN COBURN

The plot was somewhat convoluted, involving a surgically enhanced impostor posing as the president and a goofy women-take-over-the-world plan using a satellite, which seems a deliberate attempt to ridicule contemporary feminism. If that was not clear from the script, it was made explicit after the movie came out. On this topic of sexism, you probably know that a major speech in the climax of the movie was cut out, much to Jim's disappointment. He felt it damaged the theme.

JOHN CORK

On the other hand, it contains Flint reacting with horror and disgust, saying the immortal line, "An actor as president?" That was an oft-quoted line during the Reagan years. But these are not films I love as pieces of brilliant cinema. I love them because of what they reveal about the *Bond* phenomenon and the thoroughly warped values and attitudes of the era. In many ways, the bigger-budget *Bond* knockoffs like *Flint* and *Matt Helm,* the Eurospy films, and even the serious fare like *The Spy Who Came In from the Cold* are all reminders of just how brilliant those first four *Bond* films are.

ROBYN COBURN

There was some talk of a third *Flint* film, but the scripts were terrible and he declined. Periodically people at Fox had approached him for various *Flint* iterations, including a TV series, but none of them appealed to him.

Perhaps a less well-known Coburn film, but more impressive cult classic, is the satire *The President's Analyst,* in which he plays a therapist to the president of the United States whose knowledge is coveted by spy agencies from around the world.

ROBYN COBURN

The movie's plot has the title character becoming increasingly paranoid and delusional. Upon discovering that his fears are justified, he runs off and eventually hides out in a hippie commune with a rock band. Coburn spoofed both *Flint* and his own public persona, playing a gong with the band in a wild, drug-fueled love-in scene, before being grabbed by one of the international agencies desperate to learn the president's secrets. The climax of the movie has the chillingly prescient concept of the true bad guys being The Phone Company, their cheery robotic representative happily monologuing about their plans to keep everyone under constant surveillance.

Even The Beatles got into the spy game, with their delightful 1965 spy romp, *Help,* directed by Richard Lester. Meanwhile, on the small screen, Mel Brooks and Buck Henry created their own classic bumbling spy Max Smart in the legendary *Get Smart,* played by the brilliant Don Adams.

JEREMY DUNS

I absolutely loved *Get Smart* when I was a kid. For some reason that showed on TV wherever I was and I used to absolutely love that show. And I got into that way before *James Bond,* so that seems kind of weird.

Meanwhile, across the Bond, er, Pond, filmmakers were cashing in on the popularity of the spy craze with films like 1967's *Operation Kid Brother,* which starred Neil Connery, Sean's brother, as well as a litany of veterans from the official *Bond* movies, including Lois Maxwell, Daniella Bianchi, Adolfo Celi, and Bernard Lee. Other *Bond*-inspired films included Mario Bava's kitschy but wonderfully entertaining *Danger: Diabolik,* the 1968 romp inspired by a popular Italian comic book. In terms of television series, espionage thrillers like *The Man from U.N.C.L.E.,* for which Ian Fleming had created the character of Napoleon Solo, and *I Spy,* starring Robert Culp and Bill Cosby as spies gallivanting around the world under the guise of tennis pros, were big ratings winners.

ROBERT MEYER BURNETT

(director, *Free Enterprise*)

Everything that I wanted to be when I was kid was in *Danger: Diabolik*. It's directed by Mario Bava, one of the great Italian genre directors. He directed *Black Sunday*, one of my favorite horror movies of all time; *Planet of the Vampires*; and *Bay of Blood*. This film is based on a European comic book about an antihero super thief, and this movie is definitely inspired by the *Bond* films. Diabolik's cave lair is the ultimate man cave. It's a great example of pop filmmaking at the time. As audacious as Sergio Leone was at the time, Bava does something similar with *Diabolik*. This is not highbrow cinema in any way, shape, or form, but it's so much fun. When I was a kid, all I knew was I wanted a curvaceous Italian girlfriend like Marisa Mell. She was fantastically beautiful and it's a hoot. Unfortunately, it's been made fun of by *Mystery Science Theater*, which I'm not a fan of. The Beastie Boys evoked this in their music video for "Sabotage." It's one of two great movies produced by Dino De Laurentiis in 1968; the other is *Barbarella*, based on another European comic book, that also stars John Phillip Law. It was a great time for pop Euro-cinema. It was fantastic.

JOHN CORK

I also love *Danger: Diabolik*. I love a lot of the kind of weird homages to the world of James Bond.

MARC CUSHMAN

(author, *I Spy: A History and Episode Guide to the Groundbreaking Television Series*)

[Actor] Robert Culp and [producer] Sheldon Leonard both knew that NBC was eager to get a *James Bond*–type series onto the air. The network was developing *The Man from U.N.C.L.E.*, which Culp turned down, so that series and *I Spy* were in a race to see which one could get on the air first. *U.N.C.L.E.* won this race by one season, because Leonard had to figure out how to film his series around the world, and this caused it to take longer, even though the pilots for both were filmed in the same year—1964. The one thing Leonard and Culp absolutely agreed on was not to do espionage clichés in *I Spy* with 007-type spy gadgets—meaning, no pens firing poisoned darts, no cars that could become boats or airplanes, no evil organizations like SPECTRE or THRUSH or KAOS, and no Dr. No types. They wanted the humor in *I Spy* to be organic, and the characters believable and fallible.

FRED DEKKER

I never fell in love with any of them. I saw a little of everything but the stuff that was clearly *Bond* rip-offs, like *The Man from U.N.C.L.E.*, was just sort of like, why have a TV dinner when you know where the steaks are?

MARC CUSHMAN

I Spy came about because of *James Bond*. Robert Culp came up with the idea, which then inspired Sheldon Leonard's take on it, and all because of the sudden and massive popularity of *James Bond,* with *Dr. No* and *From Russia with Love* in release, and *Goldfinger* on its way. The networks were after Culp to do another series and he'd already turned down *Checkmate*, *The Virginian*, and *The Man from U.N.C.L.E.* He liked the idea of playing a spy, since James Bond was suddenly hot, but he found the pilot script for *U.N.C.L.E.* to be too camp. So he wrote his own pilot script—called *Danny Doyle*. Culp wrote himself as an American undercover agent working for the Department of Defense, and an amateur athlete, who travels the world. He showed it to Carl Reiner, who passed it along to Sheldon Leonard. Leonard, at this time, was one of the top producers in TV, but all his shows had been black-and-white half-hour sitcoms, such as *The Danny Thomas Show, The Dick Van Dyke Show, The Andy Griffith Show*, and, just getting started, *Gomer Pyle*. He was itching to do something else—an hour show, in color, and he wanted to travel. When he read Culp's script it gave him an idea—to have Culp's character travel the tennis circuit as a celebrated amateur, and to give him a partner, who would also be his trainer. This partner would be black.

Leonard had actually been wanting to come up with a show for Bill Cosby, who was a hot new stand-up comic with one comedy album out at the time. But network TV wasn't going to star a black actor in his own show, not in 1964. However, they might be willing to have the black actor play second to a white. And all three networks wanted Culp, badly. And NBC wanted Leonard, badly, because all his shows were on CBS. And they all wanted a spy show. So, Leonard pitched the three things he knew NBC wanted the most—a spy show to rival *James Bond,* starring Culp, and with him as executive producer. He added two things that he wanted—that it shoot around the world and be in color. He didn't mention Bill Cosby until *after* he had a deal.

As it turned out, Leonard pulled the plug on *I Spy* after three seasons and 82 episodes. He and Culp had cocreated the series—which is why there is no "created by" credit, only the opening proclamation, "Sheldon Leonard Presents"—and he and Culp were having creative differences. Everyone was also exhausted, because *I Spy* shot almost the entire year on the road. So it ended, even though NBC wanted two more years. Reports at the time that it was being canceled are entirely erroneous. That was the spin. The truth is, Leonard had had enough, and, as the primary owner, he could call it quits, which he did.

At the height of its popularity, *I Spy* was so popular that even the hit series *Get Smart* parodied the series.

MARC CUSHMAN

Get Smart, a wonderful show, was routinely doing theme episodes which would parody other series, as they did with a takeoff on *The Avengers* and *Ironside*, and on films such as *Rear Window*, and so many others. It only made sense that *Get Smart* did this because it was a parody to begin with, on *James Bond* and, even more so, *Man from U.N.C.L.E.* So, of course they would have to do an *I Spy* takeoff, just once. And how wonderful that Culp agreed to do a cameo in it—a whole comedy sequence, in fact. Culp was a brilliant comedian in his own right, although he mostly played drama. *I Spy* proves his versatility as an actor and writer, and that *Get Smart* episode surely showed off his comedic chops.

Robert Culp wrote an episode of *I Spy* called "Court of the Lion," which was his nod toward *James Bond*, in which Godfrey Cambridge played a Zulu Goldfinger. In another Culp-written episode, "So Long, Patrick Henry," [Cosby's] Scott recruited a bellboy named Mickey at the Peninsula Hotel in Hong Kong to help them spy on Ivan Dixon, playing Elroy Browne, a US athlete who had defected to Red China. The kid was very gung-ho and boasted that he'd seen *Goldfinger* 27 times, and counting! He'd send messages and sign them "007," which would nearly give Kelly a heart attack.

Even after the heyday of spymania in the '60s, *Bond* parodies and films inspired by the 007 films continued to endure, such as *Austin Powers* and Tom Cruise's reinvention of Bruce Geller's *Mission: Impossible* series, but perhaps none more memorably than when Roger Moore played Seymour Goldfarb Jr., driving an Aston Martin DB5 in *The Cannonball Run*.

SIR ROGER MOORE

(actor, "James Bond")

Well, you know, that was a holiday for me, because on only three occasions do all the principals meet. The rest of the time we're all in separate cars. So I was ordered to shoot my piece in a week and I had two months off in the middle of it. I love that. I wish I could've worked like that all the time. On *Bond,* you have to work every day.

ROBERT DASSANOWSKY

Austin Powers seems to have grown more from the *Matt Helm* series and its constant barrage of sex jokes. The opening mod party in *Goldmember* seems heavily inspired by the one in 1966's *Murderers' Row* and the running joke that the obvious Los Angeles hillsides are supposed to be English countryside, which comes from the problematic style of the *Matt Helm* films. For instance, the Spanish-influenced mansions of Bel Air, California, standing in for Denmark in 1968's *The Wrecking Crew.* It is the *Austin Powers* films themselves that seem to epitomize the post-millennial view of a limited and cliché "Swinging Sixties," with translated elements from *Casino Royale* 1967 and in rethinking Peter Sellers' multiple characterizations and his velvet-suited, Beatle-haired Viennese psychiatrist Dr. Fritz Fassbender from *What's New Pussycat?* That is too distant in terms of originality and authenticity.

JOHN LANDIS

(director, *Spies Like Us*)

One of the things I found so odd about *Austin Powers* movies is it was like, "Oh, how clever. It's a spoof of *Bond* and England." Hello. There are thousands of them. That's what they all were. I really enjoy all the totally wacky Italian ones the most.

E

(editor, *Die Spy Kill Kill*)

I'm always up for a good spy caper. Some I really like include *Kingsman, The Man from U.N.C.L.E., The Ipcress File, Charade, The Long Kiss Goodnight,* and *Hopscotch*, to name a few.

S

(sound editor, *Die Spy Kill Kill*)

I have a big crush on *Where Eagles Dare,* and while we both really like the *Mission: Impossible* series, I'd go as far as to say that since *Ghost Protocol,* the *Mission: Impossible* films are more consistently entertaining and worth watching than the *Bond* films are now. Big call, I know. But when *Bond* begins to ignore its own formula that kept it afloat for 50 years, it's only a matter of time before another series that works harder comes in to take the crown. Has that happened yet? Who can say?

ON HER MAJESTY'S SECRET SERVICE (1969)

"Who is George Lazenby?" It's a question that could–and likely has–come from the lips of Alex Trebek on *Jeopardy!* Any true *Bond* fan knows Lazenby was the one-hit wonder ("hit" being a relative term) who starred in the most unique of 007 films that those same fans either love or loathe, *On Her Majesty's Secret Service*.

The seeds for the film in many ways were planted with Sean Connery's frustration with typecasting and lack of financial parity with Broccoli and Saltzman, and the fact that James Bond himself had taken a dramatic backseat to the gadgets and stunts. Prior to the shooting of *You Only Live Twice*, Connery had given an interview to *Playboy* in which he commented, "All the gimmicks now have been done. And they are expected. What is needed now is a change of course–more attention to character and better dialogue."

As Maxwell Smart might say in *Get Smart*, "Missed it by that much!"

Had the actor remained in the role for the sixth film, *On Her Majesty's Secret Service*, many believe that it could have resulted in the best 007 film ever.

RICHARD MAIBAUM
(screenwriter, *On Her Majesty's Secret Service*)

If Sean had played it, that picture would've been the greatest grosser of all time, because it was the best novel and the best script, and there are a lot of people that think it's the best of them all.

CHARLES HELFENSTEIN
(author, *The Making of On Her Majesty's Secret Service*)

I don't subscribe to the "Connery in *OHMSS* = best ever" theory one bit. In my mind, a *Bond* actor's performance is based on three pillars: action, romance, and dialogue. Would Connery trump Lazenby's physicality in the action scenes? No way. Would Connery trump Lazenby's chemistry with Rigg and improve on the love scenes? Doubtful. Let's call it a tie. Would Connery trump Lazenby's expository dialogue scenes? Yes, he's clearly a better actor. So in my mind, the love scenes would be equal, the dialogue scenes would be improved, but the action scenes would suffer. And that equation does not improve the film. The "Does it change the direction of the films?" conundrum is a critical point that people often overlook. Had Connery been in *OHMSS*, Diana Rigg would *not* have been cast. It would have been Brigitte Bardot, or another French actress.

The other way Connery radically alters the equation is the fact that he would not have put up with director Peter Hunt's perfectionism. Connery's early *Bond* films only took three or four months to film. Later ones took six months and he was balking at *that* schedule, because it didn't allow him to do other films in a calendar year. He simply would not have stood for Hunt's nine-month-long *On Her Majesty's Secret Service* shoot.

GUY HAMILTON

(director, *Goldfinger*)

They asked me to do *Thunderball* and I said, "No, I've got no fresh ideas. I mean, I've done a *Bond* and I've got to do something else. But if you ever do another one, I'd like to do *On Her Majesty's Secret Service,* because there, Bond falls in love. It's about a French girl, and the hottest French girl is Brigitte Bardot. Sean and Brigitte Bardot would make a great double act, plus it's quite a good story." And they said, "Hey, that's a hell of an idea." They shot off and I never heard anything at all until about a week later and they said, "It's the most stupid idea you've ever had. Do you realize that if we start having a star playing the lead opposite Bond, it's going to cost us a fortune?" They don't mind paying for the effects, but, Jesus, "The girls pay us." Then they said, "Do the one without Sean," and they did endless tests all over the place, but I wasn't very interested in the tests, because whoever was going to be Bond was not my decision. It was obviously the franchise.

The film would ultimately be directed with a singular stylistic flair by former *Bond* editor and second-unit director Peter Hunt, who wanted *OHMSS* to be the most faithful adaptation of one of Ian Fleming's novels ever attempted.

PETER HUNT

(director, *On Her Majesty's Secret Service*)

I was finished with editing; I wanted to direct. I had been working with Dick Maibaum on the script for *On Her Majesty's Secret Service,* so it wasn't an abrupt change. It was a great story and it was a Fleming *James Bond* book, so we didn't have to deviate. I didn't want to put gimmicks and tricks in it. It didn't need making better, because it was all there. It is a marvelous adventure story with Bond surviving by his own physical skill and ingenuity.

STANLEY SOPEL

(producer, *On Her Majesty's Secret Service*)

When Peter Hunt wanted to direct *On Her Majesty's Secret Service,* there were problems. It was a natural move for Peter to become a director, though I suppose one of the problems always is that to move an editor who's at the top of his class to the directing field on a picture that's going to cost between $6 and $9 million is not always the decision of the producer. I'm sure both Harry and Cubby would have given him the break earlier, but we had to worry about the money boys. They said, "It's a big investment; let him cut his teeth on a million-dollar movie first." It's all credit to Harry and Cubby that they were able to persuade United Artists to let Peter do *On Her Majesty's Secret Service,* particularly with a new actor. If we would have had Sean to do it, or if we would have gone at that time with Roger Moore, it would have been easier for Peter. It was very difficult. I think he came out with a marvelous picture, a fantastic *action* picture.

PETER HUNT

One of the reasons why I stuck my neck out and wanted to do—in fact, was delighted to do—the film is that in my opinion *On Her Majesty's Secret Service* is one of the best of the *Bond* stories. It involves many facets of Bond as a person rather than Bond simply as an agent—a crash, bang, wallop man who gets, or loses, his man and finds out the information. I thought, for once, here is a *Bond* story which is not just an adventure, which we have done well in the past. Here is a James Bond who is going to fall in love. Instead of just more kiss-kiss-bang-bang, he is going to really kiss and find himself involved for the first time in his life and, indeed, he marries the young lady in question.

CHARLES HELFENSTEIN

The *On Her Majesty's Secret Service* scripting process was the most prolific and lengthy of the entire franchise history. There were a wide range of drafts spanning five years—ones where Connery was still attached to the project in 1964; gadget-heavy ones (featuring items such as an aquatic Aston Martin, Blofeld projecting himself holographically, laser weapons, etc.); plastic surgery drafts in 1967 to explain the actor change; and last but not least, drafts where Bond befriends a chimpanzee in Blofeld's zoo, and the simian helps Bond escape. Richard Maibaum's earliest treatment from 1964 is pretty faithful to the novel, and as time went on, the drafts veer away from that fidelity and venture more into the fantastic. Peter Hunt coming on board as director definitely reined in the story back toward Ian Fleming's work.

RICHARD MAIBAUM

On Her Majesty's Secret Service was the best of the Ian Fleming novels. It was more of an actual novel than any of them. It had a beginning, a middle, and an end, and yet it had a wonderful relationship between Bond, the girl, and her father. The whole damn thing was so interesting. I'm proud of several of the scripts I've written for the films, and this is one of them.

PETER HUNT

It gave me two stories interwoven: one a *Bond* adventure and the other an emotional relationship which culminates in marriage. This, to me, was a great challenge, because I didn't think it was easy to do. But oddly enough, maybe in my conceit, I wasn't that worried about the changing aspect of Bond. I had been sufficiently immersed in *Bond* films over the previous six years that this didn't concern me half as much as getting across the story points. I knew that if I got the right person to play the role, I would be able to maneuver him and make him do things in the *Bond*ian manner.

And *that* was the challenge. While these days it remains a media event, it's nonetheless more commonplace to witness a changing of the Bonds. *On Her Majesty's Secret Service* was the first time this happened and it was a *huge* deal. The subsequent transition to Roger Moore with 1973's *Live and Let Die* was also highly significant, but by the time Timothy Dalton, Pierce Brosnan, and Daniel Craig took on their own licenses to kill, it wasn't a tremendous shock. Yet *this* was different: how the hell was *anyone* going to follow Sean Connery?

ALBERT R. BROCCOLI
(producer, *On Her Majesty's Secret Service*)

It was a bit of a surprise and a bit of a disappointment when Sean Connery announced he was leaving. No more than that, because, after all, you have to continue as long as Bond is there. There's no reason why we should stop the series because he left. We have proven that Bond is here to stay for a long time.

JOHN CORK
(author, *James Bond: The Legacy*)

I think we all regret not seeing Dick Van Dyke as 007. Can you fathom it? You have to remember the competition was Dick Van Dyke and . . . Adam West. Seriously. They were both considered at one point to replace Connery.

ADAM WEST

(actor, *Batman '66*)

In the Sixties, there were the three Bs: Batman, Bond, and Beatles. I was asked to play Bond after Sean Connery for *On Her Majesty's Secret Service*. It didn't feel right, though. James Bond shouldn't be an American.

GLEN OLIVER

(pop culture commentator)

A few years back I caught *Colossus: The Forbin Project* for the first time. A tremendous picture by Joseph Sargent, who also directed the original *Taking of Pelham One Two Three*. I was quite taken by its lead—Eric Braeden—and said to a number of folks at the time, "He totally should've been James Bond." I dug into the matter, and quickly discovered this was, apparently, actually under consideration at one point. Like so many other actors considered for 007, it didn't work out for him. So sad. Between his presence, looks, intelligence, and intensity, he would've been a tremendous Bond.

ERIC BRAEDEN

(actor, *Colossus: The Forbin Project*)

Cubby Broccoli had me and my agent to lunch and asked if I still had a British passport. I said no. At that time I had a *German* passport, and that was the end of that. Imagine if James Bond had been played by a German—I think there would have been a revolution in England. So that fell through because of that. A lot of people always thought I was somehow tied to the British Commonwealth or whatever. But they were definitely serious about it.

GLEN OLIVER

Braeden did land a critical role in the original *Planet of the Apes* film series, though—and over 2,700 episodes of *The Young and the Restless*. These didn't afford him the high-profile visibility Bond would have, but he found a substantive and impressive career nonetheless. And good for him.

ERIC BRAEDEN

At that time I wasn't interested in *James Bond* films, to be frank with you. I wanted to do a film with Ingmar Bergman or Fellini or one of those guys. I wasn't interested in the *James Bond* thing at all. Plus, Sean Connery was the best. Period. There's no one like him, and to do anything afterward is secondary.

JOHN CORK

The thing that constantly amazes me is the repeated serious consideration of American actors to play Bond. I am happy those stars never aligned. I could see Richard Burton as a very serious Bond, and he was strongly considered. Cary Grant would have been a strange, but delightful Bond. Gary Cooper was in discussions for an Americanized version of the role in a 1960s iteration of *Casino Royale* late in his life. Many of the *Bond* team thought that Christian Bale would make a good Bond before Daniel Craig was cast, and that would have been fascinating. I will forever be grateful that Mel Gibson turned down the role.

STEVEN JAY RUBIN

(author, *The James Bond Films*)

Broccoli and Saltzman had narrowed the field down to five actors. Besides Lazenby, they were considering John Richardson, who had recently starred alongside Raquel Welch in *One Million Years B.C.*; and three young English actors, Anthony Rogers, Robert Campbell, and Hans De Vries. Elaborate action tests began in April 1968 when the full crew was assembled. Both producers were already aware that United Artists wanted to see some fighting footage of the Bond applicants. The archetypal *Bond* fight is spectacular and, although over in seconds, it is generally choreographed like a ballet, with shots of the stuntmen and stars intermixed, and edited tightly. His performance in the test fight won Lazenby the role of Bond.

PETER HUNT

Broccoli and Saltzman were notoriously known for not making their minds up, and I think we were like two weeks off of shooting, when one had to say, "Who are we going with? We're supposed to be starting, but we haven't got a Bond yet." So it got almost to the last moment before the decision was made. The decision to use Lazenby was not left in my hands, but they did say to me, "Can you work with him?" and I said, "Yes, I can. Let's just get somebody we all can agree on," because Broccoli, Saltzman, and United Artists were the ones who had to say yes or no.

DAVID V. PICKER

(president and chief executive officer, United Artists)

Replacing Sean was not going to be easy. As in hiring Sean initially, it was essential to cast a performer who would agree to multiple options, and that would be hard to do if the actor was well established. So it was pretty much back to square one. Everyone had ideas. Mine was John Newcombe, the Australian tennis player. He was handsome and had a great serve. I often wonder if he ever knew he might have been James Bond. But in the end, the two producers strongly recommended George Lazenby, another Australian (I knew nothing about his serve). All I knew was that he looked good, his experience as a male model gave him style, and if the producers felt he was the best shot, who were we to argue with the success they had created? They were the experts, self-appointed, appointed, and otherwise. So Lazenby it was.

PETER HUNT

Lazenby was very good. I had a bit of a job directing him, even though he seems to think he wasn't directed, and it was quite a job to make him Bond. But he took it and did it, and that's the important thing. I'm not questioning how difficult it was, because that's part of the director's job. You don't just stand up there and say, "Cut, action," and that sort of thing. You've got a lot more on your plate than that. It was a difficult job, but the answer for me was that it worked, and it worked for the producers as well.

Born September 5, 1939, in Australia, George Robert Lazenby spent his early years in the Australian army before working as a car salesman and mechanic. In 1963 he moved to London hoping to win the heart of the woman he'd fallen in love with. There he became a used-car salesman, which led to his being discovered by a talent agent who talked him into giving modeling a try, which worked out well for him.

There are several stories about how Lazenby was cast in the role, some of which are clearly apocryphal. While Lazenby explains that he conned his way into the Eon offices after spending time on an Eliza Doolittle transformation into a *Bond*ian rake, it seems the truth was slightly more mundane, with Broccoli and Peter Hunt having first seen the actor in a commercial for Big Fry Chocolate, which followed Broccoli catching a glimpse of Lazenby at his barber, which the actor says he personally engineered. Arriving for an audition in a Savile Row suit he bought that had been made for Sean Connery but never picked up, and going to the same barber as Connery at the Dorchester Hotel, Lazenby attempted to transform himself into the perfect Connery doppelgänger, which can be considered both a success and a failure, as the most successful 007s would later make the role their own rather than attempt to emulate what had come before. No one would confuse Roger Moore with Sean Connery in his interpretation of the character, just as Daniel Craig forged his own unique take on the iconic part, whereas Lazenby, no matter how much you may or may not embrace him in the role, could only come up short compared to Sean Connery in the thankless task of being the first actor to succeed the world-famous actor.

GEORGE LAZENBY
(actor, "James Bond")

I was a used-car salesman in Australia and there were no intentions of leaving. I mean, I didn't even know where England was, let alone planned on going there. But then the love got me. You know, I was in love with this girl and I couldn't live without her, but she moved to England. I didn't want to go out with other girls. I was sad all the time. When the mail stopped, I tried to get in touch with her and couldn't find her. Then, when I got to England, she was up in Oxford with the captain of the Oxford cricket team. And remember, we didn't have cell phones or anything, so I couldn't find her. Then a friend from my hometown saw her in town with these cricksters who came down to London to play. And that's the luck of the draw. Next thing I knew, I could see her platonically. That was in 1964.

CHARLES HELFENSTEIN

Lazenby was the highest-paid male model in Europe at the time. He jokes that signing up for Bond was actually a pay cut, and I believe it. He was in so many advertising campaigns in the mid '60s—clothing, shoes, cameras, beer, toothpaste, mattresses, car parts, candy, etc. So he had a mental leg up on his competition. He didn't need the job. That cockiness came across throughout his interview process. That cockiness is a Bond-like trait. Bond isn't meek. When casting agent Maggie Abbott called him about the role, Lazenby asked why she thought he was right for the part, and she told him it was his arrogance that made her think he'd be right for Bond.

PETER HUNT

I had a very clear-cut idea of what I wanted. I don't think our producers did, but I definitely did and, for want of a better expression, and I have said this before, what has Sean Connery got? What is this magnetism? What Sean Connery had was what I would term "sexual assurance." You cannot interpret that in any foreign language, I am afraid, because it becomes something quite different, but in English it means this man can walk with assurance. It meant that this man has a sexual ability with women that gives him such an assurance that it is not vulgar. Nothing other than masculine. But it adds up to something more than just a masculine person and that, in fact, is what Sean Connery had—certainly as James Bond. So my first thought always, whenever I interviewed anybody, was, does he have this quality? Now I interviewed hundreds, all sorts of people—actors, models, musclemen—anybody who was a likely character, and it was quite by chance that we came across George Lazenby. There was no doubt in my mind, once he walked into my office, that this man had what I was looking for. He had sexual assurance. You do look at him if he walks into the street, and so do the girls.

CHARLES HELFENSTEIN

Lazenby wasn't afraid to embellish tales to improve his chances, lying to producers about previous acting work in Germany and Hong Kong. He also tapped into that part of human nature that wants what we can't have, and told them they better act fast, because he had a lot of advertising gigs lined up. And finally Peter Hunt was Lazenby's biggest champion. They had looked at hundreds of actors and models, and none had the combination of bravado, physicality, and what Hunt described as "sexual assurance" that Lazenby had. While Broccoli and Saltzman were cautiously optimistic about Lazenby, United Artists was pretty skeptical. Hunt fought hard for Lazenby, and while acknowledging his inexperience, the director said, "Let's be bold! Let's go with him."

PETER HUNT

We looked at hundreds of people for Bond and went through a whole range of discussions saying, "What would the new Bond look like? Should we make him a modern Bond?" And it was agreed by practically everyone that, no, what we wanted was another Sean Connery. This guy, George Lazenby, certainly did look good and could move very well, which is the style we were looking for. We had already brought Diana Rigg aboard, and I spoke to her and said, "I want you to meet this boy. I'd like you to be very honest with me and tell me what you think afterward." Then I was delighted when she rang me and said, "I think he'd be fine." At that moment, we had our leading man.

JOHN GLEN

(editor, second-unit director, *On Her Majesty's Secret Service*)

George did a commercial here that was really famous for Big Fry Chocolate, and it was a picture of him being surrounded by all these lovely girls chasing him. He's got a big box of these Big Fry Chocolates on his shoulder, and he's leaving this ship. It was all very macho and he was paid a lot of money for it. He had a very good career. He's an extremely handsome guy, but acting as James Bond and playing a commercial are quite different things, as you have to have a bit of discipline. When I worked with him I was trying to keep him on the straight and narrow.

GEORGE LAZENBY

After the Big Fry commercials, every photographer in town wanted me and I never had a spare moment. Finding even the time for a haircut was a problem, but I happened to be getting one and who should be sitting in the next chair but Cubby Broccoli. I didn't know that at the time, of course, but that was where he first saw me and thought of me as a possible replacement for Sean Connery. When my agent rang to say they wanted me to test for Bond, I was absolutely stunned. I'd never acted before and didn't think I stood a chance. But I played a fight scene and made love with a girl, and they told me I'd got the part. I went to see the director, Peter Hunt, and he took one look at me and said, "You're the new James Bond—but we will have to convince them in America. Oh, by the way, what's your name?" I eventually told Peter Hunt the truth. I said, "Peter, I've never acted before. I just told them a whole lot of bullshit, and when you test me you're going to find that out." And Peter's response to me was, "You've fooled the two most ruthless guys I've ever known—you've got to be an actor! Just stick with your story, and I'll make you the next James Bond." I never understood at the time why he did it, but Peter's thing was that if he used a nonactor, he would get all the credit. That was explained to me years later.

PETER HUNT

Many people said to me, "How are you going to make him an actor?" There's a great difference between a film star and an actor. There have been a lot of very good film stars, very good personalities who do the same parts perhaps in every film, learning certain technical things as they go along. And there are a lot of actors who can also be film stars. But with a great knowledge of technical know-how as well as the human element, the necessary elements to encourage, coax, and bully them to do all the other necessary things, you can get a performance. Films, after all, are made up of small pieces of film, and very cleverly edited together it is possible to make a performance. I'm not saying "great," although sometimes you can even make a great performance, but it is possible to make a performance from anybody.

GEORGE LAZENBY

I look back at the early days of all this, and I used to live pretty much moment to moment. I didn't sit and wonder what's going to happen; that wasn't part of my character. But they [the producers] kept me busy for four months during the testing. I mean, every nighttime I'd have to go out with them socially. I'd go out with Broccoli and his family one night, and then Harry and his family another night, because their wives didn't get along, so we couldn't all go out together. That was a test to see what I was like socially, I guess. I met famous people, because they'd always go to the best restaurants. Sammy Davis Jr. came up to me in a restaurant once and sat on my lap, and I said, "What's this?" He said, "I know something you don't know!" I hadn't been announced yet, but he knew that I was top pick for being James Bond. I ran into Diane Cilento, Sean Connery's ex-wife, once. She comes running down an alley to come into this party, looked at me, and said, "I feel sorry for you," and walked past me. I sat there thinking, "Jesus, what am I getting into?"

I just didn't know what to think. I didn't say very much at the time, because I didn't have much to say. I mean, who cares that I was a motor mechanic or car salesman? These people were famous actors and whatnot. I hadn't gotten famous yet; that was prior to Bond when I was testing. I actually never went to the studio until the last test I did. They always tested me at Harry Saltzman's house in case they'd be the laughingstock of the industry testing a male model for James Bond.

One of the real questions about this new James Bond, once he was chosen, was how exactly he was going to be introduced on-screen. For some time there were elaborate plans that included the idea that James Bond had undergone plastic surgery to fool his enemies, but that decision, thankfully, was dropped. What they *did* do took place at the conclusion of the pre-credit sequence, where, after Bond saves the damsel in distress, she drives off, leaving him on a beach, holding her shoes. Looking at the camera he says, "This never happened to the other fella," and we cut to the opening titles.

CHARLES HELFENSTEIN

The plastic surgery idea lasted for a few drafts in 1967 to explain the lead actor change, but the idea never had any significant traction. Maibaum later admitted the idea was a bit too comic-book gimmicky. It isn't in the novel, so Hunt was not keen on filming it. The production team decided a throwaway line during the pre-credit sequence would suffice. It went through various iterations, including one where Sean Connery is explicitly mentioned, before finalizing on, "This never happened to the other fella." Lazenby has claimed credit for coming up with the line, but Maibaum is the author, as it is present in his drafts before Lazenby was even involved in the casting process.

GEORGE LAZENBY

It wasn't my idea, but what happened was I was doing my own stunts. I was jumping off a bloody helicopter 20 feet in the air, and started realizing that I bet the other fellow didn't have to do this. I kept saying that over and over again.

PETER HUNT

Everyone had different ideas about how to handle Sean's exit from the role. Finally, Dick Maibaum said, "Why are we playing around with this? Why don't we just take it as a matter of course?" We were all scratching our heads about how to start it, and I believe it was Dick who came up with the line, "This never happened to the other fella." We all agreed that we should just get on with it right away, because no matter what you do, you come back to the same thing—you're changing the actor, not the character. We weren't changing the style of film nor the stories, so we figured the more quickly we got it out of the way, the better.

The new leading man was only one of the changes that were being made to the franchise with *On Her Majesty's Secret Service*. For starters, Blofeld is back, but this time there are no volcano lairs, toppling of missiles, stunning blond Soviet agents looking to defect, or underwater battles with spearguns and mini-submersibles. Instead, Blofeld is looking for validation of his ancestral title as Count Balthazar de Bleuchamp, and Bond goes undercover as genealogist Sir Hillary Bray of the College of Arms by donning a pair of glasses, a kilt, and the dubbed voice of George Baker that would put even Clark Kent to shame. Of course, you have to get over the fact that Donald Pleasence now looks like Telly Savalas (who, despite his many film roles, will forever be known for his TV portrayal of Kojak) and fails to recognize 007 when he meets him again one film after *You Only Live Twice*.

Even the plot isn't as far-fetched as the usual world-in-peril drama, with Blofeld planning to release a bacteriological agent to destroy vital crops using a coterie of brainwashed beauties as delivery agents unless his demands are met. Among the so-called Angels of Death are a number of actresses who would later achieve a measure of fame, including, most notably, Joanna Lumley, who appeared in *The New Avengers* and, lest anyone forget, *Absolutely Fabulous*; while the late Angela Scoular, who played Ruby Bartlett, also played Buttercup in 1967's *Casino Royale*; and, of course, Catherine von Schell, who would later go on to play the shape-changing Maya in the second season of Gerry Anderson's *Space: 1999*—the same Gerry Anderson who had initially developed a treatment of *You Only Live Twice* for Eon.

PETER HUNT

In the story of the film, Blofeld has developed a virus. The basis of the blackmail element of Blofeld is germ warfare—we've added a certain element to it, which I think is better, that of a sterilization form of germ by which he is threatening to make extinct great herds of cattle, flocks, crops, and things like that.

RIC MEYERS

(author, *For One Week Only: The World of Exploitation Films*)

Telly Savalas is actually my favorite Blofeld, because I could believe him as a callous businessman with domination desires, as well as a willingness to lead an international crime syndicate with an iron hand. Everything Blofeld did, from boardroom electrocutions on, I could easily believe Telly Savalas would sign off on. Donald Pleasence and Charles Gray hardly had the same gravitas, but, by then, I felt the producers were actively, albeit perhaps subconsciously, undercutting anything to do with the whole Kevin McClory, SPECTRE, Blofeld legal fustercluck.

RICHARD MAIBAUM

My only problem with the film is that I don't think Telly Savalas was very good as Blofeld. He should have had an accent or something, but I couldn't convince Peter Hunt or anyone to get him to use one.

PETER HUNT

We never saw Blofeld in the first lot of films. There were always the cats, because I shot the damn cats. You see, *You Only Live Twice* should have come after *On Her Majesty's Secret Service*. Unfortunately, owing to a different arrangement that was going on, which is a long, boring story, they did it first and then I did *On Her Majesty's Secret Service* afterward. So, in fact, I always think of Telly Savalas as the first one. I wasn't very keen on Donald Pleasence as Blofeld, I'm afraid.

GEORGE LAZENBY

I had been given a per diem of $1,000, but I was up on the mountain with nowhere to spend it. So I pulled out a briefcase full of cash in front of Telly Savalas one day, and he said, "Hey, kid, do you play poker?" So he's got half my money. Harry Saltzman, who used to be a professional gambler and had to quit because he lost everything, comes in one day and he sees what Telly's doing to me and says, "Move over, kid!" And Telly said, "No, Harry! No!," and he got all my money back and said to Telly, "Leave my boy alone."

More significantly than Savalas, until Eva Green there was probably not a better *Bond* Girl than the brilliant and resourceful Diana Rigg, if you can even get away with calling her a girl. Rigg, like Honor Blackman before her, was coming off of the British TV series *The Avengers,* where she had played Emma Peel. She would, of course, go on to a highly acclaimed career that most recently has included HBO's *Game of Thrones*.

Countess Teresa di Vicenzo (known more commonly as Tracy) is probably the first real woman to appear in a *Bond* film: beautiful, capable, smart, and arch. It's no wonder Bond proposes to her midway through the film. Rigg represented a genuine evolution of the *Bond* Girl up to that point, and in a sense laid down the groundwork for how things would go–albeit slowly–in the future. Tracy is the first counterpart to Bond who has a genuine arc over the course of one of these films. When we meet her, she's suicidal and, despite her best efforts, is thwarted from her path of self-destruction by Bond on a number of occasions. Eventually, as Bond comes into contact with her father, Marc-Ange Draco, head of the Corsican crime syndicate, the Union Corse, he and Tracy reconnect and actually fall in love.

GEORGE LAZENBY

Before we were in Switzerland, I was in Diana Rigg's place, and she's with a boyfriend who asked, "Do you play chess?" I said, "Sure," and before you know it I'm saying, "Checkmate." He sets it up again and we played. I played him again. Well, he threw the board up in the air, and that's the first time Diana took any notice of me. Next thing I know, I'm in Switzerland, and she says, "If you have nothing to do with any of the other girls, we may get something going." So here she's giving me these instructions, and I lied. I was fooling around with a receptionist in the stuntman's tent. That tent is full of mattresses, and we're just about through getting a little cuddly. As Diana's walking past, a stuntman lifted up the side of the tent . . . and I'd only been there a week on the set. Next thing you know, she goes, "Oh my God, there he goes again."

DIANA RIGG

(actress, "Tracy")

They got me on board, because I was the gravitas to George Lazenby. They had to have an *actress* on board, because Lazenby was totally inexperienced. I had no illusions at all that that's why they got me, and I did what I could. I have to say, though, that the money was wonderful. It was a mammoth production, an epic, and I'd never done an epic before, so I rather wanted to know what it was like to be in an epic.

JOHN CORK

Diana Rigg is one of the great actresses of her generation. She out-acts everyone else in *On Her Majesty's Secret Service*. She both lifts the film up every time she's on-screen, and illuminates how ill-prepared George Lazenby was for taking on the leading role in a motion picture. Any actor thrown into that situation would be ill-prepared, and I really think Diana Rigg tried to help George every way she could. But she's only in a relatively small part of the film with him.

CHARLES HELFENSTEIN

The movie is remarkably similar to the book. Minor differences here and there. No chronology jump/flashback, but if I were to point out the biggest deviation, it would probably be Tracy. The casting of Diana Rigg changed the script a bit, specifically adding the fight scene at Piz Gloria between her and Grunther, because of her fighting prowess demonstrated in *The Avengers* TV series. She's a bit more capable, a bit less damaged than the Tracy of the book.

LISA FUNNELL

(author, *For His Eyes Only: The Women of James Bond*)

The women in Bond films *have* changed over time, which only makes sense because you're interacting with different politics, right? You have the Women's Movement in the '60s, the feminist backlash of the '70s and '80s, and you've got post-feminism in the '90s. You see Bond and his relationship with these women changing as the broader politics for women are changing.

DAVID F. WALKER

(author, *Reflections on Blaxploitation: Actors and Directors Speak*)

I've joked for years that the worst form of venereal disease is having sex with James Bond, because you have sex with him and there's a better than 50/50 chance you'll be dead.

JOHN CORK

The role of women in the *Bond* movies constantly evolves. Despite the attitude of the era, Fleming wrote complex characters. Many times for the women, that complexity was overshadowed by the sexuality. Most viewers remember Honey Ryder walking from the sea, but don't talk about her tale of being raped and murdering her rapist. Tatiana in *From Russia with Love* is sexually exploited by SPECTRE. Domino in *Thunderball* has sold her soul for the access to luxury and security that Largo provides, and the underlying sadness in her character certainly enriches the film for me.

LISA FUNNELL

The women in the Brosnan era are a lot more, I would say, physically empowered. I love Michelle Yeoh. You watch her as Wai Lin in *Tomorrow Never Dies* and she kills it on-screen. She is, in my opinion, a superior agent to James Bond, which is why she only appears for about half the film, because if she appeared for the whole thing, it wouldn't be a *James Bond* film, it would be a Wai Lin film, because she's *that* awesome.

GLEN OLIVER

It's a foregone conclusion that the #MeToo movement will impact how *Bond* Girls are conceived and presented in the future. However, this had been stirring within the franchise for some time, so the shift isn't entirely attributable to #MeToo. Obviously Lois Chiles' character in *Moonraker* and Barbara Bach's Anya in *The Spy Who Loved Me* portended this evolution as far back as the late '70s. In the Brosnan era, notably, *Bond* Girls shifted toward more proactive, generally stronger characterizations overall—a trend which more or less continued into the Craig years. Women became less of a target for Bond's conquest and more of a challenge for him—more of an equal—without 007 ever losing his flirty edge. He was still a horndog, but he was a horndog who didn't always get his way and could actually be put in his place.

LISA FUNNELL

One of my biggest frustrations about the Daniel Craig era, and specifically *Skyfall* and *Spectre,* is that the women are very disempowered.

JOHN CORK

Clearly Bond's behavior in some of the early films is completely outrageous. The rape-conversion of Pussy Galore is a scene one would be unlikely to tolerate in a modern film. But Bond's behavior is designed to be shocking. He was on the vanguard of the sexual revolution, a man who unashamedly enjoyed casual sex, who pursued women, and who used sex in his arsenal of weapons, as do many of the women in the films. If characters played by Scarlett Johansson in *Lucy* and *The Avengers* can exploit their sexuality to basically lure the enemy to his death, Bond certainly can exploit his sexuality. And make no mistakes, he is a sex object in the films. The filmmakers find a way to get Sean Connery shirtless in all of his *Bond* films. Roger Moore is shirtless in all but two of his *Bond* films (*Mooraker* and *For Your Eyes Only*). The filmmakers were adamant that the writers find a way to get Brosnan shirtless in *Die Another Day,* and if you ever watched *Casino Royale* with a large audience, you can hear some women's reaction to Daniel Craig in the nude torture scene. That atmosphere of sexuality is part of the human experience, part of *Bond*'s universe. As long as it is a two-way street and consensual, let's hope it doesn't disappear.

JOHN LANDIS
(director, *Animal House*)

Pussy Galore was the most interesting *Bond* Girl to me because she was so capable in the twisted Ian Fleming way. I mean, she's clearly a gay woman, who Bond converted in her Flying Circus of dykes. It's just so silly.

LISA FUNNELL

People have said that Madeleine Swann in *Spectre* is the best female character in the whole franchise, and I'm, like, "No!" Not only because of her decision to say, "I want to walk away," which was not respected. She tried to walk away and then she was kidnapped, so her choice is taken away. She becomes the princess in the castle way up high. She has to be physically lifted by James Bond, who rescues her like the damsel in distress, and she falls in love with him. There's something very regressive about this type of fairy tale. Even Disney films are not like that anymore. Even Disney Princess stories are, like, "We need to have empowered female characters who are fighting for a whole variety of reasons, and not just to get married." Disney's moving away from this, and the *James Bond* franchise is, like, "You *can* be a princess in a castle." You did *not* want to be in the theater when I watched *Spectre*.

GLEN OLIVER

This kind of thinking is essential on several levels. We do live in different times, so how women are approached in the franchise has to be factored in as both a moral and commercial consideration. Especially in a post–*Fast and the Furious* world, and especially given that the franchise's approach to women was somewhat questionable all along. Sure, there were archetypes and stereotypes and "that *Bond* vibe" to consider. But, when stepping back and viewing many female *Bond* characters through a clear lens, there was most certainly objectification afoot as well.

LISA FUNNELL

For the actresses playing the *Bond* Girls, it's a very high-profile role that gives her a lot of exposure globally. Now does that actually translate into, say, other opportunities and roles? That just depends on the particular actor who's in the role, but it's also being put into a role where you're being set up as a predetermined sex symbol. It is a very specific type of role, and when you do have something like that, it's going to define your career. Your persona's going to be associated with this image and I think that some of the women have been comfortable with that, with their presentation, and have really embraced being a *Bond* Girl. There are others who look back and say, "I'm not too happy with the way that I was represented, the type of role. I wasn't really comfortable with what I saw." Maud Adams has been the most vocal about that, looking back on her stuff and being, like, "I'm not too comfortable with what I saw or how I was treated as a woman in film." It just depends on the particular woman.

GLEN OLIVER

Removing arguments of right or wrong, intention or happenstance, misogyny or era-specific appropriateness, the simple truth of the matter is that 007 narratives will only be strengthened through the presence of stronger female characters. And, if attention is paid to writing and directing, it's very, very possible to have some fun with the "Bond as a ladies' man" conceit in a number of conceptually provocative ways which have yet to be explored. Ways which will only enrich his character, or our understanding of it at least, tremendously.

LISA FUNNELL

You watch Diana Rigg on *Game of Thrones*, and I'm, like, "It's Diana Rigg, you better listen to her!" For me, Diana Rigg made *On Her Majesty's Secret Service* successful. She reminds me of Vesper Lynd in the fact that she was a multidimensional character. She had an emotional development over the course of the film, and it was brilliantly acted. She was also someone who showed a lot of great courage and vulnerability at the same time. That vulnerability's actually a strength and not a weakness. It's a very positive and endearing quality in a character, and you saw her get into the heart of James Bond and really enliven that film.

There were also some interesting, and surprising, moments between Tracy and Blofeld that had some interesting acting going on between Rigg and Savalas.

RAY MORTON

(senior editor, *Script* magazine)

Simon Raven was brought in to polish some of the dialogue—seemingly another case of someone being brought in to "English up" Maibaum's script, which he did successfully. Raven's work is most noticeable in the scene between Tracy and Blofeld, most notably the poem Tracy quotes to distract him, which is quite lovely. His is not a major contribution, but certainly a welcome one.

PETER HUNT

The scenes forming between Telly Savalas and Diana Rigg were designed to make the dialogue a little bit sharper, a little better, a little more intellectual.

Playing no small part in the enlivening of the film is also the action, much of it taking place in the Swiss Alps and involving ski chases, battles on bobsled runs (including a battle between Bond and Blofeld), and even an avalanche. But what feels different about *On Her Majesty's Secret Service* compared to many of the other films in the series is that the action feels organic, born out of the situation rather than something the writers came up with first and grafted a story on top of. And much of this fell to John Glen, serving as editor and second-unit director and who would, in years to come, direct more 007 films than anyone else.

MICHAEL REED

(director of photography, *On Her Majesty's Secret Service*)

Peter Hunt wanted wherever possible to shoot in actual locations and still retain the sophisticated quality of the previous *Bond* films. We discussed with [production designer] Syd Cain the matching problems that we were going to have between studio sets and actual locations. We decided that we would use as many permanent ceilings on studio sets as possible, thus losing all top light and making the action as difficult to light as it would have been if it were shot on location. Peter Hunt was also very keen to use his actors, rather than doubles, in his action sequences and to use as little process work as possible.

TOM SOTER

(author, *Bond and Beyond: 007 and Other Special Agents*)

For Blofeld's Swiss headquarters, the producers selected a resort on the Bernese Oberland at the summit of the 10,000-foot Schilthorn. The Swiss authorities gave permission, and the crew used an out-of-season ski resort for their base. The resort was futuristic enough for old-style *Bond*, and also provided the Swiss Alps as backdrop.

MICHAEL REED

Piz Gloria was the fortresslike structure selected to double for the headquarters of Blofeld. In actual fact, it was a recently completed cable car station and restaurant perched on the top of Schilthorn, overlooking the village of Mürren in the Swiss Alps. Embracing a 360-degree panoramic view of the surrounding mountain peaks, which included the Eiger and Jungfrau, it was a wonderful "find" on the part of Harry Saltzman and Cubby Broccoli.

TOM SOTER

What Piz Gloria lacked was a heliport, a reasonably important element of the story. As they had done in the past, Broccoli and Saltzman dealt with this problem by building what they needed, spending $125,000 to have over 500 tons of cement and equipment carried to the peak. The film crew also commandeered the final, 3,000-foot leg of the local cable car system for crew transportation to and from the ski resort.

GEORGE LAZENBY

When I was in Switzerland, I wasn't happy there. I was working two units and I was in the same place all the time. I was stuck on that bloody mountain day and night for six months.

STEVEN JAY RUBIN

Not only were there excellent ski runs near Mürren, but it proved to be a good location for the bobsled run, which was built on the site of an older run that had been closed since 1937.

That run would serve as something of a proving ground for John Glen, who describes his career as being in a "bit of a trough" at that point. He had directed an episode of the television series *Man in a Suitcase*, and was working in the dubbing theater of the film *The Italian Job* when the phone rang and Peter Collinson, that film's director, told him that Peter Hunt was calling from Pinewood.

JOHN GLEN

Peter Collinson turned around and said, "He wants you to have a job on the new *Bond* picture." I took the call and Peter said, "Get your ass over to Pinewood. I've got a proposition for you." I hadn't really had much to do with Peter for many years, but he said, "I've been following your career and watching your progress," as one does when you've known someone for so long. I got permission from Collinson to leave immediately to go over to Pinewood, where Peter Hunt was directing George Lazenby and Diana Rigg. He said, "Sit over there and read this sequence," and it was the bobsleigh run. So I read this thing and it was a couple of pages at the most. Next thing, as Peter's finished his shot, he comes over and says, "What do you think?" "I love it." "Would you like to direct it?"

I could hardly believe what I was hearing. He said, "I've got to square it with Cubby Broccoli and Harry Saltzman, but I'm pretty certain everything will work out," and, sure enough, on Monday I was flying first class to Switzerland for a whole new career, if you like, in the big league.

Glen and Hunt met at Mürren on the Bernese Oberland and walked around the bob run, which was actually melting away as it had been a very mild winter. But then it began to snow heavily and Glen went to work. Two or three weeks later, he had an unexpected guest on the set: Cubby Broccoli.

JOHN GLEN

He came down to see the bob run, and that was the first time I'd really met him. He said, "I'd love to have a ride on the bob run," and I said, "I'd rather you didn't," because he's quite a heavy man. We got him on the four-man bob and he sat in the middle with the driver in the front and the brakeman in the back, and he went down, did one of the fastest runs because of his weight. The heavier you are, the faster they go, and he did this fantastic run down, which he never, ever forgot about. He *loved* it. He said it was the most fantastic experience, and I was just thankful that he survived it. Quite obviously I didn't want to go down in history as being responsible for killing Cubby Broccoli.

The bobsleigh run was the setting for an integral part of the film, which saw Bond pursuing Blofeld in it and the two of them getting into a battle with each other.

JOHN GLEN

Frank Capose came over and introduced me to his protégés, Heinz Leu and Robert Zimmerman. Heinz, who was to double for Bond, was a champion bobsled driver and Zurich businessman. Robert was brakeman for the national team and an Olympic skier. Their enthusiasm nearly caused their downfall. We had progressed to the shots of Bond and Blofeld fighting on the one sleigh. The first take had been too tame. If I had known a little more about bobsleighs, I would have realized the difficulty of negotiating Stone Curve while having a punch-up at the same time. I asked them to be more animated if they could. Unfortunately, I couldn't see their reaction over the radio, though they agreed to try. They were animated alright, fighting and punching away while going very fast. Halfway through the curve, the frontrunner went out of the run and an arc of splintered ice came from the top of the wall as they both swerved sideways. Heinz was thrown into the run and proceeded along on his backside, still traveling at the rate the bob was going when he fell off, while Robert fought to keep the bob from falling onto him. When the bob did drop back into the run, Heinz got up without a scratch. Robert was not so fortunate. He got caught in the machinery, suffered injuries to his face, and was flown to the doctor, where he had stitches inserted inside his mouth. Two hours later, a swollen-faced Robert reported back for duty.

The scene toward the end of the bob run sequence, in which Blofeld's head gets caught in a tree branch overhanging the run, was proving to be very difficult to shoot successfully. Our stuntmen were putting their faith in a cable attached to [stuntman] Joe Powell's back by means of a harness, with a shock absorber anchored to a tree. It looked terribly dangerous to me and much too complicated. On the take the cable broke from the harness, and Joe smacked the tree with a terrible bang and fell on his back into the run. None of us fancied trying that one a second time. Peter eventually solved the problem with front projection. Shooting with the camera reversed, he had the artist lowered down from the branch in front of one of our moving plates and finished with a frame cut right there. This rather brutal scene got a good laugh in cinemas, because the excitement had built to such a pitch that the audience welcomed something to release the tension.

On Her Majesty's Secret Service presented what would be the first of several ski chases in the films (*The Spy Who Loved Me, For Your*

Eyes Only, Octopussy did as well), but this one was particularly innovative.

JOHN GLEN

I worked with Diana Rigg and Lazenby. We made up a sledge, which Lazenby would kneel on, and then I would do all the skiing scenes, the avalanche scenes, and things like that. That would be given him for two or three days, and we'd go to Kleine Scheidegg, which has a wonderful three-mile slope, and I would get all my expert skiers around and we'd put George on the sledge, on his knees, and I would have Willy Wagner, who was my cameraman, shoot him. Willy was a wizard at skiing with a camera that he held, and he could ski backwards and forwards equally well, and also his skis had points on both ends, believe it or not. He could get very realistic scenes of skiing handheld, and then I would have other skiers zoom in on the sides, just out of shot, throwing ice and snow in front of the lens of the camera. It made it very realistic.

But because I was working the principals and doubles separately, most of my action scenes would be done with doubles. When I *did* get the principals, Diana and George, I had to show their faces. I couldn't have big doubles on the leading actors, otherwise they could be anybody. So it was a question of goggles up, goggles down. At the start of a scene, I would say, "Lift goggles!" They'd be skiing around and the villains would start firing at them or something, so goggles down. If you look at that scene, you'll see goggles up, goggles down all the time, but it was common sense to me that you had to see their faces, otherwise you could, again, be working with anyone.

RIC MEYERS

Physically, George Lazenby and *On Her Majesty's Secret Service* was Peter Hunt unleashed, with John Glen as second-unit director and George Leech as stunt arranger. Bob Simmons was nowhere in sight and, according to the credits, Lazenby, an increasingly insecure amateur who masked it with arrogance, was doubled by at least four people. It ultimately mattered, but at least during the production, Lazenby's youth and willingness to create kinetic fights seem to predict the best of mixed martial arts decades later.

JOHN GLEN

The only thing that worried me about George Lazenby was that he was so keen to get on the skis. Can you imagine? I was responsible for the three days that I was working with him; responsible for his welfare. Next thing I see, I look around and he's got skis on and he's with all the world champion skiers and he's trying to ski. If he breaks a leg or breaks an arm on that, we're buggered, aren't we? The film could be put on hold for three months, I'm fired, and that's the end of my career. So I was very concerned. I was quite pleased after three days when he actually went back to the first unit and my responsibility was over. But I did enjoy working with him.

The highlight of the film, and the thing that genuinely separates *On Her Majesty's Secret Service* from all others (except perhaps to some degree the 2006 *Casino Royale*), is the fact that James Bond not only truly falls in love, but ends up getting married. The marriage is short-lived and tragic, though, when Irma Bunt (nefariously played by Ilse Steppat, who, sadly, died at 52 just days after the film's premiere) kills her via machine gun in the film's melancholy coda. The aftermath features Lazenby's best scene as he cradles the dead Tracy in his arms and tells a policeman not to worry, that they have all the time in the world–just before the haunting Louis Armstrong (who was ill and would shortly thereafter pass away as well) song of the same name plays over the closing credits.

Director Peter Hunt has talked about the fact that he thought the film could have ended with the tracking shot of the Aston Martin leaving the wedding as M, Moneypenny, and Q, along with Tracy's father (played by a superb Gabriele Ferzetti, who almost steals the film with his morally ambiguous character of Marc-Ange Draco), watch Bond drive off into the horizon. The pre-title sequence of the following film could have been Blofeld assassinating Tracy. One can only wonder how the happier ending might have improved this film's box-office fortunes, although we'll never know.

PETER HUNT

I thought the perfect ending for the film could have been the marriage. After the wedding, I go right up on a crane as they drive off, and then you could have started the next *James Bond* film with them driving, the honeymoon, stopping to take the flowers off the car and her getting shot, and then the titles. You could have gone on from there. That was dramatically how it *should* have been. It would have worked beautifully well.

CHARLES HELFENSTEIN

Peter Hunt has mentioned this idea a few times in interviews as something that was considered, but none of the production documents, script drafts, or any other written evidence exists that suggest it was going to happen. And taking away the gut punch of an ending would negate the entire emotional journey of the film.

PETER HUNT

I always had a definite idea about the way the wedding should be conceived. From all the action and what have you, we wanted to take a breath in the film, which gave us the opportunity for Bond and Tracy to look at one another and become emotionally involved. In the script it was the idea that she would propose to him, but I didn't like that idea. I thought that Bond should always be the stronger character and should be the doer. And with the supposed animosity between the actors, and the annoyance or whatever, there was certainly nothing when we were shooting the scene.

I wanted to film it in Portugal, and I wanted the film to go from the cold climate of Switzerland to a very sunny, warm climate, which gives it a wonderful juxtaposition and change. We needed a flat beach bordered by a road that they would be driving on when Tracy is killed; this was one of the scenes that is in the book. Now it is not very easy to find this anywhere. You can find it in the Mediterranean, but I said I didn't want Mediterranean waves. I had a very dramatic scene and I wanted big waves. I was told I couldn't put it into the Atlantic, and of course what I really wanted was the best of both worlds between the Atlantic and the Mediterranean.

Well, I found that in Portugal. I somehow had an instinct and a knowledge that one would be able to find it just between the area where the Atlantic joins the Mediterranean; indeed, we found the only place I should think of in Europe where this great long beach runs parallel with the road. Most other places in Europe are vacation spots with promenades, and that's always difficult, because they're not isolated. They have tourists around. Indeed, we sent a production manager all over Europe to try and find a location. In the end, we sent him to Portugal.

The death of Tracy proved difficult for Lazenby, who feels that he was pretty much left to his own devices in terms of approaching that dramatic moment in the film, though there was a bit of lightness as well.

GEORGE LAZENBY

I'll tell you one thing about the final scene. I had learned a little bit about acting and Diana was biting my leg while she was in my lap, and I said, "Why are you biting my bloody leg?" And she said, "To make you feel sad." "Well, it's starting to turn me on, would you stop?"

PETER HUNT

One of his best moments is when she's shot. We got up there at eight in the morning. I insisted he was on set, and I sat him in the car and made him rehearse and rehearse all day long, and I broke him down until he was absolutely exhausted, and by the time we shot it at five o'clock, he was exhausted. *That's* how I got the performance at the end of the film. He thought it was me being unpleasant to him, but I couldn't say, "Now listen, George. I'm going to do this because it's the best way to get you to react." Maybe I did things like that all the way through, because I knew how to get emotions out of him, but he didn't seem to think that that was fair.

GEORGE LAZENBY

I read the book again just before I did the scene to give me the feeling. And it did. When I did that scene in the car at the end, I had tears rolling down my face and he said, "Cut!" I thought, "Jeez, I was doing that scene well," and he said, "James Bond doesn't cry. Do it without the tears." That scene would have been heavy duty with the tears.

Behind the scenes there were personnel problems as well. According to Lazenby, he didn't get along with Peter Hunt, the two of them having a major falling out early in production. And then there were rumors of trouble between him and Diana Rigg, to the point where she reportedly ate garlic right before their love scene (though some played this off as a joke).

GEORGE LAZENBY

When we were on set, the first assistant gave me a loud-hailer and said, "As a favor, just say into the loud-hailer, 'Anyone that's not needed on this set right now, could you please leave?'" I didn't know what I was doing; I just did it. Then Peter Hunt arrives and said, "How dare you?" I said, "How dare I what?" "They were all my friends and you told them to leave." He never spoke to me again; he would get the assistant director to pass his comments down to me.

PETER HUNT

I don't know why he should say that, because it's quite untrue. You can't possibly have a new, young guy who has never been an actor and not talk to him. You simply can't do it. I had to tell him where to go and what to do. The whole thing with him is that he changes his mind all the time. But he had to do what I wanted him to do. Indeed, we had long conversations during and before we even started shooting. I wouldn't have gone with him if Diana Rigg hadn't assured me that she liked him enormously at that time before we started shooting, and that she would do everything to help and work with him.

DIANA RIGG

I did the best I could, but, oh dear lord, he had a perfectly good chance, and he wasn't bad in the film, was he? It was perfectly good, it was just that he was impossible to deal with. That is a classic example of somebody who doesn't know how to deal with fame and got it wrong.

GEORGE LAZENBY

Well, she's got her problems. You can't talk down to her, or talk at her, you've got to talk *up* to her, and this is the same with Telly Savalas and everybody else. Everyone bad-mouthed everyone else. Peter was bad-mouthing the producers, the producers were bad-mouthing the director. I found on the whole picture, the only one you could get any honesty out of at all was from the guy who was supposed to be the most evil of all: Harry Saltzman. Harry Saltzman is the straightest shooter of all of them, and because of his being a straight shooter, he's the most disliked. He's got no diplomacy. He doesn't come in and say, "Just a minute, excuse me, can I talk to you?" He comes in and says, "This is what we're gonna do over here," and it doesn't go down well with these people, because they're all so egotistical. I thought I was the only one with an ego—I was the guy who was supposed to have the big ego.

JOHN GLEN

He was his own worst enemy. I didn't know him that well, but I'd worked with him for three days and I'd gotten along with him. I was at the music session with John Barry, and this fellow comes into the music stage when I was there and he kept looking at me and grinning. I thought, "Who the hell is that?" He looked like he'd been sleeping rough somewhere. He had a full beard and he was looking very scruffy, but he kept grinning at me. He said, "You don't recognize me, do you, John?" I said, "George?" And Cubby got *so* angry, because he was trying to promote this chap as James Bond and he's looking like a tramp. He says he was asked to continue with other films, and it's possible, but I was around at that time and I don't think he was *ever* going to do a second *Bond* film. He should've been a bit more disciplined, but that's his character. He's a wild Australian guy.

PETER HUNT

I think it's a measure of the man's personality. He changed about all over the place when it all went to his head. You must remember that he was an ordinary little guy from the backwoods of Australia and he was suddenly thrust into a very sophisticated area of filmmaking, and it was very difficult for him.

JOHN GLEN

George and Diana had a bit of a run-in at the end, but she did everything she could to help George. She was the consummate professional actress. She was *so* professional and George was the opposite. He didn't take it too seriously and she did. It's a shame they fell out the way they did; there was all that business about garlic on their breath and all that stuff during the love scenes. All of that was bad publicity, really, if there is such a thing.

A big part of the problems Lazenby faced was from the fact that midway through production he decided that *On Her Majesty's Secret Service* would be his one and only *James Bond* film. He simply refused to sign a contract for additional cinematic adventures.

GEORGE LAZENBY

I had the feeling that somewhere along the line, this has got to slow down, but it didn't. I kept saying to myself, "I'll learn my lines a little quicker tomorrow night and get some time to myself." But it never worked out that way. Whenever they saw I had some time to myself, they'd throw me in with some reporter, or take me to some dinner party to publicize something. I was in and out of doorways, planes, and restaurants without ever touching the ground. I never made a friend in the whole period; I was never standing in one place long enough.

On top of that, they got me to sign a letter of intent, then after the movie when I wouldn't sign the contract, they did a privy council, which is when they have a fake court hearing to see who would win. And I would have won, because I'd never been an actor before. And signing a document that I'd never seen, which was the contract, was meaningless. So I have them over a barrel. That's why they offered me a million dollars and any movie I wanted to do in between *Bond* movies. But they made the mistake of not letting me read the contract before I signed the letter of intent. If I'd have been an actor before and had signed a contract like that, I would have lost.

Ronan O'Rahilly was the guy that talked me into it. He started Radio Caroline that launched all these English pop groups, and he said, "There's a guy called Clint Eastwood. He's doing a Western in Italy. It takes him a month and he gets 500 grand. You can do two of those movies in two months and get a million dollars." And I believed him. Then, United Artists invited me to their office and Ronan came with me. They had a room full of books and they said, "We have the film rights to all these books. You can do any one of them in between *Bond* movies. We just need you to sign the contract." I said, "No," because Ronan said no. He was waving his hands behind them saying, "No!" And then, when we walked out, I said, "Why won't you let me sign that?" He said, "If you'd have signed that, they wouldn't give you anything but *Bond*-type movies in between *Bond* movies. They wouldn't ruin the image of Bond." I said, "Fair enough." So, anyway, I believed I could make money in Italy or anywhere.

There was another part of it as well: with Ronan O'Rahilly whispering in his ear, Lazenby was convinced that James Bond was out of style and just *this side* of being considered passé.

GEORGE LAZENBY

I was out one night and some guy called out to me, "Waiter!" I look around and everyone else has got long hair, bell-bottoms, and flowered shirts. The hippies had come out. I also found out that it was very hard to get laid in the suit. I thought, "What's the point of doing James Bond? What's life all about?" Later, I felt sorry for myself when I was running around Europe with a pregnant lady, who became my wife, and my daughter, and having no money. And I thought, "Jeez, I should have done another *Bond* movie," but then things started to happen. I went over and saw Bruce Lee and he gave me some money, but he died three days after he did so, so I couldn't do the movie with him that I was going to do. I *did* do three movies with his company. Then I got back on my feet again.

I also felt it was Sean Connery's gig, you know? I can't do it better than him, because he created it on his personality, and I had to copy his personality, basically. So it wasn't me, it was me trying to do the best I could playing Sean Connery playing James Bond. They changed my accent not to a Scottish one, but to an English, and changed my walk, and then let me loose. I just did it the way I did it.

On Her Majesty's Secret Service opened to mixed reviews on December 18, 1969, grossing a little over $22 million domestically–about half of what *You Only Live Twice* pulled in and indicating that the franchise was seemingly in a downward spiral. Nonetheless, it not only ultimately turned a profit, but over the years many have reassessed its strengths, and George Lazenby has certainly inspired fervent support among some fans.

RIC MEYERS

It's hard for me to truly picture what the action in *On Her Majesty's Secret Service* would look like if Connery's had stayed. Given Connery's age, 39 at the time I believe, *Bond*-weariness, and general, shall we say, mass, I doubt Peter Hunt would have deviated too much from the gladiatorial machismo of the Bond that had been. But with Lazenby being 10 years younger—and certainly slimmer—sharp, kinetic, at times acrobatic fight scenes resulted. It is the one area of his performance that no one I know of faults. Sadly, the same could not be said of his taste in clothes, behavior, accent, and line-reading. It was as if someone had let an eager Aussie stand-in do all Bond's scenes as a favor (and, by the way, I don't consider "Oh come on, Ric, he really wasn't that bad" to be high praise).

RAY MORTON

Along with *From Russia with Love*, Richard Maibaum's screenplay for *On Her Majesty's Secret Service* is the best cinematic adaptation of an Ian Fleming novel. Had Connery stayed with the series, it would probably be considered the best *Bond* film or at least the best of the thriller *Bond*s. With Lazenby's amateurish performance, it's been reduced to an also-ran. But it's still a terrific movie based on a terrific screenplay.

GLEN OLIVER

The chief issue with *On Her Majesty's Secret Service* isn't Lazenby—it's the confluence of asking audiences to settle into a new Bond (which is always a funky and sometimes lengthy acclimation at best) while also asking audiences to invest in a highly atypical, uncharacteristically emotional *James Bond* story. These two demands are disparate, and were difficult to reconcile at best. Thus, the picture was hamstrung by a perceptual disconnect or distancing. Taking Bond on this particular journey was challenging enough given how the franchise had developed the character up to that point. Piling a required adaptation to a new Bond on top of that? Probably wasn't a stellar notion, was a great deal to ask of an audience, and was never destined to unequivocally connect narratively.

JOHN CORK

All of the trappings around Lazenby were so lush and he looks the part so well, but when you watch the master cut, you realize how scared and fish-out-of-water he looks in those shots. How utterly unprepared he is to be in that role. If you watch the documentary *Becoming Bond*—they call it a documentary, but it's 80 percent a reenactment—he is the proverbial dog chasing the car and he actually catches it, and is being dragged along behind it. The thing he said to me, and he may say it in *Becoming Bond,* is, "The reason I got the role is because I wanted it more than anyone else." And you could probably get that same line from him if you spoke to him today. He *did* work harder for it, but if you look at that scene where he goes into his room and Diana Rigg has got his gun, it's, like, "What if I want to shoot you for the thrill?" And you look at the way she knows how to hold herself as an actress, you look at the way she knows how to move, and the confidence with which she's playing that character, and you believe she is this woman who is right at the edge of being completely unhinged. And he doesn't. He has no idea how to respond to that scene.

GEORGE LAZENBY

There were moments there where Peter Hunt saved me, and there were moments there where I was blank and I shouldn't have been; where I thought I could fake it, and get away with it. There were other moments where I thought, "This is a great movie." I wish I had known more about this business before I did the goddamn movie and I could have put more into it. It's a shame, really, that they take $10 million and let a guy walk around starring in a movie that's never been an actor. But that's what they think of actors.

JOHN CORK

You can look at the way he plays that scene . . . compare it to Sean Connery playing the scene in *From Russia with Love* where he realizes Tatiana has betrayed him and Kerim Bey is dead. He loses his temper and he hits her. He's trying to figure out, in this moment of, "How the hell do I deal with this situation? This is no longer a game, this has real consequences and people are dying. And I'm sitting here literally in bed with somebody who's likely to cause great damage to everything I believe in."

Connery's performance in that scene . . . everything that's going through his mind . . . on his face, the incredibly subtle changes that he's doing. And Lazenby, he didn't have that background. That wasn't who he was. Basically a lot of leading men play themselves. Lazenby is playing himself in *Majesty's* and Lazenby is a guy who was in way over his head. That's what you see on his face throughout the film, to me. And this is no knock to George Lazenby, who's a charming, amazing, witty, wonderful guy on so many levels. He's got all that in spades and he's lived a lot more life now and has been through a lot more. When you watch him in a film that he did well after *Majesty's*, there's really interesting elements in the performance he gives. But in *Majesty's* there's a reason that Peter Hunt had Lazenby redubbed for a huge section of the film. And, of course, that undercuts him, and there are other things in the script that undercut, like playing gay but you're not really gay—that doesn't work for Bond.

GLEN OLIVER

If *On Her Majesty's Secret Service* had been put together with any established Bond (even if, in some alternate reality, it had been the third or fourth Lazenby *Bond* picture), it would unconditionally and without reservation be the best 007 movie ever made. As is, and on the whole, I believe it still manages to be the best of the *Bond* films—but not unconditionally, and despite itself. This is based chiefly on the raw vitality of its filmmaking, and the fact that—despite the adaptive obstacles mentioned above—it is so unique in its essence. It also helps that Lazenby didn't entirely drop the ball—although the argument that the same story should've been with a more established and tuned Bond will always overshadow the picture.

FRED DEKKER

(director, *RoboCop 3*)

On Her Majesty's Secret Service is one of the five great ones. First off, I'm a huge Lazenby fan. He's my third favorite Bond; I think he's terrific. He's a little young, but he's incredibly charming and I think he plays everything he's supposed to play. People talk about him being wooden and all that, and I just don't buy it. He's good. He plays the end very well. It's just that he's not Connery. If he had grown into it and done the next three or four, I think he would now be considered on par with at least Roger Moore. But it was the first one that took an emotional approach to the character, that actually said, "Okay, let's pretend that he could actually fall in love." Partly because of Diana Rigg and partly because of Peter Hunt, it just works like gangbusters.

JOHN CORK

Peter Hunt, Harry Saltzman, and Cubby Broccoli all believed they had created Sean Connery. They thought they could create another Bond out of Lazenby. That did George a great disservice. They didn't understand the hard work Connery put into becoming an actor. Connery had read everything from Shakespeare to Shaw. He had been studying movement, grooming himself passionately for years to carry a film. He had worked on the stage, on television, in many films. Lazenby got the part without the depth of experience he needed, finding himself paired with a director who was not experienced working with actors.

GLEN OLIVER

Lazenby gets dragged a lot for his performance as Bond, but I think this is unfair. There is abundant anecdotal evidence indicating The Powers That Be were never interested in simply revisiting an established "take" on the character when recasting the role. Which is fundamentally wise, and should remain standard OP in the future. Everyone sees something different in Bond—everyone *wants* something different from that character. No one Bond can be everyone's cup of tea at any given time. A problem largely addressed by shaking up the role every few years.

His take on the character has always fascinated me. Whether because of the way he approached it, or whether due to some meta spillover from being uncomfortable on set (or both), his Bond always felt a little more human to me. A little more *practiced* suave, instead of being naturally suave. A little more "holding on," a little less "on top." "Everyman" is too strong a word. "Identifiable" might be better—perhaps even "fake it until you make it." In this regard, he came across as a bit more like *Die Hard*'s John McClane, thus he was a bit more accessible. Those looking for a super agent? That's not what Lazenby's 007 was about. This is evident simply in the way he throws a punch—he's *really* hauling to land those jabs. He's not an assassinating machine like Brosnan's or Dalton's Bond. Lazenby's Bond came across as an operative who is working his ass off, slugging his way through, and trying not to get himself smoked in the process. A difficult balancing act at best. Lazenby did just fine. If someone has issues surrounding his casting, perhaps they're questioning that particular interpretation of the character rather than him.

JOHN CORK

I was friends with Peter Hunt and we socialized a little bit together in his later years. I have great respect for what he brought to not just the *Bond* films, but because of the way that his editing was so innovative on the *Bond* films that it helped shift the way movies were edited, the way action got presented on film. Peter was an incredibly sharp editor and did a lot of pick-up shots and second-unit directing, obviously, on *Chitty Chitty Bang Bang* and on *You Only Live Twice*. But he was *not* prepared to walk into the director's position on *Majesty's* any more than Lazenby was prepared to walk in as the lead actor. One of the first rules in film is you don't work with too many first-timers. You can have a hunk of them, but if you get too many of them . . . I'm not sure if there was a way to solve the George Lazenby problem. That was a Harry Saltzman issue. Cubby certainly went along with it, but with the casting of Lazenby their theory was, "We want James Bond to be the star, not the actor that plays him. It's the only way we can survive." And that premise was absolutely the right premise for them to take, but it took them *Majesty's*, Connery coming back in *Diamonds Are Forever*, and then *Live and Let Die*—really a six-year period—to make it all pay off and to actually establish that as something that was a workable proposition for *Bond*.

ALBERT R. BROCCOLI

It was a very good film. It was his first film, and we . . . didn't agree with Mr. Lazenby, and he didn't agree with us, or any of the crew, and it became an impossible situation.

JOHN CORK

I think the mistake was to rely on a first-time director with a first-time actor. Peter Hunt was incredibly talented, but he thought he could fix everything in post. He thought he could shape Lazenby's performance in the editing room. Lazenby, who has a lot of talent, needed a great actor's director, and then he needed a studio committed to selling him as the new James Bond. By the end of production, that wasn't the case.

> There's a certain irony in the fact that Lazenby made the conscious decision to leave *James Bond* behind him before he'd even finished shooting the film, yet today, 50 years after *On Her Majesty's Secret Service* reached theaters, it remains the film that he's still most known for.

GEORGE LAZENBY

You know, it never goes away. Of course, if *James Bond* films had stopped being made 40 years ago, probably no one would be talking to me now, but it's never gone away in my life. I mean, I'll be in a bar and some guy will be staring at me and say, "Are you George?" It seems like that happens to me weekly or monthly or whatever. And that's both a good and a bad thing, I suppose. One, you can't be incognito too easily. Secondly, people know you and talk to you and help you out and do all that sort of thing. You can get things done better than most people, so it does have its upside, too. Everything does. But if I'd stayed a motor mechanic, I'd have had a much simpler life.

DAVID V. PICKER

On Her Majesty's Secret Service opened to decent reviews, but most pointed out the obvious—that Lazenby was no Connery. So what else was new? I'm not sure if anyone could have survived being first out of the bullpen to replace Sean but, in any case, it surely wasn't going to be Lazenby. Business was considerably less than *You Only Live Twice*, and it was clear the franchise was in trouble.

THE SEVENTIES: GO MR. BIG OR GO HOME

"Look after Mister Bond. See that some harm comes to him."

Welcome to the 1970s, Mr. Bond. The Sixties were over. It had been a decade of seemingly limitless possibilities in which boundaries were being pushed and the placid 1950s gave way to the tragic assassination of a president and the hardening of the battle lines of the Cold War—including the Cuban Missile Crisis—only to transition to the kaleidoscopic, psychedelic era of the Summer of Love and Woodstock and the passing of the Civil Rights Act. A time in which real political and sociological change seemed within reach, and a succession of mind-blowing motion pictures began pushing the very envelope of the art form, from 1967's *The Graduate, Bonnie & Clyde,* and *Guess Who's Coming to Dinner,* to 1968's *2001: A Space Odyssey* and *Rosemary's Baby* to 1969's *Butch Cassidy and The Sundance Kid, The Wild Bunch, Easy Rider, Midnight Cowboy,* and *Fellini Satyricon*. Unfortunately, the 1970s proved the hangover with Watergate, the fall of Vietnam, the Iran Hostage Crisis, bell-bottoms, and disco. The times they were definitely a-changing and James Bond would definitely have to change with them—for better or worse.

DIAMONDS ARE FOREVER (1971)

Film number seven, *Diamonds Are Forever,* embraces all the gaudy clichés you may associate with that wretched decade. It's broad, over-the-top, tacky, and downright goofy—right down to an overabundance of shag carpeting. That said, Sean Connery's official swan song in the Eon film series (following John Gavin—an American(!)—being *almost* cast as 007) may not be a great film by any means—or even a great *Bond* movie—but that doesn't mean it's not fun—filled with innumerable small pleasures.

After the perceived failure of *On Her Majesty's Secret Service,* whose box-office take had proven unable to match the lofty heights of previous installments, director Peter Hunt was out and replaced by ever-reliable Bond stalwart Guy Hamilton, director of *Goldfinger.* Joining him was the young, mustachioed writer Tom Mankiewicz, charged with making sense of Ian Fleming's novel after veteran *Bond* screenwriter Richard Maibaum and Hamilton failed to find a meeting of the minds.

RAY MORTON

(senior writer, *Script* magazine)

Following the "relatively" disappointing box-office performance of the "relatively" realistic *On Her Majesty's Secret Service,* the producers made a decision to take the series in a more fantastic direction, using *Goldfinger*'s mix of fantasy, humor, and gadgetry as the model. These elements were not Maibaum's forte, so he was replaced after the first drafts of *Diamonds Are Forever* and *The Spy Who Loved Me,* and only called in as a last-minute pinch hitter after Tom Mankiewicz unexpectedly dropped out of *The Man with the Golden Gun,* which I think is his weakest *Bond* screenplay by far. Maibaum sat out *Live and Let Die* and *Moonraker* completely.

JOHN CORK

(author, *The James Bond Encyclopedia*)

David Picker of United Artists, the executive who had wanted *Bond* even before Cubby and Harry came into the office with the rights, found Tom Mankiewicz, whose father was one of the great writer/directors [*All About Eve*'s Joseph Mankiewicz]. I love Richard Maibaum, but I don't think there was a better writer for *Bond* dialogue than Mankiewicz. He was never a genius with story, but he knew how to write words that actors could speak. He knew how to write characters who had unique voices. He knew how to pace a scene. I never felt like there was a wasted word in his dialogue.

TOM MANKIEWICZ
(screenwriter, *Diamonds Are Forever*)

I got involved in a very strange way. I wrote the book for a Broadway musical called *Georgy!* We closed in three nights and I headed home with my tail between my legs—the show had been a disaster. I'd been working on it a year and it was suddenly over. And then I got a call from my agent saying, "How would you like to do a rewrite on a *James Bond* movie?" I *loved* the *James Bond* movies. I was crazy about them, and it turned out totally by accident that David Picker, who was running UA in those days, was one of the 1,500 people who had seen *Georgy!* before it closed. They had a script by Dick Maibaum, but Cubby said, "We need a rewrite and we need a writer who is American, because a lot of it takes place in Las Vegas, but one who can also write in a British idiom." David Picker told him that he had seen a show which had a great book by me the other night, and so I was sent up to see Cubby.

RAY MORTON

Tom Mankiewicz was the ideal writer for the *Bond*-lite era. He had a talent for concocting fantastic plots filled with colorful characters, exciting spectacle, and humor. His dialogue was witty and sophisticated and filled with extremely clever one-liners. Mankiewicz began his tenure on Sean Connery's last turn as Bond, but his style found its ideal interpreter when Roger Moore took over the role in *Live and Let Die*.

TOM MANKIEWICZ

Fleming's original novel is smaller, and I must say there's a line of tension that's missing from it. Fleming, like anyone else, wrote better books and worse books. That being said, the character is always wonderful; Bond is a great character, and Fleming is a marvelous writer.

RAY MORTON

Mankiewicz's scripts were less—often much less—faithful to Fleming than Maibaum's, but he had a much different brief than Maibaum did. Maibaum's job was to bring Ian Fleming's *James Bond* novels to the screen. By the time Mank came along, that task had been accomplished and so his job became to keep an entertainment phenomenon moving forward. At that, I feel he succeeded magnificently.

TOM MANKIEWICZ

They signed me on a two-week guarantee for $1,250 a week, telling me to do the first 30 pages. At the time they were trying to get Sean back. He had turned the script down and they had John Gavin waiting in the wings to play James Bond. They'd only had one James Bond up to then with the exception of *On Her Majesty's Secret Service*, and the audience wanted Sean back.

SEAN CONNERY

(actor, "James Bond")

I don't think *On Her Majesty's Secret Service* worked. I didn't think it was bad, but I don't think it was particularly good. The remarks I'd made about the gadgetry built up to *You Only Live Twice* where they built a volcano and you can't go much farther than that . . . apart from going into space or something, which is a whole different ball game. My feeling about the Lazenby picture was if he kept his mouth shut, he might have come out a lot better. I thought for somebody who had no previous experience, he did quite a good job. I didn't think the direction was all that hot. I didn't think it merited the eleven months it took to shoot. I think it was disappointing, and the proof was that it was not palatable.

RIC MEYERS

(author, *Films of Fury: The Kung Fu Movie Book*)

Here's what I think happened. Lazenby's on- and off-screen behavior left a sour taste in every crew member's mouth. "Operation Get Sean Back" began, but the straw that had broken Connery's back was Eon's refusal to make him a partner. But suddenly he agrees to return as long as they pay him a million, which he publicly gives to charity. Doesn't hold water. No, in my somewhat extensive experience with starring actors, what they seem to want, more than anything else, after a career of rejection, is, understandably, power. When Peter Falk agreed to return as *Columbo* and Angela Lansbury agreed to continue as Jessica Fletcher on *Murder, She Wrote,* it was only because the networks gave them creative control. Although in those cases, and many others, the showrunners and producers fought it, the star always won.

DAVID V. PICKER

(chief executive officer, United Artists)

Arthur [Krim, the then-president of United Artists] called me in and asked if there was any way we could get Connery back for one more film. I called Cubby and Harry, and although they didn't disagree with our analysis, they didn't know what they could do since their relationship with Connery was essentially non-existent and non-speaking. Non-speaking? I had heard *none* of this, certainly not from the producers, who might have thought it was something worth sharing with their partners! Getting no help from Harry and Cubby, I went back to Arthur and proposed that in exchange for doing one more film as Bond, UA should make a deal with Sean to deliver two pictures to us as producer and star of any scripts he wanted to make. We would waive all approvals on cast, director, and script and preapprove the budgets, with each picture to be no more than one million. This would give Sean freedom to guide his career in any direction he wanted. In exchange, he would do one more *Bond* film.

STANLEY SOPEL
(associate producer, *Diamonds Are Forever*)

Why did Sean Connery come back? It's very simple: money! He didn't need the money, but Sean was offered a lot of money, and at the time he was heavily involved with his Scottish International Education Trust, and had promised to give them a very large donation of cash. And he gave it. He gave them his fee on the picture.

SEAN CONNERY

I'd been three years in the process of setting up my own trust, and I decided that I would give the fee to the trust. I would never have that opportunity again, so I took a week out to decide. I was sure that in the film business, again, there would never be that opportunity to make that sort of money. *And* for eighteen weeks' work.

DAVID V. PICKER

His fee would be one million and a piece of the profits. Arthur agreed, and I flew to London to meet with Sean's agent, Richard Hatton. After hearing the proposal, he responded with two changes. First, raise Sean's fee to $1.250 million. Second, a condition of Sean's return was he wouldn't have to talk to either of the producers. After I caught my breath, I said I'd have to run it by Arthur, Harry, and Cubby, but that I would strongly recommend it. Then he added as an aside that if it was approved, Sean was going to donate his entire fee to the Scottish International Education Trust. I must admit that I was just blown away by this little throwaway from Richard. And then he added that he much appreciated our getting involved and if the producers had dealt with Sean appropriately, none of these problems would have occurred.

ROBERT SELLERS
(author, *The Battle for Bond*)

Looking at the films he made after leaving Bond—*Shalako, The Red Tent, The Molly Maguires*—only *The Anderson Tapes* was a success, so obviously he did need a lift in terms of a box-office hit. It's also nice to be wanted, especially as an actor, and the deal he was offered was just too good to refuse—not so much the fee, which he donated to a charity he had just set up, so the timing there was good; no, the real clincher was the offer by United Artists to fund two projects of his own choosing. This was very shrewd on their part, since Connery had begun to talk about a desire to produce his own movies and possibly move into directing. In the end only one of these projects was realized, *The Offence*. I also think the fact that this was a one-off return appealed to him.

STANLEY SOPEL

The fee Sean negotiated, and the percentage of the picture he got, was probably bigger than any actor or actress had gotten ever, in the history of the motion picture business. So he was content to do it on a one-shot basis. It was a romp for him, and he did two things. He gave a large donation to his favorite charity, and had a darn good time doing it.

RIC MEYERS

Yes, Sean Connery would return to the James Bond role, but only if he called the shots. Curiously, a viewer can usually tell when a crew doesn't like a star who has taken over. Suddenly the lighting is darker, the angles are less flattering, and most tellingly, the wardrobe gets wonky—the turtlenecks are too bulky and narrow, the coattails are too short. Take a look at *Star Trek V*. But *Diamonds Are Forever* breaks even that mold.

JOHN CORK

After the massive disappointment of *On Her Majesty's Secret Service*, UA called Cubby and Harry to New York for a heart-to-heart. They laid down the law: no more unlimited budgets and unlimited schedules. The next *Bond* would shoot in the US so that the studio could have more of a voice. No more depressing 007 films. Audiences wanted *Goldfinger*, and that's the tone and style *Bond* needed.

In response, Richard Maibaum had once again pushed to resurrect one of his old chestnuts, the introduction of Goldfinger's twin brother, an idea he brought up regularly on virtually every *Bond* movie he worked on. The only person who apparently liked that idea aside from him was probably actor Gert Fröbe's agent.

JOHN CORK

If the studio wanted *Goldfinger,* well, why not give them Goldfinger's twin brother? So Maibaum dutifully penned a script with Goldfinger's twin in it.

RICHARD MAIBAUM

Goldfinger had a brother who was the villain, who cooked up the whole diamond caper for his purposes. One of the things that I liked about it is that we had a line for him to say, "I think you knew my brother, Auric. Mother always said he was a bit retarded." I don't know why we dropped it, but somewhere along the line we did.

TOM MANKIEWICZ

I always thought harking back to previous movies was not great. You shouldn't bring back Sheriff J.W. Pepper and bring back Jaws. You should invent new J.W. Peppers and Jaws. Goldfinger's brother comes out of left field. We also cut out this thing with motorboats on Lake Mead.

RICHARD MAIBAUM

I was very unhappy that they changed the ending to that interminable thing on the oil rig. I thought it was much better when all of the gambling casinos who have yachts, and some of them are Spanish galleons, all got together for the good name of Las Vegas, under the command of Bond, and pursued the escaping Blofeld. It was like Admiral Nelson at Trafalgar, "Las Vegas expects every man to do his duty."

TOM MANKIEWICZ

Yeah, we cut all that out. It just didn't seem to work. I can't remember why, but it was a lot of sound and fury signifying nothing. The movie itself was not so much the challenge as it was getting in the swing of things. Here I was like 28 or 29 years old and you're trying to write for yourself, but you're also trying to please everybody else and everybody's wondering whether Sean's going to like it or not. Guy [Hamilton], I must say, at the time was very valuable. He said, "Let's just do what's best for the picture and we're going to go ahead and make this. Don't worry about all of the stuff around this, we'll just do this." At the time, it was the quintessential international action-adventure movie, so you felt a little bit like, "Oh God, I have to write something terrific here."

STANLEY SOPEL

I remember Sean telephoning me. I was in Las Vegas at the time setting up this picture. I said, "Well, are you going to do it?" and he said, "Don't tell anybody, but the answer is yes." I had this burning secret in me. I knew that Sean was going to do it and I couldn't even tell Cubby!

TOM MANKIEWICZ

Here they had this incredible, worldwide, and renowned series of films and they were scared; they had stubbed their toes a little bit. They had a chance to get Sean back and I think they wanted everything to be just as good as it could possibly be. When I had finished my draft, they sent it to Sean, who was in Scotland at the time. We just waited with bated breath. There was no question, they were going to pay Sean his million, or whatever he got, but was he going to like the script? When the word came back from Scotland, "He read the script, and he loves it," I felt like Olivier had just played Hamlet for me. For five minutes I felt like the most important writer who had ever lived. *Sean Connery loved my script, and because of me, he wants to play James Bond again!*

STANLEY SOPEL

Cubby rang me the next morning and said, "Come over and have breakfast, I have some great news for you." I shot over to his hotel and as I drove through the gates, he said, "Sean's gonna do the picture!" Of course he was delighted, and I couldn't say, "I *know*!"—you can't do things like that. I think we had champagne for breakfast to celebrate.

TOM MANKIEWICZ

I had a terrific relationship with Sean. As a matter of fact, I was really surprised because when I first met him, it was up in Vegas, the day he arrived. He had read the script, he had notes on it, and he and Guy and I sat down in Sean's suite all day and went through the script line by line. I was surprised, first of all, on how much homework he'd done on the script. The thing that was most surprising to me was that most of the notes that he had were for *other* actors, which was really odd for an actor. He would say, for instance, "Couldn't she say something better than this to that guy?" I'll never forget that. Most of the time it had nothing to do with him, and he loved that script. He really did. I was terrified in the beginning to meet Sean Connery, and to meet Bond. It was 1970, so I was 27 years old. You think, "Oh my God," and he said, "It's a wonderful script and congratulations," and it just made me feel terrific, and I stayed on the picture the whole time.

In *Diamonds*, Connery's Bond is hot on the trail of Blofeld, who killed the wife of George Lazenby's 007 in the previous film. He finds him—or thinks he does—now in the form of Charles Gray, transformed by plastic surgery, into a mincing, hirsute, Noël Coward-ish supervillain.

TOM MANKIEWICZ

I love sophisticated villains, so I wrote a lot of very piss-elegant stuff for Charlie Gray to say. Wonderful guy. I tried to make him almost like [the gossip columnist] Louella Parsons. He was a wonderful Shakespearean actor as well, so, you know, he'd say, "The world will end tomorrow; pity you won't be there to see it" just right.

FRED DEKKER
(writer, *The Predator*)

I like Charles Gray as an actor, but there's a little camp there. With Blofeld, he needs to be menacing, and Donald Pleasence, even though he's kind of short and kind of a hard-boiled egghead, he's scary as shit. Telly Savalas, because he has a newbie Bond and because we sort of know Telly Savalas, was kind of scary and his plot is pretty creepy. *Diamonds Are Forever* is kind of, like, insert Blofeld here. They didn't make a bold choice with Gray.

But this time Blofeld's done with curing allergies or worrying about stuffy titles from the College of Arms: he's on to much bigger things, creating a super laser in space refracted through stolen diamonds which will allow him to blackmail the world's superpowers, with nuclear supremacy being the prize for the highest bidder. Of course, if you're the world's number one supervillain and the leader of a diabolical evil organization, where would you find sanctuary from the world's greatest secret agent? In this case, it's in the penthouse of the Whyte House Hotel in Las Vegas, where Blofeld has taken the place of the reclusive Willard Whyte, a Howard Hughes analogue, which is an idea that allegedly came to Cubby Broccoli in a dream—which is really all you need to know about this *fakakta* film.

RAY MORTON

The first *Bond* screenplay to be (co)written by Tom Mankiewicz and the first of the lighter, more humorous and fantasy-oriented *Bond*s of the 1970s. This is a fantasy *Bond* that employs the traditional 007 formula with gusto. Maibaum came up with the story's central gimmick—the villain using smuggled diamonds to create a deadly super-weapon—but his early draft was a bit of a mess.

When Tom Mankiewicz was brought on, he completely restructured the story, retaining Maibaum's gimmick, but making Blofeld the bad guy and building the narrative around an idea literally dreamed up by Cubby Broccoli—that of a Howard Hughes–type reclusive billionaire who is kidnapped and whose organization is taken over by an impostor. Broccoli was a friend of Hughes and had a dream in which H.H. was kidnapped and replaced by a double. Mank increased the script's fantasy elements. The business of Blofeld creating duplicates of himself was Mankiewicz's idea and he devised a number of entertaining action sequences, a cast of colorful characters, and lots of very witty dialogue, all delivered with a light, humorous touch. In many respects, while *Diamonds* is the final Sean Connery Eon Bond, in terms of approach, it's really the first film of the Roger Moore era.

TOM MANKIEWICZ

Cubby had worked for Howard Hughes at one time and that character doesn't exist at all in the book. At the time, Howard Hughes was living in Vegas at the Desert Inn, on the top floor and *nobody* saw him. So that was a direct reference to Howard Hughes, that Willard Whyte was living on the top floor of the hotel and no one had ever seen him. We had to have some guy who was running things in Vegas. I thought it was a rather strong scene with the two Blofelds and Bond, who has only one piton left and shoots the one Blofeld after the cat jumps in his lap. The real Blofeld says, "Right idea, Mr. Bond." "Wrong pussy." Sean was great saying "wrong pussy" because he says "pussy" with a Scottish accent.

KEN ADAM

(production designer, *Diamonds Are Forever*)

I don't want to go into too many details, because Vegas, in those days, on one side you had Howard Hughes, who was up in the Penthouse, and nobody knew what he looked like, but he owned half of Vegas, and the other side was owned by mobsters. You know, the Teamsters. Cubby was a great friend of Howard Hughes, and a great friend of the Teamsters, and I was a little designer in between those two, and Cubby said, "Why don't you have lunch with a certain lawyer [Sidney Korshak] and ask him to see those great houses in Palm Springs?" I went to have lunch and he was sitting in a corner. He had a phone brought over, and he said, "I've got this young designer from England over. Show him the best houses in Palm Springs." I was met by a black limousine and I saw *everything,* and I couldn't believe it when I found this house, because I said, "This is fantastic. It's better than whatever I could think of." The man wasn't too happy. He said, "Well, who is going to pay me?" and so on. I said, "Well, I'm only the production designer. I'm sorry, but I don't do that." Of course, then I talked to my Teamster friend, and there were no more arguments about this. We shot there. Architecturally, I thought it was wonderful.

Mixed into the insane plot are the merry and gay killers, Mr. Wint and Mr. Kidd, played charmingly by Bruce Glover and Putter Smith, who are a hoot, as are some of the memorable Mank one-liners (among the most famous are when Lana Wood introduces herself to Bond in the casino as "Plenty O'Toole," a non-plussed 007 responds, "Named after your father perhaps"; and later, when a hood, played by film noir staple Marc Lawrence, drops her out a window on the upper floors of the Whyte House only to dryly retort, "I didn't know there was a pool down there").

TOM MANKIEWICZ

In *Diamonds,* Mr. Wint and Mr. Kidd were obviously lovers in the film. I don't think you could do that today, because I think you'd get pickets out in front of your theater from gay activist groups. I'm not saying they're right or wrong. But they were cute as hell together.

FRED DEKKER

I like Wint and Kidd. The politically incorrect police are going to get me, but we'd never seen anything like that and it's not that gay people are creepy, it's that *those* characters were kind of creepy and happen to be gay.

TOM MANKIEWICZ

Putter Smith, who was Thelonious Monk's bass player when Guy and I went to see Thelonious Monk at Shelly's Manne-Hole was going "dun dun dun dun" and Guy said, "He looks like Mr. Wint." And we asked him. He had never acted before in his life. Bruce helped him a lot with the acting, insofar as he acted. He was just this wonderful walrus-looking guy. He was a musician and he took his fiddle with him everywhere. A damn good bass player.

In retrospect, obviously, I wouldn't write those two characters the same way today. I don't think, even then, that you could say those characters were done with malice. I think Bruce maybe overplays his part a little bit, but there was a kind of menace about them that gives them their own kind of personality, so they don't become ciphers since they don't have a steel hand that crushes things or whatever.

RICHARD MAIBAUM

When they're in the plane and they see Tiffany sit down, one of them indicates her and the other fella says, "She's not bad-looking." The other fella looks at him as if he's hurt and he says, "For a lady." That's a charmless little joke. ABC would cut them holding hands together when they showed it at the time.

TOM MANKIEWICZ

One thing I liked very much, and Guy did, too, was the tag in *Diamonds Are Forever,* with the assassins Wint and Kidd as the waiters serving the dinner and getting thrown overboard and blown up. Guy thought it's a terrific idea to save not your main villain, but your associate villain for the end.

SIR ROGER MOORE

(actor, "James Bond")

My favorite one-liner of all wasn't even in any of my movies. It was Lana Wood playing Plenty O'Toole in *Diamonds Are Forever*, and she says, "I'm Plenty O'Toole" and Sean Connery says, "Named after your father, no doubt." That was Tom Mankiewicz. And Tom Mankiewicz gave me one that I really liked. It was in *Man With the Golden Gun,* and I point the rifle down to the nether regions of a nasty little man to get him to talk, and I say, "Speak now or forever hold your piece."

TOM MANKIEWICZ

Actually what happened, the girl says, "I'm Plenty O'Toole." And Sean said to me, "You know, that really sort of refers to a male organ. Would you mind if I said, 'Named after your father?'" He throws that line away. That was *his* line and it was actually very funny.

> There's a nifty chase through the desert in a lunar rover as well as a brilliantly choreographed, claustrophobic fisticuffs in a tiny elevator between Bond and smuggler Peter Franks (played menacingly by stuntman Joe Robinson), and Bond's mano e womano confrontation with the deadly Bambi and Thumper. But the denouement is a bust on an oil rig, which pales in comparison to the epic *Bond* battles of the past.

RIC MEYERS

How could you ever forget Bambi and Thumper, not to mention Sean's too-short pink tie and white Sansabelt slacks unless you forced yourself to forget? *Diamonds* was Bambi/Lola Larson's only credit, but not so Thumper. Yes, that was the scene that clinched my ongoing theory that the whole movie was Sean's aversion therapy on the audience. The sequence was seemingly devised to not so subtly alter, diminish, and even embarrass the character of James Bond in the eyes of any viewer. Then, after a film of James Bond mostly running away, he slaughters two gay assassins on a boat. Compare this crude, smug, out-of-shape, even unlikable 007 to any Bond who came before. I cannot believe it was an accident. Instead I feel it was a perfect storm of star anger and producer apathy.

Jill St. John, originally cast as Plenty O'Toole, makes a wonderful entrance as Tiffany Case, suggested by Hollywood kingmaker and legendary entertainment and mob attorney Sidney Korshak. Case starts out plucky and competent, dismissing Bond casually by saying "I don't dress for the hired help," but halfway through the movie there's few vestiges of that early toughness and resourcefulness and she becomes little more than a damsel in distress, most ignominiously when she fires off a machine gun during the climactic battle in a bikini, and finds herself falling overboard off said oil rig.

FRED DEKKER

I think she's one of the great bimbos of the series. She does fine with what she's given. I do *not* believe that she's a diamond smuggler, but she's *such* a bimbo, especially in the third act in the bikini, switching the cassette tapes and all that stuff.

TOM MANKIEWICZ

Cubby had a very interesting point. At one point, Catherine Deneuve was interested in playing in *The Spy Who Loved Me*, but she wanted a lot of money and Cubby said, "I never paid a Bond woman more than a hundred thousand dollars in my life. When you think about it, no Bond woman has ever been in any of our movies and gone on to be a star." Unless you count Ursula Andress, who wasn't really a star, and Diana Rigg, who was already very well known. But none of the Girls ever went on to stardom, because they were in a *Bond* movie. Cubby always believed in putting the money on the screen.

After the excitement of the volcano battle in *You Only Live Twice* and the attack of Piz Gloria in *OHMSS*, the oil rig battle off Baja, California, seems downright anemic. It's enough to make you long for the days of scuba divers and spearguns in *Thunderball*.

TOM MANKIEWICZ

We had a scene originally in which Blofeld was granulated in a salt mine, or something like that. We were going to try and shoot it down in Mexico. We left in that wonderful invention, the Bathosub. I still laugh every time I hear Charles Gray say, "Prepare my Bathosub," because you'd get whiplash in it! Bond was going to be hanging from a giant weather balloon which he had tied to the sub. There was once a chase to a beach after the fight on the oil rig, but that was cut in the script. The ending was longer, but it also was like gilding a lily. It went on and on. We thought, "God, let's just do it there on the rig." After all, you have to have an ambiguous end for Blofeld so that he can always come back.

FRED DEKKER

It's not a good movie, but it's Sean Connery as James Bond, sets by Ken Adam, music by John Barry—in fact, it's my favorite score of all time. And it's Vegas. *And* it's Howard Hughes. All of which are things that I am interested in, so, despite its flaws, I have a real soft spot for it. It has enough of the ingredients in the casserole that I love that I'm willing to go, "Okay, it's not a great casserole, but it has those ingredients."

TOM MANKIEWICZ

A big mistake that was impossible to predict was that the car chase in Las Vegas was the high point of the picture. It taught me a great deal, which was just because you have an oil rig and 47,000 helicopters, and you can blow the whole thing up, it will not bring an audience to its feet like a simple stunt—putting a car into an alleyway on two wheels. It was impossible to predict that the audience would love the car chase that much. Which is why, I guess, I loved the little end sequence with Wint and Kidd so much, because it left the picture with a big laugh. The audience roared when he tied the tails of the guy to the bomb and flipped him over on the ship. And it needed it desperately at that point.

JOHN LANDIS

(director, *Animal House*)

There's the penthouse, and Felix Leiter says to James, "Alright you stay here. I don't want you leaving this place. You keep her here for a while." I forgot the plot at this point, but he says, "I've got men stationed all over the place, two on the roof, two on the thing, three at the thing." Then, he opens this door.

There's a man standing there and he says, "This guy." He closes the door and he keeps talking. It's like a brief moment that we wouldn't even notice, except this guy is Guy Hamilton.

STANLEY SOPEL

Sean was extremely happy, and was happy all the time we were shooting. Having agreed to do it, he was going to be very professional about it. He certainly had a whale of a time the eight weeks we shot in the States. He doesn't like working in studios no matter where they are in the world, so we worked our heads off and shot the picture as fast as we could and finished it. And he even liked the picture!

GLEN OLIVER

(pop culture commentator)

Sean Connery felt "off" in *Diamonds*. They paid him a great deal to return to the role, and his performance somehow transmitted this fact. His work in the picture felt disinvested—like he was going through the motions, a proclivity which likely wasn't challenged by the film's juvenile, even base, attempts at oddness and humor. The painfully stilted and tone-deaf "simpleton sheriff" gags, the very strange, crushingly ineffective rapport between Mr. Wint and Mr. Kidd, the fucking moon buggy chase in the Nevada desert? They all suggested a film which was struggling to find an energy and identity, and was grasping at straws.

RIC MEYERS

Given what was on-screen, no one has been able to convince me that Sean Connery wasn't indulging his long simmering resentment for the series' producers with malice aforethought. His weight, his wigs, his wardrobe, his behavior . . . all made clear to me that, with either the knowing or unknowing cooperation of the jaded Guy Hamilton and jaunty Tom Mankiewicz, he wanted to make sure that his James Bond was turned from an albatross to a figure of fun at best, and derision at worst. At least, after that, no one would be seriously clamoring for him as Bond for the immediate future other than in a knee-jerk, familiar-is-best way. Great for Sean. Not so great for me and other veteran *Bond* film fans. The strong, smart, moral, even noble 007 who had saved me was no more—replaced by a callous, careless, crude clown, shepherded by world-weary, civil-warring producers who were more than willing to play mix and match with already established, proven pop culture rather than to lead the way any longer.

FRED DEKKER

Diamonds Are Forever is a *Matt Helm* movie if you had Sean Connery and Ken Adam and John Barry. It was a different era. In 1971, we were already headed for the '80s at that point. Let's not get too serious, let's have fun, let's play the disco music, let's just be cool. If you did *On Her Majesty's Secret Service* today, the sequel would be all about vengeance and character.

RAY MORTON

In my opinion, it's also the best of Mankiewicz's credited Bond scripts: his light and witty touch was a perfect match for the larger-than-life narrative. His work persuaded Connery to return to the role and resulted in one of the more consistently entertaining films in the Eon series.

RICHARD SCHENKMAN

(editor, *Bondage* magazine)

I had such mixed feelings about Tom Mankiewicz. On one hand, he was brilliant, generous, funny, talented, and successful; on the other hand, he had personally introduced some of the goofiest elements to the series, and I could never forgive him for that.

RAY MORTON

The producers decided to take the series in a lighter, more fantastic and more humorous direction in the 1970s—the stories were less realistic, there was much more fantasy and humor, and the action was less violent and much more over-the-top. Many *Bond* purists disliked/dislike this period, complaining that the '70s *Bond*s are too light and too humorous in comparison with many of the films that came before and after. This criticism might be true, but it fails to take into account one very important fact: if the series had not lightened up, it would not have survived long enough to return to relative seriousness in the modern era. By the end of the 1960s, the *Bond* formula was beginning to wear thin—it had been repeated enough times by then that what once was fresh was in danger of becoming cliché.

This is the point at which most series die out—audiences tire of the repetition and begin laughing at what they once embraced. Eon's brilliance was to head this problem off at the pass by inviting the audience to laugh with the *Bond* films rather than at them. This allowed viewers to go on enjoying the movies for another decade or so until they began to miss the more serious approach and welcomed a return to it. Whether intentional or not, this was a brilliant tactic that ensured the longevity of the series.

TOM MANKIEWICZ

I remember when *Diamonds Are Forever* opened, I was standing in the back of Grauman's Chinese Theatre, and at the beginning of the film when Sean says to the girl on the beach, "My name is Bond, James Bond," there was just *such* a roar from the audience. It was like welcoming home your son from the war.

LIVE AND LET DIE (1973)

A few years ago the authors were doing a panel at the annual San Diego Comic-Con about "The Best 007 Movies of All Time," and avuncular, African American *Hollywood Reporter* critic and podcaster Marc Bernardin captured the essence of the film perfectly by referring to *Live and Let Die* as "playfully racist" with lines like "Great disguise, Bond: white man in Harlem." We can't imagine a better description of this gonzo introduction to the debonair charm of Roger Moore as he effortlessly steps into the role of James Bond and travels from England to New York to New Orleans and San Monique, investigating the murder of the British ambassador to the United Nations only to uncover a plot to flood the United States with heroin.

TOM MANKIEWICZ

(screenwriter, *Live and Let Die*)

I remember having dinner with Sean just before we were starting to shoot *Live and Let Die*. He said, "How is the script?" I said, "Just terrific, Sean." We didn't have a Bond then and I said, "Would you like to read it?" He said, "No," and that was, I think, because he didn't want to get tempted. He said to me, "Boy-o, all they can offer me is money." And that's what he didn't need. I brought up the question with him of his "obligation" to the public to play Bond, and he said to me, "How much of an obligation have I got to them? When does that run out? Should we put a limit on it? Should it be 15 pictures over 30 years, or what? One more this year, then is my obligation over?"

PHIL NOBILE, JR.

(columnist, *Birth. Movies. Death.*)

I think Connery was largely finished with the role, but if they'd thrown him carte blanche, there was the slight chance—or maybe just wishful thinking—that we'd have gotten something a little earthier, a little more grounded or even more complex. One wonders what Connery might have done with the role in the '70s, possibly with his frequent collaborator Sidney Lumet at the helm.

Among the choices to replace Connery, who was clearly never coming back to the Eon fold, other contenders included American superstar Burt Reynolds and a young Timothy Dalton. But it was Roger Moore, who had previously been considered for the iconic role several times, a veteran of *The Saint* as well as *The Persuaders!*, in which he had costarred with Tony Curtis, who would don the tux for this film and many more to come. Moore embraced the opportunity to star as James Bond wholeheartedly and made the role entirely his own.

TOM MANKIEWICZ

Burt Reynolds almost played Bond. What was funny is, at the time we were doing *Diamonds Are Forever* Cubby [Broccoli] and Guy [Hamilton] went over to The Golden Lot to meet an actor named Burt Reynolds, who was doing a series called *Dan August* at the time. Guy thought he was charming as hell. Burt's name came up again at *Live and Let Die*. As a matter of fact, the choice was between Burt Reynolds and Roger Moore. When I say "choice," Burt's agent, Dick Clayton, had read the script and they were discussing it very seriously. He had just done *Deliverance*. I think the biggest problem would have been getting him for three pictures, or four pictures. He was a very viable choice at the time, but Cubby was the one who nixed it. Cubby really put his foot down and said James Bond has to be English; you can't do this. At the time, Burt Reynolds was, like, the hottest actor in the world.

During an appearance on ABC's *Good Morning America*, the late Reynolds commented on the Bond situation, "I think I could have done it well. In my stupidity, I said, 'An American can't play James Bond, it has to be an Englishman.' Oops. Yeah, I *could* have done it."

PHIL NOBILE, JR.

I think Oliver Reed would have made a spectacular successor to Connery. Oddly enough, you can see Reed playing the hero opposite *On Her Majesty's Secret Service*'s Telly Savalas and Diana Rigg in *The Assassination Bureau*.

TOM MANKIEWICZ

Cubby had asked Roger at the time of *On Her Majesty's Secret Service*, but he was doing a TV series called *The Persuaders* with Tony Curtis and they couldn't get him, so they decided on Roger this time. United Artists was very nervous, because they wanted to keep this golden goose alive. They thought Roger would be fine.

RICHARD MAIBAUM

(cowriter, *The Man with the Golden Gun*)

I really think that Roger's a fine actor. People adored him personally and so did audiences. I just felt there was a little bit too much fooling around and laughing. You know what they say, when the actor laughs, the audience never does. I think Sean put it best when somebody asked him how Roger's 007 varied from his: "Well, Roger comes in the comedy door, I go out it," which is perfect. Roger comes in trying to be funny. At the end of the scene, Sean just gives a look or drops a line, and there is the humor of it all encapsulated for you. Sean didn't have to do anything, because there was a kind of an inbred irony that is a part of the Scottish character that he had without trying. It was just there. In his own way, Roger was great for the series, because he made a hell of a lot of money.

JOHN CORK

(author, *The James Bond Encyclopedia*)

Live and Let Die was the end of a seven-year experiment by Cubby and Harry. In 1966, they declined to make Sean Connery a partner in Eon Productions They wagered that James Bond was the star of *Bond* films, not the actor who played the character. With massive box-office decline with *OHMSS,* it seemed like that was a bad bet. Connery came back for *Diamonds Are Forever,* and sold ten million more tickets than *OHMSS* in the US alone. Roger Moore's casting in *Live and Let Die* was a huge question mark. He was a television star. With *On Her Majesty's Secret Service,* the studio somewhat downplayed Lazenby as James Bond. They didn't hide it, but they never celebrated it. With Roger Moore, they gave him the full embrace. They based the script very much on *Dr. No,* relying on a proven formula, but adding tons more action and stunts. While box office dropped in the US, globally *Live and Let Die* brought in more money than *Diamonds.* Clearly, the transition was handled very well.

TOM MANKIEWICZ

You write to the strengths, and Roger Moore's strengths are for comedy. For instance, Roger Moore walking into the Fillet of Soul [bar] in Harlem in his proper coat in *Live and Let Die*, you get great comedy out of it, because he looks like a very proper English twit. You can get some comedy out of it that—and you'd be an idiot not to write for it—you couldn't have with Sean. Sean walking into the Fillet of Soul in Harlem would be completely different. Sean sort of carries violence with him. He's got grit in his eye. I think the audience impression as Sean walks in is, "Uh-oh, look out. Stand back, something's going to happen here." There is violence in Sean. He looks like a bastard. He really does. A very good-looking bastard, but somebody who is capable of inflicting violence on you. There's no question about that.

RIC MEYERS

(author, *Murder on the Air: Television's Greatest Mystery Series*)

Roger Moore, of course, arrived on the 007 scene thoroughly Simon Templarized, having played *The Saint* on television for seven years before becoming Bond four years after. By then he had roundhouse-punched dozens of the same stuntmen (including his *Live and Let Die* stunt double Leslie Crawford, and his future "M," Robert Brown), and obviously saw no reason to change his fighting ways.

JOHN CORK

He was the perfect Bond of the moment. In the summer of 1973, the US Senate conducted televised hearings into the Watergate scandal. In early June, John Dean announced on national television that he had frequently discussed the cover-up of the Watergate break-in with President Nixon. Spying seemed to be a dirty word, a tool not to preserve our freedoms, but to undermine democracy. Roger Moore played Bond with a wry smile and an attitude that no one should take what he was doing very seriously. Sure, he lacked the gravitas of Connery's Bond. One never believed he was terribly dangerous. His biggest weakness wasn't his fault. He could play a good line of dialogue incredibly well, but those good lines came fewer and farther between after [writer] Tom Maniekwicz left the series.

GLEN OLIVER

(pop culture commentator)

The transition was remarkably smooth, thanks chiefly to Moore being so utterly comfortable and self-assured. That stressful sense of "ramping up" toward appreciating a new 007, which seems to come about whenever casting for the role is changed, was, perhaps, at a historical low in the Connery-to-Moore transition. It just felt instantly right. An interesting side note to Moore's casting: his overall energy felt younger than Connery's, which served to rejuvenate the vibe of 007 a bit. There's an irony in this, though. While he felt "younger," Moore was actually close to the double-0 retirement age alluded to by Ian Fleming in his books.

YAPHET KOTTO

(actor, "Kananga/Mr. Big")

Roger was very good to me. He taught me about how to be an Englishman. I learned a lot from Roger. We were very close.

GLORIA HENDRY

(actress, "Rosie Carver")

He was a jewel. He hated to do more than one take, but he would if he needed to. Every morning he would hit the pool at six o'clock in the morning and so did I. He was at one end of the pool and I was at the other. Roger shared his limousine with me on all the scenes we did together. Every morning I was in the limousine with him and whenever he signed an autograph for someone, he would give it to me to sign as well. He was so gracious.

DAVID HEDISON

(actor, "Felix Leiter")

Roger was always professional and loved cracking up the crew in between takes with jokes to keep the set light. The most remarkable thing about Roger was that he knew everyone on the crew by name and was always wonderful to them.

JANE SEYMOUR

(actress, "Solitaire")

Roger saved me in the voodoo sequence. He takes me into the grave which descends into Kananga's lair. We were shooting the bit where we come down into the studio at Pinewood, and the way we got down was we were basically attached to a forklift truck. He was an older guy and I think he slipped the gear or something and the whole thing crashed to the ground from about eight to ten feet. I went flying through the air with my high heels and my white dress with a ton of hair. Roger realized that something was terribly wrong and grabbed me by the hair so that I wouldn't fall underneath it and break my leg, and I landed with my elbow, full force, on his private parts. So we didn't shoot with Roger for a few days, but he was a real hero to me.

YAPHET KOTTO

The one time that Roger ever showed a little annoyance was when there were silhouette pictures of Sean Connery around the set. He asked, "Isn't it time to remove those?" So they did. They took them away. That's the only thing I saw him get mad about.

DAVID F. WALKER

(author, *BadAzz MoFo's Book of Spaghetti Westerns*)

There are so many things about the movie that were very different, and not just the fact that this was the introduction of Roger Moore. Even the Paul McCartney song was very different than the other songs, and so much of the movie was set in the United States and in a much better way than it had been in, say, *Diamonds Are Forever. Diamonds* was the beginning of, "Okay, where is this franchise going?"

Part of the marketing campaign to launch a new actor as James Bond involved a journal, a wildly candid and, very much of its time, making-of journal from star Roger Moore.

YAPHET KOTTO

A lot of things he said, he did not say. In fact, there's a lot of bullshit in that journal. After the film was over, Roger and I came to the United States. We had heard a rumor that he and I were not getting along. He went directly to United Artists and said, "Look, this is bullshit. Me and Yaphet got along wonderfully. We're so happy to have had him."

SHANE RIMMER

(actor, "Hamilton–Voice")

Roger was a big practical joker. You never wanted to turn your back on him. The crew couldn't believe this was going on on a *Bond* picture. But that was just what Roger did, and he knew he was going to get away with it, so he did it. When he got a little bored, Roger would do all sorts of things, and he did bring a kind of a buoyancy to the film set.

JANE SEYMOUR

He realized I was terribly gullible and very susceptible and I've never forgotten it. I was in Jamaica and I would always at lunchtime go and sit down with the main cast and the director. One day I sat down with my little tray, and everybody simultaneously got up at exactly the same time and moved away to another table, leaving me totally alone. I took it personally. I had no idea what had happened. I thought people didn't want to be with me and I'm sitting there alone and was crying. Then I finished my meal and went to my trailer and my makeup came off, and the eyelashes came off. It was an unmitigated disaster. And when I read Roger's book, or at least the bit I was in, he mentions this sequence and says, "I thought it'd be a funny practical joke, but, in retrospect, I realized that I profoundly hurt her feelings and that I've always felt badly about it." I saw him a few months before he died in England, and we were hanging out and reminiscing about the old days, and he apologized to me. He said, "You know, I realized years later that I probably really hurt your feelings when I did something that I thought was funny, and obviously it wasn't funny to you." I said, "Funny you should say that, because I got a lot of abandonment issues from that."

On paper, nothing about *Live and Let Die* should have worked, as it's set against a backdrop of voodoo and the supernatural, Fillet of Soul chain restaurants with revolving walls and trapdoors and drug running. Why does MI6 agent James Bond get involved in foiling the attempts of Kananga (a sensational Yaphet Kotto in a double role as the prime minister of the small Caribbean island of San Monique and drug kingpin Mister Big) to corner the narcotics market in the United States? It probably has something to do with the assassination of the British ambassador in the movie's oddly satisfying Bond-less teaser, which leads into one of the great *Bond* opening main title songs ever, Paul McCartney's classic rock staple "Live and Let Die." There's even the surprisingly effective and atypical Solitaire voiceover as she deals the tarot cards over a series of dissolves announcing the imminent arrival of 007 at JFK Airport, "A man comes over water . . ."

TOM MANKIEWICZ

They [Cubby and Harry] asked me which of two or three novels I'd like to write—not that my choice would have been final. They sent me three books. *Moonraker* was one of them and I said, "I think you guys should do *Live and Let Die,* because it's very much an issue in the world today." We tried to do a lot of different things. Roger was new. Paul McCartney suddenly came on to write the song. Drugs were just huge in the world at the time. It was the late sixties/early seventies, and everybody was on drugs. It was probably more au courant than almost anything else. In essence, it was a very brave movie for everybody to agree to do.

JANE SEYMOUR

I never read the book. They said forget it. Don't bother reading the book, because this has nothing to do with the script. I became good friends with Tom Mankiewicz and asked, "How do you guys write the stories? Do you take the movie from the book?" He said, "Maybe, a little. But the first thing we do, we all get together and say, where do we want to go on holiday? Then when we establish where we all feel like hanging out for the next six to eight months, then we decide which book it's going to be and how we can make it." They all decided they wanted to go to Jamaica and New Orleans and so that's what happened.

YAPHET KOTTO

David Picker walked up to me in the street while I was shooting *Across 110th Street* for United Artists and asked me to do it, and I said, "Yeah." [Director] William Wyler told me I was going to be a hero because in *The Liberation of Lord Byron Jones,* it was the first time that a black man ever killed a white man on screen. That picture sort of put my name on the map, both in the business and outside the business. When I did *Across 110th Street* and found myself above-the-title with Anthony Quinn, I knew there was something happening. Then, when they came to me with *Live and Let Die,* I thought I'd be the first black villain in a *Bond* movie. Later on, I was the first black man in space [in *Alien*]. When I got the job, I said, "Here we go again. This is history."

It was the heyday of the blaxploitation era with films like *Shaft* (1971), *Blacula* (1972), and *Coffy* (1973), and *Live and Let Die* clearly showed the influence of the genre, which included casting two actors who had starred in the 1972 hit *Across 110th Street*: Yaphet Kotto and Gloria Hendry.

DAVID F. WALKER

Live and Let Die was the first movie I remember seeing in the theater that had a lot of black actors in it. At first, it was one of the most amazing experiences of my childhood, until I started to realize, "Wait a minute, they're all the bad guys. There's no good guys in this movie." As I've grown older, I kind of go back and forth with it, and I always tell people that *Live and Let Die* is in the top five blaxploitation movies that didn't have a black lead in it, Roger Moore was the lead actor, and the other ones were films like *Conquest of the Planet of the Apes.* There are all these weird movies where people are, like, "Those aren't blaxploitation movies," and I'm, like, "Oh, but they are." For me, and some of my friends as we grew older, as much as we loved *Live and Let Die,* and as much as we loved *Bond,* that's the one where we were, like, "You're going to tell me that he beat this villain? There's *no* way Roger Moore could beat Yaphet Kotto. *No way!*"

TOM MANKIEWICZ

Yaphet Kotto, who was a fairly hot black actor at the time, was not happy. I remember Yaphet saying, "I don't know, I get inflated at the end and blow up like a balloon."

DAVID F. WALKER

We were, like, "Okay, *maybe* Red Grant could have beaten Sean Connery in *From Russia with Love*, but that's it. Sean Connery might have been able to go toe-to-toe with Yaphet Kotto, but *not* Roger Moore."

YAPHET KOTTO

I didn't like it, because it didn't make sense and it wasn't done well. It's the reason why I would like to bring Kananga back. The doll didn't look like me. How is it physically possible that he would zoom out of the water? It looks as if Kananga set it up. Barbara Broccoli, in all fairness, should be calling me up and talking to me about bringing Kananga back so we can give him a little bit of dignity. Every single day thousands of fans from all over the world say, "Is Kananga dead?" It looks as if Kananga set it up.

TOM MANKIEWICZ

You have to take into account this is the time of the Black Panthers and Stokely Carmichael, so it was a very incendiary issue. I kept saying to him, "Look, Yaphet, the *Bond* movies are definitely offensive to almost everybody." Meaning women are sex objects, Goldfinger clearly is Jewish. I was trying to make him feel better. I said, "Maybe you don't go to the Cleveland opening of this." He wanted to play the part. He wanted to be in it.

YAPHET KOTTO

I read the book so there would be no stereotypes that would creep into my performance. There were a lot of stereotypes already in the script, but I said if I play this realistically enough, you will overlook the stereotypes. I wasn't in a position to say, "Hey man, this script is lousy." I don't care. I was happy to be there. You have to take the lemons and try and make lemonade out of it. Don't complain, because you don't have no power. I mean, I just did a few movies, now I'm going to tell these people how their movie should go? I had to go along with the program. Today, Yaphet Kotto would say, "Hold it, just a second. We are not doing this this way." I'm not the same guy. After a hundred movies and the name that I have now all over the world, I now will demand certain things before we start shooting—not *during* the shooting, *before* we start shooting now. Any production that has me in it, you're going to hear me talking about it before I get before a camera. By the time you get before the camera, if you open up your mouth, you're costing people money. Then you're a bad guy. Before I do any more movies, we sit down, we're going to have a script conference, or take your movie and shove it up your ass. That's the way I feel about it now.

TOM MANKIEWICZ

Live and Let Die was a terribly racist novel filled with black people going "Sho nuff" and shuffling and things. Fleming was a terrible racist and anti-Semite. If you read his books, he says things like, "He looked back at him with his swarthy yid eyes." He was the old British Raj and terrible about minorities in his books. Everybody in Harlem in Fleming's books shuffled and jived. Not much was made about the cards. Ian talked about the cards and it was a deck of cards. There was only one scene and I put the whole tarot thing in. That was not in the book. I tried to write Yaphet as a very elegant guy. Kananga was very intelligent, very elegant. In the book, every black person was just dumber than a post.

PHIL NOBILE, JR.

While it's true that the cinematic Bond has never been *quite* as racist as his printed counterpart, the residue is there: Connery snapping "Fetch my shoes!" at Quarrel in *Doctor No* is a rather gross moment, and Moore using Indian street beggars as obstacles during a tuk-tuk chase in *Octopussy* is a bit troublesome. But the films carved their own path away from the novels, doing their best approximation of "changing with the times." Nineteen sixty-two's *Doctor No,* for example, has no mention of the "Chigroes"—you can figure that portmanteau out—described in its source novel. By 1973, the cinematic Bond was bedding African American agents in *Live and Let Die,* a far cry from what passes for race relations in Fleming's novel of the same name: "One used to go to the Savoy Ballroom [in Harlem] and watch the dancing. Perhaps pick up a high-yaller and risk the doctor's bills afterwards." That happens in chapter four. Chapter Five is called "Nigger Heaven."

YAPHET KOTTO

The script was good, but a lot of the black roles were stereotypical. Look, if you don't have a black guy helping you write the dialogue, don't try to write the dialogue, because you're going to write something that's not true. To get black dialogue, you need a black screenwriter, but you can't go tell people that, because they think they're right. The thing that did offend me was the fact I thought this was a job for a black woman. I didn't expect an English woman to be playing Solitaire. That threw me a little bit.

TOM MANKIEWICZ

I had written the part of Solitaire as a black woman and the little part that Gloria Hendry played, which was black in the movie, was originally white. United Artists made me switch them. I said the best person for Solitaire was Diana Ross, and that's who we were going to go for. At the last minute David Picker, who was a wonderful man and was running United Artists at the time, said, "I don't know whether we can have a black leading lady for Bond." Now you're talking about 1972. He said, "This is going to play great in some big cities, but I have to tell you, this is going to be culture shock for an awful lot of people to see this movie, including children. Kids who go see *Bond*. And this is a major piece of entertainment."

At the time I wrote the script, it was a difficult proposition to see a black woman and a white man go to bed together on screen. Not as a fuck, you should pardon the expression, but because they really loved each other and were infatuated with each other and smitten with each other.

GLORIA HENDRY

Wonderful Tom Mankiewicz apologized to me over and over and over again and I didn't understand why. He kept apologizing, "I'm awfully sorry." And finally, I figured it out, because someone of my hue was supposed to be Solitaire, and now you're Rosie Carver. And rightfully, I'm in the wrong role, and he continued to apologize to me. I never really understood until much later.

JOHN CORK

In the novel, Solitaire is white, so as a studio executive you're not sitting around saying, "Do we want to make Solitaire black?" Now you're making that the entire focus of the film and it's going to be hanging on this one linchpin: James Bond's leading woman is a black woman. At the time, the film would just be about that. But there was no denying that Bond did not have a problem sleeping with a woman of color; there's a whole long other political history that goes into white men sleeping with black women, and particularly when the black women may feel coerced or not particularly have much of a choice in it, that I think they were blissfully unaware of when the film came out.

TOM MANKIEWICZ

I remember David Picker saying, "Come on. Don't be a Jane Fonda about this." She was completely radical. He said, "It's not going to happen." And from their point of view, they were right. They felt there was a whole market for this film that had never seen a white man and a black woman go to sleep together on-screen. Especially in what was counted as mainstream family entertainment.

JOHN CORK

When *Live and Let Die* came out, and I don't know the dates of all these films, there had already been a number of films that had played with interracial romance and sexual encounters, but *Live and Let Die* had a sequence where Roger Moore sleeps with Gloria Hendry in the course of the film. And of course the sex scenes were never explicit, or whatever, but they were kissing passionately on-screen. Nobody in the audience in Montgomery, Alabama, where I was watching, went into hysterics, ran out, screamed, and went to call the management; angry letters didn't appear in the newspapers or anywhere. I don't think that really mattered.

GLORIA HENDRY

I did get flak from it, and they blacked out my love scenes with Roger in certain theaters all over the country and even in Africa. I get a lot of flak, because I kissed a Caucasian on camera. It's ridiculous. Hell, Dorothy Dandridge did that way back in the '50s. I remember Harry Saltzman saying, "We have to stamp out this prejudice Why don't you marry Maurice Binder?" He introduced me to Maurice Binder, who did the credits for the *Bond* films. We tried to get together and went on a few dates, but it wasn't gelling.

YAPHET KOTTO

Some of my relatives were extras in Jamaica in *Doctor No*. My relatives were like, "Oh, we were in *Doctor No* in this dance sequence." Bond was a favorite of the whole family. Who could not be a fan of James Bond? My family is from Panama and the Cameroons, so a lot of them were extras in *Doctor No*. That was a big deal in our family. When I came to Ocho Rios, it was like a huge reunion. One of my aunts said to me, "Now you're caught up with us! We were in a *Bond* film first." We all laughed at that. She said, "We're not just celebrating *you* being in *James Bond*. You're celebrating *us* being in *Doctor No*." We all cracked up at how Cubby Broccoli and Harry Saltzman had brought the Kotto and Joseph families together through *James Bond*.

DAVID F. WALKER

I go back and watch the *Bond* movies periodically, and there are villains like Blofeld, Drax, or Stromberg where it's kind of unclear what they're trying to do other than destroy the world. Over and over it's, like, "Okay, you're megalomaniacal and you're suicidal, because you want everyone dead." Whereas Dr. Kananga's goals are purely capitalist. He just wants to make a lot of money off of this heroin trade that he's developing. He was just an interesting character.

JEFF KLEEMAN

(executive vice president of production, MGM/UA)

I can tell you for every *Bond* movie I worked on, and I suspect it may be even every *Bond* movie, we always wished we could come up with a villain's plot that wasn't the massive nuclear war, a nuclear blackmail, a nuclear annihilation plot. *Goldfinger* is the gold standard of, "Wow, what an interesting plot that is."

DAVID F. WALKER

Blofeld in *On Her Majesty's Secret Service* was probably the most developed we ever saw that character, but Dr. Kananga is probably the most interesting and well developed of the *Bond* villains up to that point. Dr. No was an enigma throughout most of the movie. We hear the name, but we don't see him until well into the second act, whereas we see Mr. Big and we see Dr. Kananga, and it's a while before we realize they're one and the same. He clearly has a criminal empire working with him. Knowing how these *Bond* movies were written, and a lot of them seem like they were written on the spot, it's very interesting how well developed that character and his empire is. With so many of them, you try to remember, "Okay, so what was the villain and what was his plan?"

JEFF KLEEMAN

There is a scene in the second *Austin Powers* movie that haunted me, because it was so true to what happens behind the scenes when you are developing a new *Bond* movie, where Dr. Evil and his minions are hanging around, and they're trying to figure out what he should do. They start throwing out all these ideas—blackmail ideas, kidnapping ideas, extortion ideas—and each one gets shot down for one reason or another. And at the end of the scene, Dr. Evil says something to the effect of, "Oh, hell, let's just do what we always do. Steal a nuclear bomb and threaten the world with annihilation." And I remember seeing that and thinking, "Oh my God, that's every *Bond* story conference I've ever been in." We try so hard and we so frequently end up back at that spot.

Perhaps one of the most beautiful actresses ever cast in a *Bond* film—who, along with Diana Rigg, is one of the few to see their career flourish in the wake of the often thankless role of a *Bond* Girl—was Jane Seymour. She was just at the beginning of a successful acting career when she was cast in the film at only 20 years old.

JANE SEYMOUR

I was doing television with the BBC, a period drama series called *The Onedin Line*. I was playing the villainess who was a virginal woman in the 1880s who had inherited her father's shipping line. The story goes that Cubby Broccoli called my agent after he saw the first episode and said we'd like to meet Jane Seymour. My agent told him she's not available, because she's doing the series and that was that. The following week, episode two came out and Harry Saltzman then called my agent and said, "I'd really like to see Jane Seymour." And my agent said, "She's really not available, but if you want to meet her anyway, fine." He thought the same person had called twice. But what he didn't know is that at that time, Cubby and Harry didn't speak to each other. And this was going to be a Harry film, not a Cubby film. So my agent sent me in there saying, "Go meet him anyway since even if you're not available, you might as well because they do other films." Now as we know, they pretty much never did any more films.

I went in to meet them, and at the time I was dating Richard Attenborough's son, Michael, who I later married. I hardly had any money and I'd gone to a store in England and I'd splurged and bought myself a not very expensive suede coat with a recouthe collar. It was by far the most glamorous thing I'd ever put on my body in my life. And my mother had seen it and she said, "Oh darling, you have to have the hat as well, because it goes with it." So I really splurged and bought the hat. And that was the outfit I wore when I went to meet for *James Bond*. I'd always been told by my agent that when my hair was off my face, I looked completely different from when I had it normally, which was very long, very straight, and a center part. Just straight down. And people kept saying, well, what does she look like with her hair off her face? So, I thought, this is perfect. I'll put my hair in the hat, and I'll take the coat off when I come in, and then he'll tell me to take my hat off, and then my hair will come tumbling down. And then he'll go, "She's got lots of long hair." And I practiced it, if you can believe this, in the bathroom at the Dorchester Hotel, and then I went into Harry's office, and Harry said, "Take off your coat." A very grumpy man. And I took the coat off. "And take off that hat." And I took the hat off. And my hair came tumbling down. And he sat me down and he said, "Okay, we want you to play the lead in this film." Like right off the bat. And then, he immediately said, "Come with me. I'm going to take you over to Cubby." So we crossed the street and went to Cubby's office. We get to Cubby's office and Harry brings me in and says, "Cubby, I want you to meet Jane Seymour."

Cubby pretty much half spit and basically said, "What's the matter? How come you get to see her? I called last week and I couldn't see her. How come you get to see her?" So they were sort of having a fight about me in the room. And I'm standing there like a fish out of water, and the secretary's saying, "Come here, come here." So I go out to see the secretary while they have a big fight about who discovered me. And I'm putting my hands up like a schoolgirl and I'm saying, "Excuse me, but you both saw me at the same time, because I was on television at the same time." And they were like, "Yeah, okay."

So then, Harry said, "Call your agent." I called my agent, who was the top agency at that time, and he got me on the phone and said, "Look. Get in your car. Come over now." So now I'm all nervous about everything and then I back my Volkswagen maroon blue bug into Harry's Rolls-Royce. Gently, but enough to know that that was not a good thing. And Harry was honestly so keen on having me, he decided not to notice that I'd done that. And then I drove around the corner to SoHo where my agent was, and we got out of the car, got into the office, and he sat me down. And he said, "Okay, you need a gin and tonic." I was only 20, you know, so it's legal in England, but not America.

So then he had long conversations with the BBC and the guys there were not going to let me out of my contract. My agent kept saying, "Don't you realize if she does the *Bond* film she'll be a star. And if she's a star, you'll forever be famous for being the one that discovered her." And the producer was not buying that. My agent said, "Look, talk to your wife tonight and speak to me in the morning. Just think about it. You'll forever be known as the person who discovered her." So apparently what happened is he went home and he told his wife. And his wife said, "Don't be ridiculous. Of course you can move scenes around. And then she can do your thing and the other thing, and then your thing will be worth more, because she'll now be starring in a *Bond* film." Then I went away for two weeks in New Orleans. And then I came back and I finished the series, and I went to Jamaica and then I did everything in England.

Even though Solitaire's easily duped and not exactly the most capable of *Bond* heroines, Jane Seymour is stunning and vulnerable in the part. Honestly, has Bond ever been more sleazy than when he dupes poor Solitaire by replacing a deck of tarot cards, convincing her that they are destined to be lovers, and she promptly loses her prognosticating powers after a quick snog? The man's got game, he doesn't need to resort to such crude shenanigans—although admittedly it's nonetheless a great reveal as the stacked deck slips from his hands pre-coitus to reveal they're all "The Lovers."

JANE SEYMOUR

At 20, I was the equivalent of a 14-year-old today. I was very innocent. They cast me as a virgin for almost authentic reasons.

TOM MANKIEWICZ

Jane did as well as she could and I know Jane and I like her, but she was very virginal casting.

JANE SEYMOUR

I had a very bad cold when I was doing one of the major scenes. The third scene where he says, "Red queen on the black," whatever it is. And they were going to re-voice my entire performance. [Director] Dickie [Richard] Attenborough heard about it and said, "No, no, no. She's a terrific actress. Give her a chance. Let her re-voice just that scene. I'm sure she can do this." So I looped it and thanks to me they used my voice rather than having someone else's voice in that scene, which would have been the kiss of death as an actress. I was thrilled with that. He knew I could do it. He knew I could act. He'd seen me do tons of things and then he took me aside and he said, "Darling, you are very fortunate. You have a fine instrument. Now learn how to tune it." I actually spent an enormous amount of time straight after that doing all classical theater: Shakespeare, Christie, Ibsen. I took my training very seriously after the *Bond* film.

YAPHET KOTTO

My relationship with Jane was very good; she invited me to dinner at her house and treated me with a great deal of respect. She wasn't Solitaire, but a nice lady. She did a good job with what she had to do. She was very beautiful, long, long hair that went down to the floor. She obviously was a ballerina, because she walked on all points. But Solitaire should have been a black actress.

JANE SEYMOUR

Yaphet basically acted as if he were Marlon Brando. And Marlon Brando apparently used to make himself deaf by stuffing stuff down his ears so that he couldn't hear anyone. And then he would just look at a person and when they stopped talking, he'd say his line. He never wanted to listen to the other dialogue. Yaphet did the same thing. He was a very good actor, but it was very hard to work with him, because he never heard anything you said. So his rhythm was quite different from whatever your rhythm was, but he came across brilliantly, so whatever his method was, he was fine.

Kotto as Kananga also has a terrific rogues' gallery at his disposal with the gleefully dastardly, hooked henchman Tee-Hee (Julius Harris); the sinister Baron Samedi, played by a game Geoffrey Holder; and a memorable jive-talking taxi driver in Arnold Williams. Gloria Hendry has the thankless job of being the second banana who beds Bond and turns out to be a double agent working for, and eventually slain by, an unforgiving Kananga.

GLORIA HENDRY

A friend of mine, Ken Menard, was Sidney Poitier's stand-in on *For Love of Ivy* and I was a bunny at the New York Playboy Club, and Ken said, "You ought to go out to California, because there's more work out there." So I flew out to California to check it out and my agent took me to the set of *Black Caesar* to meet Fred Williamson. I didn't know who Fred Williamson was; I didn't follow football. So I went to his mansion where they were shooting *Black Caesar* and I got cast immediately. Afterward, I got a call to do a film with Bernie Casey called *Hit Man*. And then he said, "They want to see you in New York for a *Bond* movie." I said, "Really?" He said, "Yeah, you gotta come back." I said, "Who's paying for me to come back?" He said, "You are." I said, "What? I gotta fly back here for an audition?" It made no sense since 98 percent of the time you don't get the role. Finally, I said okay. I crunched my numbers and went back to New York and I came into the office of Harry Saltzman. He saw me as I walked through the door, and here was this wonderful guy with this white hair and his dark eyes, quite stunning, and he said, "Madam," as I'm sitting down, "how soon can you get ready to go to New Orleans?" So a limousine came to pick me up at my New York apartment and I flew off to New Orleans in first class, which I had never flown. I went straight to New Orleans and I met Guy Hamilton and Roger Moore and was, like, "Whoa, Roger! Oh my God." I had dinner with them, and they took me on the set and we just talked. And he said, "Madam, we're still looking. Would you like to stay the weekend?" I said, "No. I'm too far from home." So they flew me back to New York, and I took the first plane out and went back to California, and two weeks later I got a call from my manager saying I had the role. I couldn't believe it. I never read a line.

DAVID F. WALKER

This was the first time I'd seen any of these actors before, including Yaphet Kotto and Gloria Hendry. Geoffrey Holder was the only person I knew before I'd actually seen the movie. To see them in these roles was pretty fascinating, just to see somebody up on the big screen because, for the most part, I was a weird kid and was seeing movies that were completely inappropriate for my age range. But when you would see movies that were appropriate for your age range in the early '70s, they almost always had no black actors at all. Even in *Superman: The Movie,* which was, what, five years later? There's only one black guy in all of Metropolis, and he was a pimp. What happened, and I can only speak for myself, over the years is you kind of took what you could get and it was, like, "Okay, if we're going to be the bad guys—if we're going to be pimps and drug dealers or whatever—at least let's have some character to it."

GLORIA HENDRY

Across 110th Street was a small role, but it was a significant role. I almost didn't do it, because it had a lot of drugs in it—cocaine, orgies, the whole criminal scene and being protected by a pimp. But it was a big studio film and Anthony Quinn was the star and Barry Shear was the director. Years later, Barry Shear and Roger Moore came to California after we shot *Live and Let Die* in '73. They were staying at the Beverly Hilton Hotel and Roger called me and said, "Hey, why don't you meet us for dinner?" I couldn't. I just couldn't get over there.

JANE SEYMOUR

Geoffrey Holder was my favorite. He was an incredible dancer. I used to hate sitting around for hours on end waiting for the next setup, so I'd go over to another set in Pinewood where he'd be rehearsing all the voodoo sequences. And that's why I ended up being held up high in the voodoo scene, because originally I would've probably been just dragged alone there. But I'm an ex-dancer, so we did a lift. And I used to come and try and practice and learn how to do all that voodoo dancing, which was the opposite of ballet. We became very good friends. He was also a great costume designer and a great artist and an amazing man. When I got married years later for the third time, he designed my wedding gown.

YAPHET KOTTO

It was good to work with Geoffrey Holder, because he was a friend of my aunt, Sevilla Thornton, who had a dance school in New York City. My aunt taught Marlon Brando how to dance. She taught James Dean. She taught Geoffrey Holder. There were so many people in New York City who went through the Sevilla Thornton school and worked with her. We laughed about that all the time. I loved Geoffrey. He was a great, great man.

JANE SEYMOUR

Julius Harris was lovely. I remember taking him to the English pub. He looked around and he said, "There's no one black here. I don't think I should be here." And I said, "No. Everyone's delighted to see you. It's not that way here." And he actually loved it. He felt very comfortable ultimately. I think Yaphet had different feelings about race. He didn't understand that it's a different kind of racial thing in England from what he was used to in America.

YAPHET KOTTO

Julius Harris was also a wonderful, nice guy. We did a movie called *Nothing But a Man* together three years before I did *Live and Let Die*. We got along; I had a good time with him.

JANE SEYMOUR

When I first came to Jamaica, Geoffrey asked if I wanted to know something about voodoo. I said, "Yes, I'm an actress." I learned how to read tarot cards and Geoffrey took me to a real voodoo ceremony in the middle of Jamaica where certainly no white people ever went. There were all these women dressed in white and spinning around. They were going crazy. People almost frothing at the mouth. And there were chickens. It was real voodoo . . . or as close as you'd get in Jamaica. I thought it was fascinating.

YAPHET KOTTO

I didn't go. If my rabbi caught me going to one of those, I'd be in real trouble. No way. I once called my rabbi up and I told him I was in a fast-food restaurant and he hung up the phone.

GLORIA HENDRY

Nobody invited me, but I did hang out with some people talking about the voodoo culture. I learned a lot before I even got on the set. I'm a theater person. I did my homework.

TOM MANKIEWICZ

I bought some books on it. But I must say the guy who was really helpful was Geoffrey Holder, who was into it. He was from Trinidad, but he was a hero throughout the Caribbean. He was just instantly recognizable. He was their Clark Gable or Clint Eastwood. He was a wonderful, extravagant man and he took me to a couple of voodoo ceremonies. I read books here about Baron Samedi, the man who cannot die, and all the different gods. I became an expert tarot card interpreter at the time and would read cards at parties.

We weren't exactly sure of the last shot of the movie, so we just stuck Geoffrey on the front of that train, which was kind of fun because the audience liked him, too. That decision wasn't made until halfway through shooting the movie. It was never in the script.

GLORIA HENDRY

Midway through the movie when they were getting ready to shoot my death scene, they said, "Madame, please wait. We don't want to kill you. Because we like you so much, we want to figure out how to keep you in the movie." Days went by to figure out how they could adjust the script to keep my character alive, but then they came back and said, "I'm sorry. We have to kill you, because it would take too much to redo the whole thing to keep you in there."

JANE SEYMOUR

Guy Hamilton completely intimidated me by having this very large deck of tarot cards and shuffling them and shuffling them in the air, upside down, and constantly around the room. He did card tricks. That was his thing. My hands were small, so I couldn't even hold the deck and I had never played a card game in my life. My father had three girls and he loathed anything to do with cards, sports, or anyone who kicked, hit, or watched a ball game. It was books, ballet, and opera for us. So I was completely inept at this shuffling thing and that was the one thing that I really had to apparently be able to do. I don't think I ever really got it down.

YAPHET KOTTO

It's wonderful for a director to let his actors do their thing, but Guy didn't do anything for me. Everything that I did was on my own. He just stood there and watched me. I thought that was kind of unusual. I didn't get the feeling that Guy liked me much. I didn't do anything to him, but I didn't get the feeling that he really cared about what happened to me at all. I did everything on my own. I kind of felt weird, because you need someone to say you did it good, you did it bad. He just stood there and let me do my thing, which I don't feel is directing. I think it's a traffic cop. I got the feeling that he probably wanted somebody else to play that part, and so just let me just do it.

GLORIA HENDRY

Guy would talk to me for a scene, and in the middle of the conversation, he would suddenly say, "Roll the cameras—action." He was wonderful. No shouting. Everything was just easy.

JANE SEYMOUR

One day Geoffrey and I were a little frustrated with Guy because we felt that he was not really understanding the essence of the whole relationship between the characters of his [Geoffrey's] character and my Solitaire and what was their backstory. So Geoffrey and I borrowed our costumes and we went out on the beach with the silver tops for one day. Just for us, for fun. We said to the unit photographer, will you take some pictures of us? We're going to do an interpretive dance of what Guy didn't want to hear about. We did this sort of impromptu ballet on the beach in our costumes. And those were the famous photographs of me and Geoffrey from the film, and they had nothing to do with the movie at all. They were by far the most interesting photographs ever taken of me in the *Bond* film.

GLORIA HENDRY

It's amazing. They were taking photos of us and I took off my bra and somebody said, "Gloria! Don't do that!!" I was like, "Why not?" I didn't think anything of it. I was a bunny. We all undressed in front of each other in the dressing room. As long it's done classy, I'm fine.

JANE SEYMOUR

They also subjected me to Terry O'Neill, who spent three days photographing me and trying to make me into a sex symbol. He came up with these fantastic photographs, and then a big article had said that I loved running naked through long grass. It was completely made up, but you can imagine how my father felt when he read *that*.

YAPHET KOTTO

I wanted the director to help me, because I wasn't happy about Rick Baker's makeup that he gave to me. It wasn't what I wanted. I knew Rick Baker took an exception. The only person that supported me was Roger, but I didn't feel that Baker or Hamilton did. When he was doing the makeup job, I started to mention it to Rick Baker, but I could see from his reaction this wasn't going to go down too good. At that point, I didn't think of myself as an actor who had any right to say anything. It was too big a movie. I didn't want to come off bad, so I let him do his thing. I was a member of the Actors Studio. Makeup has to internally grow from your feelings. As a black man, I knew I had to look right. It had to be real. It can't be a mask someone puts on my face from their imagination about how a black man looks. It has to come from the actor, and it didn't come from me. Reading Stanislavski's *An Actor Prepares,* I was prepared to build a character out of it. I was prepared to bring in all the things that I had learned in the Studio of building a character, and I never got an opportunity to do that. I don't think Hamilton was happy about the makeup either, because you don't see Mr. Big on screen that much. It's so brief you don't have a chance to study it.

> Meanwhile, the action set pieces are more redolent of an old episode of *Batman* than *From Russia with Love* as Tee-Hee leaves Bond stranded on an island at an alligator farm ("Trespassers will be eaten," natch) and engages in wild boat chases in which Bond eludes the clutches of Kananga's men and the redneck sheriff in pursuit, J.W. Pepper (Clifton James), who became an instant audience favorite and returned in *The Man with the Golden Gun* (incomprehensibly vacationing in Thailand with his wife). If *Diamonds* was the birth of the kitschy '70s *Bond* film, *Live and Let Die* was its early adolescence.

MATT SHERMAN
(creator, Bond Fan Events)

In *Live and Let Die,* one of the best of the *Bond* films, Bond is in Harlem and has a thrilling car chase near the Brooklyn Bridge, but was crying out to hurl some baddie from the Empire State Building or take a romantic horse and carriage ride across Central Park! And that most exotic city, New Orleans, is seen only very briefly in the film, even though 40 area locations, mainly swampy rivers, were used by the crew for filming. I feel strongly that Fleming himself would have adored New Orleans and added it to his *Bond* canon.

ELAINE SCHREYECK
(script supervisor, *Live and Let Die*)

I nearly didn't do *Live And Let Die*. I was reading the script sitting in my garden and I suddenly said to my mother, "I can't do this film! I don't like snakes!"

TOM MANKIEWCZ

I remember in the voodoo ceremony when Jane has been tied to a stake, there's a very muscular kind of guy who dances in front of her with a green snake. They had the snake wrangler on the set and he had, like, 20 snakes or whatever. And this guy who was so strong was completely terrified of snakes. The snake wrangler said, "Let's just take it right behind the head here," and they held it and he said, "If you just hold him behind the head, he can't do anything. He's fine, he's not even poisonous." Well, we roll the film and the dance started going and at the end of the take Guy said "Cut. Okay let's do it again" and the fellow had strangled the snake. He was so scared he had held him so tightly that the snake was dead. The snake wrangler was just berserk. Almost crying. One of his favorite snakes.

JANE SEYMOUR

I had a real phobia of snakes and I was literally tied up with the snakes, so I couldn't move. They had this green boa constrictor, which is apparently quite a rare breed, and they had a dancer dancing, and the dancer was obviously dancing with a fake snake. But when they came to do closer-up stuff, he was holding the real snake and they were doing a lot of takes. By then the guy got a little comfortable with the snake so he was holding it just at the head. And then being a dancer, when they said, "Cut, we're doing another one," without thinking, he passed the snake to his other hand, further down the snake. And the snake wound around and bit him on his hand. He instinctively threw the snake away, and the teeth came out. He ran off crying and the snake came slithering right toward me. At the last minute, the snake handler picked up his snake. Literally, the last second. I was freaking out. And then he was sort of crying to me and saying, "Oh, my best snake. He's lost his teeth. And now he's going to die." That dancer should've left the fang in his hand and then we could've removed him and the snake would've lived.

But then they had to replace the main dancer with just anyone who had a matching Jamaican hand, and of course this guy had no idea that it wasn't his big moment. He didn't realize it was just his fingertips and that's all that was being seen. He got terribly excited and thought it was his big break, and so the closer he got to my face, the better he'd be recognized for being the potential movie star that he wanted to be. So I had a snake literally lick my nose—and I was freaking out.

Ultimately, though, *Live and Let Die* isn't known for its snakes, but rather its crocodiles in one of the film's most famous sequences, in which Bond escapes from a pen filled with hungry crocs.

TOM MANKIEWICZ

The crocodile sequence in *Live and Let Die* happened just because we were driving by a crocodile farm with a sign that said "Warning. Trespassers will be eaten" on a scout. That was really there. Not as big as it was in the movie, but it was there. And it was run by a man named Ross Kananga.

VIC ARMSTRONG

(stunt double, Roger Moore)

This was my third *Bond* following *You Only Live Twice* and *On Her Majesty's Secret Service*. I got to work with an incredible stunt coordinator, Bob Simmons, and my future father-in-law, George Leech. Bob rehearsed the fight in this shark pen with me, breaking down a fight, where the actors were going to go, where the edits were going to come, how we do the actual stunt. It was invaluable, and it was lessons I learned on [*Live and Let Die*] I used for the rest of my career.

Another memorable stunt was the shearing off of the top of a double-decker bus during a pursuit on San Monique, driven by Maurice Patchett, a London Transport bus driving instructor. It was actually Jane Seymour cowering in the back as the bus plunged through a narrow tunnel.

JANE SEYMOUR

I wasn't given a choice. I showed up and they said, "Oh, you'll be in the bus." I said, "Where's Roger?" "Oh no, he's in his trailer." I said, "What?" He said, "Yes, we've got a London bus driver who's going to be doing the stunt." And I said, "If they can't see him, how can they see me?" "Never mind, you've got to go now." And I asked, "Has this been done?" They said, "Yes, on paper." "You mean you've never done this?" Of course, if you watch the movie, it could've been anybody. I was the size of a red gnat. It was absurd, because they didn't know if it was going to work. That was pretty terrifying. But in retrospect, of course, if you do something thrilling like that, once you survive it, you go, "Yeah. That's cool." It wouldn't have been cool, in retrospect, if something had gone wrong.

GLORIA HENDRY

When they were doing *Live and Let Die* in the studio, they didn't have a person of my hue to do my stunt, so they took a small Caucasian British guy on the crew, dressed him in my dress, painted him dark. The arm that came through the door with the gun and got flipped over was him. If you look hard at it, you'll see that hand wasn't mine. There weren't many stuntmen of our hue. In fact, in the UK, at Pinewood Studios at the time, they didn't have *any*. They were still doing blackface.

Unit publicist Derek Coyte and legendary photographer Terry O'Neill photographed extensive shoots with the stars, including Roger Moore, Jane Seymour, and Gloria Hendry. One particular photo created ongoing problems for Kotto. Although it was a quick shot of him giving the Black Power salute in an era where this was still controversial (only a few years after Olympians Tommie Smith and John Carlos controversially hoisted their fists in the air while accepting a gold and bronze medal for the 200 meter race in track and field, respectively, during the playing of the American national anthem), Kotto felt it led to him being blackballed from the film's subsequent marketing and publicity campaigns.

YAPHET KOTTO

Roger told me that I had an enemy in the United States who was really upset that I was getting so much attention. He told me who that enemy was and to be very careful of him. Let me tell you something, I got a black stuntman to be a coordinator on that film when I told Cubby, "Wouldn't it be a good idea if the black stuntman's union was a part of this?" Cubby said, "Of course." And I'm ashamed to say that it was one of the black stuntmen who was in league with an individual who was a star at the time. He called me and said, "Hey, Yaphet, what's going on?" He gave me a power salute. Roger tried to warn me he was going to die, because he saw him talking to the photographer. I inadvertently raised my hand to salute back to him. At that moment, a photographer took the picture. I looked at this dude and I said, "You know something, man? When black men do things to black men, we hurt not just the cause, we hurt ourselves." He told me who was behind it, and I just said, "Okay." It was the very same person that Roger Moore had warned me about. Someone who didn't have anything to do with the movie at all. I was tricked into it. I know who tricked me. It was a brother who set me up. I never forgave him for it. I let him just do his thing. This had nothing to do with race. This had to do with brother to brother. Why would you do a thing like that to me, man?

RAY MORTON

There's a mismatch in *Live and Let Die* between the subject matter and the execution. The core concept of the story—Bond versus a gang of international drug dealers—seems ideal for the more realistic thriller approach. However, the filmmakers chose to go the fantasy *Bond* route, and so Tom Mankiewicz filled the story with larger-than-life characters (a clairvoyant virgin, a diplomat who uses makeup to double as a Harlem drug dealer, and a character who may literally be the Haitian Lord of the Dead) and concepts (the tarot cards, the inflatable henchman, and so on). While these bits are all highly inventive and entertaining in and of themselves, they seem far too fantastic for the basic material. Mank's light, comedic approach to what is essentially pretty dark material also feels off.

YAPHET KOTO

It was good to shoot this film in Harlem. I did *Across 110th Street* there, and I was back again with *Live and Let Die*. When the film opened up, I went to a bar and did my little publicity right there in the bar. I was hurt that I was not invited to the premiere based on the bullshit photo that was taken of me. I went to Saltzman's office, because they sent me out of town for a vacation. When I came back to England, they told me how *Time* magazine was out there for an article on the film. I said, "Why did you let me go out of town?" He says, "I need to talk to you." I went to his office and he whips out this picture of me holding my fist up in the air. I said, "Is that why you guys didn't invite me?" He says, "Well, we didn't want to take any chances that negative publicity would come out." I was hurt.

Perhaps the most divisive aspect of the film, however, remains the casting of the late Clifton James as redneck sheriff J.W. Pepper, who gets involved in the pursuit of James Bond through the bayous of Louisiana.

GLEN OLIVER

It's impossible to discuss *Live and Let Die* without shoveling out a bit of vitriol for Clifton James' Sheriff J.W. Pepper character. I'm not sure I've ever seen a film derail as quickly as *Live and Let Die* did when J.W. Pepper showed up. Suddenly, what was an interesting and perfectly respectable *Bond* film became an entirely different picture, in a distracting, utterly unnecessary, bizarrely base way. James' portrayal was so excruciatingly over the top that *The Beverly Hillbillies* or Jackie Gleason's Sheriff Buford T. Justice look like *Masterpiece Theatre* performances by comparison.

RAY MORTON

Clifton James' performance as J.W. Pepper is hysterically funny, but the character of a bumbling, racist Southern sheriff does not belong in a *James Bond* movie, especially one about drug dealing.

GLEN OLIVER

Clifton James' sequences in *Live and Let Die* went on too long, were tonally out of left field, and served the movie in no other way but to create a lowbrow, embarrassing diversion from the central action and thrust of the picture's story. I'd be very curious to know why any of this was deemed necessary, and would love to have heard the conversations which justified how what—maybe—should've been a 30-second gag turned into a routine which was damn close to a B plot. This whole section may've been *Bond*'s lowest moment ever in my estimation—so much time, effort, and expense being allotted to gags which brought no discernible value to the proceedings.

JOHN CORK

You know, when you look at the stuff, *The Beverly Hillbillies* TV show played incredibly well in the South. Certainly, Andy Griffith did, too. One of my grandfather's favorite shows for a while was *Green Acres,* which had poked great fun at sort of rural folks and things of this nature. So I think most people laughed at J.W. Pepper, because there were so many wonderful layers of comic truth in his character. I don't think that *In the Heat of the Night* [with Rod Steiger as a redneck sheriff partnered with an African American police detective from the Northeast] played poorly in the South, either, which is kind of the origin of the J.W. Pepper character in its own way. This was the circus clown version of Sheriff Gillespie.

Although it was a staple of the *Bond* series that Felix Leiter, Bond's CIA counterpart, was recast in every movie, David Hedison made such a strong impression in *Live and Let Die* that he would reprise the role nearly two decades later in *Licence to Kill,* the only actor other than Jeffrey Wright to play Leiter more than once.

DAVID HEDISON

Tom Mankiewicz was a friend, and he thought I'd be good for the part. He let me read it, I liked it, and he set a meeting with the producer for me. I got the part. I read the book. Felix Leiter was written as a fairly straightforward character, not too far removed from the average American or from me except for the guns and fighting part.

JOHN CORK

David Hedison is a great guy. I enjoyed his Leiter. Tom Mankiewicz was very smart in how he let Leiter play the guy who had to go around cleaning up the messes that Bond leaves behind. The scene at the Royal Orleans where Felix is handling the angry phone call from Mr. Bleeker while Bond is meeting with a tailor is perfectly played by Hedison. He's exactly right for *Live and Let Die*.

But as dated as many aspects of the film are today, one thing that has stood the test of time is Paul McCartney's magnificent main title theme.

MADELINE SMITH

(actress, "Miss Caruso")

Roger brought in the cassette with the demo music for "Live and Let Die" for us all to listen to. He said, "Isn't this wonderful? This is going to be a great big hit," which of course it was.

BILL KING

(editor, *Beatlefan* magazine)

Bond producers Harry Saltzman and Albert Broccoli liked having contemporary acts sing the theme song of the *Bond* films, a few of which had been hit records. Broccoli reportedly had approached McCartney about doing the theme to *Diamonds Are Forever* in 1971, but it didn't work out. When they were relaunching the *Bond* series with a new 007, Roger Moore, Saltzman invited Paul to do the theme song to *Live and Let Die* early on, even before the screenplay was finished. Paul asked to be sent a copy of the Ian Fleming book. He read it one weekend during a break from the *Red Rose Speedway* sessions, and he liked it, wrote the song the next afternoon, and the next week went into the studio with Beatles producer George Martin at Martin's AIR Studios in London to record it. Said Paul: "It was a job of work for me, in a way, because writing a song around a title like that's not the easiest thing going."

PAUL DU NOYER

(author, *Conversations with McCartney*)

Paul probably knew that a *Bond* theme would guarantee the sort of mass exposure that he could no longer take for granted since leaving The Beatles. The cinema audience would be much broader than the rock crowd he was currently reaching. And in 1973 his new band, Wings, was still not really established:

their breakthrough wouldn't come until *Band on the Run,* a year later. Unlike John Lennon, Paul never fell out with George Martin and indeed they would occasionally work together for the rest of George's life. Being a *Bond* project, it would have looked quite natural to collaborate with George: in other words, it wouldn't be seen as a sign of defeat, of trying to recapture the old Beatles magic because his new career was stalling.

BILL KING

Many years later, Paul told *Mojo* magazine: "On the Sunday, I sat down and thought, OK, the hardest thing to do here is to work in that title. I mean, later I really pitied who had the job of writing *Quantum of Solace.* So I thought, *Live and Let Die,* OK, really what they mean is live and let live and there's the switch. So I came at it from the very obvious angle. I just thought, 'When you were younger you used to say that, but now you say this.'"

In *Conversations with McCartney,* he added to Du Noyer, "It might be that having to write something for a film reminded me of what degree of license you had to play around with structure. I think that probably encouraged me to think about *Band on the Run* in the same way, as a kind of epic adventure album."

BILL KING

As then–Wings drummer Denny Seiwell recalled: "Everybody thought it was cool that we were doing something for *James Bond.* I remember what Paul told us—a couple weeks before we did the actual recording, he said they wanted him to write the theme to the next *James Bond* movie, and they sent him the book to read. And we were up at the house one day and he had just read the book the night before, and he sat down at the piano and said, 'James Bond . . . James Bond . . . da-da-dum!,' and he started screwing around at the piano. Within 10 minutes, he had that song written. It was awesome, really. Just to watch him get in there and write the song was really something I'll remember the rest of my life."

FRED DEKKER

The score by George Martin is fantastic, too. Has its own unique flavor that's different than Barry, but still very glamorous and exotic and *Bond*ian. I wish he had scored way more films. I'm a big fan of *Live and Let Die.*

JEFF BOND

(editor, *Film Score Monthly*)

It made sense to use a different composer to start Roger Moore off as James Bond. George Martin was no John Barry, but he was a fantastic arranger, and with Paul McCartney he created one of the best *Bond* songs, one that was as big a pop hit as any of Barry's. He and McCartney also built a terrific action lick into that song that really serves Bond and the film well, and the score has a great attitude without ever aping Barry.

BILL KING

When Martin presented the song to Saltzman, the movie producer thought it was a demo and asked Martin, "Who are we going to get to sing it?" Saltzman was interested in Shirley Bassey or Thelma Houston. Martin told him, "That's *Paul McCartney*" singing, and added that Paul would only allow the song to be used if Wings' recording was used. Saltzman agreed. But they also decided they wanted another performance of the tune in the film, so that's how the B.J. Arnau version came to be used in one of the New Orleans scenes. The announcement of Paul doing the theme was greeted in *Rolling Stone*'s Random Notes by the bitchy comment, "So, it's come to that." Which was, of course, Jann Wenner trying to curry favor with John and Yoko. The fact is, doing a *Bond* theme was a big deal, and it gave Wings a smash hit, spending three weeks at No. 2 on the *Billboard* Hot 100. Years later, *Rolling Stone* ranked it as the No. 1 *James Bond* movie theme song.

YAPHET KOTTO

I got sick of the song. I went to France and walked into a restaurant, somebody plays the song in the restaurant. I went to this country, I went to Germany, going into another one, somebody played it. For years "Live and Let Die"—people think it's cute. Somebody from the bar will tell them, they run quick and turn the radio up, put something on. But I love that song. It's a great moving song that has a lot of truth in there. In England I was in the play *Fences*. When I went to Liverpool, where we rehearsed, I went to a lot of places where The Beatles came from, and I found out that most of their songs are about experiences they had growing up in Liverpool. "Live and Let Die" is an experience that Paul had, a philosophy, and so you can feel it. I can feel the energy behind the song, and the words behind it are very moving.

BILL KING

The fact that he included the song with clips from the movie in his *James Paul McCartney* TV special, which aired a few months before the *Bond* film even came out, would indicate he had great expectations for it. This was the first of the Roger Moore *Bond* films, so interest in it was very high. Paul knew this was a high-profile gig. And it garnered him an Academy Award nomination for Best Original Song (though it lost to "The Way We Were"). It also won a Grammy Award for best arrangement with vocals.

PAUL DU NOYER

I would guess that Paul saw the song's live potential pretty quickly, given its dramatic and theatrical character. What mattered to him most, though, was notching up some genuinely huge post-Beatle hits. He wanted his new career to seem like more than just an anticlimax. "Live and Let Die"—and *Band on the Run,* the song and the album—were vital in that process, and it's become an absolute staple of his solo tours.

BILL KING

Since he included it in the set lists of the Wings' tour of Britain starting in May 1973—the film wasn't even released until June 27—it's obvious he envisioned it as a concert piece from the start. He continued doing it on the Wings Over the World tour, starting in Britain and Australia in the fall of 1975. The Wings version mainly was enhanced with lasers and strobe lights. When he returned to touring in 1989, Paul again did the tune, this time with the flash pots that became its trademark. After Guns N' Roses started playing the song live in 1991 and released its version, Paul apparently decided to up his game and reclaim the number starting with his 1993 New World Tour, adding even more explosions to the number. Over the years, the pyrotechnics for the number have grown ever more elaborate, particularly for outdoor stadium shows, which usually feature fireworks. He also famously did it at halftime of the 2005 Super Bowl.

YAPHET KOTTO

When the film opened up, I did what I usually did, I went back to Harlem. I went to Jock's Paradise Bar and the Red Rooster. I sat down at the bar with some brothers back there. When *Live and Let Die* premiered on TV, I watched it on television at a bar in Harlem. Whenever something good happens to me, I always go back to Harlem. That helps me remember, "This is where you came from, man. This is where your people are. When this movie comes out, you need to be with your people."

RAY MORTON

James Bond is portrayed as being a bit naïve and clueless in some scenes and a bit of an ineffectual bumbler in others. This was the result of a decision to not portray Bond as superior to the story's black characters out of a fear the movie would come across as racist. The intent was admirable, but the result was unfortunate. Still, any script that contains the line "Names is for tombstones, baby" can't be all bad.

***THE MAN WITH THE GOLDEN GUN* (1974)**

After the box-office success of *Live and Let Die,* Roger Moore's sophomore outing was rushed into production, an adaptation of Fleming's *The Man with the Golden Gun.* Essaying the titular role would be a distant cousin of Ian Fleming, legendary actor Christopher Lee, who was already a *James Bond* fan when he was invited to join the cast of the film as the high-paid assassin Scaramanga after Jack Palance of *Shane* (and later one-armed push-up fame) passed on the role. And the first hour of the film is fairly satisfying as Bond is sidelined when M takes him out of action after discovering 007 may be Scaramanga's next target–a plot that turns out to have been engineered by Scaramanga's mistress, Andrea Anders (a seductive Maud Adams), in an effort to extricate herself from an abusive relationship with the man with the golden gun.

GLEN OLIVER
(pop culture commentator)

Christopher Lee, always a blast on-screen, slid quite comfortably into the *Bond* architecture. Between this, *Star Wars,* and Peter Jackson's Tolkien films, it's clear that Lee's ability to effortlessly plug himself into already established mythologies was hugely impressive. He was an underrated performer who never enjoyed enough opportunities to truly shine, or truly test the breadth of his abilities.

RICHARD MAIBAUM
(cowriter, *The Man with the Golden Gun*)

I didn't think that Christopher Lee was properly cast as Scaramanga. I thought the character should be what he was in the book, which was a South American assassin who came from a circus background. It would be a very colorful kind of thing. But Christopher Lee got in his head, and they agreed with him, that Scaramanga should be just like James Bond, except that he veered over to crime. There was really no conflict between them from the standpoint of personality. Consequently, the scenes flattened out a bit, I thought.

FRED DEKKER

(cowriter, *The Predator*)

Christopher Lee is a really interesting and cool *Bond* villain. He's a little too debonair. He's a little too trying to be Bond himself. I wish he were a little scarier.

JOHN CORK

(author, *James Bond: The Legacy*)

I love Christopher Lee, but *Bond* villains should be dressed better than a sweatsuit and trainers. Scaramanga desperately needed a scene that established his ruthlessness and his brilliance. That never really comes. At the same time, his speech about how he found out he loves killing ranks among the best villain speeches in a *Bond* film.

GLEN OLIVER

His character in the picture was a bit underutilized and underexplored. Unlike many *Bond* baddies, I always got the feeling Scaramanga was "new money"—maybe even something of a poser—who wouldn't necessarily earn himself a chair at the table should the villains of the 007 universe ever call a Summit of Evil. If this is what was intended in his characterization, it's an interesting approach, because it reinforces the notion that Bond *could* be legitimately challenged and imperiled by a less audacious foe. It reminded the audience that 007 could be potentially thwarted by a more run-of-the-mill individual, who didn't need to lean on mercenary armies and space fleets and nukes to make problems.

TOM MANKIEWICZ

(cowriter, *The Man with the Golden Gun*)

I actually begged and pleaded and banged the table to have Jack Palance play Scaramanga. I thought he would have been perfect. That was exactly the guy I thought it should have been. I just thought it should be *Shane*. It didn't turn out to be *Shane*. It should have been Jack Palance and Alan Ladd. It should be the two greatest gunslingers.

Although Tom Mankiewicz began work on the script, growing tensions between him and director Guy Hamilton made this his final credited *Bond* film, and led to Richard Maibaum's taking over screenwriting duties for the film. Additionally, with the popularity of 1972's *Fists of Fury* and 1973's *Enter the Dragon*, martial arts became an important part of the film, in much the way the blaxploitation genre had previously impacted *Live and Let Die*. With cinematographer Ted Moore becoming ill, Oswald Morris stepped in to complete work on the picture.

TOM MANKIEWICZ

It was not a successful film in any way. This is where I parted with the *Bonds*. I left that picture after the first draft. When I got over to Hong Kong where Guy and Cubby were, it seemed like everybody wasn't quite in sync. When we got back to London, Guy wasn't particularly happy with me and I wasn't particularly happy with Guy. I remember going over to Cubby's house one day and said, "Cubby, I want to leave." And he said, "Why? What?" And I said, "I just feel like I don't have anything to give right now and I want to go." And then Dick [Maibaum] came back on the script and I went off to do *Mother, Jugs & Speed* with Peter Yates.

ALBERT R. BROCCOLI

(producer, *The Man with the Golden Gun*)

Tom really didn't have anything to do with *Golden Gun*. It was Dick Maibaum.

TOM MANKIEWCZ

I thought, and this is no disservice to Dick Maibaum who was a wonderful man and probably has his name on more of the *Bond* films than anybody by far, but Dick was like a constructionist and, for the most part, on every film I can think of, was rewritten by somebody else. Dick shared credit with a lot of people or people came on without credit and polished it in terms of dialogue and so on.

It's really the second half of the film where things go off the rails. Co-opting the issue of solar energy in the middle of the energy crisis, the plot revolves around a device called the Solex Agitator, which harnesses the power of the sun (although the writers had briefly toyed with a weather machine that could control the weather as well), and culminates at Scaramanga's Thai HQ, set amongst the scenic Ko Khao Phing Kan (now James Bond Island). It is equipped with its very own massive laser, the ultimate golden gun, which is apparently solely staffed by one burly guard who has way too much time on his hands.

RAY MORTON

(senior writer, *Script* magazine)

The screenplay for *The Man with the Golden Gun* has something of a split personality. The first half—in which Bond is trying to track down Scaramanga, the world's greatest hit man, who has sent Bond a message suggesting that 007 will be his next target—is relatively realistic thriller *Bond* material. It's also written that way and so is pretty effective. However, once the Solex Agitator is introduced, the script shifts into fantasy *Bond* mode. Scaramanga suddenly becomes a supervillain with a gimmicky handgun, a flying car, and a super-weapon that he can use to threaten the world. The two halves feel like two completely different screenplays that have been stitched together, which is essentially the case.

RICHARD MAIBAUM

I admit that the Solex Agitator was my idea, because I felt there wasn't enough to keep it going. After a showdown, what was there to go to? We had to flesh it out and came up with that device. It just flatly didn't work as we thought it would.

RAY MORTON

Tom Mankiewicz was the first writer on the film and it was his desire to write a more serious thriller about a duel between the two greatest gunmen in the world. However, after Mank departed due to conflicts with director Guy Hamilton following the writing of a first draft, Richard Maibaum was brought in to do a rewrite. Feeling the cat-and-mouse game between Bond and Scaramanga wasn't enough to support a feature-length narrative, Maibaum added the material involving the Solex. Fantasy wasn't Maibaum's forte and so this portion of the screenplay falls pretty flat. Mank was brought back to do a final polish, but he wasn't able to overcome the piece's many inherent flaws. The final result of all this stitching and mixing was one of the worst screenplays in the series, albeit one that features some excellent Mankiewicz one-liners, most notably "Speak now or forever hold your piece."

Although the producers eventually shot in Thailand, which provides the requisite picturesque globetrotting in the film, early possibilities included filming in Iran, which proved logistically difficult and, ultimately, too worrisome under the Shah's repressive regime. With the seams and the budgets beginning to show, ultimately there was nothing original or exciting enough to make the film stand out, including Peter Murton's sets, which were a pale shadow of Ken Adam's memorable production designs.

JOHN CORK

Peter Murton's production design, while heavily influenced by Ken Adam, is pretty good. The location of Scaramanga's lair is one of the most spectacular in the world.

MATT SHERMAN

(creator, James Bond Fan Events)

James Bond Island, during filming for *The Man with the Golden Gun*, was an isolated spot with pirates infesting the surrounding waters. There was a genuine element of risk during filming. Today, tourists have made it a hot spot of Thai tourism. I was shocked during a recent fan event of mine when many fans said they'd rather tour James Bond Island with me than other Asian *Bond* locations and even many of the gorgeous European *Bond* spots.

The story of James Bond Island is the story of how easily 007 opens closed doors. "James Bond" are words enough to guarantee press coverage of my events or to make a middle-of-nowhere island, one of many in Phang Nga Bay, a tourist attraction called "James Bond Island." Likewise, *Casino Royale* received permission to power motorboats past Venice homes threatened by erosion, where engines have been forbidden for a century. *Moonraker* set off explosions in a wildlife-protected river in Florida, and there are many more stories of local rules thrust aside to accommodate the *James Bond* books, films, and fans.

FRED DEKKER

I was rereading *The Man with the Golden Gun* novel, which is really interesting, because in the movie he meets Scaramanga halfway through, at a sporting event where Maud Adams is killed. In the book, he meets him pretty early on in the mission. Bond finds him almost immediately in Jamaica and they drink Red Stripe beer together—in a whorehouse. I thought, "Boy, you could never do this now." It's what I love about going back to Fleming and what his vision of who this guy was.

Ultimately, Scaramanga tests his mettle against Bond in his own island fun house while Britt Ekland, as a dreadful Mary Goodnight, plays a complete bimbo who proves to be nothing but a nuisance to Bond. And as much as the world understandably loves the late Hervé Villechaize, his Nick Nack, which played as a diminutive and more avuncular Oddjob, was not a particularly effective henchman. Even Roger Moore doesn't look like he's having as much fun as he did in *Live and Let Die* and for a moment dangerously finds himself in Connery territory when he manhandles Andrea for answers about the whereabouts of Scaramanga.

TOM MANKIEWCZ

Roger's not as physical as Sean, in the sense that Sean has something in his eye where he looks like he's a bastard. When Sean enters a room, it looks like violence may happen. Roger doesn't have that look about him. I've always said that Sean could sit opposite a woman at a table, as he did almost in every movie, and either kiss her or stick a knife in her under the table and say, "Waiter, I have nothing to cut my meat with." Roger can kiss the woman. If he sticks a knife in a woman under a table, Roger looks nasty somehow. You don't like him for doing it, where Sean could get away with it. Roger could do the line, but he couldn't kill the girl. Sean looks more like a bastard. He could actually kill the girl and the audience would roar with laughter, because Sean looked like a guy who was ready to go.

JOHN CORK

Hervé Villechaize and Christopher Lee are both brilliant. Maud Adams is very good as the dark, tormented lover, but she seems like she is in a completely different film from the very charming, scattered character played by Britt Ekland.

FRED DEKKER

In the novel, there's actually a thing in there where Mary Goodnight, who used to be Bond's secretary, is stationed in Jamaica. He buys her a drink and Fleming points out that he doesn't mention that this is his fourth of the day. He's embarrassed about how much he's drinking. I love that kind of stuff, because you don't see it in the movies often. You saw it in *Quantum of Solace* where he's drunk on the plane with [intelligence agent René] Mathis, and I just loved that. I said, "This is great. I don't know whose idea it was, but this is great." He's just lost one of the two loves of his life and he's drunk.

GLEN OLIVER

If there's a prevailing weakness in the film, it's Scaramanga's fun house. It felt cheap, and scant on menace and atmosphere. It was a solid idea in principle, but it didn't deliver the visceral gusto required to make the sequences in which it appeared work. Which, in turn, dampened the menace and aura around Lee's character. I'm not clear to what extent this was ever considered, but there was at some point in development consideration of somehow utilizing Disneyland as a *Bond* set piece—which could've been very odd and fun. I'm guessing Scaramanga's fun house grew out of this notion, but it really needed more fullness and scale to work in the way it was intended. Those same scenes might've worked wonderfully at Disneyland, for example. But as is, they're a bit constrained and cheap.

JOHN CORK

James Bond's fate should never come down to whether a hapless girl in a bikini bumps a button with her butt. Scaramanga's lair ultimately becomes unimpressive when we discover the entire solar power operation seems to be run by one very lonely Jesse Jackson look-alike.

While *The Man with the Golden Gun* proves to be a mishmash of ideas and action done far better in previous *Bond* films, all is not lost. Despite the fact most people hate it, the main title theme is a lulu by Lulu and the John Barry score, as always, is quite terrific.

MAURICE BINDER

(main title designer, *The Man with the Golden Gun*)

I get very involved with the songs. On *Golden Gun,* the original idea was for a slow, placid thing, so I thought we'd have reflections in water. Then all of a sudden the singer changed to Lulu, who bangs out songs, so the rhythm changed, so then I had to change my concept.

JOHN CORK

Even though there are great moments in the score, John Barry's penny-whistle and weird fun-house pastiche music undercut the drama. And even though he is a cad, 007 should not shove a girl in a closet while he makes love to a different woman.

The film also marked the return of the crowd-pleasing Clifton James as redneck sheriff J.W. Pepper, improbably vacationing in Thailand, from Louisiana.

JOHN CORK

Many times, James Bond seems like an incidental player in a film that seems to be more about J.W. Pepper's wacky vacation to Southeast Asia and the karate skills of Lieutenant Hip's nieces.

TOM MANKIEWICZ

Yeah, nobody should ever have brought him [J.W. Pepper] back. It's just that the audience loved him so much in *Live and Let Die* they decided to bring him back. He was never in my script. I do think it was, in essence, overproduced. He felt just totally unnecessary and terrible in *Man with the Golden Gun*.

GLEN OLIVER

I think Pepper fared somewhat better in *The Man with the Golden Gun*. It's not that [Clifton] James landed his role any more adeptly—he didn't—but the film's notion of having Bond team with someone who was clearly of an entirely different ilk, and clearly playing in an entirely different league, was at least provocative. This kind of wildly mismatched approach might be fun and interesting for the franchise to revisit in a future film, albeit in a more considered, less over-the-top manner.

At a budget of $7 million, the worldwide box office for the film was $98 million, with an anemic $21 million in the United States–prompting a reevaluation of how the *Bond* films would be made going forward. If changes weren't made, it was clear that the seemingly inevitable end for 007 might be near and it wouldn't be a golden bullet that killed him.

ALBERT R. BROCCOLI

I guess the failings were purely my fault, because I had a release date to make and I chose to go along with United Artists and make the release date rather than improve our position story-wise and production-wise. For instance, in the car chase where he goes over the river, the normal thing to do, but we didn't have time, was to have the police cars also try to do the same thing, and *they* go into the river for added humor and added suspense. But we didn't have the time to do it. We were on a tight schedule.

TOM MANKIEWICZ

I had dinner with Cubby and Guy [Hamilton] after they'd finished shooting at Cubby's house and everything was fine and nice after I did *Mother, Jugs &*

Speed. I don't know that I'd blame it on Guy or that I'd blame it on me, but maybe the third in a row was just too much.

GLEN OLIVER

The Man with the Golden Gun is a very interesting idea for a *Bond* film—essentially fusing established 007 conceits with Richard Connell's *The Most Dangerous Game*.

RIC MEYERS

(author, *Films of Fury: The Kung Fu Movie Book*)

To me, *The Man with the Golden Gun* was the height of Eon's malice afterthought. It was such a great idea, especially with Christopher Lee as Scaramanga, but at the very start the producers begin giving the audience, and Bond, the middle finger. First, again a pre-credit sequence spotlighting only the villain, but to add insult to injury they spotlight him in an unconvincing, unimpressive way, using what seems to be a reject from a touring company of *Guys and Dolls* as his adversary. Then it's revealed that his henchman is a little person, which is cool in one way, but also a clear diminishment of what they consider Bond's abilities. They continually show us what they think of Bond, as the character isn't even consistent from scene to scene. First, he enacts a silly fight sequence straight out of *The Saint,* which climaxes with him sucking, complete with making a funny face, a flattened bullet out of a belly dancer's navel, then swallowing it. The production seemed to actually be teasing veteran fans by making these fun-house-mirror remakes of Sean's scenes, which seemed to say, "Forget 007's fight at the beginning of *Goldfinger,* this is your Bond now. Nya, nya, nyaaa."

FRED DEKKER

This is a movie most people hate. I saw it in the theater opening day and saw it at least once or twice more in the theater after that. I have a real affection for it, because of the atmosphere of it. Barry's three-week score is terrific. Those locales are really interesting and exotic to me. It's sexist and dopey, but there's something about it that is a throwback that I like. The pre-credit sequence is one of my favorite pre-credits of all time. I don't think you have to have Bond in the pre-credits. I'm very firm about that, but it's interesting because he's not in *Live and Let Die,* either. That island and that score and the opening, that's worth the whole movie for me. That six to eight minutes is more fun than most of the later ones. I love the *Queen Mary* with the canted room and I love Scaramanga trying to kill the other guy who's coming out of the Bottoms Up Club. It's full of little things like that, which I enjoy more than *Skyfall*.

RIC MEYERS

There was also 007's sadistically slapping Scaramanga's mistress around and threatening Scaramanga's bullet maker with a shot to the privates. Then he spends most of the rest of the film rolling his eyes, along with me, at the upper-class twittiness of Britt Ekland's Mary Goodnight. Finally, of course, Sheriff Pepper reappears, to the delight of xenophobes everywhere (including folk who like laughing derisively at southerners). And *then* there are the standard operating racism "martial arts" sequences. Even then, before I really started getting into martial arts movies in 1978, their use of this unconvincing, condescending chop suey–socky of barely distinguishable karate, sumo, kung fu, and Muay Thai was both unconvincing and fairly insulting—resulting in a flavorless mishmash, with Bond ignominiously kicking a bowing student in the face, then getting his bacon saved by two schoolgirls (one of whom is played by the future landlady of Stephen Chow's *Kung Fu Hustle*, Qiu Yuen).

TOM MANKIEWICZ

I saw it at a screening that United Artists gave and I was very disappointed. I think in many ways *Golden Gun* and *Moonraker* are the two worst *Bonds*.

JOHN CORK

This is the third nipple of *Bond* films. It's strange, kind of funny, but definitely not sexy or exciting, and no one would miss it if it just disappeared.

RIC MEYERS

The film had all the ingredients of a classic if only they played it straight, but *nooooooo.* Even what should have been a titanic final showdown between cinematic pop culture icons—Dracula and James Bond—was delivered in a flat, predictable, unexciting, unimaginative, even cheap way. It left such a bad taste in so many people's mouths, eyes, and minds that finally, thankfully, saner heads obviously started to prevail.

With Harry Saltzman and Cubby Broccoli's relationship fraying at the seams, *The Man with the Golden Gun* would be the last of the *James Bond* movies to be coproduced by Saltzman, who would ankle the series after a particularly acrimonious negotiation in which the debt-laden Saltzman sold his rights in the *Bond* series to United Artists, forever shackling the Broccoli family to the studio as in *The Defiant Ones*.

Sadly, Saltzman, who had contributed so much to the franchise over the years, did not go out on a high note. *Golden Gun*, which had almost become the follow-up to *You Only Live Twice*, is among the worst of the *Bond* films, despite being anchored by the sensational performance of Christopher Lee as Francisco Scaramanga. With Saltzman's departure, the *Bond* pictures would become the sole purview of Cubby Broccoli and, ultimately, his children: stepson Michael G. Wilson and daughter Barbara Broccoli.

ALBERT R. BROCCOLI

Harry Saltzman and I both started together and he's just as much responsible for getting *Bond* off the ground as I was. Harry, I think, felt he wanted to do other films besides *Bond*, and I can understand that. Harry sold out his interest in our company.

STANLEY SOPEL

(associate producer, *On Her Majesty's Secret Service*)

In the early days, when the budgets were small, and were kept small by the money people—and we would have terrible fights if we went over budget in those days—it was important to have technicians who understood budgets and understood schedules, and understood that salaries had to be *earned*. If we had to work overtime, there weren't big overtime payments that had to be made. I don't think it's true to say that Broccoli did a certain job and Saltzman did a certain job and I mopped up behind them. We all did what had to be done. I suppose everyone was a specialist in their own field.

TOM MANKIEWICZ

They had been alternating. At the time they did not get along very well. I would say that Cubby in effect produced *Diamonds* and Harry, in effect, produced *Live and Let Die*. Cubby in effect produced *The Man with the Golden Gun*.

RICHARD SCHENKMAN

(editor, *Bondage* magazine)

Cubby was fascinating to me; a mass of contradictions. On one hand, a warm, generous family man. On the other hand, he could be vindictive and, in my opinion, overly greedy. I thought his occasional shortsightedness regarding fans was particularly irksome; somehow he didn't seem to grasp that in those long-ago days before the internet or even home video, we were the ones keeping the flame lit.

JOHN CORK

Tom Mankiewicz put it best. He said that Saltzman viewed the success of *Bond* as a launching point for his greater ambitions. Cubby and Harry were very different men. They had problems going back to the very start. Cubby resented Harry's endless outside projects, the way Harry would make commitments for the company, would make side deals, would blow up in public, at restaurants, and on the set. Cubby felt he had to put out too many fires started by Harry. On the other hand, Harry Saltzman was a fantastic ideas man. He was filled with endless energy. He pushed people to create at their highest level. With the success of *Bond,* he became almost a mini-studio. He was involved in twelve completed non-*Bond* films during the time he was producing with Cubby. Cubby only produced two others, and one of those, *Call Me Bwana,* he produced with Harry.

TOM MANKIEWICZ

Cubby and Harry, oddly enough, even though they wound up in various fights legal and personal, complemented each other in a strange way. Harry was a very volatile sophisticate who was forever suing people and threatening to quit. Cubby was sort of the voice of the audience all the time. He would look at the script and say, "Yeah, but how do you know that? I know he says it, but how do you know it?" Harry would say, "God, that doesn't matter, Cubby, he says it and that's fine, let's get on with it." They really had a complementary thing in those days.

JOHN GLEN

(director, *For Your Eyes Only*)

Cubby was the affable one and Harry was the sterner one, the one that used to crack the whip, but I've heard from other people that deep down he was a very kind person and if someone was in trouble or someone's family was in trouble, he would be the first to help. But it worked very well for them, Cubby being the affable guy, the popular guy, and Harry being the stern whip cracker.

GLORIA HENDRY

(actress, "Rosie Carver")

They handled you with kid gloves. They wined and dined and we had fantastic dinners together—formal, informal—and the food was incredible. They had a chair for me everywhere I went. It was always there with my name on it waiting for me. They made me feel, "Madame, what do you want on the set?" If I said, "I'd like some fruit," it was there. If I wanted a glass of wine, "Which wine would you like to have?" They spoiled you. They might not have paid well, but they'd fly you first class. You had maids and butlers taking care of you in the hotels everywhere you went. Harry Saltzman was a jewel. I hung out at his mansion and he had a pool in his home. It was huge.

STANLEY SOPEL

Of course, hard work can be fun, and we had the advantage of glamorous locations, because all *Bond* pictures were made in places like the Bahamas and Japan and Switzerland, and everybody wanted to go. We looked after our people well; we fed them well, and put them in good hotels. We had to look after our people because they, in turn, look after you. Unlike a lot of producers who have problems with unions and crews, I can honestly say we never did.

TOM MANKIEWICZ

Having worked with a lot of different producers, I just have never seen somebody who's as dedicated as Cubby was to those films. He worked so hard on them and he was really proud of them.

JOHN LANDIS

(director, *An American Werewolf in London*)

He was like the King of England and became the most powerful guy in the British movie industry. He also was very well liked. Cubby was very warm. Dana, his wife, was very glamorous. She used to be an actress. I saw her a number of times. Every time she was wearing a different mink coat. She also worked on a lot of the scripts. When the script was finished, very often from a number of different people, she was the one who put it together. It was quite impressive.

STANLEY SOPEL

It was a modest operation, really. We didn't have millions of secretaries flying around like some people might. Harry and Cubby had a Rolls-Royce each, but they were entitled to *that*; they didn't have *more* than one. They did well, and good luck to them—they deserved it. We never stopped work, that was the main thing. We just carried on and kept people on the payroll.

YAPHET KOTTO

(actor, "Kananga/Mr. Big")

Cubby thought he was my father and took me everywhere. He took me to Brazil. He took me to the West Indies. I went everywhere with him. Saltzman, he was kind of a little salty guy who thought that I was naïve and that I needed to work harder. Both were like uncle and father to me. I got along with them both. I was depressed when it was over. I still feel I'm part of the family now. The whole thing was about family.

JOHN GLEN

Cubby was very much the daddy. He was the one that was very popular with everyone. He was an amazing man. He trusted everyone. He employed what he thought were the best people, and he trusted them to do the job, and he was a kind man. In Egypt [for *Spy Who Loved Me*], I remember when all the food, which had come from England, was rotten and had to be thrown away, we were pretty desperate. We were eating the local Egyptian food, which wasn't very good, and Cubby got some spaghetti and he made a huge vat of it with tomato sauce and everything for the entire crew. It was a wonderful thing to do and everyone just loved that man. He was fantastic.

In 1981, the Academy of Motion Picture Arts and Sciences honored Cubby Broccoli with the prestigious Irving G. Thalberg Memorial Award. In his acceptance speech, Broccoli was magnanimous in praising his former partner, although it seemed unseemly of the Academy not to include Saltzman in the honor, given his over a decade of producing the film series with Broccoli.

BILL CONTI

(composer, *For Your Eyes Only*)

The call from the agent was "Cubby Broccoli wants to have lunch with you." This is after John Barry recommended me for *For Your Eyes Only.* I was in Los Angeles and, of course, Cubby was in London, so I went there for lunch. It was at Christmastime, and he picked me up at the hotel. We went out to lunch and he had a roll of $100 bills. And everyone he passed—the guy that opened the door, the maitre d, the busboy, the bellboy—he gave $100 to. It was Christmas season. He just slipped them $100 every time. And, of course, he invited me and my family. We went to dinners together with my family and his family. One of my daughters got sick; his doctor came over to my apartment at Sloane Square. He invited me to New Year's Eve at his house in Los Angeles. We came in the gate, and he had snow brought in. Everything was snow. He had the pipers brought in from Scotland to do "Auld Lang Syne." He sat my wife between Roger Moore and the French actor Louis Jourdan. She was in heaven. He was a gentleman. He must have had somebody that didn't like him, but I never knew anyone that didn't. Everyone that knew him didn't say anything but how wonderful he was. Cubby Broccoli was bigger than life. He was a rich guy. He treated everyone wonderfully.

CHARLES "JERRY" JUROE
(publicist)

"Join *Bond* and see the world," we used to say. I was everywhere on the *Bond*s. There's a business class and there's *Bond* class. First class, and then there's *Bond* class. *Bond* class was a world unto itself.

DAVID V. PICKER
(president and chief executive officer, United Artists)

Harry Saltzman was a whole different story. He was an outsider to the business, and in meeting with him it was hard to feel totally comfortable. There was, however, one aspect of his personality that touched me deeply, and that was his love for his wife, Jacqui. His deep caring for her was apparent, and through the years I always felt for him as his days grew darker. Harry changed as the *Bond* films grew increasingly successful.

JOHN GLEN

I didn't have too much to do with Saltzman, actually. I met him when we were shooting in Switzerland [on *On Her Majesty's Secret Service*]. I had dinner with him and Cubby and what have you, and while we were having dinner, the accountant came over to our table and he said, "Do you realize the stuntmen are signing the bar bill with your name?" And he showed Cubby one of the receipts. Cubby looked at it and he said, "I wouldn't mind, but they spelled my name wrong." He was a very generous man. As far as he was concerned, that was small potatoes.

TOM MANKIEWICZ

Guy Hamilton told me the quickest way to get a scene in that you really liked was to tell one of them that the other hated it. "That son of a bitch, he hates that scene? Well, that scene stays, goddammit!"

JOHN LANDIS

Guy told me the same thing. Cubby was very funny. He'd say, "Please talk about the opening sequence of the *Bond* picture with the purpose of it being to tell the audience to put your brains under the seat and say 'let's go.'"

CHARLES "JERRY" JUROE

It was a bad cop/good cop situation. They completely played United Artists like a Stradivarius. I spent more time over with Cubby and Harry than I did in my own office. They just took over my life.

STANLEY SOPEL

Harry was a great ideas man, and he'd come up with 100 ideas a minute. We'd have to throw 93 right out as being marvelously impractical, because they would cost too much or be impossible to shoot. Cubby perhaps was more practical, because he was a far more experienced producer at the time. But it was very much a team, and it's the very best team production I've ever seen in the years I've been in the business.

TOM MANKIEWICZ

Harry would get ideas in his head, and you just couldn't disabuse him of the ones that he loved. On *Live and Let Die,* he kept saying, "I've got this scene in my mind where Bond wakes up in bed and there's a crocodile next to him." I said, "But Harry, why didn't it eat him?" He said, "Well, they're asleep, the crocodile's asleep and Bond's asleep." I said, "Harry, how did it get up on the bed with its little legs?" He said, "Because they came in at night with a ramp!"

Harry would get fixated on an image and Cubby would be the one to say, "Harry, are you going to watch a goddamn crocodile walk up a ramp, for Christ's sake?" There was that kind of thing. Harry was just so mercurial. He got these brainstorms. He had a thing about Bond walking into a giant spin dryer. I don't know why, but he saw Bond at a giant Laundromat. It had nothing to do with anything that he got locked in this giant spin dryer. Harry was just obsessed with it. In the middle of *Live and Let Die,* when Bond runs down the street in New Orleans, Harry would say, "That's where he could get into the spin dryer." I would say, "No, Harry. Why would you have a Laundromat?" Harry was a shotgun of ideas and very forgetful about some of them and obsessive about others.

CHARLES "JERRY" JUROE

Nobody got along with Harry, but I did on *The Man with the Golden Gun*. Cubby was supposed to fly to Thailand and the weather was very bad, and Harry was flying over with Roger. I said to Cubby, "Don't come," because it was very bad weather, and I didn't want to have a repetition of Glenn Miller. Harry said, "You're telling them not to come?" I said, "I'm telling them not to come." I'm not that high up on the totem pole to make that kind of decision, but I did. Harry suddenly just fell in love with me. He left at the end of the movie, but he felt I showed balls. I guess that's the only answer.

TOM MANKIEWICZ

Cubby was more the conscience of the audience in a strange way. He wants to make sure everyone understands everything. I used to use an example of something that never happened: "Now, listen, Cubby and Harry. Here is what happened. Bond falls off the boat and as he is sinking underwater he meets an octopus. But this octopus has nine arms." Harry would say, "And he is bright red and on roller skates and he blows up like a balloon." You say, "No, Harry, no." Harry says, "Why not? Let's put him on roller skates. Have you ever seen an octopus roller-skate underwater?" And he would go on and on and on. Meanwhile Cubby would say, "I still don't understand what's funny about the nine arms." I would say, "Well, Cubby, octopuses have eight arms." He'd say, "Yeah, I know that. Do you think the audience is going to get it?"

TANYA NITINS

(author, *Selling James Bond*)

Tensions between Broccoli and Saltzman came to a head over the technological focus in the later films. Saltzman was concerned that the films had become "too gimmicky" and that the films shouldn't be trying to compete with the big blockbuster films that were being released at the time. Yet in terms of product placement, it was Saltzman who had the reputation of being underhanded in his dealings. For example, director Guy Hamilton complained in his commentary on *Goldfinger* that Saltzman had snuck onto the set and placed Gillette products around a scene about to be filmed after doing a deal with the company. Hamilton ended up throwing all the props out, as it was too blatant.

SHANE RIMMER

(actor, "Commander Carter")

Cubby listened. That was a great bonus. After he talked to you, you weren't afraid to open that door and go into his office and say what was on your mind. It was good. I never met Saltzman and I think that they probably stayed away from each other at that point in time. It was a family with Cubby and Dana, which was quite different from any other big film operation. It was still a family-run business and there was a lot of concern that their actors were in the right place, comfortable, and this was followed through on every picture they made. It was awfully good to work in those conditions. It was a joy to work on the *Bond* franchise.

STANLEY SOPEL

And it was by design that we put together a "family," and that was why we had virtually the same crew on the earlier pictures. At the end of a picture, people would absolutely *wait*—not take another job, but wait for the next *Bond* picture in order to be on it. Not because we paid the best wages in the business, but because they wanted to work for us. We created a very nice family. It was *fun,* and that was something Cubby and Harry were very keen on—that the pictures should be fun and not just hard work.

JOHN CORK

At some point, Harry started taking his *Bond* money and, in 1968, he started borrowing against his wealth and investing that borrowed money into a French camera company, Éclair, and around 1970, investing more into Technicolor, the lab that made many of the release prints for Hollywood movies. Both these investments proved to be disastrous. Harry borrowed more and put more money into these companies, eventually borrowing against his 50 percent share of Danjaq S.A., the holding company that had the film rights to the *Bond* novels. The bank that held the debt was UBS, the giant Swiss banking firm.

When Harry missed payments with his creditors, all hell broke loose. UBS was threatening to seize control of Danjaq. This could mean that they could force the company into receivership and sell off the assets, which was the right to make *James Bond* films, out from under Cubby Broccoli and Harry Saltzman. Harry desperately needed to sell his half of Danjaq to pay off UBS, but Cubby had veto power over any buyer. Once Cubby convinced UBS to back off the seizure, the pressure actually mounted on Harry. Cubby, of course, wanted to buy Harry's half of the company, so he said no to every potential buyer. Cubby wanted to force Harry to sell his half of Danjaq back to Cubby for pennies on the dollar.

At this point, the last *Bond* film had been *The Man with the Golden Gun*, which had sold fewer tickets in the US than any previous *Bond* film. There was no guarantee that *Bond* would ever again be a huge success. Harry resented the pressure from Cubby, so he turned to the only entity that Cubby could not legally veto: United Artists. UA ended up being very slow to pay Harry Saltzman the money he expected from the sale of his half of Danjaq S.A. Eventually, Saltzman, who thought he would end up with something like $10 million, ended up getting a small fraction of that.

DAVID V. PICKER

Harry felt that he didn't need Cubby to be successful, and began to produce films besides *Bond*. UA even financed several of these, including *Billion Dollar Brain* and *Battle of Britain*. As *Bond*'s success grew, Harry's ego grew as well, and he ventured into businesses he knew little about. His focus was spread, his ego was growing, and financial woes started to build up. The details of his buyout by UA in 1975 are not known to me, but the rumors about the incredible financial pressure he was under and his declining relationship with his partner were rampant. To survive he had to sell out, and I heard it wasn't pretty.

After his buyout and the untimely passing of his beloved Jacqui, Harry's presence in the business declined and he passed away quietly and largely forgotten in 1994. When Cubby took over the *Bond* franchise, Harry's name slowly faded away. Now in the twenty-first century with the extraordinary revival of *Bond* in the hands of Cubby's daughter, Barbara, and his stepson, Michael Wilson, Harry is no more than an asterisk. But he was much more than that. There are many people along the way that helped make *James Bond* into the most successful franchise in movie history, but if it hadn't been for Harry Saltzman, it wouldn't have happened at all.

THE SPY WHO LOVED ME (1977)

With *The Spy Who Loved Me*, Cubby Broccoli, now the sole producer on the 007 films, makes it all look absolutely effortless, but getting to that point was one of the greatest challenges of his career. After Harry Saltzman sold out his percentage in the *Bond* films to United Artists, it wouldn't have been obvious to most that rebounding from one of the least successful films in the franchise, one should throw every cent he could at the next one rather than cut his losses. One need only look at other franchises of the time, like *Planet of the Apes,* which slowly descended from the genius of the 1968 original to, four films later, 1973's nearly unwatchable *Battle for the Planet of the Apes*, whose budgets were slashed deeper and deeper with every subsequent outing.

JOHN CORK

(author, *James Bond: The Legacy*)

Cubby didn't bet the farm on *The Spy Who Loved Me*. United Artists did. UA knew that Cubby was not happy that they had rescued Harry before Cubby could force Harry to make a deal. They also believed that they were sitting on a fountain of money. Because of UA both being the studio and the producer, they were getting a 30- to 40-percent discount on their investment. Whereas previously, they had 40 percent of the profits of the *Bond* films as the financier, now they received 70 percent. It was much easier for them to make back their investment. Plus, they were eager to prove that they intended to have a good relationship with Cubby, so they happily upped the budget on *The Spy Who Loved Me*.

MICHAEL G. WILSON

(special assistant to the producer, *The Spy Who Loved Me*)

The Spy Who Loved Me was the perfect Roger Moore vehicle. We got it just right between drama and his light touch. I think in the early ones, he probably played against the script a bit, because they weren't quite written for him—they were written for Sean.

JOHN GLEN

(second-unit director, *The Spy Who Loved Me*)

The light, throwaway approach was Roger's hallmark. He never built himself up as a great dramatic actor. He was a screen personality. We'd have been fools if we hadn't gone the way we did with Roger. *The Spy Who Loved Me* was really the start of how we discovered what we could do best with Roger.

SIR ROGER MOORE

(actor, "James Bond")

My attitude was that he's sort of a ridiculous hero. Heroes to me are ridiculous and I have to play them tongue in cheek. I like the jokes, and when there's a spot that requires a joke we sometimes shot a dozen different versions and I would make up quite a few lines—all of them unusable. You can't suddenly become another person. I made up my background of how I think Bond is, how he behaves and reacts. It just happens to be the way I would behave and react.

SHANE RIMMER

(actor, "Commander Carter")

It was interesting to see both of them at work, Sean and Roger, doing two pictures with Connery and one picture with Roger Moore. You saw why they were where they were at the top of the heap. They both had something. They were electric when they started to work. Sean Connery was very serious about his contribution to Bond. Roger Moore a little less so. He liked to gag around quite a lot. Getting people in trouble and this and that. All in fun, mind you. Not serious. So it was great to work with both, because we saw that, as unlike each other as they were, there was still something very similar in both their talents. They got to the top, and they got there on their own merits.

JOHN GLEN

When I took over the series [with *For Your Eyes Only*], Roger was established in the role and what one could change was reasonably limited. But I think his personality was such that he wasn't going to change. I remember once having lunch in a restaurant and his wife, Luisa, said, "Oh, Roger, you should do this and that." And Roger said to me, "What do you think, John?" I said, "Well, you haven't been doing too badly up to now. Keep on doing what you've been doing."

> The original Ian Fleming novel of *The Spy Who Loved Me* itself was impossible to adapt given the author's insistence that only the title of the novel be used and nothing else. Not that it would have been easy to include any part of the unique story, divided into three sections: "Me," "Them," and "Him," which is told in first person from the perspective of Vivienne Michel, a Canadian woman who is looking after an isolated hotel when two mobsters arrive to burn it down for the insurance money for its owner. But prior to committing arson and pinning it on Vivienne, the two killers attempt to rape her, when they are interrupted by the arrival of none other than James Bond, gentleman agent. Only the character of the metal-toothed Jaws has its origins in the novel, and loosely at that, in the character of the steel-toothed Sol "Horror" Horowitz, one of the mobsters. Sandor, villain Karl Stromberg's other ill-fated assassin, bears a striking resemblance to the bald Sluggsy Morant bear of a man, his partner-in-crime.

CHARLES ARDAI

(editor, Hard Case Crime)

My favorite novel is no one else's: *The Spy Who Loved Me,* the one told in first-person by a female character who has the good fortune to have Bond come upon her while she's being held captive by two sadistic thugs in a North American motel on a rain-swept night. In addition to being a very sexy read for a pubescent boy, I remember the book being very much in the hard-boiled tradition—it felt like Bond had wandered into a Mickey Spillane novel, or maybe one by Raymond Chandler.

JOHN CORK

Ian Fleming strongly asserted at one point that he didn't want to have a film made of *The Spy Who Loved Me*. He had also said he didn't want the book published in paperback. He had been deeply hurt by some of the criticisms of the novel, which was very personal to him. Eon/Danjaq had to do a great deal of convincing to get the literary rights holders to let them use the title, and as part of that, they had to agree to create an entirely different plot.

CHARLES ARDAI

I remember when I discovered that a *Bond* film might literally have nothing to do with the book it was named after—*The Spy Who Loved Me* being the perfect example. That was jarring to me as a young fan: how can they take just the title and nothing more? But they did, and I just had to live with it. You just learned that the movies were their own thing and let them be that.

> Clearly fashioning an entirely original *Bond* adventure for the first time was a challenge, given the number of writers who labored on it, ranging from *A Clockwork Orange*'s Anthony Burgess to *Thunderbirds*' Gerry Anderson, comic book writer Cary Bates, Ronald Hardy, Derek Marlowe, Stirling Silliphant, Tom Mankiewicz, and, inevitably, veteran series scribe Richard Maibaum.

JOHN CORK

After the low grosses of *The Man with the Golden Gun*, UA wanted new writers. Most notably, this involved letting Anthony Burgess, author of the novel *A Clockwork Orange*, and John Landis try their hand at writing for 007.

JOHN LANDIS
(director, *Animal House*)

I went to work the first day and was introduced to Guy Hamilton, who was the director of the movie at the time and quite an interesting person. I really liked him. Then, I met Tony Burgess, who was an interesting guy. Very eccentric and he had a twitch. He had been working on it for a while. He kept going back to this idea of kidnapping the Pope, but Cubby wouldn't go for it, "No, we're not kidnapping the Pope."

RAY MORTON

(senior writer, *Script* magazine)

All of these writers worked on various treatments and screenplays for *The Spy Who Loved Me* during that film's protracted development process. None of their work was deemed satisfactory, although a few of their ideas were retained when Richard Maibaum was brought back and finally delivered a workable screenplay that was then further developed by Christopher Wood.

TOM MANKIEWICZ

They're always looking for new blood in that way, but the people who've written *Bond* the best are the tried-and-true people. There is a certain knack to writing a *Bond* picture. It doesn't make you a great writer or a bad writer if you've got it or you don't have it. But a lot of writers have great difficulty writing *Bond,* where sometimes you cram nine hours of an impossible story to follow into an hour and 57 minutes that you hope really works. It's a very bastard kind of form of writing. Some people are real good at it . . . and some aren't.

LEWIS GILBERT

(director, *The Spy Who Loved Me*)

We often scrapped whole scripts, in fact. We get something we reject totally and start all over again with a totally new idea. On *The Spy Who Loved Me,* we had quite a lot of them.

JOHN LANDIS

I'd done *Schlock* and I was up for three different jobs. One was as a writer for Dino De Laurentiis, one was for Milos Forman, and one was the *James Bond* job. I literally had meetings on all three movies within one week. Dino wanted to make what he called "a big monster movie." I asked, "When you say 'a big monster movie,' do you mean a big budget or do you mean literally a big monster?" What he wanted was a *Towering Inferno,* a monster to create disasters. I said, "Well, the ultimate archetype of this is probably King Kong," which was interesting because he had never thought of King Kong before that. We watched the original *King Kong* together at a bungalow at the Beverly Hills Hotel and I showed him *Godzilla* and *The Beast from 20,000 Fathoms* in a week. Then I met with Milos Forman, who had literally just won the Oscar for *One Flew Over The Cuckoo's Nest* like two days before. I was very excited to meet him and I saw him at the Beverly Wilshire Hotel and he had his Oscar on the coffee table. We were talking and it was actually going very well when he asked if I'd seen all his movies, and I said, "Yes." He said, "Well, which do you think is my best movie?" I said, "Well, I love *Firemen's Ball.*" And he asked if there was another movie I liked, and I said, "*Black Peter.*" At that point, he indicates the Oscar on the table and says, "What about *Cuckoo's Nest*?" I said, "Well, that was a terrific movie, but I'm really fond of that book." The bottom line is that I talked myself out of that job.

Then I saw Cubby Broccoli. I met Cubby at his house in Beverly Hills right off Sunset Boulevard. What was impressive about Cubby's house was that you went in a gate and then there was a very long drive with trees before you got to the house, which was impressive. I really liked him and he was very warm and generous. We talked about *James Bond* and we talked about ideas, and I just made up a bunch of stuff in the room, and he said, "Okay, can you leave for London next week?" So, he flew me to London and they really rolled out the red carpet. It was cold in London, and I'm from Los Angeles, and when I get there Cubby says, "Where's your coat?" I said, "I'm a *schmuck,* I didn't bring one." The next day he walks in and had bought me a coat, and they got me this gigantic apartment called Park Lane overlooking Hyde Park with two bedrooms, a living room, and a kitchen. I could walk to work, because they had offices on South Audley Street, near the Dorchester Hotel.

ALBERT R. BROCCOLI

(producer, *The Spy Who Loved Me*)

John Landis is a very bright boy. I did talk to him, and we did hire him, but his contribution would have been actually "*Animal House Bond.*" Anthony Burgess' contribution did not appear—he's a brilliant writer, but it did not appear in the work we did.

LEWIS GILBERT

I think it was around 11 or 12 writers, really, when you consider everyone who was hired to contribute in some way.

JOHN LANDIS

I had an idea for a teaser that Guy Hamilton quite liked. It was in a Latin American country, where we fade up in a very busy marketplace. At that point, the films had literally become comedies with Roger, so what I wanted to do was bloody him up. So he staggers into the shot, clearly wounded, blood dripping down his face, clothes ragged. He's being pursued. He staggers into the village making his way through the crowded market and up the stairs, and then into a church. Then these soldiers, the Federales, come and start ripping the marketplace apart, looking everywhere for James Bond. They go into this big cathedral. They go up and down the pews looking for Bond and pull people out of the confessional and put guns to their faces. After really searching the place thoroughly, they can't find him. As they leave, the camera slowly does a 180-degree to reveal, mounted on a wall above the altar of Jesus Christ, a large crucifix, and who should be hanging from it, but James Bond. That was my idea to which Cubby said, "No way."

TOM MANKIEWICZ

Danton Rissner was then running United Artists, and they'd had so many different people work on the script. Then one day, Danton said to Cubby, "Why don't you call Mank?"And he and Cubby called me up and said, "We've got the script. It needs a rewrite—and you gotta do it." They said, "You can't get any credit," because there's a thing called the Eady Levy plan [a British film subsidy] which all these pictures were made under. You were allowed three Americans and the rest have to be British unless you register an American in the beginning. I would come up to Cubby's house and have the pages typed up, but I never was on the set of that. I just did a page one rewrite.

In the end, Christopher Wood came aboard and got cowriting credit for the film with Maibaum. In the process, he also transformed the film's villain from Blofeld to Karl Stromberg (played by *The Enemy Below*'s German sub commander Curt Jürgens), as a result of ongoing litigation with Kevin McClory over the rights to SPECTRE, which precluded the use of Blofeld (other than a thinly veiled unnamed bald, white-cat-stroking villain in the teaser of *For Your Eyes Only*) in any of the films until *Spectre*, which was filmed after Eon finally had acquired all of McClory's purported rights from his estate years after he passed away.

STEVEN JAY RUBIN

(author, *The James Bond Films*)

Fearing the possibility of a legal battle with McClory, who had sole film rights to the SPECTRE organization, Broccoli had already told Christopher Wood to remove all traces of SPECTRE from the final shooting script of *The Spy Who Loved Me*.

JOHN LANDIS

I had Blofeld in it. He became a fish man in the movie, Curt Jürgens.

JOHN CORK

Initially scripts involved the revival of SPECTRE, but Kevin McClory sued, so they dropped SPECTRE. [Producer] Michael Wilson was heavily involved in developing the story arc between Bond and Russian agent Anya Amasova.

> Originally Guy Hamilton was going to reprise his role as director on the film until he left during early start-up delays to direct *Superman: The Movie* instead. Eventually he was replaced on that film by Richard Donner, leaving Broccoli to invite Lewis Gilbert to return to the *Bond* fold. Gilbert was directing his first 007 film since *You Only Live Twice*, a film to which *The Spy Who Loved Me* bears an uncanny similarity, despite producer Cubby Broccoli's views to the contrary.

JOHN CORK

When Lewis Gilbert came in, he pushed for the story to echo many elements of *You Only Live Twice*. Gilbert brought in Christopher Wood, who did the final rewrites.

RAY MORTON

Christopher Wood loved the *Bond* formula. When he was hired to rewrite Richard Maibaum's initial draft of *The Spy Who Loved Me,* his stated goal was to celebrate that formula, and I think he did so extremely well. *Spy* gives us absolutely everything we want and expect in a *Bond* film, and does so in superbly entertaining fashion. Wood had a light touch and a gift for clever and often humorous dialogue that was a perfect fit for the *Bond* films of the 1970s.

CHRISTOPHER WOOD
(cowriter, *The Spy Who Loved Me*)

Lewis Gilbert mentioned to my agents that he was looking for a writer. They recommended me. For *Seven Nights in Japan*, I would drive to his home and we would discuss the story and its development—and many other things. Lewis is a warm, friendly man, very easy to work with. Immune to pressure and tantrums.

TOM MANKIEWICZ

I think what they wanted from me was more wit and style. *Golden Gun* hadn't worked out. And where were the old kind of shameless puns? Dick Maibaum, God bless him, always used to say, "I love Mankiewicz for *Diamonds Are Forever* when they stuffed the diamonds up the corpse's ass and Bond quipped,

'Alimentary, my dear Mr. Leiter.'" That's what the pictures needed. They were a shameless kind of pun, but you could only get away with them in a *Bond* movie. Even though a lot of people don't like it, I love it when Bond points the gun at the bullet maker in *Golden Gun* and says, "Speak now or forever hold your piece." It was those kind of things they wanted on *Spy*.

Also, Curt Jürgens had to be sophisticated. He was nothing more than a German version of Charlie Gray [in *Diamonds Are Forever*]. He had a lot of "Good evening, Mr. Bond. Have some of this wonderful wine." Not like a Donald Pleasence Blofeld at all. I think that's really what they wanted, to zing it and for me to punch up Jaws. My reward for it was I was Dr. Mankiewicz who was blown up in the helicopter as they left. Although it was Dr. Markovitz in the film.

ALBERT R. BROCCOLI

We'd been going almost 18 years, so there's got to be a lot of imagination. But we never really look back and try to copy anything. The only connection, if there was one, is the fact that Lewis Gilbert directed both pictures.

GLEN OLIVER

(pop culture commentator)

It is *extremely* similar to *You Only Live Twice*—which is lazy and weird no matter how you look it at. Does this hurt *The Spy Who Loved Me*? Not really. It's a solid enough film on its own merits to overcome this inevitable, and very valid, comparison. If *Spy* hadn't been so charismatic and strong, this derivation would be vastly more troubling and damning. Besides, *The Spy Who Loved Me* is a Roger Moore movie. *You Only Live Twice* had that other guy in it.

ALBERT R. BROCCOLI

It's a very remote thing, completely. It is entirely different in the concept. I think it's a very minor point. Surely, they are always capturing something or other, aren't they? I mean villains and heroes. There has to be that conflict, where they are after something and they get it. In that case, you'll probably find that true in other stories, even more than *Bond*, where they're doing the same thing.

MICHAEL G. WILSON

I think it is difficult, in a way, to constantly be devising new capers for Bond. The limitations on the character are British Secret Service and sort of spy. This is basic, and when you get into that, you do become limited to some extent in the variations. We try to make our capers reasonably important and for that reason it's sometimes difficult. If you made them less important, then I suppose we could have more of a variety.

ALBERT R. BROCCOLI

People might say there was a train in *From Russia with Love* and there's a train in [*The Spy Who Loved Me*], and there was a train in *Live and Let Die*. But we found that those are similarities you can't really hide because it's a matter of transportation. It's like saying we won't use a plane anymore, because we had a plane in *You Only Live Twice*. It's part of the means of advancing the plot in the story and doing something interesting.

Although it is indeed a virtual remake of *You Only Live Twice*, only this time it's about submarines and not space capsules, who cares? *The Spy Who Loved Me*, which came out the same summer as *Star Wars* on July 7, 1977, is a delight from start to finish. Roger Moore has never been better as Bond and the Ken Adam sets are utterly mesmerizing, from the inside of the sub-swallowing *Liparus* to Stromberg's underwater base, *Atlantis*. The gadgets are inventive, none more than Bond's Lotus Esprit, which plunges into the water only to transform into a submarine car (which was later bought at auction by Elon Musk, who is hoping to turn it into a working submersible car—we wouldn't bet against him).

GLEN OLIVER

The Lotus is one of those elements many people seem to grouse about—but most of the people doing that grousing are very likely hypocrites, because they'd quite likely be more than happy to own a weaponized, amphibious sports car of their very own. Especially one which was given to them. Is it dopey? Sure. Is it practical? Probably not. But in a story which also features underwater cities, submarine-eating supertankers, an indestructible gargantuan with shiny metal teeth and—even more improbably—Barbara Bach as a Russian intelligence agent, why on earth would a submarine car be any issue at all?

DESMOND LEWELLYN
(actor, "Q")

Practically all the gadgets we used are real things. The jet pack in *Thunderball* was from the American army. Philips Electronics supplied us with a lot of stuff and they got great publicity from it. The submarine car actually went underwater. You'd have to wear a wetsuit and a breathing apparatus, but the car actually went 27 knots and down 450 feet. It was filmed in shallower water because it was easier. But, I mean, there you have got an underwater car.

TOM MANKIEWICZ

What's really wonderful is not that you have a Lotus underwater, but that he turns on the blinker. When the car turns underwater, the real thing blinks on and off.

FRED DEKKER
(director, *The Monster Squad*)

How much does it cost Q Division to build the Lotus? What is Q Division's budget? Who says yes? Does it go as high the PM? Can M okay the Lotus? I start to ask questions like that. I never asked about Blofeld. He's a criminal mastermind and he's got billions of dollars so he can build a base in a volcano in Japan and nobody will notice. The World Trade Center took five years or something. They're bad guys so that doesn't bother me. I'm just being a nerd now. I think Tom Mankiewicz introduced that kind of over-the-top plotting. It's not even dialogue or character, it's plotting. The audience will cheer when they see that this car can actually go underwater. Whereas in *Goldfinger*, Boothroyd shows him all the stuff it does and then he uses it. It's a magic trick. Look how much money we spent on this movie. Okay, but does it make sense? All he uses the Lotus for is to blow up the helicopter that's chasing him. He could have fired that rocket from the road.

MATT SHERMAN

Interestingly, the *Bond* film that first got me hooked, *The Spy Who Loved Me*, seems to be my least favorite lately. I adore Sir Roger Moore in the role and his *Spy* supporting cast is excellent, but things feel a bit by-the-numbers to me until the final, protracted battle inside the *Liparus* supertanker, an amazing sequence that saves the film. My feelings likely stem from how I've seen this particular film so many times, so that it holds no surprises any longer.

Above water, although clearly capable of flotation, is the gorgeous Barbara Bach as Major Anya Amasova, Agent Triple X, the resourceful opposite number of Bond in the Soviet KGB. This despite the fact that Catherine Deneuve had expressed interest in the role early on as well.

RAY MORTON

The screenplay introduces what is arguably the best concept for a *Bond* Girl in the series to date, a female version of 007, an idea that has been reused a number of times since. The tone of the piece strikes an almost perfect balance between humor and seriousness. The dialogue in the script by Wood and Tom Mankiewicz, who did an uncredited polish just prior to filming, is clever and witty, and the screenplay provides Roger Moore with two of his best scenes ever: Bond responding to Anya's mention of his late wife with "You made your point," and his later admission that, yes, he was the man who killed Anya's fiancé in the film's spectacular pre-credit sequence.

SHANE RIMMER

Barbara Bach was terrific. She was very nice, and she had a bit to think about with The Beatles sort of group around all the time. But she was good, so her time was rather split between that sort of relationship with Ringo and doing the acting bit.

In an interview at the time with *Playboy*, the now press-shy Bach, who grew up in Manhasset, Long Island, the daughter of a costume jeweler, and later became a model, who turned down an interview for this book, confessed, "I was a skinny little kid, and such a tomboy as a child. Having one brother a year older and one a year younger, I'd always been just one of the boys. When I got to be about 15 or 16, it came as a surprise to me that I was actually a girl."

TOM MANKIEWICZ

I don't think she's a very good actress. I saw Roger right after *Moonraker* and I said, "How was Lois Chiles?" He said, "The only time in my life I wished I was acting with Barbara Bach." But Barbara Bach was so breathtaking to look at. I was in England either doing *The Eagle Has Landed* or starting *Superman* when they were shooting it, because I was just finished rewriting *Spy Who Loved Me* and I walked on the set and I remember getting Cubby together with [*Superman* director] Dick Donner. I walked down to the set and it was like old home week. It was so wonderful to see all those people again, because the crew was hired and rehired and rehired [on a *Bond* movie]. Guys would look down from what we call "up high" up on the grid, and say "Hey, Mank." It was an absolute homecoming, and there in the middle of it all was Barbara Bach in a white terry-cloth bathrobe and underneath it she had a bikini or something on. I said, "Boy. Wow." I had no idea who was going to play the part and Cubby said, "Yeah, she looks great, doesn't she?"

RICHARD MAIBAUM

I'm very pleased about the reticence that we have used in the *Bond*s as far as sex and violence are concerned. I think the only nudity in the entire picture is when they got on the American submarine and she takes a shower. The sailor looks and sees her and sees just a flash of one breast as she goes in the shower. The captain of the sub says, "What's a matter, sailor? You've never saw an officer taking a shower before?"

TOM MANKIEWCZ

My favorite line I ever wrote for a *Bond* movie was never in the movie. Roger Moore meets Barbara Bach at a bar. He orders her a drink and then she says to the bartender, "And for the gentleman, a vodka martini, shaken not stirred." I'd written a scene where, and it's the only time I'm breaking my rule where I'll actually refer to somebody in a former movie, and he said, there's something about a photo of her, and she said, "The only picture we have of you, Mr. Bond, was taken in bed with one of our agents, Miss Tatiana Romanova." And Roger said, and this is in the script, "And was she smiling?" And she said, "As I recall, her mouth was not immediately visible in the photograph." And Roger said, "Ah, then I was smiling." They wouldn't let that in the movie. I think we always had some censor troubles.

> To this day, the film's teaser remains the most iconic and most crowd-pleasing of all the *Bond* pre-title sequences as Moore launches himself off a snow-covered cliff on skis and plummets for what seems like hours before a parachute billows out revealing the Union Jack. This leads into a gorgeous Maurice Binder title sequence which would not be topped until Daniel Kleinman's *GoldenEye sequence* many years later (and he had the help of contemporary CGI) accompanied by the note-perfect title song "Nobody Does It Better" by Carly Simon.

RIC MEYERS

(author, *For One Week Only: The World of Exploitation Films*)

The pre-credit sequences are a perfect example of the 180-degree change in approach. Rather, as in the prior two films, spotlight villainy and the villain, they start by establishing a threat to noble military men, establish a new kind of Moore anti-twit *Bond* Girl (complete with a boyfriend played by Michael Billington, who was this close to replacing Connery, and, of course, would have been superior to Lazenby) and then Moore is finally given the introduction as

Bond he always should have had. Everything—from the setup, lighting, dialog, wardrobe, and music—is designed to support and encourage a new approach to Moore in particular and *Bond* in general. Things are brighter, lighter, bouncier, and more colorful—befitting the new Bond's more casual, sardonic, command, as well as his expert deadpan delivery ("So does England"). He steps out into bright sunshine, Marvin Hamlisch's crazy-like-a-fox disco-tinged music kicks in, and, suddenly, finally, Sean's Bond is left behind in the powder.

JOHN GLEN

Guy Hamilton had directed the films that followed *On Her Majesty's Secret Service,* and Guy had his own people. I didn't know him particularly well, and he didn't really like second units anyway. He had his own way of doing things and he had his own editor, Burt Bates, who was a very good editor, and he didn't need me. He had his own people and that's the right of the director. I'm sure Cubby probably put a word in for me, but at the end of the day, he wouldn't stand in the way of the director having the people he wanted, so I went off and did other things.

I did a lot of very good second-unit stuff, action scenes, and I was in a bit of a trough in my career when I had a phone call one Christmas Eve from Lewis Gilbert. He said that Thelma Connell had been his editor, and she got cancer and was dying. On her deathbed, she turned around and she said, "You'll have to get someone to replace me. Get John Glen." She said that because I'd worked with her on the TV series *The Four Just Men.* She was heavily involved with the *Robin Hood* TV series and also *Four Just Men,* and she felt she owed me a favor. On her deathbed, she more or less willed me to Lewis Gilbert. I suddenly found myself out in Paris working on a film called *Seven Nights in Japan,* which wasn't a particularly good film, but I had this mountain of film to edit and I was in a foreign country. I was in France and strange assistants with French assistants and what have you, and I had to adapt very rapidly and get through this mountain of film and get it all together, which I did. I did it by harnessing the French assistants, who were fantastic. I started editing and the chief girl assistant said to me, "You cut everything yourself. Why don't you mount the film and let us cut it?"

I said, "When in Rome, do as the Romans do. I'll give it a try." We developed this system and it speeded up the whole process, so it was an eye-opener for me and I learned a lot. After that, one day Lewis [Gilbert] said to me, "Cubby Broccoli is coming over today. He wants me to direct the new *Bond, The Spy Who Loved Me.*" There'd been quite a gap since I last worked on a *Bond* picture. He had lunch with Cubby and when he came back he said, "Cubby was full of praise for you and he wants you to direct some of the second unit," so that's how I came to direct the ski parachute chase.

GLEN OLIVER

The pre-credit sequences in a *Bond* picture may be best regarded as a pre-show, if you will. A "warm up," an "opening act." They may or may not relate directly to the story which will follow in the actual film, but they sway you into the spirit of *Bond*. In many cases, they are often more compelling than the films themselves, but a few of them have risen to truly great, brilliantly encapsulated cinematic moments in their own right of which *The Spy Who Loved Me* is one.

RIC MEYERS

Director Lewis Gilbert and editor John Glen were at their best teaming to make every Moore moment count. The ski-jump sequence is a textbook example of how to unashamedly present a larger-than-life, incredible hero in a totally acceptable, exciting, credible way. Gilbert's experience directing Michael Caine in *Alfie* was much better suited to Moore's persona than Connery's, who he directed in *You Only Live Twice* immediately following *Alfie*.

JOHN GLEN

We started not only shooting the pre-title sequences, but inventing them as well, and sometimes they had nothing to do with the film that followed. They were like seven or eight minutes long and almost like a second feature. Years ago, you used to have a second feature that used to preface the film. You'd have a small film and then you'd have the main film. So in a sense, the *Bond*s took that up. They combined a second feature with the main feature.

RAY MORTON

The action set pieces are imaginative and exciting and always serve to move the story forward. That sequence, which ends with Bond skiing off a cliff and saving himself by deploying a hidden parachute, was devised by Michael G. Wilson and executed by second-unit director John Glen and daredevil stuntman Rick Sylvester, but its brilliant capper—the audience's discovery that Bond's parachute is covered with the Union Jack—was devised by Christopher Wood.

RIC MEYERS

I was lucky and happy to have been at the New York premiere of *The Spy Who Loved Me,* and when the Union Jack unfurled on the parachute, even the jaded

Big Apple crowd of critics erupted with joyful appreciation. The movie, and Moore, had me in the palm of its hand—and, thankfully, didn't let me down.

JOHN GLEN

I remember Lewis [Gilbert] saying to me, "How can you direct second unit and edit the film as well?" I said, "Watch me." It was a wonderful opportunity, and Cubby obviously earmarked me as a future director when that sequence was finished, and what was nice was that not only did I go out to Mount Asgard on the Cumberland Peninsula in Northeast Canada, but he wanted me to direct the [ski] chase as well, which I shot in St. Moritz. He wanted me to do the whole thing, which was nice, having done the last scene in the sequence [the parachute jump] which was the first shot we ever did on *Spy Who Loved Me*. It was that scene, and then the actual [ski] chase that preceded it, that was one of the last things we did, shot on a completely different continent.

MAURICE BINDER

We put Roger in the titles of *Spy Who Loved Me*, because the song was "Nobody Does It Better," and it wasn't a title song like *Moonraker* or *Diamonds Are Forever*. I thought, "Why not put Roger in and show him doing all his tricks, and show that he does it better than somebody else?" That's how it happened. He liked the idea. We worked a couple of days on the stage and did all of it.

JOHN GLEN

The shot that finished the sequence, the actual ski parachute opening with the Union Jack, and Roger Moore being revealed for the start of the title sequence was kind of a tough sequence to do, because we were on the Arctic Circle and there's this mountain on Mount Asgard which is a precipice, and it's like 7,000 feet sheer rock face, and at the top, there's a little piece of ice and snow which is like the size of a football pitch. It's quite small. It's got a slope that faces into the north where you get the north winds and it gets impacted with ice all the time. Conditions are pretty hairy down there.

You can't ever parachute coming down. Five miles an hour is about the maximum that we could have, because it blows into the face, and we didn't have a rope long enough to rescue anyone if the parachute got held up in the rock face, so it was difficult to get the conditions to actually do the shot. We were lucky. We got up there quite early and had already been on a recce [location scout] and picked all the spots where we were going to film from, and in the end we had to camp out at the foot of the mountain in freezing conditions waiting for an opportunity to shoot it. It was a tough one and it cost about a quarter of a million dollars to shoot. It was a very expensive operation, and if there'd been any telephones in Pang Batang, which was the Eskimo village, I would've been besieged from Pinewood all the time, "When are you going to come back? How much more money are you going to spend?" Fortunately, there weren't any phones.

When we did eventually get the shot, Rick Sylvester was the parachutist, and I couldn't think of anyone less like James Bond than Rick Sylvester. He was quite short and very scholarly and bespectacled and he looked nothing like Bond, but of course when he's on skis on his own, you can't really tell how tall he is or big he is in any way, shape, or form, so he was a brilliant man. Nerves of steel. He performed it beautifully. Take one and that was it. I wouldn't put him through it again.

ALBERT R. BROCCOLI

When you plan a sequence, like the ski jump, and it comes off as well as it did . . . That is *really* satisfaction, when it comes off the way it does.

JOHN GLEN

A friend of mine was in a cinema in Canada watching that sequence when he saw the film and it was in the middle of a thunderstorm, so there were all these noises of claps of thunder coming from outside the cinema during the sequence, and he said it was so dramatic, when the parachute opened, everyone in the cinema stood up and applauded. And that happened in a few places. Something about James Bond and the Union Jack meant something. It was a wonderful experience. I think you could've quite honestly said if I hadn't come back with the goods, that would've been the end of my career.

GLEN OLIVER

The ski chase culminating in the Union Jack parachute jump—which was, evidently, initially suggested by George Lazenby for *On Her Majesty's Secret Service*—and that transition into the title sequence: the slowly descending Bond, the silhouetted hands of Maurice Binder's opening credits closing in around him . . . That's pretty great cinema by any measure.

MAURICE BINDER

On *Spy Who Loved Me,* the girls on the gun barrels were actually members of an Olympic gymnastics team. They were champions on the asymmetric bars. They were marvelous; they could jump and do all sorts of things. What I had to do was paint out bars and other various things to get it to work. They were experts. We set up a whole gym on the stage with all these bars and trampolines. Everybody's jumping and flying around.

DANIEL KLEINMAN
(main title designer, *Skyfall*)

It was one of my favorite of Maurice Binder's opening credit sequences. It's got so many sorts of different, mad ideas in it. I just love the fact that he wanted a naked girl in it and that she had to be the spy, so he obviously was thinking, "How is anyone going to know she's the spy?" So he put a Russian hat on her.

MAURICE BINDER

What happened on *The Spy Who Loved Me* was I went to Egypt, and I had all these ideas for beautiful Egyptian girls with long fingernails, and beautiful headdresses. However, this came into the picture 10 or 15 minutes after the titles, and it would have dissipated the whole effect of the Egyptian sequences of the picture, so I changed it. And it didn't seem that Egyptian girls would go with "Nobody Does It Better." So, instead, four or five girls march out, and then fall down. I tried shooting that with four or five girls, but when Roger came and gave them a shove, they didn't fall down like dominoes like they should. What I did was eliminate most of them, and just used one girl, and repeated her optically. On *Spy* we cast the girls because they were gymnasts, but the others—just for their shape, their boobies, and a few other things.

This globetrotting *Bond* entry was shot in Cairo and Luxor in Egypt, Sardinia, and the Bahamas, as well as an entirely new stage constructed at Pinewood Studios. Christened the 007 Stage, it was used for the massive interior of the supertanker *Liparus*, designed and built by Ken Adam, for the massive climax in which Stromberg's men confront the freed sailors from the captured submarines in an all-out melee. The only time the action flags is when Bond needs to defuse a nuclear bomb so that he can use the detonator to storm the seemingly impregnable control room. The set was so gigantic that Adam covertly brought his mentor, the reclusive Stanley Kubrick, in on a Sunday to advise on how to best light the massive set.

KEN ADAM
(production designer, *The Spy Who Loved Me*)

I had to reduce the size of the submarines. You know, a nuclear submarine is about 420 feet. These were about 360 feet, but they had to look right, so it was the biggest interior set ever built at Pinewood, and I decided not to make the mistake of the [volcano] crater [in *You Only Live Twice*] because after we finished shooting, the locals in Buckinghamshire complained about the structure outside, so this time I built a stage around that set, and that's the 007 stage, which is still there.

RAYMOND BENSON

(author, *The James Bond Bedside Companion*)

There were many individual craftsmen who contributed to the success of the series, but Ken Adam's contribution can't be downplayed. Adam's sets were iconic and pushed the envelope in ways one didn't expect. In *Dr. No,* for example, no one expected the science fiction–style sets that dominated the second half of what began as a straightforward thriller. They helped propel the series into the "future." His volcano set for *You Only Live Twice,* in my opinion, is one of the greatest sets ever built for a motion picture. I also admire his work with Stanley Kubrick.

FRED DEKKER

Ken Adam worked on *Dr. Strangelove,* because Kubrick loved *Dr. No*. He said, "I want that guy."

KEN ADAM

I still think today that it is one of the best black-and-white satirical comedies ever made. Kubrick had an unbelievable brain, and a lot of imagination, and he was brilliant, but very difficult to work with. He was the director I had the closest relationship ever with, but that's why he became so destructive and I didn't really want to do another film for him. I got out of *2001,* and I got out of *Barry Lyndon* too, because he said, "Well, I'll have to get the next best production designer." I was very relieved, and five minutes later there was a shy, little Stanley Kubrick who said to me, "This man doesn't seem to understand why you have to have me on." I did it, but it was a mistake.

SHANE RIMMER

We had one bad situation in the control room in *Spy Who Loved Me* when somebody jacked up the explosive material. I suppose wanting to be a star overnight, I don't know. Anyway, it was too heavy, and the whole place was painted in a sort of electric white color and that just went. As soon as that explosion went, it just melted. There were extras lying on the floor of the room who had been told, "Don't move until you get a release," and some of them got burnt. It was white hot. They had to get shipped out to a hospital right away. I just followed Roger, really. He felt one person get hit and he dragged one fellow off out of the control room to safety.

JOHN LANDIS

Some of my ideas remained in the movie. The ship that opens and swallows submarines, for instance. I had actually gone with Guy Hamilton to the North Atlantic to tour a supertanker. They are *so* fucking big. It's really interesting, because what was remarkable about supertankers is they're gigantic. There's a very small crew of like six or seven people, because essentially it's a giant tank. I assume they're safer now, but you realize how fragile they were really. It's just this giant, floating thing full of fuel. The cruise liners and most big boats have propellers along the bottom so a gigantic ship can literally parallel park or make a 360 and do all kinds of maneuvers. For a supertanker, one of the things I found so fascinating was to make a turn, you had to make it like three miles before you want to actually make the turn. I couldn't get over how big they were. I felt, "This is dangerous." They used to go across the deck on bicycles and motor scooters. They're like football fields long.

KEN ADAM

The exterior of the tanker was all model. The interior of the tanker was a fullsize set. Well, not completely full size; we had to scale it down to three-quarters—otherwise it would have just been too big. . . .

ALBERT R. BROCCOLI

And very expensive!

JOHN LANDIS

I had this idea where Commander Bond goes out to this suspicious supertanker in a military helicopter. They land on deck, and he's met by the captain, who gives them a tour of the ship and everything seems completely innocuous except Bond sees a cat at one point, Blofeld's cat. They get into the copter and they're going away. Just as the ship disappears past the horizon, so they can't see it anymore, they receive an SOS that's coming from the tanker. You hear all this yelling and garbled noise and then suddenly there's a massive explosion and a gigantic wall of fire and they can feel the shockwave on the helicopter. They turn around and go right back to the supertanker, but don't see it. The sea is on fire, because there's oil everywhere. And they just see the tail as the supertanker's submerged and bodies floating on the surface. Anyway, it turns out that the supertanker, which is the same one that swallows the submarine, can also go underwater like a submarine. They just murdered some of their own crew and are lurking down at the bottom of the ocean, and now the supertanker's not suspicious anymore because it's been lost at sea as witnessed by Bond.

FRED DEKKER

Think of the inside of the water tank at the beginning of *Goldfinger,* which is only there for Bond to come in and set explosives. It's spectacular and you never see it again. That idea of building a beautiful set, this kind of Bauhaus, German expressionist, cool set, and then never seeing it again makes the whole movie just feel extravagantly expensive and spectacular and cool. Adam was a master of putting circles in ceilings. What's so incredible about that set in *You Only Live Twice* is the crater is actually canted at an angle. It's not flat, and he did that for the camera so that when you look at it, you can look out and see through it, which is just brilliant.

SHANE RIMMER

Ken Adam had as much money as he needed and he was encouraged to go blow the top off things, which he did very well. He could put down anything he wanted to, because people had a lot of faith in him. He was the ideal man for a picture. As an actor, it was as impressive to us as it was to you on the outside watching the finished movie, it just took your breath away. Everything was done in gargantuan terms. It wasn't a drawing room comedy.

KEN ADAM

[Producer/director] Alexander Korda said to me, "If you want to design for films, I advise you to have a grounding in architecture." Because, he said, "I started as a painter." Several art directors did start as painters, but he said, "I think that an architectural background is more useful." That's why I studied architecture. I never completed my studies, because the war, of course, had broken out. As a theatrical designer you've got a stage, and you are bound by the limitations of your sight lines, and the live public, and so on, so you had to invent whatever you could, which appealed to me but, at the same time, film appealed to me, too. Eventually, I think I came up with a solution, which satisfied me and possibly was one of my most successful design periods in films. I started the War Room in *Dr. Strangelove* creating completely imaginary sets, but which the public accepted as reality. There is that anecdote, which is true, actually, that Reagan, when he became president of the United States, asked his chief of staff to look at the War Room, and the same with some of my *Bond* film designs.

The film itself was an immediate smash, grossing over $180 million worldwide, making it abundantly clear that after a decade and a half in cinemas, still nobody did it better.

DESMOND LLEWELYN

I remember we were shooting in Sardinia in the most beautiful hotel and it wasn't considered good enough for Bond—they had to make it even more beautiful. The check-in girl was an absolute stunner, but not good enough for a *Bond* film. You had to have an ex–Miss World. The *Bond* films are wonderful fantasies.

FRED DEKKER

The *Bond* films couldn't help but be self-conscious, because they were so enormously successful worldwide. You go into something like *The Spy Who Loved Me* and Broccoli pulls out all the stops to give the audience what they want, and I think that's why they like it, more than whether it's good or not. It also has a villain with webbed hands who wants to live underwater. That's a far cry from even *Goldfinger*. He just wants gold.

JEFF KLEEMAN

(executive vice president of production, United Artists)

My favorite Roger Moore *Bond* movie was *The Spy Who Loved Me*. For its moment, it's a near-perfect *Bond* movie in my mind. It was actually very influential.

SIR ROGER MOORE

My particular favorite is *The Spy Who Loved Me*.

RAY MORTON

The final draft of *Spy* is one of the best screenplays in the series and, along with *Goldfinger*, it's certainly the best of the fantasy *Bonds*. The script has some weak points: the villain Karl Stromberg, who wishes to destroy the world and build a new civilization beneath the sea because he has webbed hands, is a bit too cartoonish, and his scheme is a bit reminiscent of what Blofeld was up to in *You Only Live Twice*—but everything else in the screenplay works so well that they don't much matter.

One of the most crowd-pleasing elements for general audiences, and divisive additions to true *Bond* fans, was the addition of villainous henchmen; here Jaws, played by the towering Richard Kiel, a deadly killer with steel teeth.

TOM MANKIEWICZ

I thought that it was a very good picture. I thought it had a lot of wit and style and Jaws was very original, though I did not invent him. I wrote a lot of bits for him.

RAY MORTON

The narrative construction is rock-solid—it follows the *Bond* formula almost to a T, but that is what Christopher Wood's intention was from the beginning. The end result is a wildly entertaining celebration of that formula as well as the series' second greatest (and second most iconic) henchman: Jaws.

CHRISTOPHER WOOD

Jaws was in the script that I inherited. I saw him as more of a real menace than he turned out to be. Lewis spotted the humor inherent in his performance. For the script, I worked with Lewis in London and we then discussed our ideas and what I had written with Cubby, Michael Wilson, and sometimes, Ken Adam.

JOHN CORK

Jaws developed from the novel. One of the thugs in the novel is named Sol Horowitz, who goes by the nickname "Horror." He has metal-capped teeth. When the agreement came to use no elements from the novel, they needed to change the name, and someone realized that "Jaws" was a clever idea for a name.

ALBERT R. BROCCOLI

The fans have proven that they've enjoyed it. Richard Kiel coming at him with his teeth . . . Bond finding a way to cope by turning the magnet onto his teeth . . . highly ridiculous . . . highly bizarre, but they enjoy that.

CHRISTOPHER WOOD

It was Cubby's idea to leave the fate of Jaws open at the end of *Spy*. He was a popular character and certainly one of the most memorable heavies in the *Bond* series.

The score for *The Spy Who Loved Me* was only the second in the series composed by someone other than John Barry (not counting Monty Norman's material in *Dr. No*). George Martin took on music duties for *Live and Let Die*, and Marvin Hamlisch was the composer for this film.

RICHARD MAIBAUM

John Barry is a genius. There's no doubt about it. His work on the *Bond* films has been outstanding. It's even more outstanding when you hear some of the non-regular composers. I should say Marvin Hamlisch's work on *Spy* was fine, but it wasn't anything like a Barry score.

FRED DEKKER

It's crazy that Marvin Hamlisch was nominated for an Oscar for *Spy Who Loved Me* whereas John Barry never was. He's just doing riffs on the *Bond* theme and ripping off John Barry.

JEFF BOND

(editor, *Film Score Monthly*)

Marvin Hamlisch was obviously a great songwriter and "Nobody Does It Better," like "Live and Let Die," was a perfect *Bond* song and one that almost transcended the movie by becoming a big pop hit on its own. Hamlisch could write good movie scores like *The Swimmer* and *Sophie's Choice,* and he does get into the *Bond* vibe when it counts, like his music for Stromberg's underwater lair, but a lot of the score is hamstrung by the disco movement. Still, Moore's Bond was always lighter and in some ways Hamlisch's approach might have been more appropriate than having Barry continue his sound from the Connery films.

Despite the *Bond* films being based on the legendary series of novels by Ian Fleming, *The Spy Who Loved Me,* given its lack of faithfulness to the source material, was given its own novelization by the film's screenwriter, Christopher Wood.

JOHN CORK

Each Bond film had been released with tie-in paperbacks that cross-promoted the original Ian Fleming source novel. That wasn't possible with *The Spy Who Loved Me,* because of the restriction of not using any story elements from the novel.

RAY MORTON

Christopher Wood also wrote the novelizations of his two *Bond* screenplays, and those who dismiss him as a comedy writer might be pleasantly surprised to find that both are very credible, "serious" Fleming pastiches.

JOHN CORK

Christopher Wood got his start writing novels, and early on wrote a successful paperback series of sex-farce novels, so he knew how to write in that form, and he knew how to write quickly. The novelization of *The Spy Who Loved Me* was quite successful and spawned a second Christopher Wood novelization tied in to *Moonraker.*

CHARLES ARDAI

Oh, that was astonishing to me! But it was necessary—anyone who saw the movie *The Spy Who Loved Me* and went to pick up the book hoping to read a story that had anything whatsoever to do with the movie would have been hopelessly disappointed, not to mention confused. So having someone novelize the script of the movie made a lot of sense in that case. They might have done a better job of clarifying on the cover that the novelization was a different book from the original *Bond* novel of the same title—I remember being puzzled by the whole thing when I eventually stumbled across the novelization in a rack at the library—but if you bought it at a supermarket while the movie was still in theaters, I think you probably weren't confused at all. You saw the movie poster art on the front cover and figured you'd get a retelling of the movie, and you were right. It was giving the audience what they wanted. And isn't that 90 percent of what the *James Bond* movies are all about?

FRED DEKKER

That webbed hand guy that wants to live underwater? Everything is turned up to 11 and I could sense it when I watched the movie, because I was already a huge *Bond* fan. I was like, "How far can they go before they realize they've gone too far and they have to dial back?" I was one movie off.

MICHAEL G. WILSON

The *Bond* films have evolved over the years in a variety of ways and have changed from time to time. They went from being thrillers to becoming action-adventures and their comedy went from being a rather cynical-sick humor to a more comic kind of humor. I think starting with *The Spy Who Loved Me* we had developed a style of spectacle, action, and humor in about equal amounts. You'll find that other successful pictures have used these same ingredients in about the same balance. If you see *Star Wars* or *Raiders* or *Superman,* I think that in all those films, the mix, or balance, is about the same.

RIC MEYERS

The Spy Who Loved Me remains my favorite Roger Moore 007 film. To my mind, it remains the first "true" Roger Moore 007 film—the installment when they stop laughing at him, and start laughing with him. The movie where they stop being embarrassed by and trying to embarrass him, and start introducing him as a true, credible James Bond with a character all his own. The tongue is now in Roger's cheek, not the producers'. Although obviously a remake/reboot of *You Only Live Twice,* it's a film where they are no longer remaking Sean scenes, but refashioning and redesigning them as pure Roger—playing to his strengths as Bond rather than showcasing his weaknesses.

Virtually every scene and shot seems designed to present him as a real hero, and not, as in the prior two, as a subject of derision and ridicule. *The Spy Who Loved Me* is the only one, to my mind, that truly integrates Moore's lightweight frisson into the character, plot, and action in a completely effective way.

JOHN CORK

It was a no-apologies *Bond* film, a big-screen experience. There had been a sense with *The Man with the Golden Gun*, and even with *Diamonds Are Forever* and *Live and Let Die,* that the '70s *Bond*s would be ever-shrinking, eventually more suitable as television movies of the week than for movie theaters. *The Spy Who Loved Me* re-established *Bond* as a major movie franchise.

MOONRAKER (1979)

Fans expecting to see *For Your Eyes Only* in 1979 would have to wait a little longer, despite the film's being teased at the end of *The Spy Who Loved Me*. Instead, with the blockbuster success of *Star Wars*, the Eon empire turned its attention to adapting *Moonraker*. Once again, the original novel—written in 1955 about a treacherous German industrialist's plans to wipe London off the map with an upgraded V-2 rocket—just wouldn't do. Instead, the filmmakers decided to simply remake *The Spy Who Loved Me* . . . in space. Although few would admit it at the time, it's hard to deny that's the case, as the film's plot is virtually identical to its predecessor, in which a megalomaniacal supervillain wants to destroy the world in order to create a new master race under the sea. Now, with the webbed Karl Stromberg sleeping with the fishes, it is Hugo Drax who wants to create a new master race amongst the stars.

GLEN OLIVER
(pop culture commentator)

Moonraker was originally optioned as a film property back in the mid-1950s, but the project never materialized for a variety of reasons. Presumably that adaptation would've stayed closer to Ian Fleming's source material; the 1979 adaptation bears very little resemblance to the novel.

DESMOND LLEWELYN
(actor, "Q")

When we were making *Moonraker*, someone said to Cubby, "Why are you writing a new story? Ian Fleming's was terrific." Cubby answered, "Yes, but it's so old-fashioned. It's only got a piddling little atom bomb in it."

ALBERT R. BROCCOLI
(producer, *Moonraker*)

Moonraker is an original, because the plot was about a Blue Streak rocket falling into London. We had to update the whole thing. It's so dated in its content and ideas with the Blue Streak rocket, which was obsolete right after the British made it, and since then people have gone to the moon, which Fleming never heard about because he died before all of that.

LEWIS GILBERT
(director, *Moonraker*)

It's gone way beyond anything Fleming could have imagined. I don't think Fleming could visualize 1979. The character of man has changed in these years. I don't think he ever meant Bond as a documentary character of a real spy; a real spy was never like that. He was much more like *The Spy Who Came In from the Cold*. He's just changed with the times, really.

ALBERT R. BROCCOLI

Fleming knew that these things would have to be updated. He agreed a long time ago that he had written himself out and said that we would have to update. He said, "Someday you'll have to step into my shoes and do your best."

TOM MANKIEWICZ

(cowriter, *Diamonds Are Forever*)

I was involved marginally with *Moonraker* in the beginning. After *The Spy Who Loved Me,* Cubby said, "Can you do it?" I said, "Cubby, I can't." The pictures take like a year and a half of your life. And for Cubby it's wonderful and for Roger it's wonderful and so on, but for me, it's not so wonderful.

CHRISTOPHER WOOD

(writer, *Moonraker*)

I did not like the premise of *Moonraker.* It seemed to me that we were copying *Star Wars.* I also found the idea of space slow in filmic terms. It is difficult to rush around in an astronaut's suit. Did I tell Cubby that his idea sucked? No.

TOM MANKIEWICZ

Cubby had an idea which had to do with the space shuttle, and so he said, "Can you write just six pages that we can launch this picture from?" It had to do with the capture of the space shuttle, and I remember Cubby, Michael Wilson, and I all went up to NASA in San Jose and into the simulators and the [centrifugal] spinners and so on. Lewis Gilbert came out for a couple of days and I sort of wrote like six to ten pages. Jaws wasn't in them. Rio de Janeiro wasn't in them. Most of it wasn't. It was just to sort of kick them off, because they didn't know exactly what they wanted to do. The idea for the picture when I left it was really somebody swallowing a space shuttle. And then we wanted to see where you could hide a space shuttle. But the rest of it was written after that. Mine didn't take place in outer space at all. And it wasn't really my picture. I'm a member of the family, so after I'd done the rewrite on *Spy Who Loved Me,* I was just helping out until they got it going.

RAY MORTON

(senior writer, *Script* magazine)

Christopher Wood's work on *Moonraker* was less successful than *The Spy Who Loved Me,* but it's a script that seems to have suffered from the "too many cooks" syndrome and so was not completely Wood's fault. The structure of

Christopher Wood's screenplay is solid—Wood is once again consciously using and celebrating the *Bond* formula—but in this case, the producers became too fixated on giving the public what they thought it wanted. The outer space theme and setting were famously chosen because Eon and UA wanted to jump on the *Star Wars* bandwagon.

MICHAEL G. WILSON
(executive producer, *Moonraker*)

We all thought it was a danger taking *Bond* in that direction. If we had kept going in that direction, I think it would have been the demise of the series.

JOHN GLEN
(second-unit director, *Moonraker*)

The *Star Wars* comparisons I don't think are valid, because the history was that it was shot to coincide with the American space shuttle launching, which was delayed. We, in fact, got the shuttle off before the American government.

RAY MORTON

The fantasy in *Moonraker* was often too fantastic and the humor in the piece was far broader than any seen in the series before or since. The comedy was so broad that at several points it crossed over into silliness. Wood himself is on record as having objected to many of these excesses, many of which were implemented by uncredited rewriters Ian La Frenais and Dick Clement.

DICK CLEMENT
(cowriter, *Never Say Never Again*)

To be honest, I can't remember, because we weren't on it long enough. What I do remember was, from a production manager's point of view, the most bone-chilling line you've ever seen, which said, "Note. From this point on, everybody is weightless." Ian and I looked at each other and said, "Oh, boy!" You can imagine all the guys who handled the budget saying, "Holy shit! What do we do with this?"

RAY MORTON

They did a dialogue polish on *Moonraker* and production rewrites on *Never Say Never.* One of their major contributions to the latter script was the character and name of Nigel Small-Fawcett. La Frenais and Clement are certainly very good writers, but I find their humor a bit too broad for *Bond*.

DICK CLEMENT

I remember having a very agreeable trip to Paris. We wrote stuff. Everyone was extremely nice to us, but then they changed the location so that it was one of those very different rewrites where you suddenly get a glimpse of something, but we never really got our feet wet. It didn't hurt to be doing it.

RICHARD MAIBAUM

(cowriter, *The Spy Who Loved Me*)

Thank God, I didn't write it. I didn't have anything to do with it.

ADOLFO CELI

(actor, "Emilio Largo," *Thunderball*)

I was more excited when I saw *Thunderball* than when I saw *Moonraker*. Honestly, I was a bit disappointed by *Moonraker*. They give too little importance to the relationships between the characters, it is an excess of superficiality and they pass too easily from one fact, from one episode, to another. I remember the suspense, which is now no longer present, in *From Russia with Love*, not to mention *Goldfinger*, with the laser cutting in two his testicles . . . something which they won't be able to repeat again.

TOM MANKIEWICZ

If you're going to be out in space, you're competing with *Star Trek* and *Star Wars* and so on, and you're *Moonraker* and then you say, "Well, I want to have bigger and better effects." But I think the thing the audience always really loved about Bond was the soul of his character. He was an unabashed, sexist, government employee in a very sophisticated way.

For many, *Moonraker* is the object of much disdain. Roger Moore running around in zero-gravity with a laser gun, and a smiling Jaws, who realizes he has no place in Drax's brave new world order and decides to join forces with Bond and his new blond strumpet to stop the end of the world. So yes, it's absolutely inane, but if you can overlook the absurdity of its inherently ludicrous premise and the outlandish gadgets, there's still a lot to like here. Michael Lonsdale's Hugo Drax is an enjoyable and vindictive villain (although one can only imagine how great it would have been if the producers' first choice, James Mason, had been cast), never more arch than when he and Bond go out for a day of pheasant hunting on his sprawling estate and, after Bond apparently allows his target to elude him, Drax says, "You missed, Mr. Bond," only for Bond to retort, "Did I?," as a Drax assassin drops from his shadowy perch on a tree nearby. Later, Drax dispatches his vicious Dobermans to make a meal of the treacherous Corinne Cléry as Corinne Dufour, his personal pilot, who helped Bond the previous night in more ways than one.

RAY MORTON

For all of its issues, the screenplay does contain some wonderfully witty lines penned by Wood, my favorites being: "Look after Mister Bond. See that some harm comes to him," and "James Bond, you appear with the tedious inevitability of an unloved season."

MICHAEL G. WILSON

There was some criticism of the comedy in *Moonraker*, but as far as our audience was concerned, it was our most popular one at the time. It was our own feeling, which was probably in line more with the critics than the moviegoing public, that we couldn't go any farther in that direction. You always have to take new directions or you risk becoming stymied.

The "treacherous Dr. Holly Goodhead," replacing the novel's Gala Brand, was played by Lois Chiles, ironically the original choice for Major Amasova in *The Spy Who Loved Me*. Goodhead turns out to be a resourceful CIA agent and scientist who's way more than a pretty face.

JOHN CORK

When Lois Chiles looked at Bond and asked him to take her around the world one more time, everyone wanted to be floating in that space shuttle with a partner they desired.

LOIS CHILES

(actress, "Holly Goodhead")

Because ours was set in outer space, we were on wires and it was hysterical. Blood rushes to your head when you've been up there for a very long time and you'd have this sort of thing pressing into your chest, and we were separated by a harness and they had to try to get us together manually.

Amongst the many eye-popping locations featured in the film are Guatemala, Brazil, and Italy, although the film was largely lensed in France, rather than in England, for tax reasons. Pinewood Studios provided a home for the film's visual effects unit only.

JOHN CORK

Lewis Gilbert knew the French studio system, and at the time there were serious tax issues related to shooting at Pinewood. The biggest issue of shooting in France was logistics. They could not shoot at one studio. Films tend to be mobile armies, so being on location is a common task. The base at Pinewood still existed. Derek Meddings was shooting the massive model-work and space sequences there and post-production was based there, and a great deal of the business-workings were based there. The film ran overbudget and overschedule and it had a firm release date.

BÉATRICE LIBERT

(actress, "Mademoiselle Deradier")

There was a casting in Paris where all models were invited. Model agencies sent their most beautiful girls to this casting. I went on my own—nothing to lose. When I saw all the girls, I was certain I didn't have a chance. All the girls had long black hair and were so beautiful. I had short blond hair! Albert Broccoli was sitting in a chair, looking at all the girls, and I had a "no," like many others. Just when I left I bumped into the director, Lewis Gilbert. He asked if Broccoli had chosen me and I told him he had not. Gilbert then went up to Cubby and said, "If you don't take this girl, I won't make your movie!" I got a contract for six months. We were paid per week. In total, I think I worked about three months on the movie in a time space of six months. During these six months we were not allowed to take other jobs.

ALBERT R. BROCCOLI

In *Moonraker*, the locations that we shot in Brazil, the Iguazu Falls, and the Sugarloaf Mountain sequence were an inspiration from my going there on a tour. I also make a tour with the office sometimes. I went there on a tour with Richard Kiel and a couple of girls, and we traveled around Brazil and all those places under the auspices of United Artists [for *Spy Who Loved Me*]. They felt I should go down, because we travel around and Roger goes one place and I go another place and I saw these locations. I came back to the writers and the directors, and I said, "We've got to use these locations. They are very important to the picture." So we went back again, and we did what we call a "recce" on these things, and we decided, yes, we would use it. But it wasn't because I said we've got to use them dogmatically. We'll use them if they fit in with the story. And they did fit in with the story, so we used them.

JOHN CORK

After all the shooting in Brazil under less-than-ideal conditions, often with doubles, endless close shots needed to be done with the cast, and those were put off until the last few days of shooting. Well, they did those close shots with back projection, and the system in France was substandard. The color was off, the brightness was off, the shots looked mediocre, cheap. There was no time to reshoot those scenes under better conditions.

MATT SHERMAN

(creator, James Bond Events)

Southeast of Paris, the Château de Vaux-le-Vicomte became Drax's mansion in *Moonraker,* another highly impressive film location.

FRED DEKKER

(director, *The Monster Squad*)

Moonraker was just a remake of *The Spy Who Loved Me,* which is a remake of *You Only Live Twice.* I like *Moonraker* more because of the locations and the sets. The temple in Peru that turns out to be the base in South America. That turns out to be the base for the Moonrakers. Bond comes down and all these beautiful girls come out. That's an example of over the top. For some reason, it works for me.

With a budget of $34 million, which was exorbitant in 1979, the film went on to gross over $210 million worldwide, an astounding new record for a *Bond* film, despite the criticism it received for its embrace of hokey sci-fi plot elements. Sadly, it would mark the last appearance of the late, great Bernard Lee as M, who was seemingly irreplaceable until Judi Dench was cast in *GoldenEye.* It would also be the last of Ken Adam's work on a *James Bond* film, but at least it marked a triumphant capper on his two decades of inventive, groundbreaking work for the franchise.

FRED DEKKER

I love it for two simple reasons: John Barry and Ken Adam.

KEN ADAM
(production designer, *Moonraker*)

For *Moonraker,* I went to NASA to give me some ideas what they were going to come up with, and so I knew they were using these cylinders, and sun panels, and such. The idea is to make it like a mobile so when it starts rotating to create gravity, you see different angles all the time. It worked extremely well. After that, I decided I had enough *Bonds*. I had been in space, and that was it. But we had to sort of approximate the idea for the big sets, like the space station interior or the Great Chamber; Mr. Broccoli asked me how much it's going to cost and then it was up to him to okay the cost.

LEWIS GILBERT

But usually he's built the set by then.

KEN ADAM

Fortunately, I had a very good team of people working with me, and that's something I developed over a number of years, and that gives me much more freedom to come up with initial design concepts, and concentrate really on purely the design elements.

One of the highlights of the film is the remarkable pre-title sequence in which Bond is thrown out of an airplane by Jaws without a parachute and has to steal one on the descent by skydiving and wresting one free from one of the villains as they both plummet towards Earth, only to find Jaws in hot aerial pursuit.

JOHN GLEN

It was an idea that Michael Wilson came up with. He found a lightweight anamorphic lens in Paris and he went to Continental Cameras in the States and asked if they could build a lightweight helmet anamorphic camera using this lightweight lens, and they did actually build this camera. It weighed seven pounds and it was mounted on top of the skydiver's helmet. If you put an extension on someone's neck like that, a seven-pound weight on top of your head, and you pull your parachute, there's a hell of a jerk and you can imagine what it would do to someone's neck. The cameraman devised a system whereby he put a rope around his parachute so that it would open slowly, but when you think that we were filming from about 7,000 feet, he had just seconds to get the people in frame and to do each segment, which we pre-determined. We were a small crew. My first job was to get these guys out of bed. They weren't disciplined at all in film production. The first morning shooting, I arrived and all the skydivers were all in bed! I said, "What's going on? We've got to start doing five jumps a day." I sort of had to read them the riot act. They said they had a problem because the girl cooking breakfast would take till 11:00 A.M. to get everyone fed.

FRED DEKKER

Shoving somebody out of an airplane and they're filming it for real is pretty hardcore.

JOHN GLEN

Almost all the aerial stuff we shot in America, because it was the best place to do flying stuff. It was the cheapest place, and it's so restricted in Europe and the weather is no good. You're up against it. So most of our flying stuff we used to do in the Mojave Desert. We rehearsed it on the ground and for just a two-second segment he had just enough time to get it in his frame and give them the thumbs-up, and away they went and did their little segment, which was wrestling the parachute off of him. By that time you're running out of airspace and the ground is rushing up at an alarming rate, and he had to then open his parachute slowly, so quite often he was quite close to the ground when he actually got down to a controlled descent.

JOHN CORK

It is a very weird film, but I can tell you this: when audiences saw Bond pushed out of an airplane and then go slicing through the air to take the pilot's parachute away, it was one of the most amazing bits of cinema ever witnessed by anyone.

JOHN GLEN

We had very cleverly designed parachutes with flat packs, and the wardrobe was specially designed with Velcro sections so that when they'd finished doing their stunt, they would just hand deploy and the chute would come out, having broken the Velcro sections. It got very complex, because when Bond is pushed out of the airplane, he is supposed to be without a parachute, but in fact he has a flat parachute and a reserve, so he had two parachutes. He then swoops down, dives onto a man who's in free fall, and he has a fight with him and steals his parachute and then puts it on, so he finishes up with three parachutes. The idea is crazy when you think about it, yet he did it.

Then the parachute they were fighting with had a little parachute especially made for it so it could come down to earth, because if it fell on someone's head from that height, it would kill them. In fact, one day he dropped it during the fight and it came down like a rocket. It was a crazy way to work. We only had one, and I never thought we'd lose it, so off we went on a huge search party looking for this parachute.

It was an interesting exercise, I must say, and being a film editor, I cut the thing progressively as I went along. I storyboarded it all and as we did each segment; I would do seven segments each day. I would have them delivered back to the airfield the following morning, and I would look at them, and if we needed to redo anything, which we often did, I would just recycle it into the program and cut the stuff together as I went along. Of course, the boys would get very enthusiastic when they could see it was actually working. It was a little over three weeks there filming those bits and pieces. It was probably a hundred and something jumps, since you could only do two seconds at a time. They tried to get me to jump out of the airplane. I wouldn't have any of that. But it was worth all the effort.

Less impressive was the return of popular *Spy Who Loved Me* metal-toothed henchman Jaws (Richard Kiel), who is largely played for laughs (including in the teaser in which he flaps his arms and careens into a circus tent on the ground, tainting an otherwise near-perfect pre-title sequence) in the new installment until he undergoes a remarkable transformation to the side of the angels in the third act.

RAY MORTON

Jaws was brought back, which was not a good idea, and redeemed—an even worse idea—because the producers discovered that little kids loved the character.

RIC MEYERS

It was an impressive idea—seemingly trying to outdo *The Spy Who Loved Me*'s opening parachute jump with an entire three-sided fight in midair. But I also remember being disappointed that, as the impressive sequence drew to its conclusion, the production couldn't resist getting silly. I was the head writer for the official *Moonraker* magazine tie-in from Warren Publishing, and the production gave us materials to create the magazine, which had to be ready by the time the film premiered. We had a more complete description of the opening sequence's finale. Jaws was to make a spectacular landing onto a circus big-top, and use the trapeze equipment to further slow his fall enough to survive.

Even on paper it was a ridiculous notion, and, apparently, once the crew saw the footage, they agreed. But instead of replacing it with a dubbed explanation of how Jaws could have survived the fall later on, or simply ignore it, Jaws flapped his arms as if trying to fly, then weird glimpses of the trapeze act were jumbled together, with equally weird music, giving the audience the impression that they were seeing a shadow puppet show. But my biggest disappointment was that, as with other inferior 007 installments, the pre-credit sequence concentrated on the villain, not Bond. Better to wrap up the scene having Bond doing something clever rather than Jaws doing something stupid, but it was not to be.

GLEN OLIVER

Jaws is a wonderful, iconic villain whose overall presence still stands the test of time. Over the years, I've sensed some division regarding the direction the character was steered in *Moonraker.* I think the direction they ultimately steered him was valid and interesting, but getting there was a rocky road. Some of Jaws' slapstick pratfalls in *Moonraker* very much undercut his menace—he ended up coming across as less of an antagonist or obstacle, and more of a buffoon. A tenacity which was suggested in *The Spy Who Loved Me,* but amped up to an almost shameful level in *Moonraker.* Allegedly, this happened because children didn't understand why Jaws had to be "such a bad guy"—or something to that effect—so the character was softened a bit. I've never completely bought into this rationale. Considering the overall content of any *James Bond* film, they're *really* going to be concerned with Jaws being too much of a bad guy, and *really* going to be concerned about what children say? It doesn't quite add up.

TOM MANKIEWICZ

I think the worst part of *Moonraker* is Jaws, because he's played as a kind of comedy buffoon and there was a wonderful kind of quality to him in *The Spy Who Loved Me.* I rewrote that picture without credit and I thought Jaws was a wonderful character and everything that was threatening and even genuinely funny about him didn't work in *Moonraker.* He fell in love with somebody and the malevolence was gone, and so he suddenly became this huge hulking kind of buffoon. In *Spy Who Loved Me,* there was menace even when he was fighting the shark or shaking the car at the Luxor.

GLEN OLIVER

Cornering Jaws into wrestling with a moral imperative later in that film was a stroke of genius—even though it was somewhat undercut by the silliness he'd gone through earlier in the picture. Tonally, those moments of realization, awareness, and choice might have played much more powerfully and interestingly if he hadn't been befallen by so much slapstick earlier in the movie. It would've been tremendously interesting to see how a post-*Moonraker* confrontation between Bond and Jaws might've unfolded, now that Bond, the audience, and even Jaws himself knows there are lines even that fucking huge steel-mouthed giant wouldn't cross.

The outstanding Derek Meddings miniature work here is better than ever, and John Barry's lyrical score is a career triumph despite being the most disappointing of the Shirley Bassey main title songs (both Kate Bush and Broccoli family friend Frank Sinatra were offered the gig and would have no doubt contributed superior efforts). She was a late addition weeks before release after John Barry fortuitously ran into her at lunch. The song played over another stunning sequence from *Bond* veteran Maurice Binder, which once again featured the gyrating, silhouetted nude women.

FRED DEKKER

I love the *Moonraker* score. John Barry had changed at some point—it was before the whole *Dances with Wolves* era. He was already slowing down the tempo of his scores, and if you didn't know that *Moonraker* was a *James Bond* movie, if you just heard the music, you'd think it was the score to a thriller romance.

MATT SHERMAN

Derek Meddings and the special effects crew made the space shuttle launches in *Moonraker* look incredibly lifelike. This is an amazing accomplishment, the *Moonraker* launches being created about two years before the real Columbia shuttle ever launched! The rocket sequences of the film are vivid and seem real on any size screen. And the shuttles are then flown by Bond and others into outer space, the last word in 007 locations.

MAURICE BINDER

(main title designer, *Moonraker*)

On *Moonraker* I was more careful than I was on some of the previous pictures, because what has happened is films have appeared throughout the world without [the *Bond* main] titles. In Spain, for instance, in their nonpermissive era, they cut the title sequence out of *Thunderball* and just put names on the screen. Sometimes they'd object; sometimes we would argue. Mr. Broccoli would go around and say, "Well, it's silhouetted," and so on. "If you don't know what you're looking at, you wouldn't know what you were looking at." We were a little worried about *Moonraker*, because the *Bond* schedules are so tight that when they start printing those prints, there's no stopping it. It's like a newspaper press. If the censor says, "You've got to take that booby out or cover up that behind," it's big trouble. So I'm very careful.

We had a little trouble on *Golden Gun*. The girls were in silhouette and they weren't wearing anything. We had some trouble when they were dancing and they would turn—it didn't look very good. I said, "What will we do about it?" They said, "We ought to brush it down so it [pubic hair] doesn't show in profile." So we got the hairdresser and he got some Brylcreem, or whatever it was, and just at that moment Broccoli and Roger Moore came onto my stage. They had just finished shooting, and came up and stood behind me as we were brushing. Broccoli said, "I'm the producer of this picture and I don't know what we're paying you for."

Also what would become a staple of the *Bond* films, much to the consternation of some, was the ubiquitous product placement in the film, which was the most notable it had been since Broccoli and Saltzman had last had a Russian agent crawl out of Anita Ekberg's mouth in a billboard for the movie they had recently produced, Bob Hope's *Call Me Bwana*, in *From Russia with Love*.

TANYA NITINS

(author, *Selling James Bond*)

The practice of product placement definitely ebbed and flowed during the series. However, what my research found is that cultural events such as the Cold War, the Space Race, surveillance, McCarthyism, the Soviet invasion of Afghanistan, and the threat of media oligarchy and global transmission of information were reflected in the types and level of products placed in the films. In particular, as the level of technology increased in the series, the more opportunities this gave for products to be weaved directly into the film narrative. In fact, it eventually grew to such a point that the role of Q became obsolete, as everything Bond needed could be contained in his phone (although they have brought Q back in a limited way in the later films as a nod to the origins of the series). The other major development that I found impacted upon the filmmakers' ability to place products, particularly in the background of a scene, is the rise of globalization.

In *From Russia with Love* and *You Only Live Twice,* both films were based in foreign locations—Turkey and Japan, respectively. In both films, the number of products featured and the overall number of placements in general were well below average. The only logical explanation that I could come up with for this was that at this point in time foreign locations severely restricted the filmmakers' ability to place products realistically in the background of scenes. Yet within a relatively short period of time, by the time *Moonraker* was released, numerous English billboards were able to be featured in the background of scenes featuring numerous international brands, such as British Airways and Marlboro cigarettes, despite being located in the South American city of Rio. From this point on in the series, it didn't matter where the film was located—the number and types of products continued to grow.

ALBERT R. BROCCOLI

We do listen to fans and critics, and we read what they say. We try to comply. We take that criticism, and a lot of it is valid. There was a criticism of *Moonraker* that we had too much advertising, 7UP and all of this sort of thing, and it was true. But it was not meant to be that. We were in Brazil, and every time we turned around we noticed there were certain things there, British Airways and so forth. It wasn't, as everyone assumes, a big collection of making a lot of money on these things. It wasn't that at all. We started off using a Rolex watch in the original. We not only never got a watch from Rolex, they wouldn't even loan us one. The Rolex watch we used in the picture was one that I had, which I never got back. The property department had it for continuity all the time.

JOHN CORK

I attended the U.S. premiere of *Moonraker* in New York City as a 17-year-old high school student. I will always have a soft spot in my heart for *Moonraker.*

RIC MEYERS

I met Cubby Broccoli during the New York press junket for *Moonraker* and he struck me as a combination of a benign Godfather and Santa Claus. He treated all the journalists like guests at his party, but within moments of sitting down next to me, he seemed pleased that I was an avid fan who truly wanted what I considered good *James Bond* films. So he didn't take my honesty as negative, but he did take it in stride. I explained what I considered humor from inside the movie—the *Close Encounters* theme played on the lab key pad could actually have been decided upon by the characters in the film—as opposed to humor outside the film—a double-taking pigeon—championing the former, but decrying the latter. He basically shrugged with a smile and replied, "I thought it was funny." And that was all he needed to say, really. He was the boss, but he also came off as a good boss, who seemed to appreciate that I cared, but also probably forgot about it, and me, the moment he moved on. After all, he had already weathered an inflating-then-exploding Kananga, and was about to allow "I'll buy you a delicatessen in stainless steel" in *For Your Eyes Only.*

GLEN OLIVER

Moonraker is a tremendously fun film, hugely undercut by a few jarringly stupid moments, chiefly a pigeon doing a double take, and some of Jaws' antics. *Moonraker* is diluted because it never outright owns the obliquely implied motivation of its villain. Drax wants to erase life on Earth—he's devised a way to do so which doesn't burn away the entire planet—and then he wants to repopulate our world with superior physical specimens who can look to the skies and "know there is law and order in the heavens." But *why*? There are so many wonderfully provocative, bittersweet ideas inherent in the DNA of this master plan—but they're only scantly acknowledged at best. Is he doing this because he thinks mankind, as is, is lawless and screwed up—and now it's time for something different? Is it because he believes that the current way of the world will almost assuredly catapult the human race towards ruin, so why not try to save it while addressing a few shortcomings along the way? Is it because he is really hung up on creating a perfect human, which would essentially make him a fusion of Elon Musk and Hitler? Or, is it because Drax is merely a simpering douche-nozzle who has nothing else to do with his time, because he's too Asperger-y to get laid?

In *Moonraker,* there's a hint that Drax is driven by a sweeping, grimly poetic purpose—but his Machiavellian designs are distilled into a mission statement which somehow manages to be both unfocused and ambling in, literally, 50 seconds of screen time. Through Drax, there was an amazing opportunity to bring a bit of unexpected and thought-provoking gravity to *Bond*—a different kind of gravity than *On Her Majesty's Secret Service* afforded. Even if only for a few brief moments. What *is* our world, today, and *if* Drax is even slightly correct about how far we've fallen, is it even worth trying to save? Of course Drax is categorically wrong in his belief that physical imperfection should be abolished, but under his plan, suddenly Jaws the hunter would become Jaws the imperiled or undesirable. What an amazing predicament to put a *Bond* henchman into.

FRED DEKKER

I prefer it to *The Spy Who Loved Me.* I like the girls better too.

RIC MEYERS

They had seemingly perfected the Moore formula with *The Spy Who Loved Me.* Now all they had to do was create another using the same formula. Only one problem: that formula changed depending on who was looking at it. Then *Star Wars* happened, and the plan to make *For Your Eyes Only* was postponed to make what seemed like a sure thing instead: *Moonraker.* This attempt to ride the coattails of another hit was as misguided and unnecessary as the previous attempts to bobby-pin Moore's 007 to blaxploitation—throwing off the recipe even mo(o)re, as they seemingly mixed and matched *Moon/Eyes* ideas throughout production. The film's action sequences reflected the project's patchwork insecurity.

TOM MANKIEWICZ

I think it's the worst one. Too flabby. There's no real narrative. And there are too many scenes in it for me that deal in comedy. I mean, straight-out comedy. All I remember from that film is Jaws falling in love. It was total camp.

DAVID F. WALKER

(author, *Shaft: Imitation of Life*)

Live and Let Die, for a kid, was kind of scary. It had the Baron Samedi character with Geoffrey Holder's performance. All that was just a little bit creepy. They tried some different things there, and then they started to drift back into—and they do this every time they replace a Bond—this thing where, usually an actor's third performance or so, the movies just get ridiculous. Moore I think lucked out, because *The Man with the Golden Gun* was alright, *The Spy Who Loved Me* was really solid, and then you hit *Moonraker,* and I was, like, "Oh, it's over now." They went through that ridiculous phase. *For Your Eyes Only* kind of reeled it back a bit, but then it just went back down with the remaining Moore movies.

RICHARD MAIBAUM

What happened is that they kind of veered off course with the pictures, I thought, and then in *For Your Eyes Only* we came back to a more serious approach. I think it's something that we used to do in the earlier pictures, and that is when the action would get very wild and so forth, we would deliberately do what we called pulling the balloon down, to give the audience a moment to come back to something more serious. They're willing for you to be serious, because they know that pretty soon you'll be amusing again.

THE EIGHTIES: ENDINGS & BEGINNINGS

"I hope we're going to have some gratuitous sex and violence around here again."

FOR YOUR EYES ONLY (1981)

Despite the enormous success of *Moonraker,* Cubby Broccoli, who was always prescient in anticipating future movie trends, knew they couldn't continue on the current trajectory when it came to producing bigger and more expensive *Bond* spectacles. Repeating the success of *Moonraker* was in no way assured, and after the debacle of *Heaven's Gate*, which nearly destroyed United Artists, the studio also couldn't afford another big roll of the dice. So it was back to *Bond* basics for 007, with an espionage caper about a race to retrieve a British ATAC system, which is used to communicate between the Royal Navy's fleet of submarines, and, more important, the series moves away from an overreliance on gadgets. James Bond was definitely coming back down to earth.

ALBERT R. BROCCOLI

(producer, *For Your Eyes Only*)

It was a decision we made. On the production side, we were asked by United Artists, the distributor, to do it. We felt we wanted to go back to more of a *From Russia with Love/Goldfinger* type of story.

JOHN GLEN

(director, *For Your Eyes Only*)

The actual intention was to put all the emphasis on action. To really spend our money on that rather than big lavish sets, spaceships, or press-button technology. Get back to real people, good motives, good characterizations. It results in a film where you can see where the money was spent on action.

RICHARD MAIBAUM

(cowriter, *For Your Eyes Only*)

We deliberately said, "We've got to stop this fooling around," to the extent that it went. That's why even with Roger in *For Your Eyes Only* we cut down the shenanigans a bit so that you could believe that some of it was happening. That's one of my favorites.

RAY MORTON

(senior writer, *Script* magazine)

One of the best of the thriller *Bond*s—a very good gun-and-run spy tale. The script is a marvelous example of Richard Maibaum's facility in adapting Ian Fleming's work. In this case, Maibaum, working in tandem with Michael G. Wilson, seamlessly combined two of Fleming's short stories—"For Your Eyes Only" and "Risico"—into a single, very solid narrative. Apart from the pre-credit teaser, which can be read as a deliberate farewell to a certain style of *Bond* filmmaking, all of the elements in the screenplay—especially the characters and the action sequences—are much more realistic and down-to-earth than anything seen in any of the previous films.

ALBERT R. BROCCOLI

Because we made *Moonraker* and then, of course, before that, *Star Wars* and *Close Encounters* came out, we felt we were overcrowding the public on fantasy and outer space. I found it very boring, too. It might suit somebody else, but it didn't have to be *Bond*. Everyone kept saying, "When are you going to make another *From Russia with Love* type of thing?" So we tried that; adventure, Hitchcock-ian, full of suspense, excitement, and thrills.

CHAIM TOPOL

(actor, "Milos Columbo")

The film took a different direction from the previous one. First of all, we were back to Earth and less gadgets and more handiwork, and I prefer it this way. Although I enjoyed very much "flashing," flying with the birds in *Flash Gordon*—that was fun, too. For the *Bond,* we're better off down to Earth.

With the move to a more grounded *Bond,* it's not surprising that Broccoli moved away from Lewis Gilbert, who had directed some of the more fanciful entries in the series, *You Only Live Twice, The Spy Who Loved Me,* and *Moonraker.* Attention was turned to John Glen, who had begun proving what he was capable of by handling editing and second-unit direction of 1969's *On Her Majesty's Secret Service*, as well as the pre-credit sequences in both *Spy* and *Moonraker,* which left audiences stunned.

JOHN GLEN

I was completely surprised when I eventually got asked to direct *For Your Eyes Only.* It was really strange, because it came completely out of left field. I was so amazed when he asked me to direct. I couldn't believe it. Funny enough, Cubby had been in America for a couple of years, I think, after *Moonraker,* and he came back and he asked me to have dinner with him, and the special effects supervisor, Derek Meddings; and Peter Lamont, the production designer; and Tom Pevsner, the production executive. We were all invited to the table, and then there was a series of dinners afterward, and gradually the numbers got less and less until it was just me and Cubby and Cubby's wife and Michael Wilson left there, and I thought, "Something's happening. I'm not sure what it is." Then he said, "Would you like to come back to the office?" When I went back there, they're all sitting behind the desk, and he looked at me and said, "How would you like to direct *For Your Eyes Only*?" My legs sort of went from underneath me almost. I couldn't believe what I was hearing. It was a complete surprise. It was not only a surprise to me. I think half the film industry was just as equally surprised.

When these things happen when you least expect them, the ramifications of them are huge. As far as I was concerned, I was in a spin. He said, "If you want time to think about it," and I said, "No. I don't need to think about it." I was pretty much ready for it, strangely enough. It might sound immodest to say, but I think I'd been through a few start-ups, directing a couple of things on TV and what have you, and I realized I wasn't ready. But I think because I'd been doing so much second unit on the *Bond* films and I knew what made the *Bond* films tick, I used to think to myself, if I ever got a chance to direct, I hope it's a *Bond* movie. It might sound a bit strange to start at the top. You think people start on smaller things and build out, but it's much better to go in at the top, I can assure you.

You have a wonderful crew on the *Bond* films. You've got the best of people to help you. You're not on your own, and Roger Moore was fantastic. I was so lucky I had Roger and that Roger agreed. I don't know whether he had director approval or not, but he probably did. He certainly was very helpful to me in a lot of ways; we got on very well, and there was great humor on the set. We never had any cross words at all, and we worked very efficiently.

Of course, one of the first challenges facing Glen was whether or not he would actually have Moore back as 007. The actor's three-picture contract had expired after *Spy,* and beginning with *Moonraker,* he began negotiating with Broccoli film-to-film. Given the lack of certainty on each film, the team would inevitably start looking at other actors as replacements. Whether this was brinkmanship or a genuine search for a new 007 Broccoli would never admit, but actors such as Ian Ogilvy, Lewis Collins, and the perpetual Bond wannabe, Michael Billington, were in the running. Also being considered once more was *The Lion in Winter's* Timothy Dalton, who had originally been approached for *On Her Majesty's Secret Service*.

JOHN GLEN

I was delighted and surprised to be offered *For Your Eyes Only*, but the first thing Cubby said to me was "You've got to find a new Bond. Roger's getting too old and he's getting too expensive." You know, the usual stuff. So I went out all around the world testing likely Bonds—some unknown, some known, what have you. This process took a long time. We spent quite a bit of money testing various people, and of course it got back to Roger that I was testing other people for the role of Bond. He was still negotiating, if you like, in the background, but it was a game of poker, really. I didn't realize it. I was quite naïve, but Cubby was a good poker player, and if he could convince Roger that we were looking for someone else, then it gave him a bit of an edge in the bargaining department. I didn't realize it, but I think I was a bit of a tool in this ploy. It kind of worked, because at the end of the day, Roger did the film. It was great, and then he went on and did two more with me, and I was very happy about that.

JANE SEYMOUR

(actress, "Solitaire")

Michael Billington's dream in life was to be James Bond. And so he would constantly preen himself in front of the mirror and talk every day to all of us on the set of *The Onedin Line* about how one day he was going to be James Bond. I mean, that was literally all he could ever talk about. So when he heard I was going to meet them on *Live and Let Die*, he pretty much lost it. He went, "Oh my God. Oh my God." I couldn't tell anyone for two weeks I was cast, but Michael would ask me every day, "How'd it go? Did you get it? Did you hear anything?" I couldn't tell him I got the part. Eventually, when I got the part, everybody else on the show was really sort of upset and complained that I was dead to them, but Michael was very excited, because he was that much closer to being a Bond himself. He would eventually have a relationship with Cubby's daughter, Barbara Broccoli, for many years, and unfortunately he died rather tragically. So he got as close to being Bond as you could be without being Bond.

JOHN GLEN

When Cubby told me I had to find a new Bond, I thought to myself that I've got to remind the audience of the history of Bond. Of course *On Her Majesty's Secret Service* was very much on my mind, so I wrote a scene to introduce a new Bond involving the gravesite of his wife, Tracy, him bringing flowers to it, and then devised the helicopter action scene that would follow it. The whole point was to introduce a new Bond. That was my way of doing it, but of course when Roger agreed to do the film, I thought, "It's actually a very good sequence, isn't it, to remind the audience of Bond's past? Why not?" So we kept the introduction, and it's a nice touch with Roger putting the flowers on the grave.

This would be one of the last moments in the series acknowledging the fact that Bond had been married, and his wife killed by Blofeld. The only other mention would come in a conversation between Bond and Felix Leiter's new bride, Della, in *Licence to Kill*. It's certainly the most potent since *The Spy Who Loved Me,* in which Barbara Bach's Major Amasova brings it up, triggering one of Roger Moore's finest moments of acting subtlety in response. With the reboot of the franchise with 2006's *Casino Royale*, the marriage to Tracy has been removed from canon, and therefore there are no other references.

JOHN GLEN

The original idea was to keep the continuity of character and reveal the new Bond in an exciting situation.

ROBERT CAPLEN

(author, *Shaken & Stirred: The Feminism of James Bond*)

It's actually an important moment, because I think Tracy's death is a watershed moment in the *Bond* cinematic franchise for a couple of reasons. Most importantly, it offers continuity in a world in which various actors have portrayed Agent 007. Especially in the early years, continuity after Connery's departure was essential, and producers went to great lengths to ensure that *On Her Majesty's Secret Service* had elements of past films to keep the franchise moving forward. Then, in *Diamonds Are Forever*, Bond's initial pursuit of Blofeld is out of revenge for Tracy's murder, again ensuring continuity in a franchise that again experienced a change in actors. Adding reference to Tracy during Roger Moore and Timothy Dalton's tenures links past missions to the present, despite the personnel change, and reminds viewers that Bond remains constant.

LISA FUNNELL

(author, *For His Eyes Only: The Women of James Bond*)

On Her Majesty's Secret Service ends on such a tragic and devastating note that you *feel* that loss. I like the fact that subsequent films, even though they're more episodic and stand alone, really brought that loss through to show us maybe this is why James Bond is less attached to these women, because he doesn't want to go through that again. For me, I think that that's such an important moment with Tracy being killed and to see, especially in *Licence to Kill*, Bond's sorrow. Tracy died in 1969, so you're talking 20 years later at that point. Many people might not have even seen that, and yet to bring it back to that moment and to show that sorrow and to have Bond fight for the honor of Della, who also died, but also fighting for his wife that died, is an interesting thread to keep bringing through and connecting.

RICHARD MAIBAUM

Quite frankly, I would have liked to see more of it threaded through the pictures. But the tone of the pictures was different in the middle part of the saga.

MICHAEL FRANCE

(cowriter, *GoldenEye*)

There's a moment in *GoldenEye* when Alec Travelyan comments on whether or not all those vodka martinis drown out the sound of all the women Bond couldn't save. The first version of that line was to the *woman* he couldn't protect, meaning Tracy. I would have loved for that to go in, but I guess it gets a little tricky to keep referring back to a movie that, then, was from 25 years earlier. But I like when the films have made references to Tracy, because it gives depth and backstory to Bond and a darkness you really need. And it always really works.

LISA FUNNELL

What they did with Tracy is almost what they would do with Vesper Lynd in the Daniel Craig–era films, where her presence lives on. She dies in *Casino Royale*, but in *Quantum of Solace* she's still there. You have the Vesper martini, you have the Algerian love-knot necklace, you have the Vesper theme. You have Bond being so lovesick on her that he's getting drunk on these martinis just to consume her. You see that presence that just lasts all the way through almost to *Spectre*, where you have those tapes he finds, where he can watch the interview with her and he's like, "No, I'm fine. I've moved on." That's a film arc of being heartbroken and lovesick over the loss of someone in a more continuous way, whereas in the earlier films that type of lovesickness is separated and fragmented, and almost like how you skip stones—skipping it over and across. But this is more of a condensed way, showing that the loss of someone who you truly love has that type of an impact and might then make you more of a cold-hearted spy. Tracy was the first example of this, Vesper the second.

ROBERT CAPLEN

Another reason for referencing Tracy—also linked to the continuity theme—is to reveal Bond's sensitivity and vulnerability. Despite Bond's frequent callousness and apathy, he has an emotional pressure point that can sometimes reveal itself. Anya Amasova's clinical recitation of Bond's personnel file and Bond's reaction to it humanizes him and demonstrates that Bond is not merely an agent whose entire personality and body of work can be summarized in bullet points.

In the film, a British naval vessel is sunk by an old mine and a classified British targeting computer, the ATAC, is lost at sea. The Havelocks are dispatched to retrieve it, but they are assassinated by a Cuban hit man, prompting their daughter to seek vengeance, like Elektra, while Bond attempts to retrieve the ATAC before the Russians, who are being aided by the treacherous Kristatos, played by Julian Glover.

JOHN GLEN

When détente came in, we lost a bit of our story and our ability to tell spy stories, but there were always other things, other criminals that one can concentrate on.

MICHAEL G. WILSON

I think the films are fairly political. In *The Spy Who Loved Me*, each side was played off the other until they found out about this and then joined forces. In *For Your Eyes Only*, General Gogol was quite prepared to take any advantage he could so long as he didn't get himself in some kind of public involvement. He was very content to work behind the scenes and have the Greek characters get the goods for him to purchase, *without* involving any Russians, so to speak.

JOHN GLEN

For Your Eyes Only was based on a very good Fleming short story where the girl in a revenge attack tries to kill the chap that killed her father and what have you, and that made a wonderful opening to the picture. The rest of it we made up, pinched a few bits from other Fleming books, but it's quite an interesting film.

RAY MORTON

Apart from the opening, the story and script contain no fantasy elements at all. The tone of the piece is the most serious since *On Her Majesty's Secret Service,* and the humor in the script all comes out of the characters and the situations. A good case can be made that *For Your Eyes Only* is the most realistic and believable entry in the entire series.

FRED DEKKER

(cowriter, *The Predator*)

The reset button was hit and, I think, successfully. It's a crackling thriller. Maybe Roger Moore's best performance as Bond. It's a little workmanlike for me. Doesn't quite have the pizzazz of the other films, but I like that it's grounded.

SIR ROGER MOORE

(actor, "James Bond")

The way they're constructed, they get out first of all a storyline. Then select an art director and the director, and everyone starts wandering about looking for locations, finding places. Then they come back and say "This will work," and then they change it. A script comes out, and the dialogue is not right, and I jump up and down and say, "I'm the one who's got to say it!" And it always boils down that we will change it on the floor, and we always do.

JOHN CORK

I think Roger was a very tough actor for a writer. Moore had no problem delivering a line that falls flat for everyone except him. Michael Wilson's instinct was more toward the nuts and bolts of a plot, and that sometimes pushed against Roger's instinct to treat the story as a big joke. Michael was always working in a very collaborative environment, partnering with a true great, Richard Maibaum. I think it is a mistake to underestimate Michael Wilson's contribution to the continued success of the *Bond* films both as a writer and a producer.

For Your Eyes Only marked the beginning of the collaboration between veteran Maibaum and Wilson, whose role in the franchise would only grow over the coming decades.

RAY MORTON

Maibaum and Wilson became a team when Maibaum was brought back after *Moonraker* to pen a more down-to-earth and less expensive film that would be more in the spirit of *From Russia with Love* and *On Her Majesty's Secret Service.* Maibaum began developing the story with Wilson, the film's executive producer, and eventually they decided to work directly together. The team ended up writing the scripts for all five *Bond* movies produced in the 1980s, although novelist George MacDonald Fraser contributed an early draft for *Octopussy.*

RICHARD MAIBAUM

Michael's a lawyer, an engineer, and a terrific authority on photography and photographs. He's got one of the best collections in the world of early photographs. He's an amazing guy. We always listened to anyone, no matter what their ideas are, because you never know when somebody is going to come up with something terrific. I was very pleased working with Michael Wilson.

JOHN CORK

Michael G. Wilson is a fine writer. He is responsible for the pre-credits sequences in *The Spy Who Loved Me* and *Moonraker.* Like every writer, he has his strengths and weaknesses. He was nominated with Richard Maibaum for a WGA award for his work on *For Your Eyes Only*, and that's no small honor.

RICHARD MAIBAUM

We were equal collaborators. We did a lot of conferring. When we started out, we did a very full treatment, sometimes 50 or 60 pages long. We didn't do anything like writing three pages worth of treatment on the back of a letter or anything like that. Cubby liked to know beforehand what's going to be. We lay it out very carefully. Of course, you may deviate from it if you come up with something better, or if something doesn't work, but it is laid out very thoroughly beforehand. We discuss it. Sometimes we would sit there and write it together. Sometimes, Michael wrote the first draft, or I would write the first draft, and we gave it to the other fellow and argued about it. There's an awful lot of arguing that goes on. But you know what they say, if collaborators *don't* argue, then there's one collaborator too many. When you finally settle on something, it's been through the whole process. Cubby had final approval, of course, and then John [Glen] would sometimes sit in. As I say, it's a true collaboration. In the final analysis, the writer—or writers—have to sit down and are responsible for putting all the suggestions together.

RAY MORTON

The Maibaum/Wilson screenplays were a bit of a mixed bag. The team had a talent for concocting intriguingly complex plots, although sometimes their plots were *too* complex: *For Your Eyes Only* and *The Living Daylights* are entertaining puzzles, but the plots of *A View to a Kill* and *Licence to Kill* are hard to follow, and the storyline of *Octopussy* is at times incomprehensible. Maibaum and Wilson were comfortable with the more serious aspects of Bond's world, and their thriller and action sequences are generally quite inventive, but they had little facility for humor and fantasy. Their villains tended to be bland—and there were usually too many of them—and their scripts overlong. For me, their best scripts are *For Your Eyes Only* and *The Living Daylights*—relatively down-to-earth and realistic spy thrillers filled with intrigue, clever twists, and exciting action. Their least successful ones are those that tip more in the direction of fantasy and comedy—*Octopussy* and *A View to a Kill. For Your Eyes Only,* though, was a smashing debut script from the Maibaum/Wilson team.

JOHN GLEN

I'm versed in Fleming. For instance, I think *Goldfinger* was a fantastically written book. And the short story that *For Your Eyes Only* is based on is a wonderfully written short story. I am a great admirer of Fleming. I like his style, and the way he's written scenes that I've portrayed in these films are beautifully written scenes. I've stuck to them as closely as I could.

When Fleming died, he had a very limited number of books and had a lot of short stories, and we used every bit of all his written work. We used to go through them each time we had to write a script from scratch. We used to go back through all the old scripts and all the old books and try and find any bits that hadn't been used in films to try and bring Fleming back into the story, into the mix, and we succeeded in doing that. There are bits and pieces from different books that appear in different films.

For Your Eyes Only is no exception, taking a sequence from the novel *Live and Let Die* and incorporating it. In the film, once Kristatos is exposed as being the actual villain, he has Bond and Melina keelhauled through the water in the belief that they will ultimately be eaten by sharks (sorry to disappoint you, dude!).

GLEN OLIVER

The editing and overall energy of Bond and Melina being keelhauled was surprisingly arresting for a 007 picture—and represented one of the few times underwater action in the franchise actually had a respectable pulse.

JOHN GLEN

That was a scene which has been in and out of *Bond* scripts for as long as I can remember. It's a scene no one really wanted to shoot, except for Cubby. The reason was because it was such a complex sequence to shoot, with no guarantees you were going to get it, because it was a mixture of underwater and above water. It involved four to five units shooting the material. It was very difficult to control and the cost of that part of the operation was very high. I was in Corfu shooting the sequence itself with Roger and Melina on the surface at the precise time the second unit was shooting, with Al Giddings, the underwater part of it in the Bahamas. It was all storyboarded, and it worked absolutely perfectly. That became a feature of all my films, that I would sometimes have three or four different units working at the same time at different locations around the world.

RICHARD MAIBAUM

John Glen is very, very inventive as far as stunts go. He used to be a great cutter, and he sees things in his mind visually in terms of film. When he gets an idea for something, he'd discuss it with us and we'd work on it, but actually he is very influential in that department.

The beautiful French actress Carole Bouquet plays Melina Havelock, the daughter of two marine archaeologists who are murdered by Soviet agent Gonzales after they locate the wreck of the downed St. Georges freighter.

RICHARD MAIBAUM

I thought that girl—Carole Bouquet—was marvelous, and Roger seemed to control himself from trying to be so goddamn funny all the time.

FRED DEKKER

Carole Bouquet is my top tier of *Bond* Girls. She's beautiful, but she's also spunky. A real presence in the movie. I like the Fleming-isms. Dragging them, keelhauling them with the sharks behind them is terrific. The mountain-climbing scene is also really tense and well done.

MAURICE BINDER

(main title designer, *For Your Eyes Only*)

Roger really is easy, with great gags, and makes everybody feel sort of relaxed, whoever works with him. We were doing these teaser trailers so far in advance, and in the scene with Carole Bouquet and the little Deux Chevaux [automobile] where they go off and he turns to her and says, "By the way, we haven't been formally introduced, my name is Bond, James Bond." She looks at him blankly, and Cubby said to me, "This girl, she doesn't smile. She has such a beautiful smile, and she's not smiling." I said, "I know, but that's the scene." And I said, "I do have a take where she *does* smile." And he said, "Well, why don't you use it?" And I said, "Well, the dialogue [an outtake] went like this, "By the way, we haven't met, my name is Bond, James Bond. I guess a little fuck would be out of the question.'" So what I did is, I took the dialogue from the first take and cut just the smile.

The villainy of the film is far more grounded, with no megalomaniacal villains looking to destroy the world this time out. Perhaps the most loathsome of Bond's adversaries in the film is the seemingly mute Emile Leopold Locque, played by the late Michael Gothard, a deadly killer who gets his comeuppance after he's dispatched by Bond, who kicks his car off a cliff in retribution over the death of another agent.

JOHN GLEN

The intention was at the beginning that we'd be a slightly harder *Bond* film. I can remember where Bond kicks Loque's car off the cliff with the villain inside, and Roger had quite a big discussion with me. Not an argument exactly, but he was very much against him kicking the car off a cliff. He felt that was too violent for Bond. What he wanted to do was throw back the dove, the little emblem, into the car, and because it was so balanced, even that little featherweight would tip the car off the cliff. I said, "No. I don't think that'll work." In the end, we shot it both ways. To be quite honest, it was easier to do that rather than argue about it. In the end, I used both versions. He threw the emblem in, and then he kicked it off the cliff. I think Roger in the end agreed. I just think it was too violent for him. He said at the time, "A lot of kids watch my films. I think that's a very violent thing to do." I said, "He killed your best friend [Ferrara]. He deserves it, and I think you're justified." Anyway, we did it. He was very good. He was very professional. He would let you have the last word as director.

While Julian Glover's Kristatos initially provides aid to 007 and fingers Milos Columbo, played gleefully by Topol, as the film's big bad, appearances can be deceiving. In one of the best exchanges in the film (that evokes the first meeting between Bond and Draco in *On Her Majesty's Secret Service*), Columbo tells Bond that he's not the real enemy and hands 007 back his Walther, telling Bond, "By tomorrow, we'll be fast friends." Bond levels the gun back at Columbo's chest and tells him, "We'll see." It's interesting to note that Glover, who most recently finished a run on *Game of Thrones*, had been considered for the role of Bond during previous recastings.

JULIAN GLOVER
(actor, "Kristatos")

Every time it's discussed, you can say, "Well, what's the villain going to be like this time? Will he have steel teeth? India rubber ears and laser beams in his nose? What's he going to be?" Each one has its different surprise. Blofeld was all very well, but one doesn't often see a totally bald bloke with a white cat on his lap in a wheelchair and a console in front of him. And you don't often meet them in the street, do you? But my sort of guy, and Topol's sort of guy, are multimillionaires; they're recognizable as animals. That was the idea.

CHAIM TOPOL

I went to a Fourth of July party at some American's house in London, and Dana Broccoli said to Cubby, "How about Topol for the part?" Cubby calls my agent. She didn't negotiate the deal, but she did the rest. Dana Broccoli and I were talking about it for a long time. Whenever they came up with a Bond, we were talking about the heavy, which I wanted very much to do. So I got half a heavy.

GLEN OLIVER
(pop culture commentator)

Topol is masterfully cast as a Bond ally—he classes up any film he's in, and played off of Roger Moore's energy very nicely. Two gentleman badasses—Bond being worldly and Topol's Columbo being master of his own slice of the world—working together to solve a common threat in as uncompromising a way as possible was a lovely riff on the standard MO of 007 movie plots.

CHAIM TOPOL

I had my women with me; my daughter and my wife. Making the *Bond* film was my second experience on a big production. The previous one was *Flash Gordon,* which I did with De Laurentiis. *Fiddler* was, in comparison, very little. *Fiddler* was done in Yugoslavia, and once you are in Yugoslavia, it becomes very modest, whatever you want to spend. But I found, for the first time in my life, that filmmaking can really be real fun, and Cubby does it for you. Cubby is there to have fun, and he wants everybody to have fun while making the movie. Everything is taken very easy, very professional; no rush-rush, no hustle, no bustle. Things are done in the most gentle way. I haven't been on other *Bonds*, but the combination of Cubby, Roger, and John Glen meant complete tranquility. It was absolutely a joy to work, and you're there to have fun, and I think that it comes across in the work.

The late Bernard Lee is sorely missed here, having been replaced by Geoffrey Keen as Sir Frederick Gray, the British minister of defense. Peter Lamont replaces Ken Adam as production designer, having worked with him since *Goldfinger*, and presents a more realistic look for the series, grounding the Cold War espionage in the age of détente.

JULIAN GLOVER

We missed "M" [Bernard Lee] very badly. Losing him was a tragedy. But the substitution for that was a very happy one, that duet of men in London. The appearance of "Q" as the priest is wonderful. I don't know how he got in there.

We do, however, know how Robbin Young, making a short appearance as the worker at a flower shop who interacts with Bond, came to be involved: she won a contest through *Playboy*.

ROBBIN YOUNG

(actress, "Flower Shop Girl")

I was reading *Playboy* and I was always a pageant buff, but never dreamed that I would get a role in a *James Bond* movie. Three thousand entrants, and a long process, because I didn't hear from *Playboy* for about three months. Three of us were selected to go to California for a screen test, and then I was selected. It's like a dream: a girl from Fort Lauderdale getting a part in a *Bond* film. I was there for two weeks. I did actual filming for one week, and then waited for the rushes for one week. But it was beautiful, and I got along very well with everyone. Roger Moore made me feel very relaxed. When I was doing the scene, I was nervous because I had to do a few takes, and he said, "Just remember, the public sees one." After that I just relaxed.

As John Glen explains it, one of the challenges at the start of production was a lack of preparation time. In June of 1980, there was a four-page outline from which Maibaum and Wilson were writing the film's screenplay.

JOHN GLEN

Because of a combination of snow scenes and summer scenes in the story, it was essential to start no later than September in Greece. I can remember the starting historic weather pattern for Corfu in September. It showed more rain than Manchester! One advance of sandwiching location surveys with intervals of working closely on the script was the ability to adapt action scenes to fit the locations. Our surveys must have been the shortest on record. For instance, we completed the one in Corfu in two days, finding a dozen different sites. Michael Wilson drove the hired mini-bus and only succeeded in putting us in the ditch at the end of the second day.

The cameras first turned on a mini-location in the North Sea. We picked the best three days in living memory, with blue skies and calm seas. The scene was the sinking of the fishing trawler in the Ionian Sea. I visualized the scene starting underwater, revealing the trawler as the camera rose to the surface. The box that the camera crew constructed to house the camera proved too heavy to launch and was soon abandoned in favor of a plastic bag!

PAUL WILSON

(special effects cameraman, *For Your Eyes Only*)

For a start, the trawler could not actually be sunk, even for a *Bond* film. We had to match the light and sea conditions on the exterior tank at Pinewood that a second unit had experienced in August with the real trawler in the

North Sea—and shoot in mid-November. No mean task in England that time of year, when the sun is so low that there were only two hours in the middle of the day when the surrounding trees weren't casting shadows on the backing. Derek Medding's team of model makers had to make a good job of the *St. George,* because after it was sunk in the exterior tank, it was raised and used in the 007 Stage, underwater, and shot on very closely.

ALAN HUME

(director of photography, *For Your Eyes Only*)

We had our problems. The film started shooting in September, so already the days were getting shorter, the sun lower, the rainy season nearer; nevertheless, we coped. John Glen was always willing to listen to everybody's problems, and occasions when I had to ask him, "Can I shoot in this, or that direction first?" so as to take best advantage of light conditions, he would almost always agree.

JOHN GLEN

Main shooting commenced in mid-September on the island of Corfu and the weather was super for the first three weeks. Rémy Julienne and his team of French stuntmen were hired for the car chase, and later the ski/motorcycle chase, while Arthur Wooster and his second unit were enjoying themselves turning over cars.

ALAN HUME

The schedule was eventually set for 20 weeks of shooting, which broke down to six weeks on the Greek island of Corfu, two weeks at Meterora in Central Greece, three weeks in Cortina, Italy, and nine weeks at the Pinewood Studios near London, which included underwater filming in the Pinewood tank. An American underwater filming crew was concurrently shooting in the Bahamas.

JOHN GLEN

My first choice of photographer was Alan, with whom I had worked previously on the highly successful ski parachute jump in *The Spy Who Loved Me.* Without Alan's courage in placing the cameras on the precipice of Mount Asgard in Canada's frozen north, the scene would never have been filmed. I shall never forget him disappearing over the edge and reappearing clutching an enormous rock, which was suspended under the tripod to give it stability.

One standout scene for the director took place in an ancient underwater city where Melina's father was doing work for the British government.

JOHN GLEN

It was a wonderful idea, and a lot of that was Michael Wilson, who came up with that, and Dick Maibaum. They researched it very well and it gave us a wonderful opportunity to do some very, very good scenes in the water

RICHARD MAIBAUM

We did a lot of conferring—everybody does—on the *Bond* pictures. And, of course, a stuntman himself comes up with some great ideas he'd like to try out. They'd come to John Glen, discuss it with us and so forth. The stunts may come from anyone.

JOHN GLEN

The scene where Bond and Melina enter the shipwreck to get the computer, all that stuff, we had a script conference, and we were saying that Carole Bouquet cannot work underwater. She has a problem with her ear and she can't do it. Roger is wonderful underwater, but you still don't look too good when you're soaking wet, so we made a decision that we would shoot it dry. What we did is, we used a second unit to do all the wide shots, and then when we come to the close shots of the actors, then we stick them on a stall, have an air machine blowing their hair up in the air, and shoot at 70 frames a second. It's like slow motion, and then, because of the mask they're wearing, you can't really see their lips, so you can put the dialogue on; you can play the dialogue and rough it up a bit to make it sound as though it's underwater. It worked perfectly well.

ALAN HUME

To get a realistic effect of hair movement, general slowness, and weightlessness, which is so apparent in real underwater material, Derek Meddings shot some tests, running the camera at 120 frames per second and using strong wind machines to blow the hair upward and from side to side. Also used were foreground glass fish tanks for bubble effects. Later more bubbles were superimposed into critical areas of the picture. These tests were very promising and effective, so that was the way we photographed the underwater close-ups of James Bond and the girl. Even if I say so myself, these shots proved so effective as to be undetectable from the real thing.

JOHN GLEN

Derek Meddings was our special effects guy. He was a wonderful special effects man, and what we did was we got a little bit of graph paper and we put it on the viewfinder of the camera, and we made a cross where their mouths were. Then Derek Meddings would take that little piece of graph paper over to his department and he would get a fish tank and put an air line in and create bubbles where the actual crosses were on the graph paper, and then without processing the film, so we did it on the exposed negative. We double exposed it, in other words, and then that was processed and we saw it the next day, and it worked fantastically well. It was a superimposition, but done by this mark in the graph paper on the viewfinder, and that's how we got the bubbles to come up from where their mouths were, you see, and that sells it completely. We used to use all these tricks. We didn't have CGI in those days, so everything had to be done smoke and mirrors, which is half the fun. I feel sorry for them today. They tell me, "Don't worry, we'll do it in post." It's taken a lot of the fun out of it.

The film's finale set at the St. Cyril Monastery, actually an abandoned Eastern Orthodox monastery in Greece located at the top of a rocky precipice. The sequence includes a spectacular climbing sequence, Rick Sylvester of *The Spy Who Loved Me* fame doubling for Roger Moore. Unfortunately, despite securing all the necessary permissions, the monks reneged on their agreement, presenting a unique challenge for the filmmakers.

JULIAN GLOVER

One of the finest stunts I've ever seen—the guy on the rope. I hope he was paid a great deal of money for that. All of the stunts, even the most extreme ones, were in the realm of what's just about possible, whereas in the last couple of *Bond* movies [before this], the whole point of them has been: "No way, but come on, go into fantasy land." There's no magic car this time. Even the hair-raising sequence down the bobsled run—I never thought anyone could do a ski chase again, but, my God, they did. Unbelievable. It is possible, because they did it. We said, "Who's going to do this?" Even when they were half-way down, you think, well maybe they undercranked, and things like that, and maybe it's not very slippery at all. You suddenly get a shot of the bobsled from the front. You see through that, you see the motorbikes and the ski going behind them, so you know it's real. It actually was done. But all these stunts are possible, and that's the idea with the storyline, too.

BILL CONTI

(composer, *For Your Eyes Only*)

We were in quite complicated locations and you've probably heard about the trouble we had there. It was no big deal to have fun in Corfu, because it is a fun place and that was a joy. But then in a little place called Kalabaka, a little village which is one street—you really have to be a Cubby Broccoli to know how to do it.

ALBERT R. BROCCOLI

Well, bless the monks. It seems that when we went on a recce to see these wonderful monasteries in Kalabaka, that they all agreed that we should come there. We talked to the bishop and the bishop agreed. We paid them a rather substantial sum of money to shoot there, in this particular monastery, which is the most beautiful of all. And in doing that, apparently what happened there was even though the bishop made the deal, two new monks came in and there were only two monks in that entire monastery that wouldn't permit us to come in there. The bishop tried to tell them that we were entitled to entrance, but no way. So we still went there, because we had been shooting there, and they decided they were going to screw us up good. These gentle monks, they hung all kinds of things around: paraphernalia, flags, everything to make the background unusable. And, well, we went along with that, and we kept on shooting without identifying that angle. We had taken a long shot of it and then what we did, unbeknownst to them, is we masked off on the foreground a piece, which we built so that we could shoot there, in the end sequence when the helicopter lands. So in the film business you find a way to do it. Of course they were irate, but we paid for it, we were entitled to do it.

A lot of jokes have been made over the years about the use of stuntmen for Roger Moore, but however true some of that may be, the man was very much involved with the production of the films.

JULIAN GLOVER

Roger is actually amazing. At five o'clock in the morning, having been filming all night, when you're really dead on your feet, and you keep on having to pull it out of the bottom of your trousers, he is still up and on top, joking, keeping people going.

SIR ROGER MOORE

On the ice hockey sequence I got banged up quite badly. There was a part where I had to go along across the ice, and get up and change angles, and so, instead of being knocked out, I was throwing myself in toward the camera, and I had to hit the wall. It was about 20 feet, and it's quite a long way to slide. After three takes I hadn't done it, so I thought there's only one way I'm going to do this, which is to do what I've done a thousand times, which is a shorter roll, elbow tuck and fly. I hadn't taken into account that with that jacket I was wearing, it would just slide like that forever on the ice—it pushed the acromio-clavicular and separated the clavicle. It was exceedingly painful and all my language was horrendous. And we were shooting at night and it was cold, and they whipped me off to the hospital. Nothing was broken. It was X-rayed and they said it should be taped up. I would be immobile, but that was the penultimate night of shooting in Cortina, and we would then be stuck for a week while they waited for me to take my bandages off. So I said that I would have a needle, a local anesthetic, and work the next night, which was a mistake.

Composer Bill Conti, famous for his legendary music to the *Rocky* films, replaces John Barry, a British tax exile at the time who was already busy with his brilliant score to *Body Heat*, in the latest installment with a disco-infused score.

BILL CONTI

John Barry for some reason couldn't do it, so he recommended me to Cubby. When he recommended me I was really, really thrilled. That was an honor. Because of that recommendation, I came in and was warmly welcomed by the Broccoli family: Dana, Michael Wilson, Barbara, all of those people. When Cubby said, "I have a first-time director," he told me he wanted me to write all the music in London. And I said, "Well you know, that's going to be three months, and I've got a family. I think I'd rather stay in Los Angeles, if you don't mind." He says, "Bring the family." Not only that, I brought an au pair and a girl who was going to teach my young daughters at the time. It was a wonderful three-month experience thanks to Cubby.

Conti's work on the film is probably best remembered for its wildly popular main title theme, "For Your Eyes Only," in which singer Sheena Easton is memorably depicted crooning in Maurice Binder's opening credits sequence–this after a song by Blondie, toplined by Deborah Harry, was rejected by the producers.

BILL CONTI

I never heard it, but I do know that people submitted stuff and wanted the title song. And there was no obligation to give me the song. My song was not contractual. You write the music. That's all. I thought I did a really good song for *Rocky III*, but Survivor did a better song. I'll never forget on *For Your Eyes Only* when they said, "I think we'll go with Bill's." No, I didn't jump for joy, but my heart was exploding. I didn't want to lose that.

JOHN CORK

Bill Conti's score may have some moments that have not aged well, but the title song still sounds fantastic. Have you ever heard the disco mix of Shirley Bassey's *Moonraker* title song? It was just the style of the moment. Bill Conti has nothing to apologize for when it comes to catering to the disco era.

BILL CONTI

Fashions change. Then the old fashion comes back again in another generation. So the idea of a '70s movie was stylized in the music, too. If you take *Star Wars*, you go, well, "That's in the classic form of movie writing." That style could have been done by Korngold in the '40s. Then you hear *Peter Gunn*, and you go, "Oh well, that's exactly what that is." Then you hear the disco thing that's going on and you go, "Well, that's the '70s."

I had to learn a tough lesson, because between *Rocky I* and *Rocky II*, me, the producers, Chartoff, Winkler, and Sly, we had a real disagreement. They're saying, "Oh, you need to do the same thing." I'm going, "I can't do the same thing. There's no need to do the same thing. I can just write more music." It's no fun for me to just do the same thing. Not testy, but it was like I really pleaded my case. So, I go on to do a *James Bond* movie, and when we're in the editing room, Cubby Broccoli says to me, "You know, Bill, if you don't mind," and he was really apologetic and says, "You know when James goes into action, if you'd play his theme." And I said, "Of course, I'd play his theme. I wouldn't think of *not* playing his theme."

But on *Rocky* after one film, how do you know this is Rocky's theme, and he's got to have it every time? At that time, they had been making *Bond* films for 25 years, so it made perfect sense to me. How could you not? But then I went, "Oh my God, all of that fighting for nothing." It made its point the hard way. Of course, when *Rocky* starts running, just play the damn theme.

Conti notes that when Maurice Binder met Sheena Easton, he asked if he thought she would accept the idea of actually being in the main titles, which was unprecedented when it came to singers for the series.

BILL CONTI

I said, "I think she would die to be in them. Are you kidding? There's not a person alive that wouldn't." He says, "I'm reluctant to ask her." I said, "Maurice, how can anybody say no to that?"

MAURICE BINDER

I went into Cubby's office and I looked at these tapes and I said, "My God, why did I shoot all these shots with the pretty models?" I said, "We could have used the singer, bring her out from behind." So I did, and I wasn't sure how it would work, she had never done a film before.

BILL CONTI

When they were together, they were a matched couple. I'm talking size. She was a little bitty girl. He was a little bitty man. Of course, she was just beautiful. And, of course, a great singer. A *Bond* singer.

SHEENA EASTON

(singer, "For Your Eyes Only")

The filming took one day. But the recording took a long time, because I was with Bill [Conti] and Mickey [Leeson] doing the writing. I'm not saying I had anything to do with it, but they called me in from time to time to have me sing parts of it to see how it sounded. So I felt part of it, even though I was just a bystander. And the recording took a couple of days for me to sing it and for the musicians to put it down. But the idea of being in the film didn't overwhelm me, the idea of singing the song did. If you'd asked me to put on a bathing suit and step outside, I wouldn't have been thrilled, but to sing a movie theme had always been my ambition. The *Bond* themes as a genre are the best. And just to be asked to do it, I was flattered.

BILL CONTI

In the beginning, I didn't think she was a *Bond* singer. As a matter of fact, UA was pitching her because she had a hit record called "9 to 5" (Morning Train). A little MOR pop thing that was just cute. There's no question that she's a talented girl, but I had asked Barbra Streisand to do the lyrics to a song sung by Donna Summer. So she was always in the wings, but this was this girl that United Artists wanted to use. For me though, how do you not do Shirley Bassey in those days? I agreed to have a meeting with the little Sheena girl and I'm so disappointed I can't get Donna Summer, because it meant I'd have a hit. Then Sheena comes to the door and she's tiny and beautiful and she speaks to my daughters, who knew all about her, because of that song that was on the radio all the time, and they can't understand a word she says, because of her accent. The brogue is *so* thick. But we sit down at the piano, exploring her voice where you sit at the piano, and I'm still thinking in mind of Shirley Bassey.

Now I've lost my lyricist, I've lost my star. I've got this little girl that I can't understand, but she has a wonderful voice. So I say to her, "Well, who's your favorite lyricist?" because I got to write a song. She says, "Mick Leeson." I'd never heard of him. He was a friend of hers and, at that point, I did not have a thousand lyricists in my mind. I was still so impressed with myself for trying to get Barbra [Streisand]. Now all the bets are off. So I meet Mick; we write a song. Now, the song connected with a *Bond* picture, as you know, has to have the title in the lyric. So I've got to have a song that's up the street, the soldiers are marching down. Meaning, it should end with the phrase, "For your eyes only." I do this for you, I do that for you, and I do it for your eyes only. So we write a song like that. And it's whatever, whatever, whatever, for your eyes only.

Now, I make a demo with a girl singer. Not Sheena, but a girl singer. I make an appointment with Cubby to present the song at two o'clock in the afternoon. At noon, I have a lunch with Maurice Binder at Pinewood. Maurice says, "Oh, Bill, you know, I remember the days with *Goldfinger*, and the title would come on at the same time as the song. Oh, those were the days." Now, sitting in my little coat pocket is a cassette that after three minutes *ends* with "For your eyes only." He keeps saying, "It's so nice when that happens, but I know you have your own problems to deal with." He ruins my meal, and I cancel the meeting with Cubby, and I tell him, "I'm sorry, I can't come with the tape." I call up Mick Leeson and say, "Listen, Mick, this song needs to begin with 'For your eyes only.' I don't care what you say after that. Write another lyric. Write anything, but it's got to begin 'For your eyes only.'" So then he did, and Maurice was happy. That's when he saw Sheena, and she ends up in the main title. It was a wonderful experience.

MAURICE BINDER

At one time they changed the lyrics at the last minute, and I had cut half of the titles and used four or five or six pieces of film to make it up. The voice at that point was singing, "I see your eyes in a thousand dreams," and there was a big behind going across the screen, so I had to start from scratch and retime the thing. Rearrange the pictures to the beats of music, and of course once that's done, the titles, the actual lettering. They come in on musical beats, too. Everything works with timing. And when you have about two and a half weeks to finish a title, when you've shot 25 or 30,000 feet of film, it's not easy. So you work day and night, and you're in that little cutting room that's 3 feet by 10 feet at Pinewood, on a rainy night, it's cold, windy England, you say, "What am I doing here?" and "Who's going to want to see this damn thing anyway?"

SHEENA EASTON

Maurice Binder is a walking genius. I heard that he had filmed lots of eyes and had decided to use the eyes, but then he had seen videos of me singing and thought my eyes were adequate. Then the day came and he shot my whole face, he built around that. We didn't go into great detail; I think he just found it pleasing to the eye, and maybe just from a different angle it was a good idea. I feel that it gives my song its own place in the film. If you stop the film there, it's almost like a promotional film for the song itself.

And then there's the aforementioned pre-credit sequence which opens with Moore's Bond visiting the grave of his late wife, Tracy. But as Bond takes off in a helicopter that was sent for him, an unnamed, bald antagonist (aka Ernst Stavro Blofeld) takes control of the helicopter with a remote control and tortures him and hurls bad puns at him as he flies the helicopter through narrow buildings.

JOHN GLEN

We were all scratching our heads, trying to think of a good opening sequence, because we had become quite well known for our opening sequences, and it's difficult to come up with an original idea. We all started working in different directions to try and think of a good idea. Cubby then came in from Los Angeles, and he was very tired. He came into the office and he said, "We've got to think of a good idea for this opening title." He asked if we had an idea. I came up with an idea, which is basically what is in the film now, and when I told Cubby the story of it, he said, "I don't like that very much. Think of something better than that." I think it's a good point that if someone's tired, just come back with jet leg, they aren't in the best frame of mind to be receptive to any ideas. Anyway, about a month later, we sat down again, and still no one else had come up with a good idea. We were getting pretty desperate: we were getting pretty close to shooting. I just reiterated my idea, and he said, "I think it's terrific." I said, "I told you it was." He denied it completely.

FRED DEKKER

As soon as the helicopter shows up, for me, it's okay go to the credits.

JOHN GLEN

We did some wonderful things. Peter Lamont, our production designer, was very clever, and we used foreground miniatures a lot. In *For Your Eyes Only*, the helicopter entering the shed was a foreground miniature. The helicopter in fact passed between the camera and the building, so we put up a bit of foreground building, five feet from the camera, and it just appears to go into the shed. It's an optical illusion, and we used that technique a lot in those *Bond* films. It was a fantastic way to do it. Easy. It was usually a second-unit operation. You didn't spend hours trying to match the building foreground with the building in the background. You let second unit do that. You'd spend all day there waiting for the right conditions, etc., but you plan it, and it works. It works beautifully. You've just got to give them time to do it.

PAUL WILSON

The opening helicopter sequence shot by Jimmy Davis needed our help. While Bond is fighting to gain control of the radio-controlled helicopter, it is seen to enter an abandoned warehouse, fly around, and leave again. An elaborate rig was created by special effects for the actual flying inside the building, but the model unit had to show the real helicopter flying in one end of the warehouse and out the other. Two foreground miniatures were created by the art department and carefully lined up with the real buildings. The helicopter, flying toward and down the side of the real building, appeared to be entering it, because of the foreground. All in all, I would say that I had more problems on *For Your Eyes Only* than on *Moonraker*, because I had to match to full-scale, live-action film already shot. What I shot had to be cut into those sequences without being noticed. When no one notices a visual effects cinematographer's work, he has achieved what he set out to do—fool 'em!

In the comic book adaptation based on the original script, the pre-title sequence ends with Bond taking control of the helicopter and dropping Blofeld down the chimney after he chides Bond over his cold-blooded murder of Tracy in *On Her Majesty's Secret Service* by saying, "This is the way to celebrate the latest anniversary of your bereavement," and Bond looks out the window as he drops Blofeld down the chimney and replies, "Happy anniversary."

Although the actual sequence in the finished movie itself boasts some impressive aerial photography, it culminates with Bond, who has now taken control of the helicopter, dropping the faux-Blofeld down a smokestack as the villain pleads with Bond to put him down by offering, "I'll buy you a delicatessen . . . in stainless steel" before meeting his presumed demise. These awful ADR lines, which are added in post, are usually the kind of goofy asides you come up with in post-production to amuse yourself when you're sleep deprived and mixing for days and weeks on end. They are not meant to actually go in the movie, and no line is more infamous and inappropriate in the annals of Bond history than this absurd plea from this once grand and formidable 007 villain (with the possible exception of the aforementioned diss of The Beatles in *Goldfinger*).

JOHN GLEN

As anxious as we were to mention who he was, we just let people use their imaginations and draw their own conclusions. We don't give him a name: he was just a guy with a stiff neck and a wheelchair.

RICHARD MAIBAUM

It was supposed to be Blofeld, but that line—"I'll buy you a delicatessen in stainless steel"—I had nothing to do with it. It was phoned in on the set by somebody. I don't know who. It's probably the worst line in the whole damn thing.

FRED DEKKER

How did it survive?

JOHN GLEN

That was Cubby's line. He invented that line, and we all thought it came very, very out of left field in a way. I'm not sure how amusing it was. It left a lot of people scratching their heads I think, but it was one of those statements that we used to always have, a funny line at the end of an exciting sequence to release the tension, and I guess it did that. It probably perplexed quite a lot of people as well. It was a sop to Cubby Broccoli, shall we say. He was the boss, and it was his line.

JOHN CORK

For Your Eyes Only's great opening had a fantastic reaction from audiences when Bond impaled the wheelchair of "Blofeld" on the helicopter skid. In post-production, they brought in Robert Rietty to do the voice of "Blofeld." Lewis, Cubby, and Roger Moore decided that he needed something more to say besides pleading to be put down. Cubby came up with the line, which was an old New York mob payoff, buying someone a delicatessen outfitted with stainless-steel countertops. I'm not sure even Blofeld could imagine Bond opening his own New York deli, but then again, Cubby was many things, but not a screenwriter. I think we can give him a pass for one wacky line of dialogue.

FRED DEKKER

I prefer to tune out as soon as the helicopter shows up. There's like three shots in the teaser of Bond going to Tracy's grave before that, which I love.

For Your Eyes Only, which premiered in June of 1981, would ultimately gross over $190 million worldwide, with $54 million in the United States alone. By no means an all-time high, but given the reduced budget of $28 million, a sizable haul.

JOHN CORK

For Your Eyes Only worked for audiences in 1981 during a very crowded summer filled with potential blockbusters.

BILL CONTI

It's nice to work on a project where no one is nervous, which is always surprising. There aren't that many. Bond is like that. They know what they're doing. They're not nervous, and they've got the loot to do it.

GLEN OLIVER

It's a better film than people give it credit for. The relationship between Bond and Lynn-Holly Johnson's Bibi character was an extremely clever spin on the swooning *Bond* Girl archetype. Here we had a violable young girl who actually flummoxes Bond—and whose age and demeanor forced Bond to confront his own horn-dog inclinations in some very humorous ways. Drawing Bond as both a sex object and a father figure to Johnson's character was an inspired, and damn subversive, move. The franchise could've used more of this kind of *intelligent* self-awareness.

BILL CONTI

The saddest thing about the song "For Your Eyes Only" is when it was performed for the Oscars, which is a big deal. The lead dancer, playing James Bond, broke his leg during the rehearsal and never danced again. It was my second Oscar nomination, and I was conducting the orchestra for the broadcast, and each piece of music has the title of the song, the nominee, and the name of the movie. There's five pieces of music for all the musicians. Sixty musicians, 16 singers. And when they say "The winner is," you look down to find the right one. The conductor looks up to see that everybody's found it, and you play the proper song. This all happens in an instant.

So, when you're nominated, and you're playing, there's the anxiety of playing for the show, and you see in the musicians' eyes, "Oh, I hope you win." I had already been nominated once for *Rocky* and lost that. So for *For Your Eyes Only*, they announce, "And the winner is," and it wasn't me. But the other musicians are all looking down and the director is yelling, "Music, music!" I said, "I can't. Nobody's looking at me." So it was bittersweet, but the really sad thing was the dancer who broke his leg.

One interesting side note, *For Your Eyes Only* marked the first comic book adaptation of a *James Bond* film since *Dr. No* in 1962. This time, James Bond returned under the banner of Marvel Comics and was illustrated by legendary writer/artist Howard Chaykin (*American FLAGG!*), who had previously penciled the bestselling *Star Wars* comic for the House of Ideas through its first ten issues, written by Marvel's Roy Thomas.

HOWARD CHAYKIN
(writer/artist, *American FLAGG!*)

I hated doing *For Your Eyes Only*, [co-illustrator Vince] Colletta fucked up what little good I did, and I was ass-kicked out of Marvel for years. I read the novels when I was an adolescent and dug them, but the movies never particularly interested me.

OCTOPUSSY (1983)
NEVER SAY NEVER AGAIN (1983)

It may have been the year of *Return of the Jedi, WarGames, Risky Business, Scarface, Flashdance, The Right Stuff, The Big Chill,* and *Superman III*, but 1983 also goes down in cinematic history as the Battle of the Bonds, with Roger Moore returning as 007 for the sixth time in *Octopussy* and, four months later, Sean Connery for his seventh in Kevin McClory's rival production, *Never Say Never Again*.

While *Octopussy* may not have been an "All Time High" for the 007 films and continues to get a bad rap from some fans who loathe the fact that Roger Moore dresses up as a clown in the movie, we adore this film. With a fabulous pre-title sequence in which Bond uses a miniature Acrostar Mini Jet to complete his mission in a faux-Cuban Latin American country ("So you're a Toro, too?"), the Cold War–era plot is credible and compelling. A crazed Russian general, Orlov–played with scenery-chewing abandon by an unhinged Steven Berkoff–wants to detonate a nuclear bomb on a NATO airbase to turn Europeans against the United States and pave the way for a lightning-strike Soviet invasion of Europe.

All of this takes place against the backdrop of a traveling circus, which is a front for a smuggling operation run by Octopussy (a very sexy Maud Adams, making her second and far more memorable appearance in a *Bond* film), who in turn is being manipulated by exiled Afghan prince Kamal Khan (Louis Jourdan), who is using her operation to carry out Orlov's plans. Mixed in as a kind of MacGuffin is a valuable Fabergé egg that *everyone* wants. Elements of the plot came from the Ian Fleming short stories "Octopussy" and "The Property of a Lady."

RAY MORTON

Following the success of *For Your Eyes Only,* Richard Maibaum and Michael Wilson, along with George MacDonald Fraser, again combined two Fleming short stories into a single narrative, but this time their efforts were much less successful. The overall narrative has two separate plot strands, the first involving General Orlov and his plan to detonate a nuclear bomb on a U.S. airbase, and the second involving Octopussy, Kamal Khan, and the smuggling of Fabergé eggs.

Returning as director was *For Your Eyes Only*'s John Glen, who right from the start had to deal with the fact that there was, once again, no guarantee that Roger Moore would be returning as Bond.

JOHN GLEN
(director, *Octopussy*)

Every film we did, there was always a big discussion of, would Roger be doing the next one? Of course, that was hard bargaining between Cubby and Roger's agent, but fortunately good sense prevailed and we kept staying with Roger. At the same time, he was getting a bit old, and we knew we'd have to replace him soon. We looked. We couldn't find anyone, quite honestly, who was in his class at that time. But I was very happy that he stayed on. Roger and I got on ever so well together. We had great fun, and we improvised some wonderful humor in the film. *Octopussy* is one of my favorites.

But to provide a sense of the significance of action in these films—sometimes over the leading man—all one has to do is look at the nifty coda in which Bond battles Gobinda (Kabir Bedi), henchman to one of the film's villains, Kamal Khan, on the wing of a Gulfstream jet. What Glen found strangely amusing is that he could actually shoot key sequences without a lead actor having been signed. That was certainly the case in the sequence where Bond, on horseback, is pursuing Kamal's plane, which is taxiing for takeoff. Bond leaps from the horse to the plane and hangs on for dear life as it soars into the stratosphere.

JOHN GLEN

We shot that before we commenced main shooting. We hadn't cast James Bond yet, but the favorite was a fellow with black hair, so the double had black hair. During the first week of shooting, rumors began that Roger would be returning once again, so the double was told to lighten his hair a bit. During the second week we found out that Roger *would* be coming back as Bond, so we told the double to lighten it all the way. That's what happens. You have to keep shooting even though you don't know who the actors are. All we knew was that he was six feet tall.

Naturally, Moore did ultimately return into what was a strange hybrid of the more earthbound *For Your Eyes Only* and fantasy entries like *The Spy Who Loved Me:* more realistic action, but with a definite leaning toward humor.

RICHARD MAIBAUM
(cowriter, *Octopussy*)

I thought Roger [Moore] stood off a little bit and spoofed a little bit too much. Just slightly, because he felt there was this great style he couldn't take seriously. I thought he was quite good, except for the fact that he felt he was so above it all.

JOHN GLEN

All my Bonds were slightly more realistic than other *Bond* movies. There are moments when we go into fantasy; I'm thinking of a film like *Octopussy,* where we have a car chase and the car gets all its tires shot out. And then next thing you know, it's on the railroad track, driving down into the Hong Kong Express. You are getting close to fantasy there, but it works because you actually see it happen, and it's an opportunity for some fun.

RAY MORTON
(senior writer, *Script* magazine)

The connection between the two plotlines in this film is not always clear, and the business with the eggs is often very confusing. The overall story is quite convoluted, and the structure of the piece is a mess. Exacerbating the problem, the two plotlines are written in two different styles: the Orlov plotline is written as a *Bond* thriller, and the Octopussy plotline is written as a *Bond* fantasy. So, much like *The Man with the Golden Gun*, *Octopussy* often feels like two completely different movies that have been stuck together.

JOHN GLEN

I learned a lot of things on *For Your Eyes Only* in terms of pacing. I tried to be more objective and not too emotionally involved in the action. I tried to stand back a little bit and listen to criticism. I think where it showed was, in *Octopussy* I did more work on the script. On *For Your Eyes Only,* I was brought in just before shooting began, and the script was very rushed.

A new member of the *Bond* screenwriting fraternity was thriller writer George MacDonald Fraser, a World War II veteran and former journalist who was largely hired due to his expertise on India—he had written a series of popular "Flashman" novels about the British Army in the nineteenth century. Richard Lester (*A Hard Days Night, Superman II)* had optioned the novels for movies but, having failed to get them off the ground, in 1972 hired MacDonald Fraser to write the screenplay for *The Three Musketeers* and *Four Musketeers* films he directed for Alexander and Ilya Salkind. He would later work on the script for *Force 10 from Navarone* for director and *Bond* vet Guy Hamilton. Shortly after his work on *Octopussy,* he would go on to write several drafts of *Red Sonja* for director Richard Fleischer, as well as an unmade *Lone Ranger* film for director John Landis.

JOHN LANDIS
(director, *Coming to America*)

George MacDonald Fraser was a marvelous man. Full of wonderful stories and great cheer. I loved him.

RAY MORTON

He was a great writer of historical adventure tales set in the far-flung reaches of the British Empire. Fraser wrote the first draft of *Octopussy* and is responsible for the script's Indian setting and many of the other story concepts and set pieces, including the notion of putting Bond in a gorilla costume. His original narrative was reworked by Maibaum and Wilson, but much of its essence remained. So his contribution to *Octopussy* was quite significant.

As noted, Maud Adams, who had played Andrea Anders in *The Man with the Golden Gun*, was asked to come back in the title role of Octopussy—

which surprised her as much as it did anyone. Other actresses considered for the role were Sybil Danning, Faye Dunaway, and *Star Trek: The Motion Picture*'s Persis Khambatta. Ironically, Barbara Carrera was also considered, but instead landed the plum role of Fatima Blush in the competing 007 project, *Never Say Never Again*.

MAUD ADAMS
(actress, "Octopussy")

I never thought I'd be doing a *James Bond* movie again, because as you probably know, and I knew, that they have had a policy for a long time that they will not repeat. And when I was first asked whether I would be interested in playing this part, I thought obviously they'd made a mistake. I thought the casting lady didn't realize I'd done one, but they called me because they hadn't been feeling good about the way things were going. It was a really great role. It's the first time that a woman was starring in the title role. It's a good, strong role. It's not just good loving. She has a very active involvement in the entire film. She's a strong woman. She's a businesswoman. She runs an empire.

BARBARA CARRERA
(actress, "Fatima Blush")

I was easily replaceable. I was very new in this industry and, so, to lose me was not really a problem for them. The problem for Cubby was Kevin McClory.

But unlike its competitor that year, *Never Say Never Again*, *Octopussy*, the first of the *Bond* films to be released by the newly constituted studio entity, MGM/UA, has all the *Bond* tropes from the classic "James Bond Theme" to a lush John Barry score (marking his return from tax exile in Britain that precluded his involvement in *For Your Eyes Only*), Desmond Llewellyn as gadget-master Q, and another in a series of imaginative Maurice Binder opening credits (unfortunately accompanied by a lackluster Rita Coolidge song, which had originally been planned for the late Laura Branigan, who had been topping the charts at the time with her song "Gloria").

Although the introduction of Miss Moneypenny's sexy young assistant, Michaela Clavell (daughter of *Shogun* novelist James Clavell) as Penelope Smallbone, seemed to signal the end of the road for Lois Maxwell in her penultimate appearance, she was back in the next film, *A View to a Kill*, while Smallbone was never heard from again . . . or "Miss Smallbush," as Lois Maxwell accidentally called her in a flubbed take that brought the house down on set. While the humor on the set was one thing, some fans took exception to a lot of it that ultimately appeared on-screen.

RAY MORTON

The humor in the piece is frequently much too broad and silly. There are some very good things in the piece—009's escape from the circus in the first post-credit sequence is tense and exciting, as is Bond's confrontation with Orlov and his attempt to defuse the nuclear bomb before it goes off at Octopussy's circus. Overall, however, the script is flabby and confused. *Octopussy* isn't the worst *James Bond* screenplay, but it is far from the best.

RIC MEYERS

As in *For Your Eyes Only,* the skill of the editors was laser-pinpointed by moments that linger in the memory for probably subconscious reasons. The look on the enemy officer's face just before the missile Bond has boomeranged back at them explodes . . . the moment before, and the moment after, the yo-yo buzzsaw nearly cleaves Bond in Octopussy's bed . . . the cute/clever scene where the machine-gunning Bond slides down a bannister, only to have to shoot the newel post to keep from getting castrated . . . the moment the antenna on the top of the small plane whips into the henchman Gobinda's face, sending him plummeting to his death . . . but especially the moment, as Bond navigates the top of a circus train, where he has to leap to prevent getting knee-capped or decapitated. Again, these were exceptional images cemented into my eye by the editors' expertise and a stunt team led by Bob Simmons and consisting of more than fifty people, including at least eight pseudo Moores.

So it's truly a crying shame that the image that stayed in my eye, mind, and heart, was James Bond as a total clown

Yes, Roger Moore does dress up as a clown, but it's a logical disguise given the fact he's at a circus trying to elude NATO military police, who are on the prowl for him after he stole a car and forced his way onto the base following a frenzied pursuit. The entire sequence in which Bond is rushing to stop a nuclear bomb from detonating and triggering World War III is one of the most effective suspense sequences in any of the John Glen *Bond* films. *Octopussy* is also the best looking of the Glen films, beautifully lensed by Alan Hume, particularly his travelogue shots of India. There are still a few too may lapses into slapstick throughout, and the ill-advised inclusion of a Tarzan yell during a genuinely suspenseful sequence when Bond is trying to elude Kamal Kahn's men as he escapes from his Monsoon Palace is a dud.

RIC MEYERS

I mean, whose idea was it? After all, taken at face value, with the knowing omission of a single seemingly inexplicable decision, *Octopussy* is one of the better Roger Moore *Bonds*. It had exotic locations, interesting sequences concerning Fabergé eggs and baccarat, a good villain, beautiful *Bond* Girls, some nifty gimmicks, fine details, and strong action sequences. So why do I, and virtually every *Bond* fan I talk to, lower their estimation of it in their memory?

DESMOND LLEWELYN
(actor, "Q")

This was one of my favorites. Perhaps because I had a bigger part in it.

RIC MEYERS

I think it's because, above and beyond some standard operating Moore silliness—Q in a balloon, an obedient jungle tiger, a Tarzan yell, a convertible alligator, a collapsing hospital recovery bed, etc.—there's one moment, or to be more exact, one face, that slowly, inexorably, spoils the memory rotten. If you'll recall, there's a scene in *The Spy Who Loved Me* when 007 defuses/primes a bomb. There's also a moment in *Octopussy* when he does much the same. In *Spy,* he never looked stronger. In *Octopussy,* he never looked sillier. In *Spy,* he never looked more like a hero. In *Octopussy,* he never looked more like a, well, clown.

It was as if the production crew had sat around the conference table and someone actually said, "What's the most effective way we can reduce Roger's 007 in the eyes of the audience?" Whatever the cause and motive, Moore in clown face is probably the most insidiously undermining and demeaning moment in the entire series so far. Kananga popping like a balloon in *Live and Let Die* and *Moonraker*'s double-taking pigeon happened to others. Moore's dressing up in big shoes and baggy pants happened to the man who defeated Stromberg and Drax.

MATT GOURLEY
(cohost, *James Bonding* podcast)

I love it, because he also has this strange sort of vulnerability at this time of heightened tension, where he's defusing a bomb. He's deconstructing *Bond* while being in a clown suit, while defusing a bomb. To me, it's interesting to see Bond almost in an undignified way not caring about being dignified to save humanity, while being dressed as a clown. It's fascinating, and I actually think it works.

JOHN GLEN

Roger Moore couldn't believe it. He said, "You're not serious, John, about me dressed up as a clown, are you?" I said, "It's a wonderful opportunity. What a perfect disguise. Also, it gives you such great opportunity, because you can come face to face with your identical clown. You stole his stuff, since all clowns have their own nose and makeup. You come face to face." He went along with it. The other thing was, he was in the carriage dressed in a gorilla outfit, and when Louis Jourdan says, "The bomb will go off in two and a half hours," Roger, dressed as a gorilla, looks at his watch. That got a huge laugh. Of course, Roger did that spontaneously. We hadn't even discussed it. He did it on the take. It was quite amazing. He had a great sense of humor.

RICHARD MAIBAUM

John Glen was just superb. You'll find stuff in *Octopussy* in which it's hard to find anything better in any of the *Bond*s in sheer terms of action and excitement. John is also the kind of fellow who can get a performance of sorts out of actors and he can also do this action stuff. There's always several things in there that are absolutely stunning and different.

JOHN GLEN

The crocodile or the alligator, whatever it is, on the lake. You see it swimming up toward the islands, and the front opens up like an airplane almost and there's Roger at the controls. It got a huge laugh in the cinema, and it got an even bigger laugh when it closed, so we got two huge laughs out of that, and the laughs really count for a lot. If you get a huge laugh, it's a sign of success, really. The audience is with you. I cut it a bit fine sometimes, like Roger's car swerving onto the railway tracks and losing his tires and running on the railway tracks, and then meeting a train coming the other way. That was a nod to the Keystone Kops, really. I stopped short of him going in a tunnel and coming out a smoking wreck afterward like they used to do, but I used to watch all that stuff when I was a kid, and it stays with you. You don't really steal the idea, but you kind of improvise and you adapt it. I just thought that was fun with the car. When the train actually meets the car on the track, Roger leaps off at the nick of time and the Mercedes gets hit by the train and it goes into the river.

The whole thing about Octopussy's circus was that it moves by train through East Germany, and we used the New Delhi Railway, an antique railway, but at the time we made the film, they were still using steam trains in East Germany, and they were even using them in Spain as well. Cubby loved train sequences. He always remembered *From Russia with Love*, the famous scene with Sean Connery and Robert Shaw. We always tried to do things like that.

RICHARD MAIBAUM

In all of his action sequences there are these clever things like the touch of sliding down the banister in *Octopussy* when he shoots off the pineapple sticking up there. But these happen altogether again and again in John Glen's sequences. Writers aren't always so happy with their directors, but I was just delighted at John and his work and have been from the start.

JOHN GLEN

My background as an editor is a really important part of my success, especially in the planning of action sequences. It's almost a reverse process where you take the ideas and storyboard them. To storyboard, you have to have a pretty fair idea of the duration of each shot. We sometimes use four different units simultaneously when we're making these films, so you have to storyboard very accurately. I personally find that very easy to do. I don't think I would find it easy if I didn't have a background in editing.

RICHARD MAIBAUM

There's some wonderful things in *Octopussy*. Again, *Octopussy*, like *Goldfinger*, it was one of those places where all the pins went down with a crash.

JOHN GLEN

Octopussy had so many opportunities for humor. There were scary moments, but Vijay Amritraj was quite good. He was a friend of Cubby's and they used to play tennis together at his house in Beverly Hills and he said, "I'd love to be in one of your films." Cubby came to me and he said, "What about Vijay? Can we use him?" So we wrote him into that scene as their man in New Dehli. He was good. He hated snakes; he was scared to death of snakes. I got him down to the studio at Pinewood, and we got Jimmy, our snake wrangler, to come down with a load of snakes and we draped them all around Vijay and it was such a funny day. He overcame his fear of snakes. He had this python wrapped around his neck. He couldn't stand snakes, and he was a snake charmer.

JOHN CORK

When *Octopussy* and *Never Say Never Again* were coming out head-to-head, I was all for both of them. I wanted two great *Bond* films. All I got was about half a great *Bond* film from *Octopussy*. At a certain point, I got a hold of the *Octopussy* script. I can't say reading about James Bond disguised as a gorilla or putting on clown makeup did much for my hopes for the film, but when I saw it, I quite enjoyed the movie once it left India.

FRED DEKKER

(cowriter, *The Predator*)

It didn't completely hold together, but I just saw it again recently, and I liked the spy plot. I start to like anything that's from Fleming, like the Fabergé egg. It sort of falls apart toward the end. I hated it when I first saw it, but I don't even mind Bond dressed as a clown, except for the logic of how long it would take him to put that makeup on.

MATT GOURLEY

I think *Octopussy* is the penultimate step in the arrival of *A View to a Kill*. So I'm fascinated in that trajectory. *Octopussy* still has a little bit of the groundedness left in it. It's got a little bit of that gravity in it that *A View to a Kill* really doesn't have. I love *A View to a Kill* because it's so ridiculous and campy. But I love both elements of *Octopussy*. I do think it blends it pretty well.

FRED DEKKER

Steven Berkoff is great. A really good presence. When the bomb is defused, I kind of wanted the movie to end. The siege on Octopussy's palace with Q and the balloon is not even *Diamonds Are Forever* fun, it's just kind of dopey.

Throughout production of *Octopussy*, and particularly when it was nearing its June release date, always on the horizon was *Never Say Never Again* and the one thing that Eon *didn't* have: Sean Connery. The real question was how the public would react to the notion of two 007s.

MICHAEL G. WILSON

We didn't want the public to be confused, to think that this other film is our film. We planned a campaign to distinguish ourselves from the other film and to identify our product. Certainly you and other people are aware, but you're talking about millions and millions of moviegoers who are *not* aware so much of the intrigues behind the scenes. They just know James Bond.

MATT GOURLEY

I don't remember *Octopussy* in the context of it being a Battle of the Bonds. I just remember it being this Summer of Bond. I do remember that Connery was back for Bond, but I had no concept of the official production of Eon's *Bond*. Even though I knew that Roger Moore was Bond, I knew Connery was also the first Bond. It just seemed almost like a Festival of Bond, more than a Battle of the Bonds. To me, it was, like, everybody wins!

If you weren't alive in 1983, you can't begin to appreciate what it was like during the lead-up to the so-called Battle of the Bonds. Fans lapped up every nugget of new information about Sean Connery's return to the role he made famous over two decades earlier. Acolytes of Roger Moore and the Eon series wondered how their hero would fare against the returning champion, still beloved by moviegoers the world over, who, much like the actor himself, never thought the day would come when he would play the role of 007 once more. It had all the excitement and suspense of a heavy-weight boxing title fight.

JOHN GLEN

When I was about to go to India on the recce [location scout] originally for *Octopussy*, I had the script in my car, and I parked it in the garage outside of the *Never Say Never Again* office. When I came back to the car, the boot [trunk] had been forced open and my script was gone, along with my passport, and I was leaving the next day for India. It sounds as though they knew what they were looking for. They took my bag with my script in it, and that's what I think was the target. You can't prove those things, but it was certainly a coincidence.

One thing was abundantly clear: like any war, neither side wished to lose this battle. Knowing Kevin McClory's *Thunderball* remake was an existential threat to the future of their lucrative and long-running franchise, MGM/UA and Eon made sure *Octopussy* would stand out. When Roger Moore made noises about ankling the role he had made his own, they made sure to pay up to get their man. Going into battle against Connery with a new, untested actor seemed like suicide . . . and Moore and his agents clearly knew that as well. Ultimately, the budget overages and delays in getting *Never Say Never Again* to the screen led to the film debuting months after *Octopussy*. Despite Connery's welcome return, it seemed clear there was only one winner: *Octopussy* with a worldwide gross of $184 million as compared to *Never Say Never Again*'s $160 million.

DICK CLEMENT
(cowriter, *Never Say Never Again*)

I wasn't aware of it. I'm sure everybody else was but, again, I think the race was finishing a movie—*Never Say Never Again*—that is not going to be a disaster. They had big problems. In the end, it obviously was releasable, and it has some merit, actually.

RICHARD SCHENKMAN
(editor, *Bondage* magazine)

I regret how young I was when I entered Kevin McClory's orbit. I simply wasn't sophisticated enough to manage the politics, and I ended up getting blackballed by Cubby Broccoli for a number of years when he felt betrayed by my interest in McClory's films. But how could I not have been? The man had a court-ordered interest in the Bond IP he had helped create, and was talking about launching a series of films, starting with one he had cowritten with Ian Fleming. *And* he was saying he could bring Sean Connery back! Nowadays it would have been much easier to do better research on him before my first interview with him, but you have to remember that the *Bond* bookshelf was pretty bare back then, which is honestly why I started the fan club and the magazine in the first place! Anyway, he was always lovely to me, a true gentleman, and he even allowed me to visit the set of *Never Say Never Again*. Unfortunately, I couldn't get a Connery interview, but I had a great time hanging with Barbara Carrera and Klaus Maria Brandauer. I was sorry that it wasn't a better film,

JOHN CORK
(author, *James Bond: The Legacy*)

Never Say Never Again just ended up being a mess, despite the incredible talents involved. I loved Barbara Carrera, but not much else in the film worked for me.

RAY MORTON

The screenplay for *Never Say Never Again* is an extremely disappointing missed opportunity. When Kevin McClory and Jack Schwartzman announced they were making the film, they went to great lengths to put down the Eon series—to say that Broccoli's *Bonds* had become too light and comedic and fantastic—and to say that since they had secured the "real" James Bond by signing Sean Connery to star in the film, they were going to do a "real" *Bond* film—something more down-to-earth and serious; more faithful to Fleming;

more in the vein of *From Russia with Love* and *On Her Majesty's Secret Service*. Instead, all they ended up doing was making a weak copy of the later Eon films—a fantasy *Bond* filled with over-the-top characters, far-out situations, and broad comedy, and none of it done nearly as well as even the weaker Eon entries.

Never Say Never Again traces its origin back to the mid-1970s, when perpetual Eon thorn-in-the-side Kevin McClory first began developing *Warhead* with author Len Deighton and Sean Connery. That script, based on the original *James Bond of the Secret Service* idea that McClory collaborated on with Ian Fleming and Jack Whitingham in the 1950s (which served as the inspiration for the *Thunderball* novel), never materialized as a film due to protracted legal battles with Eon and a lack of financing. It wasn't until attorney and producer Jack Schwartzman stepped in and was able to untangle the byzantine chain of title issues going back to the original *Thunderball* settlement that McClory was allowed to finally bring the long aborning project to fruition.

JOHN CORK

Kevin McClory had a 10-year non-compete clause in his deal with Cubby and Harry to make *Thunderball*. He developed a script with Len Deighton and Sean Connery in the mid-1970s, just as that non-compete clause came to an end. Deighton, of course, actually wrote the screenplay. Sean and Kevin provided some ideas, but neither were writers. Kevin diligently shopped his script. Cubby felt the script was far more than a remake of *Thunderball*, and as various production entities announced that they were developing Kevin's *Bond* film, Danjaq would file a lawsuit.

Added to this was Kevin's special sauce: he was smart, charming, energetic, but he could be quick to anger, unreliable, had very little discretion, and he had a drinking problem. After nearly six years, a lawyer, Jack Schwartzman, got involved and took over the project. He realized that the way out of court and into movie theaters was to keep the film focused as a *Thunderball* remake, retelling the story with only cosmetic changes. The original script was tossed aside, and a new script was written based very much on the novel, elements from the screenplays developed by McClory in 1959 to 1960, and the completed 1965 film. That was legally solid ground for McClory, but he was again shunted to the side as Schwartzman put together the film. Without Schwartzman, *Never Say Never Again* would have never been made.

DICK CLEMENT

They must've thought, "Who's going to remake it?" Then, Kevin McClory suddenly held up his hand and said, "I own the rights to a *Bond* film."

ROBERT SELLERS

(author, *The Battle for Bond*)

It was remarkable that Eon gave 10 years for the rights for *Thunderball* to go back to McClory. They didn't think they'd be making *Bond* films in 10 years. They had no idea that *Bond* would still be going in the '70s. McClory kept his head down for 10 years, and then in 1975, *pop*! Out he comes again, trying to make another *Bond* film, which eventually became *Never Say Never Again* in 1983.

KEVIN MCCLORY

(producer, *Never Say Never Again*)

Ten years was up, so we wrote a screenplay based on the copyrights we owned. I can't go out and write any *James Bond* story; I can write a *James Bond* story using all the usual *Bond* characters. Len Deighton was an obvious choice as writer. One other *Bond* novel had been written by Kingsley Amis [*Colonel Sun*], but I don't think that quite worked. I think he's a good writer, but you know . . . Len Deighton I've always liked as a thriller writer. He's a little complicated, a lot of people find. He's a complex man, too. He was living in Ireland, so I called him and asked if I could talk with him one day about *Bond*, and I did. I said, "I'd like you to collaborate with me," same as I did with Fleming, really. He's kind of had his fingers burned in the film industry. He coproduced a film once and . . . (*he laughs*). He said okay, it intrigued him, so he came under contract to our company, to work on the screenplay.

Sean Connery wrote a lot of throwaway lines in the *Bond*s, an awful lot, and he contributes enormously to the screenplays of any film he works on, for which he's never really had credit. I felt we needed a little more humor. Sean's kind of humor. Sean is a naturally funny man. He's got an interesting sense of humor, a Scot's humor, but he uses throwaway lines in regular conversation. You start laughing, and he says, "What are you laughing at?" It is a very natural thing with him, so I said to Len, "Listen, think we'll bring Sean in as a writer, if he'd like to. He told me he wants to write, and I think his contribution will be pretty good." It was in that area of humor more than anything, at that time, that I was interested.

McClory traveled to Marbella, Spain, to talk to Connery about potentially writing, to which he agreed. The three men—McClory, Deighton, and

Connery—began doing so "all over the place," in Ireland and Marbella, among other locations.

RAY MORTON

It was McClory's idea to create an all-new story for the first *James Bond* film rather than adapt one of the novels, so without him there never would have been a *Thunderball* story and therefore no *Thunderball* novel or 1965 *Thunderball* film or 1983 remake in *Never Say Never Again*. As to the story itself, it was McClory's idea to set the story in the Bahamas and to have it climax with an underwater battle. He also devised a number of additional narrative elements and scenes. So his contribution to the *Thunderball* story in all its versions was quite significant, although he did none of the actual writing on any of them. He was an idea man rather than a writer. Fortunately, many of those ideas were good ones. McClory functioned in much the same capacity on the 1970s *Warhead/James Bond of the Secret Service* script. Working with Sean Connery and Len Deighton, he contributed many creative ideas, although Deighton did the actual writing on the project.

KEVIN MCCLORY

I would liaison between the two of them, and eventually out of that came *James Bond of the Secret Service,* as it was named. The title came out of one of the early Fleming 1959 scripts. Later, the other side objected to it because of the similarity of the name to *On Her Majesty's Secret Service*. In any event, I particularly like one-word names. I personally think it's more effective, so their objection didn't bother me much. They felt it was too similar, and the law was valid, even though this was a Fleming title. *Warhead* was my title. We found it wasn't registered, so we registered it for our company.

I must say, by the way, it was really a tremendous experience working with Sean as a writer, because he did not contribute just throwaway lines, he also got involved in the construction of the plot, and he's a very good storyteller! Therefore, he's a good story writer, and he writes visually. He made enormous contributions, and we all got on very well.

DICK CLEMENT

I think this was his way of Sean saying "Fuck you" to them [Eon]. "I can do it without you." Rightly or wrongly, that part made his career. He's an awfully good screen actor. He really is. He's got a fantastic presence.

ROBERT SELLERS

The script they came up with was *Star Wars* underwater. It had these mechanical sharks with bombs on their backs. I mean, it was more *Austin Powers* than *Austin Powers*. There was a big helicopter fight on the Statue of Liberty at the end. It would have been incredible. Stupid, but incredible. But there were certain aspects of the script that veered too far away from *Thunderball*. That's why it was never made, because it was *too* original. It wasn't what *Never Say Never Again* became, which was a retread of *Thunderball*.

RAY MORTON

Len Deighton did the initial screenplay for *From Russia with Love*, which was discarded. Richard Maibaum was then brought in to start over from scratch, so Deighton's contribution to the finished film was at best minimal. Years later he wrote the initial draft of *James Bond of the Secret Service/Warhead*. Deighton is obviously a terrific writer, but since *Warhead* was never made, Deighton's contribution to the *Bond* films would appear to be negligible.

ROBERT SELLERS

My only regret with *Warhead* is that I wish they'd made that rather than *Never Say Never Again*. It would have been the ultimate '70s *Bond* movie.

Eon may have gone after McClory legally when he made his intentions public in 1976, but the law works both ways, and McClory certainly had a legal impact on the official *Bond* films.

STEVEN JAY RUBIN
(author, *The James Bond Films*)

Only a short time before shooting on *The Spy Who Loved Me* started in Sardinia, Broccoli received word that Kevin McClory was filing an injunction against the film to hold up production immediately. In what was to become another long and complicated legal battle, McClory claimed that the final Broccoli script was unusually similar to McClory's own *Bond* project.

KEVIN MCCLORY

As far as I'm concerned, I entered into contract with them in good faith, and they have that contract, and they've read it, and signed it, and that contract, believe me, is what I've related to you. And that contract says that all rights come back to me in order for me to make a second and subsequent films. Also, in that contract is the fact that if we do make a second film, that uses substantial material from the *Thunderball* film, Broccoli and Saltzman (now Broccoli and UA—Danjaq) get 20 percent. That's written in the contract.

I can't answer why they thought they could stop me; I will say they could not. They could try. You could try anything; I can go downstairs and stick my foot out and trip someone up—it doesn't say I've got the right to do it. Let them live with their consciences if they have them. When I think that *Thunderball* is the most successful of all of the *Bonds* . . . it was most successful because it was an original. It was written from a screenplay; it wasn't written from a novel.

STEVEN JAY RUBIN

Fearing the possibility of a legal battle with McClory, who had sole film rights to the SPECTRE organization, Broccoli had already told Christopher Wood to remove all traces of SPECTRE from the final shooting script of *The Spy Who Loved Me*.

In the script for *Warhead*, written by novelist Len Deighton (*The Ipcress File*), the screenplay opens with a plane approaching the "Devil's Triangle," only for a laser beam blasted from an unseen location to knock out its power and force an emergency landing. The plane itself is dragged to the ocean floor, which is littered with wreckage of other planes and boats, and it is brought to an underwater kingdom. The city of Arkos under the rule of Blofeld. 007 arrives in Arkos intent to challenge Blofeld's henchman, Largo, in a backgammon championship, but first must defeat a robotic shark, one of the many that protect the underwater kingdom. Meanwhile, Blofeld has unleashed real sharks with nuclear weapons mounted on them to threaten the great powers into fighting pollution. Little does Blofeld know, Largo has his own plans in which he intends to send a shark to New York City to destroy the Statue of Liberty and kill New Yorkers by unleashing the killer sharks in the sewer systems.

While the script was mercifully dead on arrival, it did lead to Sean Connery agreeing to actually reprise the role of James Bond on screen, a character he had sworn to never play again after completing work on *Diamonds Are Forever*.

KEVIN MCCLORY

I don't think he intended to play it for quite a while, and then I think eventually it was his decision to come in. I think the challenge of it interested him. He's a much more mature actor than he was when he originally played Bond. To me, it's like Muhammad Ali when he's at his most fit, when someone else is champion of the world, throwing his hat into the ring; whatever happens, you know and I know that Sean is a champ. I didn't see it as a contest as such, but I think he made that decision, and I was obviously very, very pleased when he did. This was not written for Sean, so it had to have a little rewrite on it.

Originally among those considered to direct were *On Her Majesty's Secret Service* veteran Peter Hunt.

PETER HUNT
(director, *On Her Majesty's Secret Service*)
I would have offended Cubby if I had done it. That whole situation was very poor in their thinking, and I think if I had done it, they would have thought I was a traitor. We had talks about it, but I wouldn't have taken it for that reason.

BARBARA CARRERA
I had met Kevin McClory, because one of my first films was an Irwin Allen disaster film, *The Day the Earth Ended*. It had some of the greatest living actors in it, but the film was atrocious. Burgess Meredith introduced me to Kevin McClory on that film. It had so many amazing stars: Paul Newman, Jacqueline Bissett, Burgess Meredith, William Holden. We all had these little villas to stay in when we were making it, but Paul and Jacqueline were the best cooks, so we would hang out after filming with them at night. There was a contest to come up with a new name for the movie, which ended up being called *When Time Ran Out* . . . but William Holden liked to call it *The Day Our Careers Ended*. Kevin McClory, in fact, told me that I would be the perfect villainess for *Bond*. I loved Kevin, actually. He felt very attached emotionally to *Bond* since he had collaborated with Ian Fleming.

Eventually, the filmmakers hired director Irvin Kershner, who most recently had directed the blockbuster *The Empire Strikes Back*, after a series of smaller films like the *Eyes of Laura Mars*. With Kershner onboard to direct and Lorenzo Semple, Jr., writing, *Never Say Never Again* seemed to have all the right elements to become a classic, from Max von Sydow as Blofeld (sadly, in a glorified cameo, although much of his performance was left on the cutting room floor) to *Mephisto*'s mesmerizing Klaus Maria Brandauer as Largo, Kim Basinger as Domino, and Barbara Carrera as an even more unhinged version of Fiona Volpe, Fatima Blush.

BARBARA CARRERA

I was going to do *Octopussy*, but then I was invited by George Hamilton to go to this festival in Manila in the Philippines put on by Imelda Marcos. I'd escape some evenings, and when I was looking for a place to hide, there was Kersh [Levin Kershner]. He was scouting locations with his location manager. And I said, "Kersh," because I had met him before and he had wanted me for a film I did not do. I said, "Kersh, can I sit with you? I have to hide for a bit from Imelda Marcos and George Hamilton and the whole crowd there." So then he ordered me a beer and we sat and then I said, "Well, what are you doing here?" And he said, "Well, you know, we're scouting locations. We're doing another *Bond* film and Sean Connery is coming back for it."

Then he added, "As a matter of fact, there's a wonderful character, the villainess, that you would be perfect for." So he more or less told me about this character. I was fascinated, not so much about the character but the fact that I would be working with my hero. Sean Connery was my Bond who I grew up with, and I said, "Oh, that would be fantastic to work with my hero." So he told me, "I want you to meet him when you get back to L.A." I said, "Well, there's just a little problem. Cubby Broccoli is doing *Octopussy* and he wants to hire me." And he said, "Oh, did you sign a contract?" I said, "No, not yet." And he said, "Don't worry about it." So we got back and I met Sean Connery and they called my agent later and made an offer. God, I was so elated.

DICK CLEMENT

She looked great, and she looked sexy, and she looked dangerous, which was great. There was a moment in the dailies: one of the first things I noticed was that there's a scene in a garage where Bond is down, and she's got a gun, and they're facing off on each other. What I noticed in the dailies was what a bloody good screen actor Sean was, because I was looking at him in her lines, where it was his reaction to her lines, and there was always something happening in that face. He was certainly not phoning it in. I had great admiration for him.

BARBARA CARRERA

I'd never played a villain before. I wasn't quite sure how I would play a villain, you know? But when she did come to me, finally, I knew her. I knew her absolutely. And I knew that she was a sociopath as well as a psychopath. She was lethal. I couldn't believe how everybody loved this bad character who reveled in killing. But I understand that now. I do understand it, because I loved what I was doing. When I went to kill, I couldn't think, "I'm gonna go and kill this person." What I did was I saw myself as the mythical character of Kali, the Hindu goddess of destruction. What Kali does, it's not what she destroys is evil, she destroys all negativity. She replaces it with life, and so she would come and destroy things in the most harsh and horrible way. But, while she's doing that, she's giving new life. This was part of my formula. I thought every time I had to go out and kill someone, I'm going to give them a new life. Elevate them. With Sean, for instance, I was going to annihilate him. I used a praying mantis as an example. The praying mantis or the black widow spider would seduce their prey first. And when they're in that state of ecstasy, they kill them.

DICK CLEMENT

We did have a good relationship with Sean. I think he trusted us. Sometimes, it helps that there's two of you. It's like if one of you screws up, the other one can pick up the ball and throw a diversionary pass or whatever. We did speak the same language. The fact is that we weren't worried in the way that everybody else was worried. It was not our problem, therefore we were in that neutral corner. We could keep a sense of perspective about the movie and a sense of humor about it, to some extent. I remember saying to Sean, "Oh, boy! Look, you go scuba diving and have sex, and then you have sex in the evening with somebody else." I said, "That proves something," and he said, "Aye, it proves it's a movie."

BARBARA CARRERA

[Assistant director] David Tomblin said, "Fatima should have a pet." Then someone else said, "Yeah. Why not a snake? A cobra." Mind you, up until then, I couldn't even look at a picture of a snake, much less work with one. But by this time, everybody knew Fatima, and they all loved Fatima. When I got to set, I said, "Listen, I'm no longer Barbara. When I come on the set, I'm Fatima." And they loved it. It's what made it fun. That's how she was developed. From day to day, someone would come up with an idea, the scripted scene would be there already, the dialogue would be already there. She had an incredible energy that came right through the screen. I know where that energy came from. But that's another story.

The day we were going to shoot the snake scene, I arrived in the studio and there was a cage with all these cobras. They were frightening looking. There was no way that I was going to even go near one of these things. So they came up with the idea of having a baby boa constrictor. It was only eight feet long, but very docile because of the weather. You know, they usually go into hibernation. Anyhow, I fell in love with it because, when we did shoot the film, I was in the frame, I was Fatima. I was literally Fatima. So I wasn't scared of snakes when we started this scene. So everything I did with that snake was not rehearsed at all. It just came to me and I just did it, you know, because I felt comfortable with this snake. And whatever the dialogue was I was ad libbing, you know, "Darling," the kissing it, and wrapping it around. Like I said, before the movie, I couldn't even look at the snake, not even in a photograph.

And yet the movie's still a bit of a mess, with a campy script from *Batman* and *Flash Gordon* scribe Semple (and yes, we know he wrote the great *Three Days of the Condor*, too) and compromised production values due to crippling budget overages. The film was lensed by genius cinematographer Douglas Slocombe, who had shot *Raiders of the Lost Ark* for Spielberg, but you'd never know from the look of it. Filming in France, Spain, the Bahamas, and on the stages at Elstree Studios in England, *Never Say Never Again* didn't make it to movie screens until October of 1983, several months after the debut of Octopussy.

After a succession of scripts from Semple, which hewed closer to the original novel, he was let go after Connery was unhappy with his work. Kershner hired writers Dick Clement and Ian La Frenais to take over after production had already begun, as the filmmakers began to worry they had a turkey on their hands.

RAY MORTON

Lorenzo Semple, Jr., was a solid screenwriter with a great track record, having written the initial drafts of *Three Days of the Condor* and *Papillon*. He had a tendency to not take genre material seriously and so added an element of spoof to many of his genre scripts such as *Batman*, *King Kong*, and *Flash Gordon*. His original draft of *Never Say Never Again* did a good job of updating *Thunderball* for the '80s while also balancing the legal demands of hewing as close to the original narrative as possible to stave off legal action, with the creative demands of coming up with something that felt reasonably fresh and original. Semple did take a light approach to his *Bond* screenplay, which was then exaggerated by La Frenais and Clement into much broader comedy.

DICK CLEMENT

Even Francis Ford Coppola had written a version of the script because his sister, Talia Shire, was Jack Schwartzman's wife. We also heard that Sean was extremely unhappy because he had had one experience once before with the movie *Cuba,* that Dick Lester directed, where he basically kept saying, "The script's not ready. The script's not ready." They said, "It'll be fine. It'll be fine." It wasn't fine. He was so furious to the point where when Sean walked into a room, Jack Schwartzman walked out, because it was that kind of toxic atmosphere. Sean greeted us with great relief, because he thought, well, at least we're like plumbers when the basement's flooded.

BARBARA CARRERA

Kersh had told me what the script and the character of Fatima Blush would be about, so I had a vision in my mind. I decided to go to the south of France a month early where they were filming so that I could prepare and have my costumes just right, because I had a vision of her. We didn't have a script yet, and I'm on the airplane on my way to London and I see this gentleman up ahead reading a script *Never Say Never Again*. And I thought, "Oh my God, it's my script." So I went over to him and I introduced myself and he was one of the special effects guys. I said, "Is that the script?" He said, "Yes, yes." He said, "It just came out. It just got finished." I said, "Can I read it when you're finished, please?" So he gave it to me to read when he was finished. Oh my God, I was mortified by the character. Semple didn't believe women could be villains, so his justification for this villainess that I was going to play was to make her totally unappealing. A bull-dyke with a bald head wearing man's clothing. I was in tears by the time I finished reading it. I couldn't wait for that airplane to land.

They picked me up at the airport and instead of taking me to the hotel, I said, "Where's Kershy?" They said, "He's at the studio." So I said, "Please take me there." And I had taken a rose from the dinner tray on the airplane and I took it with me and I was in tears. I said, "I read the script. I'm not that character. I'm not going to play that character. I'm sorry, Kersh." And he said, "Relax, we have six writers coming in. They're gonna revamp the whole script."

DICK CLEMENT

It started for us in England in Elstree, where we were shooting a television series which became a big hit called *Auf Wiedersehen, Pet*. Kershner was shooting a movie at Elstree and we ran into him. He said, "I'm preparing this *Bond* film." Ian said immediately, "Need a rewrite?" Kershner said, "Well, actually I do." A few weeks went by. We were working on a pilot that we really loathed, and we called our agent and said, "Did they ever find a writer for that *Bond* film?" He said, "I'll make a call." He made a call and he said, "No. They're still looking. Are you interested?" We said, "Yeah." Next thing we knew was they said, "Can you fly to Nice tomorrow?" We said, "Yes." We arrived in Nice, and they'd been shooting for three weeks, and the first thing they did was wheel us in to see what had been shot so far. I think it was some stuff with motorbikes which ended up in the movie. But there were some scenes between Klaus Maria Brandauer and Kim Basinger which were really turgid and not very good dialogue. Ian and I looked at this and nodded to each other, saying, "Well, that wouldn't end up in the movie." We were making bets on this sort of thing. We'd read the script, and we sat down with Kersh when we had a chance.

The first thing we learned was that it was politically incredibly complicated, because this was the only *Bond* film that was not Saltzman and Broccoli. They were terrified of being sued. Every rewrite had to go to the lawyers. They had even had one draft written where they only used the dialogue in the book, because they'd been told that that was the only way to be absolutely certain of not being sued.

BARBARA CARRERA

Of course, we, the actors, we couldn't care less what was happening. We were just interested in our work, you know. But we couldn't help but see and hear the incredible fight that was going on over the making of this *Never Say Never Again*. The press likes to sometimes create drama around what's already drama. Of course, Sean and Roger were very good friends. If you were at the studio in London, a lot of people from both films would see each other for lunch. We couldn't give a fish's tit, as they say in Liverpool.

DICK CLEMENT

I remember standing at the Nice airport, going to London, standing next to Kersh and saying, "Do you like the credit sequence?" The credit sequence was a white knight fighting a black knight, a fake-out that it's a medieval joust. Then you find out that it's one of those dinner entertainments. My main point to Kersh was "Look, your big ace in the hole is that you've got Sean Connery, the real Bond in a lot of people's minds. He's your ace, but you've got an opening sequence where you've three or four minutes of people with tin cans on their heads clanging, beating the shit out of each other, both stuntmen. Then you take off the helmet and reveal it's Sean." I said, "That's a terrible waste of an opportunity." He said, "Yeah, yeah. You're right. Have you got a better one?"

We take the flight to London. They put me up in a hotel, the Royal Garden Hotel. I get a call saying, "Can you be on the flight to Nassau tomorrow?" This is a dream situation for writers, when you get paid decent money and nobody's asking too many questions. Then we had to find [my writing partner] Ian, who was in a club. He was staying with our friends in Barnes. He staggered home. I left a message with them. Audrey Charles, who was his hostess, had to wake him up in the morning to get her three daughters off to school and say, "Ian, wake up. You're going to the Bahamas." He grumbled and she never forgave him, because she thought, "I've got to take three kids to school, and he's grumbling about going to the Bahamas."

We found ourselves in Nassau and wrote Rowan Atkinson into the movie for some comic relief. It was a completely new part that we created for the movie. We also wrote a new credit sequence, which is the one that's in the film where it's Sean against the clock. At the time, the morale of the crew was not very good, because they'd been picking up the vibes, as crews do, of the uncertainty between the producer, the director, and the star. By the way, every change also had to be run by the company that was insuring the movie. So we wrote this sequence and at a certain point Kersh put a ticking stopwatch over it. He showed it to the crew and everyone stomped and cheered and suddenly said, "Wow! This really works." It really lifted their morale.

BARBARA CARRERA

The first shot I did on the picture was driving second unit. I had never driven a stick shift and I shouldn't have even been doing it. I wrecked eight gear boxes. We were in Villefranche, which is right in the Mediterranean. They have these kiosks on carts pulled by a horse. They had all these oranges and apples and all these delicious fruits that they were selling. I wrecked one of them. I didn't know how to stop my car. This cart of vegetables was in my way and it was horrible. Of course, they took care of the old man who owned it. Production paid him. It was not funny at the time.

They had just started principal photography, and the only reason I was there was to get my costume and everything ready. I went to go and cry on Kersh's shoulder, and Sean's too as a matter of fact. So they were both sitting there and I went there and said, "Kersh! They had me shooting second unit." First of all, I told him about the accident and that I had to have the same hair that my stunt girl had, which was unheard of. I don't copy my hairstyle from the stunt girls. And so I was just going on, and when I was finished asking for their help, Sean says to me, "God helps those who helps themselves." That woke me up. I thought, "Whoa, thanks a lot." At first, I was offended. I thought, "Gosh, that wasn't very nice. He could have at least offered some help." But then I thank him today for that. Because had he not said that, I would have never taken control of my character. I wanted everything to look lethal. Our costume designer went and found the most incredible materials. Metallic materials that, at the time, people didn't know about. He got me all this metallic stuff and that incredible pillbox hat with little daggers on it. Of course, I was the only one who knew they were there and that was all that mattered.

Due to the restrictions of the film technically being a remake of *Thunderball,* the writers continued to be limited in what they could do, and vetting by the lawyers was a never-ending process.

DICK CLEMENT

It was tricky. We wrote the health farm scene, too, at the beginning, because we gave Bond a line that we wrote for a TV series which was very popular in England called *Porridge*. There's a line in it where the leading guy has a medical. The doctor holds up a flask and says, "I want you to fill this for me." He's across the room and says, "From here?" It got a big laugh. Quite naughtily, we said, "Well, let's give it to Sean." That was funny, so that sequence was definitely ours as well. There were certain things we couldn't change. The section of the film we had least to do with is the last, the third act, because, again, in a *Bond* film, once you get to track-suited extras being mown down in the dozens, there's usually not much the writer can do with it. Anyway, they're basically saying, "Leave it alone." So we didn't have a lot to do with that. It is a mess, and there was nothing really we could do. We did have quite a lot to do with post-production though.

One victim in post-production was that their nail-biting teaser was changed to accommodate a song instead. Out with the ticking clock, in with Lani Hall's dreadful "Never Say Never Again" title track, incongruously playing against the backdrop of Sean Connery infiltrating the camp of enemy terrorists in the jungles of Latin America in what is eventually revealed as a training exercise.

DICK CLEMENT

Later, in the view of Ian and me, one of the worst post-production decisions ever made was to put the bloody song on it, which completely dissipated the tension. But believe me, when that had a ticking stopwatch over it, it was tense. Then you put the song over it and completely buggered it up, which was a production decision later. It was our sequence that had replaced the bloody black knight against the white knight with tin cans on their heads. It was Sean. There he was. There's your man. Unfortunately, the main title was a signature of the franchise. There was always a song sung by Shirley Bassey or whoever. In the end, they felt they had to have one, too, and it would've been so much better off without it.

One of the signature scenes in the film remains the tango scene in which Connery's Bond dances with Kim Basinger's Domino and reveals in the center of the crowded reception that Largo has killed her brother in plain sight of the villain and his henchwoman, Fatima Blush.

DICK CLEMENT

There was a moment where suddenly Sean asks Kim Basinger to dance. Then the first thing he says is, "Your brother's dead." We thought this lacks diplomacy, if nothing else. I have a feeling that we ended up even in the cutting room trying to help that moment by saying, "I'm going to tell you something shocking." I don't know whether it's in the movie. I don't think it is. We were trying to say, "Brace yourself, because I'm going to tell you some bad news. Your brother's dead." It's something to ease us into it. That was later. The tango scene, though, was in danger of being kind of laughable, the wrong sort of laughter. I think in the end, they got away with it.

BARBARA CARRERA

I remember in that scene thinking, "My God, Fatima is the one who should be doing the tango. Not these two." I was in the mind of Fatima. So I went over to Kersh and I said, "Kershy," which is what I used to call him when I wanted something. "Kershy, how can Fatima do a tango, huh? Fatima should do a tango." He said, "Well, yeah. Why not?" He said to Doug Slocombe, our great cinematographer, "What's Fatima's next scene?" I said, "Well, she's coming down these stairs. She's just been given the order by my boss to go kill Sean's secretary." So, she was in her element. She was just very happy. So he said to Dougie, "What can we do for Fatima? How can she do a tango?" I said, "Well, I can dance going down these stairs." He said, "Yes, yes, yes. Dougie, can we?" And he just got very excited and they figured it out and she danced her way down the stairs and it was brilliant.

Among the writers' other responsibilities were doing character passes on each of the main roles, including the villainous Largo, played by Brandauer.

DICK CLEMENT

We were all the time trying to breathe some life into the dialog. Klaus Maria Brandauer is a very good actor, but he was resorting to the sort of tricks that actors do when they don't trust the text. In other words, there were these banal lines. There's a moment in the final film where Bond comes onboard his yacht and he says, "Welcome, Mr. Bond. Cigarette? A drink?" What he did with those two words was way too much. When I first saw his performance in dailies, I thought he was terrible. I respected him enormously, because I'd seen him in *Mephisto* and I thought, "This is a seriously good actor," but actors will fall back on every trick in the world if they don't trust the text. It was okay in the end, but you've still got that video game sequence, which is bizarre, really.

Poor Kim Basinger was not very well served by the script, whereas Barbara Carrera, her part had a lot of pizzazz. She did a lot with it. Poor Kim Basinger had a thankless role, pretty much, actually. I felt sorry for her, because I felt she was really exposed. There wasn't a lot that we could do to help her part, really. She was beautiful. That was the most she really had going for her. Apparently, she's someone who still will not talk about that film. She looked unhappy. Even on the plane going out to the Bahamas, she looked unhappy to me.

BARBARA CARRERA

She just had a difficult time, unfortunately. She and Kersh didn't get along. I stayed out of it. I never got involved with the drama. I found all of these things out after I finished shooting, and all the intrigues that were going on.

DICK CLEMENT

I feel a bit sorry for [producer] Jack Schwartzman in a way. There was a night that [my writing partner] Ian was having dinner with Sean, and Talia [Shire] came over and said, "Why did you decide to sabotage my husband's movie?" She was really being very ballsy about defending him. Sean is somebody who is nothing if not a pro. He expects everybody else to be a pro, as well. I respect that very much. He felt they had not done their homework in time, which I think was obviously true. It was partly because of the fact that they had three different scripts. I never saw the other scripts, thank God, but I heard about them. In fact, they never even explained why Bond was going to the Bahamas.

Perhaps the worst element of the entire film is the dreadful Michel Legrand score, which enterprising fans later replaced in a re-cut version of the film with classic John Barry tracks and the Shirley Bassey-fronted

Propellerheads song "History Repeating" for the main title in the cleverly retitled "Never Say McClory Again" cut.

ROBERT SELLERS

A lot of people talk about the music score wounding the film, and I totally agree. It's a great example actually of how important a musical score is to a film, how it changes the perception of the person watching it. Someone put up a montage of scenes from *Never Say Never Again* on YouTube a while back with John Barry music over the top of it, and the whole thing is lifted immeasurably.

JEFF BOND
(editor, *Film Score Monthly*)

Never Say Never Again, I think, was a case where they went after a songwriter—even though Michel Legrand had written some great movie scores, I think they were thinking less about those and more about what kind of song he could produce. It's a strange film with some strong moments, but a lot more of a spoof feeling, and Legrand's music was not effective in pushing the action. For a lot of the espionage/military moments he was harkening back to the approach he took in something like *Ice Station Zebra,* but where Barry's spy music could update to the period very well, Legrand's seemed dated and clumsy at a lot of points, and it's a rare *Bond* score that really undermines the film.

Not having the usual Eon tropes forced the filmmakers to depict familiar characters in unexpected ways, including Edward Fox as a disdainful M and Alec McCowen as Algernon, the armorer, who was the film's equivalent of Q. The writers also introduced a comedic ally for Bond in Nassau played by a bumbling Rowan Atkinson in one of his earliest roles.

DICK CLEMENT

I think one line is definitely ours, where Algernon says, "I hope we can rely on some gratuitous sex and violence." That was definitely us with a gleam in our eyes. It was definitely a moment when we were acknowledging, "Hey, it's Sean, and we know what the franchise is about, gratuitous sex and violence." That was us tipping our hat to the franchise in a way.

DESMOND LLEWELYN
(actor, "Q")

I was most complimented and very flattered that Alec, who I know quite well, played Q in a totally different way. It was a very funny performance.

DICK CLEMENT

Rowan Atkinson had never been across the Atlantic. We were dangerously near going over the top with his character. It did provide something for Sean to bounce off of, apart from everything else. But it was tense. I remember, we used to go to script meetings at the end of the day, and we were kind of in a neutral corner. There's Kersh, there's Sean, there's Schwartzman. At a certain point, we used to say, "Gosh, is that the time? Why don't we go and get the table organized for dinner?" You know what I mean? We would go off, organize the table for dinner not knowing how many people or who they would be and if they would turn up. It was enormous fun for us; not for everybody, but we were in the middle of this maelstrom that needed any help we could give it. Nobody saw us as the bad guys in that.

BARBARA CARRERA

Sean and I both had never scuba dived before and so we were a bit apprehensive. We didn't know what to expect. They tried to get us to practice with the underwater cinematographer, but we never made ourselves available, because we were afraid. So when we got to the Bahamas, we had not learned how to scuba dive. And we had a lot of our scenes in the water and we had to learn how to do it. The love scene was so bland but, you know, it was what it was. That's Kersh. He likes to find humor in everything. All the humor, the subtle humor that's in *Never Say Never Again,* is Kershner's idea.

GLEN OLIVER

(pop culture commentator)

Never Say Never Again is a high-class knock-off. It's reasonably well made, but . . . at the end of the day . . . it's a dispensable rehash of *Thunderball.* Which, in itself, wasn't exactly top-shelf *Bond.* And, due to legal constraints, that's all it could ever truly be—a retread with not much deviation—which made the whole affair feel a bit limited, constrained, and pointless. It was enjoyable in a "back for one night only" nostalgic sort of way, but its overall purpose felt more like a money grab than anything else.

ROBERT SELLERS

My main criticism with *Never Say Never Again* is that apart from the presence of Connery, it just doesn't really feel like a *Bond* film. I think the reason is the choice of director. Kershner was all wrong. He said he was approaching the film as if there had never been another *Bond* movie before. That was the wrong attitude. I think they should have stuck with their first choice of

Richard Donner. For me, despite all the globe-trotting and action, *Never Say Never Again* just doesn't have the visual splendour and scope of an Eon *Bond* movie; too often it resembles a made-for-TV movie, quite shocking when one remembers how much the damn thing cost. Connery is by far the best thing in it, Carrera is brilliant, as is Brandauer, and the whole thing is enjoyable to watch, but it could and should have been much better.

BARBARA CARRERA

Sean and I took it around the world. I wanted to do everything possible that I could do, you know? So I dedicated another two years of my life after that to promoting it wherever it was opening.

FRED DEKKER

I've never given it its due, because it's not the real deal. It's like when you go to the supermarket: there's Sugar Pops and Frosted Flakes and Froot Loops and then if you look on another shelf, there's the generic brand, which may actually have the exact same product in it, but it's got a bad cartoon panda bear. It's the same cereal, but it just doesn't have the brand name on it. Even though Connery plays Bond, I never gave it its due. I was really bothered by the winking. "I hope we're going to have some gratuitous sex and violence." What? You're ammunitions, you're an armorer. Have you seen movies? Any time a *Bond* movie acknowledges the *Bond* movies it drives me crazy. I don't mind the dwarf whistling *Goldfinger* in *On Her Majesty's Secret Service,* because it's sly. I have nothing really to say about *Never Say Never Again*. Video games with Largo? The truth is, *Thunderball* is a relatively generic story. It's not uniquely *Bond* really at all, but it was all Kevin McClory.

JOHN CORK

Octopussy won the Battle of the Bonds. It was the better film on every level, and it was just a mediocre *Bond* film.

JOHN GLEN

The thing is, quite a few of my friends were working on that film, and one day their rushes came to us by mistake. They were filming at Owl Street and we were filming at Pinewood, and the rushes, their rushes, came to us. I honestly didn't look at them. I had no interest in looking at them. We even paid for the car to take them over to Owl Street for them. That was magnanimous of us, I think. The editor I knew, and we were good friends. There wasn't a problem.

RAYMOND BENSON
(author, *Zero Minus Ten*)

I mean no disrespect to Roger Moore, but I was very happy to see Sean Connery back. I just remember the excitement of having two Bonds in one year, right before the publication of *The James Bond Bedside Companion*. It was all good!

DICK CLEMENT

What came out of *Never Say Never Again* for us, leading in a different direction, was that when Jerry Bruckheimer was trying to cast *The Rock*, and Sean [Connery] was basically holding back from signing because he didn't like his dialogue, there was a conversation where they suddenly said, "Oh, let's get Dick and Ian to come in and do that," so we worked on *The Rock*. Whatever we wrote persuaded Sean to sign on, which I think was worth quite a lot of money to Jerry. That was more of a polish; they didn't want us to touch the action sequences. We were thrilled, because, to be honest, it's not a lot of fun writing an action scene. I've heard that with Jackie Chan movies, they just used to say in the script "Jackie kicks ass!" and leave it to him. They didn't even attempt to say who did what to whom with what.

JOHN GLEN

We [*Octopussy*] opened in the summer with intense competition, Spielberg and everyone, but they decided not to and they opened late in the year, but they didn't do as well as us, anywhere near. They had Sean, which was a great attraction, but I'm not sure his heart was in it. He did it for the money, I expect.

DICK CLEMENT

I'm delighted we did it, because it was fascinating at the time to be in the middle of that whole mishmash. It's like, to be a fly on the wall with all this whirling around you. I wouldn't have missed it for anything.

ROBERT SELLERS

It became an obsession for McClory and he allowed it to totally dominate his life. He was given this once-in-a-lifetime opportunity, and he fucked it up royally. That's my view, anyway. He made an absolute personal fortune from *Thunderball* and could have gone on to do pretty much anything in the film world. He could have become an independent producer making films that he was passionate about and wanted to make. He could have helped set up a film studio in his beloved Ireland. No, none of that. He wasted his fortune on lawyers' fees and this absurd quixotic quest to prove that the *James Bond* movie blueprint started with him. I think he went to his grave a bitter and defeated man. His life could have been so very different.

A VIEW TO A KILL (1985)

After years of threatening that each *Bond* movie would be his last, usually as a negotiating tactic, Roger Moore's decade-spanning embodiment of 007 was finally, really coming to an end with this 1985 film, whose title derived from the Fleming short story "From a View to a Kill." Unfortunately, the 58-year old actor's swan song in the role was, sadly, a fairly pedestrian entry in the *James Bond* film series. But after the touch-and-go negotiations of *Octopussy*, there was a period of time when even the producers thought that might have been his final film in the series.

JOHN GLEN
(director, *A View to a Kill*)

He was such a pro, and he made the best of it, but it was a hard one. I really thought we weren't going to have him on that one. It was touch and go right to the last minute, and I think it was MGM in the end who had the casting vote and said, "Sign Roger—even if it is a lot of money," because he was pushing it at that stage. I'm glad he did. He was looking a bit old in the film, but he pulled it off, and the actual storyline was good. We had this business of Silicon Valley flooding and I think Christopher Walken was fantastic in the film.

RIC MEYERS
(author, *For One Week Only: The World of Exploitation Films*)

It's no secret that Moore himself thought this was his weakest Bond, and that much is clear in that the crew didn't have to disguise him in clown face to diminish him. His creaking limbs and face-lifted skin accomplished that instead. It's a shame that this had to be his, Lois Maxwell's, stunt master Bob Simmons, and nine pseudo-Moore stunt doubles' 007 swan song.

JOHN GLEN

Roger knew it was his last one. It was inevitable. I think we'd forestalled it on the last three films, considering I'd done three films with him over six years, when my instruction was to find a new Bond on *For Your Eyes Only*. We did pretty well to get through three films with him.

FRED DEKKER

(cowriter, *The Predator*)

Roger was getting on in years and it shows.

TOM MANKIEWICZ

(writer, *Live and Let Die*)

Audiences never accepted him the way they did Sean, because Sean was the first and Sean was wonderful. But Roger had his own strengths, too. Roger was much closer to Fleming's idea. The Bond in Fleming's books is very English. Not Scottish. I've always thought that the ideal bond for Fleming would have been a young David Niven.

FRED DEKKER

Has time been kind to Roger Moore as Bond? I don't think he holds a candle to my top three, but I have great affection for him and I like him in the role. It's a pleasant time watching him play it, but my favorite Roger Moore moments are the ones where he's knocked off course. When he gets out of the centrifuge in *Moonraker* and he's like, "Oh shit, I almost died." In *The Spy Who Loved Me* when he says, "This is the job we do and I killed your boyfriend." The moments when he actually plays the role as Fleming would have written it, he's great. I wish that the movies had serviced that a little bit more.

RIC MEYERS

By almost any criteria, *Octopussy* should have been Moore's last *James Bond* movie. Just as *On Her Majesty's Secret Service* probably would've been better with Sean Connery, *A View to a Kill* probably would've been better with Timothy Dalton, or Pierce Brosnan—or pretty much anyone who was younger than Roger at the time.

JOHN CORK

(author, *James Bond: The Legacy*)

Does anyone think that *A View to a Kill* would have been better with James Brolin? Pierce Brosnan? Timothy Dalton? Roger's not the weak link in the film.

MICHAEL G. WILSON

Yes, James Brolin was considered, but the problem with any American trying to be James Bond is that he's an American. People in foreign countries, who make up a large part of the *Bond* market, just won't accept an American in the role.

ANDREW MCNESS
(author, *A Close Look at 'A View to a Kill'*)

There's the debate as to whether an actor nearing 60 years should ever have been playing Bond; but through taking on a seventh *Bond* film, Moore did bring additional shades to his characterization. Often these emerge in his responses to the sheer force of the villainy on show: we see our debonair gent regularly unnerved by Zorin's madness and sadism. It's a surprising and effective touch. Similarly, look at his responses to the "woman in need," Stacy: he's gallant, and never slips into the realm of the patronizing. He respects her decency. It would seem nigh impossible to deliver a line like "Good girl, you're nearly there" without on some level appearing condescending. Moore never slips toward it. And so, what *A View to a Kill* demonstrates so well is how its Bond responds to the quirks of the new mad men and the new women that is often so revealing of character. Delving into Bond's history is not the only way.

JOHN CORK

It is easy to give *A View to a Kill* a lot of grief. Yet the film still has a lot of great ideas in it, and some great visual moments. There were so many very talented people working on the film. This is a movie that actually staged a fight atop the Golden Gate Bridge, had someone jump off the top of the Eiffel Tower, even staged a murder of a city official in the actual San Francisco City Hall where Harvey Milk had been murdered in 1978. Yes, it's a film that doesn't quite work, but I prefer to remember it for the parts that do live up to the highest standards of the *Bond* movies.

MATT GOURLEY
(cohost, *James Bonding* podcast)

You should love any *Bond* film. They're all good tasty meals. Some are junk food, some are a little more nutritious, but we all like our nutritious food and we all like our junk food. Don't begrudge anybody their love of a shitty *Bond* film.

ANDREW MCNESS

There is typically a degree of "same ol', same ol'" accompanying the release of a *Bond* film. I think what was particular to the vitriol greeting of *A View to a Kill* was the sense that Moore had done one Bond too many. But I think that raises something particular to each and every audience member: Do you mind, or do you not, if the Bond actor is well outside the mid- to late-thirties "ideal"? I didn't object to an excursion with this older Bond, but a notable drop in box office—adjusted for inflation, a quarter less in worldwide earnings than its immediate Eon predecessor, *Octopussy*—may suggest that a substantial number did. In any case, I think it was a creatively inspired move to place this older Bond against a markedly younger super-villain who appraises our agent most dismissively. The stakes, and the subtext, are immediately interesting, particularly coming at a time when *Bond*'s cultural currency and longevity was facing considerable scrutiny.

RAY MORTON

(film historian, senior writer, *Script* magazine)

The script for *A View to a Kill* is pure fantasy *Bond*. As mentioned previously, fantasy was not Richard Maibaum's forte, nor apparently was it Michael G. Wilson's. The film was also full of humor, which was also not their forte. The result is the worst *Bond* screenplay Maibaum ever wrote and the worst *Bond* screenplay the Maibaum/Wilson team ever wrote.

RICHARD MAIBAUM

Even Shakespeare wrote *Two Gentleman of Verona*.

The film's absolutely ludicrous premise is sadly redolent of 1978's *Superman: The Movie* in which Lex Luthor wants to drop the West Coast into the sea to create some priceless beachside property. Here, Christopher Walken's Max Zorin wants to destroy Silicon Valley to corner the market on microchips in Project Main Strike, not to be remotely confused with Goldfinger's Project Grand Slam. Actually, maybe it should.

RAY MORTON

The plot is a weak combination of the plots of *Goldfinger* and *Superman: The Movie* and every element in the piece—from the characters to the dialogue to the jokes—all fall flat.

ANDREW MCNESS

In terms of basic structure, I think comparisons to *Goldfinger* are germane; in terms of tone, less so. Like *Goldfinger*, the villains of *A View to a Kill* give the film its principal flavor. But it's a markedly different flavor: more stylish, debauched, and cruel. Not that Goldfinger and Oddjob were exactly nice guys.

JOHN CORK

Zorin's plot in *A View to a Kill* has a stark similarity to Lex Luthor's plot in *Superman: The Movie*. Both films also feature the Golden Gate Bridge prominently in their climaxes. Setting off an earthquake would wreak havoc, but the complex plot revolving around microchip manufacturing, electromagnetic pulses, and oil wells is absurdly complex. Further, we don't get to see a huge, devastating earthquake. I think for movie buffs, the similarity was disappointing. I think most moviegoers were not invested in the plot enough to notice.

ANDREW MCNESS

A cursory glance at the film's synopsis might have led some filmgoers to surmise they'd seen it all before, but, in realization, *A View to a Kill* impresses in its ability to evoke the anxieties surrounding the San Andreas fault line, and in its demonstration of another uniquely scary way to activate catastrophe.

TANYA ROBERTS
(actress, "Stacey Sutton")

I asked them if I could make a few changes to the whole big speech about the plan to flood Silicon Valley and they said absolutely not, because Cubby Broccoli's son [Michael Wilson] wrote the script and there was no way that I could change a word, but it didn't make a lot of sense to me. It just kind of went over your head and you kind of accepted it. They're so caught up with the action and the beauty of the locations that you just kind of take it as it is.

Roberts, who stars in *A View to a Kill* as Stacey Sutton, a brilliant geologist who helps uncover the plot to sink Silicon Valley, first became one of *Charlie's Angels* in 1980 where she joined the once immensely popular show as Julie Rogers following the departure of Shelley Hack near the end of its run. In 1982, she starred in the cult classic *The Beastmaster*, with Marc Singer, and in 1984 toplined Sheena as the titular heroine, which, along with *A View to a Kill*, earned her a very much uncoveted Razzie Award as Worst Actress.

TANYA ROBERTS

I had done a [*Playboy*] layout with the wild animals from *The Beastmaster*. They thought it would be a great idea to have me pose with the animals, so that's what we did. Cubby evidently saw it and thought I'd be right. So he brought me in and we just said hello to him and I said hello to Barbara, his daughter, and we chatted for a few minutes and that was it. There was no screen test, no reading, no nothing.

ANDREW MCNESS

I think that along with Kim Basinger's Vicki Vale of 1989's *Batman*, Tanya Roberts' performance as Stacey Sutton fits the blockbuster mold of "spunky heroine, ultimately out of her depth." I think she's a good fit for the film: she's suitably freaked out by Zorin's madness. There are critics and fans who feel she is too timid and straightforwardly virtuous a heroine; but with Zorin and Grace Jones' May Day presenting such a vivid and offbeat portrayal of amorality, the genuine and principled Stacey almost operates as a tonal balance. The same goes for Patrick Macnee's Tibbett in the film's first half.

TANYA ROBERTS

I thought it might stop me from getting other roles, because none of the *Bond* Girls have gone on to do anything else. But it was a good part, and I said to my agent, "Will I ever get another job or will anyone take me seriously?" He said, "Meryl Streep would take it if they offered it to her." That's how prestigious a kind of a role and a franchise it was. I did it and it was fun and I had a great time.

RICHARD MAIBAUM

Tanya Roberts was awful. I was at a screening for that film and I remember when it premiered, people were literally doubled over with laughter, falling off their seats, over the way she delivered her lines. It was just embarrassing. You look at some of the great actresses we've had—Jane Seymour, Honor Blackman, Diana Rigg . . .

MATT GOURLEY

(cohost, *James Bonding* podcast)

My dad would always say, "Wait until you see Ursula Andress. Boy, everybody went crazy about her." It's just that I see her as a beautiful woman from another era. Obviously she's a beautiful woman, but it's almost like looking at Veronica Lake or Jayne Mansfield to me, where it was just the grain of the film and the cut of the fabric and everything, it feels like it's generations away. I'm not knocking these women, but I was a boy. I couldn't understand the sexiness of it. I could inherently, but Tanya Roberts did more for me than Ursula Andress because it felt contemporary.

JOHN CORK

Tanya Roberts is the least of the problems of *A View to a Kill*. Does anyone really think that Meryl Streep could have done much better with that role? There are only so many times you can have a character yell for help before they seem like more of a burden to a film than a plus. That wasn't Tanya Roberts' fault.

GLEN OLIVER

To pick on Tanya Roberts' performance would be incredibly unfair. When viewed on the whole, a number of *Bond* Girl performances were lacking, and a number of them represented far greater missteps than Roberts' efforts. *A View to a Kill*'s greatest problem was that it felt strangely disinvested—there wasn't a sense that either the actors in the picture, or the filmmakers themselves, gave a shit about their story. And that malaise jaundiced a plot which wasn't all that interesting to begin with—so audiences had nothing to latch on to. There was nothing left for viewers to do but go through the motions.

MATT GOURLEY

She has a lot of surface traits that I like. She's a geologist and that kind of thing, but ultimately her character just becomes a damsel in distress screaming, "James, James, James."

RIC MEYERS

At least Maud Adams as *Octopussy* looked age-appropriate with Moore, but the casting of Tanya Roberts only served to remind everyone just how old Roger was and, worse, looked. They might as well have brought back *For Your Eyes Only*'s Bibi Dahl—oh, I get it now . . . *Baby Doll*! It's a very bad sign when the lighting crew can't hide a star's age. It's usually the indication of a crew's dislike when that happens, but it's easier for me to believe that the traffic director John Glen was becoming just didn't care all that much.

By this time I was a TV and movie columnist for *The Armchair Detective* magazine, and had been nominated for The Mystery Writers of America's Edgar Award for two nonfiction books about TV detectives. In fact, I had an entire chapter on *Charlie's Angels* in the second one, *Murder on the Air*, so the rumors of Roberts' "difficult" reputation were known to me. But even if any of that affected the production, it was ultimately irrelevant considering the unfocused, tired action and dialogue.

Christopher Walken stars as the villainous Max Zorin in an underwritten role with a superfluous backstory that's never explored, as a kind of second-rate Khan Noonien Singh from *Star Trek*. That he's a product of Nazi eugenics experimentation isn't fully realized. He plays the role as a full-out psychopath, which is a nice change of pace from the usual understated menace. He's also a former KGB stooge who's abandoning the Motherland to pursue his own capitalist agenda, which was a chance to wedge Walter Gotell's General Gogol into the proceedings and anticipate the rise of Trump.

Aiding Walken's Max Zorin as his aide-de-camp was one of the most memorable henchpersons to be featured in the series since Jaws, the formidable Grace Jones as May Day, played with gleeful malevolence. Although the film perhaps makes no more egregious mistake than having Jones abandon her boss to switch sides a la Darth Vader when she utters these immortal words, "I thought that creep loved me," before sacrificing herself to save Silicon Valley from certain doom.

RICHARD MAIBAUM

I thought he would have been one of my favorite *Bond* villains, but he was only okay. Maybe we loaded that part with too much. Maybe it was enough that he should have been the unscrupulous kind of financial wizard. He didn't have to have been concocted by somebody like a mad doctor. That got crazy. I don't know why we thought of it, why we thought it was necessary. It happens.

ANDREW MCNESS

The plot may not do much with the physical advantages that eugenic enhancement would bring an individual—and where we do see it, we see it more with May Day—but Walken certainly embodies the psychotic side effects. Nazism aside, I actually find the plot point an amusing rationalization: oh, these corporate psychopaths couldn't possibly be authentically human!

The corporate beast, it would seem, was still a phenomenon we were getting our heads around. The eugenics plot point also ultimately generates one of the film's best moments, I think. As the dastardly Zorin is about to fall from the Golden Gate Bridge, one could reasonably surmise a righteous moment is being set up for the audience. So many action-oriented films, after all, are driven by themes of vengeance. But in a moment that amounts to genre subversion, Zorin's creator, Dr. Carl Mortner, realizes the inevitability of his "child's" demise, and in crying out "Max, Max!," gives us a rather jolting reminder that the super villainous, too, have their families—and can be rocked by the imminent death of one of their flock. *A View to a Kill*'s climactic confrontation is quite unique, if not refreshing.

FRED DEKKER

Christopher Walken is money in the bank.

TANYA ROBERTS

He was okay looking when I worked with him, but he was so beautiful when he was a young man. He looked like a girl, he was so beautiful. I remember I saw him at a show in New York and I just fell in love with him. I wanted to go backstage and meet him, but I couldn't. I wasn't an actress at that point. He was in a show called *Kid Champion* and he was just fantastic.

ANDREW MCNESS

In a flamboyant and often fun manner, Christopher Walken delivers a genuinely unsettling evocation of corporate cronyism. His Zorin is jovial, but eerily dead-eyed. Perhaps such things are a little closer to home than one might wish for from a two-hour-plus slice of *Bond*ian escapism?

GLEN OLIVER

Walken's Max Zorin character is said to be a product of Nazi medical experimentation—which is a compelling and charged concept holding a great deal of promise for a *Bond* film. But the point is not followed through on any consequential level and doesn't seem to connect to any particular extent to Zorin's plan to go all Luthor on Silicon Valley. It's kind of a hodgepodge-y, disconnected mess.

ANDREW MCDNESS

Zorin is certainly the angel-faced madman of the series—and a memorable "Man With A View For A Financial Killing"—complete with a glowering bad woman by his side. Grace Jones' performance as May Day, a female variant on Oddjob, can be summed up in one word: presence. Even when she's in the background, out of focus, she exudes presence.

TANYA ROBERTS

Grace Jones was off the wall. She was great, she was fantastic, and she was a great, really fun, nice person. I really liked her a lot. In fact, I ran into her a few months ago and she was the same old Grace. I went to one of her shows and she did a hula-hoop thing that was all the way across the stage, not dropping it once. This woman is still in shape; she looked exactly like the days we did the movie. She's amazing and she's the sweetest, funniest, most terrific woman I have ever met. She had a great part and she played it to the hilt.

JOHN CORK

Christopher Walken is five years out from winning an Oscar for *The Deer Hunter* when he does *A View to a Kill*. He's a brilliant actor. It's just not a fully-developed role. Grace Jones is a fantastic presence on-screen, but she, Walken, Roberts, and Moore all have no chemistry together. It is like they are in completely separate movies.

TANYA ROBERTS

Walken was a little crazy and fun and coming on to all the chicks. He was a real kind of a womanizer—or at least that's the way he talked. Other than that, he was a nice guy, but we didn't spend a lot of time together. We only had two scenes together. I would be working for three weeks sometimes, and he wouldn't be working for three weeks, and so you wouldn't spend that much time together. I'd spend most of the time with Roger.

JOHN GLEN

When we were in the forest doing the horse scenes, Christopher had a habit of wandering off, so when you're ready to shoot, you can't find him. He's gone wandering off somewhere. We used to have to get an assistant whose sole job was to stand by Christopher and watch him all the time, with his walkie-talkie. The moment we asked for him, we could get him, and it became a bit of a game. Christopher used to watch, and the moment the guy took his eye off of him, he was gone. He's a bit live, that Christopher. Fantastic guy. I loved him.

MATT SHERMAN

(creator, BondFanEvents.com)

Another billionaire's place in *A View to a Kill;* one of the best subtle jokes in the film series is delivered when Bond asks the henchman Scarpine about the palatial buildings on Max Zorin's estate, which was in real life France's Château de Chantilly.

"By the way, the preview is in progress at the main stables."

"Is that [gigantic edifice] it?"

"No, no, those are the *servants' quarters*. The [equally massive and ornate] *stables* are over here."

There's is an otherwise impressive pre-title sequence in which Bond eludes his Russian pursuers after retrieving a microchip in Siberia, which is unfortunately undercut by the inclusion of a cover of The Beach Boys "California Girls" when Bond ski surfs his way out of danger.

ANDREW MCNESS

The *Bond* team were seemingly acknowledging—and making fun of—007's cultural impact. Better to make fun of yourself, lest the commentators get in there first. This was not endorsed by all; particularly—the conjecture suggests—by steadfast fans of Fleming's novels and the first wave of films. Anyway, the "California Girls" inclusion adds up to an absurdist moment; but a Roger Moore film can pull it off—and proceeds to do so. I think it's a superb teaser, although I think they're all pretty superb.

JOHN CORK

With "California Girls," fun fact: a David Lee Roth cover version charted in 1985, zipping up the *Billboard* Hot 100 chart to #3 in the U.S. Of course, that's not the version of the song used in the film. They got a soundalike band to cover the 1965 Beach Boys version. It just wasn't what audiences wanted to hear.

ANDREW MCNESS

Thoughts were the opening teaser ranks amongst classic *Bond* teasers, including the ham-fisted use of "California Girls" in the middle of a nail-biting action sequence. While often criticized, the inclusion is very much of a piece with a movement in *Bond* cinema that had been gaining traction since 1971: that is, the series' play with pop-cultural references and self-reflexive jokes.

RIC MEYERS

My criticism criteria of "humor outside the film" and "007 being a reckless endangerment"—denoting a lesser installment—were well in force here, what with "California Girls" blaring during the "Bond invents snowboarding" pre-credit sequence, and Bond threatening public safety in Paris as his car is impossibly cut in two. But *A View to a Kill* adds a third warning label: it's a lesser 007 film when more than one major action scene is based on Bond running away. The action scenes, which had been just barely credible in previous Moore outings, now became an exercise in spotting Moore's actual face amid a small army of stuntmen. It actually made me grimace in sympathy while watching Moore trying to go just a few steps up the Eiffel Tower's stairs.

GLEN OLIVER

The 007 films—particularly in the '70s and early '80s—seemed determined to undercut themselves in some hugely anachronistic, shockingly clunky ways. The pigeon doing a double-take in *Moonraker.* The use of the *Lawrence of Arabia* theme in *The Spy Who Loved Me*, the *Magnificent Seven* theme in *Moon-*

raker, and "California Girls" in *A View to a Kill*. I've never understood this proclivity. It suggests the people making these films were bored with the process, and/or didn't believe in their own material, and/or were trying to appeal to some lowest common denominator audience demographic who would've been better left ignored. At the end of the day, using tracks like these felt jarringly anachronistic. The *Bond* "universe" is just that—a universe. A style. Pointedly evoking other genres and elements of popular culture unnecessarily broke the "*Bond* illusion."

LEWIS GILBERT

(director, *Moonraker*)

Very little of it is in the original script. I think sometimes we get an idea on the floor; I think the *Close Encounters* thing in *Moonraker* we definitely came up with on the floor. The *Lawrence of Arabia* music came after the film was completed, and in fact one of the boys in the cutting room put it on as a joke, and it seemed so funny and so apt that we decided to keep it. There are a lot of references to other films; I don't think that will be continued in future *Bonds*; it's just a passing phase. Just a little joke to make people laugh.

JOHN GLEN

We always used to do things like that. We used music quite a bit in our films and the audiences are so quick to pick them up straight away, aren't they? One of the villains presses the code to get into the secret chamber and it's the *Close Encounters* theme. We snatched a bit of that, and the audience got it straight away. It was unbelievable. We tried it out on a cutting copy when we have a couple of screens and it works.

But like any sub-par *Bond* film, it's not without its own distinct pleasures. First and foremost there's an inventive and memorable score by John Barry, along with Duran Duran's justly beloved and chart-topping title track seamlessly interweaved within the score as well.

JOHN CORK

The *Bond* films have never been the great generators of hit songs. Sure, they've had some, but it has never been easy or certain, even if you have the biggest names in popular music of the moment. There is an inherent conflict between the conventions of a pop song and a *Bond* title song. "Goldfinger," which is a great song, was a hit more because of *Bond*-mania in 1964 and '65 than because it reflected the sound of the era. "Live and Let Die" perfectly captures the ethos of 007's world and is a great pop rock song, but that took Paul McCartney (and his cowriter Linda) to pull off that combination. "Nobody Does It Better" is a great song, and perfect for *The Spy Who Loved Me*, but it lacks the sense of danger and menace that most artists try to work into their *Bond* songs. Duran Duran was an ideal match for "A View to a Kill." They had a massive following of teen girls who were not the general demographic of *Bond* movie-goers, and they are skilled musicians.

GLEN OLIVER

The opening titles sequences to *Bond* pictures—and the songs which accompany them—are strange and almost paradoxical beasts. On the one hand, objectively, the title sequence to any movie doesn't (and shouldn't necessarily) make any difference to the film's overall ability to convey its story. Plenty of films open with no title sequences at all, for example. A *Bond* movie could start this way, easily. On the other hand, sometimes title sequences are calling cards—they are tone-setters—and there is no greater example of this than in the 007 movies. They are almost like identifiers . . . or birthmarks . . . for the picture's overall existence. While, at the same time, being largely separate considerations from the movies themselves. It's wild.

JOHN CORK

I don't think it is important to have a hit song attached to a *Bond* film. "Thunderball" got some airplay, but wasn't a hit. That didn't hurt the film's box office. "Moonraker" didn't chart, but that didn't stop the film from becoming the top-grossing Roger Moore film. *On Her Majesty's Secret Service* had two UK hit singles from the score . . . but they didn't chart until the 1990s. "We Have All the Time in the World" became a hit in 1994 and the David Arnold/Propellerheads version of the main theme charted three years later.

GLEN OLIVER

I vividly remember seeing *A View to a Kill* on its opening night—half the audience got up and left after the opening title sequence had run. They weren't there for Bond, they were there for Duran Duran. On the other hand, it is a *Bond* tradition that each film's actual score is largely determined by—and even driven by—the melody line established by the song featured in the film's opening. As such, the *song* . . . while not necessarily reflecting the narrative of the film itself . . . still impacts the film through the subsequent use of its melody lines throughout the picture. There are a number of other *Bond* songs which are more remembered than, or are more distinctive than, the films they accompanied. But everyone knows they're a *James Bond* song. Perhaps more than anything else, the songs are a statement of the identity and presence of a *James Bond* picture. A "stamp"—or prompt—heralding the arrival of each new story.

FRED DEKKER

Another great score. I think *A View to a Kill* is the best Barry *Bond* score after *The Man with the Golden Gun.*

ANDREW MCNESS

To contemplate whether *A View to a Kill* is one of Barry's best *Bond* scores is muddied by the fact that his sixties *Bond* scores were such groundbreakers. *From Russia with Love* and *Goldfinger* were stunning for their boldness and brassiness, while *You Only Live Twice* and *On Her Majesty's Secret Service* had an unforgettable sweeping romanticism. By *Bond*ian standards, Barry's eighties scores were low key. Does that make them lesser scores? They certainly stir the soul, and Barry's score for *A View to a Kill* is, I think, a fantastic melding of the foreboding with the majestic. To me, filmmaking doesn't get much better than the moment where Bond is given an impromptu tour of San Francisco, via the mooring rope of Zorin's blimp, and Barry accompanies these fanciful dramatics with a doomy rendition of the film's tinkling, melancholic romantic theme.

MATT GOURLEY

I love the score. I just love what John Barry did with it. I love Christopher Walken as a villain. I love May Day. Grace Jones is amazing. I know Roger Moore is like 57 when he made this thing, but I still love Roger Moore. And I love the setting in San Francisco. It feels decidedly un-*Bond* in a way that almost feels *Bond*. It almost feels like a stand-in for London in a way, because you're dealing with this great monument of the Golden Gate Bridge, the City Hall, which is a great civic, old, marble building. I admit 90 percent of it is nostalgia, but I love the level of campiness and the places it goes.

Unfortunately, there's also the indignity of a police chief in San Francisco confronting Bond, who confides that he's "James Bond of the British Secret Service," only to have the policeman retort, "And I'm Dick Tracy," before Bond hops onto a fire truck and a chase commences through the streets of San Francisco like something out of a Keystone Kops film.

FRED DEKKER

What? Not only do you know who he is, you know he's a character in movies that are from the comic book genre.

TANYA ROBERTS

That was great fun. That's when Barbara Broccoli said, "Tanya, you should be doing comedy." I don't know why she said it, but that was great and eventually I did with *That 70's Show,* which was the most fun I had in my career.

JOHN GLEN

It was a very unusual chase, wasn't it? A car chase with a fire engine. It was something we always liked to do, something original. I don't think even the Keystone Kops would do that with the ladder swinging all over the place in the streets of San Francisco.

TANYA ROBERTS

John Glen couldn't give a goddamn about the actors. Roger had been in the part for so long and he was very witty and funny and that's the way they wrote the role for him, and it allowed him to ad lib when he wanted. So for him there was no problem, but for the women, he just didn't give us a thing. Not a thing. It was just weird. So many strange things happen in show business that, you know, you're so preoccupied with so much else that's going on, on the set and with wardrobe, and with hair, with makeup, with publicity, that you're really not focused in on it. But now that I look back at it, he was a terrible actor's director.

MARYAM D'ABO

(actresss, "Kara Milvoy")

John is very relaxed and he could cut reaction sequences in his head really easily. He's a lovely man, John. He's not an active director, that's not his forte. But he was great as a director on *Bond* movies. He understood how to shoot a *Bond* movie. He was really great. I enjoyed working with him. He is an action director, but he also really gives freedom to an actor, to do his thing. But you're not dealing with Sam Mendes.

RICHARD SCHENKMAN

(editor, *Bondage* magazine)

I met John Glen several times, both on location and at press events, and he was always friendly, humble, and open. What he wasn't, however, was a particularly good director. Technically, of course, he was more than proficient, and he knew how to construct a scene after years of editing and second-unit action directing. But he had no idea how to speak to actors, and he was utterly incapable of drawing a performance from an inexperienced thespian, nor did he know how to control a scenery-chewer. He brought nothing to the table but a workmanlike competency, and that's not how you make a great movie, especially when the screenwriters aren't particularly inspired, either. It's terribly unfortunate that he directed so many of the films, but he was a very, very nice man.

ANDREW MCNESS

One thing I particularly want to highlight with Glen's directorial style is his care in ensuring that a steady sense of buildup—and a sense of the ominous—precedes each burst of action. He doesn't deprive us the foreplay, if you'll pardon the analogy, something I feel can often be bypassed in the realm of action-oriented films. He's also interested in the personality of the conflict between hero and villain: if there's something offbeat in that dynamic, he doesn't shy away from it. And he knows what a special effect he has in Christopher Walken and Grace Jones, not rushing us to the action beats, but instead giving us ample time to observe them in all their stealthy, mysterious glory.

TANYA ROBERTS

The fire in the elevator was just hot. It wasn't that close to me and it was totally safe, but it was close enough to feel it. They didn't take any chances with the talent and they made sure that everybody was safe. We were at City Hall for about three nights. We had a long scene in the mayor's office, which they cut out, because I was too aggressive. I was really fighting for what I believed in, and they cut out most of it. I have no idea to this day why they did that. I think I was just too strong and aggressive to be in *Bond* at that time.

Perhaps the highlight, though, of the film is the avuncular chemistry between Roger Moore and retired *Avenger* Patrick Macnee, who banter charmingly throughout. The denouement atop the Golden Gate Bridge also has some phenomenal stunt and miniature work. Sadly, the rear projection moments, which hadn't improved much from Alfred Hitchcock's *Saboteur*, mar an otherwise impressive sequence.

FRED DEKKER

You have *some* good ideas. The set piece over the Golden Gate Bridge, Hitchcock would be smiling in his grave over because of the rear-screen projection and all that stuff. It's old school British stuff and it just doesn't quite work.

RIC MEYERS

I had come full circle with Roger Moore. At the beginning I worried how the baby-fat-coated Ken doll would survive the few stunts he actually did, and now I rolled my eyes at this old man pretending to be the James Bond of *The Spy Who Loved Me*, *For Your Eyes Only*, or even *Octopussy*. And I was especially annoyed that the *Bond* producers were unintentionally holding John Steed of *The Avengers* up to pitiful ridicule, and an ignominious, dismissive end.

> For every great pun like Christopher Walken remarking of one of the men who objected to his caper, "He had to drop out," after he plummets to his doom from the airship high above San Francisco Bay, there are moments like the unfortunate clumsy wedging-in of the title into dialogue. As Zorin and May Day stare at Silicon Valley from their dirigible, May Day remarks, "What a view," prompting Zorin to say, "To a kill." It really doesn't get much worse than that.

GLEN OLIVER

I've seen this film a number of times, and every time I see it I feel like I've been kicked in the nuts when that damn sequence rolls around. *Really?* No one, at any point, stopped to think this through? It's an astonishingly lazy and desperate moment—one of the poorest title integrations of a film's title into the dialogue of not only a *Bond* picture, but any film.

ANDREW MCNESS

With more than a half century under its belt, the *James Bond* film series has amply demonstrated that it is a self-correcting one. If the popular commentary advocates for *Bond* to return to Earth, or to cast him in a younger mold, or to bring the series back toward a more straight-faced tone, the producers will ensure it happens. All I can say is, once the dust has settled, these missteps can emerge as gems—I certainly find this the case with *A View to a Kill*, showing us how a series can be experimental, playful, and offbeat while closely adhering to the genre elements.

MARYAM D'ABO

I was living in London at that point and *Bond* was so big under Roger Moore. There was all this publicity, and *Bond* was even bigger in England. I did go up for a cameo role, for the role Fiona Fullerton got. It was a scene in a hot tub. It was uncomfortable going up for that role, but John Glen and Debbie McWilliams, who was the casting director, remembered me. I didn't think anything of it. I never expected in a lifetime to get a role in *Bond,* because I didn't fit the mold of what I imagined being a *Bond* Girl, which was 5′10″, Amazonian-looking, you know. The character that I eventually played [in *The Living Daylights*] was more realistic-looking.

D'Abo wasn't wrong. The original choice for the role of the Russian spy who came in from the cold–and into the Jacuzzi–in the film was originally offered to the voluptuous Barbara Bach to reprise her *Spy Who Loved Me* role as Anya Amasova, Agent Triple X. But now married to legendary Beatles drummer Ringo Starr and semi-retired, she passed.

THE LIVING DAYLIGHTS (1987)

What a difference three decades make. In 1987's *The Living Daylights*, the Mujahideen in Afghanistan prove to be a vital and trusted ally against the Soviets; they would eventually spawn the Taliban and al-Qaeda. This in turn dates this movie worse than bad rear projection in a Connery *Bond* film ever could. It also marks the emergence of Timothy Dalton as one of the most polarizing actors to portray James Bond, loved and loathed in equal measure.

Throughout his short tenure, Dalton emphasized his desire to get back to the essence of Ian Fleming's work and abandon the lightness that had characterized the Moore years. Unlike Connery, who professed to have only read two of the books, neither of which he particularly liked, Dalton immersed himself in the entire canon several times–and he wasn't shy about telling you. That's why *The Living Daylights* is a bit of a mixed bag, the more serious espionage plot harkening back to classic Cold War thrillers like *The Spy Who Came In from the Cold* and even Harry Saltzman's *Funeral in Berlin*. It features the defection of a KGB officer, General Georgi Koskov (played by Jeroen Krabbé), which is really a false flag operation for a more sinister capitalist conspiracy spearheaded by the most milquetoast of *Bond* villains, Whittaker (played by Joe Don Baker), an arms dealer with a literal Napoleon complex. Its crackling good and well-plotted storytelling is from writers Richard Maibaum and Michael G. Wilson, who had briefly toyed with making the film a *Bond* prequel.

RAY MORTON

(senior writer, *Script* magazine)

The Maibaum/Wilson team rebounded from the catastrophe of *A View to a Kill* with another solid gun-and-run spy tale, extrapolated from an Ian Fleming short story. The plot is overly complicated and sometimes hard to follow, and the main villain is not very interesting.

RICHARD MAIBAUM

(cowriter, *The Living Daylights*)

It always helps to have a solid story, and the Fleming short story on which it's based is such a springboard. In it, Bond is assigned to protect a defector coming across, and then sees a girl, who is a member of a girl band, going across the street with a cello case, and as he takes up his post and waits day after day for the time that the defector is going to dash across, he realizes that the assassin, who is attempting to stop him from defecting, is actually the beautiful girl with the cello that he had seen earlier. So he refuses to shoot her, and that, to me, also seemed refreshing, and very *Bond*ian. Bond won't kill a beautiful woman for no reason at all, and also because he likes beautiful girls. So that was a good springboard, and we had to say to ourselves, "How can we make a two-hour story out of this?" The idea was determining the identity of the defector, what was he supposed to do, and so forth. It was not easy to write, but it was a lot of fun to write.

CHARLES HELFENSTEIN

(author, *The Making of The Living Daylights*)

I think the guts of the short story are definitely present in the film—Bond acting as countersniper against a female cello-playing assassin. The defection is altered and complicated a great deal, but it is the same reason to start the adventure as the short story. Saunders, the "by the book" agent on location, is obviously based on Sender from the short story. You've even got some of the same vehicles; for example the Land Rovers from the pre-credit sequence are mentioned, as one is altered to backfire at a certain time in the short story to provide a distraction. So while it isn't a word-for-word adaptation, I think a significant amount of the story is used, especially compared to films where almost nothing is used, like *Octopussy* or *Quantum of Solace*.

RAY MORTON

The supporting henchman, Koskov, is terrific, and all of the other elements—characters, dialogue, etc.—are sturdy. With the exception of the defection-by-gas-tunnel, the action in the piece is realistic and believable, as is the overall tone. The script's humor is subtle and comes out of the characters and the situations.

JOHN CORK

(author, *James Bond: The Legacy*)

The Living Daylights is a film where everyone seems to be focused on making a great *Bond* film. One of the weaknesses of the later Roger Moore films is that Michael Wilson, Richard Maibaum, and John Glen were writing very much for Roger. That's different than writing for James Bond. With *The Living Daylights*, they didn't know who would play Bond, so they were mapping out a film about James Bond, not Roger Moore as James Bond or Pierce Brosnan as James Bond, or even Timothy Dalton as James Bond. This comes through. You feel the character there, not the actor.

JOHN GLEN

I think your lead actor really dictates to a large degree how you make your films, what treatment you give them. With Roger Moore, we used a light comedic touch, which was something Roger was very good at. *The Living Daylights* wasn't really written for Timothy Dalton specifically, although during and prior to shooting we did change a few scenes to accommodate him.

RICHARD MAIBAUM

As a matter of fact, we weren't sure that Roger wasn't going to continue. The real trick of it is to find the villain's caper. Once you've got that, you're off to the races and the rest is fun.

CHARLES HELFENSTEIN

Dr. No wasn't written for Connery, *On Her Majesty's Secret Service* wasn't written for Lazenby, and *Live and Let Die* wasn't written for Moore. So Dalton was following in his predecessors' footsteps in that his first *Bond* film script was not tailored to him. Had they known Dalton would get the part from the beginning, conceivably they could have trimmed the one-liners and focused more on the drama, but I don't think it would have changed much. It's still a fantastic debut.

ALBERT R. BROCCOLI

(producer, *The Living Daylights*)

I had been to Russia, and they invited us to go there, but it's a strange thing about the Russian invitation that I had. They were very nice to me, but when I said, "Fine, we're interested in coming over here and we'd like to shoot here," they said, "Of course you can shoot here," and I said, "Do we have to show you a *James Bond* script?" They said, "Oh, James Bond, oooh!" Then they said, "We have a very good idea we'd like you to do here, and it's about this very famous American who came over here and was buried here in Moscow." I'm not going to bury James Bond in Moscow. I can't do that sort of thing, but they wanted me. And then they submitted another idea to me; they called it "Cowboys and Cossacks," which is a good property actually, and I considered doing that. But I'm so involved with doing *Bond,* and they don't want us doing *Bond* over there, and so I see no purpose in going.

RICHARD MAIBAUM

In fact, early on there we were thinking the film would take place in China. One of the other shows, we had done something about a warlord in the Golden Triangle who was also mixed up in drugs and so forth. We thought it was all very colorful. Then we thought that we could incorporate that into a story that was basically in China. They also went there and looked for locations, and they spoke to the Chinese government. But they decided it was all too difficult and expensive, so we had to come up with the story that we did. As a matter of fact, we did two treatments set in China. We had a lot of good stuff in it, but you have to let it go when you decide for business reasons that a thing can't be done or shouldn't be done.

ALBERT R. BROCCOLI

I talked to the Chinese delegation. They were my guests when I was in California, but that never worked out either, because of housing facilities for our crew, and we have to go with our own crews. You can't do these things with local crews. It's a bit of a problem, as I've gathered from other people that had been there. We're traveling with about 150 to 200 people. And that's why our costs are so high, but they're people who know what they're doing . . . the *Bond* family.

CHARLES HELFENSTEIN

The early *Daylights* drafts revolved around a young James Bond, fresh out of the Royal Navy, directionless, getting into trouble, who then gets tapped to enter the secret service by M. He's brash, making mistakes, getting into trouble. And finally he gets jailed, and his grandfather says you need to get your act together, and Bond visits him at their ancestral castle, which was sort of like *Skyfall*, three decades before that film, and the grandfather explains this great naval tradition the Bonds have had. They fought at Trafalgar and Jutland, and it's up to Bond to continue that legacy. And he puts Bond in touch with someone that used to date his aunt, and it turns out to be M.

M teams Bond up with an elder 007. Burton Trevor, described as a cross between Richard Burton and Trevor Howard, is a senior agent, and Bond is a junior agent, and they team up to fight a villain who is after the Manchu Hoard in China. The old 007 dies during the mission, and Bond assumes his number at the end. Some of the drafts even make the story a direct prequel to *Dr. No.*

While the story is interesting and there are some cool action sequences described, it didn't really feel like "*Bond*" to me. Cubby Broccoli wasn't really impressed either, and he vetoed the idea of a prequel with a young Bond. Broccoli felt that moviegoers pay to see a fully formed James Bond, a professional, not an amateur learning on the job. I also think the whole "One 007 passing the torch to the other" idea would have been challenging to market. Two 007s? That's getting into *Casino Royale* 1967 territory. So while they flirted with a reboot in 1986, it would take two more decades before they would actually go forward with one.

The Living Daylights may be best known for being the one that got away for actor Pierce Brosnan, who had been cast as Bond, only to lose the role when his option on a new (and final) season of *Remington Steele* was picked up by NBC after his association with Bond became public. Hopefully, he fired his agent for that one. Ironically, the film seems tailor-made for Brosnan with its mix of gritty action combined with understated humor and suave charm. They considered a number of potential actors, ranging from Sam Neill, whom Cubby Broccoli vetoed, to Mel Gibson, Lambert Wilson (*The Matrix Reloaded*), Christopher Lambert, and perpetual Bond also-ran Michael Billington (*The Spy Who Loved Me*).

JOHN GLEN

When Timothy Dalton came along, we really had someone who had tremendous potential. Those possibilities really hadn't been open to us before to do a harder type of film. *The Living Daylights* was a transitional film. When we started writing it, we just didn't know who Bond was going to be. It had been decided Roger wasn't going to do it anymore, but at the same time we weren't sure who it was going to be. Pierce Brosnan was the most likely prospect at the time. We saw Pierce as being in the [Moore] tradition: not-too-heavy, slightly good-humored entertainment, so we didn't really change our star dramatically on that film. It was written with Brosnan in mind. Dalton wasn't cast till within six weeks of shooting. We had to do quite a bit of rewriting.

CHARLES "JERRY" JUROE
(publicist, Eon Productions)

I was with Pierce when he was told that he was no longer going to be Bond. I got the call from Cubby in Hollywood and had to pass the phone to Pierce. It wasn't easy. He was just destroyed. With reason. Wouldn't you be?

JOHN CORK

The casting of Pierce Brosnan in 1986 to play James Bond was a complete meltdown. Had it been handled properly, no one would have even known Brosnan was in the running until the option ran out on his returning as *Remington Steele*.

CHARLES "JERRY" JUROE

It was NBC. They thought Cubby would agree to him being Bond *and* being Remington Steele. Cubby said, "No way!" People who grew up and were motion picture people looked upon television as if it was what it literally was, the small screen. Nobody wants to see a guy playing a spy on TV every week, even if it's a lighthearted spy, and then turn around and be James Bond at the same time. That doesn't make any sense. There's no way that Cubby would have accepted that, and he was correct.

JOHN CORK

It was an unfortunate situation with the entire drama playing out in public. The person it hurt the worst was Dalton. No matter what, he was going to look like a second choice for the role, and that did not help him with audiences.

JOHN GLEN

We had a meeting about it and I turned around and I said, "What about Timothy Dalton? You did talk to him once about it and he wasn't interested when he was much younger." I think he felt that he was more going to pursue a serious acting role rather than James Bond. Anyway, he didn't fancy it, but I think life had played its course and he was more inclined to go for it at that stage in his career. *And* he was a good choice. I still say he's very, very similar to Daniel Craig in his portrayal, the more serious Bond.

RICHARD SCHENKMAN

Like most people, when Timothy Dalton's name was announced as the new Bond, I said, "Who?" But after just a little looking into his work and career, I thought he was an inspired choice. I only wish he'd had better material and a better director to work with, and that his tenure as Bond didn't arise during a period rife with studio politics and financial shenanigans.

LISA FUNNELL

(author, *For His Eyes Only: The Women of James Bond*)

I have so many issues with Timothy Dalton, because he's just *so* serious and not everything has to be so melodramatic. I always call him the Shakespeare Bond, because everything is so over the top. It's interesting that the more serious Bonds of the past are not the ones that are as popular. Even though there's people who will go and rumble with me over their love of Dalton, which is fine, it's interesting that the Craig films have done so well with such a serious hero, but for the nature of those films it works.

JOHN CORK

Timothy Dalton brought 007 back to Fleming. He understood the literary Bond very well, but having met Dalton on a couple of occasions, he is an immensely charming man. That charm does not follow him on-screen in his two *Bond* films. Whether through his own acting choices or via John Glen's directing, he becomes the world's angriest secret agent. At a time where Sylvester Stallone and Arnold Schwarzenegger were creating these hyper-masculine heroes, Dalton brought a needed physicality to the role. You believed his Bond didn't need a stunt double.

JOHN GLEN

He's a very rugged kind of guy; very physical in his approach to the part. At the same time, he has a tremendous depth as an actor. There's nothing he can't attempt. The more dramatic type of film suits him better, so the stories will tend to be more dramatic. He was a fantastic actor, Timothy, and didn't seem to work in America for some reason. I don't know why, but I think he was a little before his time, probably.

GLEN OLIVER

Dalton was a very solid Bond, who got off to a great start in *The Living Daylights* thanks to John Glen pulling his head out of his ass and actually appearing to at least partially give a crap about the material he was shooting—which was a very spotty proposition for Glen, given how many of these films he directed.

RICHARD MAIBAUM

We weren't concerned with bringing in a new Bond like we had been with George Lazenby with *On Her Majesty's Secret Service*. First of all, Timothy Dalton was so much better known than Lazenby, who wasn't known at all. We made no excuses about that at all. He was just there, and he was called James Bond, and that was it. I'm awfully glad that on *On Her Majesty's Secret Service* we *didn't* go with all that stuff we'd talked about, with a facial operation and surgery. Instead, we just faced the audience bravely and said, "We're not trying to kid you that it's the same guy."

FRED DEKKER
(director, *The Monster Squad*)

I wanted to love Timothy Dalton as Bond and I don't know why I don't. As weird as it sounds, it's because I don't think he's sexy. I don't buy him in that part of the role. The guy that walks into a room and all the women turn their heads and all the men go, "I wish I was him." He doesn't have that. As fine an actor as he is. Unfortunately, he's playing it straight in a John Glen *Bond* movie. If he played it straight for another director who had a little more nuance, he might be terrific. I don't like his hair. He should have worked out more. He doesn't look formidable physically. I don't know if that's a movie critic or a filmmaker critique, but with Connery, Lazenby, and Craig, I've walked out of the theater pretending I was him. I've done it with McQueen, I've done it with Eastwood, I've done it with Cary Grant. Timothy Dalton is not one of those actors.

RIC MEYERS
(author, *Films of Fury: The Kung Fu Movie Book*)

Timothy Dalton's Bond, sadly, doesn't register as a physical or fighting presence at all. His entire performance, including his fisticuffs, was permeated by what seemed to be his angry, resentful approach to the part, which read to me as stubborn petulance bordering on barely contained rage and/or disdain.

GLEN OLIVER
(pop culture critic)

Dalton proved an expectedly fine Bond. Perhaps not as eminently engaging as many of the others—more introspective, perhaps more brooding. More of an air of distrust, and less relaxed when he did trust—which somehow lent him an air of pathos or sweetness. The way he operated felt "real"—as much as any big budget thriller feels real—the hint of espionage and trickery running through the film was a welcome change from the increasingly mundane "thwart the bad guy" plots the franchise had recently been relying on.

MARYAM D'ABO

Working with Timothy was very good. He is an absolute professional. Probably because he's a man that comes from the theater, classically trained. It's ironic: I was cast when Pierce Brosnan was going to do the role, so I was cast with him and he got his contract renewed and he couldn't get out of it. So they approached Timothy. He said if they could make it a different style, and not the attitude they had. Because every actor brings their own kind of quality to Bond, and the producers work around them. So Roger Moore was more the humor, the gadgets, and all of that. Timothy wanted to go back to the books, the more classic Bond. So that's the style they brought in *The Living Daylights*.

Working with Timothy, he's a very supportive actor. Very supportive, because he's a pro. He was wonderful to work with on the set, very professional. Timothy, probably the thing he did not like was the whole press side. That was really not his thing. He did not like the whole system of the press. All of that side, it's not his thing. He likes to be quiet. But he had that a bit going against him. Definitely. And it probably made him more tense and less relaxed.

RIC MEYERS

Not surprisingly, but somewhat tragically, Dalton's "ach-torly" approach infected the fights as well. Because he was so simmering all the time, his every action was just a bit more than required, giving me the impression that he hadn't completely finished his self-defense studies, was always slightly unknowledgeable, and even a little out of control. The result was that his physical presence hardly registered on the eyes and mind—like a film run slightly out of focus and/or sync. It's a shame since Paul Weston, the fine stuntman who did many of Moore's most memorable doubling, was promoted to stunt arranger in Bob Simmon's absence. He and fellow stuntman supreme Simon Crane even played soldiers in the pre-credit sequence. So, while the horse, snow, vehicular, and, especially, B.J. Worth's aerial action was memorable, any actual fisticuffs were instantly forgettable, leaving no way to really understand what kind of fighter Dalton's Bond was—something I could not say about Connery, Moore, and certainly not Lazenby—fighting was the one good thing his Bond could do. In fact, the best fight scene in the movie—a battle between henchman Necros and MI6 bodyguards in a defector's safehouse—didn't even include Bond. *Not* a good sign.

> Where the film is even less effective is in juggling the lighter elements that remained from the pre-Dalton drafts as well as the requisite Bond beats that Dalton just can't do justice to. Despite a solid teaser, in which the double-o's are being assassinated in Gibraltar, it's clear from the moment Dalton lands on the yacht of a bored, sunbathing lovely that the actor's going to do anything he can to escape the formula elements of a *Bond* story, and this is where he fails, tossing off his "Bond, James Bond" introduction with a rushed indifference.

RIC MEYERS

Dalton's Bond is given a fine introduction in the tradition of *On Her Majesty's Secret Service*, and it's clear, especially during his time on the top of a careening jeep, that he wouldn't require anywhere close to the number of stunt doubles Roger Moore had. But then it became time for him to speak the magic words—to say the magic name. Bondjamesbond. He rushes them, mutters them dismissively like an afterthought. Bondjamesbond. *Oooooookay,* I thought. What's that all about? Even if his Bond doesn't think his name is important, or, worse, the woman he's intruded upon isn't important, then he should have just said "James." Or "James Bond." There's no reason to say "Bond . . . James Bond," unless you're making a point of it. Unless you want to make it clear and memorable to whoever you're saying it to. All righty then. Tim, I thought, is this the kind of self-indulgent "ach-tor" approaches you're going to be trading in from now on? Turns out: yup.

TIMOTHY DALTON

It wasn't a throwaway. I thought it was integral and a proper way to treat that line in the movie. It's not a line that stands outside from the movie, it's part of the scene. He's on the phone, he's got something to do. There are dead men littered about the mountainside and he's trying to get through to headquarters. The girl interrupts him, saying, "Who are you?" So, that's his name, but his main purpose is to get on with getting his message through. You don't suddenly stop acting, turn to face front and go, quote, "Bond . . ." If I'd stood outside the movie to do it, we'd have been back in another kind of film. My decision is to play it for the movie and the way that is right for the scene, so that we stay in that movie.

RIC MEYERS

I instantly had the mental image of John Glen listening in silent, maybe even rapt, respect as Dalton explored his thespian options. Glen was, to put it mildly, clearly far more comfortable with the technical aspects of the *Bond* moviemaking machine. Glen kept the train running on time. And Dalton, after all, was a Royal Shakespearean actor. And make no mistake: this, and many of Dalton's subsequent choices, were pure "ach-tor." Dalton behaved the way an unrestrained, unquestioned "artiste" thought a secret agent should behave, only with his emotions so raw and close to the surface that he seemed ready to pop at any second. He appeared so disgruntled and dissatisfied that he wasn't a pleasure to watch. He truly gave me the impression that his James Bond simply didn't want to be there. That's a pretty Catch-22, shooting-off-your-nose-to-spite-your-face position to take and choice to make.

That much was especially apparent in his interactions with, and reactions to, Maryam d'Abo's *Bond* Girl Kara Milovy. There wasn't a moment I could find after meeting the admittedly simpering, needy, seemingly lovesick character that he more than tolerated her, and, at times, actively restrained himself from rolling his eyes.

MARYAM D'ABO

He was really thinking of the character in Bond. He was very much wanting to do what the books represented. But I also think Timothy really had a hard time with the press and the exposure. I think that might not have made him relax. For the performance, he really wanted to make him classic, serious. But I think, because we started doing press, before we shot, it might have spilled in a little bit. But that's just my projection. We did a huge press conference in Vienna, literally a couple of days before we started shooting the movie. So that was a bit daunting. And then, you'd have press that would come on set. So as the last pick on board, if you're going to be the new James Bond, and it's not your personality to act like a movie star, it might have worked against him.

Dalton, who after a prestigious career in theater made his cinema debut as the the king of France in *The Lion in Winter*, had since played leading roles in the following films: *Cromwell; The Voyeur; Wuthering Heights; Mary, Queen of Scots; Permission to Kill; Sextette* (a sexploitation movie starring Mae West in her twilight years)*; Agatha; Flash Gordon; Centennial; Chanel Solitaire;* and *The Doctor and the Devils.*

RIC MEYERS

Finally, we had a "real" actor to play the part, unlike Lazenby, so the promise of going back to what I considered the golden early days was assured. Right? After all, I was a fan of Dalton's ever since seeing him in his first screen role, as the king of France in 1968's *The Lion in Winter.* I've always joked that if he played Bond the way he played Philip II—a cunning manipulator with a wolf's smile and shark's eyes—he'd still be 007.

Prior to the beginning of production on *The Living Daylights* was his role as "mystery man" Basil St. John, the title character's main love interest in the quickly forgotten *Brenda Starr.* He was on location in Puerto Rico, working with Brooke Shields, when it was announced that he would play 007 in *The Living Daylights* and only had days to prepare before beginning work on the film.

TIMOTHY DALTON

As an actor, I was busy, I was working. I was approached in the spring, and asked if I'd be interested in doing it. And I said, "Well, there's no way, because I'm busy." The schedules clashed. I'd been asked many years ago if I'd be interested in taking over the role when Sean Connery relinquished it. Very flattered to have been asked, indeed. But at that time I think I must have been only 24 or 25. And I can remember thinking, "Too Young!" But Connery was terrific. He was tremendous, and not only did I think that I was too young, I thought it was a pretty dumb move to take over from Connery. I had a very good career going in films as a young actor. But, I mean, Connery was superb! He created, originated the role. I couldn't have taken over from him at that time. So this just came up out of the blue. They came along to me and said would I like to do it, and so I said, "Yes."

JOHN GLEN

It's a very physically demanding job to play Bond and Timothy was the perfect age. He was 40 when he started. Timothy was very physical and did a lot of stuntwork himself. He's very professional. Dalton had tremendous experience as an actor and great depth.

TIMOTHY DALTON

Usually, if there's any research to be done, I do it. In this case, one's very lucky. There are the books of Ian Fleming. I think they're terrific. As far as genre books, they've been overtaken by other writers. But even as we were making the film, I occasionally dipped into some of them. One is re-astonished by just how good a writer Fleming was. How crystal-sharp, detailed, and exciting he could be.

RICHARD MAIBAUM

John Glen is very, very inventive as far as stunts go. We have a lot of car chases, and so does everybody else, but our car chases always have some novelty in them that excuses them. They're not the same type of chase that you'll find elsewhere.

Unfortunately, Dalton's disdain for the fun of a *Bond* adventure is palpable, and so when he's put behind a new tricked-out '80s Aston Martin, something feels genuinely amiss. It doesn't help that the movie was produced at the height of the AIDS scare, and Bond is virtually monogamous in the picture. Maryam d'Abo is a wonderful *Bond* Girl as Kara Milvoy, the cello-playing would-be assassin who 007 scares "the living daylights out of," and is more enamored with the whiny Koskov than Bond.

MARYAM D'ABO

She's definitely naïve in the *Bond* world, the spy world. She was more gauche, more innocent. But there was a change happening with Kara where there was more of a relationship with Bond. When I came in, there was so much work to do. Learn how to mime the cello, horseback ride; there was so much to do to prepare for the shoot.

JOHN CORK

Unlike Barbara Bach or Lois Chiles, Kara Milvoy seemed a throwback of a very vulnerable *Bond* Girl who needed Bond's protection as a shining knight. Was this something the '80s had already outgrown, as evidenced by the decision in the next film for Lowell to be a very empowered, seemingly kick-ass CIA agent? Kara is a world-class musician who has fallen in love with a very bad man. For a good hunk of the film, she believes her lover has sent Bond to bring her to him, and she is rightfully upset when she finds that Bond has lied to her so that he can get closer to Koskov and kill him. She has one of the great moments of empowerment in the film. Bond ends up in the back of a truck headed into a Soviet airbase. She demands that Kamran Shah, the head of the Mujahideen, try to rescue him. Shah looks at the risk and says there is nothing he can do. She takes a lone gun and charges off on her own. That's a great moment. Kara is my favorite *Bond* woman of the '80s.

MARYAM D'ABO

I was asked if I wanted to screen test for the lines for the *James Bond* that was auditioning. At Pinewood Studios, they were doing a proper screen test with Barbara Broccoli and John Glen directing a scene out of *From Russia with Love.* I was not actually up for the Girl's part, but I would be seen by Barbara Broccoli. And if I did well in the screen test, I might eventually along the line go up for a *Bond* role. So I did the screen test with a French actor called Lambert Wilson, who is completely bilingual, like me. And he was very good, actually. And I just played Daniela Bianchi's scene in *From Russia with Love,* and that was it. Then, I went off to start doing a movie, a Nabakov novel, *Laughter in the Dark*, with a first-time director. We were shooting in Munich, with Maximilian Schell and Sandy Dennis. And then the film collapsed. But, it was set in 1930s Berlin. I had my hair cut short, in a bob. I looked very different. And the film collapsed.

When I did the screen test for James Bond, it was, I think, in February. And when I came back to London . . . The film collapse was at the end of summer. And I looked very, very different. United Artists saw the 15 minutes of the film that was cut by the director, that I did in Germany, to see if he could get some money from studios. They were looking for a character who was a Czech/Slovakian, to play a Czech/Slovakian role. And they saw me, and at the same time, I bumped into Barbara Broccoli in London. She saw me and did a double take. She didn't recognize me, because I looked very different. I lost some weight, I had a very different look, a much more Slavic look. And they brought me in. I didn't know anything about what might have stopped the movie, or whatever. And they couldn't find their actress, so they brought me in. And that's how it all happened. Barbara had liked me in the screen test that I'd done six months earlier. Even though they thought I was too young. And that's how it all happened; in light of artistic greed, I suddenly got a call from my agent saying, "Guess what? You got the part."

It was really sort of a coincidence. I probably wouldn't have gone up for the role if I'd still had long hair and a couple of pounds more. I don't know. I suddenly looked more like a woman. I think I looked very young, and like a girl, when I did the screen test at the time for *James Bond.* The irony is, the actor who I screen tested with didn't get the role, but I did.

Ultimately, *The Living Daylights* would have benefitted from a more stylistic lensing and a jettisoning of some of the more goofy elements, such as a zaftig pipeline worker who is seduced to facilitate Koskov's escape from Czechoslovakia to the West through the Trans-Atlantic Pipeline.

In addition to another fine and, unfortunately, final *Bond* score from John Barry, the misdirect involving John Rhys-Davies' General Pushkin is handled adeptly, and he would have made a great recurring character to replace the aging Walter Gotell as General Gogol in his final appearance in the role. The confrontation between Bond and Koskov's henchman Necros (Andreas Wisniewski), who is clearly obsessed with Chrissy Hynde of The Pretenders, onboard a cargo plane over Afghanistan is a terrific and nail-biting action sequence, although the final confrontation between Bond and big bad Whittaker is a bust and a complete anticlimax.

The film, which had a pre-production period of six months, would shoot for 19 weeks in six different countries and would mark the elevation of several members of the *Bond* crew.

ALEC MILLS

(director of photography, *The Living Daylights*)

I was working in the States on a film called *King Kong Lives* for de Laurentiis when the call came. They said there was a chance I would get the *Bond* film. I thought that was the biggest joke of the year. You don't expect to get the *Bond* until you've been lighting about 10 or 15 years. Alan Hume, my predecessor, couldn't do it. He was committed to another film. So it happened and I can tell you it's one of the big highlights of my career. My predecessors were big-time cameramen like Freddie Young, Michael Reed, and Alan Hume. They've set very high standards with the *Bond* films over the years. The opening sequence was basically second-unit work shot in Gibraltar. They started two weeks before us, and we had to match all our close work with the artists to what [second-unit director] Arthur [Wooster] had shot—the boot was on the other foot there. It's no problem usually, because we sit down and discuss what we're going to do.

MARYAM D'ABO

We had a great shoot. It was wonderful. We had a great crew. It became like a big family, because we're together for five months, everywhere you go.

Production began in Vienna for ten days of exteriors, including the Hotel Im Palais Schwarzenberg, a palace begun in 1697; the Sofiensaal Theater, where Johann Strauss played; and the grounds of the Palace of Schönbrunn, a favorite of the Hapsburgs. Whittaker's Villa shot at the Forbes Museum in Tangier and Pinewood Studios. However, the most iconic location might have been the Wiener Prater–Vienna's largest amusement park, the home of a giant Ferris wheel called the Riesenrad, that Joseph Cotten confronted Orson Welles in, in *The Third Man*, the Carol Reed film, which was one of the earliest films a very young John Glen ever worked on.

ALEC MILLS

John did say in the beginning, when we were discussing the look for the film, that he wanted to keep it a little *Third Man*, which is not easy to do because it was black-and-white. When we printed down, we were trying to re-create some of those moody feelings in Vienna, like when Bond comes into the sweet shop and goes upstairs in the bedroom armed to protect the KGB agent—we wanted it not a little spooky, but moody.

PETER LAMONT

(production designer, *The Living Daylights*)

The biggest problem was an early script and a late start abroad. We had to make contingency plans. Supposing that the Moroccan government doesn't come through, what are we going to do? And if the units start to catch up, we have to make sure we are always abreast of what they are doing so we don't hold them up. It's a constant battle and we sometimes had to rearrange the schedule. We had to rearrange it within artist's contracts, what I can do and what has to be achieved. We never spend very long on any set—maybe two or three days. It's very expensive. The big problem is building, shooting, striking, and rebuilding. It's time-consuming. We did some clever revamps and I don't think anyone saw them.

Lamont's biggest challenge remained building the Hercules plane which sails into the air, ultimately leading to that climatic battle between Bond and Necros hundreds of feet above Afghanistan.

PETER LAMONT

I suppose our biggest chore was to build a complete Hercules interior with an executive cabin in it that had removable bulkheads. We built the cockpit, the whole cargo bay, and exterior around the cargo bay. The cargo door worked. We also built the exterior of the flight deck. We built the whole thing on C stage on an all-way rocker. It looked quite good, and it later cut in with the work the California aerial unit did. To the credit of the editors and the director, I defy anybody to say actually how we did it—what kind of process we used. I will say this, it was done real-for-real in the studio and the air.

ANDREAS WISNIEWSKI

(actor, "Necros")

Dangling in the net hanging out of half a Hercules plane that had been built on the sound stage in Pinewood Studios in order to match the parachuting stunt, which had already been shot, after about half an hour Tim said, "I'm knackered already." We had no idea we would be spending three more days right there! Hard work indeed.

TIMOTHY DALTON

If there was something dangerous, I wouldn't be allowed to do it. And besides, it's the sort of question one really shouldn't be involving oneself in. Because people should go to the cinema and believe the magic. You've got to believe the guy does it. One shouldn't be talking about whether it's me that jumps out of an airplane, or gets blown up in a car. If you think about it, it's obviously not. But in terms of the film, you've got to believe it's the guy.

PETER LAMONT

People must never forget—all these *Bond* pictures are a huge team effort. We are only as good as one another. It's all a big team. We rather like to leave people thinking, "How the hell did they do it?!"

MARYAM D'ABO

One of the big highs was going horseback riding with all the actors in the desert. I was the only girl. We spent a couple of hours in the desert. That was pretty wonderful. I did have a phobia, which fit the character, of explosions and loud bangs. Driving the Jeep, while there was an explosion going on in the background, I jumped and I put my fingers in my ears as I was driving, because it was so loud. When I was sliding down in the cello case, they put little things, tiny little baby explosives, underneath the snow as we slid through. That was a bit not exactly enjoyable for me. I'm the one who was steering the cello case. That was also not the most enjoyable thing, because Timothy was heavier than me, so I couldn't keep it going in a straight line as we were going downhill. I did have a stunt double for when the horse goes rearing up in the air.

Whatever its flaws, 30 years later, *The Living Daylights* is looked back upon fondly by most *Bond* fans and in many ways presaged the later, more "dangerous" Bond, epitomized by Daniel Craig.

GLEN OLIVER

This iteration of *Bond* was feeling very tired by the time *A View to a Kill* came along. It was definitely time for The Powers That Be to hit the reset button—which they did very nicely with Dalton. Ironically, though, the Dalton *Bond* pictures represented a generally correct general approach aimed toward grounding the franchise in a more real-world universe facing more accessible perils—but they were about a decade ahead of their time.

JOHN CORK

When they made the film, they could not know that the Soviet Union would collapse two and a half years after the movie opened. For certain folks, that may date the film. Not me. When I watch the films, I'm well aware that they are time capsules of the era in which they were made. I think the film very well reflects its time, just as *Live and Let Die* reflects the era of blaxsploitation films, black chic, and the rising drug culture, or how *Thunderball* reflected anxieties about nuclear proliferation and the risks of atomic blackmail.

GLEN OLIVER

The Living Daylights is a very interesting case study. While the *Bond* franchise was, and is, no stranger to tipping its hat to current events—nuclear weapons gags and solar energy, for example—*The Living Daylights* was the first and only instance in which significant plot mechanics were allowed to significantly hinge on contemporary affairs. In this case the situation in Afghanistan, the Mujahideen, and some lip service regarding what it's all about and what it's like there. Resulting in a *Bond* which very quickly dated itself, while also providing a tantalizing glimpse into what a more "relevant" *Bond* might look like and feel like.

RICHARD MAIBAUM

I had been feeling for some time that we'd been getting a little too far out, and I like to pull the balloon down every now and then and ground it so that there is a greater sense of reality involved in what's happening. It's easier, I think, for the people to identify with. You can have all the magnificent action in the world, but if you don't care about the people involved with the action, as far as I'm concerned, then something is lost. This was one opportunity where we saw that Bond was not a thoughtless killer, who they pushed a button on so that he would go out and kill somebody. This is one picture where a man wants to be convinced before the man he is assigned to kill is killed. It was kind of a departure for us, as James Bond would be trying to avoid assassinating someone before he has a damn good reason to do so.

GLEN OLIVER

When *Bond more fully* embraced our "real world" in *The Living Daylights*—when it was clear to audiences that Bond's world was no longer stylized and fanciful, but he could be out there . . . right now . . . trying to solve problems we hear about on the news every day, there's a resonance to that. Maybe even a poignancy, which realigns who and what Bond is. And that he's not just fighting to save *his* uniquely crafted world, but the same world we're all in. That changes how the audience relates to the character a bit. With this in mind, *Living Daylights* worked very well. But the franchise couldn't, and can't, have it both ways. Bond is either a part of our often distasteful, confusing, and rotten everyday reality—or he's a part of his own stylized, rule-driven universe. The two notions can't fuse, can't coexist, and can't wobble between films.

TIMOTHY DALTON

I thought it was really exciting. I was pleased watching it. It was also gratifying to see it with an audience. I saw it in New York, and was not prepared for the whoops and cheers and very vocalized delight that the audience took in it. In truth, I don't think the audience saw the best film. We have to get it down to a certain time for distribution, and I think the film was never better than when it was about seven or eight minutes longer. In fact, it seemed shorter; had more little moments and breathing spaces. But I was obviously delighted that it went down so well with audiences.

The missing scenes Dalton refers to include a long sequence dropped from the section in Tangiers involving a "flying" carpet as well as Nadim Sawalha's bumbling chief of police, a Moroccan J.W. Pepper, who ends up, of all things, falling into a giant vat of paint.

PAUL WESTON

(stunt supervisor, *The Living Daylights*)

That was tremendous. Tim did some wonderful stuff. As it was, we took him over the roof and jumped him from roof to roof, jumping on the aerial, when he swings down onto the other building. The sequence that was cut out came at the end of that. He puts a "flying carpet" on some wire and goes fifty feet over the Casbah. It was fabulous. Tim was actually up there doing it; it took a lot of courage. As he's sliding down on the carpet, they put a banner across the road for a festival, and he goes into the banner, gets knocked off the carpet, swings down on the banner, and there's a guy going along on a motorcycle with all vegetables in the basket on the front. He swings down, drops onto the passenger seat, behind the driver, opens it up and does a wheelie through the Casbah, through very narrow alleyways. Tim did all that, then took it down some steps. He jumped off the back, said "Thank you very much," and got away. But that bit was cut out, which was a shame, because it showed what Timothy could do himself.

TIMOTHY DALTON

Well, I was pleased that went. We did have a very long movie and stuff had to go, so you have to decide. It was an episode that had a lot of nice moments in it, but ultimately it was not necessary for the film. Given what was happening in the rest of the film, it was slightly out of place. I think it was a good decision to remove it.

CHARLES HELFENSTEIN

There was a scene after the magic carpet ride where he scrambles down inside a building and he's in a gorilla cage. And the gorilla takes a liking to Bond and, in that sense, I can see Roger and a gorilla getting along, but I can't see Tim and a gorilla getting along. But then the policemen chase him and one of them falls in and the gorilla rips off the toupee from the policeman. And there's also a baby gorilla and Bond has to hand the baby gorilla off to someone for changing. It does not belong in *The Living Daylights*. It's amusing, but I scratch my head as to what they were thinking. It was Maibaum's fascination and obsession with gorillas, trying to get them in there, and I'm very grateful it was never filmed.

A scene that was more to Timothy Dalton's liking was his confrontation with Pushkin, played by John Rhys-Davies in a role originally written for Walter Gottell as General Gogol. The actor was ill and the script revised to showcase Dalton's harder-edged Bond.

TIMOTHY DALTON

Originally they were just to sit across the table having a glass of champagne with each other. One made an endeavor to try and get them to change it so that it was a little tougher, a little more as one would expect. I thought John Rhys-Davies gave a fabulous performance in that scene.

MARYAM D'ABO

All of it seems so far away now. Like another life. It was a fabulous shoot. I have a romantic notion of it, because it felt very like old Hollywood movies.

A big family. It's very rare now to be on a shoot where you get that kind of a lovely family atmosphere. A lot of shoots are very impersonal. And this was on a location, and we ended up getting to know each other well. It was a very romantic shoot with a lot of location work, and the Broccolis, and Michael Wilson, are very caring. They're like the old, elegant Hollywood producers. And you don't get that on many movies. Trust me.

RIC MEYERS

Living Daylights was a decent installment, with ample promise. So now, if only Dalton could settle down, settle in, and make his Bond someone we wanted to hang with and root for rather than tolerate and roll our eyes at, his future as bondjamesbond was assured. Yeah . . . right. Little did even I know it was about to get worse. A lot worse.

GLEN OLIVER

This would've been an excellent template for "down to Earth" *Bond*s to come—*if* The Powers That Be had actually learned anything from what made this film work. Evidently they didn't, because we got *Licence to Kill* as a follow-up.

LICENCE TO KILL (1989)

Licence to Kill, originally called *Licence Revoked*, was shot largely in Mexico for budgetary reasons. This 16th *James Bond* film was one of the lowest-grossing 007 films ever in the United States, despite earning over $155 million worldwide, and is by far the cheapest-looking installment of the series since *The Man with the Golden Gun*. Some would argue that could be because it was released during a summer in which Sean Connery continued to dominate theaters, only this time as Indiana Jones' pop in *Indiana Jones and the Last Crusade*. Another popular franchisee hit the wall (or the galactic barrier) that summer as well, *with Star Trek V: The Final Frontier*, with William Shatner making his directorial debut, also getting caught in a gravity well of critical negativity.

JOHN CORK

(author, *James Bond: The Legacy*)

There were a number of factors that hurt *Licence to Kill* at the box office. First, they wrote for Dalton, and they felt Dalton should be the anti–Roger

Moore, a serious, angry 007. Dalton in person is an incredibly charming man, and I think writing the character that way hurt the film. Although Richard Maibaum is given cowriting credit, he was basically not involved past writing the treatment because of the Writers Guild strike of 1988. Personally, I think the script needed a couple more drafts, even if they were done by Michael G. Wilson, who knows how to write well. There was just too much slack in the script that went before the cameras. Budget constraints I think also limited what John Glen could do. It's a big film that ends up feeling small, and Glen had to move through scenes fast, too fast. Shots are not well composed, and I think it is the worst-lit *Bond* film in the series.

RAYMOND BENSON

(author, *The James Bond Bedside Companion*)

With *Licence to Kill,* a lot of the material came from the novel *Live and Let Die* and the short story "The Hildebrand Rarity." In 1989, when the movie came out, I felt it was exhilarating, because we were seeing Fleming material accurately portrayed—edgy and gritty. Perhaps it was too soon to do that in 1989, especially after the Roger Moore years. It didn't totally fly with audiences at the time. Many appreciated it, though, especially fans I know who are really into the books.

RAY MORTON

(senior writer, *Script* magazine)

Such missed opportunity. The notion of Bond going rogue is great (although at this point it has been used so often I'm dying to see a movie in which Bond *doesn't* go rogue), but the script developed from that premise is very disappointing. Adapting *Yojimbo* and having Bond play the villains off against one another probably seemed like a good idea on paper, but as the narrative developed, the result was that 007 ended up taking a back seat to the bad guys much of the time. The storyline is convoluted and often hard to follow. Apart from the pre-credit sequence, the action is mundane and unremarkable. There isn't much humor, there are too many supporting characters, the dialogue is generally flat, and the whole piece just isn't very much fun.

JOHN LANDIS

(director, *Coming to America*)

Years later, after I become a successful director, Cubby asked to see me. I went to his house in Beverly Hills and he introduced me to Timothy Dalton. He was about to make *Licence to Kill* and they offered me the movie to direct. We got into a disagreement about the script, because I thought the script was terrible. The bottom line was that I was afraid at that moment to do it, because the director really has no power on a *Bond* film at all. The early ones did, but the producers are very, very controlling, and I was mostly concerned about final cut. I have mixed feelings about that, because I did not like disappointing Cubby. He was a sweet and generous man. In retrospect, I see how remarkable that was. At the time, though, I was thinking, "Boy, what the fuck am I gonna do, because there's no way this can become a good movie?"

In the film, the first of the *Bond*s not to use the title of an Ian Fleming novel or short story, Bond has his license revoked and engages on a personal vendetta against drug lord Franz Sanchez (Robert Davi) for maiming Felix Leiter and murdering his wife. Potentially intriguing and well-suited to the more-dour Dalton approach to Bond, right? Yes, except the move is blandly shot, horribly cast, lethargically paced, and the Mexico-lensed production looks unforgivably cheap. And to add insult to injury, the studio-mandated coda, in which a beaming Felix Leiter, who's apparently suffering from amnesia over the fact his wife was recently brutally murdered, calls up Bond teasing him that Her Majesty's Secret Service wants him back is absurd.

Although the film has been disparaged as *Miami Vice Lite*, *Licence to Kill* was originally conceived as a far different tale, set in China, with action set pieces planned atop the Great Wall and amongst the Terracotta Army. Once plans to shoot in China were abandoned, the story was reconceived for a faux Panama-like city of Isthmus, in a fictional country that could easily be doubled in Mexico. In the midst of working on the script, Richard Maibaum was sidelined by a WGA strike, leaving producer Michael G. Wilson to finish work on the screenplay.

MICHAEL G. WILSON

(cowriter/producer, *Licence to Kill*)

We wrote two treatments in China. It involved the treasures of China and was quite a different story. There was a question of whether we were getting a good result, though, and how expensive and what problems there might be working in China.

CHARLES HELFENSTEIN

(author, *The Making of The Living Daylights*)

Maibaum would frequently dust off discarded drafts as a starting point for the next film. China was alluring, because Bond had not visited the country in any of the previous films, and there were picturesque landmarks like the Great Wall and the Terracotta Army at Shaanxi. Additionally, the Chinese government was open to the idea, especially since it would bring in a lot of money. Some treatments were written and locations scouted, but in the end it would have been too expensive. United Artists wasn't increasing the *Bond* budgets for an entire decade, as all the films between *Moonraker* and *Licence to Kill* were budgeted in the $30 to 40 million range. The production team needed to shave costs, and so Mexico was chosen instead of China.

RICHARD MAIBAUM

(cowriter, *Licence to Kill*)

We had wanted to pick up on a warlord in the Golden Triangle from a previous film who was all mixed up in drugs. As a matter of fact, we did two treatments laid in China. We had a lot of good stuff in it, and so forth.

MICHAEL G. WILSON

I feel that in the popular cinema it was an issue that hadn't been addressed. It's usually people in the United States working with drug dealers and drug users and what goes on stopping drugs. This, however, is an effort to say if you look at what's happening to the countries where drugs are grown and exported, it's not true you're not hurting anyone when you do them. *Live and Let Die* dealt with it in a vague way, but it'd really only been dealt with in journalism and documentaries.

ROBERT DAVI

(actor, "Franz Sanchez")

What they came up with instead was *Hamlet*. The story is a revenge play. It becomes Bond having to face someone close to him that's suffered. When Shakespeare wrote his plays there were tremendous swordfights and a sense of humor. If he wrote for the screen today, I'm sure he would have a character very *Bond*ian. Franz Sanchez would be his Richard III. Now, Bond, besides having the classical type of adversary that he's faced in the past, is meeting someone who's not so fantastic. He's grounded in reality.

RICHARD MAIBAUM

We had seven pictures with Roger, and they became airier and airier. What I mean is they became lighter, especially with the way Roger attacked them, and you could not become too serious about them. But I thought that was beginning to wear a little thin, and what we had done with *Licence to Kill* was to make it more serious. Of course, there are all the usual light moments and so forth, but the humor is more ironical than funny. I think it was about time we did that. It gave us an added interest and impetus to the unfolding of the film. I think that, in a way, Dalton's personality and character was a good fit for us and gave us a fresh angle to think. Or certainly a more serious one.

ROBERT DAVI

In a chapter called "The Nature of Good and Evil" in Fleming's *Casino Royale,* you see the dichotomy which Bond faces, within himself. In the same way, Sanchez and Bond are the same people. To me, the character of Sanchez is an existential nihilist, and, in a certain way, so is Bond—we're both killing people.

RICHARD MAIBAUM

What was determined, especially since we ran out of the Fleming novels, and even the short stories, we had to pick up what the area of evil was. We had to go with what was contemporary. Of course, the thing which was the Great Satan then and the great evil is the drug lord. However, in tying into this, for the first time we have Bond becoming personally involved to a much greater extent than he's ever been in a picture before, with the death of Leiter's wife and the maiming of Leiter himself. This starts him off on a purely personal seeking of vengeance, but as he gets into it, and as he realizes what Sanchez' role in the world was, he became more and more involved with stamping out as much as he could of the drug business. It was not so much just what he started out with originally, which was to avenge what Sanchez had done to Leiter and his wife. It seems to me that this had a little more of a social context to it, so that by the end of the picture, his own personal revenge is almost secondary to the feeling that he has to stamp out this terrible scourge that is in the world today.

ROBERT DAVI

Franz Sanchez would be Donald Trump if he were born in New York. Cocaine happens to be a commodity and a means to an end. It's a way for a guy from his status in life to rise above the muck.

And while Talisa Soto, as Davi's mistress, Lupe Lamora, who suddenly takes an unwarranted interest in Bond, is embarrassingly laughable, albeit quite stunning, in the role, so are the staggeringly leaden performances from Frank McRae as Sharkey, Cary-Hiroyuki Tagawa as Kwang, and Grand L. Bush as Hawkins. Even the ever-reliable Everett McGill, who was sensational in *Twin Peaks* and *Dune*, is a dud as the treacherous DEA agent, Killifer. Far more impressive is Robert Davi, who embraces his role with gusto, *Bond* Girl Carey Lowell, and David Hedison, returning from *Live and Let Die* as Felix Leiter (the best since Jack Lord), who are all terrific.

ROBERT DAVI

You think of Hollywood as a kid when you're watching the *Bond* films and you want to be in them. You dream to be inside them. Here Cubby Broccoli was telling me how fucking terrific I'd be for this movie—it's like in *King of Comedy*. It was happening without even having to kidnap anyone.

CAREY LOWELL
(actress, "Pam Bouvier")

They put me on tape and I was asked to go back and meet with Broccoli, John Glen, and Michael Wilson. I was asked back to meet with the president of MGM and I went to London the next day. The following week they made me an offer. It really happened in two weeks. I read a scene where Tanya Roberts is describing how they're going to flood the San Andreas fault. I just went on the impulse of being very strong and straightforward. I never thought of myself as a *Bond* person. My perception of what a *Bond* person is was tied to what we'd seen in the past.

ROBERT DAVI

When I met John Glen, I got the feeling they wanted me for the part. But first it was, "Let's round up all the usual suspects." I heard that this one was interested, who was a name, and that one, and it got back to me that the casting director thought I had gained weight, said I was "puffy." Now, I hated this casting director for a week until I found out it came from Cubby Broccoli. I went back to the gym and started boxing again. I dropped 12 pounds. It was a cute thing that wasn't meant in a negative way, but I blew it up in my mind.

RICHARD MAIBAUM

I liked him. He is a *Bond*ian villain. He is a fantastic actor. I know I was watching a thing on television called *Terrorist on Trial: The United States vs. Salim*

Ajami. I went into the studio the next day, and I saw a copy. I said, "I know who could play Sanchez," and Cubby said, "Davi. I was watching it, too."

ROBERT DAVI

The first meeting we had together was in Cubby's office. I thought it was just going to be with Cubby and Michael Wilson, but Timothy was there and he and I just looked at each other for what seemed like ten minutes without saying a word. It was as if Joe Lewis and Ali saw each other before a fight. He's delightful and giving as an actor. I think we became friends. After all, he likes tequila and Shakespeare—and so do I.

CAREY LOWELL

I was delighted that my role was someone who was very capable, confident, and competitive with Bond, and also on the side of the law. It was a very welcome change for me. Pussy Galore was more masculine in her way, even though she was beautiful. That was why she probably was so susceptible to Bond's charm. I can be resistant to Bond's charm and I don't have to be gay.

ROBERT DAVI

I looked at all the films again and a couple of the novels. I loved Robert Shaw [in *From Russia with Love*], Gert Fröbe [in *Goldfinger*], Joseph Wiseman [in *Dr. No*], and Klaus Maria Brandauer [in *Never Say Never Again*]. More important than seeing what was past, though, was reading everything I could on drug lords and getting in touch with a Colombian who was from Medellin and knew about the cartel.

I wanted to be palatable and understandable. Not stereotypical. I went into the documentaries about Noriega, Escobar, and Carlos Lederer, and then I got into the music of the country to give me a certain style of movement, feeling, and repose. He was a terrifically drawn character and I added little things that made me more comfortable. Michael Wilson, who was on set, and director John Glen were both very open to suggestion.

JOHN GLEN

(director, *Licence to Kill*)

The two girls we had in *Licence to Kill* were fantastic, actually. They were different. Carey Lowell was lovely and a good actress. Dick Maibaum came up with the name Lupe for Talisa Soto's character. He's quite good with names. And I believe there used to be an old Hollywood actress, Lupe Vélez. She wasn't an actress. She was a model, but she did pretty well. She was beautiful.

TALISA SOTO
(actress, "Lupe Lamora")

I was one of the first that they saw for the role and then a month later I got some feedback.

JOHN GLEN

We approached the role internationally: French girl, English, Spanish, Mexican. We found some very good actresses, but we didn't find anyone that was quite as nice as Talisa, who also had that kind of freshness we were looking for. I was very impressed with her on the interview and on the test. She had good ideas and responded to direction very well.

TALISA SOTO

We did three scenes [on the screen test]. We did the casino, and we did the one where James Bond comes into the room thinking it's Krest, but it's actually me, and the one where you see the whip marks on her back. We did quite a few.

JOHN GLEN

We did them in two days on tape. It's thc first test I've ever done on tape [as opposed to shooting them on film].

TALISA SOTO

It was such a production. I mean, the whole crew was there.

JOHN GLEN

Originally, we submitted the script to the people at MGM/UA and they came back to us and said, "The Lupe character is a little sketchy, underwritten. We don't know who she is." And so we developed the character a bit more. We made her the kind of girl that has to have a man around. She's always up to her little tricks. You know, if the boyfriend gets killed virtually in front of her, it would be one second of silence, and then, "Who's next?" She's a survivor.

TALISA SOTTO

That's right, a survivor. It hurts, you know, to see people hurt. That's why she wants to get away from it all. On purpose I did not go back to do any research on the other *Bond* Girls, because I wanted to create my character from scratch. I didn't want any influence from other characters. These characters were really different; they both had a lot to do. James Bond wouldn't be able to do what he did without the help of Pam or Lupe.

I really focused on her being a well-known blackjack dealer. And I did some research there, because in that scene where I do a fan and bring it back up? I was practicing that every single night. I can tell you that I had four days off and flew to Las Vegas, because I had never been in a casino before in my life. So, in order to look like I know what I'm doing, I went to Las Vegas and went to this one card-dealing school. It was a two-hour crash course for blackjack dealers. Then that night I went to gamble. I got beginner's luck, and then I started losing. Then I broke even and I thought, "It's time to go home." But I learned a lot looking at the dealers and seeing how they react.

FRED DEKKER
(writer, *The Predator*)

Anecdotally, I used to go to this restaurant on Melrose, and my friend and I were walking in and Talisa Soto comes out and my jaw dropped. In person, she's a looker. She walks past another guy, I don't know who he is, total stranger, he turns to me and he just goes, "I know." It was a great moment.

Sadly, the *Wiseguy*-like dynamic between Davi and Dalton isn't plumbed for nearly the dramatic depth it required so that Bond's betrayal would be that much more impactful, a la the heartbreaking reveal that Vinnie Terranova is a Federal agent after he becomes a surrogate brother to mobster Sonny Steelgrave in the first season of CBS's *Wiseguy* two years earlier. By the time Sanchez learns who Bond is, Bond's betrayal doesn't have the dramatic weight it requires since the two haven't really known each other that long.

JOHN CORK

Licence to Kill has a great premise, inspired by the Japanese classic *Yojimbo*, that is almost identical to the highly successful John le Carré novel and miniseries *The Night Manager*. Bond infiltrated the villain's organization and sows discord from within. See how *The Night Manager* handles that story, right down to the seduction of the villain's mistress, and you can see that there was a great film in there. Yet, as with *A View to a Kill*, it felt like they were shooting from a very rough first draft, not a well-honed screenplay.

RAY MORTON

Maibaum and Wilson usually did a good job on thrillers, but their collaboration on this one was interrupted by a WGA strike—after finishing the treatment,

Maibaum was forced to withdraw from the project, and Wilson, who was not a WGA member, wrote the screenplay on his own. The result was a misfire.

JOHN GLEN

Tim's got terrific depth in his performance. He feels very strongly about this friendship he has in the beginning of the film, which is disrupted by the villain Sanchez in such a horrible way. We'd researched the background of these villains, these drug barons. And they behave just like this. They devise the most horrible way to torture people and to maim them so that they're living testament to what happens if you cross them. You see a cripple in the street and say, "That's what's gonna happen to you if you open your mouth to the police."

TIMOTHY DALTON

The first one was a much more complex story. It operated on lots of different levels. *Licence to Kill* is much more direct and it is a different kind of *Bond* story. It involves Bond on a mission of personal vengeance and, therefore, he's probably less objective, less professional, less clear than he would be if he was on a job. It's personal. It's a different kind of story, but that's as it should be. I thought a good step was taken in *The Living Daylights* away from a certain kind of *Bond* movie into something that was more involving, exciting, and believable. And I think we went a step further in *Licence to Kill.*

JOHN CORK

Bond seems to fumble his way through the first half of the film, getting fellow agents needlessly killed and injured and generally making a mess of things. And he's angry about it—very, very angry—in every scene. Bond's suave, debonair, cool façade is nowhere to be seen in the film, and I think if you strip that away, for most film audiences you no longer have a *Bond* film.

RIC MEYERS

It was a disconcerting experience seeing *Licence to Kill.* Going in, I had concerns about Dalton's overearnest performance in *Living Daylights*, but, at the same time, I had great hopes for him and the series to course correct. Surely they'd see what they had, and bring *Bond* back to serious sanity, wouldn't they? No such luck. As a veteran reader of Ian Fleming, I recognized some of the plot inspirations, but was taken aback by the telltale costume choices. *Licence to Kill* had the worst taste in Bond wardrobe since *Diamonds Are Forever.* I mean, powder blue tuxedos and white pants? Not a good sign. Usually that denotes a crew's dislike of the star they're dressing. But then, as the film's lurid visuals continued, and the high-strung story kicked in, my heart sank, and sank, and sank.

As Dalton's performance continued, I could better understand why the wardrobe was weird. Virtually every word he said was either sneered, snarled, and/or spitted. He glared and glowered. In a role that was supposedly designed to reflect Bond's sublimation of his own wife's murder, it wasn't so much that Dalton played it serious. In actuality, he seemed almost mentally and physically constipated with barely contained, unreasoning pique. Most of the time, he didn't look so much angry as petulant, like a spoiled, frustrated child who only wants his own way. Worse, his bureaucrat-with-a-bug-up-his-bum Bond was so full of smug righteousness that he behaved unprofessionally, and, at times, downright stupidly—resulting in the multiple deaths of his colleagues. Virtually all, if not flatly all, of the multiple fellow agents who died in the line of duty did so as a result of 007's overripe behavior.

GLEN OLIVER

The chief issue was not that it tried to be "something other than we'd expect for a Bond film"—that's exactly what a franchise of this age and flexibility should be doing. The problem was that it did it so clumsily, and derivatively. It was not derivative by way of self-repetition (in the way *The Spy Who Loved Me* pretty much aped *You Only Live Twice*); it was derivative because it relied on a formula which had already been rolled out, tested, driven, and beaten to a pulp by a number of other titles. Revenge piece, drug lord, earthier settings, blah blah blah—it's all the stuff of countless *Miami Vice* episodes, and god knows how many lower-budget, straight-to-video shootsploitation pieces. What was unique here was not the subject matter, it was that *Bond* was so willingly diving into this already clogged and smelly cesspool—and was doing so in poor form. And this is where Glen's failings enter the picture. Little effort was made to turn this relatively tepid and hackneyed story concept into anything more. It all felt tired, it all felt desperate, and the effort to reinvent the franchise . . . at that point, at least . . . felt unclear.

Subplots involving Hong Kong intelligence–including Bond's apprehension by undercover Hong Kong narcotics agents and subsequent rescue by Sanchez, which may be one of the series' most underwhelming action sequences ever filmed–and Don Stroud's Colonel Heller both go nowhere.

CAREY LOWELL

What John [Glen] didn't give me, Timothy did. We worked it all out, and John was free about allowing us to change the dialogue if it wasn't exactly what you might say. Glen's forte is his ability to direct action. Luckily, Timothy was helpful, because he's very into character and ready to discuss it. He is always thinking about how he's going to make it better and what it all means, and that helps everyone working with him, because there's a constant delving into what you're doing and why you're doing it. He was always there when things needed to be rehearsed or changed. We would often do a scene and realize the dialogue wasn't as we would really say it, and we'd work together to change it.

GLEN OLIVER
(pop culture commentator)

John Glen was a frustratingly inconsistent director. When he was on, he was a capable—if unremarkable—filmmaker. When he wasn't on, he wasn't on, and the result was often a bit painful. Some of the best moments in the '80s *Bond* films came about from his time with the franchise, no question about that. But so did some of the franchise's most breathtakingly inane moments.

DESMOND LLEWELYN

He's a very good director. Not only a good action director—I think he's one of the best—but he's extremely good with actors. It's funny, because I don't think John particularly likes actors or the dialogue. He wants to get on with the action, but his patience is terrific. An actor is always slightly unsure with his part, and when you're saying your lines, you don't quite know if you've got them right. If John says it's right, I accept it.

ROBERT DAVI

John Glen is known for his action, but I found him very keen and protective of what we were trying to do with the character. I loved working with him. I think he's underrated when it comes to handling actors, because in a lot of films he's taking unknowns and getting performances out of them. Maryam d'Abo was pretty good in *The Living Daylights*.

GLEN OLIVER

The main issue with Glen's direction was a general sense that he wasn't particularly invested in the material. Whether or not this was actually the case, I cannot say, but his work often felt like an exercise in "point and shoot" rather than an effort to create more fully realized cinema. The results often felt as if he were merely trying to get material on film, as opposed to shaping that material into a more transcendent state. And at no point was this inconsistency and disparity more evident than in *Licence to Kill.*

CAREY LOWELL

He's not really interested at all in the character's history, and he doesn't want to discuss much of it. The acting sort of took second place to the special effects and the action and momentum of the story.

JOHN GLEN

You don't go and watch it for the acting really, do you? It's mainly actors interspersed with action, and the action is very important in *Bond*, and the humor and the writing. It's a big adventure. It's a lot of fun. It's a lot of fun to make.

GLEN OLIVER

I do think there are worse James Bond films like *Diamonds Are Forever*, but *Licence* would certainly land on the lower tier. Dalton wasn't the problem—I'd strongly argue that Dalton's Bond was a very good Bond, perhaps even destined for legendary status if he'd had better material to work with.

It may be the fifth and final film to be directed by John Glen, and his worst, but like any *Bond* movie it isn't without its own small delights, including M crying out to his snipers during Bond's escape through an empty Hemingway House in Miami not to fire at him, "because of too many people."

JOHN GLEN

It was my idea to use that place. When you scout a place like Key West, you look for what's interesting from the camera's point of view or a dramatic point of view. I was fascinated by the plants. It was phenomenal. And they've got all these six-toed cats there, and they're all rather strange and emaciated-looking things. I love animals, and I love animals in films. I think they're great. And they're spooky, too. When you see all those cats in the foreground, you wonder what's going to happen.

We had to get in there before the hurricane season: it already was on the edge of hurricane season. The strange thing with films is, we have to go to resorts when it's low season, because in high season we can't get accommodations. And if we can, it costs us a fortune. Also, it's much better if we go there when the place isn't busy, so we can create what we want to create.

As noted, the film also marks the return of *Live and Let Die's* David Hedison as Felix Leiter, who has left the CIA to join the DEA. Hedison, as always, is a welcome addition to the proceedings.

DAVID HEDISON
(actor, "Felix Leiter")

I was having dinner with [my wife] Bridget and another couple at what was then the Bistro Gardens in Beverly Hills when Cubby and Dana Broccoli stopped by our table on the way out to chat and catch up on what we were doing. The next day I got a call for a meeting to play "Leiter" in *Licence to Kill*. It's amazing that things like that do happen—being in the right place at the right time.

Anthony Zerbe also gives an enjoyable, smarmy performance as the sniveling Milton Krest, who ultimately gets his come-uppance after Dalton's Bond engineers a clever double-cross, framing Krest for robbing Sanchez after previously eluding him in one of the film's better action scenes.

JOHN CORK

I think there are a number of excellent performances in the film. Robert Davi is fantastic as Sanchez, and he has all the best lines in the film. Benicio Del Toro is great in every scene [as his henchman]. Anthony Zerbe is a fine comic actor, and I like him in the film. I think Talisa Soto does a good job with what she was given.

JOHN GLEN

There's a great deal of laughter on our sets. There's no shouting or screaming. I hate a noisy set. I don't think you can work well when you're under that kind of pressure, and you're frightened or intimidated by the people who are on the set. It helps to have a laugh now and again. It relaxes everybody. We were doing this scene where Anthony Zerbe is explaining what happened with the airplane taking off. "This guy came out of the water . . ." And Don Stroud was listening to this, and I was watching his close-up reaction, and he's so funny . . . I couldn't stop myself.

DAVID HEDISON

I enjoyed Mexico and Key West with Timothy—fabulous locations. Benicio Del Toro was at the hotel in Key West. He was relatively unknown then, and he struck me immediately as a great guy, and a really good actor, charismatic and with a good sense of humor. We had a good time together.

However, unforgivable for a *Bond* movie, the villain, Sanchez, gets all the best one-liners here, including when a henchman asks what to do with hundreds of thousands of dollars soaked in the dead Krest's blood, and Sanchez cracks, "Launder it."

JOHN GLEN

I think the humor in our film is basically black humor. When Krest gets blown up in the decompression chamber, and the guy turns around and says, "What should we do with the money, Patron?" "Launder it." I mean, to me, that is pretty good *Bond* humor. Most of the good lines do seem to go to the villain. It's a reflection of the story. It's very difficult for a man to be doing what Bond's doing and be flipping lines out.

RIC MEYERS

Director John Glen seemed to be letting his entire eclectic cast flounder in whatever thespian hell they chose—from Robert Davi's brooding Brando to Benecio Del Toro's James Dean–ery to Wayne Newton's Vegas show to poor Talisa Soto's mannequin woods. To say the cast was all over the map wouldn't be fair to compasses. They were adrift on a rocky cinema sea, with no ship's captain in sight, about to go under.

The action, not surprisingly, was equally off-balance. If Dalton's Bond couldn't control his temper and facial ticks, he certainly seemed to have little control of his fists, legs, or even balance. Several times in the heat of battle he actually seemed tipsy, as if playing the part slightly drunk, or literally deciding to use the emotions and equilibrium of a big baby as his inspiration.

The final truck chase through serpentine desert roads is a triumph of physical stunt work, but Maurice Binder's last main credit sequence is a rehash of previous work he did far better in other movies, and the less said about Michael Kamen's anemic score, the better. Bless your heart.

RICHARD MAIBAUM

John Glen captured tremendous stunts in the film. It's hard to find anything better in any of the *Bond*s in terms of sheer action and excitement.

JOHN GLEN

I think the truck sequence is a unique kind of a piece. It's a scene I'm very proud of, because I'd been developing it so long. Like eight years. But eventually I managed to get it on the screen. We spent a million dollars on trucks; it was very difficult to do. But we pulled it off, and I think it provided a wonderful platform for drama at the end of the movie. The truck sequence, I think, is one of the longest extended action scenes in any of the *Bond* films. It goes on for about half an hour. It's an amazing sequence, and those trucks, they were played for real. I tell you, if you fell under one of those, you'd had it. Originally, I had devised it as a pre-title sequence, and got it out of the files and dusted it off. It was a horrendous operation, because of the nature and cost of the trucks. I mean, $100,000 a throw, and we needed ten.

JOHN CORK

The action scenes, with the sole exception of Bond's underwater escape and takeover of the drug plane, feel slow and lumbering. The first time you see a tanker truck explosion, it's pretty spectacular. The third tanker explosion? Not so much.

GLEN OLVIER

There were two great moments in the film. Sanchez' "jailbreak" in the armored truck, the causeway in the Florida Keys leading to the underwater breakout, was clever and well executed in terms of action and imagery, and the big rig action at the end was interesting enough—although it felt like it belonged in an entirely different film.

ROBERT DAVI

I was underwater all day. All of a sudden, chained and waiting for scuba gear to come, I realized the moment was a little too Harry Houdini–ish for me

JOHN CORK

When you look at Sanchez' escape on Seven Mile Bridge near Key West and compare that to, say, the rescue of Jamie Lee Curtis in *True Lies* on the same bridge five years later, you can see why *Licence to Kill* didn't connect to audiences the way that modern blockbusters were delivering action scenes. There is a windy mountain road chase in *Lethal Weapon 2*, which came out in the summer of 1989. I don't like the *Lethal Weapon* movies much, but that chase, which has a number of similar elements in it to the tanker truck chase in *Licence to Kill*, is cut much tighter, and, even without the big explosions, it worked better for audiences.

RIC MEYERS

Ironically, every decision made in pre-production was right. But, painfully, every way they executed it was wrong. It was right to make the action more modern, but it was wrong to do it by making it more garish, sweaty, and especially bloody. It was right to try to make Bond tougher, but it was wrong to do it by turning him into a quick-tempered, irresponsible, narrow-minded prig.

JOHN GLEN

I suppose the main thing is the planning, the writing and the planning, because the latter *Bond*s, all my *Bond*s, all we had was a short story, a couple of short stories, and not very much in terms of what one could write about, and we had to develop those stories in a script stage, and what I loved was Dick Maibaum and Michael [Wilson], they left a gap and they'd say, "There was a car chase." Fill in the gap. It's a challenge to try and invent something original, and I was always trying to get something original. Didn't always succeed. Sometimes it was an idea that had been used years and years ago and I developed it in a different way, as in *Octopussy* with the car on the railway track and things like that, but it wasn't a conscious thing. It was something that was in my subconscious, if you like, as a kid watching all those Saturday-morning films in the cinema with all the kids. It all stays with you, and if you think hard enough, sometimes these ideas come back and you develop them in a different way. That's what I loved about it, the development and the planning of the film. When I went into production, I used to think that the film is just about made. The rest of it is just pure pleasure. It was. It turned out that way. Timothy wasn't quite as much fun as Roger was, but that goes without saying. They're completely different people.

The film itself decamped from the traditional 007 stages at Pinewood Studio, but unlike *Moonraker,* which shot on tiny French soundstages in Paris, *Licence to Kill* found itself based at Mexico's Churubusco Studios, the biggest filmmaking facility in Latin America, much to the consternation of production designer Peter Lamont. Sanchez' palatial home was shot in Acapulco, while the climatic truck chase involving giant Kenworth trucks, a deluxe Maserati sportscar, and Pam Bouvier's commandeered crop duster was shot on the dangerous, winding roads of Mexicali. Globe-trotting was kept to a minimum with additional weeks spent in Key West for the film's early sequences.

MATT SHERMAN

(creator, BondFanEvents.com)

Licence to Kill is also low key on American locations, but for the sake of the story. Bond is not trying to seem glamorous, drawing attention as he often does, rather he is working quietly, covertly, to undermine his enemies. The Florida Keys take over the first act of *Licence to Kill*, including infamous and renowned local hot spots, but Bond is too busy wreaking havoc to savor the more heralded sights, like the famous Key West sunset.

JOHN CORK

Licence to Kill felt like a cheap Mexican import *James Bond* film rather than a high-class, top-shelf, bespoke British product. That's no knock to Mexico. The opening shot of *Spectre* looks more expensive than the entirety of *Licence to Kill*. The film did not get lost in the shuffle of summer blockbusters. It just didn't work.

JOHN GLEN

It was a whole new experience for us. Mexico is kind of a charming place, but it's not renowned for being particularly reliable in terms of getting your things on time when you ask for them. But the craftsmanship on the sets is wonderful. The finishing and construction is superb.

MICHAEL WILSON

We had a situation where our movie was set in that part of the world, so we saved perhaps 15 percent over what we would have spent in London to do the same film.

JOHN GLEN

It was uncomfortable at times, but we were out at sea quite a lot and it was very pleasant. But we got shipwrecked a few times. We used to go to work in these fast boats. And you know the waters around there are pretty hazardous: one minute you're in 100 fathoms, and the next, you're not. We used to race back at night from location. Had a lot of fun in those boats doing around 60 miles per hour. Racing one another back. It was great fun. One night we were coming back and it was a really dark, black night. Suddenly, we stopped. We were in two inches of water, 100 yards from the shipping lane. We'd gone all over this mud. We got out and tried to refloat it, but it was hopeless.

TALISA SOTO

I remember that. Everyone in production was freaking out. The whole crew was out at sea.

CAREY LOWELL

It was the most peculiar and most difficult thing I've ever acted in. It was pretending you're on a boat at sea. We're rocking back and forth and there was water spraying, and wind, but we were really surrounded by people on a cement stage with a big fan blowing water from a hose. It's playing-acting, not just saying lines and having a relationship with another. It's a different kind of acting.

LISA FUNNELL

(author, *For His Eyes Only: The Women of James Bond*)

Carey Lowell as Pam Bouvier is a pilot, sort of the traditional *Bond* Girl, and she, too, goes from being strong and tough to then undergoing her makeover to being assaulted by Bond in bed where he reaches up her skirt and takes out her gun and threatens her to just fall in love with him and being disempowered. Both women go on the exact same trajectory of falling for Bond and being disempowered.

RIC MEYERS

For a film that maintained it was trying to be modern, Bond's constant, heated chivalry-slash-chauvinism toward Carey Lowell's Pam Bouvier was misplaced to say the least, and inexplicable—even inexcusable—to say the most. He's constantly demanding that she not be included, like she was a hapless damsel in distress rather than a trained CIA agent who constantly showed she was smarter and sharper than he was.

LISA FUNNELL

To me, that's happened as part of a much broader trend when it comes to representing women in any sort of heroic role. Romance or heterosexual romantic love benefits male heroes, because it's a way to validate their masculinity. This notion of virility that women are attracted to bolsters you in the film, but for women it is actually something that detracts from their representation as a hero. It leads to broader notions of domestication. You become sexualized. When women are sexualized, they're not taken as seriously. For me this is just part of a broader path or trope that disempowers women through romance and it happens in action narratives that are starring women, and it happens when they are playing more supportive roles. Shouldn't Bond be able to work with really powerful, strong, vibrant women, and wouldn't it be great if these women want to be with him just because he's awesome and they're awesome? Why do we have to have women constantly, in essence, being disempowered in order to be with him?

GLEN OLIVER

Carey Lowell's Pam Bouvier was utterly unbelievable as a CIA operative. I've often hammered the franchise's lackluster casting of its Felix Leiters—due to a propensity to cast actors whose gravity doesn't embody the nature of the role at hand—and the same applies here. She felt like a sitcom mom, almost a movie unto itself. Her presence was bizarre, didn't mesh at all with Dalton's Bond, and was a distraction more than a hindrance.

RIC MEYERS

James Bond wasn't behaving the way a seasoned, experienced, well-trained secret agent would. He was behaving the way a self-righteous, overly dramatic artiste would. But it really is screen acting 101, as Michael Caine learned from Laurence Olivier. If you want to communicate inner anger, the trick is to try NOT to show it, rather than let it burst through every pore every seething second. Dalton's Bond clearly went to the Monty Python School of Biting the Heads Off Wickets. Sadly, as I was to learn in no uncertain terms over the next 133 minutes, childish, churlish behavior is not remotely endearing or attractive in a hero.

GLEN OLIVER

The presence of Wayne Newton's "Professor Joe Butcher" was also bewildering—he was never maniacal enough, or substantial enough, to resonate as a character or foil in any regard. He lived in a megachurch equivalent of a classic *Bond* villain lair, which seemed totally at odds with the tone the film had set to that point. Butcher and his "world" came across as a wasted opportunity on an epic scale. This said, Bond versus a megachurch—with a Joe Butcher–esque prophet as the Big Bad (a la Pryce in *Tomorrow Never Dies*)? That's probably what this movie should've been all along—there's a ton of thematics and material to exploit in the notion. And, unless I'm not remembering something, I don't think anyone's ever done a movie quite like it. Perhaps *Bond* will someday circle back around to it?

JOHN CORK

A little shout-out to Michael Kamen's score. There are sections where his rousing build-ups of "The James Bond Theme" really lift the proceedings.

JEFF BOND

(editor, *Film Score Monthly*)

Michael Kamen had just done *Die Hard,* which was the biggest action movie of the era at the time, so it seemed natural to bring him on a *Bond* film. After the last few Barry scores, which were kind of arthritic to go along with aging Roger Moore and his stunt doubles, Kamen got into Dalton's physicality as a more serious, deadlier Bond, and his score is tougher and more nimble. But just as the movie is a bit deglamorized for a *Bond* film, Kamen's score is less flashy than the Barry scores, and the most memorable material seems to be his guitar music for Robert Davi's villain.

GLEN OLIVER

Michael Kamen, whose overall body of work was very well considered, often smartly propulsive and iconic in *Die Hard* and the *Lethal Weapon* films, seemed like an incredibly smart choice to score this picture. But he was woefully off game here, delivering one of the least effective *Bond* scores in the franchise's history, and one of the least admirable works of his immensely impressive career.

RAYMOND BENSON

The screenplay was nominated by Mystery Writers of America for the Edgar Allan Poe Award. I thought it was a superb script with a clever Bond-on-the-inside plot. I understand what some fans think are weaknesses with the picture, but if one examines the two Fleming pieces used in the film that I mentioned, it becomes apparent that this was a pretty spot-on depiction of the literary Bond.

FRED DEKKER

I actually really like *Licence to Kill,* starting at about the halfway point. Not until that. The pre-credits is ghastly. It looks cheap. Felix and James are all buddies and they're wearing these formal hats. It just feels off. It feels wrong somehow. About midway through when Bond and Carey Lowell are in the bar and there's that chase and he's on water skis, it starts to get good, and I like the second half. Benicio Del Toro is a great henchman. We don't get enough of him. Unfortunately, Davi played a whole bunch of villains in those days in other movies, so he wasn't as special as he could have been. Whenever they get nervous they steal. Like with *The Man with the Golden Gun*, Kung Fu movies; *Live and Let Die*, blaxploitation movies; and what happened was they said, "We need to be edgy." So they looked at *Miami Vice*, and it looks like an episode of *Miami Vice*.

RAYMOND BENSON

I feel *Licence to Kill* is very faithful to Fleming's novels, having taken several elements from the author's material to fashion that screenplay. *Licence to Kill* is controversial, I know, but it perfectly captures the literary character the way Fleming wrote him. I'm constantly bewildered by fans who don't recognize that.

MATT SHERMAN

I've favored *Licence to Kill* more and more as the years have passed, because it's a quirky blend of Fleming's Bond, with Timothy Dalton looking and sounding like the James Bond of the novels, and things that are not Fleming's Bond at all. In the book, Bond went happily to a meal and the mission after Felix Leiter gets eaten by a shark, rather than quitting the Secret Service to wreak private vengeance. The *Licence* mix includes much of what makes the Eon *Bond* films evergreen standouts, such as incredible stunts performed without CGI, beautiful people and also bizarre people, a cast of highly skilled character actors, and a villainous plot that is larger than life while remaining possible, believable.

RICHARD MAIBAUM

After all, when a series has been running for as long as ours did, it's not as exciting as it used to be. It's only here in the United States where it seemed to fall off somewhat. A change in the James Bond actor always sort of affected the gross somewhat. Although I must say that when Timothy Dalton came in, the grosses were fine.

GLEN OLIVER

Licence to Kill is a mess and represents the last *Bond* film to be directed by John Glen. It's easy to drag Glen for his numerous missteps over the years, and doing so wouldn't be entirely unjustified. However, it's also important—and fair—to equally recall the things he did right. *Licence to Kill* just wasn't one of them.

Licence to Kill would mark the end of an era for *Bond* and usher in a new one. Not only was it Albert R. Broccoli's last film as a "hands-on" producer, but it would prove to be the last film for franchise veteran John Glen as well as longtime screenwriter Richard Maibaum. It was the demarcation point between the end of the original era of *Bond* and the next generation of filmmakers who would take over with *GoldenEye* after a six-year hiatus during which litigation put the very future of the 007 franchise in peril.

JOHN GLEN

I was incredibly lucky to be in the right place at the right time, and Peter Hunt had a big influence on my career the same way that Roger Moore did. I think Cubby Broccoli appreciated me as an action director, certainly, and I think that I was very fortunate to work with Lewis Gilbert. I love Lewis. He's such a good director, and he says, "You know what you're doing. Go and do it." He doesn't try and dominate you in any way. He allows you the room to be creative, and I just think I was fortunate.

When I was starting in the industry when I was 15, I was the messenger boy; I went through all the departments. I had every opportunity to go into any department, really, and I chose editing, and I went through every editing stage including sound, so that was a great, great training to be a director, particularly when you come to do action scenes where you can actually visualize each cut and delegate it to other people. Delegation and presentation are the secrets, I think, to success in films. I just think I was very fortunate to live in the time I did and work in the time I did before CGI, before it's become what it has now. I'm sure the people who practice today take full advantage of CGI and what have you, but I still think the real stuff looks better.

RIC MEYERS

One film later, the production would get the update in realism and toughness they were looking for. But, you'll notice, they had a far more assured hand at the helm—one who would ultimately go on to make what is probably the best *Bond* film so far.

RICHARD MAIBAUM

We knew that they were going to use some new people. That's all I can say. I didn't object. They had a right to do that. I have to be honest: I think these films have lasted a long time, and they've had a wonderful run. I've enjoyed and am proud of my work with them. After all, 13 films, including the first four, I think I set the tone for the whole series. So I wasn't upset about it. I just wished everybody in the whole enterprise well. And that's about it.

THE NINETIES: GOLDEN YEARS

"Christ, I miss the Cold War."

Despite the lackluster box-office for *Licence to Kill* in July 1989, the expected beginning of pre-production commenced on what would have been the seventeenth film in the series, once again to star Timothy Dalton (who was completing work on the last film in his three-picture contract). A billboard for the film even adorned the outside of the Carlton Hotel along the Croisette in Cannes for the 1990 Cannes Film Festival. But despite the outward appearance that it was business as usual, the *Bond* family was beginning to fracture after the franchise's first outright failure. It was announced that both screenwriter Richard Maibaum and director John Glen, who had directed the previous five films, would not be returning.

RICHARD MAIBAUM
(cowriter, *Dr. No*)

I think what was happening was much overhyped. I have no comment to make on it. Neither Mr. Glen or myself had any commitment to do anything beyond *Licence to Kill* and so the company was free to do whatever they wanted. It was by mutual consent, I must say. I wished them all well and I hoped they would make a lot of successful pictures whether I'm associated with them or not. After all, when a series has run as long as ours did, it's not as exciting as it used to be.

Given the success at the time of films like *Lethal Weapon* and *Die Hard*, Broccoli was intent on hiring a new director; among his choices, *First*

Blood's Ted Kotcheff, *Scandal's* Michael Caton-Jones, and, once again, John Landis. The script was being written by his stepson Michael G. Wilson, along with Alfonse Ruggiero, Jr., who received considerable acclaim as part of the creative team for the CBS TV series *Wiseguy*. Sadly, he was one film too late to make a difference. Production—which would bring aboard such writers as *American Graffiti* and *Indiana Jones and the Temple of Doom*'s Willard Huyck and Gloria Katz—was set to begin in 1990 in Hong Kong, with an anticipated release in 1991 by MGM/UA.

STEVEN E. DE SOUZA
(writer, *Die Hard*)

I was offered the opportunity to write the film; I had dinner with Barbara Broccoli about doing it. But several weeks go by and I asked my agent, "What happened with that?" He said, "I blew them off. They wouldn't pay your price." I go, "What do you mean they wouldn't pay my price?" What the agent is always trying to do is get you more than the last time; whatever movie had just come out had done well or something. He said he was trying to get my quote up and I said, "I would have paid *them*! I would have done scale!" I ended up firing my agent over that. As it turned out, the opportunity got lost, because this was right before they had that legal problem and they didn't make a *Bond* movie for four years. This was after Dalton had done two, and it would have been the third Dalton movie.

That "legal thing" was the acquisition of MGM/UA by the French-Italian broadcasting group Qintex, owner of the French production company Pathé, which merged with Pathé Communications Group to create MGM-Pathé Communications. Pathé CEO Giancarlo Parretti planned to finance the acquisition in part by selling off the television and home video rights to what remained of the studio's once vast catalog (most of MGM's most high-profile titles had gone to Ted Turner and later Warner Bros in the '80s, so what remained was largely United Artists films) so he could use the advance payments to finance the deal. For Albert R. Broccoli, this was unacceptable, given that Pathé would be selling the rights to the lucrative *Bond* film library at a vastly discounted rate just as their lucrative deal with ABC was expiring. This lead to Danjaq suing Pathé for violation of United Artists' distribution agreements with the producers made back in 1962. It would take several years, new owners, and a new studio president in John Calley to resolve the disagreement and save the *Bond* franchise from the lawyers.

In 1990, Michael Wilson told the authors that rumors of a potential Danjaq sale were a possibility, in which the film rights to *Bond* would be sold outright. Said Wilson, "It's a financial restructuring, I would say is the best and simplest way of putting it. You do have a family involved and there are all sorts of estate planning considerations. Mr. Broccoli is eighty-one years old, hale and hearty and still sharp as a tack, but it would be unrealistic not to consider the financial ramifications of it. There is no desire to stop producing *Bond* films. The thrust of it is to keep the creative management in control and intact, and the story has kind of gotten overdramatized in the press when we engaged an investment banker to explore the possibilities of a sale. It is still just a possibility and an exploration. I think that primarily it's the bottom line ownership of one of the great cultural icons of the twentieth century and something whose future is certain and unlimited. There's no telling what will be happening ten, twenty, thirty years from now, and I'm quite confident that the prices being discussed now someday will be considered to be extraordinarily modest. There is a cash flow and a tremendous synergy in having a library of 16 films, and they continue to have an extraordinary life." Perhaps one of the great understatements of all time.

Meanwhile, with the litigation between MGM/UA and Danjaq dragging on for several years and Kevin McClory still threatening to have the rights to make competing *James Bond* films based on his *Thunderball* rights, an unlikely spin-off of the 007 franchise briefly emerged, the short-lived animated series *James Bond Jr.*, chronicling the adventures of James Bond's young nephew created by none other than *Bond* producer Michael G. Wilson along with Andy Heyward and Robby London. Among the cartoon's rogues' gallery were improbably several iconic Bond villains including, not surprisingly, Jaws, voiced by actor Jan Rabson.

TERRENCE MCDONNELL

(writer, *James Bond Jr.*)

The built-in history of the *Bond* films, and even a few of the already-established characters who appeared in both the films *and* the animated show, automatically helped to give the show a pedigree that organically connected the two very different worlds of action movie and animated kids show. Some things *didn't* change from the *Bond* movies, like having big stories, the need for unique gadgets for each adventure, and the clever names for whatever new *Bond* girl James Bond Jr. might encounter. Neither did the action sequences; if the areas of action might have seemed familiar to the viewer—say, in an underwater chase scene—then we as writers had to devise a good payoff that *Bond* fans hadn't seen before. A few things *did* change between the films and the animated series, however. For instance, the deadly SMERSH and SPECTRE organizations were now replaced with S.C.U.M. (which stood for Saboteurs and Criminals United in Mayhem, of course).

Villains who had been killed off in the earlier films miraculously reappeared, including Dr. No, Goldfinger, Jaws, and Oddjob, but there were now new ones as well, including modern sea pirate Walker D. Plank, a mad scientist-cyborg named Dr. Derange, and an international terrorist Baron Von Skarin. Goldie Finger, Goldfinger's equally corrupt daughter, made a few appearances, and a figure called Scumlord ran it all. So in terms of some of the exotic locations and some of the villains, there was a certain continuity, too. As for the good guys, well, James Bond Jr.—according to the show bible—was the prep school nephew of 007. Among his best friends were Gordo Leiter (the son of CIA operative Felix Leiter) and IQ, who, like his grandfather Q, devised the fabulous gadgets.

I think the biggest challenge of writing *James Bond Jr.* was to devise a story line that sounded like it could have made a decent *Bond* movie. One was called "Avalanche Run" and was set during a winter vacation for James and his friends in the Swiss Alps. The *Bond* girl in this one is a young woman named Bunny Slopes, whose father is the engineer on the express train that is scheduled to take James and his friends back. The train is hijacked under the direction of Scumlord, with Jaws and Nick Nac at the controls, in order to crash it into a nuclear power plant. To make things worse, Jaws and Nick Nac abandon the runaway train with Bond's friends aboard after Jaws bites through the brake line and there's no way it can be stopped.

To this day, the *James Bond Jr.* cartoon remains an obscure piece of the *Bond* legend and is relatively unknown even amongst most *Bond* superfans.

TERRENCE MCDONNELL

The fact remains that after almost 30 years, this show about James Bond—or rather, his nephew—has never officially been released on DVD to the public as far as I know. If it's true, that says a lot. Maybe someday everyone will get a chance to see it, maybe not. Maybe the owners want to "leave it and let it die" a quiet death. I will admit that I've only seen the two episodes that Jim and I wrote, and the animation in one was okay, not so good in the other. Hardly what we've come to expect from the spare-no-expense franchise. Also, since we received no character designs while writing the episodes, I was shocked to finally see that Scumlord looked nothing like the "Blofeld-type" we had imagined but instead resembled a cross between The Shadow and one of the pimps from "Superfly." They'd also given Walker D. Plank a talking parrot with an eyepatch *and* a peg leg, perhaps just to be sure every five-year-old got hit on the head with the alleged joke.

With the series ending its run in 1992, another movie still seemed further off than ever as the lawsuit dragged on. Despite that, Eon remained active in developing a script for the next Timothy Dalton 007 film. Saul Cooper, who handled publicity for Eon and the Broccolis at the time, related to us, "Al *Ruggiero* did work with Michael Wilson on a script, and, as has happened with every Bond film in history, there will be other writers engaged, but no one has been engaged so far. It's more a forming the underlining basis of future development. Which I would like to emphasize and make a strong point of, because it's created a lot of unpleasantness because of the way *Variety* put it. And it's been exaggerated in other stories. It's been phrased that John Glen and Richard Maibaum have been fired or sacked or something of that sort, and that's very unkind for two men who have given a major chunk of their lives to the *Bond* pictures and who we have obviously been very happy with. This kind of puts a bitter taste on it. The fact [is] that they were not going to work on the new *Bond* film; they were never engaged or promised the new *Bond* picture. These things go in cycles. I think the whole trick with James Bond, which is obvious, is that we are making the 17th *Bond* film, not counting anyone else's *Bond* film, and its been kept alive for 30 years by very astute knowledge and adapted itself to the times. No one is saying in this film James Bond is going to be dramatically different, because that's not necessarily the point at all. These shifts take place from time to time. At one point it was how can you make a picture without Terence Young or Peter Hunt."

Wilson added of the failure of *Licence to Kill* in 1990, "I think that the film was launched at a difficult time. To come out with *Batman* and then *Lethal Weapon* opening in the preceding two weeks is really stacking the deck as high against you as you probably can. And if you're paying attention to what is happening in the movie business this summer, there's definitely a big rethink about this pattern, which started in the last couple of years, which was very dramatic last year and again this year, in which the companies put out, week after week, films which have the potential of playing for months and months, but end up killing each other."

The proposed *Bond 17* film, which was to be set in Hong Kong and feature animatronic creations from Walt Disney Imagineering, would have had set pieces that reportedly included a monster truck chase through Las Vegas, a love scene on white water rapids, and a raid on a secret arms cache inside the Hoover Dam. Additionally, Bond would encounter an array of characters, including a gay assistant called Jennings, a formidable henchman named Rodin, and a contemporary in the Hong Kong secret service, Denholm Crisp.

As they had in the past, when faced with diminishing box-office, the producers returned to the familiar tropes which had energized their most successful outings. Despite all the rumors, writer/producer Michael G. Wilson was willing to assure fans (and the authors at the time) that there remained only one certainty: "The only absolute tangible is that Timothy Dalton will be back as James Bond."

GOLDENEYE (1995)

JEFF KLEEMAN

(executive vice president of production, MGM/UA)

For [studio president] John Calley and myself, Timothy Dalton was *never* in the picture. For the Broccolis, he was. The Broccolis are very loyal. They knew the Timothy Dalton movies were not the most successful *Bond* movies, but they loved Timothy, and they believed that there should be another shot with him. Initially they were very resistant to casting somebody else. John and I loved him as an actor, and oddly in person he feels more like James Bond than he does on screen. He's charming and funny, but somehow that didn't translate to the screen. We just were not excited. That thing that was making us feel excited about making a *Bond* movie didn't include him. There was a meeting, and Cubby was still well enough at the time to attend. We debated it with Barbara, Michael, and Cubby. At the end of the meeting it got to a certain point where it got pretty heated. We were really at loggerheads. Then Cubby, who had a walking stick, raised it and lightly tapped it on the ground. Everybody stopped and turned to Cubby. Cubby very simply said, "Let's go with Pierce," and that was that. The king of *Bond* had spoken, and so we went with Pierce.

But first, there were other issues to deal with. As Kleeman explains it, when the "[Giancarlo] Parretti mess was over," it left them with another complication in that the studio was now owned by the French bank Crédit Lyonnais, who had no interest in being in the picture business.

JEFF KLEEMAN

Based on U.S. banking laws, Crédit Lyonnais had to sell us by a certain date. I don't remember the exact date, but it was around 1997 or '98. We knew that we were at a company that had limited funds, since how much money was Crédit Lyonnais really going to give us to spend if they knew they were going to be disposing of us? They were already looking for buyers, and within a few years we would have completely new ownership. Who knew what that new ownership would be and what they could do with us? It was a strange place to be. It was, as John Calley put it at one point, "Our job to put rouge on the corpse."

That was the outward, external circumstances, but internally, we weren't looking at it on the UA side. I can't speak to the MGM side, but on the UA side in terms of John Calley and Becky Pollack and myself—Becky and I were the two senior executives under John [at United Artists]—we weren't looking at it in a mercenary or calculated way. We were looking at it more as we have more limitations than any other studio. We are the last stop on anybody's list. As John also said to me after he became chairman of Sony, "Nobody ever brought us a film with a Tom attached to it"—meaning Tom Hanks or Tom Cruise—"at UA. Now all the movies have a Tom attached to them." We had very limited funds, and there was a lot of skepticism that within a couple of years, knowing that we were about to be sold, that we could actually accomplish anything.

JOHN CORK

(author, *James Bond: The Legacy*)

In 1993 when the air cleared after MGM's near-death experience, there was a new force in Danjaq: Cubby's daughter, Barbara Broccoli. Barbara and Michael [Wilson] were put in charge of developing the new *Bond* film. Cubby was still involved, but on a much smaller scale.

MARTIN CAMPBELL

(director, *GoldenEye*)

GoldenEye was the first one with Barbara and Michael in the lead positions, because Cubby was very ill. He was, like, 86 or something at the time and wasn't a well man. I met him very briefly. He had nothing to do with *GoldenEye,* because he'd just had his operation and had handed the mantle off to Barbara and Michael.

JOHN CORK

I was around a lot during that time, and I saw the struggle that went on to try to find the right tone for *James Bond* in the post–Cold War world. On one hand, a lot of folks seemed to want Bond to die or change beyond recognition. *Entertainment Weekly* published a piece where a reporter asked how to revive *Bond*. There were the usual clichés about turning Bond into a woman or altering his race, but the tone of all the coverage was heavily laden with skepticism. The studio, of course, wanted more input and control. They had pushed for multiple writers to be hired, with the idea of making multiple films back-to-back.

PHIL MÉHEUX

(director of photography, *GoldenEye*)

What I found in the previous *Bond* films, which worked very well in the past, was a glossy approach, more high-key, and an approach about beauty. The nature of action films changed a lot over the years, heading much more into reality. So what we tried to do is retain the elements of Bond as a fantasy character in a sense, but also to bring it into the '90s with a more real approach in terms of the way we filmed it. Our approach is for more of a sense of reality than possibly the previous *Bonds* were. Nowadays, people travel all over the world and they see exotic spots. When *Dr. No* was made in 1962, people didn't go to the Caribbean, so for all of us in those days it was very exotic. Now *everyone* has traveled all over the world, and that, to them, was no longer an excitement. *That's* what made us change the way the films are made. It's a move from the exotic place to more of an action-packed story. To give them their due, Michael Wilson and Barbara Broccoli and all the people said, "It's your film, do with it what you want." We wanted to preserve the old Bond-style character and the nature of his way of life, because we liked that stuff anyway. We preserved all that, but tried to make the shooting of it much more real, grittier.

JEFF KLEEMAN

It was a period we looked at as an opportunity to experiment and to say, "Let's break the rules. Let's do the most eclectic slate of films imaginable. Let's try things." John was wonderfully adventurous. Some of those things, which now in retrospect seem like, "Of course they would work," for many reasons seem like the least likely movies of their time, like *The Birdcage* or *Bond* or *The Thomas Crown Affair,* to become massively important for the company and ultimately for the sale. Some of them, like *Wild Bill* or *Tank Girl,* may not have worked, but you have to respect the fact that John and all the executives were out there saying, "Let's take risks. Let's not make cookie-cutter movies. Let's not just try to be lowest common denominator or make the same movies everybody else is making." It also led to some fabulous things which everybody knew were really risky. Even retrospectively, this probably seems risky, but was, again, incredibly meaningful. Things like picking up *Leaving Las Vegas,* which every other studio had passed on, because no one believed that would be a road to success. In fact, it was fantastic. *Those* were the circumstances.

With Bond specifically, it was not even a discussion point for Frank Mancuso, who was chairman initially, and for good reason. The last truly successful *Bond* movie had been one of the Roger Moore movies. I think it was *Octopussy.* The Timothy Dalton movies, regardless of what one may think of them or not think of them, were commercially unsuccessful. They did no real business. In fact, the business was so bad that normally you would say, "That's the death now of the franchise." In many ways, it was. The franchise went into hibernation, and some years later, when Alan Ladd, Jr., was at MGM, prior to John and Frank Mancuso coming over—this was under Parretti—he began to develop *GoldenEye* with the Broccolis, with Cubby and ultimately Barbara and Michael. But it wasn't a script that was really going anywhere. It never got packaged up in any kind of real way; there was never any start date behind it. There was more of a sense of, "We're doing it to do it," but there was no reality behind making it.

JOHN CORK

At one point, MGM execs became irritated with the slow progress and they optioned the *Quiller* spy series of novels and threatened to churn out a *Quiller* film series just to prove they could. When they arrived at a *Bond* script that they liked in the spring of 1994, the challenges actually mounted. MGM wanted rewrites and did not want Dalton to continue in the role. They needed a director, and a director generally will have his own changes he would want taken onboard.

While the follow-up to *Licence to Kill* was in development, everything came to a crashing halt when 007 super-fan James Cameron's epic espionage adventure, *True Lies,* was released by 20th Century Fox in 1994, prompting MGM and Eon to rethink their entire approach to the aging super spy in the era of the blockbuster high-octane action film.

JEFF KLEEMAN

One of the first things Frank Mancuso did when he came to MGM was look over the assets, which, of course, included *Bond,* and do some research. He had a marketing survey done about *Bond,* and what the marketing survey revealed was that because it had been over a decade since there had been a *Bond* movie that the audience cared about, the younger generation of filmgoers—the generation which studios are always seeking—was completely oblivious to *Bond*. Teen boys, who were really what were considered the core audience for action movies, had one of two responses: "Who's James Bond?" or, "Oh, that's that guy my dad likes." Neither response being impressive to MGM.

MICHAEL G. WILSON

We didn't feel the same kind of pressure the studio did. I guess we're consumed by the daily challenges and focusing on that. When you first start out, you have a sense of having to make this one good, but if you remember Truffaut's *Day for Night* in terms of making a film, he says, "You start off wanting to make the greatest film ever. By the end of the film, you just hope that you complete it." There is something about that that's true. After you set it up, it becomes a task to make it the best that it can and you stop thinking about every detail. There are production issues, staffing issues, personalities, money. Decisions that have to be made.

JEFF KLEEMAN

The feeling was that *Bond* was a wonderful franchise for its time, but the times had moved on. Cameron, Spielberg, the Wachowskis—they hadn't made *The Matrix* yet, but it was on the horizon. Things were moving in a direction where stylistically, tonally, in terms of who that hero is, the sophisticated British hero had now morphed into the sophisticated British villain as in *Die Hard* and others. Brits were now more easily cast as the antithesis of the blue-collar American hero than as the hero themselves. That *Bond* was just a thing of the past. If we were wise, we would get with the program, and we would be making *Lethal Weapon* or *Die Hard* or, ultimately, *The Matrix*. John Calley had loved *Bond,* as manifested in *Never Say Never Again*.

BRUCE FEIRSTEIN

(screenwriter, *GoldenEye*)

I think the formula needed updating. For me, the scene where the movies left the ranch was in the Roger Moore film *Moonraker*. Roger Moore is in a gondola and it comes out of the water and he goes through the plaza. *He's a spy!*

Of course it's not right to look from today at what they did in 1979, because in their time those movies did really well. At the time we did *GoldenEye*, it had been six years since they'd made a movie. Martin Campbell was in a position to start over again from scratch.

JEFF KLEEMAN

There was nothing about *Bond* that looked like it would appeal on paper to younger males or younger females. Every statistic, every data point went in the opposite direction. The only argument John and I had to make was, it worked for us when we were young. We believe that human nature doesn't change so drastically over so short a period of time. That if we presented a truly good *Bond* movie, that it would work again.

When we were at Paramount, the exhibitors used to say, "Always take Paramount's *other* movie," meaning whatever movie appeared on paper to be the big hit usually flopped, and whatever movie appeared like nobody would pay attention to it, say *Ghost* or *Naked Gun* or *Pet Sematary*, turned out to be a huge hit. I think a lot of it is, again, running counter to what conventional wisdom was, and often finding success there. Strangely enough, making *GoldenEye* was counter to the conventional wisdom at the time. Mancuso wasn't willing to give us a lot of money. He gave us $49 million, all in, which was less than the budget for *Birdcage*, which is four people in a room talking, as opposed to *GoldenEye*, which we were shooting in six countries around the world.

BRUCE FEIRSTEIN

I think the six-year break was good. Everyone agrees that although Timothy Dalton was good in his time, the series needed to be reinvented. With *GoldenEye,* what everybody working on the film did was to see how *Bond* could be updated. When I got to the script, Martin Campbell and I met and talked and we realized that the world had changed, but *Bond* hadn't. Every scene in that movie is filled with that conflict. Bond is kind of wandering through that movie in a way, where M tells him he's a sexist, misogynist dinosaur; all of the villains he runs up against look at him as if he's a relic from the past. It was a way of turning the Rubik's Cube slightly to find a new way to approach *Bond*.

JEFF KLEEMAN

The way we put it together did not give Frank, or the industry, for that matter, any more faith in the project. We loved Pierce for it, and we knew the history where Pierce had once been Cubby's first choice for Bond, but subsequent to that, Pierce's TV show had been off the air for a long time. Now, he was playing second fiddle to Robin Williams in *Mrs. Doubtfire* and second fiddle to Warren Beatty in *Love Affair.* He was essentially seen as an ex–TV actor who was now straight man to everybody in features. And *not* cut out as the big hero that is going to sweep the world.

MICHAEL G. WILSON

When you introduce a new Bond, it's *always* a challenge. Pierce was not an established star. He was a well-known figure in the sense of being recognized, but in the sense of being a star that has a following at the box office, he wasn't established at that point. So you just didn't know what was going to happen.

RIC MEYERS

(author, *Films of Fury: The Kung Fu Movie Book*)

Pierce Brosnan looked like the illegitimate child of Sean Connery and Roger Moore. He was also a great karmic choice since he had been previously cheated out of the role by NBC, the network who forced him to stay with the sinking ship *Remington Steele*. It was a what-goes-around-comes-around "happy ending" for him. And under Campbell's watch he never looked, acted, or fought better. Campbell reined in Brosnan's tendency to overdo his "showing effort and pain" performances, which sadly, steadily, got less credible and more obviously forced as his *Bond* films went on. He also shepherded as good a scene of Bond's tormented introspection as there's been in the series. Ah, if only the subsequent directors had carried on Campbell's tradition of Bond being smart, sharp, cool, and capable rather than just another student of John Wayne–style closed-fist, roundhouse punches.

FRED DEKKER

(director, *The Monster Squad*)

I think Pierce is a very engaging performer and actor. He's a wonderful actor in everything I've seen, and engaging. I feel like he's the first actor—maybe Dalton had this a little bit—who you can't get it out of your head that he knows that he's playing James Bond. I think he's better in *GoldenEye* than the other ones. You can tell he can't detach from the myth to just play the part. I'm not sure he made a choice of what he was playing. So many actors just brought themselves, and he said, "Well, I guess I'll do that, but wait . . ." Then he has, what, four years of *Remington Steele,* which was kind of a *Bond* rip-off, *Bond* light. I've read interviews with him, and I don't know that he would disagree with me. If we were buddies and got drunk, he might go, "Yeah, you're totally right."

MARTIN CAMPBELL

It wasn't a fait accompli with Pierce. As you know, he was tested before that, but due to circumstances, Dalton got the role. As luck would have it, it worked out better for Pierce to come in on *GoldenEye,* because he was very young at the time of *The Living Daylights*. I remember seeing the rest from when he was going to do it before, and I remember thinking, "Christ, he looks young." Very handsome, but young. So when he came onto *GoldenEye,* it was the right age.

MICHAEL G. WILSON

Pierce was absolutely the right choice. He has the looks, the charm, and the sophistication the part requires. But Bond also has to be a veteran—an experienced secret agent—and Pierce plays that perfectly.

PIERCE BROSNAN

(actor, "James Bond")

For me, it was an emotional and fulfilling experience, filled with a healthy sense of trepidation. I think I was more right for the role as a man of forty-two than I was back in '86. There's a maturity there as a man and as an actor. I didn't have the fear that I had back then. I could stand there and just fill the shoes and not feel intimidated by who's been there before me—Sean, Roger . . . especially Sean. I didn't feel I had to conquer that one. Sean did it his way and did it brilliantly.

MARTIN CAMPBELL

It had to be Pierce, although we did interview some other people. But everyone was lobbying for him. And he came in because he wanted the part. He really sort of loved the part. And he came in ready-made for it. I don't even remember him having doubts or worried about it at all. As much as it was with Daniel Craig at the beginning, it was just right: "I'm going to go in there and I'm going to fucking well do my best." And his best was great. In both cases, there is that thing and all the responsibility, but, oddly enough, you don't give a fuck about responsibility. That all goes out the window. You just make the goddamn movie. The *best* movie you can make. I never once, with either of those Bonds, thought, "Oh, fuck, this is a burden. What's the public going to think? Is it going to be successful?" I never think anything; it never occurs to me, because you're so involved in making the picture.

PIERCE BROSNAN

I feel for Tim [Dalton]. He's an acquaintance; we know each other, and I thought he was courageous in what he did. I didn't see *The Living Daylights;* I saw a little bit of it on a plane once. But I didn't see his films, because it was a very frustrating time for me. This had been kind of a thread through the tapestry of my life, as it were. My late wife was in *For Your Eyes Only;* in '86 I was offered the role, but couldn't do it because of the *Remington Steele* contract; and that it should have come back is remarkable. I wasn't expecting it. I thought, "Tim is off and running, he's going to do it." I would hear reports from people, "You might have been, you could have been, you should have been," and I thought, "My God, this is really going to stick with me for the rest of my life—the man who could have been James Bond." When it came up again, I said to my agent, "Look, I want this resolved as quickly as possible. I want them—the studio, the company—to either say yes or no or else I'll move on. Because it's bullshit. I've got a career. I'm quite happy. I don't *need* Bond in my life, but if they want to offer it to me, I'll definitely do it, because it's like unfinished business in my life."

JEFF KLEEMAN

There was a certain pragmatism in going with Pierce. When we were looking around at who would play Bond, one of the names that kept surfacing was Mel Gibson. It was the height of his fame and career and popularity. If we had hired Mel, we would have had two problems. One was, we'd probably pay him $20 million for the first movie. How much would the second or third or fourth movie cost? The other problem was, if the first movie succeeded, Mel had an incredibly busy schedule. We might have to wait three or four years before we could get a slot to make the next movie. You say, "Do I want to hire the biggest name who's going to cost me the most and not necessarily allow me to have a consistent release for the franchise and success, or do I want to hire somebody who I know can be affordable two, three, four movies down the line, and who will also be available for two, three, four movies in a row?" It's complicated. There's a lot of reasons behind the way the Broccolis hired the way they hired.

And for Pierce—as well as the audience—just as important as being brought on as Bond was the moment everyone was waiting for: identifying himself as "Bond, James Bond," for the first time.

New Zealander Martin Campbell, prior to being signed to direct *GoldenEye,* had directed the films *Criminal Law, Defenseless,* and *No Escape,* and the acclaimed BBC series *Edge of Darkness.*

JEFF KLEEMAN

John and I loved his British six-hour version of *Edge of Darkness*. We loved his work on *Reilly: Ace of Spies*. We looked at *No Escape*, and we were incredibly impressed by how much he got on-screen for the budget. We knew we needed a director who was going to really maximize our $49 million. The problem with Martin is, he had directed three features, and all three of them—*Criminal Law, Defenseless,* and *No Escape*—had flopped. We were saying, once again to Mancuso, "This guy did great work in television, and his features *look* really good, but none have been successful. And, yeah, we've got a guy who is a TV actor, but is not really a feature leading man; and we've got a franchise that nobody cares about anymore. But believe us, this will work. This will be great!"

MICHAEL G. WILSON

Martin had been living and working in Europe for the past twenty years, and I think that's important to a *Bond* film; it gives a certain texture and flavor. He's also an excellent director when it comes to working with actors and he's certainly good with action. He was a natural choice.

RIC MEYERS

Campbell clearly seemed to sweat the small stuff, from the casting to the action. He had cut his teeth in UK television miniseries, winning awards for *Edge of Darkness* and, perhaps more importantly, *Reilly Ace of Spies,* where he got nose-deep into real espionage and historically accurate secret agentry. So when he got to *Bond,* he knew how a top operative should behave, as well as how to far more effectively fight. And he also had a Bond and a stunt crew who were willing, even eager, to take direction.

MARTIN CAMPBELL

It's not that I was consciously going out of my way to make the film different; I just made it the way I thought it should be made. Not to denigrate the previous directors, but I think I gave it a lot more pace. The approach was to make the action tougher and hard with more of an edge. There was a tendency to have a feeling of contrivance when it came to some of the stunts in the previous films. "Gee, this is a good place to put a stunt." To a certain extent, you have to do that in some ways with *Bond,* because the stunts are important. The stunt arranger is superb, a man called Simon Crane, and there were one or two spectacular moments, but they came out of something. In the old days, I think those stunts were what *Bond* was about. I think you could get away with those stunts and everyone would talk about the big stunt of the film. It had a hell of a lot of mileage, if you think about it, in terms of the success of the movies. That's really the difference.

For writer Bruce Feirstein, there were many examples of *why* Campbell was the right man for the job, but one in particular stands out in his mind.

BRUCE FEIRSTEIN

There was a moment where budgeting created necessity when we realized we needed a shot of pilots rushing out to Russian MiG fighters when being attacked. What Martin Campbell did is he went back to '40s moviemaking where he created this thing where, just forty feet outside the doors of the studios, he had the set department build the *tails* of three MiGs. Some Russian pilot rushes to the door, breaks the door open. In the background you see just the tails of three MiGs and he runs to that. Then next time you see it, it's a shot of them in the air. It was brilliant in the sense of, for relatively little money or no money at all, there's enough there and it's within the budget and it works. A Michael Bay action movie would probably have an overhead shot or some crane shot of six pilots running out to the MiGs and the MiGs taxiing out to the runway and taking off. Martin accomplishes the whole thing with one shot that cost relatively nothing. He was always really good at that; Martin was incredibly resourceful.

What's particularly interesting about the hiring of Campbell was the fact that it broke with tradition in that the Broccolis tended to promote from within, such as was the case with Peter Hunt and, later, John Glen. They had never really hired "A-list" talent in the past with the movies themselves serving as a farm system for talent.

JEFF KLEEMAN

The first thing is why the Broccolis hired the way they did. One reason, the less kind way of putting it, would be control. The kinder way would be consistency. There is a very strong belief that as much as they didn't get along, it was the combination of Harry Saltzman and Cubby Broccoli that really made a *Bond* movie. You see it get solidified in *Goldfinger.* There's that moment when you can see how they've been trying and testing different things, and they hit on the formula. It's, like, "We've figured this out. Let's not mess it up." To that end, by the time we came to work on *GoldenEye,* the Broccolis had a 55-page bible of who the character of James Bond was down to the kind of underwear he wore, and what a James Bond movie looked like and was.

To jump ahead, when Roger Spottiswoode came on board *Tomorrow Never*

Dies, he suggested using smoke in some scenes. Smoke is often used, not in a way that's apparent when you watch the movie, but there's a light layer that you put in that you shoot the scene through. It gives it an atmosphere. It gives it a kind of textured, darker look. To the point, while pretty much every contemporary action movie was using smoke, it had never been used in a *Bond* movie. It was a month-long discussion and debate over whether it would be good for *Bond* to use smoke in the shooting of a scene, or whether it would actually be making *Bond* generic, too homogenous with other action movies and losing its distinction. Its uniqueness.

RIC MEYERS

Martin Campbell had obvious skill and taste, but also knowledge. Probably the two biggest roadblocks to good screen action are producers' unwillingness to allow the time to create it, and filmmakers' limited knowledge of *how* to create it. Making films is tough even in the best circumstances, so it's understandable that producers don't want to add time—and therefore money—to carefully designed action scenes so that they integrate, support, and enhance the rest of the film. And while I appreciate that, I usually, with the rest of the audience, just tolerate the result when producers simply hand over the action to the second unit. In a huge majority of the cases, the resulting action scenes become physiology-free, uninvolving, even dull; empty movement that can be removed from the film without affecting the plot, or affecting the viewers, in any way. But when you have a knowledgeable director who sweats the small stuff, you usually have a superlative movie.

Kleeman agrees that Cubby, Michael, and Barbara did tend to exert control, but in fairness to them, they were also very aware of the vision they had for what *Bond* was *and* they were ultimately the keepers of that vision.

JEFF KLEEMAN

Studios were going to come and go, but they were going to be consistent in terms of how to maintain it. Part of that was hiring people who they felt logistically were very reliable and responsible, but would really collaborate with them and be keepers of the flame. Part of it financial. *Bond* is maybe the most lucrative franchise in Hollywood, because, traditionally, no actor or director is given back end. There are a number of A-list actors and directors who will not accept a deal when they have no back end. They're compensated by a big up-front fee, but it was almost unheard of by the time we were doing the *Bonds* that you don't give them back end, but we didn't.

By the way, on Martin Campbell, the Broccolis were 100 percent behind him. Martin completely fit the bill for everything they wanted pragmatically. He was logistically impeccable, he had a background in Britain, even though he was from New Zealand, with his TV work. He was not looking for back end. He was not somebody who was so successful he was going to wrest control of the movie. He was, in their minds, a perfect choice. So there was no problem there at all.

The screenplay was perhaps a little more challenging. The new era for *James Bond* began with screenwriter Michael France, a longtime 007 fan—who sheepishly acknowledges that as a teen he published his own fanzine, *Mr. Kiss Kiss Bang Bang*—who had scored by writing the script for Sylvester Stallone's *Cliffhanger*. That film featured a midair action sequence involving the transfer of money from one plane to another that felt like it had come out of a classic *Bond* film.

MICHAEL FRANCE
(writer, *GoldenEye*)

I sold *Cliffhanger*, and it was five or six months away from release when the producers were looking for a new writer. I went in to talk to them in January 1993, met them at a restaurant, and they said I was the first one they talked to, and I ended up being the last one they talked to. I had *Cliffhanger* behind me, so it was easy for me to get them to read it. I was in the best possible position I could be in, because I had a high-profile spec script sale, the movie had been made, and it was just about to be released—plus there were no reviews out on the movie.

When I started on it, my assumption was that Bond would be Timothy Dalton, although that was uncertain at the time. Six years had passed and we didn't know what the situation would be. I kind of wrote it that way, not very funny, not very verbose, kind of a dark, quiet character. What happened with a lot of the revisions, of course, is that it was being tailored more toward Pierce Brosnan. More of a sense of humor; I thought Dalton was terrific, but he was a different kind of Bond.

MICHAEL G. WILSON

Michael France pitched it. In essence, he pitched the plot before he started to write it, and it's pretty much as it is in the film. The story changed, but the basic plotting has stayed pretty much the same. At the time there were reports that *True Lies* forced us to make changes to the script. I read that and was very surprised. I don't know where that came from. We do a treatment to get the beats right and the story, then we put the dialogue in. The first treatment felt like the plot didn't have much pizazz, but three weeks later, when the revised draft came in, everyone was over the moon with it and very excited. I think for some short period there was some discussion about whether or not the picture should be postponed or something, but whatever happened had nothing to do with us. We didn't change a thing based on any other film.

MICHAEL FRANCE

The most daunting thing about taking the job on *GoldenEye* was trying to come up with more and more stunts; things that hadn't already been done in the first 16 movies. As it turned out, I came up with a few too many; there were some that got rolled over to the next few films. My intent was to make sure that the action was bigger than it's been in some of the other pictures. Not so much that it was bigger than *Bond*, but other mainstream American action movies, most of which I don't think are very good and which have unimaginative action scenes. I wanted to make those as big as possible, because I knew these were the producers who could pull it off. As far as Bond's character, I wanted to bring out a little more of the darker stuff from some of the Fleming novels and present a Bond that is exactly like the Bond of *Goldfinger*. You're entering a fantasy world, but while you're watching the movie it seems real. Two hours after you watch *Goldfinger*, you think, "There's no way any of that can happen," but while you're watching it, you believe it. You *want* to believe it. I wanted to make sure this was grounded enough in reality, with the breakup of the Soviet Union and what was happening in the world of spying at the time. I wanted to have enough of that reality in the picture. If you believe that, then you're willing to go along with the bigger parts of it, which are the action scenes.

As conceived by France, the villain of *GoldenEye* would be fellow agent of Her Majesty's Secret Service Alec Trevelyan (aka 006), who, in a quest for personal vengeance against the British government (while getting rich in the process), plans on utilizing a electromagnetic-pulse satellite to send the country, and therefore much of the world, into financial ruin. That idea of a pulse satellite was as up-to-the-minute a concept as France could conceive of at that time.

MICHAEL FRANCE

When I was pushing to get the job of writing the picture, I did as much research as I could regarding high-tech weaponry. When I hit on that, I said,

"This is very nice, but how can I work out a *Bond*-type scheme? How can you make money off this or use it to private advantage?" I worked it out, walked into the office with it, and they liked it.

MICHAEL G. WILSON

We thought we'd send every yuppie quivering to his foxhole to know that his cell phone was going to die out. But seriously, you can imagine how bad it would be if we lost all of our electronic capabilities.

RAY MORTON

(senior writer, *Script* magazine)

For better or for worse, I feel that Michael France's major contribution to the series was to reinvent the *James Bond* films as a mid-nineties action movie, a series of big action set pieces loosely connected by a loose but largely inconsequential plotline. At the same time, this was probably a very necessary thing from a commercial point of view, but in terms of producing a quality *Bond* film, the results both in *GoldenEye* and the films that followed were quite mixed. Many of the action set pieces France came up with—including the escape from an underground nuclear storage facility and an attack by a helicopter equipped with tree saws—did not make it into *GoldenEye,* but did show up in later movies, so his contribution to the '90s *Bond* was considerable.

MARTIN CAMPBELL

When I first came on to *GoldenEye,* I was given a script by Michael France, who was the writer at the time. I just found the script indecipherable, and we ended up going with another writer named Jeffrey Caine.

When Jeffrey Caine was brought on to the project, he says he was provided the basic thrust of the story–the electromagnetic-pulse satellite–but he added the whole first act set at the Russian nerve gas factory.

JEFFREY CAINE

(writer, *GoldenEye*)

I established the relationship between Bond and Trevelyan. I also added additional characters, like the Russian general, Ourumov; Boris [Grishenko]; and a lot of scenes. My brief was to bring in as much character material as I could and work out story problems. What I wanted to do was bring in some new characters, try to add some wit, and fill in the spaces between the stunts. Sometimes it gets away from you. The powers that be decide that what we need here is yet another stunt, so some of your best stuff gets chopped out. Some of my best stuff ended up getting cut by other writers who came in after me, Kevin Wade and Bruce Feirstein. One scene that comes to mind is a particularly good one between Bond and Alec. It was a tension created by two men in a room and a particular situation that was every bit as tense as a helicopter chase or a tank chase. A lot of stuff that survives from Michael France is in terms of the thrust of the story. Not a lot of individual scenes and very little dialogue.

RAY MORTON

Jeffrey Caine did a page-one rewrite of France's original script, and is the writer most responsible for the structure of the final story. Caine is a very talented novelist and screenwriter, but I have mixed feelings about his work on *GoldenEye*.

JEFFREY CAINE

The whole idea of doing this film was to get something back of the flavor of the early *Bond* films. If you rewatch *Goldfinger* or *From Russia with Love*, there's a lot more character stuff and dialogue scenes without bigger-than-life action. My criticism is not just for *Bond* films, but all action movies, which have all become so action-oriented, so special effects/stunt–oriented, that they are less a writer's field than any other kind of film. They're really a director/stunt team's film. What they need a writer for is the basic story, basic characters, and dialogue. The rest is up to them, so they take over. And that trend had gone a little too far. I wanted to see that pulled back generally, to have more story and character dialogue, development, and interplay. Just a few less helicopter chases and stunts that become tiring. You've no sooner got him on the ground after ten minutes of breathless action, straight away something comes at him again. When's it going to stop? That's what I said going in, what I would like to take care of, and everybody agreed, including Martin Campbell. But little by little it was eroded and replaced by much more stunts and action than I envisioned.

MARTIN CAMPBELL

Jeffrey Caine was a nice guy, who at the time was living in Ireland. He came across and we developed a script with him, but it was still not there.

RAY MORTON

Kevin Wade is a very good writer, with particular expertise in the romantic comedy genre. I like his 1981 play *Key Exchange* very much, and really loved his screenplay for *Working Girl.* Since then he's done mostly assignment and rewrite work, as well as TV. He's strong with story construction, character work, and dialogue, and has a good sense of humor. My understanding is that he worked three weeks on *GoldenEye,* mostly streamlining and focusing Jeffrey Caine's draft of the screenplay, especially the Russian sequences. And his last name was given to the character of Joe Don Baker's character, Jack Wade, although I don't know if that was his idea or someone else's. But because he only worked three weeks and did not feel his contribution was a major one, he did not ask for and wasn't given credit.

MARTIN CAMPBELL

We had Kevin Wade for exactly one month. It was very funny, because he said, "I'm hired for one month; I will do a month's work on this." And frankly, he broke the back of the narrative. It was completely different from Jeffrey Caine's. He was a skilled writer. The bizarre thing I can remember is that he literally left on the month and the hour; I actually calculated the time and it was almost to the minute that he left. However, having said that, he did break the back of the script.

Bruce Feirstein had begun his career in political advertising before moving into actual advertising and later became an acclaimed satirist and bestselling author with his book *Real Men Don't Eat Quiche*. Eventually, though, he decided he needed to have a more creative outlet and decided to write a screenplay. It sold, and while it was never produced, the sale was enough to keep him "idiotically thinking you might succeed one day" while he began working as a journalist.

BRUCE FEIRSTEIN

I worked my way up and went from *Glamour* magazine to eventually end up writing editorials for *The New York Times*, *Spy* magazine, *The New York Observer* and *Vanity Fair*, but I had gone to the point where Hollywood stuff was selling, but nothing was getting made. I was in New York when Barbara Broccoli read some of my scripts. She called and said, "Would you like to come over and do a few weeks' work on the dialogue for this movie we're making called *GoldenEye*?" I'd read an early draft of *GoldenEye* and said, "Absolutely. I'd stab myself in the back to do it." And I did have one idea when I read the script, which was the sense that the world has changed, but Bond hasn't.

JEFF KLEEMAN

Bruce Feirstein was an accidental discovery, really. We were deep into pre-production on *GoldenEye*. One of the things we felt was that it wasn't as witty as we wanted it to be, yet. Barbara Broccoli had the idea of bringing Bruce on. I think Barbara knew him from social circles or social literary circles on the East Coast. We paid him very little money with the idea of, "Hey, come on in and just punch it up." And we figured if we got a couple great jokes or lines, terrific. And if we didn't, no harm, no foul. And Bruce came in, and he changed the course of *Bond*.

BRUCE FEIRSTEIN

At this point, Michael France had done the first draft and Jeffrey Caine had done the second. And both of them did *amazing* work. Michael France came up with the idea, the EMP stuff; and Jeffrey Caine did all the Russian stuff and brought it all along. Nothing I did could have been done without the two of them, and I deserve no more credit than they do.

MICHAEL G. WILSON

Bruce brings a lot of different elements. He has the voices of the characters and their relationships down very well, and that counts for a lot. Understanding them really makes the process of creating the script a lot easier. And he's a very gifted guy, and very good for Barbara and I to work with—chemistry is important.

MARTIN CAMPBELL

Bruce Feirstein did a lot of work and basically added all the texture to it. He did a *terrific* job. And Bruce and I worked on the script for a long time. *GoldenEye* was the final result of that. Bruce has a great sense of humor, and he worked bloody hard on it, too. He really worked very, very hard and deserves a lot of the credit for that film. He contributed character, and structurally it had been set up by Kevin, but the third act Kevin didn't really get a chance to house clean, so that needed a lot of work and Bruce did that. We had time to work it and we did, and that was the script that we shot.

BRUCE FEIRSTEIN

In keeping with the idea of modernizing things, there's the scene where Bond is fighting Xenia Onatopp and at one point she says, "You don't need the gun, Commander Bond," and he says, "I suppose that depends on your definition of safe sex." What that line is about, and why that line is there, is to nod at the audience and say, "We're aware of AIDS. We're aware of the year we're in." It was to very subtly modernize the script. The first time Bond meets with Jack Wade, there is a moment where he says something about, "Yeah, I read all about you in *The New York Times*," which had to do with the CIA leaks at the time. One of the things to do was to make the movie modern and to not get stuck in amber, and to have these tiny little things where, for example, Moneypenny turns and says, "This could be defined as sexual harassment." He says, "What's the penalty for that?" She says, "Someday you have to make good on your innuendos." You could never do that today, but at the time, this was pre–Harvey Weinstein or pre-MeToo, and you can't judge. I don't think it's fair to judge movies made in a different time. But that was an acknowledgment that it was definitely in the air at the moment, and so it was going through the script and doing all that stuff.

JEFF KLEEMAN

Bruce also helped really refine the voice of Pierce's Bond. Each actor who's taken on Bond successfully has had a slightly different kind of Bond. And that's one of the tricks when you move an actor into an established role, which is, how do you tailor the role to the new actor while still keeping the role recognizably the role? And Bruce and Martin Campbell really worked in tandem here. Martin actually had a list of mannerisms that he'd seen Pierce perfect during *Remington Steele* and in some of his feature work, that he decided he was going to make sure he eliminated. And essentially give Pierce a new version of those things, so that you knew you were watching Pierce Brosnan, obviously, but you never felt like you were watching the *Remington Steele* version of Pierce Brosnan.

PIERCE BROSNAN

GoldenEye is a good narrative, and there's some good character there. Bond's relationships are good. There's a lovely scene between Bond and M; the relationship with Izabella is good. There's a sense of vulnerability to him in the sense that he's being betrayed by his best friend. For me, this Bond is a killer, he's the professional man, he's the commander, and he's got the thing with women, the car, the martinis and all that. But then there's this man who's kind of adrift, somewhere in here [*points to his head*]. It's how you play. It's what you *don't* say. You know, people were always saying, "How is your Bond going to be different?" You just don't know. The stock answer is you take a bit of Sean Connery, a dash of Roger, and a lot of Pierce Brosnan, and somewhere in there you get Bond.

BRUCE FEIRSTEIN

Pierce was the perfect post–Cold War Bond. It's an unsettled time where the question is, is any of this relevant anymore? The threats are different. Russia's not going to nuke us anymore, and we're not going to nuke Russia at that particular point, and it's an unsettled world. It's an unclear world in regards to where the dangers are coming from. What are the big threats at that point? If you look, what you've got in that first movie is a rogue MI6 agent who's gone into business with a rogue Russian general. Then you have a media baron in *Tomorrow Never Dies,* and the oil world and the gears grinding over the future of energy in *The World Is Not Enough.* You were not dealing at that point with a guy with a nuke.

RAY MORTON

For me, Feirstein's greatest contribution to the *Bond* films he worked on was his strong feel for the character of 007 in general and for Pierce Brosnan's interpretation in particular. The *Bond* films made during Brosnan's tenure were mostly action spectaculars, with the plots taking a back seat to nonstop set pieces. The films were so busy that Bond could have easily been lost in all the chaos. But thanks to Feirstein, 007 remained distinct and vibrant in all of the Brosnan *Bonds* Feirstein wrote and is sorely missing from the one that he didn't, *Die Another Day.*

JEFF KLEEMAN

And at the same time, while Martin was working on the physical, Bruce was working on the voice. And Bruce gave Pierce a certain kind of elegant, but not fey, wit, and more self-awareness, to some degree, than previous Bonds had had. More willingness to occasionally call himself out. There was an exchange at one point in *Tomorrow Never Dies,* where Michelle Yeoh was talking about having grown up in a tough neighborhood. And Bond's response was, "I never grew up at all." It was hotly debated as to whether it was crossing the line to be too self-aware. But that was the line that Bruce was walking with Pierce. That, again, made Bond a more contemporary Bond, without having to let go of who he was. It wasn't Bond shirking off all those things we loved about Bond, it was just Bond acknowledging them a little more. In a witty, fun, clever way. Bruce and Martin had a fantastic mind meld in the way they took it on, which again had not been the intention, but was the happy accident of it all, of how do we tailor this role to Pierce? How do we really make it Pierce's in a way that's distinctive from Lazenby, from Dalton, from Connery, but still hopefully giving everybody a Bond that they say, "This is not Jason Bourne. This is James Bond"?

PIERCE BROSNAN

Sometimes if you don't articulate it well at a press conference, it comes out, "He wants to get into the deeper, darker side of James Bond," and you get ridiculed for it. I *do* think it's certainly worth exploring, but still have the humor. Still be able to weave in and out of the dark and the light.

MARTIN CAMPBELL

I think that's true, and there are elements to put in, but ultimately *Bond* is an entertainment. It's not *Hamlet*. The point is that people go to be entertained; they go to see a hero—even if he's something of an anti-hero—they go to see *Bond* for what *Bond* is about. Indeed, I think Pierce is right, but I equally think that the most important thing is not to turn it into *Hamlet*. Which is not to say there can't be certain elements in the films.

PIERCE BROSNAN

Part of the trick was to keep it as simple as possible, as honest and truthful as possible, and not pushing it. Just being there, standing there in those shoes, just looking them in the eye. Martin was a great asset in that department. He gave me great confidence to stand there and do that. There's a tendency when you do something like this to gild the lily too much, but this felt like a fresh beginning.

That fresh beginning was felt everywhere, including casting, notably with Judi Dench stepping in to take on the role of M, Bond's boss at MI6. Needless to say, this was seen as pretty evolutionary, given that the part had been played by actors Bernard Lee, for decades, and later, Robert Brown.

JEFF KLEEMAN

Martin [Campbell] is the one who had the idea of making M a woman. And not just simply making M a woman, because that, I think, alone, would not have moved the needle very much. But giving her the voice that Judi Dench had, which is what makes her, I think, such a special character in the annals of *Bond* films.

BRUCE FEIRSTEIN

Martin liked to get to the studio early, so we met at 6:00 one morning and he's looking across at me and states, "What are we going to do about the M scene?" I looked him and said, "I don't know. It's just a bunch of white guys sitting in a room talking," and it's funny that I actually used those words. Martin said, "Why don't you try her as a woman?" I went off and wrote, with the exception of one word, what you now see was Judi Dench's lines.

MARTIN CAMPBELL

The thing we kept talking about was how we were going to make this thing relevant, and the first thing I thought to do was to make M a female. In fact, I wanted another actress for the part, I didn't even think of Judi Dench. But John Calley said, "If you're going to have a woman, get a star. Get someone who is bloody good. How about Judi Dench?" So I think it was Calley who came up with that idea. We offered it to Judi and she took it. So that was the first step.

JUDI DENCH

(actress, "M")

I was absolutely delighted when I got the call, because I've been a huge *Bond* fan for years, and Bernard Lee, who originally played the part, was a great friend of mine. I can now refer to myself as a *Bond* Woman, and will indeed for the rest of my career. I enjoyed playing M. She adopts quite a tough line in this movie, but, then again, how would you become head of MI6 by being anything but tough?

JEFF KLEEMAN

Bond couldn't have the same somewhat chauvinistic, sexist approach to the world in the 1990s that he had had in the 1960s. Times had changed. That may not have been apparent to Harvey Weinstein, but it was apparent to us. And so, we definitely needed to mellow that on Bond, though we still wanted to acknowledge that that was part of Bond's origins, but he was having to step up to new times. So we needed somebody who'd call him on it. And who better than a female boss, who clearly adores him as a person, but also does not accept any of his behavior without calling it out? And that was all Bruce. And it was brilliant.

PIERCE BROSNAN

She just nails him, and it adds a distinctly different slant to Bond's relationship with M. As an actor, working with Judi was certainly one of the highlights of the movie for me. She's a magnificent actress, a great lady, and a wonderful person.

RAY MORTON

Bruce Feirstein was the key *Bond* screenwriter of the 1990s. He did the final rewrites on *GoldenEye* and, based on a suggestion by Martin Campbell, was the writer who transformed M into a woman with a groundbreaking characterization who would recur in the series for the next seventeen years. He is also the writer who perfectly defined the dramatic hurdle Bond needed to overcome with audiences when M described Bond as "a sexist, misogynist dinosaur; a relic of the Cold War," an impression 007 manages to put to rest by the end of the picture.

MARTIN CAMPBELL

That was a scene we absolutely needed to address what the audience was thinking, that Bond was a dinosaur. With it, we were able to get ahead of the critics, and it was a deliberate thing. Bruce wrote that scene and did a terrific job of it. Because you've got an actress like Judi Dench, who's one of the best, if not *the* best, it gives that scene an awful lot of clout. She did for us what people were worked up about, so we got over that problem.

MICHAEL G. WILSON

In the film, Alec says, "James Bond, Her Majesty's royal terrier," and M calls him a dinosaur. He's got everyone kind of jumping on him, just like one of our critics. Just take the stuff the critics have said for years and throw it into the script. You don't have to write the dialogue, just use the reviews.

Rounding out the cast was Polish-Swedish actress Izabella Scorupco, the only survivor and eyewitness of the GoldenEye attack on its control center in Severnaya, who ends up aiding Bond in his quest to stop Trevelyan; Dutch actress Famke Janssen as Xenia Onatopp, Trevelyan's henchwoman, whose particular means of killing her opponents is to crush the life out of them with their thighs; and British actor Sean Bean as 006, who fakes his death at the Arkhangel'sk nerve gas facility in the pre-credit sequence, only to be revealed nine years later as the head of the Janus crime syndicate.

MARTIN CAMPBELL

For the character of Natalya, we went over all the European countries. The only one I hadn't been to was Sweden, so Debbie McWilliams, who is a terrific casting director, said, "I'm on the plane tonight." Next morning, she rang me and said, "I've got your girl." So Izabella came over, and I think within thirty seconds we knew she was right. She was a pop singer; she had a gold record or something.

IZABELLA SCORUPCO
(actress, "Natalya Simonova")

I loved the part of Natalya. She's very strong and very brave, and she has a lot more energy than I've ever had—always on the run and escaping. And I don't mind being called a *Bond* Girl; I take it as a compliment. I've always loved the *Bond* films—the glamorous locations, the extraordinary situations—so even if they had me running around on high heels and sighing, "Oh, James," I would have done it. For me, it's being part of a legend. It's just fantastic.

MARTIN CAMPBELL

The strength of Izabella is that you could feature her in sequences *without* Bond and she was so interesting. It begins when she gets caught in the planes that hit the facility and everything explodes, and she has to crawl out of the wreckage. Then you see her on the train, where she meets Alec Trevelyan, and she's so strong in each of them.

BRUCE FEIRSTEIN

Natalya was fun to write, and Izabella was a joy to work with. She had a great sense of humor, and, though I could be wrong, I think she went to Martin Campbell and said the relationship between she and Bond feels unresolved. She probably also went to Barbara, who is the one who pushed this. I get called back from London and told I've got to do this scene on the beach where the two of them talk about who they are in their relationship. So I wrote that whole scene about boys with toys, and that Bond's attitude is what keeps him alone.

There was the feeling that there needed to be a deeper emotional connection between Natalya and Bond. We already had the scene in the hotel room, before the two of them flew off to the satellite dish, but there just wasn't enough "there," they said. So I flew back to London to write it. When I arrived on the set at Leavesden, they were shooting the EMP attack on Severnaya, where Izabella is crouched under the satellite control desk as the room explodes around her. Fun stuff. As they reset to shoot the scene from another angle, Martin said, "Write something for them on the beach," and sent me off with Izabella to talk about what she thought was missing, and how to make the relationship more believable and modern. "Try to write something good this time," he teased. "And do it fast."

So the two of us went off and talked about how walled off Bond is, and that there had to be more than just physical attraction and danger to bring them together. Later that afternoon, when I began to write it, I hooked into Ian Fleming's idea that Bond can't commit to a relationship because he doesn't trust anyone, and—at the same time—won't allow anyone to fall in love with him, to spare them the hurt, as he could die tomorrow. This led directly to the interchange where Izabella (as Natalya) challenges him and, as a smart, strong woman, calls him on it: "It's what keeps me alive," he says, and she replies, with a flash of anger, "No. It's what keeps you alone." And as in so much of the writing I did on *GoldenEye,* I just got lucky that afternoon, and came up with the stuff about "boys with toys," where she nails him on the futility of war, and needless death, in the post–Cold War era.

With a few tweaks—improvements—from Michael, Barbara, and Martin, what you see on the screen is pretty much what I wrote that afternoon. Martin staged it beautifully, Phil Méheux shot it wonderfully, and Izabella delivered a really terrific performance. Whatever I wrote, they made better. I'm too close to judge it. But I'm always flattered when I hear people talk about the way the scene resonated with the audience, and made the relationship feel believable, modern, and adult.

FAMKE JANSSEN
(actress, "Xenia Onatopp")

When I was cast, I had just started production on the film *Lord of Illusions,* and the producers and director of *GoldenEye* were in town to meet people, and I met with them. They had done the script and were rewriting it, and it was a good meeting, although they had nothing to go by and asked to see some footage of *Lord of Illusions* once we were shooting, and they sent it off and asked me to screen test, which I did with Pierce.

I think I've always wanted to *be* James Bond, not any of the women in the movies, and I thought Xenia came as close to *being* James Bond as you could come without being him. She really enjoyed the same things that he did—she loves to drive cars fast; she loves the men, he loves the women. And the way she kills people—using her thighs to crush the life out of them—I just thought that was so typically James Bond; it's so ridiculous and over the top, and such a male fantasy that fits perfectly into a *James Bond* movie.

MARTIN CAMPBELL

I have to give all the credit to Famke, because she just grabbed that part by the balls. She really went for it and was terrific. The combination of the two girls works very well. And the truth is, Bond's relationship with the women had to change. In the past, the women were fodder for Bond, basically. Possibly not *On Her Majesty's Secret Service,* because he marries her and Diana Rigg was a wonderful actress. But usually they were window dressing.

FAMKE JANSSEN

It was frightening as well as exciting to take on the part, because I know the whole cliché about the Bond women, but the thing I liked about it, of course, is I was playing the villainess and not the girl hanging on his shoulder. I also think the script was very nicely updated without losing James Bond's fun character, and I think they had a great cast, which made it stand out from previous *Bond* movies.

SEAN BEAN

(actor, "Alec Trevalyan")

I was in Russia when they were casting, in the Crimea doing something else, and I got a phone call from my agent saying they were thinking of me for the part of the *Bond* villain. I said, "Great, that would be good," and everything, but then I didn't hear anything. They came back again, but I was doing another film at the time, so we tried to make it work around that, and fortunately that was possible. And I was really pleased to be involved in it. It's a legendary thing, isn't it, to be a part of *Bond*?

Alec is a character who felt like he had been betrayed. His parents were Cossacks in Russia during the war, and they were betrayed by Stalin after the war, and the British executed quite a lot of them. He comes to find this out, or maybe he already knows, but from then on he uses this as a weapon, and this forces him to turn his back completely on everything he's been brought up to believe in and go in the other direction. And he genuinely believes he's fighting for the right to betray the people who betrayed his parents. I don't think villains do things to be wicked or evil; they have some kind of aim and they believe in what they're doing. Otherwise, I don't think they'd do it. If you're playing it, you've got to believe you're doing it for some reason, otherwise you're just acting evil, which doesn't work.

MICHAEL FRANCE

The notion of personal betrayal was something we had from the start of the story. We'd never really gotten a serious look at other 00 agents. Usually they're just the guy who gets knocked off at a certain point in the picture after helping Bond out for fifteen minutes. I thought it would be interesting to get a look at a friendship and a betrayal and just think about what would happen if one of these guys went bad. Somebody who had the same training as Bond, and was just as clever as Bond, and decided to put that knowledge to work for himself. It's not something you've seen. There hasn't been a lot of emphasis on what's going on in the Secret Service. The personal relationships we've seen have primarily been the father relationship with M, the flirtatious relationship with Moneypenny, and the screwy old uncle relationship with Q. It seemed there would be a very strong bond—sounds like a pun—or a strong tie between these guys who go out on life-or-death missions.

SEAN BEAN

Trevelyan retained some of the qualities that he had when he was an agent with Bond, but unfortunately he turned in another direction, sort of trying to build an empire, but he's a very clever fellow, and so he matches Bond with his intellect, his training and aggression. And Bond appreciates that he's an equal. He understands that and knows that if he drops his guard, I'll be straight on him.

Although the intention of the production was to shoot, as per usual, at Pinewood Studios in England, it turned out that the facility couldn't accommodate *GoldenEye* due to other productions on the lot at the time. The search began for a new home base, and it was eventually found in Leavesden, England, at an abandoned wartime plane factory and airfield owned by Rolls Royce. A deal was finalized and Eon was given permission to change whatever was necessary to make production happen. Years later, George Lucas would shoot the *Star Wars* prequels there, and then, Warner Bros took it over for the filming of all eight *Harry Potter* films. Currently it serves as a *Harry Potter* museum/tour, and has been home base for production of the *Fantastic Beasts,* superhero films based on DC Comics, *Spider-Man: Far From Home*, and the adaptation of Broadway's *Cats*, among many others.

One of the biggest challenges faced by production designer Peter Lamont and his team at Leavesden was re-creating the streets of Saint Petersburg, Russia, for an elaborate tank chase, with Bond at the controls of the vehicle. It took 175 workmen a little more than six weeks to complete the set. Sixty-two miles of scaffolding were used to support the fabricated street that was constructed over an area of two acres. They outfitted the set with authentic Russian-style telephone kiosks, statues, advertising, and street signs.

MICHAEL FRANCE

The producers had sent me out to Saint Petersburg before writing the script, and Moscow, to do Russian research. I thought they did a pretty good job of re-creating Saint Petersburg. When we decided to set a big part of the movie in Russia, because Bond has never really gone there before in movies—*From Russia with Love* is in Turkey—I told them that I needed to go and see these places to work out the action scenes, and also to look for the kind of Russia that you're not used to thinking about, which is very cool, sophisticated places Bond could go. I ended up seeing a variety of different things, a lot of picturesque places and Saint Petersburg. And also things like airfields where they have planes stored. I worked out a way to break into KGB headquarters that didn't quite make it into the movie.

MARTIN CAMPBELL

The tank chase, the special-effects guy Chris Corbould came up with. Again, it was, "What *haven't* we done before? We hadn't seen a tank thundering through Saint Petersburg, so why don't we do that?" You just keep an open mind to anybody who comes up with ideas. What's funny is you come up with ideas that get held back to a later movie. For example, there was a scene where under a helicopter there was a giant saw. That appeared in *The World Is Not Enough*. We couldn't afford it, but the idea was there.

JEFF KLEEMAN

Building Leavesden wasn't that expensive. What was expensive was when things didn't quite go perfectly, such as when we got kicked out of Saint Petersburg. Or more like we *fled* Saint Petersburg. We had made a deal to shoot there for the tank chase. We had all of our permits. We had all of our arrangements. Every film has security. You go to a film shoot in Los Angeles, you're going to see some off-duty cops hanging around, just watching, making sure nothing gets stolen, nobody gets messed with. It's all taken care of. For Russia, we had very heavy-duty security. We had heavily armed military guys who traveled with us wherever we went. We start shooting the tank chase; we shoot for a day or two.

We show up on location and the Saint Petersburg militia is there. Our Russian security, as soon as they see the Saint Petersburg militia, they get in their cars and they leave. The militia explains that they have orders to shoot anybody who tries to roll film. We had a fixer who had arranged everything in the first place. We called him and he went over to the mayor's office. He said to the mayor, "Excuse me, but we've got all the permits." He showed him all the paperwork. "I don't understand what the militia is doing there, and why they're preventing us from shooting." The mayor said, "I granted these permits before I fully understood the extent of what you were doing. Now that I see the extent, I realize we have not charged you enough." Our fixer said, "How much are you thinking?" The mayor said, "I think we need three million dollars more." The fixer said, "That's a problem, because I'm only authorized to give you $30,000 more." The mayor said, "I'll take the $30,000." But we knew that this was not a problem that was going to go away. Or at least we suspected it wouldn't. That may have bought us a couple of days, but we aren't getting through this whole tank chase without the militia showing up again.

MARTIN CAMPBELL

There was another part of this. I was five days behind on *GoldenEye* and we had to pull back with the budget and everything else. The idea was first and second unit were going to Saint Petersburg. They came to me and said, "How are you going to sort this all out?" I don't think I was actually five days behind, but it was the equivalent in money of five days behind, because of other stuff that had gone over budget. So I said, "Okay I'll tell you what we'll do. We'll build Saint Petersburg here at Leavesden."

JEFF KLEEMAN

It was the "Thank God we had Leavesden" moment. It was the moment when suddenly Leavesden, instead of having a problem in that we didn't have Pinewood, was a blessing. We had all this space that we weren't using that we could essentially turn into a Saint Petersburg street, and we could run that tank up and down that runway and make it look like we were going up and down through Saint Petersburg. It was brilliant.

MARTIN CAMPBELL

That pulled us back the five days, and we came in on schedule and budget. Second unit went to Saint Petersburg, they shot all the bits with the tanks, but we built these big streets and everything on the lot.

BRUCE FEIRSTEIN

One of the delightful things about being a part of the *Bond* films is that it was like working in the middle of a circus, and it was hilarious. I would sit in my office on the third floor of what is now Warner Bros Leavesden. Sitting there all day long, you would have MiGs flying over the building as they were doing their thing, and you would look out the window and there was a tank that was crushing Russian cars, trying to find the most most aesthetically pleasing crush for what would eventually become that incredible tank scene. And I remember one morning Barbara Broccoli pulled up to the studio and there were people there from the Ministry of Defense. It turned out they had overflown the studio and seen all of these Russian planes and military equipment on the ground, and wanted to know what the hell was going on.

Beyond Leavesden, after the moribund *Licence to Kill*, James Bond returned to globetrotting around the world, and the production shot in, among other places, Puerto Rico, Switzerland, Saint Petersburg, and the French Riviera.

TOM PEVSNER
(executive producer, *GoldenEye*)

I think this was the most complicated shoot we've ever accomplished. It involved more than an average amount of relatively short foreign location shoots, and each foreign location is difficult to organize, regarding of the length of time you're there. The sheer number and diversity of the locales made it a very complex operation.

MARTIN CAMPBELL

The problem, organizationally, is keeping straight in your head what everyone else is shooting at any one particular time and knowing how it's going to cut into whatever sequence *you're* working on.

The pre-credit sequence, in which a Soviet nerve gas facility was partially shot in Switzerland at the Verzasca Dam, involving stuntman Wayne Michaels' bungee jump off the top of the dam—a world's record for a leap against a fixed object, which was 750 feet of concrete.

WAYNE MICHAELS
(stuntman, *GoldenEye*)

It's pushing the limits of what can physically be done. The loading on the ropes is extreme and the body is traveling at such a high rate of speed that it puts a great deal of strain on you. You're trying desperately to hit a pocket of air that will take you away from the wall, and the winds that are whipping around the bowl of the dam toss you like a leaf. At the end of the jump, I only had milliseconds to pull out a gun to complete the scene, and there was *nothing* that was going to stop me from getting that damn gun out.

MARTIN CAMPBELL

We knew we were introducing Pierce in the pre-credit sequence, and I said, "It's a new Bond, why don't we introduce him upside down in a toilet?" I remember thinking, "What a great way to introduce Bond," right? At least that sets the tone—he's upside down in the bathroom of some chemical plant in Russia.

JEFF KLEEMAN

One of the things we loved about *Bond,* that we wanted to retain even if it seemed old fashioned, was as much as possible doing the stunts practical. And we really threw those cards on the table in the opening sequence of *GoldenEye,* when there's the bungee jump off the dam, which was done completely practically. It was shot in a way to leave no doubt for audiences that this was done completely practically. And it was breathtaking. We had actually planned to do the motorcycle chase and plane off the cliff practically, too. When you talk about missteps, it's not so much a misstep, but a great disappointment, that we didn't manage to pull it off practically, because that had been our intention. It bothers me every time I think about that movie, that ultimately, we had to use some green screen.

MARTIN CAMPBELL

When the plane goes off the edge with the bike behind it, *that's* a real shot. I think we used seven bikes that we lost. So that was actually for real, and it was a very tricky shot to do; to time the plane and the bike at the same time. That was second unit that did that shot.

JEFF KLEEMAN

The reason we weren't able to pull it off [practically] was the wrong airplane was sent to us on the day we had to do the stunt. My aeronautics knowledge is minimal, so I may slightly be misstating this, but it was a plane where the engines could be reversed. Which meant that once the pilot took the plane off the cliff, he could slow it down, which would give our stuntman on the motorcycle—and there really was a stuntman on our motorcycle following that plane off the cliff—time to skydive and catch up to the plane and catch on. But the plane we were sent did not have the reversible engine. And we were on that tight $49 million budget shooting schedule, there was no, "Oh, let's just stop. Everybody stay in this location or return to this location later when we can get the right plane." That was impossible to do. So we actually did try the stunt for real, and see if we could do it with a real plane. And it was shot with the plane going off and the guy on the motorcycle going off after it and trying as hard as he could to catch up to that plane. It didn't quite work, so a lot got green screened in. But the intention was always, with those first two movies, never green screen, never CGI, always try to do it practically in complete antithesis, say, to *Mission Impossible*.

RIC MEYERS

There's something that happens in the pre-credit sequence of *GoldenEye* that, by all rights, should have been the central characteristic of Pierce Brosnan's Bond from that moment on. It's a little thing—it takes less than a second—but it is not only memorable, it distinguishes him from any other actor who has played the role. If the following directors had embraced it, it would have made Brosnan's somewhat sabotaged 007 run more distinctive.

It was, if you'll excuse the expression, a head cock. Not a head jerk. The difference between a knowing cock and an involuntary jerk makes all the difference—all puns intended. As Bond preps time bombs to blow up a Russian installation, a bullet hits the top of the doorway he's crouched behind. He reacts to the ricochet by sharply, but calmly, nodding his head to the side to avoid any shrapnel while, just as importantly, not slowing his bomb-prepping or changing his expression in the slightest. Shrapnel is all in a day's work for this new Bond.

This one quick, simple, action marks him as a consummate professional—a well-trained agent who knows how to remain cool and capable under pressure—and silently and simply eradicates the previous four hours of twitchy, pouty, seething sulk of the Bond who came before him. It's hard to definitively attribute this telling detail. Could have come from the new *Bond* producers Barbara Broccoli and Michael Wilson. Could have come from the new *Bond* screenwriters Jeffrey Caine and Bruce Feirstein. Could have come from stunt coordinator Simon Crane, a veteran of the Dalton years. It could have even come from Brosnan himself. But I'm betting it came from one man . . . Campbell, Martin Campbell . . . who, for my money, is the twenty-first-century James Bond's not-so-secret weapon. If he had only done one *Bond* like a certain Australian model I could mention, I might never be sure, but he did two, and, from an action standpoint, at the very least, they are the best *Bonds* made so far. Even more evidence is that as soon as he left the series, both Bonds he worked with started floundering save for a couple of arguable instances, and their films were never as good again. Coincidence? I think not.

Like the pre-credit sequence, one of the highlights of the film was the climax taking place at a satellite installation and culminating in a hand-to-hand battle between Bond and Trevelyan.

PHIL MÉHEUX

The climax of the film builds and builds, but the difficulties with this is that the location is an observatory in Puerto Rico. It's a huge, fantastic-looking place, but the problems with it are that it functions as an observatory and therefore we can't just walk in and film all over there. It's also huge, vast. The disc that sits under it, they wouldn't like if we had fights and battles and trampled all over it. So what we've had to do is split this down to a combination of indoor sets, outdoor sets, model work, and optical effects in order to create this continuing moving piece. Throughout the climax, the tension mustn't drop, everyone has to be caught in the action and it must build to the inevitable climax. We mustn't catch them off guard with any piece that we do that doesn't fit. The biggest problem was fitting all the pieces together, like a jigsaw, and retaining the element of location and the tension of the action.

There were three units working on this. Second unit worked on the real dish, model unit had three units working on this, our unit works the actors' part of it. You have to homogenize all those different elements. That's the most I've ever had to do with all those different elements coming together and retaining some continuity of the lighting and look in the way we all tackle everything.

MARTIN CAMPBELL

006 being the villain is an interesting twist, even though we do end up in the inevitable control room at the end. But it's very different. It's about two men. They have a fistfight at the end, for which I went back to the *From Russia with Love* idea of hammering each other. The two actors do it marvelously. It goes on for almost the same length as the *From Russia with Love* fight, about a minute and ten seconds. Which is really a lot. They really go at it, too. It brings it down to a human level where you're not relying on gadgets, and just getting it done with the bare fists fighting. I always thought the fight scene in *From Russia with Love* was the best one ever done.

SEAN BEAN

Connery and Shaw was a good combination, wasn't it? In this film, in that scene, it's not just about fighting, it's about seeing it in the eyes. It's seeing that link between them, and as they fight to the death, you see the advantage going from one to the other, and who's going to win? It just keeps you on the edge of your seat, even though the audience, in the back of their mind, knows Bond will win, but I'd like to think they might have forgotten that. Martin Campbell had told me that it was more of a psychological battle between them than an actual physical one.

JEFFREY CAINE

That's a *wonderful* fight. It gained tension from the fact that they were in a train about to go into a tunnel, and you know that when it goes into the tunnel, Red Grant is going to make his move. He's such a formidable adversary anyway. Robert Shaw was so believable as that killer. Even though you knew James Bond would have to win the encounter, you still weren't sure that Bond was going to be the one who was going to come out alive, because Grant was so formidable. That's the kind of tension I'm talking about that comes out of character foremost and not hardware. That tension is a good one. It's an outcome that isn't certain, which is why Alec Trevelyan is a good choice as adversary, because he's believable. 006 would have been trained with exactly the same standards as 007, so he has to be every bit as good as Bond. It's only Bond's virtue that makes him a winner. And the fact that it's his movie and not Alec Trevelyan's. Which is why he's such a good adversary.

GoldenEye proved to be a rejuvenation of the franchise in almost every respect, but the singular area where it fails is the score by Éric Serra, a frequent collaborator with Luc Besson, who more or less refused to utilize the "James Bond Theme" and created a score that was dramatically removed from the John Barry sound that had characterized the series for over three decades

JEFF KLEEMAN

We were all on board hiring Éric Serra to score the movie. *GoldenEye* was a tightrope of how to maintain everything that anybody who had ever loved *Bond* loved, while making *Bond* interesting and contemporary enough to appeal to a new generation as well. There's a lot of moments in *GoldenEye* where we made choices to reflect that one way or the other, sometimes successfully, sometimes less successfully. The idea of let's get Éric Serra to score this felt like a way to do that. When we hired Éric Serra, we believed that the "Bond Theme" would be fully incorporated into the score. We *didn't* think it was going to be wall-to-wall "Bond Theme." In fact, we thought choosing a moment to really introduce the "Bond Theme" was going to be super important, that we shouldn't just lead with it. We had to make it an event so that it could live within a more contemporary kind of film score. Having that balance would be nice. But when we saw our first cut of the movie with Éric Serra's score, there was no "Bond Theme," and we were stunned by that. There was a lot about the score we loved. There were a lot of scenes where it worked really well, but we were horrified that there was no "Bond Theme."

MARTIN CAMPBELL

The music got criticized a lot, and the thing is that he had worked for Luc Besson. I had asked John Barry to do it, but he didn't want to. Then I went to Bill Conti or someone like that, and *he* didn't want to do it. Then I thought, "You know what? We're trying to reinvent this thing." I'd seen Éric Serra's stuff on *Léon: The Professional*. It was great stuff. So I said, "Why don't we get him? Why don't we just change it? Let's put something in the '90s, something completely different." So everybody agreed, but I thought the score was disappointing. I thought he could have done a better job of it, but that's what we were stuck with. Now I loved John Barry's music, and what he did with the "Bond Theme." It was disappointing that Eric didn't use it.

JEFF KLEEMAN

Thus began a big discussion about the fact we had to have the "Bond Theme." Where do we put it? How do we balance this out? How do we make it mesh? Ultimately we did. It may not show up there as much as we would have liked. The score may have pushed a little further away from *Bond* than would be ideal, but I don't ultimately think the score is a disaster. I think we did get the "Bond Theme" in there. With David Arnold on *Tomorrow Never Dies,* we reset the balance and we learned what we needed, which allowed, I think, us to guide David Arnold to the right place in subsequent films. There's a lot of *GoldenEye* which benefits from Éric Serra's score, and future *Bond* films benefited by being able to see how far you could push and where you needed to pull back.

MARTIN CAMPBELL

And then what happened was that Serra, in his wisdom, had given us a track for the tank chase that was exactly in the same register as the fucking tank—

so the music disappeared. So, in desperation, I rang up [re-recording mixer] Graham Hartstone, who was doing the mix, and said, "Oh my God." He had just done a quick run-through to check the music. He said, "We can't hear a fucking thing, because the tank is in the same register. There's no way." So I rang Serra and said, "Look, there are problems here." I tried to explain and he said, "Well, take the effects down." Just didn't want to know. So I thought, "Fuck you!" and slammed the phone down.

JEFF BOND

(editor, *Film Score Monthly*)

This was another case of taking a trendy composer and going after something cutting-edge as they started up with a new Bond, and unfortunately Serra just can't seem to come up with anything memorable in terms of characterizing Bond. The tank chase arrangement of the "Bond Theme" was done by someone else [Serra's orchestrator John Altman], and the techno stuff that Serra came up with for the rest of the film just doesn't have much life outside the film.

MARTIN CAMPBELL

Now first of all, Serra was reluctant to ever use the "Bond Theme," and that's because he doesn't get paid royalties on it. I said to his assistant, "This has got to be straight-out *Bond*. It's got to be the "Bond Theme," it has to be percussion, it has to be horns. We just go through all huge effects and everything else." We went through the sequence and I said, "You've got five days to do it." This was on a Wednesday, and we had to hit the mix on Tuesday. And he did a great job. He came up with it. And Éric Serra has never spoken to me since.

JEFF BOND

The movie is such a good launch for Pierce Brosnan that Serra really can't hurt it—so it's definitely superior to Michel Legrand's *Never Say Never Again,* but mainly just because it's unobtrusive and doesn't make you stop and scratch your head in the middle of the action scenes.

An updating that *did* work exceptionally well was Daniel Kleinman coming in to take on the main title treatments in the aftermath of the April 9, 1991, death of Maurice Binder. With a background in television commercials and music videos (including Gladys Knight's main title song for *Licence to Kill,* which put him on Eon's *Bond* radar), he brought a whole new series of techniques to the iconic *Bond* title sequences, which brought with them a modern sensibility. Born December 23, 1955, in Britain, Kleinman got swept up in Bondmania as a kid, buying bubblegum cards, toy versions of the Aston Martin, and finding himself drawn in by various graphics associated with the series.

DANIEL KLEINMAN

(title sequence designer, *GoldenEye*)

I was always interested in art and my mother was an artist. With Maurice Binder's titles, there was an element of fantasy and excitement and sexiness and humor that are in a lot of the early *Bond* titles. One kind of forgets how fresh that was at the time; now it's quite ubiquitous when it's used to suggest a spy thriller or something of the like. And it's kind of become a cliché. In one of the first meetings I had with Barbara Broccoli and Michael Wilson, Michael asked me whether I thought it was a good idea to keep the women and the guns, or just to lose them altogether. I said I thought it would be a big mistake to lose them, because in my view there are certain things within the title sequence that make you know you're seeing a *Bond* film. You take all those things away, then there's a certain expectation that you might well disappoint people. But the challenge is to try and reinvent those tropes or themes and make them be relevant to the film, but also tonally work with the age, the style, or whatever, and not make them feel gratuitous. And luckily I came in to doing them just at a transition point in the technology of creating film graphics. I was able to jump on the back of new technology, which certainly helps give it a different look and feel.

But the other thing I was very keen on is to lose any kind of gratuitous sexiness and to bring a narrative to the sequence, so that rather than just sitting and watching a kaleidoscope of vaguely sexy, interesting images, and a load of names, you're actually learning something about the film. Or at least it's giving you a sense of what's going to happen: the first few reels of the movie, before the titles, were set in one time period, and the second, when you come out of the titles, it was in another time period. It was an opportunity for me doing a sequence which sort of says in an abstract sort of way, time is passing, and also suggests what politically might've been happening, and how the world had changed from the opening of the film to the next part of the film.

As a result, it wasn't necessary to have some subtitle saying what had happened, but in the titles you've seen Communist icons being smashed up and falling, and you get the sense that, okay, after these events, then the Soviet Union split up, and things changed and Western values became more prevalent. In my mind I kind of felt the idea of having girls in lingerie smashing up the statues and whatnot actually made it even better, because that was sort of saying that Western values—things like jeans and underwear and sexy Western exuberance—was part of what undermined the Cold War Soviet milieu, or whatever was happening at the time. And people in the East wanted what they saw in the West, they wanted bubble gum, they wanted jeans, and that was why, in the end, the whole regime fell to bits. And being able to do it with these girls doing it, I got both things in, I got a bit of the political message, if anyone wanted to see it, and also we've got a bit of sexiness in there, which was part of the trope and the language that Maurice had set up.

The first glimpse that the audience got of Pierce Brosnan in *GoldenEye* came in the form of the teaser trailer, which began with Brosnan approaching the camera and asking, "You expecting somebody else?" The crowds went insane.

JEFF KLEEMAN

Again, going completely contrary to all the data, Joe Nimziki had this idea for the "You know the name, you know the number" teaser trailer. There were a lot of people who doubted him at MGM and really questioned the wisdom of that. As far as I know, the whole idea of that trailer was his. He came in and he directed it. He was really hands-on, and when that trailer went out, the response was *enormous*. It was beyond anything anybody could have hoped for. Certainly anything anybody believed possible. It was the moment when both internally at MGM and externally in terms of the industry, everybody suddenly said, "Wait a minute. Maybe *GoldenEye* is going to do business," which was great, because we were on the verge of going over budget and we needed a few extra dollars.

What we were trying to do with *GoldenEye* was re-launch *Bond* with a studio that didn't initially believe *Bond* was viable. Pierce had never been Bond. Martin had never directed a *Bond*. None of our writers had ever written a *Bond*. Barbara and Michael, who really became the lead producers, had been there for many *Bonds,* but they had never been the lead producers without their father really highly present. John Calley had been involved with *Never Say Never Again,* which was certainly a *Bond* movie, but it wasn't exactly the kind of *Bond* movie we were trying to make. And I had been an ardent fan, but I had never worked on a *Bond* film before.

So, in a way, it was a movie where the odds were stacked against us. And the real question wasn't could we make a perfect *Bond* movie, if that even exists. But could we make a *Bond* movie that could prove that there was a contemporary audience for James Bond, and he was still a viable hero for our world and franchise for our industry? And to that end, we succeeded. So, it *is* a success. Are there things that, as we were doing it and after we had done it, we felt we could've done better? Or not could have done better, but we wished we had been able to do better? And are there lessons learned? Absolutely. I'm a big believer that it's really easy to attack someone for a bad movie or a flop. But sometimes you have to make the bad movie or the flop to learn what you need to learn, to then make the great movie that everybody loves next. And you see that with *Bond* movies throughout. I can't claim that all *Bond* movies are equally good. There're, for me, peaks and valleys.

MARTIN CAMPBELL

The time you get a bit nervous is when you finish the film, put it all together, and preview it. It had a good preview, not a great preview, but one of our problems was that there was no digital in those days. Now, after a preview, you can quickly put in background and it's not perfect, but it's enough. In those days, you couldn't. So there is Bond on the top of the needle, fighting 006, and he's got a bloody green rope and all sorts of safety lines, and the audience laughed. Of course they laughed. There's all these safety devices on green screen and the audience hoots. The movie was also ten minutes too long, and I knew exactly what to take out.

RIC MEYERS

For this first Brosnan Bond, at least, the series was running on all cylinders, because they had a captain who knew what he was doing, what he wanted, and how to get it from his cast and crew. Campbell was on duty when Judi Dench became M, and also oversaw the return of Ian Fleming–esque character names, as well as the spot-on casting of Famke Janssen as Xenia Onatopp. And there has rarely been as independent, competent, and believable a *Bond* Girl as Izabella Scorupco as Natalya Simonova; nor as formidable and effective a villain as Sean Bean as Alec Trevelyan . . . that is, until the next Martin Campbell–directed *Bond*.

The action throughout snapped, crackled, and popped—from Bond's memorable, well-structured tussle with Xenia in a steam room, through the awesome tank chase through Russian streets, to the climatic confrontation in a satellite dish's engine room. That fight between "00" agents was the best, most professional, most authentic mixed martial arts so far in the series, and both

Brosnan and Bean went above and beyond realizing it—only being doubled twice during the multi-minute fight. And it was a fight that actually served a distinct purpose to further the plot and characters—an extremely rare occurrence in action films in general and the *Bond* series in particular—evidenced by Bean's concluding comment: "You know, James . . . I was always better."

JEFF KLEEMAN

With *GoldenEye,* it certainly isn't a valley. I think it's a peak. But I know there were certain things, that when we finished *GoldenEye,* we said, "Wow. Um, wouldn't it be nice if we can take this further?" Some of them were obvious. Like, with *GoldenEye,* there are what I would call Bond accoutrements. And what I mean by that is, Bond is first and foremost a spy. And if Bond didn't have to deal with some kind of international espionage, there would be no Bond story. But what makes Bond distinctive are all the things around him. And some of those are his attitude, some of them are how he dresses or the situations he's in, some of them are the villains. Some of them just having M and Moneypenny and Q and gadgets.

GLEN OLIVER

(pop culture commentator)

At face value, there's nothing hugely remarkable about *GoldenEye.* It is, in essence, a straight-up *Bond* film, its most notable deviation being that one of the big bads was a former double-0 agent. But the filmmakers took those tried and true formulas and simply gave them all . . . heft. The story was *Bond* all the way, but felt more "real world" in its aesthetic and vibe. Little moments, like Gottfried John's Ourumov flashing a smile of respect, amazement, bewilderment, and frustration as Bond escapes, very simply, and smartly, humanizes a character which might otherwise have been a cardboard cliché.

JEFF KLEEMAN

There's always calibrations on the things that are a part of Bond's world. We knew we wanted to give Bond a car that did stuff as part of the gadget list. We knew that was one of the things that, if previous *Bond* fans watched the movie, they would be hoping for, expecting. So, we gave him a car that did stuff, but in the process of getting the script and the budget to where it needed to be, everything the car did was essentially eliminated. Which left us with a conundrum. We've given Bond this car, it does all these cool things, and we want that, but we have no space for it to actually do anything. So we created, pretty last minute, that moment when Joe Don Baker shoots off the missile accidentally from the car. Which doesn't really have a plot function, or function in an action sequence, but it's just to say, "Yes, we know, the car does stuff, and at least let's get a little beat out of it." But we always had on our checklist: Next movie? We've got to make good on that. If there is a next movie, we have to deliver on it.

So going into *Tomorrow Never Dies*, one of the things at the top of our list was let's have a car that does something. And to that end, it was really [director] Roger Spottiswoode who came up with the idea of that car chase, which happened in the parking garage. It's one of my favorite things in the movie for many reasons. Two of which being that it breaks the rules. And these were things that were argued about vehemently. One was having it in a contained, not particularly geographically interesting space, a parking garage. It's not a traditional *Bond* car chase. Usually it's, you know, in a moon buggy going across Las Vegas. Or it's jumping over crocodiles in *Live and Let Die*. Here, we didn't have any restaurants for it to run through, any people to hilariously disturb. We were in what was probably the least conventional choice for a *Bond* car chase.

And then, we went even a step further. Bond didn't drive the car from the driver's seat. He sat in the back with a little remote control game board. And today I think that wouldn't be so crazy, but back in 1995, gaming was not in the place it is today and there were a lot of people who felt, "You can't have Bond be passive. He's going to seem really passive here. It's, in some ways, emasculating, to have him do it this way." This is why it's helpful that the idea came from the director, because the director had in his mind a way of shooting it and a way of executing it, that I think, when you watch the car chase now, you never think, "what a boring landscape" or "what an emasculated Bond."

GLEN OLIVER

Phil Méheux's photography had grit and depth and that distinctive "big budget film of the era" style, but also very clearly evoked the *Bonds* which had come before. There was so much . . . balance . . . evidenced throughout this movie. So much awareness of formula. Acknowledgement of a need to tweak, of the need to address "X" and "Y" factors, but a measured restraint and pointed effort not to take a re-jiggering too far.

RIC MEYERS

This was the *Bond* I had been waiting for, and of course I kept my fingers (and toes and eyes) crossed that the fine style would continue—little knowing that the next installment would be the start of seven years of bad luck for the new 007, and the saddest secret fustercluck in *Bond* series history.

FRED DEKKER

It's the definition of a reboot. Let's shake it up, let's start again and make it cool. There's something fresh about *GoldenEye*. There's something to me really kind of special about it, because it's doing the tropes, but it's not doing them by rote. I think Campbell is a very gifted director. He made some great choices.

PIERCE BROSNAN

It's a lovely feeling to have people's warmth come at you, but it makes you very responsible for getting it right. There was a lot of pressure when we began, but that pressure alleviated. Everyone felt good, that we had come through the other end of it.

RAY MORTON

The screenplay of *GoldenEye* is a mixed bag. On the one hand, it does a terrific job of re-introducing the Bond character and repositioning and contextualizing him for the post–Cold War era. The script also has a great pre-credit sequence, it reimagines M as a woman, and it features one of the better henchmen—or in this case henchwoman—in Xena Onnatop. On the other hand, the story doesn't make much sense (006 puts his plan to avenge his people by setting off an EMP over England in motion by getting captured, faking his own death, and then spending nine years becoming a black-market arms dealer?). It is also poorly structured (the first act has Bond accidentally stumbling across the villain's plan through pure coincidence, which is seriously poor screenwriting. Coincidence is the opposite of drama). The script also has an oddly self-conscious tone and spends far too much time apologizing for Bond.

GLEN OLIVER

At the end of the day, the vibe I got from *GoldenEye* was . . . love. The filmmakers seemed to be clearly saying, "We love you, James Bond! We'd love to take you to the salon for a makeover, but you'll always be just who you are to me."

MARTIN CAMPBELL

Connery was always wonderful, because he is an incredibly tough man who doesn't put up with fools easily. He's a total professional and God help you if you're not. Pierce has all of that. He turned out to be a really good Bond. Sean never really had class; by that I mean there was always a touch of blue collar in him. You never quite believed he went to Eton or what the original Bond of the book had done. You didn't get that at all, though you got a hell of a lot of pluses on top of that. I think Pierce has all of that, plus he's very good at action. Apart from that, he's a bloody good actor, which was another surprise at the time. I'd seen a couple of movies he was good in, but having done television for so long, one tended to base it on *Remington Steele*. But he's a terrific actor, and he surprised everybody.

PIERCE BROSNAN

The *Bond* films represent an enormous legacy, and you cannot turn away from them. You cannot *not* acknowledge them. As an actor, you can't be scared of them or intimidated by them. In '86, I was. I didn't feel I had enough under my skin. Since then I lost my wife, I've lost jobs. Losing Cassie was very significant. Not a day goes by that I don't think of her; certainly in relationship to this, because she wanted this so much for me and it just didn't happen. But in '86, I remember the script sat by the bed through all those weeks of negotiations, and I thought, "I'll read it once the ink is dry on the pages." But the pen never saw the paper, really. I remember *not* feeling the weight. I feel weight in life now, as an actor and as a man. Whether it was up on the screen in *GoldenEye* is for others to decide. When the job came in and the phone rang, and all the negotiations had happened, and all the opinion polls were taken, I just went on with the gardening at home, took care of the lads, planted trees, and then the phone rang and they said, "OK, you've got the job. Congratulations." I said, "Good, right. Let's do it." For a long time I still couldn't celebrate. I couldn't really let loose, because I'd been there before to the gate and had it snatched away from me.

TOMORROW NEVER DIES (1997)

Two enormous pressures on the shoulders of *GoldenEye* was whether or not *Bond* could be relevant in the post-Cold War '90s, and just as importantly, whether or not 007 could continue without the guiding hand of Albert R. "Cubby" Broccoli. The man who had launched the series with Harry Saltzman over 30 years earlier passed away from heart failure at the age of 87 on June 27, 1996. Outside of being the final word on whether or not Pierce Brosnan would be James Bond, he actually had very little to do with the film, acquiescing control to his children, Barbara Broccoli and stepson Michael G. Wilson. On both counts, the answer was a resounding yes.

That being said, Pierce Brosnan's sophomore outing as James Bond—*Tomorrow Never Dies*—is a polarizing installment of the 007 series. So much so that even the authors of this book have diametrically opposing opinions of the finished film. While Gross considers it a high-water mark for the Brosnan films, Altman despises the movie. Suggests Altman, "A perfect example of the movie's ineptitude is the brilliant teaser in which Bond has to escape with a nuclear warhead before cruise missiles rain down on an isolated encampment where hi-tech weaponry is being auctioned to the highest bidder. Great scene, great action, wonderful David Arnold score and what's the supertitle? A Terrorist Arms Bazaar. Do we really need to have this identified and, if so, calling it A Terrorist Arms Bazaar in a milquetoast font is just so . . . Dr. Seuss." Gross, however, adores the film saying: "Is it deep and nuanced? Not really, but the action is tremendous, there's some emotional weight provided by Bond's connection with Paris Carver, it looks great, David Arnold's score captures the flavor of Barry but takes it forward . . . Too much stealth boat, but overall I'm able to go back to it over and over again."

PIERCE BROSNAN

(actor, "James Bond")

GoldenEye busted open wide doors in many avenues of life, professionally and personally. But it came with a price, being that you don't have enough time to do all the things you want to do. The price is you have intrusions into your privacy at the hands of the media. But having been an actor for so many years, and with a success like that, you adore it. You relish it. At the same time, you keep in your mind that sometimes these things can be short-lived. But it was wonderful to see *GoldenEye* be a magnificent success and James Bond back up there in the landscape as it were, and to have a whole new generation embrace the character.

JEFF KLEEMAN

GoldenEye was a far bigger success than the studio ever imagined it would be. And there was something else that took the studio by surprise, which exponentially increased its success, which was the Nintendo *GoldenEye* video game. Because there had been a deal with Nintendo to do a video game and, frankly, nobody took it seriously. Again, we're in 1995, video games, yes, we all get it, but they weren't quite the phenomenon they are now, or would become later. And certainly movie studios weren't obsessed with the ancillary marketing of creating video games off their movies. It was nice, and they were doing it, but it wasn't that big of a deal.

So Nintendo does this *GoldenEye* video game. And the video game is a *monster* success—in its own way, as successful as the movie, at least on its terms. And as you may remember, there'd been that marketing survey where teenage boys did not know who James Bond was. Well, what happened, thanks to the Nintendo video game, is those sixteen-year-old boys who went and saw *GoldenEye* and loved it also bought the video game. And when they played the video game at home, their younger siblings, who had not been allowed to go see *GoldenEye,* became obsessed with the video game, too. And so now you had six-year-olds, seven-year-olds, eight-year-olds who were suddenly *GoldenEye* and James Bond fans, even though they'd never seen the movie. And this just sent the studio into stratospheric joy.

And on top of *that,* the discovery was made that when a studio releases a new entry in a series that is fresh, innovative, and does well, it breathes new life into all the previous iterations of the movie.

JEFF KLEEMAN

(executive vice president of production, MGM/UA)

So it's not just a revenue stream from *GoldenEye,* it's from all the previous *Bond* movies. And back when home video was a very, very big deal, what you would see is every time a new *Bond* movie—*GoldenEye, Tomorrow Never Dies, The World Is Not Enough, Casino Royale*—came out, MGM/UA would repackage all the *Bond* movies. There would be the special high-definition new version, there would be the Blu-ray version, there would be the whatever version. And they *all* resold. And in that moment, the combination of *GoldenEye*'s box office success, the Nintendo halo effect, and the rejuvenation of a really substantial piece of the library, MGM/UA suddenly realized, particularly as it was preparing for a sale and needing to find a buyer, well, if we can prove that this is an ongoing concern, we can ask for a much higher selling price than we would normally have ever been able to.

This would in turn have a direct effect on the next 007 adventure, *Tomorrow Never Dies,* in terms of not only the need to rush it into theaters within two years, but the studio's desperate need for it to duplicate the kind of success that *GoldenEye* achieved.

JEFF KLEEMAN

So, *GoldenEye* came out in 1995 and we were given a date in 1997 without a script, without anything, to have *Tomorrow Never Dies* in the theaters. Again, not missteps, but more, what can you do better? There was suddenly this sense of, "Oh and by the way, you have an open checkbook, you know, go for it. You know, blow it out. Go bigger, funner, better than *GoldenEye*."

MICHAEL G. WILSON
(producer)

How do you deal with that? It only means to us that they tended to be very supportive, which was helpful. You don't start out saying, "We're going to make this one at half-speed." I think you make every picture as well as you can, and hope that you come up with a good script and hope that the elements all work together. If the studio supports you, great. On the other hand, we seemed to be the road show for them, so they pulled out all the stops, which is great.

PIERCE BROSNAN

You can really enter into the whole realm of what is riding on your shoulders, or you can look at it in very hard, practical terms in the sense that I did my job. I went in there and made *Tomorrow Never Dies* and my job was over. There wasn't much I could do about it beyond trying to sell the movie. I cannot take on the responsibility of the studio or anyone's job at the studio. My job is acting the role and that is what I did.

Brought on very early in the process was Canadian director Roger Spottiswoode, whose previous credits include *Under Fire* (1983), *Shoot to Kill* (1988), *Turner & Hooch* (1989), *Air America* (1990), and *And the Band Played On* (1993). On the surface, the choice seemed a little odd, but it apparently made perfect sense to the people who worked with him.

JEFF KLEEMAN

There was a debate we had at UA with the Broccolis about *Bond* directors. This isn't why we brought Roger in, but there was an interesting debate, which was the auteur versus the non-auteur. We understood why you didn't bring in auteur *Bond* directors, why you brought in really competent wonderful directors. Someone like Lewis Gilbert was a great director. You look at his body of work and it's phenomenal. Maybe of all the directors of the Connery, Moore, Lazenby, Dalton era, Lewis really does have an amazing body of work. He bridged them from *You Only Live Twice* through *Moonraker*. But most are really strong, competent directors who are not auteurs. When John Calley and I became involved with the *Bond* movies, particularly after *GoldenEye*, at one point we proposed a theory to the Broccolis. We were getting calls from every major director in town saying, "We want to do a *Bond* movie. I'll do a *Bond* movie"—Spielberg told us, "I'd love to direct a *Bond* movie." We proposed, what if we went for it? What if each *Bond* movie was a different auteur? What if Spielberg directed one, and then Scorsese directed one? If the Spielberg one worked, which it probably would, because it's Steven Spielberg, great. But if it flops, a) *Bond* movies have recovered from flops before, and b) if it flops, won't everyone be really curious to see what the Martin Scorsese version is? So they'll show up again. By the way, if the Scorsese version doesn't work, then they'll really want to see what the David Cronenberg version is and they'll show up for *that*.

PIERCE BROSNAN

There's no reason they couldn't do different genre type *Bonds*. A thriller *Bond*, a scary *Bond*, a science-fiction *Bond*, a horror *Bond*. It *can* be done, but you put it in cold print and people say, "Oh my God, what's he talking about?" But I know it can be done somehow. Now would they be willing to stray from the formula? God, no, they'd be terrified. Just saying that out loud and putting it in print they'd be, like, "Lock him up, put him in the jacket." But why not? You have all the tools there: the character, the music, the women, the martinis, the gadgets, M, Q—you take those people and put them in a setting which is very different. It's exciting to think about. You set the whole piece in London. You do a character piece. Martin Scorsese *has* said he would love to do one. Can you imagine that? Try saying that to Michael Wilson.

JEFF KLEEMAN

In a way, by having an auteur, it makes it flop-proof, was our point of view. Also, because John and I come from an auteur philosophy. It makes it flop-proof, because each new auteur creates a new curiosity about what the movie is. What's the Wachowski version of a *Bond* movie going to be? But Barbara and Michael didn't like this plan for all the reasons we've discussed earlier. They aren't necessarily wrong. I don't necessarily disagree with them. The process of good collaboration is one where you can really argue and bring up all of these ideas and a lot of them get shot down, but you ask the questions.

MICHAEL G. WILSON

Looking at his best work, which I think is *Turner & Hooch* and *Under Fire*, as well as some of his more recent television work of the time, we felt Roger as a filmmaker had the ability to tell a story. He was extremely good at editing in post-production, which we needed in order to get through our schedule.

We had the most horrendous and short post-production schedule and it was a miracle that he brought it off. Those were many of the considerations, and he did a good job.

JEFF KLEEMAN

Roger had begun as an editor and this ultimately became a lifesaver on *Tomorrow Never Dies*. We had the shortest post-production for *Tomorrow Never Dies* of any *Bond* movie I believe in the history of *Bond* movies. Certainly in the history of contemporary *Bond* movies. I may be off on this, but I think it was about 14 weeks. The DGA mandates a 10-week director's cut. Most movies that are studio movies have somewhere around 30 to 40 weeks of post, if not more. Particularly if they had special effects. Particularly if, as with *Tomorrow Never Dies,* you're shooting six different units simultaneously.

MICHAEL G. WILSON

Six units shooting in different parts of the world, and things involving boats, underwater, skydiving—a whole list of elements, and whereas you usually have *one* of those factors, in this one we had *all* of them.

JOHN CORK

(film historian; author, *James Bond: The Legacy*)

Roger Spottiswoode got a beautiful sense of movement in the action scenes. The scene where Bond and Wai Lin are both breaking into the Carver headquarters and have to escape is one of the best constructed action sequences in any *Bond* film. Sure, there are no big stunts or explosions, but that scene oozes everything I love about *James Bond*.

JEFF KLEEMAN

Roger never batted an eye at this schedule. And the schedule was necessary to make the release date. I don't believe we could have delivered that movie on that post schedule to the degree of quality it is at, without somebody as competent in the editing room as Roger and who, while he was shooting, was able to cut it as well as he was able to do it. There are very few directors I've ever worked with who can do that. A lot of directors, particularly contemporary directors, shoot a lot of cameras and they shoot a lot of footage, and they figure they're going to select it in the editing room. The editing process can become very long, because there's a lot of selecting, a lot of playing. Roger was really precise. He knew what he wanted, he knew what he needed. He had editors who he had worked with before, he had a shorthand with. He would be working with them by night while he was shooting by day. He was covering all six units. At one point, he was getting Robert Elswit, the DP [director of photography], to show up at the second unit and while he wasn't officially shooting the second unit, guiding the second unit. It was a level of editorial coordination that was a necessity, but is very hard to come by.

ROGER SPOTTISWOODE

As a director, you try and bring a vision of the film, what the film will be. In my case, I wanted to change it a fair amount and keep some of the best of the old. You come to make a very interesting version of something people know and love—quite different and quite the same. It's a tightrope you walk along, but a very interesting one.

JEFF KLEEMAN

We considered Roger an incredibly smart filmmaker, and yes, an auteur, particularly if you looked at movies like *Under Fire,* which I think is a wonderful movie. But not someone who was going to, from the outside, go AWOL or basically have some radical "it's my way or the highway" approach. He was also an energetic filmmaker and we liked that, in a way. While he is not at all Martin Campbell, he had similarities to Martin in terms of the muscularity he brought to his filmmaking, which the Broccolis always like. And our meetings with him were great. Roger had fantastic ideas, like the car chase. But there's a great lesson I learned from the Broccolis, and it is this: Barbara and Michael, who I always refer to collectively as the Broccolis, don't see eye to eye on everything. In fact, I would say on a tremendous number of creative and production issues, they disagree. But you would never know that, dealing with them from the outside. I was lucky enough to be let into their inner circle, and they have what may be the single best working relationship amongst themselves and their inner circle that I have ever seen in Hollywood.

Which is, you show up in the morning at E Lot, and pretty much until about 5:00 in the afternoon, you will argue. You debate *everything.* When Bond enters the room, does he flip the light switch up? Does he flip it down? Well, he would never flip it up, because of this; well, he would never flip it down, because electrical engineering wouldn't allow it to go like this; well, he would . . . And you argue it all out, like the world depended on it, and it gets heated. I mean, it gets *really* heated. And amongst everybody. It's not versus Barbara and Michael. It's Barbara arguing with Michael, it's Michael arguing with Barbara, it's me arguing with one or both of them, it's the director arguing with them. You have a break, we all go to lunch together, the argument ceases for lunch. But then it picks right back up again, and then around 5:00 usually Barbara goes into a little section where there's some alcohol and pours drinks for everybody.

And by the time we all leave, we are all smiling and friendly and patting each other on the shoulder. And we have come to some kind of resolution, and it's not a resolution that we all agree with, necessarily, but it's the resolution we feel we can all live with. And when anybody, whether it was the people I worked with at the studio, or a journalist, or a writer, or a director, or an actor, or whomever, asks a question, we all speak with one voice.

PIERCE BROSNAN

It was certainly different working with Roger compared to Martin Campbell. Martin works at a much higher frequency than Roger does. Martin is highly prepared—not that Roger isn't, but Martin has his storyboards down. He's like this powerhouse when he's on the set. He controls the set; it's *his* set, it's his world. You either dig in or it drives you nuts. I love the guy and I would go out on any other movie with him in a blink of an eye. Martin had everything buttoned down completely, so when you went in, you knew exactly what the day's work was. Not that you were short-changed as an actor, because he loves actors and is very good with them and has a wonderful ear for dialogue. You have a 120-day shoot or something like that, and you just have to know where the camera is going to go.

Roger, on the other hand, was a little more improvisational and he worked closely with his DP. They really worked on the shots, so it was a bit more time-consuming. Robert Elswit, the DP, really created a look and was given the time and space to do it. It makes things a little harder, because you have to keep up the momentum.

MICHELLE YEOH

(actress, "Wai Lin")

Roger Spottiswoode was *so* hands-on. I've done a lot of action movies, but he taught me a lot about being the character, being a person rather than doing it just for the sake of doing action. It's very important or else it's just another action movie. He gave our characters a sensitive side, but at the same time keeping it in the style of a *Bond* movie. That's very important, because at the end of the day people will have a preconception of what a *Bond* movie should be like, and you don't want to give them too much of a culture shock. But Roger was able to do that; to take the characters one step further. I enjoyed working with him.

JEFF KLEEMAN

Once we had Roger, the focus became the script. I'd always been aware that there was a sort of literary history with *Bond* screenplays. Anthony Burgess wrote a screenplay for *The Spy Who Loved Me,* which I have always begged the Broccolis to let me read, and they have never let me read it, but I really want to. I have like five or six screenplays I've always wanted to read that I've never been able to read, and that's one of them. I have a real penchant for *You Only Live Twice,* which Roald Dahl wrote on. And, again, while I don't know what Dahl contributed or didn't contribute, there are things in *You Only Live Twice* that I really like to believe were thanks to Roald Dahl having brought his particular wit and point of view to it that makes it special, as far as I'm concerned.

The first writer brought on to the project was legendary mystery and noir novelist Donald Westlake, who had written over a hundred novels and nonfiction books, including *The Hunter,* which was adapted into the classic 1967 film *Point Blank,* with Lee Marvin, *The Outfit,* and *Two Much*. He also wrote the screenplay adaptation of Jim Thompson's noir, *The Grifters,* for which he was nominated for an Oscar.

JEFF KLEEMAN

I had grown up always loving Donald Westlake. And the thing that intrigued me about Westlake is he wrote *Tough Guys* under his Richard Stark pseudonym incredibly well. His Tough Guy character is as good as it gets in terms of tough male crime stories. And he also wrote humor, the flip side of the Parker coin being Dortmunder, incredibly well. And he wrote really interesting sequences. That heist mind of his was phenomenal. And so I thought, what would a Donald Westlake *Bond* movie look like? So I reached out to Don and he flipped for the idea. So, we brought him out; he met with Barbara and Michael. We hired him to write a treatment. Westlake is a travel nut; we had an interesting opportunity, which was Hong Kong was being handed over to mainland China in 1997. What if we made a *Bond* movie that was the first *Bond* movie that was grounded in a current event? A current international event. And we set it during the handover of Hong Kong to mainland China.

We wanted to get Bond back to Asia; it had been a while, and that just seemed like another way to take Bond and make him contemporary, but still allow him to be Bond. And we were all fascinated by what was going to happen with the handover, anyway. So, Don went off and he wrote a couple of treatments that had some amazing stuff in them. Really cool. Really what I would call *You Only Live Twice* kinds of things. Ultimately, though, Don did not, as you know, write the screenplay. But Don then went and wrote a novel inspired by the treatments he'd written for *Tomorrow Never Dies,* which was published by Hard Case Crime [*Forever and a Death*].

So at this point, the clock's ticking. The clock was ticking when we started with Don, but one of the reasons I'd liked Don is he's fast. This is a guy who's turned out more novels than most people could humanly read, because he would sometimes be turning out five or six original novels a year. I was not worried about Don keeping up with the schedule. But when it *didn't* work out, we were now really behind, and we'd lost a lot of time. So, we called in Bruce Feirstein, who, while he had never written a *Bond* script from scratch before, we had great belief in him, because of the work he'd done on *GoldenEye,* and we knew we had the voice of Bond with Bruce. And Bruce had a lot of really good ideas. They were *great* ideas.

RAY MORTON

(senior writer, *Script* magazine)

Bruce Feirstein's original draft of *Tomorrow Never Dies* centered around the British handover of Hong Kong to China, but when it became obvious that the handover would be old news by the time the movie came out, the decision was made to keep Feirstein's villain, a megalomaniacal media mogul, but to devise a new scheme for him to carry out.

BRUCE FEIRSTEIN

The picture is greenlit and Spottiswoode comes on board. And one question that comes up is, can we actually do Hong Kong in '97? The handover of Hong Kong from Britain to China was supposed to be in May of '97. The picture would have been coming out at Thanksgiving of '97. Henry Kissinger was on the board of directors of MGM and he advised against it, because while things might go right, what happens if things go wrong and then you're stuck with a picture that's in an alternate universe? Everyone thought about this, and it made sense. So at that point we knew we were going to have a media mogul as the villain. That didn't change. The idea, which I came up with, was that it's going to be about creating a war for news.

BRUCE FEIRSTEIN

What I *really* wanted to explore was the idea that somewhere Bond had had someone he was madly in love with. That's where the character of Paris came from. Pierce very much, as he said after *GoldenEye,* wanted to peel away the layers of the onion. When we started talking about *Tomorrow Never Dies,* I had three sentences on the blackboard. The first sentence was, "Words are the new weapon, satellites are the new artillery." The second sentence was, "I'm not going to end up with you in some raft again." And the third one was, "Contrary to what you believe, the entire world isn't made up of madmen who can hollow out volcanoes, fill them with long-legged women, and threaten the world with nuclear annihilation."

Those three lines were the crux of the movie. Elliot Carver is words are the new weapons, satellites are the new artillery. Paris, in a very early draft . . . I wanted him to run into a woman he had run into before who said to him, "I'm not going to end up floating in some raft with you." And through various machinations, she ended up being the villains' wife, the Teri Hatcher character. Her name was Paris from day one. In the normal process of working these things through, what we ended up with was, in many respects, entirely different, but in some respects exactly where it should have been. That's the way it worked. Then you work out all kinds of things. It's a long, involved process. I started working on *Tomorrow Never Dies* just after *GoldenEye* came out. On January 6, 1996, I was in London. I finished the first draft in August 1996, we went into pre-production and Roger Spottiswoode was hired to direct in September, and we went into production at the end of September. Several other writers came in and played around with what I did, then I came in to put all the pieces back together.

RAY MORTON

With only a short time left before the film needed to start shooting, United Artists flew six Hollywood screenwriters to London for a week-long brainstorming conference. A number of key ideas generated in that session were incorporated into the revised storyline.

JEFF KLEEMAN

The clock was ticking. The normal time a studio gives for a first draft of the script is 12 weeks. In our case, we wanted to be able to hire a department head, start location scouting, start working on stunts, start working on casting long before we'd lost three months. Because at this point, we were under two years out from having to have this thing in theaters. The idea was to create a brainstorming session that would hopefully crack enough of the plotting of the script and the sequences so that Bruce could go off and write, having maybe saved what could have been five or six weeks of solo work. It was, as far as I know, a first. It certainly was long before *Transformers* or any of those writers' rooms. I did know the practice in television, but at that point TV was sort of half writers and half freelancers. So we gathered a bunch of writers, and they were great writers. Intentionally eclectic writers. They included Nick Meyer, Dan Petrie, David Wilson, Leslie Dixon, and Kurt Wimmer, who did not know each other at the time, but would—to some degree, because of this writers' room—end up writing *The Thomas Crown Affair* remake with Pierce.

But what we did was we gathered in London for a week and Roger Spottiswoode was there. It was a phenomenal week. It wasn't easy. It was a lot of grueling work, a lot of arguing, a lot of really smart passionate people valiantly defending each of their ideas wonderfully articulately, but not always right or at least what we wanted. It was pretty much 24 hours a day, because even when we were not in the Eon offices working, we took all of our meals together. We went out to breakfast, lunch, and dinner together. It was almost like *Bond* summer camp. It had that feel, because everyone was there because they loved *Bond*. They were kind of thrilled to have an all-expense-paid trip to London and be in the *Bond* offices and just imagine what Bond might do in his next movie. And a lot of things sprung from the writers' room.

BRUCE FEIRSTEIN

That was where the Michelle Yeoh character of Wai Lin kind of got invented. Roger was fascinated with Michelle Yeoh, so I came up with the idea of a Chinese spy that Bond is going to deal with. We would fit that in. And the Teri Hatcher role was a rethinking of the role of the woman in my original script set in Hong Kong, because I had that line where she slaps him and he says, "Is it something I said?" and she says, "I'll be right back."

Now I don't want to sound like an asshole here, but the writers came in, pitched all sorts of ideas, but then I went back to my original script and kind of tweaked and rewrote it, because we knew we had to move. The plot came from me and we went forward. Roger, though, was under enormous pressure, and I was replaced after I turned in my draft, because they felt they wanted a fresh voice.

JEFF KLEEMAN

We needed things moving quickly, so for a while we decided to keep David Wilson on and have him and Bruce divide up sections of the script. They would write simultaneously, since everybody knew where we were going, and Bruce could always finesse David's dialogue to match his dialogue, it would give us a big jump-start for them to be writing at the same time. So there were a number of sections that David wrote and then Bruce would make sure they had the Bond voice to them. Bruce was writing other sections, which let the script move forward much more quickly.

BRUCE FEIRSTEIN

There was a writer named David Wilson—not related to Michael—who was brought in to do some action scenes, and that apparently didn't go anywhere.

JEFF KLEEMAN

Roger Spottiswoode's brother-in-law was actually Nick Meyer, and so Roger suggested that Nick come on to polish some stuff. Nick is a brilliant writer; no one is going to say no to that. Nick came on board.

Nicholas Meyer is generally credited as the man who saved *Star Trek,* in that he was the one who finessed the second big-screen version of the classic series, 1982's *The Wrath of Khan,* that infused new life into the franchise. His previous credits included *The Seven-Per-Cent Solution* and *Time After Time,* and he would later go onto direct films like 1998's *The Deceivers* and 1991's *Company Business* as well as the *Trek* sequel *The Undiscovered Country.*

NICHOLAS MEYER

I should state at the outset that I was never a fan of the *James Bond* franchise. I prefer my spy fiction less cartoonish, favoring Hitchcock and le Carré over Ian Fleming, therefore I cannot claim any sort of passion for the material. But I had three intimate points of contact with the film in question, which made it difficult for me to turn down the invitation to participate. In no special order, they were my friend and protégé, Jeff Kleeman, who was the UA executive on the film; my friend, the star, Pierce Brosnan, who I had directed on *The Deceivers,* a Merchant Ivory production we shot together in India; and the director, my friend, Roger Spottiswoode, who is also my brother-in-law once removed (his brother is married to my sister, whom he met as the result of my longtime friendship with Roger).

To the best of my recollection, I got a call from either Jeff or Roger, possibly both, asking if I would be willing to fly to London along with several other writers to participate in a roundtable brainstorming session regarding the script, which was originally, and more sensibly, called *Tomorrow Never Lies,* a title which at least had the virtue of relating to the story. The villain of the piece was inspired, like *Citizen Kane,* by a certain newspaper baron (*Tomorrow* was the name of his flagship newspaper). The specific question we were all asked to address was, "What does the villain want?" And, in an emphatic parenthesis, we were reminded a) that previous *Bond* villains had already wanted the gold in Fort Knox, atomic weapons, control of the oceans, control of outer space, etc. And b) "keep it simple." I flew to London, pondering this question. We were generously housed by Eon at the Dorchester Hotel. There had been roughly twenty *Bond* films before this one, and the Broccoli family knew how to make them.

JEFF KLEEMAN

I adore Nick, I have worked with Nick, Nick is an incredibly close friend, but it was, in retrospect, the wrong time to bring Nick on. What I mean by that is we should have either brought Nick on at the very, very beginning, so he could have been part of the truly original conceptualization. Or we should have brought Nick on at the very end, so it would be a very surgical, we need this particular scene strengthened in this way. Instead, Nick came on at the midpoint. We had a script, but it wasn't fully working yet. So it needed an overhaul, but we still had enough stuff underway that we couldn't afford to have the baby thrown out with the bathwater.

BRUCE FEIRSTEIN

Nick Meyer threw out the script and did a whole entirely different treatment about population control. I never saw it. I just know he turned it in, had a huge fight with Barbara Broccoli, and was gone.

NICHOLAS MEYER

I am certain that memories of what follows diverge from others: the inevitable *Rashomon* effect, but I remember my own participation thus: at some point I had an uncharacteristic brain wave (perhaps it was jet lag), and in a room at the Eon office on Piccadilly, with perhaps thirty people in attendance, seated in a large circle, I spieled my idea.

JEFF KLEEMAN

Nick, who is very fast, would go off and he would come back two days later with sections of the script that were so wholly different from anything we had been talking about or imagined, regardless of whether they were good or bad, that it pretty much caused everybody's head to explode.

NICHOLAS MEYER

In many ways, the *James Bond* films are as rigid in their format as an English sonnet. The prologue consists of an amazing stunt sequence, followed by dazzling credits and familiar music, followed by Bond in M's outer office, exchanging banter before receiving his assignment from M. This is followed by several action sequences, introduction of a femme fatale, exotic locations, etc., before Bond finally encounters Mr. Big in his lair, who explains, "No, Mr. Bond, it's not about money. It's about . . ." And here you may fill in the blank.

JEFF KLEEMAN

Nick is very good at defending his own work, and one of the reasons he's very good at defending his own work is he is very smart and he doesn't write anything without very strong reasons. Every word, he has a reason and thinking beyond.

NICHOLAS MEYER

Now imagine all this has taken place and Mr. Big goes on to explain that everything that has happened thus far, all the attempts to kill Bond, etc., were a test to see if Bond was really the right man for the job Mr. Big has in mind. "I think you will find," he goes on to say, "that fundamentally I'm a 'people person.'" Meaningful pause. "There's too many of them." Pause for gasp from the room. Mr. Big then turns on all the monitors in his lair, and each reveals a horrifying instance of overpopulation, from famine in Ethiopia to gridlock in LA. Mr. Big explains he's trying to address a planetary crisis no politician is even willing to *mention*. "Even lemmings know what to do when they grow too numerous, do they not, Mr. Bond? 007, that's some kind of license, isn't it? Tell me, Mr. Bond, how much game are you allowed to bag with that license? Will you help me, sir? Will you help me to save planet Earth?" Mr. Big goes on to explain, in my spiel, that he wants to shrink Earth's population by starting a war between India and China, the two most populous nations on the planet, and Bond agrees to do this.

JEFF KLEEMAN

There was, for those of us who attended it, an infamous, but also to me on a larger scale beyond Bond in terms of what I do in this industry, fascinating meeting where Nick had handed in pages in which all this stuff was going on. Barbara and Michael said, "Nick, this is not what we asked you to do. This is not what the scene was. This does not feel like who Bond should be in this movie. We don't understand why you're giving us these pages."

NICHOLAS MEYER

Needless to say, thirty folks in the room were riveted. I went on to explain, "Bond has finally found a foe worthy of his steel. Mr. Big is wrong, but *why* is he wrong? It's horrifying that we actually agree with Mr. Big. Every word he says. His logic is irrefutable, but when Bond says he'll use his license to kill to help we're horrified, but of course the smarter members of the audience will assure themselves that Bond will ultimately defeat Mr. Big and those suckered in will be pleasantly astonished by his volte-face." "There you have it," I concluded. "It's not been done before and it's simple." In my recollection, I later went back to the Dorchester, mightily pleased with myself, only to return the next day to find that my scenario was off the table. "It's too serious," Barbara Broccoli explained.

JEFF KLEEMAN

Nick said, "You've hired me because I have skill and I have a proven track record as a writer. That includes taking very well-known and beloved characters, whether it's Sherlock Holmes or *Star Trek,* and bringing them to an audience in ways that are exciting and fun, and great for the audience, and that ultimately gets cheers. You've hired me because I have that expertise. You want me to give you that expertise. So my job is not to be a stenographer and just give you back what you already want, because you don't need me to do that. My job is to give you what is best for you, whether you know it or not. Whether you'd be able to think of it or not, because that's why you hire me in the first place. That's why you pay me so much money in the first place."

NICHOLAS MEYER

That was my crash course in understanding how the *Bond* franchise worked. It was of crucial importance that nothing be real in the *Bond* stories; it was all about locations, action set pieces, and babes. How dense I had been *not* to perceive this! In my recollection, I made several other attempts to supply dialogue or scenes while I was in London, but all these were rejected and shortly thereafter I flew back to Los Angeles with my tail more or less between my legs.

JEFF KLEEMAN

I believe it was Barbara who essentially said to Nick something along the lines of, "Don't confuse being smart and talented with being a silkworm, in which everything that comes out of your ass is gold." That really was the end of Nick's involvement with *Tomorrow Never Dies*.

After Nick flamed out, Roger had worked with Daniel Petrie, Jr., in the past a lot, so he asked that Dan come in and do some writing on the script. Dan in some ways is the opposite of Nick. Dan was president of the WGA at the time, and Dan is a consummate diplomat. Amazing diplomat. So he navigated Roger and the Broccolis as well as anybody could at the time. He provided one thing. I would say 90 percent of the script is Bruce Feirstein, and wonderfully so, but Dan Petrie did provide one thing, which is just superb, and again it's one of the things that I think make *Tomorrow Never Dies* a special movie. That's the assassin played by Vincent Schiavelli. Yeah. That character, that whole scene, that is all Dan. I think it's lovely.

RAY MORTON

Pierce Brosnan still felt the piece was too disjointed and needed a lot of work. Bruce Feirstein was then brought back to pull the whole thing together in his final draft.

BRUCE FEIRSTEIN

At the time, I thought this was crazy, where I did the drafts, then they had this meeting. Then I got fired. Then they had other writers and they threw out their stuff. And then they came back to me, and at the time I thought that this was just insane. But what I came to realize is that, no, this is what was actually happening on every movie at that point. And in the press, it was written up as unusual and crazy, but in fact this was going on in big action movies then. They were throwing lots of writers at pictures. So, kind of like the way to describe this is that I rode the horse into town. I got knocked off the horse for a while. And then got back on the horse and rode it across and finished the race on it.

ROGER SPOTTISWOODE

At the very beginning of the process, the studio was—rightly so—very concerned, because the original script in October was centered around Hong Kong going back to China, and because they felt the film wasn't going to come out early enough; it might become terribly dated very quickly, so we had to really change it rather quickly and come up with a new storyline while keeping the same characters. It was a big, complicated thing to do and deliver it within a year.

PIERCE BROSNAN

The script went through a few changes. The studio wanted it as soon as they could get their hands on it, so we went out the door with a script which, under normal circumstances, should not have taken off. But having said that, sometimes when you're dealt that kind of pressure, people either rise or fall to the occasion and realize the script needs work. Scenes that may have been three pages long and full of extraneous dialogue became one and a half pages of very lean dialogue that had much more bite to them. And I was involved with more of it this time than I was on *GoldenEye*. I worked with the writer, the writer would visit, we would talk about what needed to be done. Roger was very open and sharing with the film that he had already shot, and was excited by it, and consequently generated a wonderful air of excitement about the film. A lot of people weren't quite sure what was going on, if the style or look of the film was going to work.

BRUCE FEIRSTEIN

So all the sleuthing about who did what and all that, there's not a lot of truth in any of it. It's all overblown. And when you look at the picture, you had a guy who worked in journalism, who had been on CNN, who also worked on *GoldenEye*. It's not as if it was some medical drama where somebody who had never had any dealings with medicine suddenly leaves, a whole bunch of other doctors come in, fix the script, and then you get credit for something you didn't know about. I mean, this was my world. So, was it difficult? Were there lots of grinding of gears? Absolutely. One of the things was that it had a very short production schedule; there were big deadline pressures on it. And 20 years later, I think that Roger Spottiswoode did a terrific job. Roger had this vision; he wanted to make a fast-paced *Bond* movie and deal with some current-day issues, because, don't forget, he had made *And the Band Played On*, and things like that. While he and I might not have agreed on small points here and there, overall we both wanted to do a movie about a media mogul.

ROGER SPOTTISWOODE

They wanted it not to be political and I didn't want to make a political film, because these films are entertainment. The finished film, which is hopefully entertaining and nothing more, is nonetheless much more contemporary than one would have expected, and was much more about current events because of events in the world leading up to it, most notably the death of Princess Diana and Dodi Fayed. And because it is a media mogul who feels if the news isn't there, you'd better do something about it, even if it means a certain amount of invention. He wants a Gulf War–like situation between England and China, or something like the Spanish-American War. Enough of an incident where he will get some things out of it and in the meantime, he will be particularly well placed to cover it. Ted Turner didn't start the Gulf War, but the Gulf War sure helped CNN. It had been there for five years, but nobody was watching. But it was made by the Gulf War. Our character is a man who is in need of a bit of a boost. It had enough connections and Jonathan Pryce played it with enjoyment.

PIERCE BROSNAN

Roger Spottiswoode works in his own wonderful fashion, and sometimes it's not clear to everybody what he is doing. But people had the confidence in seeing the footage to let him go with it. I kind of liked working like that as well. The schedule moved around constantly, which was a bit of a hardship on the heads of departments. It was hard work in that respect, trying to bring the story in, but ultimately we got a very streamlined story, a great baddie, and a very timely piece dealing with the media.

ROGER SPOTTISWOODE

It's an extension of reality, as all these films are, but because we had a more contemporary subject, it didn't feel as far-fetched. *GoldenEye* had a clever and simple plot about a brilliant man who perceived an easier way of achieving his end, and you sort of had fun with him. He was a smart, interesting villain, and I hope that's what we achieved without making a political drama at all.

Politics aside, there was real drama generated by reports of dissension on the set, crewmembers threatening to walk, Spottiswoode and

Feirstein no longer speaking, and so on. Based on the coverage during production, *Tomorrow Never Dies* was self-destructing and was promising to be a disaster. The irony of the coverage, given the film's subject matter of those in power trying to manipulate the news, was not lost on anyone.

MICHELLE YEOH

People who were not there will read what reporters have to say about it and think that that is what is happening, because that is the only way they can be in touch with what is happening on the set. It's unfortunate that so many negative things were coming out, which were so untrue. It's a very family-oriented thing, and when you are doing a movie, not everybody is going to agree with everybody else at the same time. And that's good, because it's healthy disagreements.

ROGER SPOTTISWOODE

Trust me, the irony was not lost on me. Of course I felt that. Invitations for journalists to come to the set before they wrote about it, or to ask other people to verify their story, including the people named, were met with, "We have our sources, we don't need to check anything." It was all hokum, although we did wrestle the script into existence. Obviously we had discussions and arguments at times about it, but everything was within the framework of what always goes on in the making of films. Thank God it does, because if it wasn't, you could be sitting on a terrible turkey. If you don't investigate, explore, tear it apart, rebuild it, and sort of punch it around until it's working, you're a lunatic. And these things are very hard to do, to get a modern, contemporary thriller where the people sound real and are real. It's a difficult animal to make work, but you can't make these films until you love your actors, and your actors love you, because you're asking them to do so much. If you don't get on, I wouldn't even know how to do it.

MICHAEL G. WILSON

I think the film sort of hooks into misgivings that people have about what was happening with the media and this concentration of media in the hands of a few. And the power it gives them. It hooked into the misgivings of the public and taking it into the fantasy world that Bond inhabits. It is based on reality. I think in the Cold War days you could base it on some vague fear people had of the uncertainties of the superpowers and their positioning and their political stability. The challenge with *Tomorrow Never Dies* was finding other areas where there's a certain discomfort and concern that the public may have that we could adapt into one of our stories.

Ultimately, the film is the story of media mogul Elliot Carver (*Miss Saigon*'s Jonathan Pryce) who is seeking to obtain the exclusive broadcasting rights in China for his Carver Media Network–an evil version of Ted Turner and a version of Rupert Murdoch with a little William Randolph Hearst thrown in for good measure.

In the film, Carver sends the British fleet off course by manipulating a GPS signal using a GPS encoder invented by a ham-fisted terrorist, played by the late Ricky Jay. Brosnan's Bond is on the case thanks to the fact he used to sleep with Carver's wife, Paris Carter, played by Teri Hatcher, who, at the time, was starring as Lois Lane in the TV series *Lois & Clark: The New Adventures of Superman.* Monica Bellucci (later to appear in *Spectre*) and Sela Ward both auditioned. Additionally, the presence of Hong Kong chopsocky star Michelle Yeoh as Colonel Wai Lin, an MSS spy, is a welcome reprieve from the *Bond* damsels in distress of yore. There's even a terrific nod to *The Defiant Ones* as she and Bond race through the streets of Vietnam on a motorcycle, handcuffed together, while being stalked by a helicopter pursuing them in the skies above. Jonathan Pryce is also terrific as the slimy and malevolent media mogul, although one can't help but wonder how the producers' original choice would have been–Anthony Hopkins, who turned down the role.

BRUCE FEIRSTEIN

The thing I do really like and am proud of about *Tomorrow Never Dies* is that Elliot Carver is a very much of the moment villain who is *not* out of the history of *Bond.* If the character is based on anyone, it's Robert Maxwell, but it's definitely *not* Rupert Murdoch. Elliot Carver is a man who can influence world events. I think where this came from was that while we were working on *GoldenEye,* right before it came out during that summer, I was in London doing some final lines. The thing was, I was watching a CNN report on Bosnia or something and was thinking, "God, this is really even better than what Charles Foster Kane said in *Citizen Kane,* 'Send me the pictures, I'll provide the war.'" Somebody can do that much quicker and faster now than anyone else before, so that was kind of where the idea came from. You don't know whether anything you watch on TV is true at all; it's just manipulation of the media. I take pictures in, let's say for lack of a better example, Jerusalem, and I only decide to show one side of it. Who knows what's true? In *Tomorrow Never Dies,* his plan involves creating a worldwide crisis in order to up his media ratings. He instigates an international incident between England—which is why Bond is in the movie—and China.

JONATHAN PRYCE
(actor, "Elliot Carver")

The character is based on some kind of truth, not any particular media mogul but someone with that kind of power that is being explored by him. A lot of research was done by Bruce Feirstein. I have met with people who wield enormous power, and that goes into the research. Nothing specific, other than what we see around us all the time. That's the beauty of the character; he's *so* recognizable.

BRUCE FEIRSTEIN

There's a very funny wink at the end. M is with Moneypenny and they're putting out a press release. M says something to the effect that Elliot Carver died going overboard on his yacht, or something like that, in the Mediterranean. That's *exactly* how Robert Maxwell died. I always wondered if anybody would pick up on it.

PIERCE BROSNAN

In a *Bond* movie, to have someone as flamboyant and charismatic as Jonathan Pryce playing this Ted Turner/Rupert Murdoch type character to create World War III is a hoot. Also quite real. His personal agenda is he wants to get rich, he wants to rule his own empire, and ultimately, of course, the world. He is enamored with power, but in a very doable fashion. It also answered the question that was being asked time and time again: with the Cold War over, what is James Bond going to do? Well, Bond is still relevant in world events, as it were. He's still viable as an action hero and it felt good working on such a story surrounding the media.

JONATHAN PRYCE

Elliot Carver points out the danger of putting the power in one man's hands. And he has fun as well. It's not one long political tract; ultimately he *is* a *Bond* villain who does dastardly things and who doesn't kill Bond as quickly as he should. He's not really that efficient.

BRUCE FEIRSTEIN

Elliot Carver is a wannabe megalomaniac and he is larger than life, gregarious, a media mogul who was born in Hong Kong, the illegitimate son of an English person in Hong Kong and very much resents the British turning Hong Kong back over. His signals, not unlike a lot of media moguls' signals, have been blocked from going into China and he kind of sees this as a two-for-one shot. He gets back at England for handing Hong Kong back over, and he gets back at China for not letting his signals in.

JEFF KLEEMAN

Until the writers' room, the female lead was an American woman. It was during the writers' room that we changed her to Asian and created that role, which ultimately Michelle Yeoh was going to inhabit. We talked about Michelle for that role in the room. I already knew Michelle and had always wanted to do something with her, so once the role became Asian, I brought up Michelle and there was talk, then we went and looked at clips of Michelle and we got excited about her. I'd actually been introduced to Hong Kong movies and Michelle Yeoh by David Byrne of the Talking Heads, who was a Jackie Chan fanatic and took me to the Nuart [art house theater in Los Angeles] to see a Jackie Chan film festival. *Police Story 3* was playing, with Michelle Yeoh jumping the train with a motorcycle. It was, like, "Wow, who *is* she? She's amazing." And Michelle has the first full action sequences—really standalone action sequences—of any female hero in a *Bond* movie, and she's got two of them that are wonderful. Robert Elswit and Roger brought a look to the *Bond* movie that was in keeping with *Bond,* but added some contemporary elements like the smoke we'd talked about.

BRUCE FEIRSTEIN

Moving along from the track in *GoldenEye,* instead of the typical bad girl villainess, the person Bond chooses to work with is a Chinese secret agent who is every bit his equal. We took the idea of Bond in the '90s and expanded on it. It's not what you would often see in these movies, and you saw in *GoldenEye* where you take the beautiful girl and make her a computer programmer. In this film we had a smart, intelligent, feisty, capable Chinese secret agent, played by Michelle Yeoh, who teams up with Bond. It was one more way of continuing along the path of Bond facing the new world. Well, in the new world it's a media villain who's the madman, and Bond has to team up with a woman who is every bit as capable as he is.

MICHELLE YEOH

I describe Wai Lin as Bond's female counterpart. At the beginning, both of us are, like, "No, *you* better leave; I can handle this on my own." But out of respect for each other, because we recognize a lot of things that are very similar in terms of character and the way we work and handle people, we work together. The time was right for that. She holds her own and doesn't take any shit from anyone—especially not from Bond. Actually, the role was very similar to a lot of the roles that I've played before in Hong Kong. I always played the very strong female roles, but to do so in a *Bond* movie was a different thing. It was like a recognition on the part of not just the producers, but the audience, that women empowered Bond. That's was a very big step.

LISA FUNNELL

(author, *For His Eyes Only: The Women of James Bond*)

The women in the Brosnan era are a lot more, I would say, physically empowered. I love Michelle Yeoh. You watch her as Wai Lin and she kills it on screen. She is, in my opinion, a superior agent to James Bond. She has her own spy gadgets, and that's probably the reason why she only appears for about half the film, because if she appeared for the whole thing, it wouldn't be a *James Bond* film. It would be a Wai Lin film, because she's that awesome, right?

MICHAEL G. WILSON

In my mind, using Michelle was never a risk. In the mind of some of the people on the film and some of the people who had to market the picture, the question was, it would help us in the Far East, but she was kind of unknown in the West. But in the end I think her performance was so endearing to the public.

ROGER SPOTTISWOODE

Pierce had a tremendous costar in the film in the form of Michelle Yeoh and they worked terribly well together. They're kind of equal partners in the second half, so that gives him other areas to go in. It wasn't more of the more conventional *Bond* women who kill you with their thighs or bury you in their cleavage.

LISA FUNNELL

The two of them were able to really operate side by side as counterparts in separate ways, and I wish that was true with the ending of *Tomorrow Never Dies*. I felt there was no romantic connection between her and Bond, and that that was just thrown in at the end with the two of them kissing.

JEFF KLEEMAN

Pierce has elegance, he has wit, he has strength, he can be scary, you only need to look at *Long Good Friday* to know he can be tough, he can be scary. He seemed to us sort of like a wonderful amalgamation of Sean and Roger. What Pierce was yearning for, and we were acknowledging as well, was to add another emotional layer to Bond. To move toward those moments where it may not be what the movie is fully about, but you feel that there are some things beyond country and mission and vengeance that Bond cares about, that touch him deeply. And Pierce can play that really well. So with *Tomorrow Never Dies,* the creation of Teri Hatcher's character was a move toward that; a move toward saying, can we get away with giving Bond some backstory and some emotion here?

TERI HATCHER
(actress, "Paris Carver")

Paris and Bond have a relationship in the past, before this movie starts. It was meaningful and emotional, which I think is different from relationships he's had before in other movies. But she and Bond couldn't go the distance, because of his job.

PIERCE BROSNAN

In regards to Paris Carver, I'd asked at the beginning that if he was going to get involved with someone, that it would be someone who was meaningful to the man and not some woman he picks up at the beginning of the story that he doesn't know. Someone from his past. So they took that and used that, and it came in the package of Teri Hatcher. She is a woman that he really loved, but she just got too close and he left. He bailed out. Now he meets her in this story and she's married to Elliot Carver, but Bond still has something for her and her for him. We went to a place that I don't know if Connery ever went to, because Sean did it his way and I did it mine. Just two completely different men with different styles of Bond. There's an emotional chord there that has a certain resonance throughout the piece, which is good. I'm glad they put it in.

TERI HATCHER

Being married to Elliot Carver, she's settled for a safe life, so she's a little disappointed in herself. I think she's a really strong, smart woman, but her life has sort of gotten away from her a little bit and isn't what she would have wanted. But because of the character's background, I think she adds a little emotional weight to the Bond character as well. The part is fairly small, but I'm fine with that. It really consisted of two or three pivotal scenes that are significant toward moving the plot along, and those were a lot of fun to play, because of who the actors are in the scene with me.

JEFF KLEEMAN

It was probably the first move in the contemporary *Bond* era toward what Daniel Craig movies have become, without completely capsizing the story. It didn't fully manifest in *Tomorrow Never Dies,* because Pierce and Teri got off on the wrong foot. On the very first day they were shooting together, there was a major misunderstanding between them, and it affected the entire rest of the shoot between them. It was a misunderstanding that, when the smoke eventually cleared, I think they both felt very badly about, because, truly, each fully misinterpreted what was going on with the other.

TERI HATCHER

When the producers asked me if I would be interested in doing this part, it was perfect, because I was pregnant and only wanted to work for a few weeks. It just seemed like it was meant to be, in the sense that it was a fun part, it was a fun movie, I was excited to be in it, and the timing worked out for me physically.

JEFF KLEEMAN

Barbara and Michael and I were actually in the horrible position of seeing it unfold and knowing the truth. But because of certain personal confidentiality issues for both actors, we couldn't go to the other actor and say, "Look, this is what's really going on." And it was very, very frustrating. I am a believer, as much as I deeply care about every movie I work on, that you have to put the people first. No movie is really worth doing something that is devastatingly hurtful to another human being. So, we were not going to try to go against someone's wishes about their personal life with someone they had themselves not made the choice to share it with. But at the same time, it created a huge cloud over all of their scenes. And while I believe, in another world, if the timing had been different or the personal issues hadn't been there, they would have been beautiful together, just phenomenal together, we never hit that emotional layer we wanted to, because they were getting increasingly angry and frustrated and confused by each other.

TERI HATCHER

My husband had said to me, "You have to do the movie, because I have to live out my fantasy of being married to a *Bond* Girl." Well, I guess that was the least I could do for him. Now when I'm 80, I can be a grandmother saying, "I remember when I was a *Bond* Girl. . . ."

Perhaps the film's most successful new addition to the *Bond* family was the arrival of composer David Arnold, who John Barry had recommended after hearing his re-orchestrations of classic *Bond* songs and themes for *Shaken and Stirred: The David Arnold James Bond Project*, a CD of *Bond* cover songs. Arnold not only pays homage to John Barry throughout, but forges his own musical identity that honors the franchise and almost makes one forget about the musical missteps of the previous film . . . almost. Sadly, k.d. lang's terrific song, "Surrender," was moved to the closing credits when the studio requested a more prominent artist sing the main title, hence Sheryl Crow's "Tomorrow Never Dies."

JEFF BOND
(editor, *Film Score Monthly*)

I think with David Arnold the *Bond* producers recognized that they needed to acknowledge the classic *Bond* sound, yet somehow move forward without John Barry. And David Arnold has to be the greatest success story in attempting to do that. Arnold came out of big action movies like *Independence Day*, so he knew how to write on a big, bold canvas, which is something I think some of the other non-Barry *Bond* composers weren't always great at. Arnold also made a very astute study of John Barry and he knew how to bring the flavor of the Barry scores to the series while still doing his own thing. If there's a downside to Arnold, it's that his action music can be frenetic, which is in keeping with the style of modern composers like Michael Kamen. With Barry, the action music always seemed to be about how graceful and unflappable 007 seemed under fire, whereas if you're writing in the late '90s/early 2000s action style, it's so hyper you get the feeling that everyone is panicking, even Bond. For me the pinnacle of Arnold's work was *Casino Royale*, where he introduced a powerful new theme for Daniel Craig's Bond that fits in perfectly with Barry's approach and also superbly characterizes Craig's tougher 007—and he's also able to reflect Barry with his very silky, romantic approach to the Vesper Lynd scenes.

Returning to handle the titles was Daniel Kleinman, who admits that the second time around wasn't as enjoyable as the first, much of it having to do with his collaboration—or lack thereof—with director Spottiswoode.

DANIEL KLEINMAN
(title designer)

This was a tricky one. It was also coming after *GoldenEye* and felt like the second guard. What I wanted to do was create an idea of digital overload, where you've just got all this stuff coming at you. It was the beginning of people's appreciation of the internet, and understanding about what digital information is going to be, and manipulating the news, and all that sort of thing. So I tried to make it sort of become pretty busy, intense.

And Roger, he's not a very nice man. He didn't have any ideas of his own; he only ever really said he didn't like anything. But he never really said what he did like or offer anything alternative, so we didn't get on all that well. Directing is all about communication and everybody being on the same page, and being motivated, and being creative together, and all that sort of thing, but unfortunately those are not streams in Roger's oeuvre. Anyway, he does what he does, but it wasn't a great film, and I don't think it was one of my best title sequences, because it was created with not an enormously fantastic atmosphere.

Overall, production on *Tomorrow Never Dies* was *not* easy, but despite the difficult shoot, there were moments of fun to be had behind the scenes—though perhaps not everyone would recognize them as such.

JEFF KLEEMAN

I was always so impressed by the way I would sometimes know that Barbara vehemently disagreed about something, or Michael vehemently disagreed about something, but when John Calley would call up and ask them, they would just both defend whatever had been agreed on, as though they were both equally passionate about it. And Bruce was great with this kind of debate. So was Martin. Roger was not. Roger had an uncanny ability to suss out what it was that would most upset somebody on the deepest, emotional, psychological level, and then say or do it. And at one point he did this with Barbara. And I took him aside that evening after the shoot, and I said, "Roger, you can say anything you want to Barbara, but you cannot say *that*. Not only is it not true, but there's no good that comes from it." And he said, "I know, I just can't help myself. It's like the scorpion and the frog."

And what would happen is two things. In the debates and the arguments, Roger would pull his secret weapon out. He would say something that would just cause people to go nuclear. It took him three weeks until the end of production to find my trigger. But he found it. Barbara and Michael, Bruce, and Roger and myself are sitting around a table, because we're still working on the final three weeks of the script. It was a script that was really written as we were shooting. Roger says, "I've come to the conclusion that we need to stop production, that we can't finish the movie yet. We need to wait. We need to postpone the release date." At which point I am told by witnesses that there was a little red spot that started right here, below my ear, and just started to creep up over my face until my entire face became red. And I then, in no uncertain terms, said there is no way production is stopping on this movie. You know, *you* may not be finishing production, but *somebody* is going to finish production on schedule, it will be released when it needs to be released. And afterward, after Roger left the room, Barbara, Michael, and Bruce were just laughing like crazy about this. And I said, "Guys, why didn't any of you say anything? Why did you just wait and let me do that?" And I can't remember if it was Barbara or Michael, but one of them looked at me and said, "Because we just wanted to see what you were going to do. It's so much fun!"

And Roger knew what the answer was. He knew we weren't stopping production, but he had just figured out the way to stir me. And so a lot of difficulty . . . Well, the difficulties with Roger came from the fact that the Broccolis had a way of debating and then unifying that Roger, for whatever reasons, didn't sync up with. He couldn't argue with them in a way that at 5:00 every afternoon we could all be friends again and agree on having a united front, which led to, at one point, him actually shooting a sequence without telling them. Just went behind their back. We had wrapped for the day, and then he secretly gathered some crew and the actors and shot it, and nobody knew the sequence existed until we suddenly saw it in a cut in post-production.

It did make the movie. And look, much like the Nick Meyer conversation, it leads to an interesting debate. Which is, you're a director. You're making a movie. There is something you believe is genuinely good and important. There is something the producers do not want to do. They have told you not to do it. You can pull it off without affecting the budget or the schedule, but you know you aren't going to be allowed to do it, but you do, genuinely believing in the end it will be useful. Do you lie, and do it for the good of the movie, figuring you are not harming anybody in the process of doing it? But in a way, you *are* breaking a covenant with the producers, you're going behind their back. You're asking other people to break their covenant with them. Or do you go along, thinking that the movie is not going to be as good as it could have been? I get that internal conflict, and in some ways I can argue both sides of it, but that isn't the way it works best with *Bond* movies and with Barbara and Michael.

And there was also the fact that Jonathan Pryce liked to stir people up. Something that Martin Campbell started, which was great, was on *GoldenEye*; a few weeks into the movie, he decided to have the editors cut together some of the footage that had been shot, and he showed it to cast and crew and everybody got excited.

When the same thing was done on *Tomorrow Never* Dies, it became apparent that Roger Spotiswoode might not be able to take as good as he gave.

JEFF KLEEMAN

Our shoot was over 100 days long, and we were initially shooting six to eight weeks on *GoldenEye*. So that kind of morale booster was huge, because all these people did not know what a *James Bond* movie was going to be these days. Roger did the same thing with *Tomorrow Never Dies,* and the day he had the footage to show everybody was the day Jonathan Pryce arrived. So, Michelle and Pierce are going into Pierce's trailer to watch the footage, and Jonathan shows up and they say, "Jonathan, Jonathan, come along! We're about to see some footage!" So Jonathan comes along, and they watch the footage, which was great, spectacular. And Michelle and Pierce are so happy, and Jonathan is just silent. And finally Pierce turned to him, and says, "Jonathan, what did you think?" And Jonathan says, "I didn't realize you were going to play it like *that,*" and walks out of the trailer. And he was just stirring things up. But he would do it to everybody, including Roger.

So we're on the stealth boat, and it's a scene between Jonathan and Michelle Yeoh on this stealth boat, and Jonathan walks into the scene in his full suit, but barefoot. And Roger says, "Jonathan, don't you think you should put some shoes on?" And Jonathan says, "Why? My feet aren't going to be in the shot are they?" And Roger says, "No, your feet aren't going to be in the shot, but, you know, you're doing a scene with another actor, and it might help for the authenticity, and the reality, and the feeling of the scene and performance if you were actually fully dressed like you were in the scene." And Jonathan looks at Roger and says, "Oh, you're confusing me with an actor who gives a shit." And again, Jonathan actually *did* care, but he just knew that this was the way to get

Roger. And he did it with *everybody.* Jonathan did it to amuse himself. Roger did it because he couldn't help himself. It was a volatile situation, but it's a better movie because they're both in it. Jonathan Pryce is a great *Bond* villain and Roger really brought things as a director that were fantastic, ranging from sequences to performances. He did some improv stuff with Pierce and Michelle which led to amazing chemistry between the two of them.

BRUCE FEIRSTEIN

There was an instance where Michael Wilson and I are in Thailand, in Bangkok. Michael was staying in this suite at the top of the Shangri La Hotel, which is endless. It's got like four hundred bedrooms, a kitchen, and all this. We'd just had a really tough day shooting; it's been 105 degrees. So Michael invites me up to the suite for a drink. It's around 5:30 or 6:00 in the afternoon and we're on the 40th floor of this hotel, standing on a balcony, and it's kind of like a moment of silence. Jane Wilson, Michael's wife, is also there. Suddenly a breeze comes up the building and we look off and there are two helicopters chasing each other up the river. We watch them go off and turn in the distance, and there's an explosion. You see some smoke come up somewhere in the distance, and I turned to Michael and said, "Are those ours?" Without missing a beat, Michael takes a sip of his drink and says, "I hope so" . . . Honestly, I just have huge affection for him. I watch Michael and Jane bring up their kids, and I always think that he was the father I'd like to be. I can't pay a man a higher compliment than that.

Tomorrow Never Dies was, indeed, polarizing to *James Bond* fans, but the truth is, it grossed only about $20 million less than *GoldenEye* at the global box office; it was once again proof that 007 was here to stay, the franchise's viability in the 1990s no longer in question.

GLEN OLIVER

Tomorrow Never Dies is underappreciated. Spottiswoode brought tremendous "oomph" to his direction—this was a *Bond* for the *Die Hard* generation, and its gusto somehow conveyed more truthfully than the franchise had felt for some time.

JEFF KLEEMAN

One of the things we could have done better with *Tomorrow Never Dies* is not have such a lengthy stealth boat finale. We spend far too much time on that stealth boat at the end, but that is really a factor of, we have built the stealth boat sets and we didn't have a script. We were getting closer and closer to the end of production, so we just put a lot more script on the stealth boat, because we had those sets built and accessible to us. If we didn't have a hard release date, we wouldn't have had to do that. But on the business side, because it is this dance between art and commerce, on the business side we had an unavoidably hard release date, and so we had to make adjustments.

GLEN OLIVER

Brosnan's Bond tended to have a bit more "action hero" bravado than the other Bonds, which worked incredibly well on the whole—largely because this bravado portrayed Bond's unwavering determination. This is pointedly evidenced in this picture. "We're trapped," fears Michelle Yeoh's Wai Lin. "Never," says Bond with icy conviction. In many ways, this exchange sums up the Bond character in two lines. It's a great insight into 007, and one of my favorite "in your face" moments of the franchise.

RIC MEYERS

Wai Lin's fighting shows little of the fluidity and skill of Michelle Yeoh's other work—retreating instead to standard stiff, muscle and anger-driven punches and kicks with many an exaggerated "hi-ya!" And the opportunity for Wai Lin and Bond to teach each other a thing or two is completely wasted—the film even going so far as to have the villain mock Lin's skills without giving her the chance to correct the error of his attitude. Instead, by the finale, Brosnan's Bond is in full roundhouse punch mode, and the climax reduces Wai Lin to Paris Carver–level damsel-in-distress helplessness. Well, at least Yeoh got the reward of being the first Asian actress to be a full partner in all the subsequent promotion of the film in cinemas and on Madison Avenue.

JOHN CORK

For years I've quoted Carver's line—written by Bruce Feirstein—"The distance between insanity and genius is measured only by success." It is, to me, the best line of dialogue in a *Bond* movie. The last act is somewhat of a mess, but the first two-thirds works like gangbusters.

MICHELLE YEOH

The *Bond* movies are such a legacy, so working on a film like *Tomorrow Never Dies* you're working with a lot of history, you're working with a family, with people who have dedicated a lot of years of their lives to it. There's such pride in making the movie; everyone involved was so dedicated and I had a lot of fun. For me, at the end of the day you have to enjoy what you're doing or else it's a struggle. But having done it, you're a part of history. You're immortalized. What's better than that?

RAY MORTON

The result of the rather chaotic and time-pressured writing process on *Tomorrow Never Dies* is a loose remake of *The Spy Who Loved Me,* in which Bond teams up with a female agent from an enemy power to stop a madman from unleashing World War III. The villain of the story—the megalomaniacal media baron Elliot Carver—is solid and his scheme is both timely and satirical. Wai Lin is an appealing female lead. The narrative structure is strong, although the plotline sometimes gets a little lost amid an excessive number of action set pieces. The script plays with an interesting notion—what becomes of the *Bond* Girls after their movies are over? Not much is done with this idea, although Paris' murder does provide Bond with a nice emotional stake in the story. The action is imaginative, the pacing is brisk, and there's a light-on-its-feet quality to the piece that makes this the most purely entertaining *Bond* screenplay in quite a stretch.

ROGER SPOTTISWOODE

One concern I had at the beginning is that one doesn't want a string of meaningless stunts that don't really connect. I think action like that is completely pointless and it doesn't even work; nobody quite enjoys it. You have to be invested, you have to go for the ride, you have to be involved with the characters, it has to work in that way. Otherwise it's a meaningless gun-fest, shooting-fest, murder-fest or body count–fest, or whatever the current vogue is in town. Now if one succeeded in that goal, other people will tell you. I can only tell you what I *wanted* to do. Those are one's concerns going into it, not to make a meaningless fantasy of endless action and silly women running around and gadgets bumping in for no reason. If it doesn't all work together, it isn't a movie.

What you have to do is make a really good entertaining movie—that's at least what I tried to do—that connects, has characters and a story that you're interested in that allows you to go for a tremendous ride, and afterward you think, "Yeah, all those things I used to like about them were there, but they weren't added on as bells and whistles. They were integral." Who knows if we did it?

THE WORLD IS NOT ENOUGH (1999)

Unlike a fine wine, *The World Is Not Enough*–the final *James Bond* film of the 20th Century–does not age well. Stepping in as director is Michael Apted, who incongruously helmed such films as *Gorillas in the Mist* and the legendary *Up* documentary series, which chronicles the lives of several British kids every seven years into adulthood. The 1999 007 film has the unlikely origin of having been inspired by a TV documentary on oil drilling in the former Soviet Union in Azerbaijan, which was seen by Barbara Broccoli.

Ultimately, the film written by the team of Neal Purvis and Robert Wade, and a returning Bruce Feirstein, is a pastiche of several ideas, including the assassination at MI6 of an old college friend of M's, Sir Robert King; a Patty Hearst-like kidnapping story, and Istanbul being menaced by an impending nuclear meltdown to drive up petroleum prices worldwide. Purvis and Wade would become the twenty-first century Richard Maibaum, subsequently working on virtually all the *Bond* films thereafter after having impressed Barbara Broccoli and Michael Wilson with their work on *Plunkett & Macleane*. They would leverage their success with the *Bond* films into several other series, including *Johnny English* and writing the aborted *Bond* spin-off *Jinx* after *Die Another Day* was a financial hit.

JEFF KLEEMAN

(executive vice president of production, MGM/UA)

Post–*Tomorrow Never Dies,* we talked about doing a prequel that was just about the Vincent Schiavelli character, Dr. Kaufman, before he meets his demise with Bond. The other was a Michelle Yeoh spinoff. They didn't happen for a combination of two factors. One is we were diving into *The World Is Not Enough*, because MGM/UA was obsessed that we get another *Bond* movie out in 1999, so the amount of head space any of us had to pursue two other movies simultaneously was slim. I was already pursuing *Thomas Crown Affair* in that interim. Then the other was the sale happened. MGM/UA was sold and that took up a lot of time and space.

As was the case with *Tomorrow Never Dies,* they began seeking out a director immediately. Before Apted was signed, one person given serious consideration was *Harry Potter and the Prisoner of Azkaban*'s Alfonso Cuarón.

JEFF KLEEMAN

I will say, somewhere enough of the auteur reasoning did seep in to the point that when we got to *World Is Not Enough*, we took a run at Alfonso Cuarón. We got into very serious discussions with Alfonso about it and thought we were actually going to do it with him. Then Alfonso decided he wanted to do *Speed Racer*. Then, of course, he didn't end up doing *Speed Racer*, but we moved on at that point. So there were a couple months of, "We're going to make a *Bond* movie with Alfonso Cuarón," which I still wish I could see how that movie would have turned out. But things worked well with Michael Apted.

MICHAEL APTED

(director, *The World Is Not Enough*)

I suspect the whole idea of my doing this is something that my agent thought of. I mean, I suddenly got a call from them asking if I would be interested in doing the next *Bond*. I don't know if they suggested this to the Broccolis or if the Broccolis had suggested it to them, but I had to go through a whole audition process. I had about five different meetings with the Broccolis, some at the studio, and at different levels with the studio people. I mean, they were seeing other people at the time, and it took about three or four weeks before I got the job. But I have to admit that I was surprised when I was offered the job, as *Bond* had been very much the province of action directors. I thought it was a joke when I first got the call, and I was thrilled when it wasn't.

MICHAEL G. WILSON

Michael Apted is a dramatic director who focuses on the characters, and he's a good filmmaker. So were Roger Spottiswoode and Martin Campbell, but he brings something special to it. He gets a lot out of the actors, and I trust him. They work *for* him.

DENISE RICHARDS

(actress, "Dr. Christmas Jones")

When I thought to myself, "I have to do *Bond*, because it's a huge movie," it was more about the opportunity for me to work with Michael Apted, who I think is a great director; an actor's director. He brings a nice element to *Bond*, because of the films he has done. He hadn't done an action movie, which I think is great, because he brought that other element to it. And also to work with Pierce, and to be in a cast like that was just a great opportunity.

MICHAEL APTED

I wanted the job once I thought about what I could bring to it, which *wasn't* 120 minutes of wall-to-wall pounding action—which I had gotten the feeling talking to them that they *didn't* want. They wanted something more than that. They felt they wanted something with maybe more emphasis on story and character. And, of course, in this particular story there was a woman right in the middle of it, and I've done a lot of work with women, so I imagine those were the elements they wanted in it. On top of that, I thought I could learn a whole shitload more stuff. I'd never done big action. I've done action, but never of this scale, and I thought I could learn a whole lot more about computer work, about running a film, and I also thought this could do my career good. I could have a blockbuster under my belt, which would make life a bit easier for all the things I wanted to do. I could see it could be mutually to our advantage.

JEFF KLEEMAN

Michael Apted was, in some ways, you could say, a choice toward the lines of, let's keep deepening the *Bond* characters and the emotions and the thoughts here. He was, of course, British and Commonwealth, which is good for the cultural aspect of *Bond*. He was a grown-up in terms of there was not a logistical situation you could throw at Michael that would faze him. And particularly on the tight schedule, as we learned with *Tomorrow Never Dies*, we would be faced with lots of logistical issues.

MICHAEL APTED

It turned out to be very intimidating in the beginning, because there was so much of it—especially in the preparation. You prepare the film for four or five months, and you're being asked to make decisions in November about stuff you won't shoot until June. There was a time in pre-production where I thought, "How will I ever get through it?" Because there's huge crews and everyone wants decisions all the time, but it was just a question of once we started shooting, things fell into place and all of that sorted itself out.

JEFF KLEEMAN

By this point, with the two Pierce *Bond* movies that preceded, we had developed a very strong second unit and effects unit and action unit. So while both Martin and Roger were obsessed with guiding second unit, it used to be a joke that if the second-unit director backed up five feet, they'd bump into Roger.

And it was essentially true, and it was just as true for Martin. They somehow found a way to always show up at second unit, regardless. There was also the belief that after two movies, our second-unit group could compensate for whatever lack of action experience Apted had, because now we had a group that had been working together on two movies, and very well. Michael was probably the closest thing to a throwback to the original *Bond* directors, in that sense.

MICHAEL APTED

When I went in on it, I thought, "God, this will be a can of worms here; there are eighteen films before this; there's going to be tons of baggage." But that absolutely wasn't true. It was a very congenial atmosphere; the Broccolis run a very congenial ship, there are lots of generations of people there, the stunt men, the special effects guy, his dad did it and his brother did it. . . . So it was a very congenial atmosphere. On top of that, Pierce Brosnan was very supportive and collaborative, and the cast was good. So while I didn't really know what I was getting into, to be honest, it turned out alright.

At the outset the decision was made to make the villain of the piece—the true villain, unlike the suggestion of villainy that surrounded Maud Adams' title role in *Octopussy*—a female, in the form of the unhinged Elektra King, ultimately to be played by Sophie Marceau.

BRUCE FEIRSTEIN
(screenwriter, *The World Is Not Enough*)

Pierce wanted a more serious movie and more depth to the Bond character. Purvis and Wade provided the launching point for a character with Elektra King, who was age appropriate, and who was damaged, and who was *not* a character seen before in the *Bond* canon.

JEFF KLEEMAN

The thing we started with that we were really intrigued by, was what if we could have a strong female villain. We were always looking for what we could do that wouldn't break the *Bond* universe, but pushes the series into a new direction in one way or another.

BRUCE FEIRSTEIN

Elektra wasn't a character sitting there saying, "Oh, James." She was a very tough, smart, damaged woman and the kind of character that Pierce wanted, so you had an opportunity to, as he so often said, peel back the layers of the onion.

JEFF KLEEMAN

You want to either do something we haven't done before or do something we haven't done for a really long time. And again, without necessarily screwing with who Bond is as a character, looking at ways to give more contemporary values to the world, and to what Bond is wrestling with. To never just make it feel like, "Oh, you're seeing a pure throwback to the '60s." So we loved the idea of having a female villain.

MICHAEL APTED

Every film is a worry, and with so much in the way of expectations riding on a new *James Bond* film, there was so much more to worry about. I didn't want to repeat what others had done; I wanted to deliver the goods while at the same time making it a little bit different. There was a lot of anxiety attached to that.

JEFF KLEEMAN

And, we also—I can't remember why this was, except maybe it had just recently opened and we were enthralled with the architecture—we're obsessed with having a sequence in Bilbao. With the Guggenheim. We were obsessed with that. The other thing that was really interesting, and I can't remember whether it was Barbara or Michael, but I kind of think it might have been Barbara who hit upon it, was Baku, and that there was this region that none of us had ever heard of, and did not seem to be particularly in the news, but was so vital in terms of the world oil supply. And in many ways created such an interesting international situation. On top of that, we were so enthralled with Judi Dench and wondered if we could we give her a bigger role to play. Could we do more with Judi Dench as opposed to having her just say, "Hey, here's your mission, Bond," and maybe check in with him once or twice? And of course, that idea of, can we make things a little more emotional since we have Pierce, you see playing out with the relationship with Sophie Marceau and Judi Dench in *World Is Not Enough* as well. So you can see there are certain ideas that start to become fleshed out there, that don't necessarily manifest very well, but that we're starting to play with and experiment with, and that are on our minds going into *World Is Not Enough*.

RAY MORTON
(senior writer, *Script* magazine)
Neil Purvis and Robert Wade first showed up with *The World Is Not Enough.* They've devised the plots of every *Bond* film from *The World Is Not Enough* to *Skyfall*, although, with the exception of *Die Another Day,* the final draft of their pictures have usually been done by others. The results have been mixed. The one script they have sole credit for, *Die Another Day,* is terrible. *The World Is Not Enough* and *Quantum of Solace* are both middling, but *Skyfall* is pretty darn good, and *Casino Royale* is terrific.

BRUCE FEIRSTEIN
I think when the ultimate history of *Bond* is written, you're going to look back and say the most influential writers on *Bond* were Maibaum and Neil and Rob. And Neil and Rob deserve a tremendous amount of credit for carrying it forward for all those years. When people ask why I wasn't brought back, well, actually they found guys who lived in England, who truly understand the series, the franchise, and worked on it consistently to bring it forward, including writing the largest grossing *Bond* movie in history.

JEFF KLEEMAN
They ultimately became in-house guys for Barbara and Michael. They became the sort of trend with the *Bond* movies, where they would write a couple of drafts, and then Bruce would come in and polish them up. And I think in a way, they had this thing with Barbara and Michael where Barbara and Michael would really enjoy the brainstorming process with them. And they were very, very easy to work with, and so they felt like they could turn out a sort of basic draft pretty fast with them, but their drafts never fully delivered what we needed delivered, at which point you bring in Bruce, who can always deliver what we need to deliver on the *Bond* movies.

BRUCE FEIRSTEIN
In the case of *The World Is Not Enough*, the film was about to go into production and Barbara and Michael called and asked me to come back, look at the characters, and straighten out some story problems. I went to work with Michael Apted, who was great and wonderful, and spent three or four months working on it. I worked on Pierce's character, on the Elektra King character and the actual mechanics of what happened. But Purvis and Wade basically got the movie up, and then it was just coming in and fixing this, that, and the next thing.

RAY MORTION

They left the series after *Skyfall,* but were then called back to rewrite John Logan's first drafts of *Spectre,* and so must share the blame for that mess of a screenplay. Purvis and Wade remained on board to write the script for *Bond 25,* but their work was put aside when John Hodge was hired to write the script for an alternate *Bond 25* based on an idea by director Boyle. Then Boyle left and attention was turned back to the Purvis and Wade script.

BRUCE FEIRSTEIN

This is a note about screenwriting in general: if your name is in the credits, you contributed significantly. So on *The World Is Not Enough*, if you were thinking that they built it, I came in and I fixed some things and changed some things, and at that point it was clear that I had contributed significantly to what you see on the screen, that doesn't take anything away from them. So when you hear that, for example, Paul Haggis wrote this or John Logan wrote that, that may be true, but the *other* truth of it is that the underlying structure and the basic idea and all of that, and the movie, comes from them. So Purvis and Wade have had an extraordinary impact and influence on the series.

JEFF KLEEMAN

Purvis and Wade would make the Broccolis feel really comfortable, and Bruce made them feel comfortable, too. I mean, Bruce was Barbara's original guy. Bruce really had a way of navigating directors, hearing them, executing what they needed while keeping Bond, Bond, and bringing the script up to the level it needs to be at.

RAY MORTON

Dana Stevens did several rewrites on *The World Is Not Enough,* primarily to develop the character of Elektra King and her relationship with M. So Stevens can be credited for playing a key role in bringing the first female main villain in a *James Bond* movie to the screen.

Elektra King was played by French actress, director, screenwriter, and author Sophie Marceau, whose previous acting credits include *Revenge of the Musketeers, Braveheart, Beyond the Clouds, Anna Karenina, Lost & Found,* and *A Midsummer Night's Dream.*

MICHAEL APTED

One of our issues was how can we make the film more interesting about women and more interesting *to* women, so that women aren't just seen as sexual decoration? In developing Elektra, we looked at stuff about Patty Hearst—that may seem kind of bonkers when you're doing a *Bond* film, but we took it seriously. We tried to engage the actors' minds.

PIERCE BROSNAN

(actor, "James Bond")

Michael Apted and I met before this film and sat and talked. We talked about character, and who this character is and what is his relationship with Elektra. What do they mean to each other? What if she gets close to his heart? I think Bond does fall in love with her; he is very seduced by her.

MICHAEL G. WILSON

The interesting thing about the Elektra character is she's not *born* evil. It's almost as if M participated in shaping her, so it all kind of folds in on itself. It's not clear cut, but the situation *is* and it needs to be dealt with. I think that's the fascinating part of the story.

JOHN CORK

(author, *The James Bond Encyclopedia*)

To me, the greatest single thing in *The World Is Not Enough* is Sophie Marceau. She turns in an amazing performance.

MICHAEL APTED

What I saw in Sophie, because it's a fantastic and a difficult role, and it's something that the whole story succeeds or fails on, is that you have to believe you can fall in love with her. *And* you have to believe that you don't want to kill her, all within seventeen minutes of screen time. What I thought was that she was incredibly adorable; when you sat with her, you *did* fall in love with her. But she had something else, which was kind of a little weird. She had this sort of child-woman thing, that you could see she was an elegant child. She had a kind of childish spitefulness, a kind of retro thing about her. She has something that some women have, which is she can be a child one moment and then a woman in the next. I thought that was the key to Elektra when I met her. I knew that was what I wanted; you couldn't have a woman who was just sophisticated, or just mature. There had to be a certain immaturity at work so you could believe she was childlike and crazy. There had to be a certain craziness that you could build into it.

SOPHIE MARCEAU
(actress, "Elektra King")

The *Bond* women have gradually evolved over the years and now are very much at the central core of each story. Years ago, Bond would not have had a female boss, but movies are based in reality and should move with the times. I've always loved being physical in movies, and Elektra was a gift, because she's a very feminine character in an action film. There was a lot I could do with her.

LISA FUNNELL
(author, *For His Eyes Only: The Women of James Bond*)

The thing I like about Elektra King is that she's the first sort of female arch villain who is pulling the strings, and we really didn't have anybody like that. I mean, we've had villainous henchwomen who are interesting and fascinating, but we never really had a woman manipulating Bond. That's something I really appreciated about her.

MICHAEL G. WILSON

The key is whether or not the relationship between Sophie and Pierce works, because if that doesn't work, it's a disaster. So the issue there was writing it and casting it. We fought for Sophie Marceau, because we didn't want to have someone who was well known to the American public or anyone outside of England or France. If you cast someone who's a famous actress, like a Sandra Bullock or something, they're going to hate you and you're going to lose the audience. If you cast someone who's an instant villain, like Sharon Stone, everybody says, "Bond, look! Wake up! You can't trust her!" so you cast someone who is a great actress but doesn't come with all that baggage. I think the casting is *so* important. To bring that off, that's what Michael Apted did. He brought off the relationships. That was part of why we wanted him; that's the essence of having a good dramatic director. We could always supply the action, but he's actually very good at action in the sense that he knows every action sequence needs a narrative, and he directs that part of it very well.

At the outset, the audience isn't convinced that Elektra is the villain of the piece, believing that it could be Robert Carlyle's Renard, who happens to have a bullet lodged in his brain, resulting in his being unable to feel pain (except of the heart, as he obviously loves Elektra). Prior to *Bond,* the actor's film credits include *Trainspotting, Carla's Song, The Full Monty,* and *Plunkett & Macleane*.

ROBERT CARLYLE
(actor, "Renard")

Bond was always going to be delicate, because you just never know with these kinds of movies, though it seemed to have worked out alright. I'd say the most fun part was working with Pierce Brosnan. I know it sounds boring, but that's true. Pierce is without a doubt just one of the loveliest men you could meet, so he made me feel very much at home. I confessed to him how nervous I was in the first scene, because I had a two-page thing with him. He said, "OK, imagine how nervous I felt on *my* first day." So he made me feel great and it was a lot of fun working with him.

MICHAEL APTED

Robert Carlyle is like a firecracker who brought a lot to the character of Renard. He created moments that you feel sympathy for him that were as important as the times you hated him. He had a real drive as the underdog, and that made him a different kind of *Bond* villain.

ROBERT CARLYLE

Playing the villain in a *Bond* film has to be the ultimate. You can be as evil as you can possibly be. You look back at all the great actors who have played villains in the previous movies—Robert Shaw, Christopher Walken, Donald Pleasence, folks like that—and it's an honor to be a part of this little piece of history.

MICHAEL APTED

There were many arguments with the studio. They were annoying. They're unreasonable only insofar as they want, for instance with Renard, the biggest male movie star in the world. They'd say something like, "We want Tom Cruise to play Renard"—obviously that didn't happen, but we had to go to Tom, to his agent, and talk about it, and the agent saying, "Yeah, well, make us an offer," so then the studio would say, "We'll offer you a million dollars," and we would say, "What the fuck are you talking about? We can't afford his usual $20 million price, so why would you propose this in the first place?" It was that kind of thing.

MICHAEL G. WILSON

I think the character was pretty effective. You realize that he, too, has been manipulated by Elektra, so I guess it builds her up to see that she can manipulate Bond *and* Renard.

Denise Richards is improbably cast as a brilliant nuclear scientist, Dr. Christmas Jones (although Tiffani Thiessen and Spice Girl Geri Halliwell, both contenders for the role, wouldn't have been much better), and there's not much she can do with some of the insipid dialogue that's slipped into her mouth. While *Trainspotting*'s Robert Caryle is the presumed villain of the piece as the anemic Renard, it turns out that the true villain is the unhinged Elektra King, played by a sexy and superb Sophie Marceau. Carlyle inherits an affectation that was supposed to go in *Tomorrow Never Dies* in which the villain could feel no pain. While that was jettisoned from Otto Götz's character in that film, it was given to the pitiable Renard.

RIC MEYERS

What was the point of having an antagonist with a bullet in his brain that makes him impervious to pain, as well as increasingly stronger, if none of that—*none* of it—is utilized? Instead, there's a sloppy tussle in a sinking submarine (a locale that is equally pointless) that ends simply because the script says so. What I was hoping for was a climactic battle for the ages, with the villain's gimmick front and center. For example, because Renard feels no pain and is getting stronger as the lodged bullet sinks, Bond is forced to start breaking Renard's bones. Even though Renard can't feel the pain of the broken bone and keeps fighting, a broken arm simply won't be as useful as an unbroken one. Even so, Renard eventually is moments away from strangling Bond no matter what Bond does, so, as a last ditch effort, Bond plunges a thumb or forefinger into Renard's bullet wound, forcing the bullet into the brain. Done smartly and effectively, it would've been a hell of a climax (as opposed to one of the groaningly poor finale puns in the series), but, to my eyes, pretty much everyone—from director Michael Apted to stunt coordinator Simon Crane—fell victim to a wildly schizo formula mix, which, like 007 himself, swung dizzily from good ideas (and *Bond* Girls) to bad ones—a problem Brosnan's Bond was far from finished with.

If there was a truly polarizing aspect of *The World Is Not Enough*, it's probably the casting of Denise Richards as nuclear physicist Dr. Christmas

Jones. Prior to her escapes with Bond, she had been seen in the films *Starship Troopers, Wild Things*, and *Drop Dead Gorgeous*.

MICHAEL APTED

I wanted Denise from the minute I saw her, and the woman who casts all my films had cast her in *Wild Things*, so I knew about her. With Denise, there was a sort of sassiness about her. In some ways, she's the most conventional of the *Bond* Girls; she's the jiggle vision, she's the *Bond* babe, but, again, we tried to give her some weight. It's perfectly believable that someone like that—maybe not as good looking—could do that job. I thought she wouldn't be kind of passive, which is important, because she had a lot to do with Pierce with a sassiness I liked.

DENISE RICHARDS
(actress, "Dr. Christmas Jones")

I met with a studio executive and read the script, and then I went and read for Michael Apted. They flew the girls they were testing, myself included, to London to screen test for it. And then, luckily, they cast me. Obviously I knew *Bond* was big, but I didn't realize how huge a movie it was until the day I found out I was cast and it was literally on every news station. And then I was, like, "Oh, God, this is a *big* movie!" Which scared me even more. It was kind of overwhelming.

JEFF KLEEMAN

In retrospect it was a really bad idea, but obviously nobody enters into a bad idea, well not nobody, but usually you don't enter into a bad idea thinking it is such at the time. There is, I think, with every franchise movie a little bit of pendulum swing. And there were some people who had felt that we had moved very far away from the traditional *Bond* Girl in *Tomorrow Never Dies*. Particularly because we had leaned into it so much with both Izabella and Famke on *GoldenEye* and Michelle Yeoh in *Tomorrow Never Dies*. Boy, was she wonderful in every way, but there was a camp who felt that we needed someone who was a really traditional *Bond* Girl. And we didn't want to do that with the female villain. We felt that in some ways that would be diminishing the female villain—I mean, there's nothing diminishing about Honor Blackman in *Goldfinger*, but nonetheless it didn't feel like, in 1999, that was what we should be doing. So with Sophie Marceau we were casting an incredibly reputable actress who could also be Bond's equal and who, when you saw her, yes she was very attractive, but you didn't objectify her in the way that *Bond* Girls are traditionally objectified. As I say, though, there was a camp that said we need the *Bond* Girl who is still fulfilling the role of traditional *Bond* Girl expectations.

DENISE RICHARDS

Doing the movie I was terrified, but I was also so excited. Then I was, like, "How am I going to do this? To work on a film where there's so much history?" But everyone was so welcoming and encouraging and very helpful. And as far as people saying the whole *Bond* Girl thing, it was up to me as far as what I did after that, and the choice that I made. It wasn't even a question in my mind; it was all that other people were talking about. I didn't even think, "Oh, if I do this movie, then this or that will happen." I didn't even go there. It was definitely an opportunity that I couldn't let pass up, working with the director, Michael Apted, and the cast. It was just such a wonderful experience and a good opportunity for me no matter what would happen after that.

JOHN CORK

Denise Richards came onto the film at MGM's insistence. There is, of course, a trope of casting beautiful young actresses as accomplished scientists. Elisabeth Shue played one in *The Saint* two years prior. Holly Goodhead certainly fits the mold. I think Denise Richards gives a credible performance, but she is not credible in the role. She's hampered by the Lara Croft outfit and that she has no character arc or outside life at all. The audience simply never believes she is a nuclear disarmament specialist, and nothing the filmmakers do helps convince us that she is.

BRUCE FEIRSTEIN

The Christmas Jones character clearly, as people have written about it, is problematic. The casting came from MGM and I had tried to address the obvious red flag, which was a nuclear scientist walking around in short shorts with a tank top. It was a decision made above my head, above my pay grade. At one point I actually talked about maybe Pierce should actually say to her, "You don't look like a nuclear scientist," and she could, in turn, point out that he was too handsome to be who he claimed to be in the film while undercover, but it went nowhere.

RIC MEYERS

Denise Richards was coming off an impressive hat trick. After almost a decade predominantly in television, she appeared in *Starship Troopers*, *Wild Things*, and *Drop Dead Gorgeous* just before 007 came knocking. Her vocal enthusiasm for her *Bond* Girl role was widely disseminated, especially the idea that Dr. Christmas Jones had "depth of character, in contrast to *Bond* Girls in previous decades." Oh, that old, inaccurate, saw again. I find every actress who maintains that, or something like it, must have been very selective in their viewing. It certainly doesn't reflect the likes of Honey Ryder, Pussy Galore, Kissy Suzuki, Tracy Bond, Agent Triple X, Wai Lin, and many others.

BRUCE FEIRSTEIN

As I said, when you work on *Bond* movies, there are a lot of decisions made at higher levels that you're not privy to or why. And I will defend Denise. This is not about Denise. This was about, Denise tried her best and really gave her all. She was great to work with and lots of fun, and so the criticism I've read of her in the role, I think, is unfair, because it's like one of those things where they blame the screenwriter for something that he had nothing to do with.

GLEN OLIVER

(pop culture commentator)

There is no way around this: Denise Richards isn't a particularly good actress. But let's be brutally honest here: she's not cast in roles because of her ability to interpret lines or instill nuance into complex characters. Commensurate with this notion is the inescapable truth that, especially back in the day, the acting requirements of a *Bond* Girl weren't terribly stringent. So, *in theory* there's no reason whatsoever Richards shouldn't have acquitted herself at least adequately as Christmas Jones. But for whatever reason—*wow*—this didn't happen. Christmas Jones was perhaps one of the most gratingly misguided performances ever to find its way into a *James Bond* movie. Jesus, can you imagine a Rik Van Nutter/Denise Richards film?

LISA FUNNELL

When we have my "Gender and James Bond" course, it's always like, "Who's the worst *Bond* Girl, Christmas Jones or Stacey Sutton?" It is a debate in my class where my students fight it out to try to tell me who is worse.

JEFF KLEEMAN

We didn't want to make two movies in a row where people just start saying, "Okay I get it. So you've stopped doing *Bond* Girls." Also with Michelle Yeoh, again with *Tomorrow Never Dies,* we couldn't give her a particularly *Bond* Girl–ish name. We would be falling into really incorrect Asian double entendre that would, again, be a throwback to *Breakfast at Tiffany's* type Asian trope, and we did not want to do that. So we moved so far away that there was this, "We'll make her Christmas Jones," which is a little more *Bond* Girl–ish type name, even though it's not really double entendre to the same degree as Pussy Galore. Cast her with someone who really feels like a modern-day version in terms of appearance of a traditional *Bond* Girl. But we're still forward thinking 1999, we don't want to make her some helpless ditzy female persona, we want her to be smart and competent. So we say, "We gotta make her smart and competent and useful. She can't just feel like we're shoehorning her in there just to have some eye candy," so we make her a nuclear scientist. Was this ultimately the right decision? No. Did it happen with the best intentions? I think yes.

GLEN OLIVER

From her first line of dialogue, anything she attempted to communicate was every bit as half-baked and unconvincing as the worst lines ever delivered in an Ed Wood movie. It made her *Starship Troopers* performance feel like Oscar fodder in comparison. That her *The World Is Not Enough* performance made it to screen—that someone didn't slam on the breaks and recast the role—still astonishes me to this day. But it's nowhere near as astonishing as the question her very presence in the film raises: How is it possible to screw up being a *Bond* Girl?

RIC MEYERS

It was suggested that Richards entered the production complaining that she wanted to be taken seriously as an actress—a desire apparently extending to virtually everything she could comment on. The place it showed on-screen the most was in her wardrobe—especially after they dressed her up as Lara Croft for her character's introduction. From then on, she allegedly wanted to dress as modestly as a scientist might.

MICHAEL G. WILSON

A friend of mine collects war relics from Afghanistan and he goes to all these different places. He went to New York City and met this woman there who was a collector of these things; she was a Russian atomic physicist about thirty years old. When she graduated, she went into the Special Forces, and whenever they have a plane go down with atomic bombs on it, even if it's outside the country, they have this group that parachutes in and they disarm the bombs. She was on that team and she was very much like the Denise Richards character, and I thought that was kind of interesting. She was beautiful, an athletic type, like you'd have to be if you were in the Special Forces. And it's an interesting thing that a woman ended up in that business. And you can only do it in your twenties, because after that you have to retire.

Naturally Pierce Brosnan was back for his third turn as 007, delivering a performance that in some ways felt more nuanced. Look at him in the pre-credit sequence prior to the boat chase—there's a maturing in his portrayal that's abundantly evident as the actor seemingly becomes more comfortable in the role.

PIERCE BROSNAN

I like to think that we captured some of what happened in the days of Sean Connery in terms of character and mood. We came out the door with *GoldenEye,* and I felt like I was a baby at the time. There was some action and some character work there, but I think by *The World Is Not Enough* my confidence had grown and my assuredness with the role had grown. I wouldn't have expected less of myself. I think that the same could be said for Connery if you look at Connery in 1962 with *Dr. No,* and then to his third, being *Goldfinger.* There was that whole mystique about the third *Bond,* the actor really gets into his stride.

MICHAEL APTED

I think with this film, Pierce was leaving his mark on it as he'd been doing each time he played Bond. He's more vulnerable here; I think he has that nice balance between being very vulnerable and being very mean. He's a real killer, there's no doubt about that. He has no compunction about offing people, even Elektra, and yet he's more vulnerable.

MICHAEL G. WILSON

People from time to time have speculated on why we don't try this, why we don't try that, and certainly Pierce had speculated about those things. But when he got down to working with Michael on *The World Is Not Enough*, I think he saw he was getting it just right. We had in mind the type of picture we wanted, and so we would get a director and talk to him and see that we're all making the same picture. That's the key, and our relationship with Michael worked well because we were all making the same picture and going in the same direction.

MICHAEL APTED

Once I started shooting, the hardest thing, which really shook me up, was that I had to pay attention to what everyone else was doing. There were occasions where there were three or four other units shooting; the opening title was being shot, and I had this out-of-body experience where I was shooting a shot and the phone rang, and it was the model unit in the Caribbean who were actually doing the very next shot in the movie—an eight-hour time difference and 8,000 miles away—at the same minute we were doing consecutive shots. So not only did I have to pay attention to what I was doing, but I had to watch what everyone else was doing to make sure it was all making sense and that they were doing what I wanted them to do. I knew I had the very best people doing everything, so they would often go off in their own track.

Sadly, the beloved Desmond Llywelyn would make his final appearance as Q, paving the way for his successor, played by John Cleese. Although there was talk of him returning despite his seemingly definitive farewell to 007, after an emotional send-off as he reprised the role of Q for the last time, the jocular actor tragically died in a car accident on December 19, 1999, at age 85.

BRUCE FEIRSTEIN

One of my most gratifying experiences was meeting Desmond Llewelyn on *GoldenEye*. He came to lunch one day, and meeting him was like meeting Santa Claus. You're sitting there and there's Desmond, who you remember from *Goldfinger*, and he's got big hands and he's telling you that he's a complete Luddite and that all this stuff is beyond him. At that point he knew he was getting on in years, and he began to send me handwritten seven- or eight-page scenes of how he would be written out of the movies. It's not that he wanted out, but at that point he was in his 80s. On the days that he shot, it was wild. All these grips who couldn't care if there's a fireball going on, and all of the crew who were kind of nonchalant about all this stuff—where driving a tank through a brick wall is a normal day's work—when Desmond showed up, they all brought their kids. And Desmond sat on the set between takes, never went to his trailer, and just was the *Bond* Ambassador. He was incredibly gracious and kind and welcoming, which actually dovetails into the story of how I actually *did* write him out.

On *The World Is Not Enough*, I was told to go off and write the scene. I thought long and hard about it, about what is it that we're really saying here, and the line of description in the dialogue is the two of them look at each other, knowing this might be the end, and Bond is Arthur and Q is Merlin. They say good-bye and Q says, "I've tried to teach you two things. First, never let them see you bleed. Second, always have an escape plan," and he's lowered out of frame on that platform. The affection everyone felt for Desmond was just palpable, and what a sweet man to work with.

For Daniel Kleinman, creating the title sequence for *The World Is Not Enough* set to a Shirley Manson song that was anything but garbage was not much less disappointing than its predecessor, but for entirely different reasons.

DANIEL KLEINMAN

(main title designer, *The World Is Not Enough*)

I was trying to be quite psychedelic. But out of all of the sequences that I've done, that was probably the one I felt worked the least. I think that's because, again, I was battling with the technology to create the images. The computers had moved on quite a bit so that even though on *GoldenEye* I was using computer technology, I was limited to a certain number of layers, and CG wasn't really an option. It still had a foot in the analog world. Whereas by the time it came to *The World Is Not Enough*, the CG stuff had moved on, and I think I was sort of pushing the technology a little too far, too fast. But some of things, I felt, didn't quite work. But there's some nice images incorporating oil that work.

Like any 007 film, *The World Is Not Enough* is more than watchable, however. The first 20 minutes are superb, with a terrific sequence in Bilboa, Spain, where Bond confronts a Swiss banker in his office and escapes using his wits. Shortly thereafter, in what is the longest *Bond* pre-title sequence ever, Bond pursues the assassin who killed Robert King on a superb speedboat chase down the Thames, which is a logistical tour de force culminating in Bond watching the sultry Grazia Cucinotta off herself rather than be captured by 007.

RIC MEYERS

The pre-credit scene serves as a good barometer of the subsequent film's flaws, with Bond serving again as a reckless endangerment to public safety, nonsensically straightening his tie underwater (it would have worked after surfacing, not during the dive), and surviving a ridiculously high fall onto sloped steel.

There's a notable lack of classic *Bond* set pieces. Although there's the welcome return of a ski chase, shot in Chamonix, France, a later scene in which Bond and a returning Robbie Coltrane as Valentin Zukovsky are stalked by a helicopter wielding blades at a caviar factory looks exactly like what it is: a bad set and action sequence that hadn't made the cut of several previous films.

RIC MEYERS

Oddly, the production seemed to want to constantly leave Brosnan hanging. He is literally at the end of his rope in the pre-credit sequence, as well as a set piece inside an exploding tunnel. Then there's the five circular saws that hang like chandeliers from attacking helicopters to chop 007's car clean in half—one of the most ludicrous, unlikely, ineffective, and unacceptable weapons ever to appear in a *Bond* film. Also straining the audience's credibility levels was an equally unlikely gadget from Q branch: a deus ex machina ski jacket that transforms into an avalanche protector ball.

BRUCE FEIRSTEIN

I've spoken to Michael Wilson many times over the years and have always been so impressed with him, his approach to this stuff and the fact he can approach it with a sense of humor; he can make fun of things that are goofy and be serious about the things that work great. One fun example: I was brought back to punch up, fix, and tweak *The World Is Not Enough*. You have this opening sequence, which is kind of over-the-top absurd. I have to laugh, because I love the opening sequence, but I also recognize there are certain parts of it that are just slightly implausible, like a woman wearing a red leather jacket in a speedboat with a 50-caliber machine gun mounted on the back deck. In the middle of the Thames on a Tuesday afternoon outside MI6 headquarters. But it's a *Bond* movie, so you go with it.

But one thing I noticed is that the way it's written, it's just a chase down the Thames and the whole thing is about he's chasing after this woman, he gets off the boat, climbs up after her, and she ends up blowing up the helium balloon. So I look at this and it's incredibly innovative and original, but I see one small problem with it, which is: What is Bond doing? Why is he chasing her? So I write in this thing where Bond says, "I can help you; I can save you." And I write in that helicopters are coming in to kill her. In other words, what was missing was what Bond was trying to accomplish. I'm sure Purvis and Wade had thought of that and maybe it got cut. Who knows? But I was brought in to look at funny stuff like that and fix it. Later, Michael says to me, "You've got to see the opening sequence. So I walk into a room at Pinewood and Michael and I are sitting at the table and I'm watching the opening sequence, which is 27-minutes long at this point and it's gonna be cut and all this, but all of a sudden I see something that is not in the script, which is that Bond is chasing her down the Thames and suddenly is firing torpedoes at her.

I look at Michael and say, "This doesn't make any sense. Where did this come from? He's trying to save her. Why is he firing torpedoes at her?" Michael gives me a look and Michael says, "They're non-lethal torpedoes." We look at each other and we just start to laugh, and what's unstated there is that the torpedoes *aren't* coming out. We need the torpedoes, because we need some kind of action bump here, but it's, like, I loved that Michael knew exactly what I was talking about. So, should they have been in the movie? Of course they should. Do they make any sense? No, but it doesn't matter.

JEFF KLEEMAN

There is a cut scene, which was cut in terms of self-awareness and crossing the line. Bruce wrote a marvelous exchange for M and Bond that did not make it all the way into the movie. M's meeting with her billionaire pal, and Bond comes in, and the billionaire leaves. Bond's a little distrustful of him. Bond's questioning him. And M says, "James, contrary to your opinion, the world is not filled with megalomaniac billionaires who hollow out volcanoes, fill them with bikini-clad women, and threaten the world with nuclear annihilation." There's a pause and Bond says back to M, "It only takes one." It was a wonderful exchange. It did not make it into the movie, but again, there's always that pressure of how fine a line are we walking here? But it was just so much fun to have it written on the page and seeing it performed, even if it never ended up in the movie.

BRUCE FEIRSTEIN

That was the line I'd written on the board early on with *GoldenEye*. It got cut, but it's on the DVD as an alternate scene. But I was sitting in a meeting with Barbara and she looked at me and said, "There's no way that line is going in." I think she felt that moment took you out of the movie, that it was too self-referential. That it would be like suddenly making Goldfinger jokes.

I'll tell you, though, there *is* something funny in the movie that's really weird that, years later, came into play. There was a scene missing where Judi Dench as M has any reaction to MI6 getting blown up. So I wrote this scene which begins with her telling everyone that this will not stand. I see her on the set that morning and asked, "What do you think?" And, and this was the only time I ever got any real criticism from her, she said, "A little Churchillian, don't you think?" And I said, "Yes, but I have a feeling that in that kind of national emergency, that's what they would do." She replied, "Okay, fine," and went and did it. Two years later, the jets fly into the World Trade Center, and what does Tony Blair say? "This will not stand."

RAY MORTON

The script for *The World Is Not Enough* breaks new ground by presenting the first female lead villain in the Eon series. Unfortunately, too much attention was paid to Elektra King and her relationship with M that Bond takes something of a back seat to these two characters for long stretches of the story. The second act is unnecessarily complicated and is not always easy to follow, and the stakes in the third act aren't always as clear or as emphasized as they should be. There are several strong character moments for Bond in this film, especially when he kills Elektra, but overall the script is too long, not always well-focused, and a bit plodding. And the final double-entendre is arguably the worst in the series.

BRUCE FEIRSTEIN

One of the things I always found funny was the reaction to the movies. I'll give you a perfect example. There's a scene in *The World Is Not Enough* where there's a line someplace that has Pierce commenting on a vacation spot. I remember we're on a stage at Pinewood, we've built a set at the bottom of a nuclear reactor. Pierce is in a blue jumpsuit, Denise Richards is with him, and he's about to use some device that shoots out of his watch that lifts the two of them out of the hole. So he passes some remark about a nice place to go on vacation. I'm standing on the set huddled with Pierce

Brosnan, Michael Wilson, and Michael Apted. Now I've written this line which something about a vacation, but using the word holiday, because I know the British word for vacation is holiday. Apted turns to Michael and me and says, "Are you sure you want to use holiday?" Michael Wilson says, "No, maybe we ought to go with vacation, because two-thirds of the world aren't going to get it." Michael turns to me and says, "What do you think?" and I say, "Your call." Pierce says, "International picture. Let's go with vacation even though holiday is right."

So the picture comes out and what are the reviews? The reviews say, "Bruce Feirstein is an idiot who doesn't understand British vernacular." And, of course, all the blogs and stuff like that claim I'm a moron who shouldn't be writing these movies, because I don't understand something as fundamental as that. You never know not so much *who's* responsible for what, but you never know the decision-making process that goes into things. The difference between now and when those movies came out is that now I can look at that and laugh. Back then, reading it in some newspaper about what a fucking idiot I am, you get pissed.

RAY MORTON

Purvis and Wade came up with a clever narrative twist—they introduce a character in Renard who we think is the film's principal villain, only to reveal that he actually subordinate to the film's real big bad, the character we originally think is the film's leading lady. However, the twist is telegraphed early on in the piece and so is never quite the big surprise it's meant to be.

BRUCE FEIRSTEIN

When I came on to *The World Is Not Enough*, through Neil and Rob's script they'd decided on the villain, most of the action sequences, and the plot. So the difference on this one is that on *GoldenEye* I really had significant input. On *GoldenEye,* Martin Campbell and I imposed a discipline on the script, which was, "OK, we're going to go back and look at every scene now and make it that the world has changed, but Bond hasn't." So every scene in that is the old Bond coming up against the new world. That's how come Zukovsky looks at Bond in *GoldenEye* and laughs and says, "You're still fighting the Cold War. It's over." M says, "You're a sexist, misogynist dinosaur." And Trevelyan says, "We risked our lives, for what?" And Bond is *still* a knight fighting under the old code. So in that one I really did have a larger role in building on the terrific work that had already been done by Mike France and Jeffrey Caine—and it's important to use their names, because the three of us do have credit on that film.

Tomorrow Never Dies is a different situation, where I did the first draft and the second draft, and then other writers were brought in and some of the talent then believed that everyone thought we should go back toward what the earlier draft was, and I went back in. So in that case it was less a question of creating anything new or fixing anything than it was just restoring what was there within a very short time frame. So, *Tomorrow Never Dies,* my input there was trying to get the final script back to what the producers and I had originally wanted to do with the character of Elliot Carver. We didn't get as far as we wanted, but we got close enough. What I had hoped for was more character stuff. But the film did well and the audience seemed to like it. I think that ultimately the box office response speaks to itself on the movie. On *The World Is Not Enough,* I had considerably less involvement, and part of it had to do with a certain continuity of not tone, but just continuity. Part of the problem is it takes a while to get up to running speed on Bond. Everyone thinks they know who he is, and then you start writing it and you realize you *don't.* I was brought in at the end to just look it over and to polish and to touch things up. That's it.

JEFF KLEEMAN

Of the three *Bond* movies I worked on, *The World Is Not Enough* was the movie that I am most disappointed by, and most disappointed by myself, because it's the one I'm most disappointed by. I don't love it as much as I love the other two, and the other two have lots of flaws, I'm very well aware of. But *The World Is Not Enough*, whether it was exhaustion after four years of *Bond* movies, or the release date, or a number of factors that just conspired to make it, for me, and I'm saying only for me, not up to the standards I was holding the other two to. I don't know. But whatever my contributions were to it, I feel like they should have been stronger or more forceful or more creative than they ultimately were. That being said, the opening sequence, through that chase on the Thames, I adore. And if the whole movie had been at the level of the pre-credit sequence, I would be thrilled with it.

PIERCE BROSNAN

I think we had hit a certain chord with *The World Is Not Enough* that wasn't in the two previous films. That comes from my performance, the writing, and from having a director like Michael Apted, who is so versed in storytelling and narrative, in drama, in character. Not an obvious choice, maybe, for this kind of action movie, but I think, as we've all seen, it has a style of storytelling and character that certainly wasn't in *GoldenEye* or *Tomorrow Never Dies*. Not taking away from the other guys, but we hit a good partnership. It was a good foundation to build on.

MICHAEL APTED

When I made the film, I didn't sit down and watch all the other *Bond* movies; I watched Pierce's. I know what I tried to do, which was to make a coherent story. I tried to make the opening of the film relate to the end of the film, so the opening just wasn't some piece of action stuff up front. I tried to make the characters complicated; I tried to make Bobby Carlyle's character complex and to stop making characters caricatures. I tried to stop things from being black and white. *That's* what I tried to do, which is what I try to do in my movies, so I was bringing what I do in my movies to the *Bond* films, but knowing with *Bond* I have to deliver certain icons. I have to deliver the babes, I have to deliver the action, the gadgets; and so there are certain things the audience expects, and I have to do that. But on top of that, there was room to do certain things without obscuring the intent of the film.

JEFF KLEEMAN

We were wrestling with the *Austin Powers* aspect of, "Oh shit, let's just do what we always do, get a nuclear bomb and threaten the world with nuclear annihilation problem." With Jonathan Pryce, Bruce, who comes from the media, had said, "Let's really do a media-based villain and talk about the power, in our own, quiet, entertaining way, of the media and its own bias in world events, when it's supposed to be objective." Which we all know it's not. We felt like, okay, we're fine then. Yes, he is trying to create World War Three as most *Bond* villains do, but we're finding a way to give him some interesting shading. With Sophie Marceau, Robert Carlyle, Baku, and the oil, we were once again trying to walk that line—but we didn't walk it successfully.

Again, the intentions were good, but it's also the frustrating thing of being on the two-year production schedule. If we had a lot more time to develop the script, I think we would have figured most of this out. We were in this conundrum, which is either we say we gotta make a movie every other year and therefore let's just make them cookie cutter and not take any risks at all and not try to push the envelope, but just do yet another version of X. We see some franchises that do that. Or we say, "Gosh, we don't have as much time as we'd like and we could probably do this even better if we had a lot more time, but how can we not try?" And with each movie—*Goldeneye, Tomorrow Never Dies, The World Is Not Enough*—they all have flaws, but a lot of those flaws come from trying to push the envelope a little bit with time and production constraints that don't allow for fully cooking the script. And yet, none of us wanted to just turn out the complete formula version.

THE 2000s: BOURNE AGAIN

"You think of women as disposable pleasures, rather than meaningful pursuits. So as charming as you are, Mr. Bond, I will be keeping my eye on our government's money, and off your perfectly formed arse."

DIE ANOTHER DAY (2002)

Welcome to the twenty-first century, Mr. Bond.

Although *Die Another Day* is considered by many to be the worst of the *James Bond* movies, it's a somewhat unfair characterization of a film that is more woefully schizophrenic than anything else. For its first hour, *Die Another Day*, which was conceived as a celebration of four decades of *James Bond* movies for the franchise's then 40th anniversary, is filled with a litany of wonderfully satisfying moments. The teaser, in which Bond infiltrates the DMZ on an assassination mission against a rogue North Korean colonel, is crackerjack, and his subsequent incarceration and escape from a North Korean gulag is all first-rate—provided you're not a representative of Amnesty International. While Madonna's song has its many detractors, we're not among them.

In the sensational first hour of the film, Bond is then exchanged in a prisoner swap for his nemesis, Zao, in a suspenseful and stylishly crafted sequence. By the time a rogue 007 enlists the help of the Chinese and Chang (Ho Yi), a Chinese agent moonlighting as a hotel manager, who shares some witty bon mots with Brosnan, the film is firing on all cylinders. A subsequent trip to Cuba accompanied by a terrific David Arnold score keeps things humming, and Emilio Echevarría is marvelous as Raoul, a sleeper agent in Havana, who could have easily become a beloved recurring character. By the time a voluptuous Halle Berry, as NSA agent Giacinta "Jinx" Johnson, emerges from the sea off the coast of Cuba in a barely there orange bikini in an homage to Ursula Andress, we have all the elements in place for a really great *Bond* movie–which at times feels more *Harry Palmer* than *Bond* when Bond finds himself at a mod sci-fi body modification clinic, but that's all part of the fun.

But all good things come to an end, and by the time Gustav Graves invites Bond to "a little scientific demonstration in Iceland," the wheels begin to come quickly off the Aston Martin. The film literally self-destructs an hour in after the film's biggest highlight, a masterful fencing scene in a private club between Bond and the film's villain, played by a snarling Toby Stephens, which is interrupted by the welcome presence of Rosamund Pike, in one of her first film roles, as the treacherous Miranda Frost. Sadly, beginning with Graves' aforementioned invitation, the film builds to a succession of escalatingly absurd set pieces culminating in a moronic and embarrassingly executed paragliding scene in Iceland, as Bond narrowly escapes the space laser Icarus' obliteration of the ice caps near the villain's secret lair, a palatial ice palace. It truly left the audience wondering if they were watching *Bond* or an *Austin Powers* film. Not only does it showcase some rather shoddy looking CG, but director Lee Tamahori also leans on a dated bag of early twentieth-century editing tricks, such as an abundance of speed ramps (rapid zooms to amp up the action) and step dissolves that don't help the film either. And we haven't even mentioned the invisible car yet. Or the fact that at one point Graves is wearing an electric power suit that makes him look like a video-game character, and *nobody* comments on it (and Bond usually comments on *everything*).

TOBY STEPHENS

(actor, "Gustav Graves")

You know, I have *no* idea what that was about. That film was truly one of the strangest audition processes I ever went on. It was a North Korean who is made to look American, and I was asking, "Uh . . . do you want me to speak in . . . a . . . Korean accent?" The whole thing was made with new script pages being slipped under the door during the night.

When Roger Moore derides the film, as he did artfully in *The London Times*, you know you're in trouble. Said Moore at the time, "I thought it just went too far—and that's from *me*, the first Bond in space! Invisible cars and dodgy CGI footage? Please!" Nobody said it better.

Despite whatever critical barbs the film received, it was a smash success at the box office, and Halle Berry's character of Jinx, an NSA agent, was immediately embraced, prompting an attempted spin-off. Eon hired regular *Bond* stalwarts Neil Purvis and Robert Wade to begin work on the script for MGM, only to see the movie abandoned by the studio, much to the anger of the *Bond* camp that had put extensive time and resources into developing the project as the first of a series of films that would have extended the *Bond* cinematic universe.

New Zealander Lee Tamahori, who had previously directed such films as the superb *Once Were Warriors* (1994), *Mulholland Falls* (1996), *The Edge* (1997), and *Along Came a Spider* (2001), as well as three episodes of *The Ray Bradbury Theater* and a second season episode of HBO's *The Sopranos*, was brought on early as director.

LEE TAMAHORI
(director, *Die Another Day*)

It's a funny old road. *The Sopranos* I wanted to do, so I sought that one out, but things like this, the *Bond*, all come through your agent. Your agent calls and says, "Do you want to do a *Bond* movie?" I'd never actually thought about it, but it didn't take me long to decide to take it. I thought it would be a great idea, because I'd been doing kind of hard-edged, dramatic pictures for a while, and I thought it would be nice to do something a little light. It's not that *Bond* is light, but it is one of the more enduring genres we've ever seen, and I thought it might be nice to do lighthearted big action for once. Also, I wanted to test myself on the size of a movie; it helped me break out of a kind of pre-conceived shoebox that people were going to want to put me into.

PIERCE BROSNAN
(actor, "James Bond")

He was wise enough to know that if he got all his ducks in the right order, it will take off like gangbusters, and, obviously, that brings in more work.

LEE TAMAHORI

When I was asked, I said to them myself, "Come on, what made you guys choose me?" because I was as surprised as they were. What they said is they're always looking for someone new and a little different. A lot of people actually call them up and want to do these movies, and a lot of people who are actually in the action genre call them up, but they're not particularly interested in the action specialists. They always know the action will be taken care of one way or another, perhaps finding someone who has a different take on it, who perhaps might reinvigorate it and see it in a new light. Hence Michael Apted, and certainly Martin Campbell. So it surprised even me that they would even consider me, but they're very interesting like that. They sit around and look at what people have done, and don't necessarily analyze it in view of the genre they're working in. They think ultimately, and you'd have to ask them this, that they either like or dislike the movies that the people make, and if they like something that someone's made, they're quite shrewd in their judgment of technical craft versus good storytelling. I think it comes down to something like that. And if you sit and talk to someone in a room for several hours, you do learn a lot just talking to people. And people will either stand up and tell you they're going to change the entire genre and shoot it all like this, and do it all like that, or you can get stuck in the story elements, and what you like about it and what you think you might change about it, which is kind of what I did.

BARBARA BROCCOLI
(producer, *Die Another Day*)

We had to find someone who could get their head around the franchise and the expectations. Lee Tamahori's body of work is amazing. *Once Were Warriors* is one of the greatest films made in the last fifty years. He has great energy and visual sense. We felt he had a very strong vision for the film and could take it to another level.

PIERCE BROSNAN

When you look at his work—with *Once Were Warriors,* he came on the scene with that picture and it was so powerful and so distressing and so reality based. That in itself he had going for him. He was not going to pull any punches, and I liked that, because he would be able to bring this "down." I mean, at that point it had gotten so away from what used to happen back in the days of Connery. I wish I could get the same money and then just keep Connery's schedule. That would be great, but they had become so fantastic that you could lose a character in there for the guy who is playing the role. And I was playing the role, so I always said to them, "Just what is the character about? Where's the character? What's the interaction between them?" Anyway, Lee was a good man for pulling it down, I think, and keeping it a reality-based, character-driven piece. He was hungry for it and he'd made some really fine films. He has an edge to him. It's like Martin Campbell. They're not dissimilar; both New Zealanders and both have that kind of ferocious appetite for film.

LEE TAMAHORI

When Barbara, Michael, and I met, we got along famously. They have a unique and different way of dealing with a movie, which I found refreshing. But the way it happened, I came over and met them, and in one weekend I literally arrived, we met on a Sunday, and by Monday evening I was back in New Zealand on a plane and they had already decided that they wanted me to do it. That was a very quick decision, I thought. It was something to do with just meeting and our dialogue. I think they already liked the movies I had done and wanted to reinforce, just for themselves personally, that I wasn't a maniac and the film would be in good hands. *I* wouldn't have hired me. You've got to understand the history of this: It's all very well for Barbara and Michael to want me to make the film, but MGM was very reluctant. Quite wisely, I think, because if this is a "wife-beating" director from New Zealand who may turn our favorite franchise into . . . who knows? So those things do get discussed. I'm very fond of saying—and I mean it—I would play devil's advocate, if I had been in their shoes, sitting in Los Angeles, and I would have made the same decision about me, so credit to them, all of them, for giving me this chance, and I appreciate it.

As he explains it, Tamahori has always loved the *Bond* films, though he did feel that the franchise occasionally tended to become moribund, and there was always the hope of reinvention, in the vein of what Martin Campbell had done on *GoldenEye*.

LEE TAMAHORI

Here we were making this very big deal about *Die Another Day* being the 20th movie in time for the 40th anniversary. But I always felt these movies used to be great thrillers, and then they became big event pictures with special effects during the Roger Moore years. But when it was the Connery era—*From Russia with Love*—they started off always as little excellent B grade thrillers that became something else. So I got to this movie and I said what we should endeavor at all cost is to make this a damn good thriller, and then all the rest of the stuff would be pasted on top of it: big action, girls, gadgets, and all that stuff. Now that may sound like what you should do anyway, but sometimes I have the feeling that things can get a little lost, and these things can turn into giant event movies in and of themselves, full of pyrotechnics and explosions, and then you can lose your way.

Returning from *The World Is Not Enough* to write the screenplay for *Die Another Day* was the team of Neal Purvis and Robert Wade, only this time there wouldn't be a Bruce Feirstein in the mix. This film, insofar as they were concerned, would be their only *Bond* they would get sole credit on (despite their names being attached to each subsequent film of the next two decades) becoming the "Richard Maibaums" of *Bond's* most recent era of films.

MICHAEL G. WILSON

(producer, *Die Another Day*)

Working with the writers is a group effort. We brainstorm for weeks kicking around ideas until we come up with some kind of plot.

BARBARA BROCCOLI

We always start off with the topical aspect. What is the world worried about now or in the next couple of years? And what is James Bond's position in that arena? With *Die Another Day,* we talked about the places in the world that still had an aura of mystery and intrigue. And North Korea is one of those places. Then we discussed how a villain could be introduced into this scenario and what journey could we take Bond on that he hasn't been on before. What challenges could we greet him with? It was quite a long process.

PIERCE BROSNAN

When you get the script in advance—which I did six months before we started shooting—they were so busy just trying to flesh out the story that in that version there is not much character there. There's not much of a rapport between the characters. It's an impressionist script, so to speak. As you get closer to it, and as they get more comfortable with the structure of the story, *then* you come to what's the character and how does the character really move within it, and what is at stake for the character. *That's* when you make suggestions. That's when you speak up. At least that is the way I have done it.

LEE TAMAHORI

I thought the concept was a great idea, but I could see it had some kind of fundamental problems in telling the story, so we needed to work on that—I was just throwing out some ideas. But it's a funny thing, because you come into it and you go, "I wonder if I can actually comment on this, because this has been written over a period of two years." One presumes that the producers and the writers have gone into this in great detail, but while that is true, it's never gone into with *that* much detail. They're always waiting to attach a director before they *really* go in, like any script, and pull it apart and fine tune it. It used to be a mystery to me before I started making movies as to what point a script is turned over to a director and it changes. It's a writer's worst nightmare, but the public doesn't seem to be well educated in that. They all think we're a bunch of madmen who just want to put our own idiosyncratic brand on a script and call it our own and steal the credit. And certainly my few years then of working in America had been kind of a self-taught exercise. What you found was that your job was to tune these movies up. And I now see I have an ability and an instinct to look at a script and see what needs to happen to make it better.

MICHAEL G. WILSON

We decided that with *Die Another Day* Bond would be captured and thrown into military prison. Pierce really responded to that. He was always looking for some new aspect of the character to explore. There are two aspects to Fleming. One is character—James Bond and the people in his world—and the other is story. When we're preparing a *Bond* film, we always look back to the novels and the Fleming material for that.

BARBARA BROCCOLI

Character is most important. Bond is so complex and multi-faceted that you can always tap in to some new aspect, particularly with Pierce. He had such humanity and vulnerability, and we could go into areas we hadn't been. In *Die Another Day,* he's captured and tortured, and yet survives to fight another day.

LEE TAMAHORI

We were pushing Bond into a range he's never been in before. Half the script is Bond outside MI6, operating on his own. There's betrayal and double-crossing going on. Pierce and I worked on pushing the envelope and trying new things without running too far from Bond's essence. We wanted the series shaken up, but not at the expense of what people inherently like about the character.

ROBERT WADE
(writer, *Die Another Day*)

Our key task was to make Bond a character rather than a caricature. We were trying to draw out his darker side. We consider Pierce the perfect actor to draw out the complex combination of emotion and cold blood.

NEAL PURVIS
(writer, *Die Another Day*)

He's vulnerable without being weak. You want to push him, put him through a journey. We wanted the action and scale to flow naturally from the story and the characters.

LEE TAMAHORI

Once we started pulling the script apart and putting it back together again—and remarkably it survived very intact—we kept tuning up everything for seven months, even while we were shooting, just to make sure. I just hate these movies where they have logic holes and big plot holes and people just say, "That's okay, the audience will understand." I've never underestimated the intelligence of an audience, because I think they're far too smart, and these pictures should be no different. And if you *do* make one of these and people say just cut to the explosion and everyone will be fine, that's just so lazy. So in some ways I wanted to get back into that kind of old-fashioned tough thriller, and then in the back end of it I wanted to drive it into the twenty-first century with a kind of new aggressive post-production and cutting and technique.

PIERCE BROSNAN

We'd gotten Halle Berry, who is beautiful and someone who I actually had been watching for some time. Not only is she beautiful, but she's a hardworking actress and she is an *actress*. That had been my thing: "Please get an actress. Get someone who you can act with; one who is going to just give it back to you."

MICHAEL G. WILSON

Halle Berry is an incredible human being. Working with her was one of the great experiences of our lives. She and Pierce had wonderful chemistry. She's very beautiful and very professional, and she is so natural. She was wonderful in the movie, the ultimate *Bond* woman in many ways.

HALLE BERRY
(actress, "Jinx")

I like Jinx. She's really strong, and I like the fact she's the next step in the evolution of the *Bond* woman. Year after year, they've gotten a little stronger, a little smarter, and more equal with Bond, while still retaining their sexiness. Now they're Bond's intellectual equals and physical rivals—and Jinx was one more step in that evolution.

LEE TAMAHORI

With Jinx, we had this dynamic character, almost a female James Bond, and I knew Halle would be perfect. Halle was really up for it. You know exactly who Jinx is in this adventure. We gave her a lot of kick-ass action and other extraordinary moments. Halle stepped up to the plate and did it.

HALLE BERRY

The character is super feminine, very witty, as quick as Bond with the comeback lines, and as tough as nails. That's the most empowered woman to me—someone who can be sexy and tough at the same time. Jinx has many layers to her character, and they were enormous fun to play around with. And I was comfortable with most of the action scenes. Knife combat, gun play, propelling off wires—I was able to do all that and look professional. But there was one stunt that nearly beat me. Pierce and I had to run alongside a moving plane before hauling ourselves up into the wheel bay. It was only going about 15 miles an hour and I was sure I could cope with that. But you don't realize how fast that is when you're trying to catch a moving plane. By the fourth or fifth take, I was exhausted. Pierce did it effortlessly, but even though my legs were running, I was going nowhere.

PIERCE BROSNAN

Then you have Toby Stephens, who played this character, Graves, and that's a really fascinating role with a kind of duality to the character.

TOBY STEPHENS

It was an enormous buzz to be cast, but then you suddenly realize the responsibility of playing a *Bond* villain is quite big. The films have an enormous following and such enormous expectations, and, inevitably, the *Bond* villain is a catalyst and engine of the movie. If you don't have a good villain, you won't have a great film, really. I do have really good lines, but I was disappointed that I never got to say, "Goodbye, Mister Bond." Most *Bond* villains get to say that. I actually said it in my screen test; I felt that even if I didn't get the part, at least I got to say that line.

ROSAMUND PIKE
(actress, "Miranda Frost")

Die Another Day was my first feature film. The fact that it was a *James Bond* film made it even more nerve-wrecking. You have a responsibility to create another fantastic *Bond* character and live up to all the expectation. But it is brilliantly exciting. I had to train in fencing for the role, and I had to learn how to handle a gun. I had never held a gun before. I was pretty gun shy. But I felt like a kid in the school playground acting out a scene from a *Bond* film.

In many ways, the character of Zao, Graves' right-hand man, was a throwback to classic *Bond* henchman, his face, following events in the pre-credit sequence, being disfigured and embedded with diamonds as a result of an explosion instigated by Bond.

RICK YUNE
(actor, "Zao")

It was one of the most painful—*and* ticklish—experiences of my life. Every scene I was either glittering or glowing. I was also completely hairless. It was the first time I had to work with something like that and it wasn't very comfortable, but I am grateful for the experience.

And then there's the new MI6 Quartermaster, with John Cleese reprising his role from *The World Is Not Enough*, taking over for the late Desmond Llewelyn; as well as Judi Dench playing M for the fourth time.

JOHN CLEESE
(actor, "Quartermaster")

The hope was that Desmond and I could have worked together for another two or three films. Sadly, that was not to be. Like Desmond, I despise technology in all its forms. I can never make things work. I have trouble with ordinary pencils, so I wasn't really qualified to play the role, but I got it anyway. And like Desmond, I had terrible trouble learning the lines dealing with high-tech gadgetry. I've always thought anybody seriously interested in technology has something wrong with them, something missing in the emotional part of them. The funny thing about learning gobbledygook is that some bits come very easily and others not so. I couldn't get "target-seeking shotguns" out clearly—maybe it's a tongue twister—but "tiny cameras on all sides project the image onto a light-emitting polymer film," *that* was quite simple.

JUDI DENCH
(actress, "M")

M is more complicated with each film, and she and Bond have grown gradually closer since their initial confrontation in *GoldenEye* when she referred to him as a misogynist dinosaur. I think M cares a great deal for Bond, although she doesn't show it too much. She's knows he's the best. Personally, after all those years in the theater, it was a breath of fresh air to do something completely different. That's what I look for all the time. You play Queen Victoria, and suddenly you get to play the head of MI6. That's very exciting.

For his part, Brosnan was returning to play Bond for the fourth and, as it would turn out, final time.

LEE TAMAHORI

Pierce knows all the quirks and foibles of the Bond character. It's great when I would say, "Pierce, I don't know what to have Bond do in this scene," and he would say, "I know exactly what to do," and then punches some guy and straightens his tie afterward. Classic Bond.

PIERCE BROSNAN

Bond has always been about the circus. *Bond* has always been about the high theatricality of the film in terms of who is going to play the role of James Bond, will he come back as James Bond, who is going to be the *Bond* Girl, the gadgets, the locations? Cubby Broccoli set the benchmark there with Harry Saltzman all those years back, and Cubby, being the ringmaster, knew how to set up a show and leave the audience wanting more. As an actor, coming into it, you have to be fully aware that it's many roles you play, because you have to deal with the media: you have to be strong enough to be able to live with it on a day-to-day-existence and year-to-year existence, probably for the rest of a career. I mean, Connery is still Bond. Roger is still Bond. I would be happy to wear that mantle in years to come and I am very proud of it. It takes an energy and it takes a certain grace and just doggedness to do it, because it is repetition, and if you do get it right, and you are successful in the role, which every actor wants to be, then you have to do it again and again and again.

NEAL PURVIS

After three previous *Bond* films, Pierce had a great understanding of the character. He has changed things on occasion, because he doesn't believe Bond would react in a particular way. There was an instance when he had a gun trained on the villain when one of the girls put a gun to his head. His instinct was to spin and shoot the girl instead of the villain, and that was the right thing to do. It wasn't the way it was written, but it's what Bond would do in that situation.

PIERCE BROSNAN

When I got to the fourth, I promised myself that I was going to look back at the first three films I'd done, just to see if there was any growth, any relaxation and confidence. The confidence was there, and if there was one thing, I didn't want to have to try as hard. This is a man who is seasoned anyway. He knows the game of life. He knows what the missions are about. He lives a good life, and I'd had a good life playing the role. I knew what the role was about.

In the end, *Die Another Day* is such a strange hybrid of commercial success and creative failure. Yes, it broke all 007 records, scoring nearly $432 million at the global box office, but there is such a sense of disdain about the film, particularly its last third.

JOHN CORK

(film historian; author, *James Bond: The Legacy*)

The mood out there was that it was time for a big, absurd *Bond* of the scale of *The Spy Who Loved Me*. There was also a conscious decision to make a film that paid tribute to all 40 years of 007. To me, the film becomes more of a game of "name that homage" than a fully engaging *Bond* film, but it has its charms.

BRUCE FEIRSTEIN

(writer, *GoldenEye*)

When I was working on the films, the things I tried to stay away from are control rooms, countdowns, guys in orange suits. That was my constant fight. Invariably it's, like, 30 guys in camo gear come out of nowhere bristling with weapons. No longer orange jumpsuits, but the idea is there. I just want to know one thing: is there a union of nameless, faceless mercenaries? I've always said that I just want to see the job interview. Basically the guy comes in and says,

"I'm looking for fifty or sixty hardcore mercenaries." "What are you doing?" "I'm going to plan world domination." The guy across the table says, "I hate to say this, but I've kind of seen this in movies before. I get killed and you die." "Yeah, but think of the wardrobe." But we all think the same things: At the bottom of these huge office buildings there are at least 30 guys watching video screens, hunched over like paratroopers about to go out a window. At night they have nothing better to do, so they rappel down the side of a building. I remember watching *Bad Boys,* and at the end there are 300 guys with weapons. What was the game plan here, guys? "Mayhem ensues"—it's my favorite line to write.

JEFF KLEEMAN

(executive vice president of production, MGM/UA)

There's something I've noticed historically with *Bond* films, which I'm not quite sure why it is. The longer someone plays Bond, the more they seem to start to move toward the *Austin Powers* side of the spectrum. And I'm not sure why. I mean, Connery doesn't move all the way there, but Connery certainly gets a little goofier as the *Bond* movies go on. Roger Moore absolutely does. And while I'd left before the final Pierce movie, that definitely . . . when you get to the point you have an invisible car, you're starting to get into pretty goofy territory.

LEE TAMAHORI

The shooting of the movie tended to look conventional. When I say conventional, I mean '90s conventional *Bond,* because both Roger Spottiswoode and Michael Apted, I think, were very much following the template that Martin Campbell set. And in some ways you have to stay with this thing, but it's a tricky one, because I'm sure if you spoke to Roger and Michael, they would say they went in there with all the best of intentions to make a new *Bond,* but somehow it ended up looking the same. So they are very tricky, because you have to deal with girls, gadgets, big action, Q, M, and all that stuff, and you can't do a dogma version of it. These things are very expensive set pieces, so you can't get out and change it so radically.

GLEN OLIVER

(pop culture commentator)

Die Another Day is essentially two movies, both representing wildly different interpretations of a *Bond* story. The first half is an engrossing, sometimes gritty political/espionage thriller. The second half is, essentially, a comic book.

The first half is commendably smart in direction, writing, and the performance of its leads. The second half is less concerned with such elements. Neither interpretation of *Bond* is fundamentally inappropriate, though it's safe to say 007 tales are usually at their strongest when they're not going for cheese and frivolity.

JEFF KLEEMAN

I was not there for *Casino Royale,* but I suspect Martin gets a lot of credit for this: He didn't try to do the Pierce Bond with Daniel Craig. He recognized that Daniel needed to be a very different kind of Bond, with a different kind of voice and a different kind of physicality. And so, there again, you see how the actor, in conjunction with a good director and good writing, can define a Bond.

GLEN OLIVER

The issue with *Die Another Day* is that the basic tonalities driving the two halves of the picture are so disparate. They essentially fracture the movie. The later half craps on all the good will and real estate so potently earned in the first hour of the film, but also fails to stand on its own *because* of the first hour of the film. As a result, *Die Another Day* shorts itself out.

RIC MEYERS

(author, *Murder on the Air: Television's Great Mystery Series*)

Considering what Spottiswoode was rumored to be up against on *Tomorrow Never Dies,* he should have gotten a medal, but it's little wonder he didn't sign for a follow-up. Apted, long hailed as more of a documentarian than a budget-bursting action director, may have simply decided to get the increasingly fast train he was stuck on into the station anyway he could—subtleties be damned—then get off for good. And then there was Lee Tamahori, a wild card director if ever there was one. But he originated in the same country as Martin Campbell, so what could go wrong, right? So he was signed to helm what should have been a celebration: the 40th anniversary, 20th film in the *James Bond* series.

The skeleton was fine. The cast, save for the unfortunate stunt-casting cameo of a singer whose acting had always been famously cringe-worthy, was solid. The action, led by legendary vet Vic Armstrong of *Indiana Jones* and *Superman* fame, looked great on hovercrafts, in fencing schools, and on crashing jumbo jets. The first third gave Brosnan what he said he wanted: more challenges and depth to his Bond—echoing what happened to the book Bond when he was brainwashed and sent back to assassinate M at the start of *The Man with the Golden Gun* novel. So they should have made an exciting, involving celebration of the series and character for the remainder of the running time, yes? But, instead, for some reason, the final two-thirds segue into a flat, erratic, self-conscious, near satire of themselves, with some of the worst dialog and special effects since *Plan 9 from Outer Space*. That should be an exaggeration, but upon recent viewing, it is uncomfortably close to the truth.

RAY MORTON

(senior writer, *Script* magazine)

The first act of *Die Another Day* sets up a marvelous premise for a terrific *Bond* thriller. While on a mission, 007 is betrayed by an unknown operative. This betrayal results in him being captured. He then spends a year being tortured in an enemy prison until he is released in a prisoner swap. Disavowed by MI6, he sets out to discover the identity of the person who betrayed him. However, once this premise is established, nothing is done with it and the narrative instead veers off into a lot of pseudo sci-fi and action movie nonsense featuring some of the most leaden *Bond* fantasy elements ever. After such a promising start, the script turns into one of the worst *Bond* screenplays ever and provides an extremely disappointing finale for Pierce Brosnan's tenure as 007.

RIC MEYERS

After seeing *The Crow* in 1994, I coined the phrase "city of assholes movie" to describe the kind of film where everyone is trying to act tough or look cool. You know; the kind of flick where everyone is posturing, speaks purposely, and says really lame or nonsensical things in an attempt to seem hip and with it. Only *Die Another Day* takes it one step further. The dialog between Bond and Jinx, especially, is so forced and unnatural that they either don't seem to actually be talking to one another, or else they seem to be conversing only in spy passwords.

This staid, unnatural approach tied inexorably in with how the film played. There was no excuse, but there must have been a reason for the remarkably shoddy look of the film—especially the visual effects, specifically Bond's parasailing and Jinx's high dive, both which looked like they were done by a freshmen computer class. And a bad freshmen computer class at that. Other special-effect-driven movies that came out that year were *Lord of the Rings: The Two Towers*, *Men in Black II*, *Harry Potter and the Chamber of Secrets*, and even *Star Wars Episode II: Attack of the Clones*, so it wasn't like decent digital effects weren't available to them. And it was also a hell of a time to stumble in the genre, what with *The Bourne Identity* and Vin Diesel's *xXx* also premiering the same year. But stumble they did, repeatedly, until they all but fell over.

JOHN CORK

There is a point where *Die Another Day* loses its audience, and that is the makeshift kite-boarding scene. The movie begins with shots of real surfers riding very real giant waves. Placing a CGI Bond on a CGI wave later on can't ever look real when you've just shown the audience what real surfing looks like. Tamahori, who is skilled with a certain kind of film, just wasn't the right guy for this job. The pacing is wrong. The camera is often in the wrong place. The performances are tweaked so that they are too over the top. And it is a great cast. Every actor in there has buckets of talent. But the film opts for manic energy over cleverness. It is the Jolt Cola of *Bond* films.

RIC MEYERS

Better people than I have tried to figure why, but I looked to the same place I did when the *Bond* movie was good: the director, cinematographer, and editor. David Tattersall, fresh from the *Young Indiana Jones* TV series, was the director of photography. Five years before he had been DP on *Con Air,* and three years before that he had filmed *The Phantom Menace,* the first *Star Wars* prequel. *Die Another Day,* however, was to be his only 007 film. Andrew MacRitchie and Christian Wagner were credited as editors. It was MacRitchie's second credit following *The New Adventures of Pinocchio* three years before, although he had been first assistant editor on the previous two Brosnan *Bonds*. Wagner, however, had been editing since 1985, including such similar projects as *Mission Impossible II* and *Spy Game*. But in both cases, neither editor worked on a *James Bond* film again. Meanwhile, the companies credited for the digital effects were Cinesite, originally affiliated with Kodak; Framestore; and an uncredited Double Negative—both British companies—who have all gone on to notable work with *Inception, Interstellar,* the *Harry Potter* film series, the *Dark Knight* trilogy, and the *Captain America* movies. Not surprisingly, none of their sites tout their work on *Die Another Day,* considering how obvious and shoddy the results were.

LEE TAMAHORI

I didn't feel intimidated by the film. I knew what I was getting into and was under no illusion. A *Bond* movie falls into a specific genre and you have to provide certain elements. You must respect the fact it's essentially about girls, guns, gadgets, and big action. Once you've got those in place, you can do a lot of things. My only pressure was not messing it up. These movies are giant monsters. Huge filmmaking machines. You better keep on top of all that well-oiled machinery, or else. In the end, I had absolutely no regrets about taking the reins. Seeing the film, I was happier than ever that I took them. I've always thrived on high-octane, intense filmmaking, and this was as intense as it gets. I tried pushing the envelope on every level—massive action sequences: the Ice Palace is the biggest *Bond* set built since the submarine dock on *The Spy Who Loved Me*.

GLEN OLIVER

If the tone and styling of the first hour or so of the picture had been maintained throughout, this would've been regarded as one of the finest, smartest *Bond* films ever made. In the same vein, even if it was not everyone's cup of tea, if we'd gotten a *Bond* film *solely* devoted to the comic book-y, almost superheroic trappings we saw in the second half of *Die Another Day*? I firmly believe that film would be regarded as a bold, ballsy, self-confident, and bat-shit crazy interpretation of the franchise that people would be discussing and debating for years. The fusion of the two approaches into one film resulted in a confused and confusing hybrid offspring with an aggressively marginalizing identity crisis.

MATT GOURLEY

(cohost, *James Bonding* podcast)

I've started to like *Die Another Day* more, and people can't understand it. I'm like, well, it's because it goes so far in one direction. At least it's almost consistent. Where *GoldenEye* is consistent in its tone, *Die Another Day* is as well in its crazy tone. It's almost in the *A View to a Kill* category for me, where I like watching it because it's so bonkers. The other two in the middle [*Tomorrow Never Dies* and *The World Is Not Enough*] want to have your cake and eat it, too, and I just don't like it.

BARBARA BROCCOLI

I'm often asked how we keep the series going. We have over 300 people out there shooting the movie—*that's* what keeps it going. My father started making the films in the sixties, and we have a really dedicated crew of people; generations of people who care about their work and *James Bond,* and every single person contributes to their success.

LEE TAMAHORI

James Bond is an outrageous concept that somehow withstood the test of time. A lone guy with a touch of sophistication and a dash of humor saves the world all the time. My first one was *From Russia with Love*, and it's probably still my favorite, although *Goldfinger* runs a close second. I always loved *From Russia with Love*, because it was the only Cold War movie they ever made. A real spy story. I remember I was about ten or eleven and I didn't know what sex was, and there were these filthy Russians filming people through the mirror, and I thought, "Oh, this is racy." So it's a great opportunity to come in and do one of these, because I guarantee you that every director, certainly the last four . . . talk to any of us, we knew what we were getting into and we were all very careful about protecting it. None of us would have wanted to just do it as a job; I think we were very aware that we were being handed a previous jewel of the crown, and you do not want to be the guy who screws it up.

During the Pierce Brosnan years, there was a lot going on behind the scenes of the *James Bond* franchise legally, but unlike the situation between *Licence to Kill* and *GoldenEye*, production and development didn't come to a halt while the parties resolved their differences. Most notably, John Calley, who had been the head of MGM/UA, left to run Sony Pictures in 1996. Two years later came word that Sony had teamed up with Kevin McClory for what was announced as a new series of *James Bond* films based on his *Thunderball* rights. Said Calley in an interview, "I think we can put through a number of very exciting *Bond* movies. We feel the rights we acquired will support those ambitions.

Needless to say, Eon and MGM didn't agree and filed suit.

Another player McClory had sucked in prior to the announcement was *The Godfather* producer Albert S. Ruddy, who announced that, again based on these supposed rights, he was going to produce a 100-episode 007 TV series. Contacted at the time of this announcement by the authors, and queried as to if McClory's rights would allow such a thing, he replied, "Well, that's the argument we're going with." Needless to say, Ruddy was dropped in lieu of the potentially more lucrative Sony deal.

MICHAEL G. WILSON

(producer, *Casino Royale*)

On *Thunderball*, Kevin McClory was producer, Cubby and Harry were executive producers, and he had a 10-year restriction. He couldn't make another *Bond* film for 10 years, and then when that was up he started saying he wanted to make another film. He made *Never Say Never Again,* and then that didn't do so well, and so then what happened was that in 1967 Columbia Pictures had made *Casino Royale* as a farce. So when John Calley went over to Sony, he knew that there was a problem with Kevin McClory from when he was working at MGM, so he went and he said, "I can get the McClory rights. You guys at Sony have *Casino Royale,* right? Let's start our own series, because with two novels we could claim a series, right? You've got series rights." So we had another lawsuit.

BEN FRITZ

(author, *The Big Picture: The Fight for the Future of Movies*)

John Calley's announcement in 1997 that he had obtained the rights for Sony Pictures to make its own competing series of *James Bond* movies has to go down as one of the sneakiest and most suspect moves in the history of modern Hollywood. And that's a very high standard.

Calley knew 007 from his days running United Artists and he was familiar with the convoluted rights surrounding 1965's *Thunderball* and its 1983 remake, *Never Say Never Again*. Those two films are the only ones not produced by a member of the Broccoli family, and so their producer, Kevin McClory, claimed they weren't part of the deal Danjaq had with United Artists and its parent, MGM. It wasn't totally crazy, since *Never Say Never Again* had in fact been distributed by Warner Bros., not United Artists.

Calley was newly installed atop Sony Pictures, and one of his first moves was to make a deal with McClory for a parallel series of *James Bond* movies. It was pretty insane. Audiences would obviously be confused by two different versions of James Bond in their own franchises with different creatives in control. And it took approximately five minutes for MGM's CEO Frank Mancuso to file a lawsuit. He called McClory's ownership claim "delusional" and said Sony had been "duped."

MICHAEL G. WILSON

John Calley is a legend and all that, and, of course, we didn't get on with him. He's passed away now, so there's no point in kind of dwelling on it, but he had a responsibility as being president of United Artists/MGM, a corporate responsibility, and was in a position of trust. Then to go to another studio and violate that is typical of John Calley. It's one of the things where you just get the luck of the draw with these guys at the studio. There's plenty of guys that were just as bad as he was, but there were plenty of good ones. If you stay long enough at MGM, you kind of run through all the guys in Hollywood.

DEAN DEVLIN

(writer/producer, *Independence Day*)

After the success of *Independence Day*, Roland Emmerich and I signed a deal to do *Godzilla* and other movies for Sony. One of the first things John Calley came to us with was *James Bond*. He said the studio now has the rights to do *James Bond* movies and we'd like you to do one. We were very excited about doing a *Bond* movie for them if we could do it as a period piece and have it take place in the 1960s, but those conversations didn't get very far.

JEFF KLEEMAN

(executive vice president of production, United Artists)

At the time, I was at United Artists, but I was still going over and having lunch with John at Sony, and then he makes a deal with McClory, which is a direct assault on MGM and Frank Mancuso, with whom he had a falling out. So there's no love lost between the two of them. And as soon as he makes the deal with McClory, Barbara and Michael rightly feel utterly betrayed. And I'm in the middle of this triangle, and because I'm the executive who not only worked the closest with John on the *Bond* movies, but also was really the only executive other than John to work on the *Bond* movies, I'm put in the middle, and a lot of depositions followed. It was a very sad time for me. It may have also, to some degree, affected my feelings about *The World Is Not Enough* since I felt like I was always in the depositions and knowing every word you're saying is affecting somebody who matters to you. That was tough. And then ultimately it went away. Sony got *Spider-Man*, which was a little disappointing to me, because I was actually planning to work on *Spider-Man* at MGM/UA. And we got *Casino Royale* and *Never Say Never Again*, so that was incredible.

Eventually, Sony, Eon, and MGM/UA would come to a settlement which involved a complicated deal in which the studio gave up its claims to make a competing *James Bond* franchise, transferring its rights not only to the underlying intellectual property of the original *Casino Royale* novel, but all rights to the 1967 film as well as *Never Say Never Again*, owned by Jack Schwartzman's Taliafilm. In exchange, MGM quietly gave Sony its rights to its part of the web of *Spider-Man* rights it had claimed as a result of its acquisition of the defunct Cannon Pictures and aborted the James Cameron version, which Sony had attempted to untangle for many years.

BEN FRITZ

The true brilliance of John Calley's move came when the two sides went to the negotiating table and it turned out that producing more *Bond* movies wasn't actually his endgame at all. For him, the disputed *Bond* rights were merely a chess piece. What he wanted were the free-and-clear rights to *another* character the two companies were fighting over: *Spider-Man*.

Sony had recently acquired the rights from Marvel to produce to produce new *Spider-Man* movies and release them in theaters, but MGM claimed it held some rights to the character under a deal with a shady B-movie producer named Menahem Golan that it had set years earlier.

In March 1999, the two companies announced they had reached a settlement over the *James Bond* rights: MGM would pay Sony $5 million, and in return it would be the one-and-only home of *James Bond* movies. But behind the scenes, there was another secret piece of the agreement: MGM had also agreed to drop all its claims to *Spider-Man*.

The deal ended up working brilliantly for them both. *Bond* movies have prospered for another two decades to come and most of their profits have flowed back to MGM (though Sony, ironically, ended up releasing several of the most successful in the late 2000s and 2010s for MGM). *Spider-Man,* meanwhile, is the most profitable movie franchise in Sony Pictures' history and was directly responsible for the creation of Marvel Studios and the nonstop deluge of super-heroes at multiplexes today.

Did John Calley ever *really* intend to make those *Bond* movies? Or was it entirely a ploy to get the *Spider-Man* rights? He died in 2011, so we may never know for sure what was in his mind. But it's hard to believe he was ever too serious about *Bond,* since he gave up the rights to a character who at that point had a long and successful box office history in return for a comic book character who had never been on the big screen before.

Now, after several decades, the rights to Ian Fleming's first James Bond novel had finally come home. What producers Michael G. Wilson and Barbara Broccoli were going to do with them soon became abundantly clear and would change the Bond franchise forever.

***CASINO ROYALE* (2006)**
***QUANTUM OF SOLACE* (2008)**

Is there such a thing as the perfect *Bond* movie? The answer is a resounding no. There never has been and there's unlikely to ever be, but *Casino*

Royale—and its deadly card battle between Bond and Le Chiffre—*sure comes damn close to being nearly flawless.* In 2002's *Die Another Day,* the familiar end credits tag promised James Bond would return, and in 2006's *Casino Royale* he did, but looking considerably different than he did four years earlier. Now portrayed by the steely Daniel Craig, Barbara Broccoli's gambit of casting the bad-ass blond Brit as the iconic, polished secret agent paid off big time. While there are some echoes of Timothy Dalton in his performance, Craig evidences a charisma, sadism, and wit in his portrayal of the role not seen since the heady days of Sean Connery. If Pierce Brosnan was the heir to the Roger Moore era (and that's a compliment, by the way), Craig proved a perfect fit to the tailored Tom Ford tuxedo as Sean Connery's successor as the gritty, fierce, and unforgiving secret agent with a license to kill. *And* not reluctant to use it.

It's fascinating to see the series go through its most dramatic reboot since Bond fell to Earth after the bloated and insipid (albeit, enjoyably kitschy) *Moonraker* in 1981's overrated *For Your Eyes Only,* a film which *Casino Royale* easily puts to shame while having the most emotional resonance for the character since the justifiably lauded *On Her Majesty's Secret Service.*

Craig, fortunately, is no George Lazenby, and despite his unapologetically mediocre turn as Lara Croft's love interest cum villain in *Tomb Raider,* the Craig who shows up in *Casino Royale* is the one who displayed so much promise in *Layer Cake* and Spielberg's masterpiece, *Munich,* a far more polished and interesting actor than his early career choices may have implied. And while this Bond may be the man women want to be with, he's not necessarily the man men want to be. He's arrogant, unhappy, and unpolished, a bit of a cipher (and Fleming's "blunt instrument") who still doesn't know if he wants his martinis shaken or stirred. Unlike Brosnan, who looked suave and debonair in a tux, Craig looks uncomfortable, with a face that looks like a pugilist who's taken a few too many uppercuts. But then, despite Ian Fleming's protestations that he wanted an actor like Cary Grant or Noel Coward (!?!) to play Bond, which fit Roger Moore and Brosnan to a tee, it feels like Craig really is Fleming's creation come to life.

RIC MEYERS

(author, *Films of Fury: The Kung Fu Movie Book*)

If a head-cock was the defining moment of Brosnan's *Bond* in *GoldenEye,* then virtually the entirety of Paul Haggis and Martin Campbell's *Casino Royale* was the defining moment of Daniel Craig's *Bond*, and essentially the entire series. Despite Richard Maibaum, Johanna Harwood, Terence Young, and Sean Connery creating the movie Bond from Ian Fleming's exceptional literary foundation, this *Casino Royale* was so exceptionally, tastefully, expertly, and insightfully made, it doesn't even seem to belong to the *James Bond* film world that came before.

DANIEL CRAIG

(actor, "James Bond")

In *Casino Royale*, James Bond is a darker character, which is how Ian Fleming originally wrote him. We start right at the beginning of Bond's career, when he has a lot of rough edges, and he doesn't like to get involved with people. As the movie goes on, though, he becomes more refined.

MARTIN CAMPBELL

(director, *Casino Royale*)

Casino Royale is the book where Bond becomes a double-0. He was prone to making rash judgments and thinking more with his heart than his head. He drank too much, smoked 70 cigarettes a day, and was very misogynistic. In the course of the story, he has a serious romance, and by the end he becomes the Bond we all know and love. His evolution is really what the book's about, and that's what this movie is about, too.

JOHN CORK

(film historian, author, *James Bond: The Legacy*)

With *The Spy Who Loved Me*, the *Bond* novels and short stories ceased to be a primary inspiration for the Bond films. Sure, there were references, an unused scene from *Live and Let Die* in this film or that; a character named dropped here or there, but no one was seriously looking to base a film off of Fleming's books. With *Casino Royale*, that changed. While the first half of the film only makes small references to the novel, the second half is a legitimate film version of the first *James Bond* adventure. Fleming was a brilliant writer, and *Casino Royale* is a powerful story that sets up the Bond we know and follow. It was great to see how that novel reinvigorated the series.

PHIL MÉHEUX

(director of photography, *Casino Royale*)

Fleming wrote *Casino Royale* as a straightforward thriller. The book has some very ugly scenes in it. The producers and Martin all felt some of the more recent *Bond* films had gotten slightly off track and too wound up in visual effects. The man is a government-hired assassin, but the series was becoming unreal.

MARTIN CAMPBELL

Once you get to an invisible car and that sequence of snowboarding off a fucking iceberg or whatever the hell it was—which was done digitally and looked awful—in *Die Another Day,* for Barbara and Michael that was the end of it. They had to rethink it, obviously.

JOHN CORK

When I met with Michael and Barbara to pitch to get a job writing for them in 1993, *Casino Royale* was the first thing I brought up. I believe it was the first thing Purvis and Wade brought up. I think nearly everyone wanted *Casino Royale* done in some way, yet the rights were not available. With the settlement of the Sony lawsuit, and bringing the distribution rights to MGM films, it was a perfect time.

It also became the perfect time to essentially reboot the series, transitioning from Pierce Brosnan to Daniel Craig and from a 007 well-established in his career to one first getting his license to kill. Of course, to listen to Brosnan tell the story, he received a phone call from Broccoli and Wilson (*a phone call*?!?) admitting that they didn't know where else to take the series and needed to start over, so they were moving on. The reality, according to others, is that the actor's agent was pushing for a $40 million payday, reportedly proclaiming that without Brosnan there was no Bond.

BARBARA BROCCOLI
(producer, *Casino Royale*)

We were very happy obviously with *Die Another Day.* It was the most successful film we'd had. We loved Pierce and he had made four great films for us. We then sat down to figure out what we were going to do with *Bond 21.* Michael and I felt at the end of *Die Another Day* that we had sort of taken Bond along a sort of fantastical journey and that we had kind of reached the point of no return in terms of a little bit too much CGI: the invisible car and things like that.

MATT GOURLEY
(cohost, *James Bonding* podcast)

I like *GoldenEye* a lot. I really do. And I like Pierce Brosnan as an actor quite a bit, but I knew him as Remington Steele, in the same way that people probably knew Roger Moore as The Saint. For me personally, the films after *GoldenEye* just weren't for me. They seemed like too much of a rehash, without bringing anything new. The issue I take issue with in the Brosnan run is not all that much to do with Brosnan. It's more to do with them kind of trying to strike a tone balance between Connery and Moore, feeling like they said, "We understand there's good in both. Let's take both of the good of those." But those things, those are oil and water to me. They don't work. The way they'd go campy and then ask you to believe in the sincerity of the darker moments were nose-bleedy to me. They would just jar me.

MICHAEL G. WILSON

We'd had writers start on the next picture. We also were having problems with Pierce's agent. He had recently changed agents. And I was sitting there—and we'd just read the newest draft of the treatment—and Barbara said to me, "What do you want to do?" We had just won the lawsuit and now we owned *Casino Royale* and I said, "I'd just like to start all over again. I'd just like to make *Casino Royale* and clear the whole thing out." She said, "Exactly what I want to do. Let's do it." And she got on a plane and said to the studio, "We want to start all over again and do *Casino Royale*." And they're kind of, like, "What? You know, that's a big risk."

We just started with Sony and went over to see Amy Pascal, then head of Sony. She said, "Oh, it's going to be so great working with you." You know, she's very enthusiastic. "So, when are we going to have *Casino Royale*? Who are you going to have as Q and Moneypenny?" "They're not going to be in it." "Oh," she said. "Well, what about the girl?" We said, "Girl dies in the end." She said, "This is a *Bond* film?" "Yeah, it's a *Bond* film." "Oh my God, no, no, no." I said, "This is what we've got to do, because we've just gotten too fanciful with the invisible cars and all that stuff. We've got to bring it back down to Earth." And to their credit, the studios all went along with us, both Sony and MGM. Our feeling was that if we kept going the way we were going, it was going to kill off the franchise

BARBARA BROCCOLI

Casino Royale was the first book that Fleming wrote about James Bond, and when my father and his partner, Harry Saltzman, had gotten the rights from Ian Fleming, *Casino Royale* was not available, so they couldn't do that one. Which was a shame, because they really wanted to. So they ended up doing *Dr. No*. They started there, and in fact later on *Casino Royale* was made by Columbia as a spoof. So we got the rights to *Casino Royale* in the '90s. We really wanted to make it, and Michael said, "Let's just do it now." So, Michael and I sat down and we said, "You know, I think that this is the thing that we've got to do." And that's what we set out doing.

MICHAEL G. WILSON

The same thing happened with *Moonraker.* We stuck with Roger, but we just couldn't keep going with that. We had to change direction, because it was getting ridiculous. So we had to change, but *Moonraker* was the most successful picture, and the next pictures weren't as successful. But it was important to change.

GLEN OLIVER

(pop culture commentator)

Stripping out the "introducing your new James Bond!" elements, *Casino Royale* could have worked very nicely with Pierce. In fact, it might have even worked *better* with Pierce, as the picture could have leveraged his history in the role to create a stronger perceptual frame for his relationship with Vesper. In the same way *On Her Majesty's Secret Service* would have resonated more fully if we were following a Bond we'd already acclimated to.

BARBARA BROCCOLI

Because it was Bond's first mission, it couldn't be someone who had played the role before. So, I mean, that was the kind of difficult part to it, because it meant that we had to make a change. We did discuss it with Pierce, and he was very gracious about it, and he's a great guy. He was a great Bond and he did four wonderful films for us.

JOHN CORK

After *A View to a Kill*, when Michael and Richard Maibaum knew they had to cast a new 007, they developed the idea of looking at Bond's origins. That idea was to introduce Bond as a very young agent, early 20s, just breaking into the service. Cubby nixed that, and that was a good call on his part. By the time they came to develop *Casino Royale,* they knew they had to introduce Bond as a more seasoned agent, and that worked well.

RAY MORTON

(senior writer, *Script* magazine)

I think the part of the script that works least well is the "young James Bond's first mission" element. *Casino Royale* is Fleming's first James Bond novel, but it is not the story of Bond's first mission. Apart from the fact that *Batman Begins* was an influential hit at the time the script was being developed, I'm not sure why Eon felt it necessary to make this the story of "how Bond became 007," and I think these elements are the film's weakest.

To begin with, they significantly alter Bond's background and therefore his character. The Bond of the novels and the other movies is an upper class (or at least upper middle-class) sophisticate well associated with the finer things in life and comfortable moving in the higher echelons in society. Although it's never specifically stated, the Bond in the *Casino Royale* screenplay comes across like a slightly thuggish fellow from the lower classes who has to be introduced to things such as martinis and tuxedos. (In this respect, it feels like the writers misinterpreted the famous Fleming description of Bond as a "blunt instrument" as a description of his character rather than his function.) The Bond of the novels and other films was a naval officer; this one is a special forces commando. The Bond of the novels and the other films is a man who is always supremely in control. This Bond is a man who is barely in control of himself. None of these are bad elements in and of themselves, but they're definitely not the Bond we know and love. This Bond is more of a standard modern action hero than the 007 we're used to and lacks many of the qualities that make Bond a special and unique character.

GLEN OLIVER

Despite Hollywood's trends to the contrary, there is no need *whatsoever* to steer toward young James Bond stories, Jane Bond movies, and what not. Much like *Star Wars* and *Star Trek,* there are more than enough ingredients in the mix to tell perfectly suitable, it not extraordinary, 007 stories as is. The *Bond* franchise has always, and should always be, about tweaking and refining and experimenting, and this is a nearly perfect vehicle for which to do so.

007 isn't even confined to any *one* genre. These are spy movies, sure. But they're also action pictures, they have strong streaks of humor, some of them are thrillers, more than a few of them have considerable science-fiction elements, and every once in a while there's some gushy stuff. That's one helluva a palette to work with. The flexibility provided by the nature of this almost undefined genre should afford creators any number of opportunities and luxuries, and ensure that a hard reboot of the franchise will never be required.

Despite the fact he had turned down numerous opportunities to direct the post-*GoldenEye films in the series,* director Martin Campbell was more than willing to return for *Casino Royale*, given the nature of the film and the forging of a new James Bond actor.

MARTIN CAMPBELL

I came back simply because it was so different. It was going back to the books, which is what was so great about it.

DANIEL CRAIG

Martin fires everyone up. You obviously need that level of energy in the action sequences, but it's equally valuable in quieter, dramatic scenes like the poker tournament.

JUDI DENCH
(actress, "M")

I did my first-ever *Bond* with Martin, and it's good to come back to work with him again. He is very enthusiastic and knows the conditions that actors like to work within. He knows that when you are doing repeated takes, you need to have an atmosphere of suspended calm and quiet, so you can get to the next take quickly while everything is still clear in your mind. There's nothing worse than an enormous break between takes, with people relaxing and wandering about. Martin is encouraging, gentle, and excitable. And he knows the *Bond* scene very, very well.

MADS MIKKELSEN
(actor, "Le Chiffre")

Martin is very specific. If I come in at six o'clock in the morning, he will have been there since four o'clock rehearsing by himself. Very energetic person, very in love with this business and in love with the film he is doing. He is also listening, and if you come up with an idea, he would definitely try it out. So he is a man that is willing to work with you instead of just dictating you.

MARTIN CAMPBELL

Part of the appeal is that Barbara and Michael are great and they give you your freedom. The only time they'll pull you in, and quite rightly, is when they feel you're stepping too far outside the *Bond* movie. There were a couple of things on *Casino Royale*, tiny moments, where Barbara got a little bit upset about a couple of things, but both remained in the film. One of them was the scene when Bond and Vesper get to the casino and they're in the hotel room and she's getting all made up. Bond, full of attitude, comes in and hangs up her dress and says, "I want you to wear this, because I want the players looking at you and not at their cards. A distracting technique." It was chauvinist as hell. Then he goes back in and, my God, he sees this beautiful suit laid out. I remember Barbara saying, "You can't have that. You can't have that. Bond has his own suit." I said, "But he's not Bond yet." And who better than someone as gorgeous as her? Tit for tat, you know what I mean? It's a perfect scene, and in the end Barbara was fine with it.

The other was at the beginning when he breaks into M's apartment. She comes in and she's all pissed off with the way he's just sitting there. Anyway, they're talking and he says, "Oh, I thought M was just a letter, but then I realized . . ." And she cuts him off and says, "One more word and I'll have you shot." Which I thought was terrific. I loved it. But Barbara felt that's not the way that Bond went. Other than that, I was left entirely alone, and they're marvelous as producers. They let you do what you're there to do. Michael Wilson is wonderful, too, because he has a very dry sense of humor. He's very calm, focused, and just relaxed about it all. He's somewhat of a writer himself, tweaking and stuff. He'll come up with stuff and sort of suggest things and so forth. He's just very practical.

MADS MIKKELSEN

Barbara and Michael [Wilson] were on the set all the time. That might sound as if, "Uh-oh," but they were there for us fetching coffee, asking if everything was alright, whenever we played poker there would be a little knock and Michael Wilson would be out there coming in with his four little chips. It really fast became a little family. It sounds like a horrible thing to say, but it did become a family. I was so surprised. I had come from small films and I go to this enormous budget film and I anticipated a lot of screaming and people getting fired and drama. It was just like being on a small Danish film, though of course there were 400 people running around you, but you tend to forget that. They were definitely the main reason for us feeling that way, Barbara and Michael.

The early drafts of the *Casino Royale* script were written by Neal Purvis and Robert Wade (the sole writers on *Die Another Day*), and it was obvious to Campbell that another voice needed to be added to the mix. That voice was Paul Haggis, whose Academy Award–nominated credits include *Million Dollar Baby* and *Crash*, and who was also the creator of the TV series *Due South* and cocreator of *Walker, Texas Ranger.* At the time he was first contacted, Haggis was on vacation with his family in Italy when he received word from his agent that Broccoli, Wilson, and Campbell were interested in him rewriting the *Casino Royale* script. Unfortunately, he had promised his family he would take the month off, so the mountain, in essence, came to him.

RIC MEYERS

Purvis and Wade, who have never shown any skill remotely close to what is seen/heard here, most likely cobbled the pieces together, but clearly Paul Haggis turned it into an actual script with the best dialogue and structure of any *Bond,* while Campbell clearly turned it into a movie with the best *mise-en-scène* in the series. His taste, style, and appreciation for kinetic, comprehensible, exciting action permeates the experience.

MARTIN CAMPBELL

I want to put this delicately, but I personally don't think Purvis and Wade do much service to *Bond.* What happens with them, I guess, is they lay the basics and always another writer, inevitably a Paul Haggis or a Jez Butterworth, or whoever, comes in and completely redoes the script. That seems to be the pattern now, where the director comes in and sort of then wants his own writer. Barbara and Michael, to their credit, always do it. They don't disagree.

PAUL HAGGIS

(screenwriter, *Casino Royale*)

Before they arrived, they sent me the script to read. Purvis and Wade are good writers; I was a big fan of *Let Him Have It,* but I felt that they hadn't really redefined this character. My understanding is that they wanted us to redefine Bond, and the script had problems. Anyway, Barbara, Michael, and Martin came to the town of Balsina, a little town, and we talked. I seem to remember saying something like, "The script has many sins, only one of them is unforgivable. You don't have an act three. Would you like one?" That was a big, complete asshole move. And they said, "Yeah, of course." But at this point they have already built this giant set; they were building all the sets, including one for the sinking house at the end.

In this version, if I recall, once they get to Venice, Bond goes out shopping or something, then he comes back to the hotel room and finds Vesper dead on the bed, having slit her wrists. There's a note that says, "Watch the TV." So Bond sits down and puts a video cassette in the television, and for a couple of pages sits there and watches Vesper's taped confession, telling him the entire plot, that she had betrayed him, blah, blah, blah. It ends with a man we've never met, who's across St. Mark's Square picking up money at the bank and ends up at the sinking house with these other guys. Bond kills them and gets away, and *that's* the end.

MARTIN CAMPBELL

I wanted Paul Haggis, because, frankly, I think the script with the two boys deviated so much from the book, if you see where I mean. Massive action sequences, and I remember there was a huge action sequence on a dam, of all things. God knows I can't even remember what context it was, but I suggested Paul Haggis and Paul went right back to the book. That's what he based it on and completely rewrote it from start to finish.

It was Haggis' thought that once he's been betrayed, Bond is going to want to kill *Vesper;* that *she* is the one he's actually after.

PAUL HAGGIS

He doesn't give a damn about the money or the *Bond* villain. It's her, and that betrayal, that's most important to him. He traces her, she and the villain are going to run into the sinking house, she's going to somehow lock herself into something, then she's going to drown. Bond is going to realize, as his beloved is drowning, he's going to try and save her. He's going be unable to do that, and he's going to be haunted by that forever. After that, he becomes James Bond. And they said, "How are you going to do that?" and I said, "I don't know. Go away." So they went off and they were really, really lovely to me. They trusted me.

MARTIN CAMPBELL

In the case of *Casino,* there were two sequences from Purvis and Wade: the chase at the front was a five- or six-line paragraph that basically said, "Now we're going to have the best parkour sequence ever filmed." Which I understand. No point in writing six pages of a particular parkour sequence. You might as well just put that in there, because between the director and the stunt arranger, and your second-unit guy, you're going to make a sequence. So that was their idea, the parkour. And the sinking house at the end. The action within those sequences is completely a combination of myself and Gary Powell, the stunt arranger.

PAUL HAGGIS

So I wrote act three and sent it to them. It started on, I think, page 70 or something and went through to the end of the movie. And they liked it. But then they said, "Quick, what's next?" So I ended up writing act two and sent it to them. Then they said, "Paul, Paul, Paul, we need an act one, we're going to go shoot." So likely the production got pushed by a couple of weeks, because of the casting. So I was able then to write act one and sent it to them without ever having read the entire script together.

RAY MORTON

(film historian, senior writer, *Script* magazine)

Paul Haggis did the final rewrites on *Casino Royale*. He did a great job tuning up the dialogue and creating a new third act and finale for the story set in Venice. And so, along with Purvis and Wade he can be credited for rebooting the *Bond* series in spectacular fashion.

PAUL HAGGIS

It was great fun doing it, though I didn't expect it to be me, because although I've always loved *Bond*, that's not the kind of writer I am. But I did love just disappearing into that character and reinventing the dialogue and treating him like a human being rather than the Bond we've come to know who was larger than life. What I needed to do was create the characters and really dig in under the skin of Bond and Vesper. I was really curious as to how Bond became Bond. What was his relationship to women? How did he turn out this way? In the readings that I've done, for example, he would only sleep with married women. Wow, what kind of man is *that*? And I wondered what would happen if that man actually fell in love and really opened up. Then I had to ask myself a lot of questions, like, "Why do we fall in love?" And I said, "Well, for me, often I need a person who can see through all my armor and see who I really am." And Bond has a lot of emotional armor, so someone who can see him through that, who will call him on that, *that's* going to be really attractive to him.

The key to this reboot, of course, was the casting of Bond himself; Barbara Broccoli is the one who immediately locked on to Daniel Craig, and found herself in the position of having to convince just about everyone else.

MICHAEL G. WILSON

I guess we spent about a year and a half or two years looking for someone: looking at over 20 people in the UK and former British colonies and looked at innumerable films, and we had some film tests. In the end we chose Daniel. He was the only one we offered the film to. There's been some speculation that we offered to other people, but that's not accurate.

BARBARA BROCCOLI

We're in the movie business and so you're always looking at people. He's just been one of those actors. He's an astounding actor and he is very charismatic, and he has an amazing screen presence. We just thought from the very beginning that he was the guy, and when we approached him he said, "Listen, I'll keep an open mind about it, but I'm not going to make a decision until I see a script." From the time we gave him the script to the time that we announced him, I think, was three or four weeks. So all of the stuff that was going on in the press was speculation, and I won't comment on who we met or didn't meet. That's like saying, "Who did you sleep with before you got married?" The thing is that we always wanted him, but obviously we didn't know if he was going to do it. So, we met other people, and we looked at other people, but we never offered it to anyone but him. We offered it to him. He read the script. He said yes and we announced it.

MARTIN CAMPBELL

What happened was we tested eight people for Bond. Daniel came in and the poor bugger had just literally done the red eye or something from Baltimore. So he had to fly overnight. I felt so sorry for him, because he was obviously wrecked in terms of God knows how many hours he'd been up. I test everybody, and they do a very thorough test on Bond. It's a lot.

MICHAEL G. WILSON

When we audition for the role of Bond, we ask actors to do the scene in *From Russia with Love,* where Bond meets Tatiana Romanova for the first time. That scene has everything you want to know about a potential Bond: drama, romance, and action.

MARTIN CAMPBELL

They *always* choose that scene. It's where Connery comes into his hotel room, takes off his jacket, his gun, throws them on the sofa, turns the bath on in the bathroom, then senses a presence. Goes out across the terrace and into his bedroom, and there is the blond girl, from *From Russia with Love*. He then sits down and the scene is Connery, on the one hand, and he needs information about the Lector decoder. On the other hand, she, of course, is an agent who has been sent out to snare Bond and is working for Rosa Klebb. So he has to seduce her. In other words, it contains all the elements of Bond in a funny way: seduction and the digging for information. I shot that with every one of them.

RIC MEYERS

It's no secret that, during the *Casino Royale* casting process, Campbell preferred Henry Cavill, who would go on to become both Superman and The Man from U.N.C.L.E., but was deemed too young by producers. It was reportedly Barbara Broccoli who held out for Daniel Craig, much the same way her father had held out for Pierce Brosnan, Timothy Dalton, and then Pierce Brosnan again.

MARTIN CAMPBELL

We tested Henry Cavill, who did a really good test. The guy out of *ER*, Goran Visnjic, and Sam Worthington are the ones who come to mind. And then Daniel came in and Daniel was obviously by far the best actor. He's not conventionally handsome like Pierce Brosnan or anything. Ironically, what he is, is very much more like what Fleming conceived. He always said Hoagie Carmichael was the model for that. Anyway, to cut a long story short, they all went off and Barbara was pushing for Daniel. She really liked the idea of Daniel, and what we all had to do was look at the test, meet in a room at the back of Harrods—I'll never forget that—and it was all very democratic, I must say. There was myself; Barbara; Michael; the casting director, Debbie McWilliams; Amy Pascal; I think Howard Stringer, the chairman of Sony, was there. We had to say who it was, right? Daniel Craig was the frontrunner at this point, because Barbara had been pushing for him. I was unsure, because I was steeped in Pierce, the good-looking Bond.

BARBARA BROCCOLI

He just seemed right for now. He just seemed like he was a man who is a twenty-first century Bond. This script was very complex and we needed an actor who could handle all of these things, because he has to be agile physically, tough, you've got to believe that he can kill people; but in this script, as you saw, you also get to see inside of him. He has to be vulnerable, but remain tough, and I think that he's done a hell of a job. I think that he's fantastic.

MARTIN CAMPBELL

I have to say, I was on the fence about him, because Daniel was not the conventional Bond. He was a superb actor, but I remember saying, "I have to think about this." I had to get my head around it. Every Bond had been the sort of handsome Bond that we all kind of knew. This was on Friday, and on Saturday I watched *Layer Cake,* which he's superb in. I thought, "He's great. He's absolutely great." And he had a sense of humor in that film. There was also a twinkle in his eyes, and I thought, "Barbara is absolutely right." And she was.

PAUL HAGGIS

Barbara and Michael read the draft of the script I'd written; they liked it; they sent it to Daniel Craig, who was their first choice, I believe, at the time. Barbara had asked me my opinion of him, and, having seen *Layer Cake*, I said, "Oh, he's the guy to go for." She took my advice, and was obviously very good at casting.

DANIEL CRAIG

It's a simple reason why I wanted to do it. There's no kind of bullshit attached to it: The script was great. I got it, I read it, and I said, "I'd be a fool not to have a go at this." I really had that in the back of my mind; hindsight is a very easy thing to say this with, but I was going, "If you don't do this, you're going to regret not having a go at it." He's one of the biggest and most iconic figures in movie history, and I'm an actor. This is what I do for a living, and if I don't take on challenges like this, then what's the point? And work was going well; it'd been going very well for me. I'd been very happy with what I was doing, but I didn't expect Bond to happen. I had other kinds of plans in my mind maybe of what I wanted to go and do, and how I wanted to carry on, but *this* carried on. Barbara Broccoli is very persuasive, and she made me an offer that I couldn't refuse.

JOHN CORK

Daniel Craig had been known as villains and for his role in *Layer Cake. And* blond. Now it's a stroke of genius, but then? Casting a new actor as 007 is a fraught proposition. There is no sure thing. Martin Campbell was very skeptical of Daniel Craig even weeks into shooting. But it turned out to be a brilliant decision to cast him. He had the experience, the physicality, and the talent to make Bond his own.

DANIEL CRAIG

I was in Baltimore when I got the news, on my own, so I went out alone to have a drink and celebrate. Of course I couldn't very well start telling people in the bar, "I'm James Bond!" They probably would have thrown me out or called the hospital to collect me. As soon as the reality of the situation sank in, I wanted to start preparing physically. I wanted to do as much of the action work as I could so that the audience could see it's me and it's real. I feel like I became a sports nut of sorts, and that meant acquiring injuries and carrying on, bashing through to the next level of pain. Although Gary Powell and his stunt team did fantastic work to make sure everything was as safe as possible, if you don't get bruised playing Bond, you're not doing it properly.

MARTIN CAMPBELL

It didn't take long for me to realize that Daniel would be a revelation for the audience. He combines toughness with charm and a sense of humor, and because this is a much more character-driven story, his depth and gravitas were a perfect match for the role. At the same time, he was in great physical shape and proved himself to be excellent in the action scenes.

MICHAEL G. WILSON

Daniel was very reluctant, and we kept asking him to come in, talking to him, and finally he says, "Well, *if* I do it, I'll do it one hundred percent; I'll totally do it." So then, when we hired him, he went into a six-month physical thing that really transformed his body. I've never seen anything like it. He must have added, I don't know, ten inches to his thighs and the whole chest. He actually transformed himself. And he kept at it; he eats this scientifically controlled diet all the time and he goes to bed at nine o'clock at night when he's making the movies. He's like a monk.

DANIEL CRAIG

I didn't do anything special. I went to the gym and I pushed weights and I ran about. It was intense and I had to do it every day. I was doing an hour and a half a day, maybe. I would work out, and we increased the weight quite rapidly, because that was the only way that I was going to fill out, and I had a high protein diet. At the end of the workout, I would do twenty minutes on the bike to try and keep the fat down. There is no real secret to it. You can find it in any health magazine. I had a good trainer, which helped and encouraged me.

JUDI DENCH

Daniel has a wonderful presence. He's very handsome and strong, but at the same time, you wouldn't want to be on the wrong side of him. Those are all perfect traits to have as an actor. He seems to have relaxed into the role. I'm sure it gave him some anxiety, as it would any actor, but he doesn't show it on set.

DANIEL CRAIG

The biggest difference on a movie set like that one is when you walk on and you're doing a huge stunt sequence and you get an understanding of how big the scale is. You sort of see all the many more people on set, but when you're doing a dialogue sequence, whether I was doing it with Eva or Mads or Judi, it's all scaled down. You're trying to do the same thing that I was doing in *The Mother.* You're just telling a story, and you're acting with other people. I don't differentiate between the two, and that was important when we were doing the film. I didn't want us to be sort of shooting two movies. I didn't want to be shooting an action movie and a love story, or whatever the story is—I wanted it to be absolutely seamless. I wanted it to be that I could see the storytelling going on in this.

JUDI DENCH

He has a great sense of humor, and I always find a shared sense of humor is the first clue to working well with an actor. He also has a kind of self-deprecation about him that is very attractive.

EVA GREEN

(actress, "Vesper Lynd")

He's a gentleman and he's strong, and he's not mannered. That ruggedness is attractive and probably quite dangerous. He is sexy and not self-conscious, which is very important for a man, and he has a sense of humor—another plus.

DANIEL CRAIG

I didn't go out of my way to make Bond likable in this movie. I didn't go out saying, "Please like him." I wanted to show someone who changed. I did not want him to be the same person at the beginning of the movie that he was at the end, and I wasn't thinking beyond this movie at the time. But I *was* thinking that if we ever did another movie, we needed to have somewhere to go. I wanted to see a fallible human being, someone who made mistakes, and someone who an audience watches and goes, "This might turn out good. This might turn out really bad." And sometimes it did. But I wanted him to be fallible, because, dramatically, it's much more interesting. If I play any character, I want to see a weakness within them, because I want to see how they cope with that and deal with things. I don't want to watch any two-dimensional character. I want to watch a rounded person make decisions, and I can't believe it when they make decisions and they're Teflon-coated. That was not interesting to me.

Craig may not have worried about whether or not the public "liked" Bond, but he certainly had faced widespread criticism upon being announced in the part, ranging from the familiar internet bric-a-brats to the tabloid media.

MADS MIKKELSEN

It was difficult to see that feeling on him, but I am sure there was a lot going on inside. It wasn't something that we went around talking about on the set, because that wouldn't benefit anyone, but I am sure that he felt the love and respect for him as an actor on the set all along. The only thing he could do was focus on the work and do his best. You couldn't listen to all of that gossip about being blond; it is really hard to take it seriously, but if I went to work—any kind of work—every day reading in the paper that I am crap at it, that is a hard day.

BARBARA BROCCOLI

It was bizarre. I mean, I was perplexed by the whole thing. We were in the Bahamas and we'd been shooting for a month and all this stuff was coming out, and I thought, "How can people be judging something that they haven't seen?" It's the most bizarre thing. I think that it died out because everyone did start to think, "Well, wait a minute. What are they basing these comments on?" They hadn't seen him play the role.

DANIEL CRAIG

Look, it *did* affect me. I will not lie to you. I went, "You know what, what can I do? I can't answer it." I couldn't start getting on to internet sites and talking back. I get the passion that people feel for this, and I understand that. I make films, and normally when I make a film we wait until we get to the premiere and we get so the audience sees it, and *then* I start getting reviews. It was, like, "See the fucking movie and then you can say what you like about it, but watch the movie." So that's my answer There was no point in getting in tit for tat arguments about the way that I looked.

MADS MIKKELSEN

I am sure that he didn't read it, but it was hard not to be aware. It was all over the place all the time, and I understand to a certain point why people reacted, because it was Bond. And he was interesting as a new Bond like a new president. But the things that they came up with, like, as I said, being blond, it's ridiculous and you can't work with that, but I am sure he had a hard time. He is breathing much easier now, I guess.

EVA GREEN

In the makeup trailer in the morning, sometimes you read the tabloids and you see, "Oh, he's blond. He can't act. He can't drive cars." But what can you do? I mean, I knew his work before and I always thought it was fantastic. But the thing in England is that Bond is like the Queen, so he was worried; he wanted to be so good. Now I think he's relieved, because people appreciate him as Bond.

BARBARA BROCCOLI

When my father and Harry hired Sean Connery, everybody from Ian Fleming to everyone else was saying, "Oh, what about . . . ?" Even the studio, when they received the screen test for Sean Connery, said he was too much of a common man and that they should keep looking. Try again. Ian Fleming was surprised, but once he saw him play the role, he then said, "Wow, he's fantastic!" And when Sean sprung on the screen, at the time in post-war Britain when everything was dark and sort of black and white, suddenly Sean Connery exploded on the screen in these Technicolor movies that were sexy and funny and dangerous. Then everyone said, "God, he's great."

Once he came to terms with the reactions of the media and some of the fans, Craig focused on the task at hand: becoming James Bond.

DANIEL CRAIG

When I was signed, I read most of the books. I watched all the movies and then I kind of put myself there. There is a huge lineage, a huge history of the books and the films, and to ignore it would be stupid. So I soaked it up and got as much of it as I could, and I had them in my trailer. I would go to relax and would put one on and check it out. I didn't want to miss a trick; I wanted to do something good.

Next to Diana Rigg's Tracy Vincenzo in *On Her Majesty's Secret Service*, it's difficult to think of another *Bond* leading lady that plays as significant a role, not only in the film but in terms of her impact on Bond as a character, as Eva Green's Vesper Lynd.

BARBARA BROCCOLI

When you look at the early films, the women were very extraordinary for the '60s. They were pilots, and tough and strong women who did extraordinary things; who were sexual and had an equal sort of sexual appetite. They weren't the wilting flowers. I think that what happened was that maybe in the '70s and '80s it became more window dressing. We had groups of girls in bikinis sitting around swimming pools, and I think that's where we got that sort of attention. And they're all beautiful women and great women and they all contributed to the glamour and beauty of the movies.

EVA GREEN

When they approached me, they didn't give me the script, just sent me the sides, and asked me to audition in London. My agent was, like, "Be careful, it's a *Bond* Girl." I was concerned, too. If it's just the beautiful girl for Bond, I didn't want to do that. They kept asking me to come in and audition, but I had this other project. Two weeks before it collapsed, they gave me the script and I read it. I was, like, "Oh my God!" I really liked it. It's so different from the other roles that we've seen in the past, and the character of Bond is much more human and realistic and trashy, and more emotional. So I thought, "Why not?" I went to Prague, I met Barbara Broccoli and Michael Wilson and Daniel, of course. We did that scene; it was very low key, very casual.

BARBARA BROCCOLI

We had seen Eva Green in *Kingdom of Heaven* and *The Dreamers* and we thought that she was fantastic. The thing is that this character of Vesper, the way that it was written in the book and in the screenplay . . . I mean, in *Bond* lore she is the most important character because she affects his life forever. So we had to cast it really well. She had to be alluring and beautiful. She had to be a great actress, but she had to have this kind of mystery about her. She has to be a kind of enigma, because he falls in love with her and instinctively he knows that there is something missing; there is something wrong, and he can't quite put his finger on it. It's a very difficult role to cast, and we'd seen Eva and we called up and they said, "No, she's not available. She's doing a film in France."

We started looking at a lot of people and no one just seemed right. I kept saying to the casting director, "Just ring her agent every week." And this went on for months and months. She wasn't available. She was signed to do another film, and I just kept saying, "You have to keep calling every week." Eventually they said, "Well, the film may not happen." And all of this stuff. It was one of those European finance films and sometimes they're tricky to get together, and so I said, "Please, please get her in." And I felt like she had to do it. It was just fate that at the end, her other film, the dates moved and we were already shooting. She came to Prague and we were all kind of anxious, because sometimes when you meet someone it isn't exactly what you thought. She walked in and Martin and Michael and I went, "Oh, my God. She's it." Then she came in and read with Daniel and he was, like, "Oh, we've got to have her." So it was fate that things shifted and she was able to do it.

MARTIN CAMPBELL

The relationship between Vesper and Bond is the spine of the story, and we needed an actress who could hold her own against Bond. There is no doubt that this is the best female role in all of Fleming's books, so we tested extensively to ensure we cast the most suitable actress. Again, we tested six or eight girls and we just weren't happy. We just didn't feel it was there. And then we talked about Eva Green, who was so gorgeous and great in *The Dreamers*. So we met her, and she had quite a heavy accent on her English. She said, "Look, I can lose this accent. I'll always have the accent, but I can really lighten it."

EVA GREEN

There was some mumbling at the screen test, that's not a good sign, then I went to New York, four days after, and my agent called me and said, actually you have to come back straight away to Prague and audition again, because they're not fully satisfied. So, I was crying. It's very stressful, and I didn't know what was wrong, but they eventually said, "It's just the English, darling; you just have to work on the English." But I'm sure it was not really that; it's always a pretext, they're not sure, they just want to be, you know, certain, so I had to do it again in costume, and on the real set with Daniel. It was very formal, and they called me a week after, and I got the part.

DANIEL CRAIG

I know there was a lot in the press about who was going to do this and whatever, but when she came in, there was no decision for me. She brings something to it that's great. She's got a mystery about her any way that you look, and the character had to have a mystery. She's beautiful and she's a great actress, which is a really important thing. It needed to be someone that I think he could fall in love with, and she does such a fantastic job. She is the heartbeat of this movie and that was crucial, that we got that love story going, because everything else sort of slots into place around it.

EVA GREEN

It was one of the best scripts I'd read in a long time. It's deep, with lots of twists and turns, and the love story moved me. Vesper is a complex person. She is full of secrets, and I think that is why James Bond is attracted to her, because he can't really see through her. She is like a sphinx. She has many layers: she's sharp, sassy, quick-witted, but also vulnerable. She and Bond spark off each other; they are always bantering and they understand each other on the surface.

MARTIN CAMPBELL

So Barbara and myself, we really liked the idea, but the studio *didn't*. Sony didn't want her, because they were worried about the accent. So she went away for two or three weeks and we played a game with the studio, which was we kept saying we were considering other girls as we started shooting. Then we said, "Look, fuck, we're up against time. We've got to take her. There's no other option." That was by design. Then, she came in while we were shooting. Actually it was the scene in M's apartment, and that's where we tested her. And she had indeed lost a lot of her accent; she did what she said. We shot a scene with her and sent it to the studio and they were fine with it. So that's how we managed to get her.

DANIEL CRAIG

Once she did the screen test, there was never a question about it. She's just got this innate mystery about her. She's got something going on and she's a fine actress. That sequence on the train, which was part of her audition process, and we really put her through the ringer—we had a day's filming of where we had to do that scene over and over again, and the point was that it should be fun, and she just nailed it. Absolutely nailed it. I mean, it's incredibly important that we got that right, and she absolutely made that her own, and therefore all that plot and all that love story I think works fantastically because of her.

LISA FUNNELL

(author, *For His Eyes Only: The Women of James Bond*)

Vesper Lynd really breaks down the *Bond* Girl mold. She is *the* woman the way that Irene Adler is to Sherlock Holmes. Eva Green is divine, but her performance and just the presence that she has in *Casino Royale,* for me, was something different than I had seen before, and it was more than just Halle Berry kicking butt in *Die Another Day.*

EVA GREEN

Vesper is not the classic, iconic *Bond* Girl, wearing a bikini, being sexy, and firing guns. There is more to her than that. She is the first woman Ian Fleming wrote about, and she has a great impact on Bond's life. She is the root of all the *Bond* women who follow and explains why he behaves the way he does with those women. I also love the way she evolves throughout the whole movie, because she's so strong and sassy and very clever, and he's not expecting that. We know Bond is a big seducer and can read through people, but he can't read through her. I mean, he's trying hard. I like the fact that she slowly opens up and becomes more and more vulnerable. They're very similar in their way.

With everything about *Casino Royale* being far more rooted in reality than many of the predecessors in the series, finding an actor to bring that realism to the villain was just as important. The answer came in the form of Mads Mikkelsen.

MADS MIKKELSEN

They wanted me to audition and they called me up when I was shooting a Danish film in Prague and couldn't make it. I didn't have the time, so I told them that and didn't expect to be called back again—I thought that they probably had a couple of thousand people that I was one among. But they *did* call back and they were willing to pay for my flight ticket as well. That sounded serious, so I eventually did it. I came over there, got dressed and ready to shoot the scene with Daniel, but they didn't have the time, so they gave me the part like that. It was kind of intimidating. On one hand, I was glad not to audition, because audition situations are normally strange; standing with a machine gun in your hand, shooting at a chopper that doesn't exist. On the other hand, I also wanted them to see me before they said yes, but I understood that they had seen me in a lot of films and they did have a conversation with me before.

BARBARA BROCCOLI

With Mads, our casting director Debbie McWilliams travels around Europe a lot and meets with a lot of international casting directors. She came back from Scandinavia with this film called *Open Hearts,* which is a very bleak dogma type film; a very, very interesting film. She said, "Oh, what about this actor? He's really good." And she put it on, and sometimes if you're looking at a lot of tapes you look for like ten minutes or fifteen minutes, and you think, "Yes, maybe, no." Whatever. We put this in and we were just transfixed for two hours. "This guy is unbelievable." So we showed him to Martin, and Martin said that he was great, and in fact it was just around Christmas time and I happened to be in New York and he was here with his family. He walked in the door and I said, "This is the guy. This is him." He's so powerful, and again, he has this presence. In the book, Le Chiffre is a very kind of unattractive, ugly, sort of sloth-like creature, and we thought that wasn't going to be very right for this film. He's written as a really kind of horrible and revolting creature, and we were like, "No. We have to have someone sexy and dangerous." He has to be an equal to Bond, and I think that scene, the torture scene between the two of them, is just great. You really get it.

MADS MIKKELSEN

I'm attracted to scripts where my character might have some secrets; to be offered the role of Le Chiffre, "the cipher," a man with no real name, was perfect. Many actors say that playing the villain is more interesting than playing the good guy, because he always has a twist in his character. But I think if you are playing the bad guy, you try to show a good side to him sometimes, and if you are playing the good guy, you try to show a flaw in him, so it's not one-dimensional for the audience. My favorite *Bond* villain was Christopher Walken in *A View to a Kill.* He's got what it takes to be a good villain.

And the audience knows action films, which was another area where *Casino Royale* had to shake up the *Bond* paradigm, which was obvious with the brutal pre-credits scene that saw Bond dispatching an enemy in a bathroom; to the post-credits sequence which features a brilliant parkour foot chase, one of the series' finest action sequences; a fight that takes

Bond and his opponents down four flights of stairs; and a tense airport sequence where 007 has to prevent the detonation of a bomb on the largest plane in the world.

RIC MEYERS

The filmmakers take the Fleming description of Bond as a "blunt instrument" and give it form and function from his dramatic first appearance on. The pre-credit melee in the men's room is the most brutal and effective in the 007 film canon, but it passes the Meyers' Test with flying colors thanks to the traitor's comment "made you feel it, did he?" He did, indeed—as did we, the audience.

MARTIN CAMPBELL

There was originally a cricket game that got cut, because it just felt too laborious. The whole thing was going on too long. It just needed to cut straight into it. So when Bond breaks in the guy's office and so forth, he's there. You just have these flashbacks, and we wanted to come in on the violence of it, really, which was just to energize the thing. And I wanted that scene in black and white. I wanted to start with black and white. One of the reasons was I wanted the first color to be the blood that runs down on-screen. I put the original story of the gun barrel into that movie. That's where that came from. So that one shot where he turns, fires, and then the blood starts, and so that's the first color in the movie.

PHIL MÉHEUX

If you want to do something quite different and turn everyone around, do something in black and white. People are so used to seeing all these stunts and everything in color, and we go right into a scene of black and white with very little stunt work. Some people shoot color and get rid of it in the digital intermediate (DI), but I didn't like the look of that.

RIC MEYERS

But even the pre-credit scene, and the clever incorporation of the previously superfluous gun barrel into the actual story, pales in comparison to the extended, post-credit, parkour chase. If Brosnan's *GoldenEye* head cock hinted at his 007's expertise and professionalism, everything Craig says or does here all but writes it across the sky in fireworks. This sequence is not only the best in *Bond,* it also stands as one of the greatest fight scenes in movie history which, tragically, is actually a pretty short list.

DANIEL CRAIG

Action films have always been changing. We've got the *Bourne* series, which are superb movies. They had kind of brought things to a grittier way, but we've had those for years if we think about movies like the Michael Caine spy movies that they were doing in the '60s. We've always had that and those have always interested. I think that Bond had a lot of that in the beginning, but then that was sort of lost, then came back again with Timothy Dalton. A lot of influences for movies I put into the work that I do. The landscape has changed as far as politically and changes in the world of that nature, but I don't know if we're any less confused than we ever were. That's what I think is enduring about the character. He kind of seems to know the answers, or at least he knows where the bad guy is and he goes and gets him. That's part of the piece of escapism. That's what I wanted to see in my Bond character, the guy who knows what he's up to.

MARTIN CAMPBELL

The whole idea of the parkour sequence was not to make the action seem realistic; it couldn't be done. You can't jump off a fucking crane from one to another; you'd kill yourself, but the *perception* is that it's reality. Do you know what I mean? A lot of that running here and there wasn't invisible cars and ice palaces. It's just about two guys, one of them chasing another. The key to it was to make Bond a little bit clumsy, thinking with his heart instead of his head. So when he jumps, he really makes a fuck up of it almost, right? When he hits things, he hits with one hell of a bang, and there is a kind of a bull-in-a-China-shop attitude with that. Whereas the other guy is very sleek and thought-out and fluid and so forth. But it's the relentless energy that Bond has that gives him the upper hand, though even *then* he fucks up at the end and shoots the guy.

RIC MEYERS

Okay, how do you compare and contrast Craig's Bond with his fast, athletic, adversary? Other Bonds might have tried to duck or dodge a gun thrown at them. Craig's blunt-instrument Bond catches it and throws it back. Other Bonds may have tried to follow their enemy through a narrow window at the top of a wall. Blunt Bond goes *through* the wall. Blunt Bond knows better than to put his forefinger on his earpiece. Blunt Bond knows it's better to use a steam shovel to get past obstructions. Blunt Bond knows it's better to put one bullet in a gas tank than to take on a small army. And so on and so forth with every decision the character clearly makes throughout. So by the time the sequence is done, Judi Dench's M doesn't have to say she thinks Bond's a blunt instrument. We, the audience, already know, because the filmmakers showed us. Everything Bond does speaks of his character, and how it's different from his opponent and everyone else. Just as in great dramatic scenes you can clearly see him thinking, which most screen fighters never do. I pretty much attribute this solely to director Campbell and writer Haggis, since everything else—star Craig, screenwriters Purvis and Wade, and stunt coordinator Gary Powell—returned to the series with far less, and ever-diminishing, results.

ALEXANDER WITT

(second-unit director, *Casino Royale*)

When you think about that parkour scene, that's a great example of a group process. Martin Campbell has his idea of what he wants, and then we work closely with Gary Powell and try to come up with new ideas on how to do the stunts, which is how we came up with this French actor, freestyle runner—who also came up with ideas. But at the end, it was really Gary and I that came up with the ideas even when we were asking the free runner, "Okay, what can we do? What's cool that we can do now?" Sometimes he couldn't come up with ideas, so we had to come up with a lot of them ourselves. Even Michael Wilson and Chris Corbould came up with a couple of ideas. Not every director is open like that, but Martin in that sense was very open to change and us coming up with ideas.

MARTIN CAMPBELL

There's also a fight on four flights of stairs and we went hand-held during it. It's much more immediate and horrible when you get the camera right in there. The bad guys attack Bond and then they all go down four flights of stairs, throwing themselves over bannisters and such. We built the whole set of stairs onstage at Barrandov Studios in Prague, and on each level a doorway and window appeared to be leading to a corridor. The set went almost to the ceiling of the stage, but it was important to be able to see the whole thing and follow the fight all the way down.

PHIL MÉHEUX

It was so important to collaborate with the production designer and art department when creating the set. Originally they were going to make the stairway enclosed by four walls. I said, "That really stumps me as to where the light's going to be, because I need to look down it and up it and not see film lights." So I suggested we make each level look like there's a frosted-glass window and a corridor on the other side of that. They put in these windows made of alternating yellow and white squares that gave a very interesting effect when I lit through them.

DANIEL CRAIG

My criteria, and I know that it was Martin's as well, is are we missing a trick here, or are we doing this right? Things can get out of hand on a movie this size, because the storyline gets out of whack. We had a script and the one thing that we had to stick to was that script and that piece of storytelling. Then the sort of stunt scenes and the action sequences, they had to be a part of the story. In the action there was also a de-emphasis on gadgets. It was not a debate; that was from all of us, too. That was from Martin. That was from Gary Powell, from Barbara and Michael.

We were making a movie where any kind of gadget, any kind of effect that happened, is part of the storytelling. In the Miami airport, there were a lot of planes landing, and they were there to sort of say, "We're at Miami. Here are the planes." We couldn't have planes landing in the back of shots. That's impossible, so we have CGI to give us that, but nothing that you see in the movie stunt-wise is not happening. It's all happening then, and if it's not me doing it, it's someone else doing it and they're getting hurt. You ask a stuntman what it feels like to fall down a flight of stairs, and they'll tell you what it's like falling down a fucking flight of stairs. That's how we wanted to feel—the pain of it.

ALEXANDER WITT

Martin's approach was to do as much on camera as possible. It was something that I liked to do, too. So that's how it really came about, to leave the CG out. They still do the same thing and they try all the stunts and everything to do as real as possible. I mean, we're using more CG for other things, but the main action we tried to do practically as much as possible.

MARTIN CAMPBELL

Once again, I storyboarded the whole thing. That was a tough scene to shoot, because we had to shoot that in Prague. They gave us four days to shoot and we had a Virgin Airlines plane there. Those who are quick-witted can see Branson there; he demands that, if you have his planes, he has to be in the film. I would have actually taken that scene out; we didn't need it. It kind of breaks the fourth wall. But we had to include it because of the plane. However, he very kindly gave us two planes for four nights. We shot that four days out the back and then all the stuff where the sprinters go was studio, and then we went to a disused airport outside of London and shot all the runway stuff there. In the end, it was a great action sequence.

The main "action" of the film is actually the card game that pits Bond against Le Chiffre, the results of which will have ramifications on pretty much everyone involved. As was the case in the Fleming novel, it is the main set piece of the film, and it also plays around with the idea of Le Chiffre's villainous malformity, if you will: his eye tends to tear up, resulting in droplets of blood.

MARTIN CAMPBELL

The card game was my biggest worry on that film. I thought, "How the hell do we get over this? We have a couple of action sequences. The fight on the stairs is one. The poisoning is another, but does that sustain? Is that enough to support what essentially are three big card scenes?" Like I said, it was genuinely my biggest worry in the film.

PHIL MÉHEUX

Betting in itself is pretty boring. The audience isn't necessarily going to know the game, so if Bond says, "I'll raise you," and they turn over the next card, how many people in the audience will know if it's a good card or a bad card? So you have to deal with the drama between the characters. It's all about looks, so you never really want to be too wide, but you also don't want just a bunch of close-ups. We had a whole day of rehearsal with all the actors playing their cards and running dialogue, and then we worked out where best to seat everyone and how to shoot it. We tried to approach it with as many variations as we could within those limitations. We did one card game that was all filmed with a static camera, and we did another where the camera was constantly moving around the table. Then we did one game where the camera starts pretty far back and slowly closes in on Bond and Le Chiffre. You can fly a camera down a wire as two people are having a conversation in St. Paul's Cathedral, and it can be fun for a moment, but you very quickly start to diffuse the drama if you're just moving around them. I try always to avoid movement for movement's sake.

DANIEL CRAIG

We all said at the beginning of the movie, "If we cast actors in this, it's going to work." Mads Mikkelsen is fantastic and he cuts my job in half. All we wanted to do with the poker stuff was try not to confuse the audience, because of course there will be some people in the audience who play poker and know what's going on, but we had to appeal to everyone. So we had to have a sparring; not a sparring, but we had to "box." That, I think, was key to making that sequence work and making it not about . . . some people watching it sort of know what's going on with the hands and the flop and the river cards and things, but ultimately it's about, "I've got better cards than you." That's poker, really. It was fantastic at some point, and I know that there was no money involved, and I know that they were just chips, but when you're pushing, like, twenty-five million, going like that, you feel good. It gives you a good feeling.

MARTIN CAMPBELL

I screened every film with card games in it, from *The Cincinnati Kid* to *Maverick* to 5 *Card Stud*. Anything that had cards in it. Then I thought, "You know what? It's *not* about the game. It's about the guys *playing* the game. *That's* the key to it." If that's a mind fuck between those two, that's what is so riveting about it, and what the stakes are. What each has to lose. In the case of Mads, he would lose his life. With Bond, he would lose the whole mission, plus a hundred and fifty million dollars.

DANIEL CRAIG

Those scenes took three weeks to film and it was tricky, because if we were trying to shoot this table here, this is one of the harder things to do, because you have to shoot everyone, and that's what it was like at that table. What we did, and what was really essential, was that we made the scene about the battle that was going on, and because of that, the scene worked really beautifully. That's a testament to Martin and our editor, Stuart Baird, because it's really tricky to kind of get that intensity.

MADS MIKKELSEN

It was fun. It was three weeks, and we all thought that it was going to be tough to sit around and being concentrated for that long. What do you know? Cards and chips, and every single break that we had we played poker. After the wrap, we played poker. So it was an intensive three weeks of poker. It was really fun.

MICHAEL G. WILSON

Most of us could play poker, and, as well as rehearsing the tournament, we played poker for fun. In fact, we often ended up playing in the corridors between scenes.

MADS MIKKELSEN

Le Chiffre has a scar on his eye, and the vein starts to pump when his heart rate increases, so he casually presses his finger against it to stop, but Bond notices. It has to be as subtle as possible, of course, or he wouldn't win many power games. But Le Chiffre manages to turn this flaw to his advantage. Achieving the bleeding eye was pretty simple. They just stopped the film and placed a little dot there, and then later on they fixed it up with some CGI.

FRED DEKKER

(director, *The Monster Squad*)

Mads Mikkelsen is a great *Bond* villain, and with the blood tears—just that one little affectation makes him not your standard villain.

MADS MIKKELSEN

He also had the blind eye, and I wore a contact lens for that. It wasn't annoying; it was comfortable to wear and we liked the look of it, because I was playing a lot of poker in this film, and there is nothing more annoying than looking at a person that is unreadable, because they only use one eye. It becomes blurry and unfocused, and we really liked that detail. What was annoying was that I lost my sense of depth, because I was only using one eye. So I became the most clumsy villain in history. I couldn't see anything, all my depth perception was gone, so I just kept knocking things down. Thank God for editors.

For his part, Mikkelsen had developed some background for Le Chiffre that doesn't come from Fleming's novel or from anything in the script.

MADS MIKKELSEN

I think he was an orphan from Albania or Algiers—somewhere down there—and he had been a street kid until he turned 14 or 15. I am sure he was small, so he carried a pocket knife, and that eventually ended up in his own eye. That is why that scar is there. He has always had this thing with numbers; he played backgammon, and then he becomes a chess player, and then slightly moves into having contact with the Mob.

Straight out of the novel is Campbell's audacious translation of the infamous torture scene, which is quite uncomfortable and effective on screen. With Bond having won the money, Le Chiffre is willing to do anything to obtain it from him—the people he works for will kill *him* if he doesn't. This finds Bond, naked, tied to a chair, with his opponent swinging a thick, braided rope under the chair and into his genitals.

DANIEL CRAIG

The torture scene was the easiest scene in the movie to shoot. I hate to say, but it took a day of shooting and it was done. It was on the page and Mads is a fantastic actor. We figured it out together. I sat in the corner and listened to some music and got myself into the idea of it. We both had discussions about the scene. I said to myself that the one thing I didn't want to do, even though he was in the position that he's in, is to lose. Bond cannot lose even though he knows that he's going to die. He must never let it go. Martin, Mads, and I sat down and talked about it, talked about how we were going to do it, and then we just got on with it and shot it. It was remarkably easy. We had a hard bottom on the chair, obviously, because I would've been thrown out of the chair otherwise, and it cracked at one point and I left the room. I jumped like eight feet in the air.

MADS MIKKELSEN

It was specifically a tough situation for Daniel, sitting there for eight hours. So we just had to stay focused. We framed it up really heavily, and then once we started shooting it, we shot it all the way through. We couldn't go into the middle of it, because he has to bring that level of energy every time. So we maybe did it thirty or forty times, and it was really tough. When Daniel was done and they started filming me, he was still there giving a hundred percent in order to make this go up to that level, and thank God for that.

MARTIN CAMPBELL

He gets his balls hit with a carpet beater in the book as opposed to rope, which I came up with. It's just a nice thing to swing around. If you're going to have your balls beat, why not do it with a nice chunky rope? I thought it was the most interesting scene in the movie. I was expecting the censor boards to be really tough on it, but they weren't. Ironically, the Americans were fine and gave us a PG-13. There were a few protests about that; people felt we were being cut a bit of slack by giving it a PG-13. The English took one shot out, which is the shot where Mads is sort of walking around him and puts the rope over his shoulder and then leans into him. They felt it was a little too sexual. Americans have no problem with that.

DANIEL CRAIG

During it, I suggested to myself that after the first one, the second one wouldn't hurt as much. It was just realizing that the pain would get less, and so, consequently, the more he got hit, the more he got in control of the situation. In a book you've obviously got more time to be thinking about it. But, you know, Mads is great. He's a great actor and he got it immediately and it wasn't that we changed lines, but we improvised a lot of the physicality of it. I think it's a pretty good scene that works.

And things just continue from there. Bond and Vesper *seem* to have accomplished their mission, romance seems to have blossomed between them, but then Bond discovers she's taking the money herself, resulting in his feeling betrayed and pursuing her. This leads him to a villa under renovation in Venice, where he takes on the bad guys, during which the building starts to sink into the canal, ultimately leading to Vesper, unable to live with the fact she betrayed him, allowing herself to drown.

PHIL MÉHEUX

For a long time, people were afraid Venice was sinking, and it turned out what was making Venice sink was the fact that houses were drawing water from wells under their foundations, and when the water went out, the foundation was sinking into the empty gap. They've stopped people from doing that, and Venice *isn't* sinking anymore. But with that in mind, we fabricated the idea that this old-fashioned villa might be kept on the water line with fixed industrial balloons while it was being renovated. To distract everybody, Bond shoots a balloon, and as the house starts to sink into the canal, he manages to sneak in and hide behind a pillar. Then more of these balloons explode, and the house sinks further and further with Bond, Vesper, and the baddies inside.

DANIEL CRAIG

There was twenty feet of water, and it was a house that sank five, six, seven times a day right there into the water. It was like a roller coaster and it was all computer-driven. Then it would come out and we'd dry off a bit and would do the scene again. I think it's a *great* sequence and I've never seen anything like that before.

MARTIN CAMPBELL

The outside is models; there's no CGI. They were about fifteen feet high, those models. They built them at Pinewood. The whole sort of three, four, or five palazzos were designed by Chris Corbould, who is brilliant. And the interior was this huge, real size palazzo built on a big steel frame. You could move this thing that way and that way, and not once did it break down or have problems, which is a huge credit to Chris. Normally those things are a fucking nightmare. They're always going wrong or didn't work or they have to be repaired. Not once.

PHIL MÉHEUX

It could twist and turn and physically drop many feet down. There were pipes underneath that could shoot water up into the set to suggest the house was sinking into the canal. It was very tricky to light, because the set was built inside a large metal casing that allowed it to be tilted in different directions.

EVA GREEN

I had to learn how to control my breathing underwater. In the beginning it was scary, although of course it is perfectly safe, because there are so many people looking after you. Also, I'm nearsighted, so I couldn't really see what was going on. I rehearsed in clear water, but during the takes the water had to be murky, like the Grand Canal. I think they used broccoli to get the right color.

In preparation, I did some sessions in London, and it was just underwater in a tank and we were trying to find the choreography for it. It's more like a dance than awful and claustrophobic. It was really fine, and the ambulance was not far [*laughs*]. But I've never see anybody drowning before or committing suicide. And for the bubbles coming out of my mouth, I'd swallowed some water, but not in my lungs. It was difficult to find a way to do it, but then in doing it, it was very emotional. I remember on the third take I was crying.

David Arnold returned to score the film, marking what would be his fourth turn as composer, and, following the main credits is the magnificent Saul Bass-inspired title sequence by now-longtime series vet Daniel Kleinman. This abandons the silhouetted nude women of the Maurice Binder era, replacing it with a particularly apt art-deco animation for this film, which actually feels like it could have worked in Charlie Feldman's *Casino*

Royale. Nonetheless it's Kleinman's best work since *GoldenEye* and is as stunning as it is ingenious, despite being more Saul Bass than Maurice Binder inspired.

DANIEL KLEINMAN

(main title designer, *Casino Royale*)

I'm not always successful at it, but each time I try and kind of inject something new or different. The trick, really, is getting the variations on the theme, but without throwing the baby out with the bathwater. Trying to reinvent the whole thing and make it feel fresh. But you still want James Bond to say, "I want a martini, shaken, not stirred." With *Casino Royale* I wanted to go more graphic than I had before. I'm a big fan of Saul Bass and that sort of work, and it bears relevance to that as well. But it also came down to a narrative imperative, which was the book. The story is based around gambling and cards, and the iconography of cards. That's really where I started from, so it doesn't just come out of the blue, it came out of what the film is about. I also went back to the original book cover, because that was the first *James Bond* book, and I think the cover had actually been designed by Ian Fleming himself. It was really quite a good cover, and a reasonable bit of design, so I took that as a starting point, because it was the introduction to James Bond. And that film, *Casino Royale,* was kind of like a reinvention. It was James Bond reborn; the story is him before he was James Bond, it's him becoming James Bond. So I think, in that sense, you could get away with it being a bit different, and a bit like another starting point. It kind of refers back to *Dr. No,* which was the first *James Bond* film with the very graphic titles.

The big conundrum was whether to have girls in it, and ladies, or whatever. I probably tried to get them in at some point, but Martin Campbell said to me, "Look, I don't really think we should have girls in this, because he hasn't become the womanizer James Bond. He's still a human; he's a part of the story, he's getting his heart broken, and that's why he becomes this sort of slightly misogynistic person." That made sense to me.

Normally in a *Bond* movie—but especially when a new actor is introduced in the role—the audience absolutely *waits* for him to identify himself as "Bond, James Bond." Well aware of this, Campbell decided to save it for the very end of the film, when Bond has wounded "Mr. White" and is demanding information.

MARTIN CAMPBELL

The one thing we got away with in that film, which I was sort of amazed at, but we all wanted him to not say the name until the end of the movie. The reason for that is that he's *not* the Bond we know and love until the end of the movie, so up to that point, he's on a learning curve, you know?

Despite whatever concerns there may have been at the outset regarding Daniel Craig's being cast as James Bond, *Casino Royale* would go on to gross over $594 million at the global box office, surpassing *Die Another Day* by about $160 million. Obviously the filmmakers were doing something right.

RAY MORTON

The first screen adaptation of an Ian Fleming *Bond* novel since *On Her Majesty's Secret Service,* although this *Casino Royale* screenplay is more an expansion of Fleming's book—fitting the novel's narrative into a larger story of the young James Bond's first adventure as a 00 agent—than it is a direct adaptation. Whatever the case, it's terrific. The plot is more than solid, and the characterizations are all very strong—perhaps the strongest they've ever been in any *Bond* movie. The notion that the *Bond* series needed to be rebooted or that we ever needed to see young Bond's first adventure always seemed unnecessary to me (and still does), but this screenplay certainly does a fine job of doing both. The script fails to include some traditional *Bond* movie tropes (Q, Moneypenny, a briefing scene in M's office, etc.) and yet it is very recognizably a 007 movie. Certainly the best screenplay Purvis and Wade have written for the series.

RIC MEYERS

With *Casino Royale,* James Bond wasn't just back, he had arrived—newly born and formed—in a film that worked on every level: drama, comedy, romance, suspense, and action. It was truly a thriller, since I was thrilled by almost every part of it. The extended fight through the museum and airport was beautifully designed to elicit audience involvement and emotion. Campbell and company did the *GoldenEye* finale fight several notches better with the kinetic casino stairway fight between Bond and an African warlord's henchmen that nicely book-ended the pre-credit men's room melee.

The finale battle in Venice works well, but would have worked far better had Bond's adversaries been Le Chiffre and Valenka, the woman who almost successfully poisoned 007. Even so, I'll admit that combining his triumphant personal killing of Le Chiffre and Valenka might have blunted the tragedy of Vesper's sacrifice. But the accent is on "might have." Personally, I don't think so. In any case, *Casino Royale* remains the best-cast, best-written, best-filmed, best-acted, and best-choreographed *James Bond* movie ever.

EVA GREEN

It's an action movie and a thriller, but it's also a love story. I think women identified with Vesper and were moved by her predicament. In comparison to other *Bond* films, it's grittier and realistic and based more on characters than action. This is a different James Bond, raw and sensitive. People, I think, saw him in a different light. You see his flaws and watch him become the Bond you think you know.

FRED DEKKER

Martin Campbell is a throwback to Guy Hamilton, Terence Young, and Peter Hunt, because he's a Brit, he has a point of view, he's been in the trenches of British television with *Edge of Darkness* and all of that stuff, and he brings a vision to it that is augmented by Broccoli and Wilson, but he doesn't disappear into the movie the way the previous directors have. He's actually, like, "Here's what we're doing," and he has the confidence to do it.

MATT GOURLEY

(cohost, James Bonding podcast)

When Bond became truly interesting for me was *Casino Royale,* in that Bond is not a role model. He's a psychopath, and he's a fascinating character to watch. When I say I'm a fan of the *Bond* films, I'm not a person who's like, I want to dress like Bond and live like Bond. Actually that lifestyle kind of grosses me out a little bit, to be honest. But I want to watch this guy succeed, and I want to watch him fail. I want to watch him make mistakes. Daniel Craig has brought mistakes to this role that really reawaken the franchise.

RAY MORTON

Making *Casino* Bond's first adventure also forced the series to reboot, an idea I didn't love in the first place and that has led to a lot of confusion in the subsequent Craig films, as the character jumped from a reckless neophyte to a burned-out veteran to a guy ready to quit the whole thing without ever passing through the period where Bond was at the top of his game before he's even reached his adventure with Doctor No.

DANIEL CRAIG

By the end of the film, I think that we'd set up the idea that there's an organization out there that needs to be sorted out. And he's got a sense of revenge, that he wants to go and get them. So that's the first thing. Everybody sort of said, "This is how he becomes Bond." I think that process was still happening and it was that idea that we hadn't finished yet. We didn't. We had someone who is still maybe too headstrong and maybe doesn't make all the right decisions. I wanted to take on what we set up there.

Which is exactly what Eon decided to do with the next film, *Quantum of Solace*. The best description we've ever heard of the outlier in the *Bond* franchise is that it serves as a great epilogue to *Casino Royale*, best watched back to back. Unlike Bond's (very) brief vengeful crusade against Blofeld in the opening moments of *Diamonds Are Forever*, which was a follow-up to the assassination of Tracy di Vincenzo Bond in *On Her Majesty's Secret Service*, *Quantum of Solace* is the first true sequel in the *Bond* canon, continuing the story set up in the previous film, taking place just minutes after its conclusion.

DANIEL CRAIG

It just seemed to me when it came down to it, and we all agreed, that to my mind at the end of *Casino Royale* it was sort of the *beginning* of the story as opposed to the end of one. He had fallen in love, had his heart broken; this organization they discovered, they have started peeling back the onion skin. To do another movie and just go, "Oh, there was this chick once," seemed to be the wrong thing to do. It just fit, and that's it. I don't know when the idea came up, really.

RAY MORTON

Quantum is the first direct sequel in the series and, like the idea of rebooting, maybe doing a direct sequel wasn't a great idea. By making the focus of the film Bond struggling to deal with the trauma of Vesper's betrayal and death—rather than have him move on from the terrific final scene of *Casino Royale* to a completely new adventure—it establishes Craig's Bond as a perpetually dour, wounded character, which isn't my favorite version of the character, although thankfully Craig plays the hell out of it, which gives this version of 007 much more appeal on the screen than he has on the page.

MARC FORSTER
(director, *Quantum of Solace*)
Even though this film starts an hour after the last one ended, I don't see this as a sequel, because there's a story within it that's self-contained.

MICHAEL G. WILSON
I think the *Bonds* have been a series of films. It's true that *Quantum* is a direct sequel, and it literally takes place an hour after the last film ended. There were always references in the *Bond* films of one blending in to the other—in *From Russia with Love*, there is a reference to *Dr. No,* for example. It's been partly series, partly sequel. This is unique in that sense, but it's not too far off.

BARBARA BROCCOLI
I've also seen it referred to as a revenge movie. It's *not* a revenge movie—it's much more complicated than that. But it *is* a follow-up to *Casino Royale,* with lots of action, but also deals with the inner turmoil that Bond is facing following that film.

DANIEL CRAIG
At first we think it's vengeance, but it goes somewhere else. They've killed the love of his life, and the last thing he knows is that she was a double agent. She sold him out. The relationship that he was looking at was just a lie, so he's got this kind of spark inside him where, although he doesn't want to admit it, he needs to find out the truth. Without that he is not going to function properly. So, definitely, this movie is about beginning that discovery.

But the mistake in this movie is the perception that he's on a vendetta, and he's not. I kind of keep this whole thing about the title *Quantum of Solace:* it's actually what he's looking for. That's all he's looking for. He just does a job. He's not out to take revenge. He might be a little angrier than he was in the first one, but that's the actual point. The point at the end is that he gets a chance to do the guy, the one guy who's actually responsible. Not the bosses, but the actual guy that twisted the love of his life, and he says no.

To be sure, *Quantum* is not a great film, and much of its plot doesn't make sense due to the fact the film was rushed into production in the midst of a crippling Writers Guild strike, which led even cowriter Paul Haggis to admit that the script was a few rewrites away from being shootable. But surprisingly, like a fine wine, the film improves with age thanks to the energy and originality its director Marc Forster (*Finding Neverland, World War Z*) imbues it with (for instance, the evolving fonts of the film's supertitles are terrific—seriously). Despite starting with a chaotic car chase that's more *Bourne* than *Bond,* thanks to the quick cutting and hyper-kinetic action of the teaser, the film's super British in the best of ways and features a low-key villain played by a wormy Mathieu Almalric (*The Diving Bell and the Butterfly*).

At the time one of the shortest, albeit most expensive, *James Bond* films ever made, *Quantum* almost could have benefited from a longer running time to help explain its byzantine plot involving the hijacking of a South American country's water supply by the nefarious Quantum organization, a poor man's stand-in for SPECTRE, for which Eon had not yet gotten the rights back. Sadly, Gemma Arterton's Strawberry Fields, who's a welcome aide-de-camp for Bond, gets summarily dispatched in the most disappointing of ways when, in a replay of *Goldfinger,* her body gets found covered not in paint, gold paint; but oil, motor oil. An ineffective and clumsy homage to its superior progenitor.

Still, there's a lot to enjoy about *Quantum,* and in perhaps one of the greatest moments in any modern *Bond* film, 007 shows up at the opera where he interrupts a covert meeting of Quantum in the middle of a performance of Puccini's *Tosca*. It's a spectacular sequence, impeccably directed and staged. There's also the novelty that Bond never sleeps with, let alone attempts to bed, his costar, the vengeful Camille, played effectively by Olga Kurylenko. And it's the smaller moments, like Craig's scenes with a returning Giancarlo Giannini as Mathis, that really shine here, as do his few and far between moments with a returning Jeffrey Wright as Felix Leiter (and a pre-*Stranger Things'* David Harbour as sleazy CIA director Gregory Beam, who could easily be an apparatchik in the Trump administration had this been made a few years later) making a welcome encore appearance. And, indeed, Bond's relationship with Judi Dench's M continues to be a series highlight, much as it anchored the previous Brosnan films as well.

Admittedly an unlikely choice, Marc Forster was announced as director of the film in June 2007, and seemed as surprised as anyone else that he was approached by Wilson and Broccoli.

BARBARA BROCCOLI

We chose Marc because he happens to be one of the greatest directors around. He's a great filmmaker and he brought some tremendous elements to this film performance-wise, story-wise, action-wise. He's a great storyteller. We just desperately wanted to work with him, and we were thrilled that he agreed. He made an extraordinary film.

DANIEL CRAIG

He's a lover of films, a cinephile through and through. You look at how complex his films are, but how different his films are. That strikes me as a very brave person who can sort of say, "You know what, I'm not going to stick with it. I'm going to take subject matters at completely opposite ends of the spectrum." When he came to do this, I met with him, and one of the things that I knew about this, having done one already, is that this is twice the length of any other movie. It's three months to shoot one regular movie, a fairly regular-sized movie, and this is six months. It's six months on every location, and as soon as I met him I *knew* that he was a brave man and that he was up for doing it. I had a great time working with him.

ROBERTO SCHAEFER

(director of photography, *Quantum of Solace*)

When Marc told me he had been offered this movie, my response was, "How could you *not* do a *Bond* film?" He wasn't sure, because the script didn't really exist at that time, but I told him that to be part of a *Bond* film is every boy's dream. Our editor, Matt Chesse, said exactly the same thing. The dream of doing *Bond* sort of sucked us into the reality of it.

MARC FORSTER

I loved the *Bond* films with Ken Adam's production design. Those movies were so much about style, design, and clothing. I wanted to go back to that and yet still make a modern *Bond*. For example, one of the things I wanted to do was compose partially obscured frames. I think those sorts of obscurities increase tension, because everything you don't see is left to the imagination of the audience. It applies not just to framing, but also to characters and the things they reveal or don't reveal. That's what makes Bond so interesting: he is hidden from us.

ROBERTO SCHAEFER

That sort of goes against everyone's instincts, so we had to fight to let things stack up in the frame without people moving them out of the way. We probably didn't get quite as much of that as we hoped to, but we also didn't want the first-unit material to stand out from the second-unit footage.

DANIEL CRAIG

We're not making a kitchen sink drama here; we're making a *Bond* movie. What Marc wanted, and the producers and I wanted, is to bring back a visual flair to the movie, so every frame in every shot we see is beautiful. And there may be things exploding, but they're good to look at. We're making a *Bond* film, but we need some reality. We need to do more. It's not like we're making some sort of big action romance here. This is a *Bond* movie first of all. You have to apply the *Bond* equation, which is that we have to have as much action as we can possibly fit in with the story, which makes sense. But the reality of the situations and people's emotions is kind of important, because we want an audience to care, to get involved and stay interested.

MARC FORSTER

If you have an action sequence, you have to tell a story, because drama and action go hand in hand. And I think one inspires the other. If you don't have a story with the action, then the action is empty.

MICHAEL G. WILSON

Compared to *Casino Royale,* there are probably twice as many action sequences in *Quantum*; it's pretty much jam-packed. The important thing, which Marc has brought to it, in helping devise the script and in the shooting of it, is a sense of humanity to the characters and making an intriguing story to go with the action.

MARC FORSTER

When I got involved, the script *wasn't* set in stone. We developed it together until I was really happy with it. I've always loved action movies, especially action movies with stories. If you go back to films like *Aliens* and *The Terminator,* I was always a big fan of those. I think that if action movies are told properly, they can have some depth with something interesting to them. And if you have an actor like Daniel Craig, it's even more exciting. He's also a physical actor and not just purely a dramatic one, so you can have both aspects, which is very interesting.

DANIEL CRAIG

I got bruised up from the fight scenes, but that's part of the deal. I wouldn't have done the movie without going all the way.

MARC FORSTER

I always loved the *James Bond* franchise and the character and what he stands for. Also, how it has changed and developed over the years. *James Bond* is a part of film history, and in that sense it's something really exciting and interesting to be a part of that. In that sense, I was very intrigued. Daniel Craig took the franchise in a different direction and he's such a superb actor that I saw the possibility to explore something with him that I was interested in.

Development of *Quantum of Solace* actually began while *Casino Royale* was in post-production, the initial idea reportedly coming from producer Michael Wilson. Although originally scheduled for a May 2008 release, it was eventually pushed back toward the end of that year. The first draft script was completed by Neal Purvis and Robert Wade in April 2007, with Paul Haggis being persuaded to step back in for a rewrite, even though he was reluctant to do so.

MICHAEL G. WILSON

The title is from an Ian Fleming short story from the *For Your Eyes Only* compendium. It's uncharacteristic of most of Fleming's work. Someone at a dinner party narrates a story to Bond about a character, and he makes comments throughout. It's not typical of Fleming. It's a character study that doesn't involve any plots or anything with spies, but we thought it was an intriguing title and referenced what's happened to Bond in *Casino Royale* and what happens to Bond in this film.

DANIEL CRAIG

The title of Fleming's story refers to the nature of relationships and the fact is that if you don't have that quantum of solace in a relationship, then the person hurt the most will resort to a kind of bestial cruelty. In the film, we tried to make that bigger. Bond's lost the love of his life. He needs an answer.

MARC FORSTER

There's a reason the desert plays such a big part in the film: I feel it mirrors the psychological status of Bond. It brings with it isolation and loneliness. I think what's going on with Bond, this psychological state that he's in, is isolation and loneliness. There's a struggle to survive within him; there's a constant struggle, and that's what the desert represents to me.

DANIEL CRAIG

What happened with Vesper just doesn't make sense. The man wins at poker. He's one of the best poker players in the world, and this woman turned him upside down and lied to him to his face and made him fall in love with her. And that has popped him off, so he needs to find out.

While this gave Bond the emotional motivation for the story, there was still the plot involving Quantum—a secret organization that seems to have agents virtually *everywhere*—and the machinations of Dominic Greene.

MICHAEL G. WILSON

In developing the idea, we're always trying to think in contemporary terms. What are the real issues that are coming up? What we see in the future is a fight over natural resources, and the people that can control them will be bigger than governments or states. Our particular man here, Dominic Greene, is someone who is controlling the water in various countries, and if you remember in *Chinatown*, if you control the water you control the whole development of the country. I think that's true. Right now it appears to be oil, but there are a lot of other resources that we don't think about too much, but are all essential and they're very limited and every country needs them. Because every country knows that raising the standard of living—and populations are getting bigger—is the way we're all going, Greene has found a way to inhibit the delivery of the water system without people knowing about it. What he wants to do is get control of the distribution system, so then he'll provide the water. Fresh water is actually a pretty scarce resource.

DANIEL CRAIG

The Quantum organization is looking at places that are potentially weak politically. Let's say like Haiti. A destabilized place. The idea is that our bad guys, whatever nationality that organization is, are taking advantage of that. So we're maybe using an old idea, but there's a history of instability in South America that may or may not have something to do with larger organizations, and we're using that as part of our storyline. The bad guys are doing what they've kind of always done, and they're trying to mess around with countries and with states for their own benefit. For their own individual benefit as opposed to for the people.

Given *Casino Royale*'s nearly universal critical acclaim, it shouldn't have come as a surprise that Wilson and Broccoli were soon knocking at Paul Haggis' proverbial door. After some reluctance, he was brought in to rewrite Purvis and Wade, though he wasn't sure he was up for the challenge, particularly in the aftermath of *Casino Royale*'s reception. And thanks to that Writers Guild strike, his involvement was extremely limited, with star Daniel Craig and director Marc Forster putting pen to paper together for rewrites as they went along through production, since WGA writers were banned from writing during the strike.

PAUL HAGGIS

(screenwriter, *Quantum of Solace*)

I kept saying no and they kept coming until I finally said yes. When I started the script, I started almost completely over, because I had a different idea, and we just weren't as in sync on that one. I was taking bigger risks for me and for the character, and I don't think they were comfortable with it. In fact, during production I got a call from Marc Forster, who said, "It's going really, really well, but we cut the ending." I said, "What do you mean you cut the ending?" "We didn't need it." "Well, how does it resolve?" And he said, "No, no, it's gonna be great." "How's it gonna be great if you cut the ending?"

MARTIN CAMPBELL

I wasn't there, because it sort of comes under how many control rooms can you blow up? But it was definitely an epilogue to *Casino Royale.* The first scene was almost the follow-up from our last scene, but I don't know what went wrong with it. I know the strike had a lot to do with it. Haggis wrote the original script, and he's credited for it, but I know they rewrote him. He did a great job on *Casino* and I think it took him about five weeks. We hardly changed anything when it came in. Maybe a couple of tweaks, but a terrific, wonderful writer. I think he delivered a script to them, which I read, which I thought was pretty damn good, and for whatever reason they rewrote it all, as often happens in those circumstances.

PAUL HAGGIS

What I had done is that this was a personal journey for Bond, and we don't know why he's going through everything he is. Eventually he confronts Greene and demands, "Where?" Next thing you know, he's taking the case from the body and we see him walking away. He shows up at an orphanage and a nun lets him in, saying, "We were expecting someone else." He goes, "I know"—I can't remember the exact dialogue, but he walks upstairs and looks into a room with a lot of toddlers. She points out a child and he says, "That's her?" She goes, "Yes," and he says, "She wants you to have this," and he hands her cash and the lease on the building. The nun says, "Do you want to meet the child?" and he goes, "No, that's okay." And he walks out.

My idea was that Vesper had a child with this other guy, and *that's* why she betrayed Bond. It wasn't just blackmail; it was bigger than that. The villain had put this child in the orphanage, and Vesper just didn't know. Bond, being an orphan himself, hunted down the child's location, feeling he owed it to Vesper, and wanted to be sure the child was taken care of, although he never wanted to have anything to do with it. And with that he walked away and I thought, "Oh, that's cool." But they cut all that.

One thing that remains in the film that Haggis came up with is the relationship between Bond and Olga Kurylenko's Camille Montes, a Bolivian agent who has a vendetta of her own against Greene and the man who terrorized her as a child, General Medrano. It is *not* a romantic relationship.

OLGA KURYLENKO
(actress, "Camille Montes")

Camille is very strong and very feisty. I don't think that the others have been so feisty. She's independent. What's good about her is that she has her own story in the film. I think if Bond weren't there, she would still have her story. She doesn't need Bond to exist.

DANIEL CRAIG

I was involved with the casting process, and Olga came in and just had this kind of quiet—I don't know—toughness about her, and also something going on, this sort of secret that she's carrying with her. She was thrust into this, and we started training her, and we started getting into it and I was, like, "This is kind of what it's like." She just did a great job. I think that her story kind of ties into it nicely, and they don't get into bed.

LISA FUNNELL

I like Camille Montes, and the reason I do is that she reminds me of Gala Brand from the novel *Moonraker* in the fact that she doesn't end up with Bond at the end. Gala walks away from Bond, because she already has a fiancé, and that novel ends on this devastating note where Bond's, like, "I need to escape these people's lives and run away and be this cold hero." I mean, it's *so* melodramatic, but it's great. In *Quantum of Solace,* she realizes that Bond's heart is still connected with Vesper Lynd, that he doesn't have a place or space for her, so she walks away. For me, that is *such* an empowering representation, that you don't always have to force a relationship if it's not going to work. That you can be good on your own. I love the fact that the two of them really supported each other. She had her own trauma; she had her own revenge narrative while he was going through his own deal.

DANIEL CRAIG

There is obviously an element of vengeance in her story. Bond isn't on a mission of vengeance. He wants to find the peace within himself because he lost somebody. Olga's character is on a mission of vengeance. That's why he can step back and say, "Okay, I'm going to help you out. I'm going to help you get your goal. Understand that I don't think it's the right thing to be doing. I think you are going to screw yourself up." In fact, at the end of this movie he gets the one man who was responsible for Vesper's death and he *doesn't* shoot him. Olga's character has a strength in her.

PAUL HAGGIS

Their relationship was my choice, and it's something I really wanted. I also wanted a heroine who you *couldn't* save. Who every time you tried, she kicked your ass by rejecting your help. I thought that was a fun character. The approach with Bond is he always saves the girl, right? Well, he can save her, but she's going to save him, too. But overall, she just doesn't want his help.

LISA FUNNELL

The two of them were able to really operate side by side as counterparts in separate ways, and I wish that that was the ending of *Tomorrow Never Dies* with Wai Lin, because I felt that there was no connection between her and Bond and that that was just thrown in at the end, the two of them kissing. There's no lead-in to that. It's like *For Your Eyes Only*—there was no lead in to any of the romance there. I didn't feel it, but I like that in the case of *Quantum of Solace* that it just ended with them parting ways.

OLGA KURYLENKO

I was very happy and proud that she doesn't sleep with Bond. And it's okay. He slept with all of them in twenty-one movies before *Quantum of Solace*. But he was behaving well, so we gave him a kiss.

Not reprising his role as the contemporary Maurice Binder was main title designer extraordinaire Daniel Kleinman who, like several of the other modern Bond stalwarts, was replaced by Marc Forster's usual collaborators.

DANIEL KLEINMAN

Marc wanted to use his guys [MK12], and actually the Broccolis very, very sweetly phoned me up. I think they were a bit worried that I'd be upset, which I wasn't at all. I take each offer to do it as it comes, and I'm very grateful for it. It was his prerogative, he wanted to work with his own guys, and they're very good. I actually like that sequence. It's not one of the best *Bond* films ever made, I kind of slightly didn't understand the plot, but it had a few up points as well as down points. I thought the title sequence actually was rather good. It felt different, and quite rightly so, from what I'd do. They made it their own thing, which was cool.

In the end, the reception to *Quantum of Solace* was mixed, although the audience, still enraptured from the experience of *Casino Royale*, turned it into a blockbuster that grossed $586 million, only $13 million shy of its predecessor. Of course, at $200 million, it was also considerably more expensive.

RAY MORTON

The WGA strike of 2007 to 2008 forced the film to go into production without a finished script, which had a disastrous impact on the movie. Apparently, Purvis and Wade's initial drafts really were a direct sequel to *Casino Royale* and focused on Bond's mission to track down Vesper's fiancé, who we learn was not a kidnap victim as she thought he was in *Casino*, but was actually working with Quantum to set Vesper up. Director Marc Forster apparently did not care for this approach (although many of its elements remain in the final movie) and wanted to change the focus of the story to a Quantum plan to control the water supply in Bolivia. Paul Haggis began moving the story in this direction but was unable to finish doing so when the strike hit. That left Forster and Daniel Craig to essentially write the script as they shot, and the result is a story whose elements are under-developed and whose narrative focus is fuzzy at best. The result is a sort-of a sequel to *Casino Royale* that is also sort-of-not-a-sequel and not much of a *Bond* film either.

JOHN CORK

The Writers Guild strike hurt the film, but the filmmakers also felt the schedule was too tight. They quickly felt they needed more than two years to make films of this scope.

RAY MORTON

Because the script was essentially unfinished and the WGA strike prevented the producers from hiring another writer, director Forster and star Craig worked out the final rewrites on the *Solace* script themselves. The interrupted writing process and the final draft being completed by non-writers are the likely reasons the *Solace* screenplay turned out so poorly, although I must say I'm the biggest fan of many of the ideas Forster wanted implemented in the first place.

RIC MEYERS

The *Bond* producers certainly had their hearts and hopes in the right place, tapping mainstream drama director Marc Forster to bring his artistry to the second Craig effort. Publicity maintained that the movie was Michael Wilson's idea with a rough script by him, Purvis, and Wade—which was then handed over to Haggis, who finished his polish just moments before the greatest threat to James Bond ever descended: the Writers Guild of America strike. Apparently from that moment on, the director and his star were "forced" to give the script the death of a thousand cuts. Indeed, the finished film looked as if it had been pecked apart by ducks, or rewritten by a hundred chimps chained to typewriters. Instead of a strong, focused, logical story, Vesper's traitorous boyfriend was reduced to a minor afterthought in a vastly disappointing, anticlimatic, throwaway scene tacked onto the end, and the amorphous mess that was "Quantum" was used like putty to fill in the cracks "of Solace." The film lurches this way and that, the action scenes edited with a shredder to within a millimeter of their life—as if trying to distract the audience from the essential emptiness, even silliness, of all the pointless movement going on around them.

RAY MORTON

It's one of the worst screenplays in the series. The tone of the piece is dour, grim, and depressing. The story is uninteresting and its themes opaque. There's no adventure; no fun. The villain is dull, and his scheme is jumbled and unclear. Something about hoarding water and installing a puppet government in Bolivia. We don't care about any of the characters, including Bond, who is just miserable and unpleasant and is completely lacking in his usual charm and humor—except in the scene in which he tells the desk clerk at the luxury hotel that he and Fields are "schoolteachers on holiday . . . who won the lottery"—the only time in the entire narrative when James seems anything like his old self. Worst of all, it seems to go out of its way to *not* be a *Bond* film. It contains almost none of the elements that distinguish the series, and the few elements it does introduce that might have some *Bond*ian potential it does nothing with: e.g. the villain is hoarding water in a vast underground dam, something noted only in passing. Where's the climactic scene in which Bond blows up the dam and sends the water rushing back to the dehydrated populace? Instead, we get a fistfight in a burning hotel. Who cares?

GLEN OLIVER

Did the film's stylistic departures from the series alienate audiences? Most certainly this was a factor, but this is an issue impacting a number of fan communities beyond 007/*Quantum*. There's a vitriolic and militant tendency running through many fan communities these days—*Star Trek*, *Star Wars*, *Lost in Space*, *Doctor Who* among them—which resists any change to formatting or established conceit. This is a narrow, almost pig-headed prescription of the way things "ought" to be rather than stepping back and appreciating both the flexibility a long-standing franchise can afford, and weighing the positives which experimentation and growth of change and approach can bring about.

Ironically, sometimes this fervent resistance to change spits directly in the face of the stated intent of these franchises' creators. When this happens, product is often summarily condemned on general principle, rather than being judged on its own merit. This was very much one of the dynamics which hamstrung *Quantum*'s reception—traditionalists weren't capable of moving with it toward more contemporary stylistic sensibilities. It's a shame, really, and a bit of a double standard on the audience's part. Hollywood is incessantly slammed for being too derivative and not imaginative enough with the product it turns out, but when filmmakers attempt to head in some unexpected direction, or expand the palette upon which a franchise is painted in unexpected ways, they get hammered and condemned for trying something new. Traditionalists tend to very much place creative Powers That Be in a no-win scenario.

JOHN CORK

There are all of these films that have been influenced by others around them; that doesn't diminish the film per se. As far as the *Bourne* influence on *Quantum of*

Solace, the editor, who also worked on that, was incredibly proud of his work. He'd hold seminars and talk about the editing of that film. It's held up, but you can watch videos of people going on about action films and that the editing ruins the film. People make that argument about *Quantum of Solace*. It's very difficult to tell what car you're looking at in that initial sequence in the tunnel during the car chase. Then there's the scene where Camille is with Dominic Greene, and they're all on the boat to get a Kennedy senator over to General Medrano. She's on the boat there; Bond rams the boat. She's suddenly got a gun in her hands at a certain point, and I would ask people after they watch that movie, how did that gun get there? Where did the gun come from? And nobody would know. There's a shot of her reaching up under her skirt and pulling the gun out of a garter holster, but most people don't read that shot. It happens too quickly, you know?

The sequence at the opera is just brilliantly put together. But can anybody explain to me exactly what Mathis is talking about when he's dying? Mathis and Bond are talking to each other, but I don't know what they're saying. Is he saying he was working for the enemy? Was he not saying it? What *is* he trying to communicate here?

PAUL HAGGIS

I think Marc Forster did a fine job shooting the action and stuff, and there's a lot of my stuff still in there. There's a great deal I liked about it, but I thought it could be better.

MATT GOURLEY

I think *Quantum of Solace* was a worthy experiment and will age well. I actually think there's precedent for it in Terence Young, who in the beginning was kind of known to be a *Bond* type persona and invented a lot of the tropes of what this became. In a way, that was his own type of auteur filmmaking. These blockbusters didn't exist. There were war movies and action movies, but they weren't like what *Bond* is now. There wasn't style, there weren't travelogues. But this version of auteur filmmaking that Marc Forster and later Sam Mendes brought to the franchise was interesting to me.

DANIEL CRAIG

What sort of fascinates me is that people talk about this thing of *Quantum* being a violent *Bond*. If you watch *Dr. No* and *From Russia with Love*, especially, it's kind of just as violent. If you think about it, at the time it was probably *more* violent relatively speaking. There's just this darkness that Connery brought into it. This is a complicated character. It's not two-dimensional. This guy has a past and there is a reason that he behaves this way, and that for me was one of the reasons that I wanted to do this.

The other thing he wanted to do—but actually found himself nervous doing—was his first full gun-barrel sequence, which ended the film.

DANIEL CRAIG

That was probably when I was scared. We did that one twice. We filmed it twice. I did it over and over again. I watched on the monitor, and I think we got it right. There were ideas to fuck around and make it more graphic and things, and I was, like, "No, no, it has to be like the old ones."

And nothing would be like the old ones more than when Bond celebrated his 50th anniversary in *Skyfall*. But that's a story for another decade.

THE 2010s: IT'S YOUR SPECTRE AGAINST MINE . . .

"A gun and a radio; not exactly Christmas, is it?"

SKYFALL (2012)

Over the years *Quantum of Solace*'s battered reputation has improved with fans, while the far more popular *Skyfall* seems to have diminished somewhat due to its many plot contrivances. And then there was the ending, which some felt was too evocative of a film like *Home Alone,* in which Bond finds himself in a mano a mano confrontation with Javier Bardem's formidable Silva (hot off his Oscar-winning performance in the Coen Brothers' *No Country for Old Men*) in his nearly deserted ancestral family home in the Scottish highlands.

Director Sam Mendes, a renowned theater director and veteran film director, brings a freshness to the proceedings, but the real hero here is legendary director of photography Roger Deakins, who elevates *Bond* firmly into A-list territory with his magnificent lensing. (There is perhaps no more memorably shot scene in a 007 film than Bond's hand-to-hand fight with Ola Rapace's Patrice in the skyscrapers of Shanghai.) Everyone has upped their game here for the celebration of the 50th anniversary of the franchise, and the pre-credit teaser is another series all time high as Bond, and what will later be revealed as Moneypenny, engage in a high-stakes pursuit of the all-too-familiar NOC list of agents that's been stolen, a well-worn MacGuffin that needs to be retired as a plot device in spy movies everywhere. Javier Bardem is sensational as Silva, the ultimate rogue agent, who was betrayed by Judi Dench's M many years earlier and has now mapped out a plan for vengeance–though his caper relies far too much on coincidence and happenstance to truly be credible, as he remains one step ahead of MI6 at virtually every turn. Nonetheless, he's suitably creepy and vengeful and a classic in the *Bond* rogues' gallery of villains. Although given the thankless role of the seeming femme fatale, Sévérine–who is dispatched by Silva in another one of the film's best scenes–Bérénice Marlohe is seductive and satisfying.

Anchored by Adele's brilliant Academy Award-winning "Skyfall" main title song, a series high, along with Daniel Kleinman's magnificent opening title sequences, the film in so many ways represents the best of the franchise, even if it suffers in the third act as Bond teams up with Albert Finney (a role originally earmarked for Sean Connery, who wasn't interested) to fend off Silva and his men in that *Home Alone*-like *Straw Dogs* standoff.

That said, by the film's conclusion, all the familiar chess pieces are back on the board, including a new M (wonderfully cast with a more avuncular Bernard Lee-ish Ralph Fiennes), a terrific Naomie Harris as Moneypenny, and the return of M's pinched leather door in his office. All in all, a welcome return to form for 007 on his birthday. Surely the best of times.

MICHAEL G. WILSON
(producer, *Skyfall*)

It was our 50th anniversary and 23rd film, and the pressure was on to make the best *Bond* ever. We had an extraordinary cast, an incredibly talented creative team, and an emotionally charged script.

DANIEL CRAIG
(actor, "James Bond")

When we were doing *Skyfall,* it was about retaining what it always had; it's making movies for the audience, putting it all on the screen, and the Broccoli family is the reason for that.

MICHAEL G. WILSON

I think back to the early days when *Dr. No* was going to be released. No one really thought that we were going to get 50 years out of Bond, let alone the 23 pictures at the time of *Skyfall*. Back then, United Artists had a deal with Cubby and Harry for four pictures and, even then, they thought that was stretching it, but no one contemplated this kind of success. I think once a fictitious character becomes part of the culture, they'll come back like Sherlock Holmes does or Superman or Batman. Usually, though, it waxes and wanes and is not a continuous thing. But it's always down to the public.

SAM MENDES
(director, *Skyfall*)

There was an interview with Michael Wilson on one of the *Bond* documentaries where he said, "If it ain't broke, don't fix it, because that's a recipe for disaster." The truth is, he's right, but it takes a hell of a courageous person to know that what you've got to do is keep changing it and not make it the same. I think that has ultimately been the reason it's regenerated so brilliantly; taking the risk to take everything away in order to rebuild it, and that's why it endures, because it's *not* the same. Every *Bond* is different, and every generation needs a different *Bond*, and it's been able to move with the times. And hopefully we set it up for another fifty years.

A departure from Eon's tendency to hire journeymen directors in the past, Sam Mendes was the series' first legitimate auteur filmmaker, something the Broccolis had avoided in the past as not to cede control to their directors. That would change with Mendes, who won both the Academy Award and the Golden Globe for directing 1999's *American Beauty;* in addition to directing *Road to Perdition* and, for the stage, new, darker takes on *Cabaret, Oliver!, Company,* and *Gypsy,* as well as, more recently, the West End production of *Charlie and the Chocolate Factory*.

DANIEL CRAIG

I knew that Sam would put everything behind it. He would put all of his knowledge of moviemaking behind it, but also his knowledge and love of Fleming and Bond.

BARBARA BROCCOLI
(producer, *Skyfall*)

Ever since I saw Sam's theater work initially, and his films, I've just hoped that we would be able to entice him to come and do one of these. The enthusiasm and enormous commitment he brought to *Skyfall,* and his sort of childlike, boyish excitement, was really infectious.

SAM MENDES

I'd always been a huge fan of the *Bond* movies, so I have my own personal relationship with *Bond,* which began when I was nine or ten years old, when *Live and Let Die* came out. We happen to be living in a time when it's possible to make a big, entertaining, glamorous, escapist movie that also says something about the world we live in. With Daniel's performance in *Casino Royale* and *Quantum of Solace,* James Bond feels like a real man in a real situation again. It reminded me of the way I felt when I watched the Sean Connery movies. I thought it opened up all sorts of wonderful possibilities for the character. I love that movie.

BARBARA BROCCOLI

With his knowledge and history, he identifies with the audience. He knows what works and what an audience is expecting. And, frankly, that was great to watch on set.

SAM MENDES

I have to say that Michael and Barbara are extraordinary, because they work very well as a team. Barbara has a remarkable skill for making people feel like she knows their name and knows what their issues are, and if there's ever a crisis, she's the one who will handle it. Michael brings an enormous amount of experience and wisdom, combined with such a gentle presence on the set—he never bullies or lectures. If you have an idea and are wondering, "Has Bond done this before?" ask Michael. He knows.

DANIEL CRAIG

When we started talking about it, I felt a connection with someone who had exactly the same enthusiasm and respect for the *Bond* films that I did. And, of course, I deeply respect Sam as a director. I said to him, "This is going to be a new experience for you. Trust me, because I made two of them and it was a very new experience for me. Nothing can quite prepare you."

JAVIER BARDEM
(actor, "Silva")

As an actor, the great thing about Sammy is that he really encouraged us to approach the same scenes from different angles. I was surprised, because this was my first big movie, and I thought everything was going to be in place, but I found a great creative laboratory of performers with a great director in charge. It's not that I was afraid of it being the opposite, but it was a nice surprise. I guess he put together the ones that he considered the best, and that's what you saw.

NAOMIE HARRIS
(actress, "Eve Moneypenny")

I think Sam is very, very collaborative. So, his first thing when I got the part and we had a meeting is that, straight away, he has the writer, John Logan, there. He said, "Anything you want to change, any suggestions you have for your character's journey, just bring them on, tell us, and we'll go with that." So, he's really, really open like that.

BÉRÉNICE MARLOHE
(actress, "Sévérine")

Once I was on set, it was a really cool experience with Sam Mendes and Daniel Craig. I really liked that it was a very normal vibe on set where you could just be relaxed and try things. Sam really knows the work of actors and he's not afraid to let them try things and give them freedom. And "normal" is the best word for me, because when one thinks of a *James Bond* set, I would assume they would think it's a big, overwhelming production, but it was surprisingly normal and relaxed.

SAM MENDES

I wanted to have a huge challenge, and it was no question that they don't come bigger than *Bond* in terms of scale and expectations. I wanted to wake myself up and try something completely new, and I also wanted to come back to England and make a movie. I've never made a movie in England, bizarrely, despite the fact I'm English, and I wanted to work with Daniel and Judi Dench again, who I haven't worked with for a while. What I didn't know was I was going to have two producers who were going to encourage me in a way to make something as personal for me as all the other things I've done. My only concern going in was if I were going to be making a movie by committee, but they have an amazing way of guiding you without seeming to guide you, which is the art of producing.

The early drafts of the screenplay were written by the returning team of Neal Purvis and Robert Wade, and, as per usual, another writer was brought in to develop the script further. In this case it was playwright/screenwriter/producer John Logan, nominated for two Academy Awards in the category of Best Original Screenplay (for 2000's *Gladiator* and 2004's *The Aviator*), and once for Best Adapted Screenplay (2011's *Hugo*).

RAY MORTON

(senior writer, *Script* magazine)

John Logan did a major rewrite on *Skyfall*, focusing primarily on developing the characters and dialogue. He was the writer responsible for Silva's memorable "rat" monologue. He did a terrific job, so his contribution to the film was a significant one.

JOHN LOGAN

(screenwriter, *Skyfall*)

I felt greatly encouraged by Sam and Barbara Broccoli and Michael Wilson to make the screenplay as unique as I could, using my particular strengths as a writer. Coming from the world of theater, for me, it has always been about character and dialogue. When you look over the vast panoply of *Bond* films, things tend to emerge, like a lightning bolt: great moments of character interaction—whether it's Bond and Goldfinger, Bond and Blofeld, or Bond and Vesper Lynd. Those are the amazing scenes that just stop your heart, because they're unexpected in what's considered a genre movie.

DENNIS GASSNER

(production designer, *Skyfall*)

I believe that story always comes first when planning to design any given set for any given character. Throughout the process of *Skyfall*, I considered Bond's emotional journey and how each environment affects him and vice versa.

ROGER DEAKINS

(director of photography, *Skyfall*)

During prep on the film, Sam and I went through the script together, talking not just about the visuals, but also about character development. It was great to be involved in that interchange of ideas, because those discussions affected how the script developed.

DANIEL CRAIG

Nobody told me that we couldn't make an action film with a good story, and we always go back to Fleming when we just sit and discuss. And if you look at the novels, as an author, he's so conflicted. I mean, Fleming tries to kill Bond off at one point and backs off from it. I mean, he gets *really* pissed at the character. In truth, Bond is a killer. He kills for a living, and it's really kind of a dark place he goes to. But what I'm so proud about with *Skyfall* is that the writing is so good. And the lightness of touch is back that we wanted so much. You need good writing for that, and I think that's what we had.

We combined that element with a very emotional story that just employed me. They knew what kind of actor I was. It's their fault. Blame them. In a lot of ways, *Skyfall* is about families. This one's a little bit about families and parents and children. Not in a heavy way, just in terms of a plot that's going back to his childhood just to sort of destroy it and move on to begin again.

RIC MEYERS

(author, *For One Week Only: The World of Exploitation Films*)

I like the fan theory that between *Quantum* and this, Craig's Bond went on all of Connery's, Moore's, Dalton's, and Brosnan's missions (though minus Lazenby's, so Vesper could effectively replace Tracy in 007's heart). So by the time we see him in *Skyfall,* he has gone from a newly minted double-0 blunt instrument to the jaded and alienated automaton he now is. It would certainly explain how the Aston Martin, complete with *Goldfinger*-era ejector seat, could show up.

RAY MORTON

The story for *Skyfall* is—oddly enough—a compilation of the main elements from the Pierce Brosnan *Bonds*: Bond screws up on a mission and is cast into the wilderness (*Die Another Day*). After MI6 headquarters suffers a devastating terrorist attack (*The World Is Not Enough*), Bond returns to the service and must reprove his worth (*Die Another Day*) by facing off against a former 00 agent turned supervillain (*GoldenEye*). During the course of the adventure, he romances the supervillain's consort, who is then killed by the supervillain in retaliation (*Tomorrow Never Dies*).

Interestingly, much of *Skyfall* deals on some level with Bond's place in the world. While thematically that's similar to *GoldenEye*, in the Brosnan film's case it was a behind-the-scenes examination. In this film, it's more textually overt. Allowing an exploration of this are his relationships in the film, beginning with M (Judi Dench reprising the role for her eighth, and final, time despite a brief, surprise cameo in *Spectre*).

SAM MENDES

On *Skyfall* I had been given an enormous amount of freedom, and I've never felt constrained or hidebound by the genre or the franchise. Part of that is Daniel and Judi Dench, both of whom I already knew well. Frankly, I'd love the two of them to be in any movie I directed.

JUDI DENCH
(actress, "M")

Bond and M are two people who work well together. She's obviously very fond of him, and she's often accused of being preferential toward him—but she can also be ruthless about him. Daniel and I struck up a good relationship the first time we worked together, and the relationship has developed as each script requires something a little bit more from us. This is especially true in *Skyfall*.

DANIEL CRAIG

Their relationship is based on mutual respect. They both know that every time the chips are down, one of them will have to make a sacrifice—it's difficult to have a touchy-feely relationship with someone under those circumstances. But at the same time—and Sam was very keen on this—Bond's always had in the back of his mind that there's a bit more. It's something he never shows, but the connection is there, and I get a kick out of that as an actor, to play a life you can't show.

BARBARA BROCCOLI

We wanted to really mine the relationship between Bond and M, because it is the most significant relationship he has in his life. M is the only person who represents authority to him. You have two extraordinary actors, and we just thought, let's go all the way. It's worked extremely well. It's a very emotional story.

GLEN OLIVER
(pop culture commentator)

In Bernard Lee's version of M, the character's connection to Bond was a little more stodgy, reserved. He was the irascible old schoolmaster to Bond's behaviorally challenged student. It was a fun dynamic, but there wasn't much there in terms of subtext or depth. Lee was a lovely presence to be sure, but, realistically, the nature of his role screamed interchangeability. Judi Dench brought a great deal more depth to her approach. A gravitas that was somehow far more stern than her predecessors, but at the same time time guiding and maternal. More human. Almost—a practical iciness?—which masked deeper and more profound qualities. She played off of Brosnan's Bond extraordinarily well; there's often a sense that their conversations were unfolding across multiple layers, and that details and subtext was implicitly being communicated or understood. Which was a tremendous dynamic given the *Bond* films' intelligence/espionage setting, that somehow rang true on a human level as well.

JOHN CORK

(film historian; author, *The James Bond Encyclopedia*)

Judi Dench may be the most inspired piece of casting since Sean Connery was selected to play James Bond. Her character shifts quite a bit over the years, but Dench brings a sense of authority to the role that overcomes quite a bit. But in all honesty, she does a terrible job of running MI6. She manages to get the service involved in her personal friendships. She gets kidnapped as a result. She abandons her best agent to a North Korean prison. Her subordinates are constantly violating her edicts. She allows headquarters to be the target of terrorist attacks on multiple occasions. At one point, her right-hand man turns out to be working for an enemy organization, and on two occasions, whatever security measures she's taken still allow for high-value detainees to escape custody from her facilities. And bizarrely, she allows Bond to go in and personally confront the man who betrayed his lover. She blithely asks him after if he killed the man. That wouldn't look good at a hearing in front of Parliament. At the end of her life, she decides that she should use a flashlight when she's trying to evade pursuers in the dark. Even after her death, she's leaving secret messages behind for her agents, because she's lost control of MI6. Yet despite all this, Judi Dench made a *fantastic* M.

GLEN OLIVER

Dench being ported over to the Daniel Craig era was distracting for a number of reasons, not the least of which is having to grapple with the continuity—or discontinuity—or question marks raised by an (established?) M dealing with a "new" Bond. Her role seemed harder and less nuanced than it had in the Brosnan era, which suited Craig's sensibilities nicely, but also made settling into the transition a little more peculiar.

FRED DEKKER

(director, *Night of the Creeps*)

Bond and M have a really sort of tempestuous relationship in the Craig movies. The Brosnan movies are kind of all over the place; one minute she's telling him he's an idiot, then the next she's doing cunnilingus jokes. So there's no relationship there, but she was never a mother figure. She was never a sister figure.

RAY MORTON

Bond has sex with the girl in the beach town and with Sévérine, but the *Bond* Girl in this movie—the main focus of 007's attention and love—is M. One wonders what Bernard Lee would have thought of *that*.

MARYAM D'ABO

(actress, "Kara Milovy," *The Living Daylights*)

Judi Dench considers herself a *Bond* Girl. Her role was fantastic.

MATT GOURLEY

(cohost, James Bonding podcast)

By using M as a stand-in for a *Bond* Girl in *Skyfall,* they're not only developing their characters a little bit more, but part of it is also the enthusiasm with which the producers greeted new ideas about Bond and M and the franchise as a whole. They're playing with what the notion of a *Bond* Girl can be. That's exciting to me.

Overall the cast for *Skyfall* was an impressive one, which had a lot to do with the fact that Mendes had been brought aboard to lure A-level talent, most notably Javier Bardem.

MICHAEL G. WILSON

(producer, *Skyfall*)

Specifically, because Sam Mendes was the director, we got an incredible cast for *Skyfall.* It's the best cast we've ever had. And then they put themselves in his hands, because he's a good director. I think the performances all around in the film are outstanding.

DANIEL CRAIG

You have to take the time and the effort to find the right people, enthusiastic people. We've just been blessed with every character, whether it's Ben

Whishaw or Ralph Fiennes or Javier Bardem or Albert Finney or, of course, Judi Dench. And then the casting of the girls: Naomie Harris and Bérénice Marlohe: finding two exceptionally beautiful women who are very serious actresses and who are intelligent and work hard. For me, it was a joy.

JAVIER BARDEM

When I read the script, I was immediately drawn to the story and the character's possibilities. To work with Sam Mendes and to be a part of his incredible cast and crew, I couldn't say no to an opportunity like this. Silva is an angel of death; a very clean-shaven person who happens to be rotten on the inside. He has a very personal objective—he's *not* trying to destroy the world—and he is on a straight line to that objective. He is a man seeking revenge. It's about being focused on the one person he wants to eliminate. It's always about who's the person behind the character. When I think of a character, I always think about, I don't really care if it's villain or good or tall or short or bald or with long hair. It's always about what's behind the role that makes him more intriguing.

SAM MENDES

The key to a great *Bond* villain is to strike a balance. The performance has to be real enough, but also have flamboyance. The great ones—the Dr. Nos, the Rosa Klebbs, the Goldfingers—are ever-so-slightly theatrical and yet are all the more frightening because of it. For Silva, Javier allowed himself to be playful and mischievous, but never lost the danger, the mystery, the strangeness, the otherness. I think he did something wonderful.

JAVIER BARDEM

It would be very difficult for me to play a role that I just saw as some kind of symbol. In this case, there is a man suffering, a man full of pain and frustration, who simply wants to fix the situation. Within that journey, there was room to be funny or aggressive, but I could perfectly understand who he was, and that helped me to portray him. He's more of a broken person with a very definitive and specific goal to achieve, which is way easier to portray than a symbolic idea, which was more or less what it was in *No Country for Old Men*. That was the idea of violence, a horrible fate itself, but there was no human behind it. Here there is a broken person. Sam Mendes gave me these great notes, and we wanted to create somebody that creates uncomfortable situations rather than being somebody scary or threatening. Somebody that really creates the insecurity of something unexpected happening in front of the person who's dealing with it.

I brought in some ideas of people that I know, people that are publicly known, and we worked with it until the point where we found that it would make sense. This thing about hair or looks, they all have to make sense. I don't believe that you just do that because you want to have fun with it. You always have to make sense. When you watch the movie, rewind and you see what kind of character Silva is and how he is inside. Then you will understand the outside.

There is a moment in the film when Silva has Bond tied to a chair and seems to be flirting with him, Bond ever-so-slyly suggesting that he's had a gay experience. This sparked much conversation, though the actors believe it was considerably overblown.

DANIEL CRAIG

I don't see the world in sexual divisions. Someone suggested that Silva may be gay, but I think he would fuck anything. He's a great flirt. It's a great kind of game of cards. It's the right thing to say, and the way that Javier plays it, it's so great. What's great about Javier's performance is that he plays it for real. He plays it to the limit and he never forgets he's playing a *Bond* villain. That's a testament to how good an actor he is. I love that scene. It makes me laugh.

JAVIER BARDEM

The sexuality was something important to create a behavior, but is not the main thing. You can read anything into it you want, but, again, he's more into the thing of putting the other person in an uncomfortable situation where even James Bond himself doesn't know how to get out of it.

As played by Lois Maxwell until 1985's *A View to a Kill*, Miss Moneypenny was pretty much restricted to being outside M's office, whether it was at Universal Exports, an Egyptian sphinx, or the sunken Queen Elizabeth. She was decidedly *not* a woman of action, but that's exactly what she is (or at least attempts to be) in the form of Naomie Harris' sensational portrayal in *Skyfall*. The actress' previous credits include the second and third *Pirates of the Caribbean films, 28 Days Later . . .*, and *Mandela: Long Walk to Freedom*.

BARBARA BROCCOLI

The character of Eve Moneypenny as written was basically a field agent with a lot of sass, but it wasn't until Naomie came in that we really saw the potential that this character could be something entirely new in terms of a *Bond* film. She's very resourceful, she gives Bond a really hard time, but you still manage to have a tremendous affection for her, and there is a wonderful flirtatiousness between them. She can hold her own with Bond. She's an extraordinary actress.

NAOMIE HARRIS

I think really that any character you play fundamentally is successful because it's coming out of you. I feel like I'm a hundred different personalities. Seriously, I do. I feel like that's the reason why I have to be an actress, because I get an opportunity to air those different characters. Without that opportunity I'd probably go crazy. So, rather than looking outside of myself to find characters, I look within. Eve is definitely within me, that adventurous side, that gung-ho mentality, that running into the danger and actually finding it exhilarating to be in the midst of it. That kind of "I'm going to rough and tumble with the guys"—all of that has to be within me or I wouldn't be able to play it.

SAM MENDES

In recent years, the *Bond* films have featured two girls, one an exotic type and the other a home-grown type. Naomie manages to be both.

NAOMIE HARRIS

Eve is a brilliant field agent who's very independent, intelligent, witty, fun, and courageous. She's not afraid to stand her ground with Bond, and I think that makes her so much more interesting. Playing Eve really allowed me to highlight the more adventurous side of my personality, which was a lot of fun.

One of the most intriguing characters in the film, despite her limited screen time, is Bérénice Marlohe's noir-ish Sévérine, Silva's mistress, who at first seems to be very much in control, eventually succumbing to Bond's charms and then, on Silva's private island, is quickly dispatched by Silva for her betrayal. Interestingly, when she would rehearse for the role, she would spend a lot of time listening to Shirley Bassey sing her *Bond* themes. "She really has the vibe within her voice of the *Bond* movies to me." Berenice smiles. "Super powerful and a quality of being able to hypnotize with her voice. It's nice that Adele wanted to be faithful to that spirit of creating something that's like . . . floating."

BÉRÉNICE MARLOHE

The appeal of *Skyfall* for me was being able to create something within a *Bond* movie. It happened that I was cast as a *Bond* Girl, because, unfortunately, I couldn't have Javier Bardem's role—and at some point I was very jealous of his role, because this is the kind of thing I would like to do one day. When I auditioned for Debbie McWilliams, I told myself, "You're going to be Marlon Brando, because you already look like a woman, so you don't need to play that." And I remember trying to capture the essential Marlon Brando during the audition. I don't know if it worked, but obviously it did for the audition, so that was cool.

I was struggling in France for ten years, and during that time I was trying to prepare myself for something like this to happen. Even though this role was quite short, in a way, on-screen, I wanted to try to put more complexities and colors in to create her, so that, hopefully, on-screen the audience could feel something was appearing; that something below the line was happening. Different ways of receiving her personality and inner life.

SAM MENDES

If I could have invented a *Bond* Girl, it would be Bérénice. I wanted to find somebody with all the classic components of a *Bond* Girl: voluptuous, sexy, a woman and not a girl, mystery. She is half-Cambodian, half-French. She gives us that mystery. On top of all that, she happens to be a fantastic actress.

> On-screen there's an interesting transformation for the character in that when we're first introduced to her, she seems incredibly strong and able to hold her own against Bond. But the closer she gets to Silva, the weaker and more victimized she appears to be.

BÉRÉNICE MARLOHE

That's very true. I never thought about that, but as soon as Bond is even mentioning the name of Silva, we can see something like a switch in her go off. And it's the opposite of what you would expect: instead of seeing someone grow stronger as they go along, she gets weaker. And it's the perfect way to go to Silva and introduce the next scene.

ROBERT WADE
(screenwriter, *Skyfall*)

Sévérine is a survivor. Like many of the women in the Fleming books, she's toughened herself up, because she knows what it is to have been abused at the hands of men.

BÉRÉNICE MARLOHE

Where I tried to regain some of her strength was on the island, right before Silva shoots her. We briefly understand that she had quite a heavy past and interaction with Silva and it wasn't an easy life, but I wanted in her eyes there to be a look of dignity, even if she was afraid. I didn't want it to look like she was pleading; I wanted her to stay standing and to face her now-adversary Silva.

LISA FUNNELL

(author, *For His Eyes Only: The Women of James Bond*)

I feel that the women are still very disempowered in these films. For instance, a character like Sévérine, who was sold in the sex trade. She's a sex slave to Silva. She's asking James Bond for help and then he seals her deal by walking in on her in a shower? Her body has been exploited her whole life, so, to me, that's *not* romantic, that's exploitative. Then she's standing there and she gets shot in the head and nobody even comments on her death. Instead, they lament about the loss of good Scotch. To me, she's so disempowered and tragic. Such a regressive representation of women.

BÉRÉNICE MARLOHE

The funny thing about the shower scene is that I have a fear of drowning. We would shoot that scene for hours, and so I stayed under that shower and we had to talk under the water. And after hours you have a lot of water going into your nose and mouth, and each time they would say "Cut!," I'd be to the side coughing up water. It was very funny, because it wasn't at all in the spirit of a romantic scene.

PHIL NOBILE, JR.

(columnist, *Birth. Movies. Death.*)

As much as we move away from Fleming's pages, the vestiges of that ugly undercurrent remain. Consider the outcry over *Skyfall*'s handling of Sévérine, a typical *Bond* Girl in every sense: a woman in over her head, mixed up with bad people, who succumbs to Bond's charms and pays for it with her life. It's not a new element; that same arc more or less plays out in just about every *Bond* film from *Goldfinger* to each one of Daniel Craig's *Bond* films. But in 2012, it's as if the culture decided we should no longer be okay with this.

Rounding out the cast was Ralph Fiennes as Gareth Mallory, chairman of the Intelligence and Security Committee who, following M's death, takes her place as the head of MI6; Ben Whishaw as the new, and *much* younger Q; and Albert Finney as Skyfall's caretaker, Kincade.

RALPH FIENNES
(actor, "Gareth Mallory")

On the surface, Mallory has a charm, an old-world courtesy, but underneath there's a steel there. He is absolutely able to stand up to M and go head-to-head with her.

MICHAEL G. WILSON

You're not sure where Mallory's loyalty lies in the film—whether he's going to be a help or a hindrance to M and to Bond. He seems to ask a lot of difficult questions and be very critical. It's a very ambiguous character. And when it came to trying to reintroduce the character of Q, it made sense that he would now be a young technical genius, and the character was written with that in mind. Ben was the obvious choice, because he has this wonderful kind of openness to him, and a real intelligence and wit.

BEN WHISHAW
(actor, "Q")

Q represents one of the central conflicts in the film—the old versus the new. It's a battle and a theme that runs through *Skyfall*, between the way the world is going now and the way that the intelligence services are traditionally run.

JOHN LOGAN

When Bond meets Q, there's initial suspicion of "Who's this kid with spots and why is he telling me about my job?" But they quickly develop a mutual respect.

BEN WHISHAW

The new Q is a sort of computer genius, one of only six people in the world who has certain knowledge. He's quite a mysterious person, with a sly sense of humor.

DANIEL CRAIG

I think technology, on the whole, is boring, but what I love about this is that we brought Ben in, who is Q and is a computer whiz, and we have this clash of the two worlds, and there's a potential there to make a really great team. It just means Bond doesn't have to be dealing with technology. We very deliberately kept the gadgets simple, because we use them, but we don't just sort of put them in extraneously. My instinct about them is that we should use them when we need them, but not have them for the sake of it.

BARBARA BROCCOLI

Albert Finney is the most extraordinary man: sexy, wonderful, and delightful. I think he is going to be very well remembered as Kincade, because the relationship he has with Bond goes way back and he appears just in the nick of time. It's delightful to have him in a *Bond* film, because Cubby desperately wanted to work with him, and of course I've wanted to work with him, but we have never had the opportunity until now. He is a legend, a fantastic actor, and just funny, charming, extraordinary, and dead sexy.

There's no denying that Daniel Craig seemed completely comfortable playing Bond for the third time.

BARBARA BROCCOLI

Daniel's one of the greatest actors that we've ever had. He has inhabited the role of Bond, and he's pushed it in directions that one wouldn't have thought possible. Starting with *Casino Royale* and going into *Quantum,* and certainly in this film, he really reveals Bond's inner life in a way that we've never seen before. It's in a way that Fleming does in the books, where you really feel as if you understand the inner turmoil and complexity and conflicts. With this screenplay and with Sam, we unearthed a lot of the emotion connected to Bond's own past and mined the dramatic tension that stems from that.

SAM MENDES

Bond is actually a remarkably difficult part to play, because he says very little, and the moment you make him say too much, it's not Bond anymore. He operates on instinct a lot of the time. He has his own inner demons and he doesn't reveal them to other characters, and yet the audience needs to be aware of them, especially in this particular movie. In *Skyfall* the audience had to see him, in a sense, fall apart and put himself back together again, but none of the other characters see what's really going on behind the curtain. Daniel did that, I think, brilliantly.

From the riveting pre-credit sequence and its battle on top of a moving train to the battle at Skyfall, the film certainly delivered in the action department, though the mandate, as is often the case with *Bond,* was to not let the stunts overwhelm the character moments that are at the heart of any great *Bond* film.

SAM MENDES

If you're not engaged with the characters, the action is meaningless, however good it is. To me, you have to put the characters in a credible and believable situation; you have to make it almost impossible for them to survive—and then show how they survive. That's the challenge.

MICHAEL G. WILSON

We have an incredible team, including Gary Powell, Chris Corbould, Alexander Witt. They get together with Sam and formulate the most exciting and interesting sequences we can dream up while still telling the story. And Daniel contributes a great deal to designing the action—he's the one who really pulls it off. He does as much of it as he possibly can, and I think the reason the action works as well as it does is because he sells it. That's our one rule: it has to feel real.

NEAL PURVIS
(cowriter)

You can have as many explosions as you like, but the dramatic core has got to work.

DANIEL CRAIG

The rule we applied was that I started rehearsing those scenes well before we started shooting and the fight sequences are worked out very carefully so that they're choreographed. I'm not a fighter. I mean, I pretend to be one. It's called bullshit boxing, but I know that we try and make it look good and we talk camera angles and we talk about how to best take advantage of the situation. With that stuff in the beginning, on the train, I mean, you've also got to deal with the fact the train's going from side to side, so you're trying to stay on your feet most of the time, but it's just very carefully worked out, and Roger knows where to put the camera, and Alexander Witt, who did the second unit, he knows where to put the camera, and we have constant dialogue, we watch, we look, and we say, "This fist looks good going into this face like that. . . ." It's just a lot of work involving a lot of skilled people.

RIC MEYERS

It's interesting to compare the opening chase and fight in this to the opening chase and fight in *Casino Royale*. In the former film, Bond's energy is fresh, pent-up, inspired. But in this latter film, he seems to be going through the motions automatically—like he's done it dozens of times before—even mentally flailing a bit. The moment he takes to straighten his cuffs after tearing off the back of a train car and jumping aboard is especially inspired, since the action is automatic, seemingly almost un- or subconscious.

JOHN LOGAN

Writing action sequences is one of the great challenges and the great joys of being a screenwriter. The challenge as a writer on *Skyfall* was to find ways to make the action as "*Bond*ian" as possible, which to me means it's tough, it's real, and it's heightened.

MICHAEL G. WILSON

All of us, Sam and Gary especially, felt that we need to push this movie as far as we could. And we've always relied on the fact that we do things for real in *Bond* movies, and that's just the way it is. If it's CGI, it's just to help out, as opposed to creating the scene. Standing on top of a train, travelling at 50 kilometers per hour, fighting with Ola Rapace going over a bridge was probably a stand-out moment.

RIC MEYERS

That fight atop the train car with his quarry harkens back to the fight between 007 and 006 in *GoldenEye* in that both are equally matched and doing almost the exact same thing. Little wonder Moneypenny accidentally shoots Bond, since the fighters are essentially indistinguishable from each other. Bond had become an even blunter blunt instrument—maybe even one whose edge has dulled. But since that seemed to be the point that they were trying to get across, I appreciated it.

GARY POWELL

(stunt coordinator, *Skyfall*)

It's important to lock down the action step by step so my team can learn it like the back of their hand. After rehearsing for months on end, it gets ingrained in the memory, making it less likely to make mistakes.

SAM MENDES

Editing action is a good deal more exciting than shooting action. Shooting action is very, very meticulous, it's increments, tiny little pieces. To me, the challenge is to create parallel action so you're never locked into a linear chase. It's never just "A" following "B"; there's something else going on simultaneously, so you're following several overlapping stories at the same time.

JAVIER BARDEM

There is some physicality to the role that you have to be prepared to do, but of course mine compared to Daniel's was nothing. And he does the action scenes so easily. From the outside, watching him, I was thinking, "If I were you, I wouldn't be doing that!" I mean, I did a little bit, but nothing in comparison to what Daniel did.

MICHAEL G. WILSON

Daniel's an extremely hardworking actor, probably the hardest working actor I've ever seen. And it's not only the mental preparation, but the physical preparation. He works out like a demon, like a professional athlete. He is really committed to the role, committed to being Bond.

ALEXANDER WITT

(second-unit director, *Skyfall*)

He likes to do as much as possible, though sometimes the production doesn't let him do it because of insurance. If something happens to him . . . for instance, on *Skyfall* he twisted his ankle. He was with first unit and couldn't shoot for, I don't know, four or five days or whatever it was. On *Casino Royale,* he did pretty much everything himself, even going high in the cranes and all that. That became less and less. I don't know if it had to do with age or production saying, "Okay, you can do this and that, but not *that.*" There are people like Tom Cruise that still do their own stunts, and on the last one he broke his foot. Not every actor is like Tom, though. They'd rather have somebody else do it.

BARBARA BROCCOLI

Daniel contributes a great deal to designing the action and the fights in particular, and he's the one who really pulls it off, because he wants to do as much of it as he possibly can. We were in Turkey for the train sequence, and I had my heart in my mouth the whole time; he and Ola were fighting on the roof of a moving train and the moves that they were doing were just heart-stopping. Daniel's the reason why the action works as well as it does, because he sells it, he's up there and I think audiences know that.

One moment that gets an absolute rise out of the audience is when Bond, attempting to get M to safety, goes to a storage unit to retrieve the Aston Martin DB5 circa *Goldfinger*, ejector seat and all.

MICHAEL G. WILSON

We've flirted with other cars from time to time, but we always do come back to Aston Martin. It's a signature car for Bond and a classic one, his own personal one.

DANIEL CRAIG

This story was the perfect platform to reintroduce the DB5. The film is about Bond returning to his roots and confronting old demons, so it felt right. We get some good use out of it, too.

JOHN LOGAN

We're in love with the DB5! When you think of Bond, you think of certain things very clearly and one of them is that particular car. It is Bond's essential car, and in a movie about reorienting Bond to his past and to his future, we just had to use it—beyond the fact it's completely cool.

FRED DEKKER
(cowriter, *The Predator*)

Here's the thing about the Aston Martin. Before Bond and M go to Skyfall, he goes to storage and takes out the 1964 Aston Martin that he used in the Goldfinger affair—even though he has another 1964 Aston Martin that he won at a poker game two movies previously. It's like Mendes isn't even paying attention.

Other elements that came into play in *Skyfall* were the addition of more *Bond*ian humor, that brilliant Oscar-winning title song from Adele, and the return of Daniel Kleinman handling the stunning main title sequence.

DANIEL CRAIG

I just felt when I came on to *Casino Royale*, which showed the beginning of Bond, that we couldn't just cram in the old gags. It would have felt wrong, and I was not trying to copy anybody that had come before, because they all did the part so well. I didn't want to be just that person; I wanted it to be me in this. But it's always been a plan to get those gags put back into the movies in an original and fresh way.

SAM MENDES

We couldn't have done this movie without *Casino Royale,* because what Martin Campbell did so brilliantly in that film was to bring everything back down to sea level as well as eliminate the assumption that there were going to be those moments. So now we are able to reintroduce them with a sense of fun and mischief.

BARBARA BROCCOLI

For the title song, the only person that we wanted was Adele. She came to meet with us, she read the script, and she took it very, very seriously. With Paul Epworth, she wrote a beautiful song that delivered on every level, and of course she has the most extraordinary voice—she delivered a classic Bond theme. It was a dream come true to have her on board.

DANIEL KLEINMAN

(main title designer, *Skyfall*)

When it came to the titles, Sam Mendes is a very clever man, very interesting man. He likes to see a storyboard, and he did have ideas. He probably had more input than any of the other directors I've worked with, although he wasn't consistent. I think that's because when you're doing the movie, and you're so involved with it, you're discovering a lot as you're going along, and it's changing. It's not a fixed thing from the beginning, and now we go and film it and it has a slightly more organic process. We worked on a few ideas, and then I had to change it a bit, because he felt it no longer fit with certain scenes in the film, or themes in the film. And that's fine. It's part of the process. Actually I like that; I like being able to adapt and change and bring in new things and find solutions.

There is also, at some point, the elements of the song which come into it. That's usually quite a way down the line. I usually do a storyboard, and once everybody's okay with it, I work out how I'm going to do it. I go and film it like a normal film shoot, commercial shoot, or whatever. Then spend a few months editing and fine tuning and hoping that when the final mix of the music turns up, it all kind of fits together, which sometimes it does, sometimes it doesn't, and I have to carry on tweaking and changing.

There was a lot of hype surrounding the release of *Skyfall* and the fact that it was James Bond's 50th anniversary on the big screen. The audience certainly responded, with the film—largely critically acclaimed—being the first 007 adventure to gross over $1 billion at the global box office.

RAY MORTON

Skyfall is the most *Bond*-film film in the Craig quartet. Sam Mendes brought a marvelously elegant sense of class and style to the production, something *Bond* films desperately need in order to be *Bond* films. That was sorely missing from *Quantum* and present in just a minor key in *Casino Royale*. It also brought wit and humor back to the films, something else a great *Bond* film absolutely must have. Craig enhanced it all with his performance, which maintained the gritty characterization he established in the two previous films, but then added some stylish wit to his portrayal, along with a few hints of Connery and Moore along the way.

The story and script of *Skyfall* are both excellent, but there is one curious aspect to them both that I never hear commented on and that is that Bond fails at every single thing he attempts to do in the course of the film: he fails to obtain the hard drive from Patrice in the opening mission (and nearly gets killed in the process); he fails to prevent Patrice from killing the man in the Shanghai hotel room; he fails to obtain Silva's identity from Patrice before Patrice falls to his death; he fails to save Sévérine; he fails to stop Silva's attack on the hearing; and he ultimately fails to save M. The film has such style and high spirits and is so entertaining that it seems to be easy to overlook the fact that Bond pretty much blows it throughout the movie.

There's another aspect of the film that was disconcerting to some, that in *Casino Royale* Bond had just gotten his license to kill, while in *Skyfall* he's being considered too old for what's considered to be a young man's game.

RAY MORTON

After rebooting the series with Bond's first adventure just two films earlier, the series now skips ahead to a point where 007 is now washed-up and over the hill, and now he has to get his mojo back. And so, the screenplay for *Skyfall* essentially reboots the reboot. That odd turn aside, this script is terrific in every way: it has a great arc for Bond, a terrific villain, strong supporting characters (including great new versions of Moneypenny and Q), solid action sequences that do an excellent job of advancing the story, a marvelous third act confrontation, and an emotional climax that bids a tearful farewell to the M we have known for the past two decades and resets Bond to continue his adventures for years to come. Silva's scheme to get himself captured and then escape so he can kill M doesn't make a whole lot of sense, but the script's only main flaw is that Bond fails at his mission (to save M) and the villain succeeds in his (to kill M). This is the first time Bond has failed in the history of the series, and it's something that most people talking about the film never seem to mention. It was a very odd choice on the part of the writers and it's still not clear to me if they even realize what they have done.

FRED DEKKER

As Sévérine, Bérénice Marlohe is great, especially in that scene where she's, like, "This guy—Silva—is scary." Then Bond goes to the island and gets her killed. He gets *everyone* killed in this movie, basically. He just fucks up everything he sets out to do from the beginning of the movie, where he is accidentally shot by Moneypenny and lands in the water. You'd think he'd get up out of the water and go back to work. No, he goes to an island to drink beer and then watches TV. He sees that MI6 has been hit by terrorists, and then he goes back. But he doesn't go to his office and he doesn't call in; he goes to M's apartment and drinks her booze and he's kind of ill-shaven, and it's, like, "What's he upset about?" Is he still thinking about Vesper? He acts weird and then he takes forever to be retrained. It wasn't like he was brainwashed like in *The Man with the Golden Gun* novel. He got shot and fell off a bridge. Okay, what the fuck?

So he takes forever for his physical training, his rehabilitation, for which I don't understand why he's doing that, and then he sets out on his mission against Silva, who's ahead of him every step of the way, ridiculously so. Then, ultimately he realizes, "Okay, Silva's got it out for M, so I have to protect M." I can't remember if this is his mission as prescribed by military intelligence or if he takes it on himself, but she's fine with it. So, his idea is, "I'm going to take her away and protect her." So, he takes her to the middle of nowhere to his mommy and daddy's house where there are no weapons at all except for an old guy with a musket, Albert Finney. So you think, "This was a stupid plan, but he's Bond, so he's going to pull it off." *He doesn't.* He gets her killed. I screamed and was, like, "Is this really happening?" Here's the thing: it *seems* to be a good movie, but when you really think about it, it's not. It's just a bad spy movie. His spying is bad, he fucks everything up, and at the end he gets them killed, and then he cries. Why are you crying? *Because* you fucked up?

JOHN CORK

Sam Mendes grew up loving *Bond* films. I think he was at a point in his life where he wanted to tackle what *James Bond* meant to him, so he brought a passion. He also brought a desire to make a film that challenged the audience. Contrast the ironic use of "California Girls" or "London Calling" in earlier films with the French song "Boum" or "Boom Boom" by The Animals. They completely work in the moment. They are part of the villain's core, a man who just wants to blow up everything that hurt him. When, during the helicopter attack on Skyfall, Mendes pay homage to *Apocalypse Now,* he knows he doesn't have to go bigger. He can make his statement with one helicopter. When M quotes poetry, it is not some obvious piece, but from *Ulysses* by Tennyson. The film feels smart, and Bond's world is an erudite world.

RIC MEYERS

At the end, the new M is in his red-upholster-doored office, Moneypenny just outside. Bond is back, better than ever, and ready to take on anything MI6 has to throw at him. My contentment could have only been larger if a file marked "Dr. No" had been glimpsed on M's desk. The film series was in excellent hands and poised to move forward with style.

MICHAEL G. WILSON

The price of freedom is eternal vigilance. That's what you have to do, because if you don't, you will meander off, and when you do that, you start jeopardizing the future.

RIC MEYERS

For all intents and purposes, it looked as if the next fifty years would be even better. What could go wrong?

SPECTRE (2015)

The announcement of *Bond 24* was greeted with eager anticipation by fans who welcomed the legendary Bond villain Ernst Stavro Blofeld back into the fold. Not since 1971's *Diamonds Are Forever* had Bond's own Moriarty appeared on-screen (unless you count the unnamed bald nemesis in *For Your Eyes Only*). Now, after the death of producer Kevin McClory, who had tied the rights to Blofeld and SPECTRE up in litigation for decades, Eon quietly acquired all of McClory's purported rights from his estate. At last the SPecial Executive for Counter-intelligence, Terrorism, Revenge, and Extortion had come home.

And the *Bond* producers wasted little time bringing Blofeld back to the screen when they announced the next film in the series would be entitled *Spectre*. Despite Sam Mendes' protestations that he wouldn't return to the *Bond* fold after *Skyfall,* both Sony and Eon made him an offer he couldn't refuse, and Mendes, now more assured and comfortable at the helm of a *Bond* adventure after the worldwide blockbuster success of the previous film, was ready to bring Blofeld back to the *Bond* universe. Unfortunately, he remained equally enamored with plumbing Bond's backstory as well.

SAM MENDES
(director, *Spectre*)

So what we had here was a kind of creation myth at play with Spectre. We were not adhering to any previous version of the Spectre story; we were creating our own version. Our film was a way of rediscovering the organization and its super-villain, setting him up again for the next generation.

DANIEL CRAIG
(actor, "James Bond")

Having Spectre in the film opened up lots of avenues for us to explore. Having this organization allowed us to be both traditional while also bringing in something very new.

FRED DEKKER
(director, *The Monster Squad*)

They'd already brought in something new with Quantum. So what were they saying, "You know this Quantum secret organization we're doing? We were calling it Spectre amongst ourselves, but we couldn't tell you, because we didn't own the rights. But now we do, so forget about Quantum and just go with Spec . . ." It's like the Aston Martin: they're not trying hard enough to tie it together so that the series has a logical kind of connection.

RAY MORTON
(senior writer, *Script* magazine)

John Logan was hired to write *Spectre,* the follow-up to *Skyfall.* Along with director Sam Mendes, it was Logan's idea to reintroduce the Spectre organization and its nefarious leader Ernst Stavro Blofeld to the Eon series after an absence of 44 years (or 34, depending on how you feel about the pre-credit sequence of *For Your Eyes Only*). However, his first draft was poorly received by both Eon and Sony and he departed the project. His script was rejected, but his core idea was retained, and so his contribution to *Spectre* was certainly key, even if his contribution to the overall story wasn't. Getting involved at that point was Jez Butterworth, a playwright who had worked with Mendes on previous projects. Butterworth was brought in by Mendes to do a final polish on *Skyfall* and a more significant draft on *Spectre*. His work on the first film does not seem to be major. His contribution to *Spectre* was more significant, and so he must share the blame for that mess of a screenplay.

Perhaps there is no more disappointing film in the *Bond* ouvere than *Spectre*. While there are far worse movies, the excitement that greeted the return of Blofeld and Spectre for the first time in an official *Bond* film in decades was palpable. Not unlike *Die Another Day*, however, *Spectre* would sadly prove equally schizophrenic and ultimately disappointing—though on the surface the elements all seemed to be there. *Blue Is the Warmest Color*'s Léa Seydoux and legendary Italian actress Monica Bellucci were early cast announcements, along with *Guardians of the Galaxy*'s Dave Bautista as henchman Mr. Hinx. These were followed by word that Academy Award-winner Christoph Waltz would be playing Blofeld (following in the steps of Donald Pleasence, Telly Savalas, Charles Gray, and our personal favorite, the unseen Anthony Dawson in *From Russia with Love* and *Thunderball*). At that point, fans had become even more thrilled regarding the film's imminent production, but somewhere along the way things derailed.

The plot has Bond go from a rogue mission in Mexico City to Rome, where he meets Lucia Sciarra (Monica Bellucci), the widow of a powerful criminal assassin, and from there uncovers and infiltrates an organization no one had ever heard of, Spectre. At the same time, in London, M (the returning Ralph Fiennes) is dealing with Max Denbigh/C (*Sherlock*'s Andrew Scott), the head of the Centre for National Security, who we will eventually learn to absolutely no one's surprise is connected with Spectre and its plans to take control of the security systems of every country on Earth, shutting down MI6 in the process. Aided by Moneypenny and Q (respectively Naomie Harris and Ben Whishaw), Bond sets out to stop Spectre,and the trail leads him back to the sinister Mr. White (Jesper Christensen) and then, his daughter, Madeleine Swann (Seydoux). As the two attempt to find Blofeld, they begin to fall in love.

SAM MENDES

There's a school of thought in the movie that says, when it comes to national security, everything should be centralized. That we should be almost entirely dependent on surveillance and should let drones do our dirty work abroad. C questions whether we need to send people out in the field. MI6 is, therefore, at risk. In particular, the double-0 section.

ANDREW SCOTT
(actor, "C")

The idea is that surveillance will now be stepped up. He has the opinion that one man in the field, even someone like Bond, cannot really compete with the huge technological advances that we've made in the twenty-first century. The idea of people losing control of their digital ghost and other online legacy is central to the storyline of the film. It's something I think we can all relate to—our privacy and how much information we feel is right to keep to ourselves and how much we need to be protected. That's a big question, and it's still very relevant right now.

RAY MORTON

This script seems to have been cursed from the start. The one thing the filmmakers seemed sure of was that they wanted to reintroduce Blofeld, which was a great idea. But from the start, all the rest of the ideas seemed either misconceived or just plain terrible. At different times, Blofeld was reported to be an African warlord, and, different versions of either the Lucia Sciarra or the Madeleine Swann characters, before they finally settled on the worst idea of all—making him Bond's long-lost, sort of half brother. Hard to figure why they couldn't just make him what he has always been—the leader of an international terrorist organization. Early versions of the script also had either Bill Tanner or M himself turn out to be Spectre's mole in British intelligence, the character who eventually became C in the final film. The idea of revealing a beloved regular character to be a villain is an idea some writers just can't resist, but is always a terrible one, because it just makes loyal viewers feel sad and bad about life. After the final scene of *Skyfall* sets 007 up to head out on a classic *Bond* adventure, this film has him go rogue yet again, which at this point in the series has become a worn-out notion. And the idea that Blofeld was behind all of the villains and capers in the Craig era is an idea that probably seemed cool on paper, but comes across as horribly cheesy on film.

Not that you would get any of the filmmakers to agree with that assessment. After the success of *Skyfall*, producers Michael G. Wilson and Barbara Broccoli spent considerable time trying to convince a reluctant Sam Mendes to come back to the fold, despite the fact that the director had been fairly vocal in his belief that he'd said everything he wanted to say about 007. Eventually, though, he was convinced. And that journey, he says, began with the characters.

SAM MENDES

It all starts with character with me, and I wanted to explore all sorts of different aspects of the characters that I'd left behind in *Skyfall*. We had populated MI6 with a whole new generation of people: a new M, a new Moneypenny, and a new Q. I wanted to let those relationships develop and grow. Bond had a sense of a new beginning. *Skyfall* was an entirely reactive movie as far as Bond was concerned. In the first sequence, he was pursuing somebody with all his old focus and drive, but he gets shot before the credits even roll and for the rest of the movie he is one step behind Javier Bardem's character, Silva. You could even argue that at the end of *Skyfall* he has failed. He has not kept M alive, and though Silva's death is a victory for Bond, there are other elements that are failures. Hence, with *Spectre*, I wanted to give him a chance of redemption.

DANIEL CRAIG

We wanted to be better than *Skyfall*. It is as simple as that. We didn't have a choice; we had to be bigger and better. With *Skyfall*, we set something in motion and we wanted to go a bit further with it and experiment a bit more.

BARBARA BROCCOLI

(producer, *Spectre*)

This film is very much about the empowerment of Bond and, with Daniel portraying the character, he does this with such enormous integrity that we really feel what he is going through, emotionally as well as physically.

The film kicks off with a kinetic pre-title sequence set against the backdrop of Mexico's Day of the Dead festivities—which in itself was preceded by a breathtaking *Touch of Evil*-like opening shot. While there was the stunning cinematography by Hoyte van Hoytema, as well as a grimy and gritty first act that had Bond finding himself tracking down Bellucci's character, much of the film's bad press caught up with it and proved accurate. Thanks to the infamous Sony Pictures Entertainment hack of 2014—which saw private emails between producers and Sony studio chief Amy Pascal, as well as the film's script itself, hit the internet—it had become public knowledge (proven upon viewing the final film) that the creators of *Spectre* had struggled fruitlessly for months to crack problems with the third act. The script in question was widely disseminated (and dissected) during production.

BEN FRITZ

(author, *The Big Picture: The Fight for the Future of Movies*)

To me, the most interesting details came deep in financial documents that revealed how the two companies split the profits. MGM owned the rights to release *Bond* movies, but after emerging from bankruptcy in 2009 as a severely slimmed down studio with no distribution operation of its own, it needed a larger studio to handle that job for it. Sony desperately needed globally popular franchises and was willing to bend further backward than any studio to get 007. Or more accurately, to hold onto them, as it had released *Casino Royale* and *Quantum of Solace,* too, while MGM was spinning into bankruptcy.

In order to release the movies that would end up being 2012's *Skyfall* and 2015's *Spectre,* Sony agreed to cover half their budgets but receive only 25 percent of their profits. So on *Skyfall,* which grossed a massive $1.1 billion, Sony's profit was a measly $57 million. MGM, meanwhile, made $175 million, and Danjaq got $109 million.

Many Sony executives were mad at Amy Pascal, the studio's motion picture chief. They thought she had a history of making bad business deals in order to look good to the creative community.

Even Pascal had to admit it was a pretty crazy arrangement. "Who else is gonna make such a one-sided deal with MGM?" she asked Barbara Broccoli in an email.

Beyond the third act problems, however, the cast is underserved by a script that can't decide if it's going to play it straight or lighten up the formerly dour Bond. Unfortunately, after 007 ejects from his Aston Martin to avoid being killed by Dave Bautista's relentless Mr. Hinx—a nearly mute killing machine—it evokes unwelcome comparisons to the paragliding sequence in *Die Another Day.* And by the time Bond gets to Switzerland, we feel we've stepped into a less-well-realized version of *On Her Majesty's Secret Service.* And despite Seydoux's solid performance, there's not even a simmering amount of romantic tension between her and Bond.

By the time they both arrive at Blofeld's desert lair, the film begins to rapidly unravel as it tries to evoke the spirit of *You Only Live Twice*'s classic volcano base, but grounded in the contemporary realism of a meteor crater in the desert. Unfortunately, you can't have it both ways. By the time the film enters that troubled third act, and despite all efforts to redress the studio's concerns, it turns into a *Mission Impossible* film with Moneypenny and M all joining the fray in an attempt to bring down the sniveling C. But perhaps the most egregious misstep the film makes is its clumsy attempt to create a *Bond* cinematic universe in which everything that's happened to 007 since *Casino Royale* is part of a master plan by Blofeld ("the author of all your pain"), who himself is revealed to be Bond's own foster brother, Franz Oberhauser, an absurd revelation that doubles down on the unwanted and un-needed family drama of *Skyfall*.

None of which actually affected production, which traveled from Mexico City to Switzerland, Rome, North Africa, and London.

SAM MENDES

Given the fact that Bond is much more engaged in his own journey, we were able to play around with much more widespread locations. There is much more variety and a far greater physical and geographical journey in this movie than in *Skyfall*. We couldn't really do that in the last movie, because we were very London-based. Yes, there were sequences in Shanghai and Istanbul, but the second half of the film took place almost entirely in London and Scotland.

DANIEL CRAIG

In *Spectre*, we could work with a slightly different style from the other *Bond* films I've done. This film is very individual, but also harks back a little to what has gone before in the *Bond* films of the '60s and '70s.

SAM MENDES

I also wanted to get back to some of that old-school glamour that you get from those fantastic, otherworldly locations. I wanted to push it to extremes. And it doesn't get any bigger than Mexico City and the Day of the Dead.

STEPHANIE SIGMAN

(actress, "Estrella")

The opening scenes of the film start with Bond and Estrella celebrating the Day of the Dead in this amazing location with thousands of people. It is a beautiful scene, because it's very close to the reality of how we celebrate that day in Mexico. That was very nice for me, being Mexican, and it wasn't difficult to get fully immersed in the scenes.

MICHAEL G. WILSON

(producer, *Spectre*)

Though we have worked on the *James Bond* films for more than 35 years, Barbara and I both felt that the opening sequence to *Spectre* was something magnificent to behold.

DENNIS GASSNER

(production designer, *Spectre*)

When the Day of the Dead came up, I was extremely happy, because it's been something I've been watching for a long time, coming from California and therefore being very close to Mexican culture. We started doing our research, and when we reached the right tone and started designing it, it worked out really well. The Mexicans were absolutely wonderful to work with and are obviously passionate about displaying what their culture is invested in. Working on the Day of the Dead section of the film was one of the most exciting things I have done in my career, ever.

ALEXANDER WITT

(second-unit director, *Spectre*)

That opening sequence has a helicopter as part of it, and there's this pilot who does all the acrobatics. The authorities left and we had the two helicopters in the Zócalo, right in the middle of Mexico, in front of the Presidential House. They didn't let us do a lot of the acrobatics there. We went to an airport like an hour's flight from Mexico City. It was a new airport that was not in use yet. That's where we did all the aerials and the helicopter doing the turns and all that. I did some hand-held inside the helicopter with the fight going on.

BARBARA BROCCOLI

That opening scene is good old-fashioned filmmaking rendered on a gargantuan scale. The Mexico scenes are truly epic, and the Day of the Dead sequence stands as a reminder of what a *James Bond* film can achieve. Here we were in the middle of a foreign capital city with thousands of beautifully dressed extras and a world-class stunt team executing jaw-dropping scenes.

MICHAEL G. WILSON

We've had some amazing sequences set in the snow, and we were very conscious of what we've done in all these films. That meant we wanted to do something different from being in bobsleds or using any of the usual winter sports. Hence we had a different kind of chase with airplanes and 4×4s.

SAM MENDES

We wanted to send Bond to one of Europe's great cities at night, and we chose Rome because of the history and an atmosphere of darkness and foreboding. Particularly if you're dealing with 1920s and 1930s Fascist architecture. There is something dark and intimidating. And for the intimate part of the film, we went to North Africa, in Tangier and the Sahara. If you want this incredible immense landscape, this emptiness, then where better than the Sahara? So with all these locations, you have three tones that are quite different and quite extreme. And with London, the challenge was to try and find a way of shooting there that felt fresh and new and yet which was also a continuation of *Skyfall*. We tried to find a way to look at familiar locations and familiar places within London from a different perspective, and I think we found some great ways to do that. These five locations give you a clue as to why the movie was technically so hard to achieve, and why it was so exhausting, why it took so long to shoot, and why it has taken no prisoners.

On his journey, Bond does manage to find some time for lovemaking, initially with Monica Bellucci's Lucia Sciarra, and, of course, Seydoux's Swann.

MONICA BELLUCCI
(actress, "Lucia Sciarra")

I said yes right away, because I was very happy to work with Sam Mendes and to be part of this project. I have so much respect for the *James Bond* films in general, because I think they are such a big part of cinema history. And I respect so much all the *James Bond* Girls; I think they are beautiful actresses and talented, and it was very interesting for me to be part of this history. When Lucia first meets Bond, she doesn't trust him, because she comes from a world where only corrupt men have the power. But the chemistry and the attraction between them is so strong and she realizes her feminine power over him. Then she trusts him. He saves her and she gives him the information he needs—they find an interesting way to sign a contract with each other.

GLEN OLIVER
(pop culture commentator)

The Powers That Be deserve the highest praise for casting Monica Bellucci, albeit in far too brief a role, as a *Bond* Girl. If memory serves, she's officially the oldest *Bond* Girl yet seen in these pictures—kudos to all involved for saying "fuck you!" to the irrational and discriminatory ageism that frequently plagues large scale films, and the industry in general. It was an interesting role, which I would've liked to have seen more of, and Bellucci was still sexy as hell.

LÉA SEYDOUX

(actress, "Madeleine Swann")

The character is intelligent, independent, and she doesn't want anything to do with Bond when she meets him for the first time. She's not impressed. But the relationship softens; she understands Bond very well, because she has an insight into the world that he lives in. For his mission he needs to understand things from his past and he needs Madeleine for the information she can provide. Eventually it is a very strong relationship between them.

JOHN CORK

(film historian, author, *Bond Girls Are Forever: The Women of James Bond*)

I think Léa Seydoux is a fantastic actress with a very haunting quality. I think she was a great choice to play Madeleine Swann. I also liked Monica Bellucci. Both roles were slightly underdeveloped for my tastes. I would have rather more Monica or Léa than some guy listening to opera driving a Fiat 500.

Playing the iconic role of Blofeld was Christoph Waltz. Requisite intimidating henchmen included Dave Bautista as Hinx, who meets his apparent demise in a battle with Bond on a train transporting 007 and Madeleine to what would be Blofeld's headquarters.

CHRISTOPH WALTZ

(actor, "Ernst Stavro Blofeld")

In this film, it's the classic, and the classical, protagonist/antagonist dynamic. The dynamic is that the hero's major existential quest needs to be thwarted, and every obstacle needs to be set up to the degree that endangers not just the achievement of his quest, but endangers the existence of the hero himself. Everybody was very aware that this dynamic is, to say the least, very desirable in this context. That dynamic is what makes these stories really interesting.

LISA FUNNELL

There is that moment in the film where Blofeld tells Bond, "I'm the author of all your pain," and I'm, like, "This is *not* the Marvel Cinematic Universe where you planned four films and everything connects." I mean, Marvel takes you with breadcrumbs and you're like, "I get how everything comes together." In this case, it's like an afterthought of trying to put things together. Like, you're telling me that Silva, who's on this personal quest and vendetta of revenge, because he was handed over during the 1997 handover back to China and all this stuff, that somehow he was part of your organization? That was a deeply personal revenge narrative where he wanted to get at M and MI6. There's no trace of Blofeld in there. For me, I'm, like, where did he come from? Where would he have been? I just don't buy any of that. Blofeld to me was so one-dimensional—not even two-dimensional—and so disappointing. I was bored.

RIC MEYERS

(author, *Films of Fury: The Kung Fu Movie Book*)

By the time the revelation that Blofeld was actually Bond's foster brother, who had not only killed his parents because "mom liked you best," but also had masterminded every enemy in the series to take some sort of spoiled, tantrum-tinged revenge, my brain was already hitchhiking home. Just as well. The movie, incredibly, just got worse from there, until the only rational explanation for what happens on-screen during the finale and climax is that it was all a fantasy that Bond was having while Blofeld is drilling his brain—a la Terry Gilliam's *Brazil* or *The Twilight Zone*'s "An Occurrence at Owl Creek Bridge." This wasn't just sad, it was a travesty and tragedy.

DAVE BAUTISTA

(actor, "Hinx")

This film has something of an old-school feeling, especially when you consider the history of Spectre. They're this large, mastermind organization that is everywhere. They're very mysterious, and it's important that they remain that way. I always thought it was really cool to be the bad guy, but being a member of Spectre, specifically, is great.

GLEN OLIVER

I remember being hugely excited to learn Dave Bautista had landed a role in *Spectre*; I'd really enjoyed his work to date, and felt (and still feel) that the extent of his range had yet to be fully or properly explored. Hearing that he'd been cast as an "iconic henchman" was quite provocative, and gave rise to fun imaginings of how the current *Bond* regime might envision the notion of "iconic," given the wonderful array of memorable and "iconic" henchmen who've visited the franchise in the past. What we got was Dave Bautista looking like Dave Bautista—dressed for a semi-formal dinner, wearing a beard cribbed from Zangief from *Street Fighter*, saying next to nothing, and not even being a particularly effective henchman. Such squandered opportunity, like so much of the film.

RIC MEYERS

My eyes got increasingly bigger and my jaw increasingly slack as I watched the film unravel—until I started blinking as Bond and his contrived, unconvincing lady love wait for a private train at a stealthy station that might as well have had the announced destination of "Blofeld's Secret Spectre Headquarters." But even that hadn't made me mentally check out. No, what made me quit was the overhand ice pick. During the epic (not) train fight on the way to Spectre's meteor crater hideout—which, by the way, also makes little sense since Blofeld is supposedly awaiting Bond's arrival—Bond tries to stab Hinx with an ice pick . . . overhand. Stabbing someone overhand—that is, with the arm upraised and the weapon clutched in the fist with the blade coming down from the pinky—is as dead a giveaway that someone on the film crew doesn't know what they're doing, as a silenced revolver is. Anyone who knows anything about guns knows you can't silence a revolver. And anyone who knows anything about effective knife fighting specifically—and fighting in general—knows you should never, ever, try to stab even a barroom brawler overhand. Q, M, and any martial arts instructor used by MI6 would know that is never trained in any law enforcement organization, let alone Her Majesty's Secret Service. Yet there's James Bond—the vanquisher of Red Grant, Oddjob, and Jaws—trying to stab Hinx with an ice pick. Overhand.

The smart, effective fighter of *Casino Royale* is totally MIA. He really no longer has a fighting philosophy other than that of Wile E. Coyote. Overhand ice pick?!? That showed how everyone involved just really didn't care anymore.

Besides Spectre and Blofeld, two other returnees to the film were composer Thomas Newman (who had made his debut on the franchise with *Skyfall,* replacing David Arnold much to many fans chagrin) and main title designer Daniel Kleinman. A new addition was singer Sam Smith, who sang the song "Writing's on the Wall," which was cowritten with Jimmy Napes.

JEFF BOND

(editor, *Film Score Monthly*)

Newman was a daring choice for the *Bond* series, but so was Sam Mendes, and this was a case of getting an auteur director and having that director bring along his artistic entourage from previous films. Newman is a master of orchestral color, and his music fantastically reflects the exotic locales in *Skyfall* and *Spectre*, but he's been very controversial among *Bond* fans because he has not really genuflected toward the Barry *Bond* sound, and he hasn't created the kind of outsized personality for Bond that Arnold managed.

GLEN OLIVER

Sam Smith's opening song, "Writing's on the Wall," was one of the weaker songs in the franchise's history. His strained falsetto evoked a late night lounge act on a cruise ship more than it suggested the power of many *Bond* songs, or the "out of the box" nature of others. He lacked the vocal range to pull off that piece of music. Which is, perhaps, ironically symbolic for the overall quality of the picture.

DANIEL KLEINMAN

(main title designer, *Spectre*)

The Spectre octopus was a part of the titles, and I think that was my idea, actually. There was a paragraph of ideas for images that could be in the titles, which I think Sam Mendes had written himself. I did run with a few of those ideas, but I'm pretty sure the actual octopus, and it coming to life, was sort of my idea. I just liked the imagery of it. There's always one thing within each movie where I think there's one key image which feels like that is what I base everything else on, and do variations on a theme. The octopus was it in that one. It became a little more real than I intended. Originally I wanted it to be much more shadowy, and a bit symbolic. It became quite a literal object, but in a way that kind of gave it maybe a bit more yucky menace.

At *Spectre*'s conclusion, Blofeld, who has seen his face scarred in a helicopter crash caused by Bond, is arrested rather than killed, while 007 and Madeleine, who he rescued from his foster brother's machinations, literally drive off together, Bond apparently leaving his spy life behind. Until *Bond 25*, at least.

GLEN OLIVER

Spectre was, perhaps, doomed from the start. It was following up one of the more highly regarded films in the *Bond* franchise, which was an exceedingly tough act to follow in the eyes of many *Bond* fans. It reintroduced Spectre (the titular mega-criminal organization) into the mix, which incited no small amount of enthusiasm and anticipation amongst fans of the series—as this element had been notably, perhaps sorely, missing from *Bond* films for decades. The film's top-lining guest star, Christoph Waltz, was an Oscar-winning actor and critical favorite. It was also the 24th *Bond* film, which meant it had to work overtime to not only balance and validate all of these other weighty expectations, but overcome the threat of "*Bond* fatigue" which constantly dogs the franchise. All of this was, in many ways, a roundly predictable recipe for disaster. Although "disaster" is probably too strong a word for *Spectre,* the picture certainly ranks as one of the more misguided and under-baked 007 movies yet made.

RAY MORTON

Both the Sony hack which revealed early versions of the script to the public and complaints from the cast (especially Ralph Fiennes, if reports are to be believed) forced the story to be rewritten just before the film went into production, but I'm not sure this can be blamed—as it often is—for the script turning out as poorly as it did. I think the script's core ideas were so poor to begin with, that no matter how they were arranged, the script was never going to work. Some projects are just misconceived, and that definitely seems to have been the case from the get-go with *Spectre*.

JOHN CORK

Spectre made money hand over fist. It underperformed *Skyfall* stateside by a big margin, and that is a challenge that the studio and Barbara and Michael have to look at carefully. But *Skyfall* was an outlier. It sold more tickets in the U.S. than any *Bond* film since *Goldfinger* and *Thunderball.* If you leave out *Skyfall,* the grosses of the *Bond* films, adjusted for inflation, ever since *GoldenEye* are relatively flat, with only about a 15 percent variation between the top grosser—*Die Another Day*—and the lowest grosser—*Spectre*—of that era. *Skyfall* showed that there was a huge upside potential for a *Bond* film that really connected with audiences.

RIC MEYERS

Craig's Bond started fresh, but the ripening and rotting set in as early as *Quantum of Solace,* where he looked like a numb victim of circumstance. It continued in *Skyfall* through his inability to actually succeed at anything. And now, there has never been a *James Bond* movie that made less sense than *Spectre*. There's a difference between outlandish plotting and nonsensical plotting. *Spectre*'s story went from nonsensical to almost insultingly inexplicable.

MARTIN CAMPBELL

(director, *Casino Royale*)

At the end of the day, I was a little disappointed in the film. I enjoyed *Skyfall* thoroughly, but in *Spectre,* for instance, Blofeld, who over the series has been built up as this very powerful, enigmatic character, felt very weak. And I didn't buy the stepbrother business. I thought all that was most peculiar. And then there was something like the scene with Monica Bellucci that went off on a tangent that had nothing to do with the main story.

Marvelous opening sequence, brilliant, I loved all that. I thought the Mexican side was superbly directed and very exciting, but I felt sort of the second half of the movie just went down hill, basically. It all starts with the script. One or two good action sequences and a great punch-up on the train and so forth, but the story was disappointing. Léa Seydoux was fine—she's a very good actress—but narratively speaking, it was weak.

RAY MORTON

After finally getting *Bond* back on track after three reboot films, for some reason *Spectre* now brings us what seems to be Bond's final adventure—the one in which he walks away from Her Majesty's Secret Service, seemingly for good. Why anyone thought we wanted to see this, I have no idea, but it certainly lets all of the air out of *Skyfall*'s marvelous final scene. The script's one brilliant idea is to reintroduce Bond's arch-nemesis Blofeld after a far-too-long absence. Apart from this, the screenplay is a total whiff. It saddles Bond and Blofeld with a ludicrous backstory that posits them as pseudo-foster brothers and a ludicrous twist in which Blofeld is revealed to have been the mastermind behind all of the plots in the Daniel Craig run of the series—two dreadful ideas that are emblematic of backstory-happy, *Save the Cat!*-influenced, crappy 2010s blockbuster screenwriting. The *Spectre* screenplay is overlong and ponderous, lacking in exciting or meaningful action, and spends far too much time on a subplot involving the MI6 office staff that tries to position M as Bond's costar in the film rather than the supporting character he is and should always remain. *Spectre* had a lot of potential, but the final product is a complete dud.

GLEN OLIVER

Spectre suffers from a substantial identity crisis. The film takes itself very seriously, but its somber tone, oppressive photography, and superficially treated (but conceptually lofty) subject matter (the issues surrounding electronic surveillance) feel like a smokescreen to mask plotting that is actually wafer thin, and logic that is sometimes shoddy at best. If you look at *Spectre* objectively, it's fairly unsubstantial beneath the operatic smoke and mirrors. Its Bond/Blofeld "brother" dopiness doesn't seem to substantially register on either the Bond character, or the *Bond*-verse in general—begging the question: why bother to "go there" if the payoff wasn't going to be loftier? It just doesn't seem to matter in the grand scheme, and feels like an unnecessary distraction and convolution. This, like many of the film's serious moves, feels manufactured and clunky. *Spectre* takes itself *so* seriously, and is, at times, so over the top and over-written, that it often feels more like a *Naked Gun*/Zucker Brothers parody than a 007 film.

By the time the film was released, Daniel Craig infamously stated that "he'd rather slit his wrists than do another one." Unsurprisingly, the actor found himself donning the tuxedo once again for the latest *Bond* adventure, directed by *True Detective's* Cary Joji Fukunaga, alongside returning *Bond* Girl Léa Seydoux as Madeline Swann in what is presumed to be his own swan song (this following a brief dalliance by Eon with director Danny Boyle and writer John Hodge, who parted ways with the Broccolis over the familiar "creative differences").

MARTIN CAMPBELL

Daniel always makes remarks like that. Well, excuse me, you've earned a hundred million off the fucking movie. This is a knee-jerk reaction to this stuff. It's just very hard work for him and he gets beaten up a bit, but he's 120 percent committed to these movies and will remain that way until he stops doing them.

JAMES BOND WILL RETURN

"It's quite alright, really. She's having a rest. We'll be going on soon. There's no hurry you see, we have all the time in the world."

There are few assurances in life beyond death and taxes, but one other thing you can always count on is a new *James Bond* film. While it's been decades since they were released like clockwork every year, soon to be every two years, and later many more years in between, the release of a new film is an inevitability and one of the more pleasant joys in an increasingly unpleasant world. While the man behind the tux may change, Ian Fleming's character remains the same: a sexist, misogynist, dinosaur who is always ready to do what's right for England and the world. We can't imagine what we'd do without you, 007.

Why have these films lasted for over five decades, when so many other legendary movie franchises have expired, validating Cubby Broccoli and Harry Saltzman's gamble on the gentleman agent with a license to kill lo those many years ago? It's a puzzle that even those who have worked on the film series continue to ruminate on after all these years.

TERENCE YOUNG

(director, *Dr. No*)

It was a miracle. When you look back on it, we were just damn lucky and everything worked. It was just one of those things. It could have gone exactly the other way, and they'd have been sunk without a trace.

RICHARD MAIBAUM

(screenwriter, *On Her Majesty's Secret Service*)

One of the reasons is that they're beautifully produced. Cubby Broccoli is the driving force behind the whole thing. He has good taste; he is attentive . . . he stays with it. He is completely involved. I think the answer is that they've had a good run because they're good films.

DAVID V. PICKER

(president and chief executive officer, United Artists)

Consider this: the combined negative cost of these movies from the 1960s and 1970s—*Dr. No, A Hard Day's Night, Last Tango in Paris, Lilies of the Field* and *Never on Sunday*—was less than two 30-second spots on the Super Bowl. That's right—the entire negative cost of those movies, less than two 30-second spots on the Super Bowl. Times have changed.

OLGA KURYLENKO

(actress, "Camille Montes")

I didn't realize people loved *Bond* so much. People love it. I realize that people have collections of *Bond* movies. They have been watching them all the years. This movie has existed through the decades. It's still alive today. People are still as interested as they were before. It didn't finish, it didn't stop, and people didn't say, "Oh, I forgot it. I don't want to watch it anymore." They are still excited today.

JEAN-JACQUES DETHIER

(development economist at the World Bank and a lifelong Bond fan)

The main world threat these days is clearly linked to cyberthreats, automation of the industrial world, and artificial intelligence—and intelligence and counterintelligence services in the U.S., UK, and Europe have not found a convincing way to combat these threats. Cyberspying is a major weapon used by Russia and China. The other major threat, in my view, is the decline of democracy: the fact that existing democracies are fragile and are turning into plutocracies, and that populations seem happy with corrupt and populist regimes like Trump's in the United States or the Berlusconi/Lega/Fratelli d'Italia coalition or the Cinque Stelle movement in Italy. In both cases, cyberthreats and plutocracy, it should not be a problem to come up with a good plot, should it?

MADS MIKKELSEN

(actor, "Le Chiffre")

The *Bond* series has been developing for decades now, and every time you get a new Bond, they take another step. That is the big secret of its survival.

TIMOTHY DALTON

(actor, "James Bond")

Obviously, as a generalization, he fulfills a lot of fantasies. Men's fantasies and perhaps women's fantasies, too. But I don't think you can define what it is that makes an audience identify, or want to identify, with him, or if they do. That is a gift of any character in a piece of drama that works.

TOM MANKIEWICZ

(screenwriter, *Live and Let Die*)

Bond movies are definitely chancy. One of the things that probably has hurt some of them more than anything is that they don't offend anybody anymore. I remember people gasping when they heard Pussy Galore. Just gasping. People thought it was disgusting.

ROBERT CAPLEN

(author, *Shaken & Stirred: The Feminism of James Bond*)

On the surface, the *Bond* Girl represents pure sex appeal, a fantasy of the archetypal woman: attractive, somewhat resourceful and worldly, intriguing, and susceptible to the power of persuasion. She is, in many respects, escapism for both male and female audiences. Men want to seduce her, and women want to be her.

CHARLES "JERRY" JUROE

(publicist)

You've got to understand, there was THE *Bond* Girl and the *Bond* Girls. To those of us in the company, the *Bond* Girls were all of the girls in the picture, they were the *Bond* Girls. The *Bond* leading lady was the leading lady. It was a difference. Today, a girl is in one 10-second sequence, and she's a *Bond* Girl, with the press.

JOHN CORK

(film historian; author, *Bond Girls Are Forever: The Women of James Bond*)

I've generally been more comfortable referring to the women in the *Bond* films as "*Bond* Women." The actresses themselves refer to the sorority of actresses who have appeared in the films more as being "*Bond* Girls."

ROBERT CAPLEN

I remember watching my first *James Bond* film at a young age and enjoying the intrigue, sophistication of James Bond himself, and the beauty of his female counterparts. I didn't quite understand or appreciate the innuendo until I was a little older.

JOHN GLEN
(director, *For Your Eyes Only*)

In this day of political correctness and the fact that women's lib has taken over, there's always been a bit of a stigma attached to *Bond* Girls. They don't really go on to do many great things, usually. Diana Rigg is probably an exception, but for a lot of them, or most, it was almost a bad career move.

ROBERT CAPLEN

There has been a lot of discussion over the years about how an actress's career has been impacted by her participation in the *Bond* franchise. I'm not sure there's really much validity to it. Many *Bond* Girl actresses were relatively unknown (Jane Seymour had her debut in *Live and Let Die* and later found tremendous success on the big and small screens; Rosamund Pike debuted in *Die Another Day* and has been critically acclaimed in numerous roles throughout her career), with few exceptions (Honor Blackman, Diana Rigg, Lois Chiles), and many were established film stars in their native countries (such as Daniela Bianchi, Claudine Auger, and Luciana Paluzzi), who continued to star in European films after their *Bond* Girl performances.

JOHN CORK

The role of women in the *Bond* movies constantly evolves. Despite the attitudes of the era, Fleming wrote complex characters. Many times for the women, that complexity was overshadowed by their sexuality. Most viewers remember Honey Ryder walking from the sea but don't talk about her tale of being raped and murdering her rapist. Tatiana in *From Russia with Love* is sexually exploited by SPECTRE. Domino in *Thunderball* has sold her soul for the access to luxury and security that Largo provides, and the underlying sadness in her character certainly enriches the film for me.

TOM MANKIEWICZ

In their time, they were really fruitless parts. The picture was so much about James Bond that it was never about them. I suppose it's very difficult to get a serious actress to want to be in a *Bond* movie.

ROBERT CAPLEN

More recently, the franchise has used well-established actresses to fill *Bond* Girl roles—Oscar winner Halle Berry, Teri Hatcher, Monica Bellucci, Léa Seydoux—and their careers have not been adversely affected.

TOM MANKIEWICZ

Bond movies were, in their own way, and I don't apologize for it, quite sexist. That was part of it. It was part of the era and the time.

RICHARD MAIBAUM

The *James Bond* syndrome, of course, has become worldwide and is sort of in the *Sherlock Holmes* class now. The whole *James Bond* syndrome has just become a part of the culture, and I think that has a great deal to do with it. Although the pictures have varied in how they were acceptable to audiences, they continued on a very steady and high level, and the audience knows that they're going to get a good show. They're not going to get short-changed. I think the answer is that they've had a good run because they're good films.

MATT SHERMAN

(creator, BondFanEvents.com)

Out in the spy world, I've also worked with real-world intelligence officers—the preferred euphemism for spies—of the FBI, CIA, NSA, and KGB. These people love James Bond, and the *Bond* actors and *Bond* technicians loved meeting them, too, at my events. At Langley and at The International Spy Museum in Washington, D.C., I've heard in person from these real-life heroes. Many of them grew up with Bond as *their* hero, or writing and mailing letters to U.N.C.L.E., hoping to join Napoleon Solo at age 12, and so on. Amazing!

DANIEL KLEINMAN

(main title designer, *Skyfall*)

What's great about it, as you say, going back to the beginning, is that when you grow up with it as a child, if you're a *Bond* fan, when you're a little boy, and you're kind of sitting in the cinema and going, "Wow, that girl's got no clothes on, that's fantastic." And you're suddenly kind of part of it. It's a very family-oriented production setup, the whole thing. You kind of feel like you are part of a big family. They're very inclusive, very nice people. It's a sort of great thrill to be part of it. And it is sort of movie history. I doubt if anyone's going to remember my Guinness commercials, but they might remember the *Bond* titles, which is kind of nice.

FRED DEKKER
(director, *RoboCop 3*)

I've always harbored this dream of doing a comic book series in which Alfred disappears and Bond shows up and teams up with Bruce Wayne. And be totally true to the underlying mythology of both of those characters because they're very similar. They're two peas in a pod.

JANE SEYMOUR
(actress, "Solitaire")

James Bond is just such an amazing franchise. I think it's partly because it's sort of English and it's tongue in cheek. It's not just hard . . . Well, it's become much more kind of hard drama now than it ever was. I mean, back in the day, it really was about absurdly sexy women and a debonair English spy with ridiculous utensils. But I think the reason it sustains so well is that every era has had a different style of *Bond*. So *Bond* has actually grown up with society. It's changed. When I did it, it was definitely sort of *Austin Powers* time. Nowadays, that *Austin Powers* thing wouldn't work. When I watched *Austin Powers*, I went, "Oh yeah. That's me in the *Bond* days." That was swinging London. That was who we were and what was happening.

TANYA ROBERTS
(actress, "Stacey Sutton")

The *Bond* movie plots aren't very convoluted. But I find that the blockbusters today are and they're just too big for trying to say too much and do too much, and I find it ends up very thin.

JOHN LANDIS
(director, *Animal House*)

One of the interesting challenges is the *Bond*, and it's a problem really; Bond could always be superior to the low-budget knockoff, but then, they started doing the *Bond*. Christopher Nolan made *Inception*. There was a whole sequence taken from *On Her Majesty's Secret Service* and using the same location. Then also the *Bourne* movies, the *Mission Impossible* movies. They spend so much money on the stunts, it's very hard to impress an audience with anything anymore. That moment in *Goldfinger* and of him getting out of the scuba suit, being in a white tuxedo, is so wonderfully insane and done well. In *From Russia with Love*, they have the assassination sequence with that big billboard for *Call Me Bwana,* and in the beginning of *Dr. No,* the "Three Blind Mice" calypso music. They really had a sense of experimentation in the early days. Then it just kind of settled into greatest hits. "You have to have this, you have to have that." I don't know though, each *Bond* movie makes more than the others.

JOHN GLEN

I think to get at an original idea that's up-to-the-minute and moves fast and has got original action in it gets more and more difficult as time goes on. If someone said to me, "Dream up a scenario for a new *Bond* film," I'd think, "Christ, how am I going to start?" What do you do? At least one thing we can thank the Cold War for is it gave us plenty of ammunition on the scriptwriting front. Now it's not much fun. It's electronic, and it's just phony news and interfering in elections and things like that. It's not particularly box office, is it?

TANYA ROBERTS

Press conferences and publicity were just something you had to go through that, you know, they shoot all kinds of questions at you, most of them ridiculous, and you answer as best you could.

BARBARA CARRERA
(actress, "Fatima Blush")

I also realized that this character of James Bond will be around even after we are dead. He's a character that will survive time. I had so much fun doing it, and it did so much good for me. Today, the first thing people remember is this *Bond* film. They don't know about all the other films that I did. They just know *Bond*!

JOHN GLEN

They've kept the quality going. There's been one or so that haven't been so good. You know that, but I think the public will forgive you for one. If you did two bad ones, then I think you could be in a lot of trouble, but I think they've kept them fresh. They try to keep them topical. I think the freshness of them is something. If they'd been all Fleming, Fleming had written all the older films, they probably would've died out, because they would've been left in the '60s or in the '50s, but the fact is that we keep updating them.

DESMOND LLEWELYN

(actor, "Q")

You're sitting there and watching this wonderful world that you would love to be in. But you know, it's all much bigger than life. And I think the great thing Cubby Broccoli did was follow Ian Fleming's dictum really, which was, he was asked what makes a good thriller? And he said, "To any *Bond* story add all the advantages of expensive living. Give Bond the right clothes and the right background and the right women. Set your story in the most beautiful place and take us along at such a speed that nobody will notice the idiosyncrasies in it."

FRED DEKKER

(cowriter, *The Predator*)

When we talk about Idris Elba, or whoever the woman that they're going to cast, it's like, "No." He's a British man. He's a snob, and he's a racist. That's what the guy wrote. It's the Stephen King thing; no, they didn't rewrite my book, it's right up there on the shelf. Yes, you don't have to shoot the character that Fleming created, but I like the character that Fleming created more than what you're proposing doing with it. End of speech.

YAPHET KOTTO

(actor, "Kananga/Mr. Big")

They came to me and asked me, "Is it all right for a black man to play James Bond?" I said absolutely not. You do that, that's the end of the franchise. Bond is white. This thing about diversity is bullshit. We cannot put black guys in every goddamn thing just because it would be wonderful. It's happening all over TV and movies. Black guys in the days of King Arthur. Black guys who were Vikings. Come on man, get real. Put black people where they belong, and let white boys play the part the way they play the part. You just can't diversify and be liberal for everything. It's bullshit. James Bond is an Englishman, gentleman, a white man. That cannot happen. What I'm going to do is say, "Okay, you want a black guy to play James Bond? How about me playing John Kennedy? How about that?"

PHIL NOBILE, JR.

(editor in chief, *Fangoria* magazine)

I think the way the series treats women has been evolving since 1962. Compare Honeychile Rider of the book to the film version, or the fact that Roger Moore's Bond had a fling with a black agent. There's a faction of *Bond* fandom who always thinks the changing world is going to come for their precious 007, but the series has always been set five minutes from now, and though it occasionally hits a sour note, the franchise is more in tune with the times than people seem to think.

MATT GOURLEY
(cohost, *James Bonding* podcast)

I think where we've arrived at it now is a good evolution. It was a long arc and a long time coming. You got blips of it with Pussy Galore and Teresa, Diana Rigg. *Octopussy* a little bit and Izabella Scorupco in *GoldenEye*. But by the time you get to Eva Green as Vesper Lynd, which is ironic because you're kind of going back to the first book ever written, they're finally bringing *Bond* Girls to the point of really playing a part, not just in having their own identity and agency as a character, but playing a part in the plot and the story.

PHIL NOBILE, JR.

The 007 novels were fantasies of their time, bedtime stories for a man and an era in their twilight. Without apologizing for Fleming, it was an age that had different standards and different entitlements than we do today, and Fleming created colorful tales that, ultimately, aren't much different in their attitudes about race and gender than other pop culture artifacts of the time. Fleming's work is perhaps more scrutinized because we've been mining his work for entertainment for 60 years. What other entertainment property from 60 years ago is generating a billion dollars for its parent company? That's a seriously elite club, and one whose members are undergoing similar radical revisions these days.

JOHN CORK

If characters played by Scarlett Johansson in *Lucy* and *The Avengers* can exploit their sexuality to basically lure the enemy to his death, Bond certainly can exploit his sexuality. And make no mistake, he is a sex object in the films. The filmmakers find a way to get Sean Connery shirtless in all of his *Bond* films. Roger Moore is shirtless in all but two of his *Bond* films [*Moonraker, For Your Eyes Only*].

The filmmakers were adamant that the writers find a way to get Brosnan shirtless in *Die Another Day,* and if you ever watched *Casino Royale* with a large audience, you can hear some women's reaction to Daniel Craig in the nude torture scene. That atmosphere of sexuality is part of the human experience, part of Bond's universe. As long as it is a two-way street and consensual, let's hope it doesn't disappear.

MARTIN CAMPBELL

(director, *Casino Royale*)

I think Daniel Craig sort of opened the door a little bit for a good character actor. It doesn't need to be a Roger Moore, beautiful looking guy. Or a Pierce, very handsome looking. It doesn't need to be. It could be somebody who is like Daniel, who has a sort of rugged good look about him, but very different to the others.

PHIL NOBILE, JR.

It's my great fear that the franchise's recent penchant for serialization and continuity will translate into making canon the fan theory that I absolutely hate: the "James Bond is a code name." Rather than rebooting or retconning what came before with a recast, which is something the series was content to do for 40-plus years, this will allow them to justify a recast—including a race or gender swap—while still keeping everything "in continuity." I really hope this doesn't happen. Aside from abandoning the "nothing matters but the story we're telling right now" attitude I've come to love from the series, it's actually the most cowardly way to deliver a black Bond or a female Bond. Because that actor will always have this asterisk next to it.

TOM MANKIEWICZ

It is the most remarkable thing. I don't care what you do, there are only so many times you can go to the well. And I'm not saying the next *Bond* movie, if there's a new Bond or it's a startling story, couldn't engender four more. But that character has had a larger life as a character in continuous form than any character in the history of movies. You could probably count Tarzan over a period of 30 years but they only made one every five or six years with a different Tarzan every time, and they were pretty silly movies. *Bond* is really unique.

RONALD D. MOORE

(creator/executive producer, *For All Mankind*)

If I say "James Bond" to you, it evokes a certain image and idea, and people then want to see the next version of that. "Oh, who's doing James Bond now? What is the new cool? Can he reinvent it? Who will be the next one?" Then you get into all the arguments of who the best ones are. That's really interesting. I'm sure there's a thousand theses that have been written analyzing *James Bond* and why it's lasted this long.

RALPH WINTER

(producer, *Planet of the Apes*)

Even today, you *still* look forward to that opening sequence and what sort of bizarre things they're going to do with him strapped in a helicopter flying upside down. As a guy who makes those kind of movies, I always look forward to see what *Bond* is going to do to push the limit and make it even more fun. I'm a kid in a candy store watching those movies still.

MARYAM D'ABO

(actress, "Kara Milovy")

As long as the Broccolis, Michael Wilson, and Barbara Broccoli will be there, and the family will be involved in producing the *Bond* movies, *Bond* will exist. If the family were not there anymore, it won't be *Bond* anymore.

TIMOTHY DALTON

It is a modern popular classic of the cinema. Mr. Broccoli had the integrity to carry on this series of films with real expertise and imagination and ingenuity, which I think is rare. A lot of sequels die. They become cheap and exploitative. The quality of these films has been expanded, film by film.

MICHAEL G. WILSON

(producer, the *James Bond* films)

The first one was a success, and they then made another one, and the audience grew because they knew they weren't going to get cheated. Is there a future for *James Bond*? I like to think of us as like a member of the House of Representatives in the United States government. Every two years they come up for reelection. Every few years we come out with a picture and people go to the box office and they vote and we're either voted back in or not.

SEAN CONNERY

(actor, "James Bond")

Of course the films will go on, but who'll play me, I just don't know and can't guess.

ACKNOWLEDGMENTS

This book would not have been possible without the gracious assistance of so many in the *James Bond* community that were willing to share transcripts of their interviews, speeches, and public appearances with the authors. Unlike our previous works, which were almost exclusively based on our own interviews and personal archives, because of the large number of individuals involved with the *James Bond* series who have passed away, we found ourselves inevitably needing to rely to some extent on the additional scholarship of others to ensure that this volume would be as comprehensive as possible.

We are deeply indebted to all of them for their help and contributions, large and small. First and foremost among those is Richard Schenkman, founder of the James Bond Fan Club and editor of *Bondage* magazine, who provided several of his interviews for inclusion in this book, including interviews of Kevin McClory and Albert R. Broccoli. Special thanks to all the others who shared some of their interviews with us, including Steven Jay Rubin; Tom Soter; Robyn Coburn; Anders Frejdh, editor of the indispensable 007 website, *From Sweden with Love*; Steve Pizzello and David E. Williams of *American Cinematographer* magazine.

We are also immensely grateful to the late David V. Picker, who graciously allowed us to excerpt some recollections from his fascinating autobiography, *Musts, Maybes, and Nevers,* which spans his amazing career overseeing some of the most remarkable films and filmmakers of all time; as well as Steven A. Simak, who provided several John Barry quotes from his interview for the National Public Radio series *Music of the Cinema.*

In addition, legendary Ian Fleming and James Bond scholar John Cork provided immeasurable assistance and support throughout the process of writing this book, as did Lauren Cheung, Matt Sherman, Mike Pingel, Ryan Goldhar, talent manager Scott Ray, and the many assistants, agents, managers, and others who answered the call, literally and figuratively.

While some quotes included are from public personal appearances, press conferences, conventions, and tributes, the vast majority of the text remains culled from original interviews conducted by the book's authors for this volume. And to those who agreed to be interviewed—the list of names of whom would be far too long to feature here—our heartfelt appreciation.

A very special thanks to genius auteur Woody Allen who, despite having written, directed, and starred in a myriad of the greatest films ever made, was still willing to take the time from his busy schedule to discuss his work on 1967's *Casino Royale*—a movie he disdains—with us at great length.

Finally, we would be remiss not to thank our agent, Laurie Fox at The Linda Chester Agency, in addition to our new editor extraordinaire at Tor/Forge, Christopher Morgan, as well as his illustrious predecessor Brendan Deenan, who was always so supportive of our efforts. Also, very special thanks to copy editor Edwin Chapman for making us seem literate.

And finally, and perhaps most importantly, Ian Fleming, Cubby Broccoli, and Harry Saltzman, who started it all. Truly, *nobody* did it better.

ABOUT THE AUTHORS

MARK A. ALTMAN is a television and motion picture writer/producer/director who is currently the showrunner and executive producer of the CW's *Pandora*. He also served as co-executive producer of TNT's hit series *The Librarians*. Previous TV credits include *Agent X* (TNT), *Castle* (ABC), and *Necessary Roughness* (USA), among others. In addition, Altman has sold numerous pilots, including to USA Networks, and most recently, developed pilots for the El Rey Network and Sony Pictures Television. Altman has also sold feature scripts to such studios as Beacon Films, DreamWorks SKG, and Constantin Films.

He is the creator and host of the popular pop culture podcast *The 4:30 Movie*, which curates fantasy movie theme weeks in the spirit of the classic WABC *4:30 Movie*, along with *Inglorious Treksperts*, the only podcast for *Star Trek* with a life, for the Electric Surge Network, which he founded with producer Dean Devlin.

Altman also produced the $30-million film adaptation of the bestselling video game, *DOA: Dead Or Alive*, which was released by Dimension Films. His first film was the award-winning cult classic, *Free Enterprise*, starring William Shatner and Eric McCormack, which he wrote and produced and for which he won the Writers Guild of America Award for Best New Writer at the AFI Los Angeles Film Festival prior to its theatrical release. He is also a producer of the *House of the Dead* series, based on the video game from Sega, released by Lionsgate. In addition, he also produced James Gunn's beloved superhero satire, *The Specials*.

His bestselling two-volume series cowritten with Edward Gross, *The Fifty-Year Mission: The Complete Uncensored, Unauthorized History of Star Trek*, was released by St. Martin's Press in 2016 in hardcover to unanimous critical acclaim, including raves in *The Wall Street Journal*, *Booklist*, and *Publishers Weekly*. Their follow-up on *Buffy The Vampire Slayer* was published in September 2017 and a follow-up about *Battlestar Galactica, So Say We All*, was released in August 2018.

Altman is a former entertainment journalist. In the past, Altman has contributed to such newspapers and magazines as *The Boston Globe, Written By, L'Cinefage, Film Threat, The Guardian, The Boston Edge, Cult TV, Computer Player, Brandeis Magazine*, and many others, including *Cinefantastique*, for which he launched their independent film division, CFQ Films, which produced numerous successful genre features for DVD and VOD release.

He has also written numerous comic books for DC and Malibu Comics, including issues of *Star Trek* and *Star Trek: Deep Space Nine*. With Steve Kriozere, he cowrote the critically acclaimed graphic novel *Elvis Van Helsing*.

Altman has spoken at numerous industry events and conventions, including ShowBiz Expo, as well as the *Variety*/Final Draft Screenwriters Panel at the Cannes Film Festival. He was a juror at the prestigious Sitges Film Festival in Barcelona, Spain. He has been a frequent guest and panelist at Comic-Con, held annually in San Diego, California, and a two-time juror for the Comic-Con Film Festival. In addition to being a graduate of the Writers Guild of America Showrunner Training Program, he is a member of the Television Academy.

Twitter: @markaaltman
Instagram: @markaaltman

EDWARD GROSS has had a life-long obsession with film and TV, part of which was for the daytime television series *Dark Shadows*. That show, which he couldn't get enough of, inspired him to write his own fan fiction, which led in turn to writing reviews and, ultimately, a desire to get into entertainment journalism, which actually managed to manifest itself into a career.

That career has included positions on the editorial staff of a wide variety of magazines, among them *Starlog, Cinefantastique, Comics Scene, Femme Fatales, Cinescape, Life Story, Movie Magic, Film Fantasy*, and *Geek*. Additionally, he's written or cowritten a number of nonfiction books, including *X-Files Confidential, Planet of the Apes Revisited, Rocky: The Ultimate Guide, Above & Below: The Unofficial 25th Anniversary* Beauty and the Beast *Companion*, the two-volume *The Fifty-Year Mission, Slayers & Vampires*, and *So Say We All*. After serving as executive editor, U.S., for empireonline.com, he currently serves as film/TV editor of closerweekly.com, lifeandstylemag.com, and intouchweekly.com.

Twitter: @edgross